© Houghton Mifflin Harcourt Publishing Company
Image Credits: ©Fr. Tony Grossenburg/Flickr/Getty Images

ALGEBRA 1

Analyze • Connect • Explore

Edward B. Burger

Juli K. Dixon

Timothy D. Kanold

Matthew R. Larson

Steven J. Leinwand

Martha E. Sandoval-Martinez

Common Core State Standards © Copyright 2010. National Governors Association Center for Best Practices and Council of Chief State School Officers. All rights reserved.

This product is not sponsored or endorsed by the Common Core State Standards Initiative of the National Governors Association Center for Best Practices and the Council of Chief State School Officers.

Printed in the U.S.A.

ISBN 978-0-544-10215-6

7 8 9 10 11 12 13   0029   23 22 21 20 19 18 17 16

4500633419   E F G

Authors

Edward B. Burger, Ph.D., is the President of Southwestern University, a former Francis Christopher Oakley Third Century Professor of Mathematics at Williams College, and a former vice provost at Baylor University. He has authored or coauthored more than sixty-five articles, books, and video series; delivered over five hundred addresses and workshops throughout the world; and made more than fifty radio and television appearances. He is a Fellow of the American Mathematical Society as well as having earned many national honors, including the Robert Foster Cherry Award for Great Teaching in 2010. In 2012, Microsoft Education named him a "Global Hero in Education."

Juli K. Dixon, Ph.D., is a Professor of Mathematics Education at the University of Central Florida. She has taught mathematics in urban schools at the elementary, middle, secondary, and post-secondary levels. She is an active researcher and speaker with numerous publications and conference presentations. Key areas of focus are deepening teachers' content knowledge and communicating and justifying mathematical ideas. She is a past chair of the NCTM Student Explorations in Mathematics Editorial Panel and member of the Board of Directors for the Association of Mathematics Teacher Educators.

Timothy D. Kanold, Ph.D., is an award-winning international educator, author, and consultant. He is a former superintendent and director of mathematics and science at Adlai E. Stevenson High School District 125 in Lincolnshire, Illinois. He is a past president of the National Council of Supervisors of Mathematics (NCSM) and the Council for the Presidential Awardees of Mathematics (CPAM). He has served on several writing and leadership commissions for NCTM during the past decade. He presents motivational professional development seminars with a focus on developing professional learning communities (PLC's) to improve the teaching, assessing, and learning of students. He has recently authored nationally recognized articles, books, and textbooks for mathematics education and school leadership, including *What Every Principal Needs to Know about the Teaching and Learning of Mathematics*.

Matthew R. Larson, Ph.D., is the K-12 mathematics curriculum specialist for the Lincoln Public Schools and served on the Board of Directors for the National Council of Teachers of Mathematics from 2010 to 2013. He is a past chair of NCTM's Research Committee and was a member of NCTM's Task Force on Linking Research and Practice. He is the author of several books on implementing the Common Core Standards for Mathematics. He has taught mathematics at the secondary and college levels and held an appointment as an honorary visiting associate professor at Teachers College, Columbia University.

Steven J. Leinwand is a Principal Research Analyst at the American Institutes for Research (AIR) in Washington, D.C., and has over 30 years in leadership positions in mathematics education. He is past president of the National Council of Supervisors of Mathematics and served on the NCTM Board of Directors. He is the author of numerous articles, books, and textbooks and has made countless presentations with topics including student achievement, reasoning, effective assessment, and successful implementation of standards.

Martha E. Sandoval-Martinez is a mathematics instructor at El Camino College in Torrance, California. She was previously a Math Specialist at the University of California at Davis and former instructor at Santa Ana College, Marymount College, and California State University, Long Beach. In her current and former positions, she has worked extensively to improve fundamental pre-algebra and algebra skills in students who have historically struggled with mathematics.

Program Reviewers

Sharon Brown
Instructional Staff Developer
Pinellas County Schools
St. Petersburg, FL

Maureen Carrion
Math Staff Developer
Brentwood UFSD
Brentwood, NY

Jackie Cruse
Math Coach
Ferrell GPA
Tampa, FL

John Esser
Secondary Mathematics Coordinator
Racine Unified School District
Racine, WI

Donald Hoessler
Math Teacher
Discovery Middle School
Orlando, Florida

Elizabeth Jiménez, CEO
GEMAS Consulting
Pomona, CA

Becky (Rebecca) Jones, M.Ed.
NBCT EA-Math
Orange County Public Schools
Orlando, FL

Sheila D.P. Lea, MSA
Ben L. Smith High School
Greensboro, NC

Toni Lwanga
Newell Barney Jr. High
Queen Creek Unified School District
Queen Creek, AZ

Tiffany J. Mack
Charles A. Lindbergh Middle School
Peoria District #150
Peoria, IL

Erin Bostick Mason, MA.Ed.
Adjunct Faculty
Dept. of Language, Literature and Culture
College of Education, California State University
San Bernardino, CA

Jill Kerper Mora, Ed.D.
Associate Professor Emerita
School of Teacher Education
San Diego State University
San Diego, CA

Jean Sterner
Thurgood Marshall Fundamental
Middle School
Pinellas County Schools
St. Petersburg, FL

Mona Toncheff
Math Content Specialist
Phoenix Union High School District
Phoenix, AZ

Kevin Voepel
Mathematics & Professional Development
Coordinator
Ferguson-Florissant School District
Florissant, MO

© Houghton Mifflin Harcourt Publishing Company • Image Credits: (t) © Photodisc/Getty Images; (b) © photodisc/Getty Images

UNIT 1A Numbers and Expressions

COMMON CORE

MODULE 1 Relationships Between Quantities

COMMON CORE

MODULE 2 Exponents and Real Numbers

COMMON CORE

...sions

MODULE 4 Equations and Inequalities in One Variable

COMMON CORE

MODULE 5 Equations in Two Variables and Functions

COMMON CORE

© Houghton Mifflin Harcourt Publishing Company • Image Credits: (t) © Image Source/gettyimages.com; (b) © John Fedele/Blend Images/Alamy

MODULE 6 Linear Functions

MODULE 7 · Building Linear Functions

COMMON CORE

MODULE 8 · Modeling with Linear Functions

COMMON CORE

© Houghton Mifflin Harcourt Publishing Company • Image Credits: © Handout/Reuters/Corbis

UNIT 2B Exponential Relationships

MODULE 10 Exponential Functions and Equations

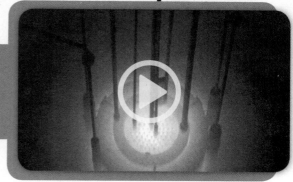

MODULE 11 Modeling with Exponential Functions

© Houghton Mifflin Harcourt Publishing Company • Image Credits: (t) © Everett Collection Inc/Alamy Images; (b) © RLHambley/Shutterstock

UNIT 3 · COMMON CORE

Statistics and Data

MODULE 12 — Descriptive Statistics

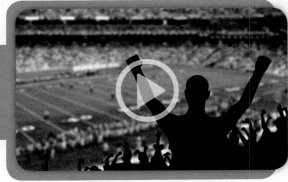

MODULE 13 — Data Displays

MODULE 14 Polynomials and Operations

MODULE 15 Factoring Polynomials

© Houghton Mifflin Harcourt Publishing Company • Image Credits: (t) © Joseph McNally/Photonica World/
Getty Images; (b) © Sergio Pitamitz/Robert Harding Imagery/Getty Images

MODULE 16   Solving Quadratic Equations

COMMON CORE

UNIT 5   Functions and Modeling

MODULE 17   Quadratic Functions

COMMON CORE

MODULE **18** Piecewise and Absolute Value Functions

COMMON CORE

MODULE **19** Square Root and Cube Root Functions

COMMON CORE

APPENDIX **The Pythagorean Theorem**

COMMON CORE

Common Core Standards for Algebra 1

Correlations for *HMH Algebra 1*: Analyze, Connect, Explore

NUMBER AND QUANTITY

Standard	Descriptor	Citations
THE REAL NUMBER SYSTEM		**N-RN**
Extend the properties of exponents to rational exponents.		
N-RN.1	Explain how the definition of the meaning of rational exponents follows from extending the properties of integer exponents to those values, allowing for a notation for radicals in terms of rational exponents.	29–36
N-RN.2	Rewrite expressions involving radicals and rational exponents using the properties of exponents.	29–36
Use properties of rational and irrational numbers.		
N-RN.3	Explain why the sum or product of two rational numbers is rational; that the sum of a rational number and an irrational number is irrational; and that the product of a nonzero rational number and an irrational number is irrational.	37–44
QUANTITIES		**N-Q**
Reason quantitatively and use units to solve problems.		
N-Q.1	Use units as a way to understand problems and to guide the solution of multi-step problems; choose and interpret units consistently in formulas; choose and interpret the scale and the origin in graphs and data displays.	15–22, 51–56, 65–72, 187–192
N-Q.2	Define appropriate quantities for the purpose of descriptive modeling.	65–72, 89–96, 255–262
N-Q.3	Choose a level of accuracy appropriate to limitations on measurement when reporting quantities.	7–14

ALGEBRA

Standard	Descriptor	Citations
SEEING STRUCTURE IN EXPRESSIONS		**A-SSE**
Interpret the structure of expressions.		
A-SSE.1	Interpret expressions that represent a quantity in terms of its context. a. Interpret parts of an expression, such as terms, factors, and coefficients. b. Interpret complicated expressions by viewing one or more of their parts as a single entity.	51–56, 57–64, 65–72, 587–594, 595–602

Standard	Descriptor	Citations
A-SSE.2	Use the structure of an expression to identify ways to rewrite it.	57–64, 65–72, 509–516, 523–532, 533–540, 541–548, 549–556

Write expressions in equivalent forms to solve problems.

Standard	Descriptor	Citations

A-SSE.3	Choose and produce an equivalent form of an expression to reveal and explain properties of the quantity represented by the expression.
	  a. Factor a quadratic expression to reveal the zeros of the function it defines.
	  b. Complete the square in a quadratic expression to reveal the maximum or minimum value of the function it defines.
	  c. Use the properties of exponents to transform expressions for exponential functions.
		337–344, 345–352, 353–360, 523–532, 533–540, 541–548, 549–556, 571–578, 579–586, 587–594

ARITHMETIC WITH POLYNOMIALS AND RATIONAL EXPRESSIONS		**A-APR**

Perform arithmetic operations on polynomials.

Standard	Descriptor	Citations
A-APR.1	Understand that polynomials form a system analogous to the integers, namely, they are closed under the operations of addition, subtraction, and multiplication; add, subtract, and multiply polynomials.	485–492, 493–500, 501–508, 509–516

CREATING EQUATIONS		**A-CED**

Create equations that describe numbers or relationships.

Standard	Descriptor	Citations
A-CED.1	Create equations and inequalities in one variable and use them to solve problems.	89–96, 97–106, 367–374, 461–468, 669–676, 563–570, 571–578, 579–586
A-CED.2	Create equations in two or more variables to represent relationships between quantities; graph equations on coordinate axes with labels and scales.	179–186, 201–206, 219–226, 337–344, 367–374, 381–386, 627–634, 635–642, 643–650, 661–668, 693–700
A-CED.3	Represent constraints by equations or inequalities, and by systems of equations and/or inequalities, and interpret solutions as viable or nonviable options in a modeling context.	89–96, 97–106, 277–284, 285–292, 293–302, 303–310, 311–318
A-CED.4	Rearrange formulas to highlight a quantity of interest, using the same reasoning as in solving equations.	107–112

REASONING WITH EQUATIONS AND INEQUALITIES		**A-REI**

Understand solving equations as a process of reasoning and explain the reasoning.

Standard	Descriptor	Citations
A-REI.1	Explain each step in solving a simple equation as following from the equality of numbers asserted at the previous step, starting from the assumption that the original equation has a solution. Construct a viable argument to justify a solution method.	89–96, 97–106, 107–112

Standard	Descriptor	Citations
Solve equations and inequalities in one variable.		
A-REI.3	Solve linear equations and inequalities in one variable, including equations with coefficients represented by letters.	89–96, 97–106, 107–112

A-REI.4	Solve quadratic equations in one variable.
	  a. Use the method of completing the square to transform any quadratic equation in x into an equation of the form $(x - p)^2 = q$ that has the same solutions. Derive the quadratic formula from this form.
	  b. Solve quadratic equations by inspection (e.g., for $x^2 = 49$), taking square roots, completing the square, the quadratic formula and factoring, as appropriate to the initial form of the equation. Recognize when the quadratic formula gives complex solutions and write them as $a \pm bi$ for real numbers a and b.
		563–570, 571–578, 579–586, 587–594, 595–602, 603–610, 661–668, 669–676

Solve systems of equations.		
A-REI.5	Prove that, given a system of two equations in two variables, replacing one equation by the sum of that equation and a multiple of the other produces a system with the same solutions.	303–310
A-REI.6	Solve systems of linear equations exactly and approximately (e.g., with graphs), focusing on pairs of linear equations in two variables.	277–284, 285–292, 293–302, 303–310
A-REI.7	Solve a simple system consisting of a linear equation and a quadratic equation in two variables algebraically and graphically.	669–676, 697–698
Represent and solve equations and inequalities graphically.		
A-REI.10	Understand that the graph of an equation in two variables is the set of all its solutions plotted in the coordinate plane, often forming a curve (which could be a line).	119–124
A-REI.11	Explain why the x-coordinates of the points where the graphs of the equations $y = f(x)$ and $y = g(x)$ intersect are the solutions of the equation $f(x) = g(x)$; find the solutions approximately, e.g., using technology to graph the functions, make tables of values, or find successive approximations. Include cases where $f(x)$ and/or $g(x)$ are linear, polynomial, rational, absolute value, exponential, and logarithmic functions.	125–132, 661–668, 701–708, 717–724, 725–726, 769

Standard	Descriptor	Citations
A-REI.12	Graph the solutions to a linear inequality in two variables as a halfplane (excluding the boundary in the case of a strict inequality), and graph the solution set to a system of linear inequalities in two variables as the intersection of the corresponding half-planes.	233–240, 311–318

FUNCTIONS

Standard	Descriptor	Citations
INTERPRETING FUNCTIONS		**F-IF**
Understand the concept of a function and use function notation.		
F-IF.1	Understand that a function from one set (called the domain) to another set (called the range) assigns to each element of the domain exactly one element of the range. If f is a function and x is an element of its domain, then $f(x)$ denotes the output of f corresponding to the input x. The graph of f is the graph of the equation $y = f(x)$.	125–132, 187–192
F-IF.2	Use function notation, evaluate functions for inputs in their domains, and interpret statements that use function notation in terms of a context.	125–132, 187–192, 227–232, 627–634, 635–642, 643–650, 693–700
F-IF.3	Recognize that sequences are functions, sometimes defined recursively, whose domain is a subset of the integers.	133–140, 213–218, 353–360
Interpret functions that arise in applications in terms of the context.		
F-IF.4	For a function that models a relationship between two quantities, interpret key features of graphs and tables in terms of the quantities, and sketch graphs showing key features given a verbal description of the relationship.	163–170, 171–178, 179–186, 193–200, 345–352, 627–634, 635–642, 643–650, 651–660, 669–676, 693–700, 701–708
F-IF.5	Relate the domain of a function to its graph and, where applicable, to the quantitative relationship it describes.	125–132, 155–162, 187–192, 337–344, 345–352, 627–634, 693–700
F-IF.6	Calculate and interpret the average rate of change of a function (presented symbolically or as a table) over a specified interval. Estimate the rate of change from a graph.	171–178, 201–206, 677–686

Standard	Descriptor	Citations
Analyze functions using different representations.		

F-IF.7	Graph functions expressed symbolically and show key features of the graph, by hand in simple cases and using technology for more complicated cases.
	  a. Graph linear and quadratic functions and show intercepts, maxima, and minima.
	  b. Graph square root, cube root, and piecewise-defined functions, including step functions and absolute value functions.
	  e. Graph exponential and logarithmic functions, showing intercepts and end behavior, and trigonometric functions, showing period, midline, and amplitude.
		155–162, 163–170, 171–178, 179–186, 337–344, 345–352, 627–634, 635–642, 643–650, 693–700, 701–708, 709–716, 731–738, 747–754

F-IF.8	Write a function defined by an expression in different but equivalent forms to reveal and explain different properties of the function.
	  a. Use the process of factoring and completing the square in a quadratic function to show zeros, extreme values, and symmetry of the graph, and interpret these in terms of a context.
	  b. Use the properties of exponents to interpret expressions for exponential functions.
		345–352, 353–360, 571–578, 579–586, 587–594, 651–660

F-IF.9	Compare properties of two functions each represented in a different way (algebraically, graphically, numerically in tables, or by verbal descriptions).	187–192, 693–700, 701–708, 731–738, 739–746, 747–754, 755–762
BUILDING FUNCTIONS		**F-BF**
Build a function that models a relationship between two quantities.		

F-BF.1	Write a function that describes a relationship between two quantities.
	  a. Determine an explicit expression, a recursive process, or steps for calculation from a context.
	  b. Combine standard function types using arithmetic operations.
		133–140, 201–206, 213–218, 219–226, 353–360, 367–374, 627–634, 635–642, 643–650, 693–700

F-BF.2	Write arithmetic and geometric sequences both recursively and with an explicit formula, use them to model situations, and translate between the two forms.	213–216, 241–242, 323, 353–360
Build new functions from existing functions.		
F-BF.3	Identify the effect on the graph of replacing $f(x)$ by $f(x) + k$, $k \cdot f(x)$, $f(kx)$, and $f(x + k)$ for specific values of k (both positive and negative); find the value of k given the graphs. Experiment with cases and illustrate an explanation of the effects on the graph using technology.	193–200, 361–366, 635–642, 643–650, 651–658, 693–700, 701–708, 709–716, 739–746, 755–762
F-BF.4	Find inverse functions. **a.** Solve an equation of the form $f(x) = c$ for a simple function f that has an inverse and write an expression for the inverse.	227–232, 241–242, 323, 375–376, 397

© Houghton Mifflin Harcourt Publishing Company

Standard	Descriptor	Citations
FUNCTIONS: LINEAR AND EXPONENTIAL MODELS		**F-LE**
Construct and compare linear and exponential models and solve problems.		

F-LE.1	Distinguish between situations that can be modeled with linear functions and with exponential functions.
	   a. Prove that linear functions grow by equal differences over equal intervals, and that exponential functions grow by equal factors over equal intervals.
	   b. Recognize situations in which one quantity changes at a constant rate per unit interval relative to another.
	   c. Recognize situations in which a quantity grows or decays by a constant percent rate per unit interval relative to another.
		171–178, 179–186, 213–218, 345–352, 353–360, 387–394, 677–686

F-LE.2	Construct linear and exponential functions, including arithmetic and geometric sequences, given a graph, a description of a relationship, or two input-output pairs (include reading these from a table).	201–206, 213–218, 219–226, 337–344, 345–352, 353–360, 367–374
F-LE.3	Observe using graphs and tables that a quantity increasing exponentially eventually exceeds a quantity increasing linearly, quadratically, or (more generally) as a polynomial function.	387–394, 677–686
Interpret expressions for functions in terms of the situation they model.		
F-LE.5	Interpret the parameters in a linear or exponential function in terms of a context.	187–192, 193–200, 219–226, 255–262, 345–352, 381–386

STATISTICS AND PROBABILITY

Standard	Descriptor	Citations
STATISTICS AND PROBABILITY: INTERPRETING CATEGORICAL AND QUANTITATIVE DATA		**S-ID**
Summarize, represent, and interpret data on a single count or measurement variable.		
S-ID.1	Represent data with plots on the real number line (dot plots, histograms, and box plots).	439–446, 447–454, 455–460, 461–468
S-ID.2	Use statistics appropriate to the shape of the data distribution to compare center (median, mean) and spread (interquartile range, standard deviation) of two or more different data sets.	431–438, 439–446, 455–460, 461–468a
S-ID.3	Interpret differences in shape, center, and spread in the context of the data sets, accounting for possible effects of extreme data points (outliers).	439–446

Standard	Descriptor	Citations
Summarize, represent, and interpret data on two categorical and quantitative variables.		
S-ID.5	Summarize categorical data for two categories in two-way frequency tables. Interpret relative frequencies in the context of the data (including joint, marginal, and conditional relative frequencies). Recognize possible associations and trends in the data.	**411–416, 417–424**

S-ID.6	Represent data on two quantitative variables on a scatter plot, and describe how the variables are related.
	  a. Fit a function to the data; use functions fitted to data to solve problems in the context of the data.
	  b. Informally assess the fit of a function by plotting and analyzing residuals.
	  c. Fit a linear function for a scatter plot that suggests a linear association.
		247–254, 255–262, 263–270, 381–386, 461–468

Interpret linear models.		
S-ID.7	Interpret the slope (rate of change) and the intercept (constant term) of a linear model in the context of the data.	**255–262, 263–270**
S-ID.8	Compute (using technology) and interpret the correlation coefficient of a linear fit.	**247–254, 263–270**
S-ID.9	Distinguish between correlation and causation.	**247–254**

Additional Common Core Standards for Grade 8

Correlations for *HMH Algebra 1*: Analyze, Connect, Explore

Standard	Descriptor	Citations
Analyze and solve linear equations and pairs of simultaneous linear equations.		

8.EE.8	Analyze and solve pairs of simultaneous linear equations.
	  a. Understand that solutions to a system of two linear equations in two variables correspond to points of intersection of their graphs, because points of intersection satisfy both equations simultaneously.
	  b. Solve systems of two linear equations in two variables algebraically, and estimate solutions by graphing the equations. Solve simple cases by inspection.
	  c. Solve real-world and mathematical problems leading to two linear equations in two variables.
		277–284, 285–292, 293–302, 303–310, 669–676, 697–698

Define, evaluate, and compare functions.		
8.F.1	Understand that a function is a rule that assigns to each input exactly one output. The graph of a function is the set of ordered pairs consisting of an input and the corresponding output.	125–132, 187–192, 227–232, 627–634, 635–642, 643–650, 693–700
8.F.2	Compare properties of two functions each represented in a different way (algebraically, graphically, numerically in tables, or by verbal descriptions).	187–192, 693–700, 701–708, 731–738, 739–746, 747–754, 755–762
8.F.3	Interpret the equation $y = mx + b$ as defining a linear function, whose graph is a straight line; give examples of functions that are not linear.	179–186, 187–192, 193–200, 201–206, 337–344, 627–634, 677–686
Use functions to model relationships between quantities.		
8.F.4	Construct a function to model a linear relationship between two quantities. Determine the rate of change and initial value of the function from a description of a relationship or from two (x, y) values, including reading these from a table or from a graph. Interpret the rate of change and initial value of a linear function in terms of the situation it models, and in terms of its graph or a table of values.	179–186, 187–192, 193–200, 201–206
8.F.5	Describe qualitatively the functional relationship between two quantities by analyzing a graph (e.g., where the function is increasing or decreasing, linear or nonlinear). Sketch a graph that exhibits the qualitative features of a function that has been described verbally.	163–170, 171–178, 179–186, 193–200, 345–352, 627–634, 635–642, 643–650, 651–660, 669–676, 693–700, 701–708

Standard	Descriptor	Citations
Understand and apply the Pythagorean Theorem.		
8.G.6	Explain a proof of the Pythagorean Theorem and its converse.	AL1–AL12
8.G.7	Apply the Pythagorean Theorem to determine unknown side lengths in right triangles in real-world and mathematical problems in two and three dimensions.	AL1–AL6
8.G.8	Apply the Pythagorean Theorem to find the distance between two points in a coordinate system.	AL13–AL18
Investigate patterns of association in bivariate data.		
8.SP.1	Construct and interpret scatter plots for bivariate measurement data to investigate patterns of association between two quantities. Describe patterns such as clustering, outliers, positive or negative association, linear association, and nonlinear association.	247–254, 255–262, 263–270, 381–386, 461–468
8.SP.2	Know that straight lines are widely used to model relationships between two quantitative variables. For scatter plots that suggest a linear association, informally fit a straight line, and informally assess the model fit by judging the closeness of the data points to the line.	247–254, 255–262, 263–270, 381–386, 461–468
8.SP.3	Use the equation of a linear model to solve problems in the context of bivariate measurement data, interpreting the slope and intercept.	255–262, 263–270
8.SP.4	Understand that patterns of association can also be seen in bivariate categorical data by displaying frequencies and relative frequencies in a two-way table. Construct and interpret a two-way table summarizing data on two categorical variables collected from the same subjects. Use relative frequencies calculated for rows or columns to describe possible association between the two variables.	411–416, 417–424

MATHEMATICAL PRACTICES

Standard	Descriptor	Citations
MP MATHEMATICAL PRACTICES STANDARDS		*The mathematical practices standards are integrated throughout the book. See, for example, the citations below.*
MP.1	Make sense of problems and persevere in solving them.	**Examples: 112, 170, 185, 225–226, 239, 394, 431–435**
MP.2	Reason abstractly and quantitatively.	**Examples: 37–42, 44, 162, 186, 226, 262, 292**
MP.3	Construct viable arguments and critique the reasoning of others.	**Examples: 36, 40–41, 206, 240, 373**
MP.4	Model with mathematics.	**Examples: 107–108, 111–112, 131, 199, 284, 291**
MP.5	Use appropriate tools strategically.	**Examples: 15, 90–92, 163–167, 178, 193–197, 269, 446, 453**
MP.6	Attend to precision.	**Examples: 7–10, 14, 16, 22, 262, 283**
MP.7	Look for and make use of structure.	**Examples: 52, 170, 218, 254, 351, 366**
MP.8	Look for and express regularity in repeated reasoning.	**Examples: 29–33, 58–60, 64, 138, 178, 344, 359–360, 393**

Succeeding with HMH Algebra 1: Analyze, Connect, Explore

Actively participate in your learning with your write-in Student Edition. Explore concepts, take notes, answer questions, and complete your homework right in your textbook!

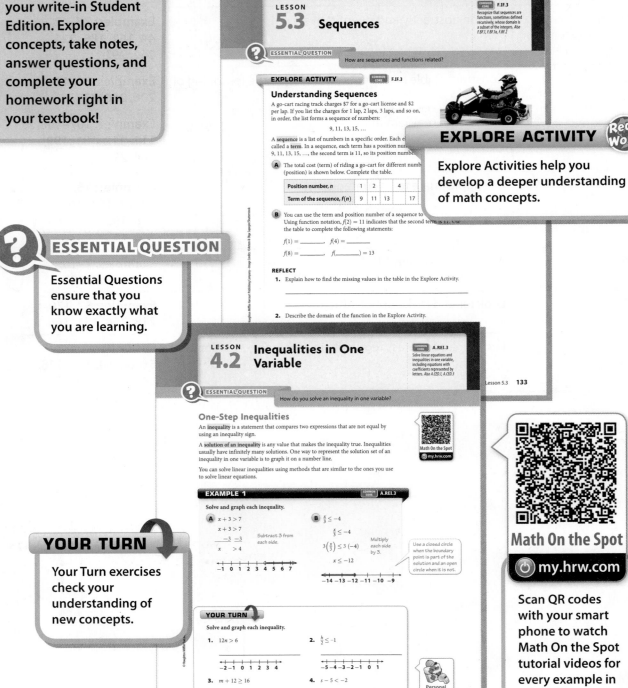

LESSON 5.3 Sequences

COMMON CORE F.IF.3
Recognize that sequences are functions, sometimes defined recursively, whose domain is a subset of the integers. Also F.BF.1, F.BF.1a, F.BF.2

ESSENTIAL QUESTION How are sequences and functions related?

EXPLORE ACTIVITY COMMON CORE F.IF.3

Understanding Sequences

A go-cart racing track charges $7 for a go-cart license and $2 per lap. If you list the charges for 1 lap, 2 laps, 3 laps, and so on, in order, the list forms a sequence of numbers:

9, 11, 13, 15, …

A sequence is a list of numbers in a specific order. Each element is called a term. In a sequence, each term has a position number. 9, 11, 13, 15, …, the second term is 11, so its position number

A The total cost (term) of riding a go-cart for different numbers (position) is shown below. Complete the table.

Position number, n	1	2	4	
Term of the sequence, $f(n)$	9	11	13	17

B You can use the term and position number of a sequence to Using function notation, $f(2) = 11$ indicates that the second term is 11. Use the table to complete the following statements:

$f(1) =$ _____ $f(4) =$ _____
$f(8) =$ _____ $f($ _____ $) = 13$

REFLECT

1. Explain how to find the missing values in the table in the Explore Activity.

_____

2. Describe the domain of the function in the Explore Activity.

Lesson 5.3   **133**

EXPLORE ACTIVITY Real World

Explore Activities help you develop a deeper understanding of math concepts.

ESSENTIAL QUESTION

Essential Questions ensure that you know exactly what you are learning.

LESSON 4.2 Inequalities in One Variable

COMMON CORE A.REI.3
Solve linear equations and inequalities in one variable, including equations with coefficients represented by letters. Also A.CED.1, A.CED.3

ESSENTIAL QUESTION How do you solve an inequality in one variable?

One-Step Inequalities

An **inequality** is a statement that compares two expressions that are not equal by using an inequality sign.

A **solution of an inequality** is any value that makes the inequality true. Inequalities usually have infinitely many solutions. One way to represent the solution set of an inequality in one variable is to graph it on a number line.

You can solve linear inequalities using methods that are similar to the ones you use to solve linear equations.

Math On the Spot
my.hrw.com

EXAMPLE 1 COMMON CORE A.REI.3

Solve and graph each inequality.

A $x + 3 > 7$

$x + 3 > 7$
$\underline{-3 \quad -3}$ Subtract 3 from each side.
$x \quad > 4$

$\begin{array}{ccccccccc} & | & | & | & | & | & | & | & | \\ -1 & 0 & 1 & 2 & 3 & 4 & 5 & 6 & 7 \end{array}$

B $\frac{x}{3} \le -4$

$\frac{x}{3} \le -4$
$3\left(\frac{x}{3}\right) \le 3\,(-4)$ Multiply each side by 3.
$x \le -12$

Use a closed circle when the boundary point is part of the solution and an open circle when it is not.

$\begin{array}{ccccccc} | & | & | & | & | & | \\ -14 & -13 & -12 & -11 & -10 & -9 \end{array}$

YOUR TURN

Solve and graph each inequality.

1. $12n > 6$

$\begin{array}{ccccccc} | & | & | & | & | & | \\ -2 & -1 & 0 & 1 & 2 & 3 & 4 \end{array}$

2. $\frac{h}{2} \le -1$

$\begin{array}{ccccccc} | & | & | & | & | & | \\ -5 & -4 & -3 & -2 & -1 & 0 & 1 \end{array}$

3. $m + 12 \ge 16$

$\begin{array}{ccccccc} | & | & | & | & | & | \\ -1 & 0 & 1 & 2 & 3 & 4 & 5 \end{array}$

4. $s - 5 < -2$

$\begin{array}{ccccccc} | & | & | & | & | & | \\ -1 & 0 & 1 & 2 & 3 & 4 & 5 \end{array}$

Personal Math Trainer
Online Practice and Help
my.hrw.com

Lesson 4.2   **97**

YOUR TURN

Your Turn exercises check your understanding of new concepts.

Math On the Spot
my.hrw.com

Scan QR codes with your smart phone to watch Math On the Spot tutorial videos for every example in the book!

© Houghton Mifflin Harcourt Publishing Company

Unit Project F.LE.3, F.LE.6, F.BF.1a

Going Down?

Construct a ramp that is at least 4 feet long. The angle the ramp makes with the ground should be 30°. Working with a partner, release a ball from various points on the ramp. Measure the distance the ball rolls and the time (using a stopwatch) that it rolls. You should perform several trials for various distances.

The quadratic equation $d = \frac{1}{2}gt^2$ models the distance d (in ___ ___lls in t seconds. Use your data and the ___ ___ the value of g. Create a report that explains your approach, ___ ___ ata in tables, and shows your calculations. You can use a ___ ___ ata to a quadratic regres___

___ m any questions you ha___

Unit Project

Apply new skills and concepts to solve real-world problems in Unit Projects and Math in Careers Activities.

MATH IN CAREERS ACTIVITY

Investigator The reaction distance, $r(\text{ft})$, is the dis___ the time the driver decides to stop until he or she app___ distance, $b(\text{ft})$, is the distance the vehicle travels once ___ reaches a complete stop. Both distances are influence___ vehicle. The stopping distance, $s(\text{ft})$, is the sum of the ___

$s = r + b$

$r = 1.47vt$, where $v =$ speed (mi/h) and $t =$ reaction ___

$b = 1.075 \frac{v^2}{a}$, where $v =$ speed (mi/h) and $a =$ decele___

Transportation departments typically use a reaction ___ deceleration rate of 11.2 ft/s² to calculate stopping ___ breaking distance, and stopping distance for a drive___

618 Unit 4

Reading Start-Up

Vocabulary

Review Words
- one-step equation
- one-step inequality

Preview Words
- equivalent equations
- formula
- identity
- literal equation
- solution of an equation

Visualize Vocabulary

Use the review words to complete the case diagram. Write an example for each oval.

One-Step Mathematical Statement

Reading Start-Up

Get vocabulary, language, and note-taking support throughout the book.

Understand Vocabulary

To become familiar with some of the vocabulary ___ the following. You may refer to the module, the g___

1. One definition of identity is "exact sameness." An e___ expressions. If an equation is an *identity*, what do you think is true about the expressions?

2. The word *literal* means "of letters." How might a literal equation be different from an equation like $3 + 5 = 8$?

Active Reading

___ Before beginning the module, create a ___ o help you organize what you learn about ___ es. Organize the characteristics of the ___ for easy comparison.

Module 4   87

UNIT 3
MIXED REVIEW

COMMON CORE

Assessment Readiness

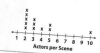

Personal Math Trainer
Online Practice and Help
my.hrw.com

1. Consider each function. Is it an exponential growth function?
   Select Yes or No.
   A. $y = 0.3(1 + 0.5)^t$ ○ Yes ○ No
   B. $y = 28(0.85)^t$ ○ Yes ○ No
   C. $y = \frac{1}{2}(2)^t$ ○ Yes ○ No

2. The two-way frequency table shows the results of a survey of a group of randomly selected students about whether they own a cat or a dog.

	Has a Dog		
Has a Cat	Yes	No	Tota
Yes	10	16	26
No	21	33	54
Total	31	49	80

   Choose True or False for each statement.
   A. Ten students in the survey own both pets.   ○ True ○ False
   B. The marginal relative frequency of students surveyed who own a cat is 32.5%.   ○ True ○ False
   C. The joint relative frequency of students surveyed who own a dog but not a cat is about 67.7%.   ○ True ○ False

3. The weights of 5 lion cubs in pounds are 19, 22, 21, 23, and 21. Is the standard deviation of the weights more than 1 lb? Explain.

4. A machine produces bolts with a mean thread diameter of 0.250 inch and a standard deviation of 0.002 inch. Any bolts with a thread diameter greater than 0.250 inch or less than 0.244 inch must be rejected. What is the probability that a bolt produced by the machine will be rejected? Explain how you know.

0.15% 2.35% | 34% 34% | 13.5%
13.5%

Performance Tasks

★ 5. The dot plot shows the number of actors in each scene of an episode of a television show. Identify the outlier in the data and determine how it affects the mean and median of the data.

Actors per Scene

Assessment Readiness

COMMON CORE

Prepare for new high-stakes tests with Common Core aligned practice items and Performance Tasks.

★★ 6. Last month, a car dealership sold 96 cars. Of the 2-door cars, 2 were hybrids and 21 were not hybrids. Of the 4-door cars, 5 were hybrids, and 68 were not hybrids.
   a. Complete the two-way frequency table for the data.
   b. Create a two-way relative frequency table for the data.
   c. For the cars sold at the dealership, is there any association between the numb___ and whether the car is a hybrid? Justify your reasoning.

★★★ 7. A college baseball coach is deciding between two pitchers to add to the team. In general, a better pitcher throws more strikes. The table shows the percent of strikes thrown per game by the two pitchers in their last high school baseball season. Which pitcher should the coach add to the team? Justify your answer by using both data displays and statistics.

Acevedo	59, 62, 71, 67, 64, 58, 68, 63, 65, 64, 59, 69
Forbes	54, 67, 51, 61, 52, 54, 52, 60, 64, 51, 60, 62

The eStudent Edition provides additional multimedia resources to enhance your learning. You can write in answers, take notes, watch videos, explore concepts with virtual manipulatives, and get homework help!

Math On the Spot
my.hrw.com

Math On the Spot video tutorials provide step-by-step instruction of the math concepts covered in each example.

my.hrw.com

$72m^{3/4}$

Real-World Videos show you how specific math topics can be used in all kinds of situations.

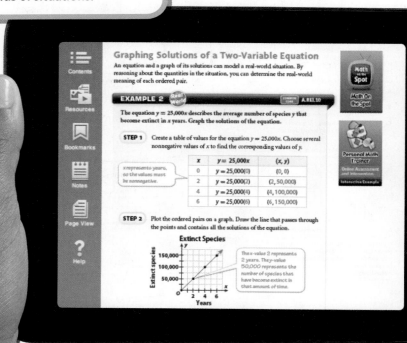

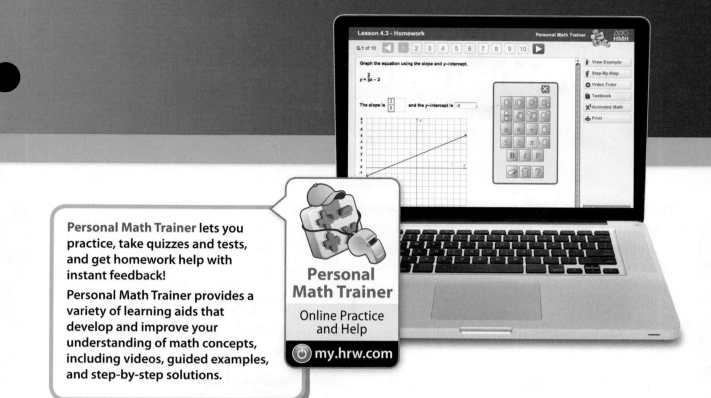

Personal Math Trainer lets you practice, take quizzes and tests, and get homework help with instant feedback!

Personal Math Trainer provides a variety of learning aids that develop and improve your understanding of math concepts, including videos, guided examples, and step-by-step solutions.

Personal Math Trainer

Online Practice and Help

⏻ **my.hrw.com**

Animated Math activities and virtual manipulatives let you interactively explore and practice key math concepts and skills.

Animated Math

⏻ **my.hrw.com**

Standards for Mathematical Practice

The topics described in the Standards for Mathematical Content will vary from year to year. However, the *way* in which you learn, study, and think about mathematics will not. The Standards for Mathematical Practice describe skills that you will use in all of your math courses. These pages show some features of your book that will help you gain these skills and use them to master this year's topics.

MP.1 Make sense of problems and persevere in solving them.

Mathematically proficient students start by explaining to themselves the meaning of a problem… They analyze givens, constraints, relationships, and goals. They make conjectures about the form… of the solution and plan a solution pathway…

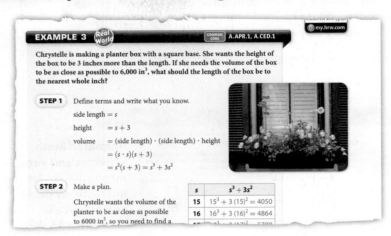

EXAMPLE 3 (Real World)   COMMON CORE A.APR.1, A.CED.1   my.hrw.com

Chrystelle is making a planter box with a square base. She wants the height of the box to be 3 inches more than the length. If she needs the volume of the box to be as close as possible to 6,000 in³, what should the length of the box be to the nearest whole inch?

STEP 1 Define terms and write what you know.

side length $= s$

height $= s + 3$

volume $=$ (side length) · (side length) · height

$= (s \cdot s)(s + 3)$

$= s^2(s + 3) = s^3 + 3s^2$

STEP 2 Make a plan.

Chrystelle wants the volume of the planter to be as close as possible to 6000 in³, so you need to find a

s	$s^3 + 3s^2$
15	$15^3 + 3(15)^2 = 4050$
16	$16^3 + 3(16)^2 = 4864$

Problem-solving examples and exercises lead students through problem solving steps.

MP.2 Reason abstractly and quantitatively.

Mathematically proficient students… bring two complementary abilities to bear on problems…: the ability to decontextualize— to abstract a given situation and represent it symbolically… and the ability to contextualize, to pause… in order to probe into the referents for the symbols involved.

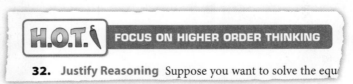

H.O.T. FOCUS ON HIGHER ORDER THINKING

32. Justify Reasoning Suppose you want to solve the equ

Unit Project COMMON CORE F.BF.1a, F.F

Focus on Higher Order Thinking exercises in every lesson and a **Project** in every unit require you to use logical reasoning, represent situations symbolically, use mathematical models to solve problems, and state your answers in terms of a problem context.

MP.3 Construct viable arguments and critique the reasoning of others.

Mathematically proficient students... justify their conclusions, [and]... distinguish correct... reasoning from that which is flawed.

REFLECT

1. Make a Conjecture How can you write the square root or the cube number *n* using an exponent?

Essential Question Check-in and **Reflect** in every lesson ask you to evaluate statements, explain relationships, apply mathematical principles, make conjectures, construct arguments, and justify your reasoning.

MP.4 Model with mathematics.

Mathematically proficient students can apply... mathematics... to... problems... in everyday life, society, and the workplace.

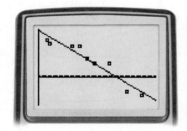
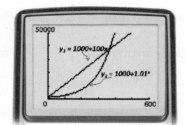

Real-world examples and **mathematical modeling** apply mathematics to other disciplines and real-world contexts such as science and business.

MP.5 Use appropriate tools strategically.

Mathematically proficient students consider the available tools when solving a... problem... [and] are... able to use technological tools to explore and deepen their understanding...

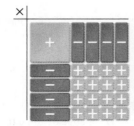

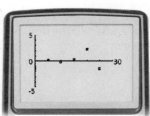

Exploration Activities in lessons use concrete and technological tools, such as manipulatives or graphing calculators, to explore mathematical concepts.

MP.6 Attend to precision.

Mathematically proficient students… communicate precisely… with others and in their own reasoning… [They] give carefully formulated explanations…

REFLECT

1. **Communicate Mathematical Ideas** Explain why $16^{\frac{1}{2}}$ is a monom $x^{\frac{1}{2}}$ is not a monomial.

Key Vocabulary

accuracy *(exactitud)*
   The closeness of a given measurement to the actual measurement.

Precision refers not only to the correctness of calculations but also to the proper use of mathematical language and symbols. **Communicate Mathematical Ideas** exercises and **Key Vocabulary** highlighted for each module and unit help you learn and use the language of math to communicate mathematics precisely.

MP.7 Look for and make use of structure.

Mathematically proficient students… look closely to discern a pattern or structure… They can also step back for an overview and shift perspectives.

$$(x + y)(x + z) = x^2 + xz + xy + yz$$

Product = a   Product = c

$$\left(\boxed{}\ x + \boxed{} \right)\left(\boxed{}\ x + \boxed{} \right) = ax^2 + bx + c$$

Sum of outer and inner products = b

Throughout the lessons, you will observe regularity in mathematical structures in order to make generalizations and make connections between related problems. For example, you can see the same structure used when learning to multiply binomials and factor trinomials.

MP.8 Look for and express regularity in repeated reasoning.

Mathematically proficient students… look both for general methods and for shortcuts… [and] maintain oversight of the process, while attending to the details.

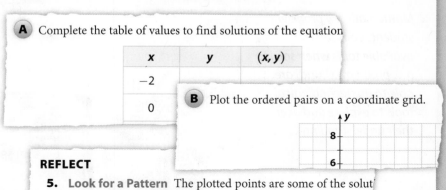

A Complete the table of values to find solutions of the equation

x	y	(x, y)
−2		
0		

B Plot the ordered pairs on a coordinate grid.

REFLECT

5. **Look for a Pattern** The plotted points are some of the solut equation. What appears to be true about them?

Examples in your book group similar types of problems together to allow you to look for patterns and make generalizations.

REVIEW OF GRADE 8 PART 1

Review Test

Personal
Math Trainer

Online Practice
and Help

my.hrw.com

1. Evaluate $(3^{-4})^6$.

_____

2. Simplify $-8\sqrt{-15+31}$.

_____

3. A passenger plane travels at about 7.62×10^2 feet per second. The plane takes 1.23×10^4 seconds to reach its destination. About how far must the plane travel to reach its destination? Write your answer in scientific notation.

_____

4. What linear function describes the relationship shown in the table?

x	$f(x)$
-5	25
-3	13
2	-17
3	-23

_____

5. A remote-control airplane descends at a rate of 3 feet per second. After 6 seconds the plane is 89 feet above the ground. Which equation models this situation, and what is the height of the plane after 12 seconds?

_____

6. Which of the following is a congruence transformation? Select Yes or No.

A. a dilation with scale factor 1
◯ Yes ◯ No

B. a reflection across the *y*-axis
◯ Yes ◯ No

C. a translation 5 units down
◯ Yes ◯ No

D. a dilation with scale factor 2
◯ Yes ◯ No

7. In the gift shop of the History of Flight museum, Elisa bought a kit to make a model of a jet airplane. The actual plane is 20 feet long with a wingspan of 16 feet. The finished model will be 15 inches long. What will be the wingspan of the model?

_____

8. What is the value of *n*?

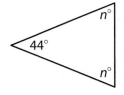

_____

9. Melanie is making a piece of jewelry that is in the shape of a right triangle. The two shorter sides of the piece of jewelry are 12 mm and 9 mm. Find the perimeter of the piece of jewelry.

_____

10. What is the distance, to the nearest tenth, from $S(4, -1)$ to $W(-2, 3)$?

_____

11. Estimate $\sqrt{285}$ to the nearest hundredth.

_____

12. Harry and Selma start driving from the same location. Harry drives 42 miles north while Selma drives 144 miles east. How far apart are Harry and Selma when they stop?

_____

13. In Hannah's science report, she says that the average distance between the Sun and Earth is about 9.3×10^7 miles. Show how to write this number in standard notation.

_____

14. A summer theater pass costs $24.75. Every time the pass is used, $2.75 is deducted from the balance. Write an equation to represent this situation.

_____

15. Describe a possible situation that could be modeled by the graph.

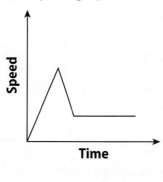

_____

_____

_____

_____

_____

16. Dilate the figure by a scale factor of 1.5 with the origin as the center of dilation. Graph the new figure below with the original figure.

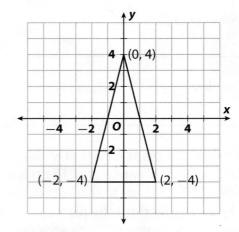

Performance Task

17. Does the following graph display a function? Explain.

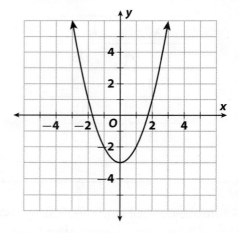

_____

_____

_____

_____

_____

REVIEW OF GRADE 8 PART 2

Review Test

COMMON CORE

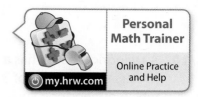

Personal Math Trainer

Online Practice and Help

my.hrw.com

1. Write the equation, in slope-intercept form, of the line shown in the graph.

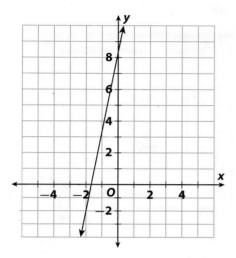

_____

2. What is the solution of
$-4c + 10 + 8c = 86$?

_____

3. How many solutions does the equation
$c + 2 = c - 2$ have?

_____

4. What is the solution of the system of equations?

$\begin{cases} y = 3x + 1 \\ y = 5x - 3 \end{cases}$

_____

5. A bicyclist heads east at 18 km/h. After she has traveled 19.2 kilometers, another cyclist sets out from the same starting point in the same direction going 30 km/h. How long will it take the second cyclist to catch up to the first cyclist?

_____

6. Which of these functions is a linear function? Select Yes or No.

A. $f(x) = 3 - \frac{x}{3}$
◯ Yes   ◯ No

B. $f(x) = 3^x + 4$
◯ Yes   ◯ No

C. $f(x) = 3^3 - 3x$
◯ Yes   ◯ No

D. $f(x) = 3(4 - x) + 3$
◯ Yes   ◯ No

7. Which function has the greatest rate of change? Explain.

- $y = 11x - 8$

- A fitness club charges a $200 membership fee plus monthly fees of $25.

- $y = -8x$

- $\{(-1, -2), (1, 2), (3, 6), (5, 10), (7, 14)\}$

_____

_____

8. You buy hats for $12 and sell them for $8 each. Describe the graph of the profits. Is it a line or a curve? Does it go up or down?

_____

9. An artist is creating a large conical sculpture for a park. The cone has a height of 19 feet and a diameter of 28 feet. What is the volume of the sculpture to the nearest hundredth?

_____

10. A cylindrical barrel has a radius of 4.2 meters and a height of 3 meters. Tripling which dimension(s) will triple the volume of the barrel? Select Yes or No.

   A. height

     ◯ Yes   ◯ No

   B. radius

     ◯ Yes   ◯ No

   C. diameter

     ◯ Yes   ◯ No

11. What linear equation best models the data in the scatter plot? Write your answer in $y = mx + b$ form, and round m and b to the nearest integer.

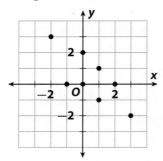

_____

12. Write a function that converts x days to y hours.

_____

13. Solve $h - 8 = 3h + 3$.

_____

14. Solve the system using any method.

$$\begin{cases} 2x - 5y = -22 \\ x + 3y = 11 \end{cases}$$

_____

15. Rewrite the equation $2y + 3x = 4$ in slope-intercept form. Then find the slope and y-intercept.

_____

16. Find the slope of the line that passes through the points $(-3, 6)$ and $(4, 2)$.

_____

17. Describe the correlation in the scatter plot and explain what it means in the given situation.

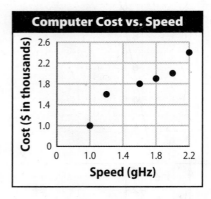

_____

_____

Performance Task

18. Use the graph to identify the slope and y-intercept. Then explain what each means in the context of the problem.

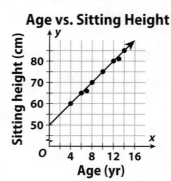

_____

_____

_____

_____

COMMON CORE

ALGEBRA 1 PART 1
Benchmark Test

Personal Math Trainer
Online Practice and Help

my.hrw.com

1. A movie theater charges $8.50 for a ticket. To help the local animal shelter, the theater agrees to reduce the price of each ticket by $0.50 for every can of pet food a customer donates. Write an equation that gives the ticket cost y for a customer who contributes x cans.

_____

_____

2. The population of a Midwestern suburb is growing exponentially. The chart shows its population for four consecutive years. Write a rule that gives the population P_n after n years. Use $n = 1$ to represent Year 1.

Year	Year 1	Year 2	Year 3	Year 4
Population	6500	7800	9360	11,232

_____

_____

3. Ticket sales for the first 5 nights of a new play form the sequence 400, 399, 396, 387, 360, ... If this pattern continues, what rule gives the number of tickets sold on the nth night?

_____

_____

4. Write each system of linear inequalities that is graphed.

A.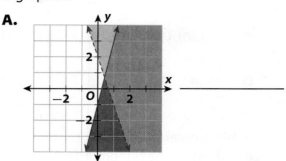

B.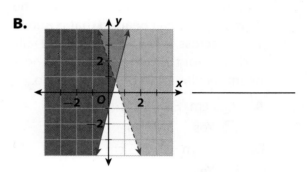

C.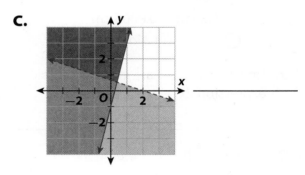

D.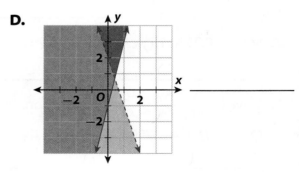

5. Which represents a price that increases at a constant rate per ounce for ordered pairs in the form (ounces, price)? Select Yes or No.

A. (8, 0.50), (12, 1.00), (24, 1.50), (32, 2.00)
  ○ Yes   ○ No

B. (8, 0.60), (12, 0.90), (24, 1.80), (32, 2.40)
  ○ Yes   ○ No

C. (8, 0.80), (12, 1.20), (16, 1.60), (20, 2.00)
  ○ Yes   ○ No

D. (8, 0.40), (12, 0.80), (16, 1.60), (20, 3.20)
  ○ Yes   ○ No

6. A micrometer used in a factory measures thickness to one hundredth of a millimeter. This micrometer is used to measure the diameter of a ball bearing that is about 1.7 cm across. What is a reasonable value and error for the measurement of the bearing's diameter? Select Yes or No.

A. 2.25 cm $\pm$ 0.05 cm
  ○ Yes   ○ No

B. 1.715 cm $\pm$ 0.005 cm
  ○ Yes   ○ No

C. 1.6713 cm $\pm$ 0.0005 cm
  ○ Yes   ○ No

7. How many terms are in the algebraic expression $2x - 9xy + 17y$?

_____

8. Solve $y = \frac{5}{8}b + 10$ for b.

_____

9. Solve $-0.25 + 1.75x < -1.75 + 2.25x$.

_____

10. Solve $\begin{cases} -7x + 5y = -5 \\ -9x + 5y = 5 \end{cases}$ by elimination.
Express your answer as an ordered pair.

_____

11. Write an exponential function to model a population of 390 animals that decreases at an annual rate of 11%. Then estimate the value of the function after 5 years (to the nearest whole number).

_____

Performance Task

12. Kristi rides her bike to school and has an odometer that measures the distance traveled so far. She subtracts this distance from the distance to the school and records the distance that remains. What are the intercepts of the function represented by the table? What do the intercepts represent?

Time traveled (min)	Distance remaining (ft)
0	5000
2	3750
4	2500
6	1250
8	0

_____

_____

_____

_____

_____

_____

_____

_____

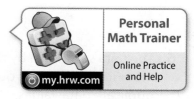
1. Aaron won $500 in an essay contest. He invests the money in an interest-earning account. The table shows how much money he has in the account. Find an appropriate model for the amount that Aaron will have in the account after t years. Then, use the model to predict approximately when Aaron will have $1000 in the account.

Aaron's Account	
Year	**Value**
1	$520.00
2	$540.80
3	$562.43
4	$584.93
5	$608.33

_____

_____

2. How could you translate the graph of $y = -x^2$ to produce the graph of $y = -x^2 - 4$?

_____

_____

_____

3. Use the number line to create a box-and-whisker plot of the data 7, 9, 11, 12, 13, 15, 12, 17, 18, 12, 9, 7, 12, 15, 18, 10.

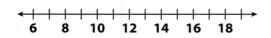

4. Explain whether $p + 4r^2$ will be positive or negative if p is positive. Is this always true?

_____

_____

_____

_____

_____

_____

_____

5. Look for a pattern in the data set. Which kind of model best describes the data; cubic, exponential, quadratic, or linear? Explain.

Population Growth of Bacteria	
Time (hours)	**Number of bacteria**
0	2000
1	5000
2	12,500
3	31,250
4	78,125

_____

_____

_____

_____

_____

_____

6. The data set shown by the box-and-whisker plot includes a single outlier and no duplicate data values.

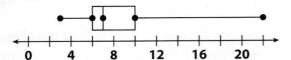

The outlier is removed. Select True or False for each statement.

A. The interquartile range increases.
○ True   ○ False

B. The interquartile range decreases.
○ True   ○ False

C. The range increases.
○ True   ○ False

D. The range decreases.
○ True   ○ False

7. Subtract. Simplify your answer.

$$\frac{x^2 + x + 6}{5x^3 + 8x^2 + 3x} - \frac{-4x^2 + 6}{5x^3 + 8x^2 + 3x}$$

_____

8. What is the coefficient of x in the expression $(5a)x - 17x^2 + 14a$?

_____

9. Consider the following box plots.

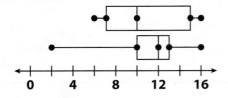

Which data set has the greater median? Which has the greater interquartile range?

_____

_____

_____

_____

Performance Task

10. The PGA tour is for male professional golfers; the LPGA tour is for female professional golfers. Earnings for the top 50 golfers on each tour in 2010 are modeled by the functions in the table and the graph. Compare earnings as a function of rank for the PGA and the LPGA.

PGA Earnings, 2010

Rank	Millions of $
1	4.95
10	3.53
20	2.87
30	2.41
40	1.88
50	1.61

_____

_____

_____

_____

_____

_____

_____

_____

_____

Numbers and Expressions

MODULE 1

Relationships Between Quantities

COMMON CORE N.Q.1, N.Q.3

MODULE 2

Exponents and Real Numbers

COMMON CORE N.RN.1, N.RN.2, N.RN.3

MODULE 3

Expressions

COMMON CORE N.Q.1, A.SSE.1, A.SSE.1a, A.SSE.1b, A.SSE.2

MATH IN CAREERS

Cave Geologist A cave geologist uses math from algebra and geometry up through higher-level math to study caves, find resources in them, or organize their excavation. He or she uses math for statistical analysis of the data he or she gathers.

If you're interested in a career in cave geology, you should study these mathematical subjects:
- Algebra
- Geometry
- Statistics
- Calculus

Research other careers that require the use of geometry and statistics.

ACTIVITY At the end of the unit, check out how **cave geologists** use math.

Prices at the Pump

GASOLINE

The Unit Project at the end of this unit will ask you to calculate and compare costs of gas at a gas station. You will collect data from a gasoline purchase. To successfully complete the Unit Project you'll need to master these skills:

- Understand precision and rounding.
- Understand and use real numbers.
- Write and evaluate expressions.

1. If the price showing on the pump is $3.799, what is the price per gallon to the nearest cent?

_____

2. If you bought 14.580 gallons, describe how the cost $55.39 was calculated.

_____

_____

_____

_____

Tracking Your Learning Progression

This unit addresses important Common Core Standards in the Critical Areas of writing and interpreting expressions and understanding and distinguishing between rational and irrational numbers.

Domain A.SSE Seeing Structure in Expressions

    Cluster Interpret the structure of expressions

The unit also supports additional standards.

Domain N.RN The Real Number System

    Cluster Use properties of rational and irrational numbers.

Relationships Between Quantities

ESSENTIAL QUESTION

How do you calculate when the numbers are measurements?

COMMON CORE STANDARDS

LESSON 1.1
Precision and Significant Digits
COMMON CORE N.Q.3

LESSON 1.2
Dimensional Analysis
COMMON CORE N.Q.1

Real-World Video

In order to function properly and safely, electronics must be manufactured to a high degree of accuracy. Material tolerances and component alignment must be precisely matched in order to not interfere with each other.

my.hrw.com

GO DIGITAL
my.hrw.com

my.hrw.com

Go digital with your write-in student edition, accessible on any device.

Math On the Spot

Scan with your smart phone to jump directly to the online edition, video tutor, and more.

Animated Math

Interactively explore key concepts to see how math works.

Personal Math Trainer

Get immediate feedback and help as you work through practice sets.

Are YOU Ready?

Complete these exercises to review skills you will need for this module.

Personal Math Trainer

Online Practice and Help

my.hrw.com

Rounding and Estimation

EXAMPLE Round 25.35 to the nearest whole number.

25.35   *Locate the digit to the right of the whole number.*

25   *Because it is not 5 or greater, do not round up the whole number.*

Round to the place value in parentheses.

1. 3.24 (tenths) _____   **2.** 0.51 (ones) _____   **3.** 35.8 (tens) _____

Compare and Order Real Numbers

EXAMPLE Compare 2.11 to 2.02.

2.11   *Align the numbers at the decimal point.*

2.02   *Compare each place value from left to right.*

2.11 > 2.02   *Because 1 > 0*

Compare. Write <, >, or =.

4. 3.01 ◯ 4   **5.** 80.2 ◯ 8.03   **6.** 9.001 ◯ 9.010

7. 1.11 ◯ 1.01   **8.** 3.2 ◯ 3.2   **9.** 0.154 ◯ 0.145

Measure with Customary and Metric Units

EXAMPLE Measure the line segment in inches and in centimeters.

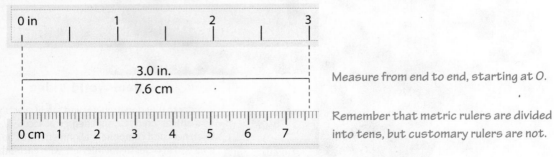

Measure from end to end, starting at 0.

Remember that metric rulers are divided into tens, but customary rulers are not.

Measure each item to the unit in parentheses.

10. the length of your foot (inches) _____

11. the width of your index finger (millimeters) _____

12. the height of your desk chair (feet) _____

Reading Start-Up

Vocabulary

Review Words

customary system of measurement (*sistema usual de medidas*)

decimal system (*sistema decimal*)

metric system of measurement (*sistema métrico de medidas*)

Preview Words

conversion factor

dimensional analysis

precision

significant digits

Visualize Vocabulary

Use the review words to complete the bubble map. You may put more than one word in each bubble.

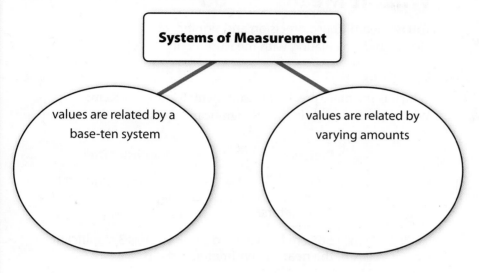

Systems of Measurement

values are related by a base-ten system

values are related by varying amounts

Understand Vocabulary

Complete the sentences using the preview words. You may refer to the module, the glossary, or a dictionary.

1. The level of detail of a measurement, determined by the unit of measure,

   is _____.

2. _____ are the digits used to express the precision of a measurement.

3. _____ is a method of determining the proper units in an algebraic solution.

4. The ratio of two equal quantities in different units is a _____.

Active Reading

Layered Book Before beginning the module, create a Layered Book for taking notes as you read a chapter. Use two flaps for each lesson from this module. As you study each lesson, write important ideas such as vocabulary, properties, and formulas under the appropriate flap.

COMMON CORE

GETTING READY FOR
Relationships Between Quantities

Understanding the standards and the vocabulary terms in the standards will help you know exactly what you are expected to learn in this module.

COMMON CORE N.Q.3

Choose a level of accuracy appropriate to limitations on measurement when reporting quantities.

What It Means to You

You will learn to use precision and significant digits when calculating with measurements.

EXAMPLE N.Q.3

Which is the more precise measurement: 5.7 m or 568 cm?
Which measurement has more significant digits: 5.7 m or 568 cm?

	Precision	Significant Digits
5.7 m	5.7 m = 570 cm is measured to nearest *ten* centimeters.	5.7 has 2 significant digits.
568 cm	568 cm is measured to the nearest centimeter.	568 has 3 significant digits.

568 cm is more precise because it is measured to a smaller unit.
568 cm has more significant digits.

COMMON CORE N.Q.1

Use units as a way to understand problems and to guide the solution of multi-step problems; choose and interpret units consistently in formulas; choose and interpret the scale and the origin in graphs and data displays.

Key Vocabulary

unit analysis/ dimensional analysis (*análisis dimensional*)
A practice of converting measurements and checking among computed measurements.

What It Means to You

You will learn to calculate with measurements to solve problems.

EXAMPLE N.Q.1

Li's car gets 40 miles per gallon of gas. At this rate, she can go 420 miles on a full tank. She has driven 245 miles on the current tank. How many gallons of gas are left in the tank?

STEP 1 Find the number of miles remaining.

$$420 \text{ mi} - 245 \text{ mi} = 175 \text{ mi}$$

STEP 2 Find the number of gallons.

$$x = 175 \text{ mi} \cdot \frac{\text{gal}}{40 \text{ mi}} = \frac{175 \text{ mi}}{40 \text{ mi}} \text{ gal} = 4.375 \text{ gal}$$

According to these measurements there are 4.375 gallons left in the tank.

Visit **my.hrw.com** to see all **Common Core Standards** unpacked.

my.hrw.com

LESSON 1.1 — Precision and Significant Digits

COMMON CORE **N.Q.3**

Choose a level of accuracy appropriate to limitations on measurement when reporting quantities.

Math On the Spot

my.hrw.com

ESSENTIAL QUESTION

How do you use significant digits when reporting the results of calculations involving measurements?

Precision

Precision is the level of detail of a measurement. More precise measurements are obtained by using instruments marked in smaller units. For example, a ruler marked in millimeters allows for more precise measurements than a ruler that is marked only in centimeters.

A measurement of 25 inches is more precise than a measurement of 2 feet because an inch is a smaller unit than a foot. Similarly, 9.2 kilograms is more precise than 9 kilograms because a tenth of a kilogram is a smaller unit than a kilogram.

EXAMPLE 1

COMMON CORE **N.Q.3**

Choose the more precise measurement in each pair.

A 5.7 m; 568 cm

5.7 m   Nearest tenth of a meter

568 cm   Nearest centimeter

A centimeter is a smaller unit than a tenth of a meter, so 568 centimeters is the more precise measurement.

B 31 oz; 31.32 oz

31 oz   Nearest ounce

31.32 oz   Nearest hundredth of an ounce

A hundredth of an ounce is smaller than an ounce, so 31.32 ounces is the more precise measurement.

Animated Math

my.hrw.com

REFLECT

1. **What if?** Suppose that Example 1A asked you to choose the most precise measurement from among 5.7 m, 5.683 m, and 568 cm. Now what would the answer be? Why?

_____

_____

_____

_____

YOUR TURN

Choose the more precise measurement in each pair.

2. 2 lb; 31 oz _____

3. 4 in.; 0 ft _____

4. 6.77 m; 676.5 cm _____

5. 1 mi.; 5,280 ft _____

EXPLORE ACTIVITY COMMON CORE N.Q.3

Exploring Effects of Precision on Calculations

A Measure the width of a book cover to the nearest centimeter.

Width of book cover: _____ cm

Measure the length of the book cover to the nearest tenth of a centimeter.

Length of book cover: _____ cm

B A measurement given to the nearest whole unit can actually range from 0.5 unit below the reported value up to, but not including, 0.5 unit above it. So, a length reported as 3 cm could actually be as low as 2.5 cm or as high as nearly 3.5 cm, as shown in the diagram. Similarly, a length reported as 3.5 cm could actually be as low as 3.45 cm or as high as nearly 3.55 cm. Find a range of values for the actual length and width of the book cover.

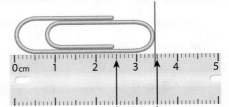

When measuring to the nearest centimeter, lengths in this range are rounded to 3 cm.

Minimum width = _____   Maximum width < _____

Minimum length = _____   Maximum length < _____

C Calculate the minimum and maximum possible areas of the book cover. Round your answers to the nearest square centimeter.

Minimum area = minimum width × minimum length

Maximum area < maximum width × maximum length

REFLECT

6. Give a range of possible values for a reported width of 21.0 cm.

_____

My Notes

Significant Digits

In the preceding Explore Activity, there was a wide range of possible values for the area of the book cover. This raises the question of how a calculated measurement, like an area, should be reported. Keeping track of **significant digits** is one way to resolve this dilemma. Significant digits are the digits in a measurement that carry meaning about the precision of the measurement.

Math On the Spot

⏻ my.hrw.com

Identifying Significant Digits	
Rule	**Examples**
All nonzero digits are significant.	37.85 has 4 significant digits. 622 has 3 significant digits.
Zeros between two other significant digits are significant.	806 has 3 significant digits. 0.9007 has 4 significant digits.
Zeros at the end of a number to the right of a decimal point are significant.	1.4000 has 5 significant digits. 0.270 has 3 significant digits.
Zeros to the left of the first nonzero digit in a decimal are *not* significant.	0.0070 has 2 significant digits. 0.01048 has 4 significant digits.
Zeros at the end of a number without a decimal point are assumed to be *not* significant.	404,500 has 4 significant digits. 12,000,000 has 2 significant digits.

Math Talk

Mathematical Practices

A student claimed that 0.045 m and 0.0045 m have the same number of significant digits. Do you agree or disagree? Why?

EXAMPLE 2 COMMON CORE N.Q.3

Determine the number of significant digits in the measurement 840.090 m.

STEP 1 Find all nonzero digits. These are significant digits.

840.090   *8, 4, and 9 are nonzero digits.*

STEP 2 Find zeros after the last nonzero digit and to the right of the decimal point. These are significant digits.

840.090   *The zero after the 9 in the hundredths place is significant.*

STEP 3 Find zeros between the significant digits found in the previous steps. These are significant digits.

840.090   *There are 2 zeros between the significant digits 4 and 9.*

STEP 4 Count all the significant digits you have found.

840.090   *All the digits in this number are significant.*

So, 840.090 m has 6 significant digits.

Determine the number of significant digits in each measurement.

7. 36,000 ft _____   **8.** 0.01 kg _____   **9.** 15.0 L _____

Operations with Significant Digits

When you perform calculations with measurements of differing precision, the number of significant digits in the solution may differ from the number of significant digits in the original measurements. Use the rules in this table to determine how many significant digits to include in the result of a calculation.

Rules for Significant Digits in Calculations	
Operation	**Rule**
Addition or Subtraction	The sum or difference must be rounded to the same place value as the last significant digit of the least precise measurement.
Multiplication or Division	The product or quotient must have no more significant digits than the least precise measurement.

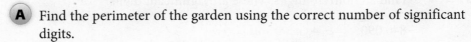

EXAMPLE 3   Real World   COMMON CORE N.Q.3

A rectangular garden plot measures 16 feet by 23.6 feet.

A Find the perimeter of the garden using the correct number of significant digits.

Perimeter = sum of side lengths
= 16 ft + 16 ft + 23.6 ft + 23.6 ft
= 79.2 ft

The least precise measurement is 16 ft. Its last significant digit is in the ones place. So round the sum to the ones place: 79 ft.

The perimeter is 79 feet.

B Find the area of the garden using the correct number of significant digits.

Area = width · length
= 16 ft · 23.6 ft
= 377.6 ft^2

The least precise measurement, 16 ft, has 2 significant digits, so round to a number containing 2 significant digits: 380 ft^2.

The area is 380 ft^2.

REFLECT

10. Justify Reasoning Why must the area have no more than 2 significant digits?

_____

_____

_____

_____

11. Critical Thinking Can the perimeter of a rectangular garden have more significant digits than the measures of its length or width have? Explain.

_____

_____

_____

12. Find the perimeter and area of a sandbox that has a width of 4.5 ft and a length of 3.45 ft. Write your answers using the correct number of significant

digits. _____

13. In chemistry class, Julio measured the mass and volume of an unknown substance in order to calculate its density. It had a mass of 23.92 g and a volume of 2.1 mL. Find the density of the substance in g/mL, using the

correct number of significant digits. _____

Personal Math Trainer

Online Practice and Help

🔄 my.hrw.com

Guided Practice

Choose the more precise measurement in each pair. Then state the minimum and maximum possible values for the more precise measurement. (Example 1 and Explore Activity)

1. 18 cm; 177 mm

_____

_____

2. 3 yd; 10 ft

_____

_____

3. 71 cm; 0.7 m

_____

_____

4. 1.5 ft; 19 in.

_____

_____

Determine the number of significant digits in each measurement. (Example 2)

5. 12,080 ft _____

6. 0.8 mL _____

7. 1.0065 km _____

A rectangular window has a length of 81.4 cm and a width of 38 cm. Use the correct number of significant digits to write each indicated measure. (Example 3)

8. Find the perimeter.

81.4 cm + 81.4 cm + 38 cm + 38 cm

The unrounded perimeter is _____ cm.

The least precise measurement is _____ cm.

Its last significant digit is in the _____ place.

Perimeter rounded to the _____ place:

_____ cm

9. Find the area.

81.4 cm × 38 cm

The unrounded area is _____ cm^2.

The least precise measurement is _____ cm.

It has _____ significant digits.

Area rounded to _____ significant

digits: _____ cm^2

10. A model car rolls down a 125.3 centimeter ramp, and continues to roll along the floor for 4.71 meters before it comes to a stop. The car's entire trip takes 2.4 seconds. Find the average speed of the car. Use the correct number of significant digits. (Example 3)

> Do not round your results before you are finished with the calculations.

STEP 1 Total distance = [ ] cm + [ ] m

= [ ] m + [ ] m = [ ] m

STEP 2 Speed = $\dfrac{\text{total distance}}{\text{time}}$ = $\dfrac{\boxed{}\ \text{m}}{\boxed{}\ \text{s}}$ = [ ] … m/s

The measurement with the fewest significant digits is _____ s,

with _____ significant digits. So rounding the speed to _____

significant digits is _____ m/s.

The car's average speed is _____.

11. How are significant digits related to calculations using measurements?

_____

_____

_____

1.1 Independent Practice

COMMON CORE N.Q.3

Write each measurement with the indicated number of significant digits.

12. 454.12 kg; 3 significant digits _____

13. 8.45 lb; 2 significant digits _____

14. 9.1 in.; 1 significant digit _____

Order each list of units from most precise to least precise.

15. centimeter, millimeter, decameter, meter, kilometer

_____

_____

16. feet, inches, miles, yards

_____

_____

17. pints, quarts, cups, gallons

_____

_____

18. **Analyze Relationships** How is the precision used in measuring the length and width of a rectangle related to the precision of the resulting area measurement?

_____

_____

_____

_____

Express each calculator result using the rules for significant digits.

19.

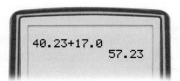
```
40.23+17.0
        57.23
```

_____

20.

```
40.23*17.0
       683.91
```

_____

21.

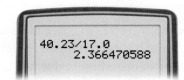
```
40.23/17.0
      2.366470588
```

_____

22.

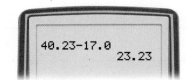
```
40.23-17.0
        23.23
```

_____

23. Write this sum to the correct number of significant digits:
34.01 m + 1940 m + 4.6 m ≈

_____

24. Measure the length and width of the pictured book to the nearest tenth of a centimeter. Then use the correct number of significant digits to write the perimeter and area of the book.

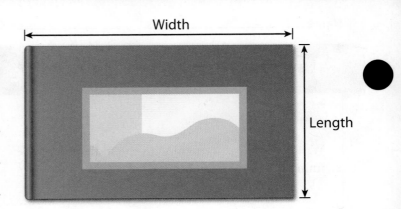

Width

Length

_____

_____

_____

H.O.T. FOCUS ON HIGHER ORDER THINKING

25. Justify Reasoning Yoshi is painting a large wall in the park. He measures the wall and finds that the dimensions are 4 m by 20 m. Yoshi has a can of paint that will cover an area of 81 m^2. Should he buy more paint? Explain?

_____

_____

_____

_____

_____

26. Make a Conjecture If two measurements have the same number of decimal places and the same number of significant digits, is it ever possible for the result of an operation performed using these measurements to have a different number of decimal places or significant digits than the original measurements? Explain.

_____

_____

_____

27. Explain the Error A student found that the side lengths of a square rug were 1.30 m. The student was asked to report the area using the correct number of significant digits. He wrote the area as 1.7 m^2. Explain the student's error.

_____

_____

28. Communicate Mathematical Ideas Consider the calculation 4.3 m $\div$ 16 s = 0.26875 m/s. Why is it important to use significant digits to round the answer?

_____

_____

_____

1.2 Dimensional Analysis

COMMON CORE N.Q.1

Use units as a way to understand problems and to guide the solution of multi-step problems; choose and interpret units consistently in formulas; choose and interpret the scale and the origin in graphs and data displays. *Also N.Q.3*

? ESSENTIAL QUESTION

How can you use dimensional analysis to convert measurements?

EXPLORE ACTIVITY   N.Q.1

Exploring Measurement Conversions

In the United States, the customary measurement system is used for everyday tasks such as finding the volume of a bottle or the length of a room. However, scientists throughout the world use the metric system of measurement. To convert between these two systems, you need to use equivalent measures such as those shown in the table.

Metric and Customary Measurements		
Measurement Type	**Metric unit**	**Customary equivalent**
Length	1 meter	3.28 ft
	1 centimeter	0.39 in.
Area	1 square meter	10.76 ft²
Volume	1 liter	0.26 gal
Mass/Weight	1 kilogram	2.2 lb

Use the equivalent measures given in the table to find the capacity of an 8-liter gas tank in gallons.

A From the table: 1 liter (L) = _____ gallons (gal)

B From the diagram, about how many liters are in

1 gallon? _____

C Will the number of gallons in an 8-liter gas tank be greater or less than 8?

Explain. _____

_____

_____

D To convert 8 liters to gallons, do you need to multiply or divide by the

conversion factor? _____

8 L = _____ gal

REFLECT

1. Analyze Relationships How would you convert from 8 gallons to liters?

_____

Converting Measurements

Dimensional analysis is a way of using units to help solve problems involving measurements. You can use dimensional analysis to convert units by setting up ratios of two equivalent measurements, such as $\frac{12 \text{ in.}}{1 \text{ ft}}$. These ratios are called **conversion factors**.

EXAMPLE 1

COMMON CORE N.Q.1

The body of a large adult male contains about 12 pints of blood. Use dimensional analysis to convert this quantity to liters. There are about 2.1 pints in a liter.

Identify the given unit and the unit you need to find. Use that information to set up your conversion factor. The given unit should be in the denominator of the conversion factor, so that it will cancel out when multiplied by the given measurement.

$$x \text{ liters} \approx 12 \text{ pt} \cdot \boxed{\textbf{conversion factor}}$$

$$\approx \frac{12 \ \cancel{\text{pt}}}{1} \cdot \frac{1 \text{ liter}}{2.1 \ \cancel{\text{pt}}} \qquad \textit{The pints in the denominator cancel with pints in the numerator.}$$

$$\approx \frac{12 \text{ liters}}{2.1}$$

$$\approx 5.7 \text{ liters}$$

The body of a large adult male contains approximately 5.7 liters of blood.

REFLECT

2. Explain the Error Elena wanted to convert 30 inches to centimeters. She multiplied 30 in. by $\frac{1 \text{ in}}{2.5 \text{ cm}}$ and got an answer of 12. What was her error?

_____

_____

_____

_____

_____

_____

 **YOUR TURN**

Use dimensional analysis to convert each measurement.

3. 3 feet ≈ _____ meters

4. 4 inches ≈ _____ yards

5. 12 kg ≈ _____ lb

6. 4 inches ≈ _____ centimeters

Converting Rates

Sometimes you will need to convert not just one measurement, but a ratio of measurements.

When working with a rate such as 50 miles per hour, you might need to know the rate in different units, such as meters per second. This requires two conversion factors: one to convert miles into meters, and one to convert hours into seconds.

EXAMPLE 2   COMMON CORE   N.Q.1, N.Q.3

A cyclist travels 105 kilometers in 4.2 hours. Use dimensional analysis to convert the cyclist's speed to miles per minute. Write your answer with the correct number of significant digits. Use 1 mi = 1.61 km.

STEP 1   Identify the rate given and the rate you need to find. Use that information to set up your conversion factors.

$$x \; \frac{\text{miles}}{\text{minute}} \approx \frac{105 \text{ km}}{4.2 \text{ hr}} \cdot \boxed{\textbf{conversion factor}} \cdot \boxed{\textbf{conversion factor}}$$

$$\approx \frac{105 \text{ km}}{4.2 \text{ hr}} \cdot \frac{1 \text{ mi}}{1.61 \text{ km}} \cdot \frac{1 \text{ hr}}{60 \text{ min}}$$

Set up conversion factors so that both km and hr units cancel.

$$\approx \frac{105 \text{ mi}}{4.2 \cdot 1.61 \cdot 60 \text{ min}}$$

$$\approx 0.2588 \text{ mi/min}$$

STEP 2   Determine the number of significant digits in each value: the distance, the time, and both conversion factors:

- 105 km has 3 significant figures.
- 4.2 hours has 2 significant figures.
- 1 mi/1.61 km has 3 significant figures.
- 1 hr/60 min is an exact conversion factor. Significant figures do not apply here, or to any conversion within a measurement system.

The value with the fewest significant digits is the time, 4.2 hr, with 2 significant digits. So the result should be rounded to 2 significant digits.

The cyclist travels approximately 0.26 miles per minute.

REFLECT

7. Communicate Mathematical Ideas Tell which of the following conversion factors are exact, and which are approximate: 1000 grams per kilogram, 0.26 gallon per liter, 12 inches per foot. Explain.

_____

_____

_____

My Notes

Personal Math Trainer

Online Practice and Help

ⓞ my.hrw.com

YOUR TURN

Use dimensional analysis to make each conversion.

8. A box of books has a mass of 4.10 kilograms for every meter of its height. Convert this ratio into pounds per foot.

_____

9. A go-kart travels 21 miles per hour. Convert this speed into feet per minute.

_____

10. A tortoise walks 52.0 feet per hour. Convert this speed into inches per minute.

_____

11. A pitcher throws a baseball 90.0 miles per hour. Convert this speed into feet per second.

_____

Math On the Spot

ⓞ my.hrw.com

Converting Areas

Dimensional analysis can also be used for converting areas. When converting areas, the conversion factor must be squared because area is expressed in square units.

EXAMPLE 3

COMMON CORE N.Q.1, N.Q.3

The area of a practice field is 45,100 ft². How large is the field in square meters? Write your answer with the correct number of significant digits. Use 1 m ≈ 3.28 ft.

Identify the given unit and the unit you need to find. Use that information to set up your conversion factor.

Math Talk

Mathematical Practices

When would you multiply by the cube of a conversion factor?

$$x \text{ m}^2 = 45{,}100 \text{ ft}^2 \cdot \boxed{\textbf{conversion factor}}$$

$$\approx \frac{45{,}100 \text{ ft}^2}{1} \cdot \left(\frac{1 \text{ m}}{3.28 \text{ ft}}\right)^2 \quad \text{Square the conversion factor to convert square units.}$$

$$\approx \frac{45{,}100 \text{ ft}^2}{1} \cdot \frac{1 \text{ m}^2}{10.7584 \text{ ft}^2} \quad \text{The ft}^2 \text{ in the numerator cancel the ft}^2 \text{ in the denominator.}$$

$$\approx \frac{45{,}100 \text{ m}^2}{10.7584}$$

$$\approx 4192.073 \text{ m}^2$$

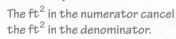

45,100 ft²

Because the given measure and the conversion factor both have 3 significant digits, the product should also be rounded to 3 significant digits. The area of the practice field is 4190 square meters.

YOUR TURN

Use dimensional analysis to make each conversion. Use the equivalent measures indicated.

12. The surface area of a swimming pool is 373 square feet. What is its surface area in square meters? (1 m = 3.28 ft) _____

13. A birthday card has an area of 29.1 square inches. What is its area in square centimeters? (1 in. = 2.54 cm) _____

14. A patio has an area of 9 square yards. What is its area in square inches? (1 yd = 36 in.) _____

Guided Practice

Use the diagrams to determine whether you need to multiply or divide by the indicated value to convert each measurement. (Explore Activity)

1. To convert 5 meters to feet, you need to _____ 5 meters by 3.28 feet per meter.

5 meters ≈ _____ feet

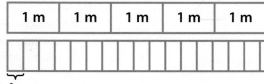

2. To convert 11 liters to gallons, you need to _____ 11 liters by 3.8 liters per gallon.

11 liters ≈ _____ gallons

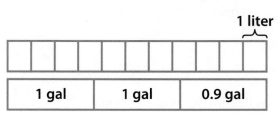

Set up the conversion factor needed for each conversion. Use the table of equivalent measures in the Explore Activity. (Example 1)

3. meters into feet

_____

4. gallons into liters

_____

5. pounds into kilograms

_____

6. A dripping faucet is wasting 0.5 mL of water every second. How many liters of water does it waste per week? Write your answer with the correct number of significant digits. (Example 2)

STEP 1 Identify equivalent measures. 1 L = _____ mL

1 wk = _____ days   1 day = _____ hr

1 hr = _____ min   1 min = _____ s

STEP 2 Set up conversion factors, cancel units, and calculate.

$$\frac{0.5\ mL}{1\ s} \cdot \frac{\boxed{}}{\boxed{}} \cdot \frac{\boxed{}}{\boxed{}} \cdot \frac{\boxed{}}{\boxed{}} \cdot \frac{\boxed{}}{\boxed{}} \cdot \frac{\boxed{}}{\boxed{}}$$

= _____ L/wk

The answer should have _____ significant digit(s),

so the final answer is _____ L/wk

7. If an area can be washed at a rate of 3100 cm²/minute, how many square inches can be washed per hour? Write your answer with the correct number of significant digits. (Examples 2 and 3)

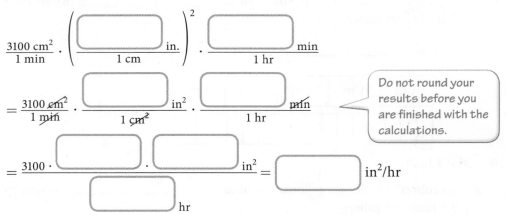

Do not round your results before you are finished with the calculations.

Because the given measure and conversion factor both have _____

significant digits, the equivalent rate is _____ square inches per hour.

? ESSENTIAL QUESTION CHECK-IN

8. How is dimensional analysis useful in calculations that involve measurements?

_____

_____

_____

© Houghton Mifflin Harcourt Publishing Company

1.2 Independent Practice

Personal Math Trainer

Online Practice and Help

my.hrw.com

COMMON CORE N.Q.1, N.Q.3

For Exercises 9–14, choose the conversion factor you need to multiply by to carry out each conversion.

A. $\frac{3.28 \text{ ft}}{1 \text{ m}}$ **B.** $\frac{0.39 \text{ in.}}{1 \text{ cm}}$ **C.** $\frac{2.2 \text{ lb}}{1 \text{ kg}}$

D. $\frac{1 \text{ cm}}{0.39 \text{ in.}}$ **E.** $\frac{1 \text{ kg}}{2.2 \text{ lb}}$ **F.** $\frac{1 \text{ m}}{3.28 \text{ ft}}$

9. feet to meters _____

10. meters to feet _____

11. inches to centimeters _____

12. centimeters to inches _____

13. kg to pounds _____

14. pounds to kg _____

Use dimensional analysis to make each conversion. Write your answer with the correct number of significant digits. Use the equivalent measures indicated.

15. A bedroom is 5.2 meters wide. Find its width in feet. (1 m ≈ 3.28 ft)

_____

16. A bag of rice weighs 3.18 pounds. Find its mass in kilograms.
(1 kg ≈ 2.2 lb)

_____

17. A giraffe can run about 14 meters per second. Find its speed in miles per hour.
(1 mi = 5280 ft; 1 m ≈ 3.28 ft)

_____

18. The cover of a photo album has an area of 97.5 square inches. Find its area in square centimeters. (1 cm ≈ 0.39 in.)

_____

19. A carpet costs $15 per square foot. (When calculating the price, any fraction of a square foot is counted as a whole square foot.) If the area you want to carpet is 19.7 square meters, how much will it cost to buy the carpet? (1 m ≈ 3.28 ft)

_____

20. Measure the length and width of the outer rectangle to the nearest tenth of a centimeter. Using the correct number of significant digits, write the perimeter in inches and the area in square inches.

Length to nearest tenth of cm:

_____

Width to nearest tenth of cm:

_____

Perimeter in inches:

_____

Area in square inches:

_____

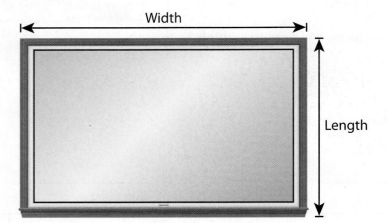

Width

Length

 **FOCUS ON HIGHER ORDER THINKING**

Work Area

21. **Represent Real-World Problems** Write a real-world scenario in which 12 fluid ounces would need to be converted into liters. Make the conversion, and write the converted measure with the correct number of significant digits. Use 1 fl oz = 0.0296 L.

_____

_____

_____

_____

22. **Analyze Relationships** When a measurement in inches is converted to centimeters, will the number of centimeters be greater than or less than the number of inches? Explain.

_____

_____

23. **Explain the Error** A student measured the area of a bulletin board as 2.1 m². To find its area in square feet, he multiplied 2.1 by 3.28, getting an answer of about 6.9 ft². Explain the student's error. What is the correct area in square feet?

_____

_____

_____

_____

Ready to Go On?

1.1 Precision and Significant Digits

Write each measurement with the indicated number of significant digits.

1. 982.1 m² (3) _____

2. 1.5244 kg (2) _____

Give the result of each operation with the correct number of significant digits.

3. 170.1 lb + 3.44 lb _____

4. 1.1 cm × 4.28 cm _____

5. A circle has a radius of 3.07 inches. Using the correct number of significant digits, find the circumference and area of the circle.

_____

1.2 Dimensional Analysis

6. Use dimensional analysis to convert 8 milliliters to fluid ounces.

Use 1 mL ≈ 0.034 fl oz. _____

Use the table of equivalent measures to answer each question.

7. A designer found the area of a wall to be 3.0 square yards. What is the area of the

wall in square meters? _____

Measurement type	Metric unit	Customary equivalent
Length	1 m	1.09 yards
Volume	1 L	2.11 pints
Mass/Weight	1 kg	2.20 lb

8. Will a stand that can hold up to 40 pounds support a 21-kilogram television? Explain.

_____

9. Scientist A dissolved 1.0 kilogram of salt in 3.0 liters of water. Scientist B dissolved 2.0 pounds of salt in 7.0 pints of water. Which scientist made a more concentrated salt solution? Explain.

_____

_____

? ESSENTIAL QUESTION

10. How are significant digits used in calculations with measurements?

_____

_____

_____

MODULE 1
MIXED REVIEW

Assessment Readiness

Personal Math Trainer

Online Practice and Help

my.hrw.com

1. Is each volume greater than 2.5 liters? Use 1 liter ≈ 0.26 gallon.

   Select Yes or No for expressions A–C.

   A. 0.5 gallon   ◯ Yes   ◯ No

   B. 3 quarts   ◯ Yes   ◯ No

   C. 5.5 pints   ◯ Yes   ◯ No

2. Choose True or False to tell if each measure has exactly four significant digits.

   A. 0.0025 millimeter   ◯ True   ◯ False

   B. 15.04 seconds   ◯ True   ◯ False

   C. 0.01225 gram   ◯ True   ◯ False

3. A silo is composed of a cylinder topped by a half-sphere. The height of the cylinder is 6.2 meters and the radius of both the cylinder and the half-sphere is 1.6 meters. Use 3.14 for π. Find the volumes of the half-sphere, the cylinder, and the entire silo to the nearest tenth. Explain how you found the volume of the silo.

4. A rectangular rug has a length of 231 centimeters and a width of 166 centimeters. What is the area of the rug in square meters? Explain how you determined the correct number of significant digits for your answer.

5. Christina swims 2400 feet in 16 minutes. Gloria swims 12 meters in 15 seconds. Whose average speed is faster? Explain. Use 1 meter ≈ 3.28 feet.

Exponents and Real Numbers

MODULE

2

COMMON CORE

COMMON CORE STANDARDS

LESSON 2.1
Radicals and Rational Exponents

COMMON CORE N.RN.1, N.RN.2

LESSON 2.2
Real Numbers

COMMON CORE N.RN.3

? ESSENTIAL QUESTION

What sets of numbers are included in the real numbers?

Real-World Video

Zoo managers must determine the amount of food needed for a healthy diet for the animals.

my.hrw.com

GO DIGITAL
my.hrw.com

my.hrw.com

Go digital with your write-in student edition, accessible on any device.

Math On the Spot

Scan with your smart phone to jump directly to the online edition, video tutor, and more.

Animated Math

Interactively explore key concepts to see how math works.

Personal Math Trainer

Get immediate feedback and help as you work through practice sets.

Are YOU Ready?

Complete these exercises to review skills you will need for this module.

Personal Math Trainer

Online Practice and Help

⟳ my.hrw.com

Exponents

EXAMPLE Write $(-5)^3$ as a multiplication of factors.
$(-5)(-5)(-5)$ *Write the base −5 times itself 3 times.*

EXAMPLE Write $21 \cdot 21 \cdot 21 \cdot 21 \cdot 21 \cdot 21$ using a base and an exponent.
21^6 *The base is 21 and the exponent is the number of factors 6.*

Write each expression as a multiplication of factors.

1. 4^2

2. $(-6)^4$

3. 12^1

_____

_____

_____

Write each expression using a base and an exponent.

4. $7 \cdot 7 \cdot 7 \cdot 7 \cdot 7$

5. $33 \cdot 33 \cdot 33 \cdot 33$

6. $(-2) \cdot (-2)$

_____

_____

_____

Evaluate Powers

EXAMPLE Evaluate $(-3)^4 - 6^2$.
$(-3)(-3)(-3)(-3) - 6 \cdot 6$ *Write as a multiplication of factors.*
$81 - 36$ *Simplify.*
45

Evaluate each expression.

7. $5^1 + (-9)^2$

8. $3^2 \cdot 2^3$

9. $(25)^0 - 5^3$

_____

_____

_____

Squares and Square Roots

EXAMPLE Find $\sqrt{49}$.
7 *Because $7 \cdot 7 = 49$, 7 is the square root of 49.*

Find each square root.

10. $\sqrt{16}$

11. $\sqrt{81}$

12. $\sqrt{10{,}000}$

_____

_____

_____

Reading Start-Up

Visualize Vocabulary

Fill in the missing information in the chart below.

Word	Definition	Example
exponent		$3^4 = 3 \cdot 3 \cdot 3 \cdot 3 = 81$ 4 is the exponent.
rational numbers	A number that can be written in the form b/a, where a and b are integers and $b \neq 0$	
	A real number that cannot be expressed as the ratio of two integers	$\pi, \sqrt{2}, e$

Vocabulary

Review Words

exponent *(exponente)*

rational numbers *(números racionales)*

irrational numbers *(números irracionales)*

Preview Words

radical expression

radicand

index

real numbers

closed

Understand Vocabulary

To become familiar with some of the vocabulary terms in the module, complete the following sentences using appropriate preview words. You may refer to the module, the glossary, or a dictionary.

1. The _____ consist of the rational numbers and the irrational numbers.

2. The _____ of a radical expression indicates which root to take of the _____.

Active Reading

Key-Term Fold Before beginning the module, create a Key-Term Fold Note to help you organize what you learn. Write a vocabulary term on each tab of the key-term fold. Under each tab, write the definition of the term and an example of the term.

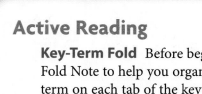

GETTING READY FOR
Exponents and Real Numbers
Understanding the standards and the vocabulary terms in the standards will help you know exactly what you are expected to learn in this module.

 N.RN.1

Explain how the definition of the meaning of rational exponents follows from extending the properties of integer exponents to those values, allowing for a notation for radicals in terms of rational exponents.

Key Vocabulary

radical *(radical)*
An indicated root of a quantity.

What It Means to You

You can rewrite expressions containing radicals as expressions with rational exponents and vice versa.

EXAMPLE N.RN.1

Rewrite $32^{\frac{1}{5}}$ as a radical and simplify.

Raising to the $\frac{1}{5}$ power is the same as taking the 5th root.

$$32^{\frac{1}{5}} = \sqrt[5]{32}$$
$$= \sqrt[5]{2^5}$$
$$= 2$$

N.RN.2

Rewrite expressions involving radicals and rational exponents using the properties of exponents.

Key Vocabulary

exponent *(exponente)*
The number that indicates how many times the base in a power is used as a factor.

What It Means to You

You can use the properties of exponents to rewrite and simplify radical expressions and expressions containing rational exponents.

EXAMPLE N.RN.2

Simplify $8^{\frac{5}{3}}$.

$$8^{\frac{5}{3}} = 8^{\frac{1}{3} \cdot 5}$$
$$= \left(8^{\frac{1}{3}}\right)^5$$
$$= \left(\sqrt[3]{8}\right)^5$$
$$= \left(\sqrt[3]{2^3}\right)^5$$
$$= 2^5 = 32$$

Visit **my.hrw.com** to see all **Common Core Standards** unpacked.

 my.hrw.com

LESSON 2.1 Radicals and Rational Exponents

COMMON CORE **N.RN.1**
Explain how the definition of the meaning of rational exponents follows from extending the properties of integer exponents to those values, allowing for a notation for radicals in terms of rational exponents. *Also N.RN.2*

ESSENTIAL QUESTION

How are radicals and rational exponents related?

EXPLORE ACTIVITY   COMMON CORE **N.RN.1**

Defining Rational Exponents

The **radical symbol** $\sqrt{}$ is used to indicate square roots. Roots other than square roots are indicated by using an index with the radical symbol. An expression that contains radicals is a **radical expression**.

Index $\rightarrow \sqrt[3]{125} \leftarrow$ Radicand

Complete the steps below to explore the relationship between radical expressions and rational exponents. Recall that $(a^m)^n = a^{mn}$.

A
$$\sqrt{4} = 4^k$$

STEP 1 $\left(\boxed{}\right)^2 = \left(\boxed{}\right)^2$ Square both sides of the equation.

STEP 2 $4^1 = 4^{2k}$ Power of a Power Property

STEP 3 $\boxed{} = \boxed{}$ If $b^m = b^n$, then $m = n$.

STEP 4 $\boxed{} = k$ Solve for k.

STEP 5 Substitute your value for k in the original equation: $\sqrt{4} = 4^{\boxed{}}$

B
$$\sqrt[3]{8} = 8^k$$

STEP 1 $\left(\boxed{}\right)^3 = \left(\boxed{}\right)^3$ Cube both sides of the equation.

STEP 2 $8^1 = 8^{3k}$ Power of a Power Property

STEP 3 $\boxed{} = \boxed{}$ If $b^m = b^n$, then $m = n$.

STEP 4 $\boxed{} = k$ Solve for k.

STEP 5 Substitute your value for k in the original equation: $\sqrt[3]{8} = 8^{\boxed{}}$

REFLECT

1. **Make a Conjecture** How can you write the square root or the cube root of a number n using an exponent?

_____

Simplifying Expressions with Rational Exponents

Definition of $b^{\frac{1}{n}}$	
General Rule	**Examples**
A number raised to the power of $\frac{1}{n}$ is equal to the nth root of that number: $$b^{\frac{1}{n}} = \sqrt[n]{b},$$ where $b \geq 0$ and n is an integer > 1.	$b^{\frac{1}{2}} = \sqrt{b}$ $\quad 25^{\frac{1}{2}} = \sqrt{25} = 5$ $b^{\frac{1}{3}} = \sqrt[3]{b}$ $\quad 8^{\frac{1}{3}} = \sqrt[3]{8} = 2$ $b^{\frac{1}{4}} = \sqrt[4]{b}$ $\quad 81^{\frac{1}{4}} = \sqrt[4]{81} = 3$

You can use the definition of $b^{\frac{1}{n}}$ to simplify expressions with rational exponents.

EXAMPLE 1   COMMON CORE N.RN.1, N.RN.2

Simplify each expression.

A $64^{\frac{1}{3}}$

$$64^{\frac{1}{3}} = \sqrt[3]{64} \qquad \text{Use the definition of } b^{\frac{1}{n}}.$$
$$= \sqrt[3]{4^3} \qquad \text{Rewrite the radicand as a cube.}$$
$$= 4$$

B $32^{\frac{1}{5}} - 81^{\frac{1}{2}}$

$$32^{\frac{1}{5}} - 81^{\frac{1}{2}} = \sqrt[5]{32} - \sqrt{81} \qquad \text{Use the definition of } b^{\frac{1}{n}}.$$
$$= \sqrt[5]{2^5} - \sqrt{9^2} \qquad \text{Rewrite both radicands as powers.}$$
$$= 2 - 9$$
$$= -7$$

REFLECT

2. Justify Reasoning Is $b^{\frac{1}{n}}$ where $b > 0$ and n is a positive integer always a positive integer? Justify your answer with reasoning or a counterexample.

_____

Personal Math Trainer

Online Practice and Help

my.hrw.com

> **YOUR TURN**

Simplify each expression.

3. $16^{\frac{1}{4}}$

_____

4. $125^{\frac{1}{3}}$

_____

5. $49^{\frac{1}{2}} + 27^{\frac{1}{3}}$

_____

6. $1000^{\frac{1}{3}} - 64^{\frac{1}{6}}$

_____

Using Properties with Rational Exponents

You can use properties of exponents to simplify expressions containing rational exponents. Recall the following properties of exponents.

Properties of Exponents

Property		Numerical example
Product of Powers Property	$a^m \cdot a^n = a^{m+n}$	$2^2 \cdot 2^3 = 2^5 = 32$
Quotient of Powers Property	$\dfrac{a^m}{a^n} = a^{m-n}, a \neq 0$	$\dfrac{2^5}{2^3} = 2^2 = 4$
Power of a Product Property	$(a \cdot b)^n = a^n \cdot b^n$	$(2 \cdot 3)^2 = 2^2 \cdot 3^2 = 36$
Power of a Quotient Property	$\left(\dfrac{a}{b}\right)^n = \dfrac{a^n}{b^n}, b \neq 0$	$\left(\dfrac{1}{2}\right)^2 = \dfrac{1^2}{2^2} = \dfrac{1}{4}$
Power of a Power Property	$\left(a^m\right)^n = a^{mn}$	$(2^2)^2 = 2^{2 \cdot 2} = 2^4 = 16$
Negative Exponent Property	$a^{-n} = \dfrac{1}{a^n}, a \neq 0$	$2^{-2} = \dfrac{1}{2^2} = \dfrac{1}{4}$

To simplify expressions with rational exponents use the properties of exponents and the definition of $b^{\frac{1}{n}}$.

EXAMPLE 2

COMMON CORE N.RN.1, N.RN.2

Simplify each expression.

A $125^{\frac{2}{3}}$

$$125^{\frac{2}{3}} = 125^{\frac{1}{3} \cdot 2}$$ Write the exponent as a product

$$= \left(125^{\frac{1}{3}}\right)^2$$ Power of a Power Property

$$= \left(\sqrt[3]{125}\right)^2$$ Definition of $b^{\frac{1}{n}}$

$$= \left(\sqrt[3]{5^3}\right)^2$$ $125 = 5^3$

$$= (5)^2$$

$$= 25$$

B $81^{\frac{3}{4}}$

$$81^{\frac{3}{4}} = 81^{\frac{1}{4} \cdot 3}$$ Write the exponent as a product

$$= \left(81^{\frac{1}{4}}\right)^3$$ Power of a Power Property

$$= \left(\sqrt[4]{81}\right)^3$$ Definition of $b^{\frac{1}{n}}$

$$= \left(\sqrt[4]{3^4}\right)^3$$ $81 = 3^4$

$$= (3)^3$$

$$= 27$$

Math Talk

Mathematical Practices

Why is it better to evaluate the radical expression first before raising to a power?

C $64^{\frac{3}{2}} = 64^{\frac{1}{2} \cdot 3}$ Write the exponent as a product

$= \left(64^{\frac{1}{2}}\right)^3$ Power of a Power Property

$= \left(\sqrt{64}\right)^3$ Definition of $b^{\frac{1}{n}}$

$= \left(\sqrt{8^2}\right)^3$ $64 = 8^2$

$= 8^3$

$= 512$

REFLECT

7. **Communicate Mathematical Ideas** Explain how you simplify any expression of the form $a^{\frac{m}{n}}$.

_____

_____

_____

_____

8. Example 2A showed how to simplify $125^{\frac{2}{3}}$. Is it possible to simplify $125^{\frac{3}{2}}$ using similar steps? Explain.

_____

_____

Personal Math Trainer

Online Practice and Help

⏻ my.hrw.com

YOUR TURN

Simplify each expression.

9. $8^{\frac{4}{3}}$

10. $25^{\frac{3}{2}}$

_____   _____

11. $1^{\frac{3}{5}}$

12. $1000^{\frac{4}{3}}$

_____   _____

Math On the Spot

⏻ my.hrw.com

Rational Exponents in Real-World Contexts

You can use rational exponents to describe relationships in real-world contexts, such as the relationship between an animal's required caloric intake and its mass.

EXAMPLE 3   COMMON CORE   N.RN.1, N.RN.2

The approximate number of Calories *C* that an animal needs each day is given by $C = 72m^{\frac{3}{4}}$, where *m* is the animal's mass in kilograms. Find the number of Calories that each animal needs daily.

A a Siberian tiger with a mass of 256 kilograms

$C = 72m^{\frac{3}{4}}$

$= 72(256)^{\frac{3}{4}}$ Substitute 256 for *m*.

$= 72(256)^{\frac{1}{4} \cdot 3}$ $\frac{3}{4} = \frac{1}{4} \cdot 3$

$= 72\left(256^{\frac{1}{4}}\right)^3$ Power of a Power Property

$= 72 \cdot \left(\sqrt[4]{256}\right)^3$ Definition of $b^{\frac{1}{n}}$

$= 72 \cdot \left(\sqrt[4]{4^4}\right)^3$ $256 = 4^4$

$= 72 \cdot (4)^3$

$= 72 \cdot 64$

$= 4608$

The tiger needs 4608 Calories per day.

B an Asian elephant with a mass of 4096 kilograms

$C = 72m^{\frac{3}{4}}$

$= 72(4096)^{\frac{3}{4}}$ Substitute 4096 for *m*.

$= 72(4096)^{\frac{1}{4} \cdot 3}$ $\frac{3}{4} = \frac{1}{4} \cdot 3$

$= 72\left(4096^{\frac{1}{4}}\right)^3$ Power of a Power Property

$= 72\left(\sqrt[4]{4096}\right)^3$ Definition of $b^{\frac{1}{n}}$

$= 72\left(\sqrt[4]{8^4}\right)^3$ $4096 = 8^4$

$= 72(8)^3$

$= 72 \cdot 512$

$= 36{,}864$

The elephant needs 36,864 Calories per day.

YOUR TURN

13. Use $C = 72m^{\frac{3}{4}}$ to find the number of Calories that an Australian shepherd dog with a mass of 16 kilograms needs each day.

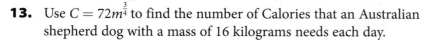

Personal Math Trainer

Online Practice and Help

⏻ my.hrw.com

Guided Practice

Simplify each expression. (Example 1)

1. $100^{\frac{1}{2}}$

_____

2. $1000^{\frac{1}{3}}$

_____

3. $32^{\frac{1}{5}}$

_____

4. $25^{\frac{1}{2}} + 81^{\frac{1}{4}}$

_____

5. $216^{\frac{1}{3}} - 27^{\frac{1}{3}}$

_____

6. $81^{\frac{1}{2}} - 64^{\frac{1}{6}}$

_____

Simplify each expression. (Example 2)

7. $1000^{\frac{2}{3}}$

_____

8. $27^{\frac{4}{3}}$

_____

9. $64^{\frac{5}{6}}$

_____

10. $64^{\frac{2}{3}}$

_____

11. $32^{\frac{3}{5}}$

_____

12. $128^{\frac{4}{7}}$

_____

13. Near Earth's surface, the time t required for an object to fall a distance d is given by $t = \frac{1}{4}d^{\frac{1}{2}}$, where t is measured in seconds and d is measured in feet. Find the time it will take an object to fall 100 feet. (Example 3)

_____

14. The relationship between the radius, r, of a sphere and its volume, V, is $r = \left(\frac{3V}{4\pi}\right)^{\frac{1}{3}}$. What is the radius of a sphere that has a volume of 36π cubic units? (Example 3)

_____

15. The relationship between the radius, r, of a sphere and its surface area, A, is $r = \left(\frac{A}{4\pi}\right)^{\frac{1}{2}}$. What is the radius of a sphere that has a surface area of 64π square units? (Example 3)

_____

ESSENTIAL QUESTION CHECK-IN

16. What does the denominator of a rational exponent represent?

_____

_____

_____

2.1 Independent Practice

Personal Math Trainer

Online Practice and Help

my.hrw.com

COMMON CORE N.RN.1, N.RN.2

Simplify each expression.

17. $25^{\frac{1}{2}} \cdot 81^{\frac{1}{4}}$ _____

18. $343^{\frac{1}{3}} \cdot 27^{\frac{1}{3}}$ _____

19. $125^{\frac{2}{3}} \div 25^{\frac{1}{2}}$ _____

20. $10{,}000^{\frac{1}{2}} \div 1000^{\frac{2}{3}}$ _____

21. $64^{\frac{2}{3}} - 81^{\frac{3}{4}} + 9^{\frac{3}{2}}$ _____

Use the equation $t = \frac{1}{4} d^{\frac{1}{2}}$, where t is the time in seconds and d is the distance in feet, to find the time it takes for an object to fall each distance.

22. 144 feet _____

23. 36 feet _____

24. 16 feet _____

25. 1 foot _____

26. Use the equation $t = \frac{1}{4} d^{\frac{1}{2}}$ to determine the height from which an object fell if it took 4 seconds to reach the ground.

_____

If a right triangle has legs of length a and b and hypotenuse of length c, then $c = (a^2 + b^2)^{\frac{1}{2}}$. Determine the length of the hypotenuse for a right triangle with the given leg lengths.

27. $a = 5$ in., $b = 12$ in.

_____

28. $a = 6$ cm, $b = 8$ cm

_____

29. $a = 12$ mi, $b = 9$ mi

_____

Write the name of the property that is demonstrated by each equation.

30. $\left(25^2\right)^{\frac{1}{2}} = 25$

_____

31. $3^7 = 3^3 \cdot 3^4$

_____

32. $3^{-2} = \frac{1}{9}$

_____

33. $\left(\frac{2}{3}\right)^3 = \frac{8}{27}$

_____

34. $2^2 \cdot 3^2 = (2 \cdot 3)^2$

_____

35. $\frac{3^7}{3^5} = 3^2$

_____

For each property, give an example that demonstrates the property. Do not use an example that has been shown in this lesson.

36. Power of a Power

_____

37. Power of a Product

_____

38. Negative Exponent

_____

39. Quotient of Powers

_____

40. Power of a Quotient

_____

Work Area

41. Communicate Mathematical Ideas Use the Commutative Property of Multiplication and the properties of rational exponents to rewrite $2.5^{\frac{m}{n}}$ as two equivalent radical expressions. Explain what these two expressions mean about different ways to evaluate $2.5^{\frac{m}{n}}$.

_____

_____

_____

_____

_____

42. Multiple Representations Show that a^6 can be written as a perfect square and as a perfect cube.

_____

_____

_____

43. Critical Thinking Use the Commutative Property of Multiplication and the Associative Property of Multiplication to show the Power of a Product Property $(a \cdot b)^n = a^n \cdot b^n$ is true.

_____

_____

_____

_____

_____

44. Critique Reasoning Jay said that by the Quotient of Powers property, $\frac{0^5}{0^2} = 0^{5-2} = 0^3 = 0$. Is this correct? Explain.

_____

_____

_____

COMMON CORE N.RN.3

Explain why the sum or product of two rational numbers is rational; that the sum of a rational number and an irrational number is irrational; and that the product of a nonzero rational number and an irrational number is irrational.

? ESSENTIAL QUESTION

What are the subsets and properties of real numbers?

EXPLORE ACTIVITY 1   COMMON CORE   Prep for N.RN.3

Understanding Real Numbers

Recall that a rational number can be expressed in the form $\frac{p}{q}$, where p and q are integers and $q \neq 0$. The decimal form of a rational number either terminates or repeats. For instance, $\frac{3}{4} = 0.75$ and $-\frac{5}{6} = -0.8333\ldots$.

An irrational number cannot be written as the quotient of two integers, and its decimal form is nonrepeating and nonterminating. Examples of irrational numbers include square roots of non-perfect squares and cube roots of non-perfect cubes. For instance, the decimal form of $\sqrt{3}$ is $1.7320508\ldots$, which neither repeats nor terminates.

Real numbers consist of all rational and irrational numbers.

The Venn diagram shows subsets of the set of real numbers. Each of the subsets includes one example of a real number belonging to that subset.

Classify each number by writing it in the most specific area of the diagram.

A -5

B 0

C $-\sqrt{10}$

D $-\frac{8}{17}$

E 8

F -12

G $\sqrt[3]{2}$

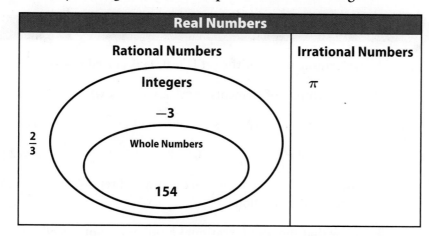

Animated Math
⏱ my.hrw.com

REFLECT

1. **Communicate Mathematical Ideas** How does the diagram show that all whole numbers are integers and that all integers are rational numbers?

_____

_____

_____

_____

Properties of Real Numbers

All real numbers have the following properties with respect to addition and multiplication.

Properties of Real Numbers	
Commutative Property of Addition	$a + b = b + a$
Associative Property of Addition	$(a + b) + c = a + (b + c)$
Additive Identity	The additive identity is 0, because $a + 0 = a$.
Additive Inverse	The additive inverse of a is $-a$, because $a + (-a) = 0$.
Commutative Property of Multiplication	$a \cdot b = b \cdot a$
Associative Property of Multiplication	$(a \cdot b) \cdot c = a \cdot (b \cdot c)$
Multiplicative Identity	The multiplicative identity is 1, because $1(a) = a$.
Multiplicative Inverse	The multiplicative inverse of a for $a \neq 0$ is $\frac{1}{a}$, because $a\left(\frac{1}{a}\right) = 1$.
Distributive Property	$a(b + c) = ab + ac$

A set of numbers is **closed** under an operation if the result of the operation on any two numbers in the set is also a number in that set.

EXAMPLE 1

COMMON CORE N.RN.3

A **Determine whether the set {−1, 0, 1} is closed under addition.**

Add each pair of elements in the set. Check whether each sum is in the set.

$-1 + (-1) = -2$ [✘] $\quad$ $-1 + 0 = -1$ ✔ $\quad$ $-1 + 1 = 0$ ✔

$0 + 0 = 0$ ✔ $\quad\quad\quad$ $0 + 1 = 1$ ✔ $\quad\quad$ $1 + 1 = 2$ [✘]

The sums −2 and 2 are not in the original set, so the set {−1, 0, 1} is not closed under addition.

B **Show that the set of irrational numbers is not closed under addition.**

Find two irrational numbers whose sum is not an irrational number.

$\sqrt{3} + (-\sqrt{3}) = 0$ $\quad\quad$ *0 is not irrational.*

The set of irrational numbers is not closed under addition.

REFLECT

2. Give an example that shows the set of integers is not closed under division.

_____

My Notes

3. Give an example that shows the set of irrational numbers is not closed under multiplication. _____

4. Communicate Mathematical Ideas Under which operations is the set of whole numbers closed? Not closed? Explain.

_____

_____

_____

_____

YOUR TURN

5. Is the set {–2, 0, 2} closed under addition? Explain.

_____

_____

6. Give an example that shows the set of irrational numbers is not closed under division. _____

Personal Math Trainer

Online Practice and Help

 my.hrw.com

EXPLORE ACTIVITY 2 COMMON CORE N.RN.3

Proving that Sets are Closed

The set of integers is closed under addition and multiplication. Complete Steps 1–5 to prove that the set of rational numbers is closed under addition. Begin with the definition of rational numbers a and b.

STEP 1 Let a and b be _____ numbers.

Then $a = \frac{p}{q}$ and $b = \frac{r}{s}$, where p, q, r, and s are integers and q and s are not 0.

$$a + b = \frac{p}{q} + \frac{r}{s}$$

STEP 2 Find a common denominator.

$$= \frac{p}{q}\left(\frac{s}{s}\right) + \frac{r}{s}\left(\frac{q}{q}\right)$$

STEP 3 Multiply.

$$= \frac{\boxed{}}{\boxed{}} + \frac{\boxed{}}{\boxed{}}$$

STEP 4 Add the numerators.

$$= \frac{\boxed{}}{\boxed{}}$$

© Houghton Mifflin Harcourt Publishing Company

EXPLORE ACTIVITY 2 *(cont'd)*

STEP 5 Conclusion: Because the numerator $pq + qr$ and the denominator qs are both ______________, $\frac{ps + qr}{qs}$ is a rational number.

Summary: For each set of numbers in rows A–D, enter "Yes" if the set of numbers is closed under the operation. Enter "No" if the set of numbers is not closed under the operation.

	Closure of Number Sets				
	Set	**Addition**	**Subtraction**	**Multiplication**	**Division**
A	Real numbers				
B	Irrational numbers				
C	Rational numbers				
D	Integers				

REFLECT

7. **Critique Reasoning** In Step 5, how do you know that $ps + qr$ and qs are integers?

____

____

8. **Critique Reasoning** How does $a + b = \frac{ps + qr}{qs}$ prove that the set of rational numbers is closed under addition?

____

____

____

____

9. **Draw Conclusions** Given that the set of rational numbers is closed under addition, how can you prove that the set of rational numbers is closed under subtraction?

____

____

____

____

N.RN.3

Complete Steps 1–8 to prove that the sum of an irrational number and a rational number is irrational.

STEP 1 Let a be an irrational number and let b be a rational number.

Then $b = \frac{r}{s}$, where r and s are _____ and $s \neq 0$.

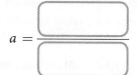 This proof is called a "proof by contradiction." This is when an assumption is made at the beginning, and if the logical outcome is false, then the assumption must be false.

STEP 2 The sum $a + b$ must be either rational or irrational. Assume that the sum $a + b$ is rational.

Then $a + b = \boxed{}$, where p and q are _____ and $q \neq 0$.

$$a + b = \frac{p}{q}$$

STEP 3 Subtract b from each side. $a + b - \boxed{} = \frac{p}{q} - \boxed{}$

STEP 4 Substitute $\frac{r}{s}$ for b. $a = \boxed{}$

STEP 5 Find a common denominator. $a = \frac{p}{q}\left(\frac{s}{s}\right) - \frac{r}{s}\left(\frac{q}{q}\right)$

STEP 6 Multiply. $a = \dfrac{\boxed{}}{\boxed{}} - \dfrac{\boxed{}}{\boxed{}}$

STEP 7 Subtract. $a = \dfrac{\boxed{}}{\boxed{}}$

STEP 8 Because $ps - qr$ and qs are integers with $qs \neq 0$, $\frac{ps - qr}{qs}$ is a rational number. But in Step 1, a is given as an irrational number. This means

that the assumption that _____

was incorrect. So the sum of an irrational number and a rational

number must be _____.

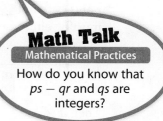 **Math Talk**

Mathematical Practices

How do you know that $ps - qr$ and qs are integers?

REFLECT

10. Justify Reasoning Use the results of Explore Activity 3 to justify that the difference of an irrational number and a rational number is irrational.

_____

_____

_____

Tell whether each set is closed under the given operation. (Example 1)

1. {0, 1}; multiplication _____   **2.** {0, 1}; addition _____   **3.** even integers; addition _____

4. Prove that the set of rational numbers is closed under multiplication. (Explore Activity 2)

Let a and b be rational numbers.

Then $a = \frac{p}{q}$ and $b = \frac{r}{s}$, where $p, q, r,$ and s are integers and q and s are not 0.

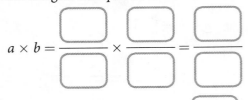

$a \times b = \dfrac{\boxed{}}{\boxed{}} \times \dfrac{\boxed{}}{\boxed{}} = \dfrac{\boxed{}}{\boxed{}}$

Because pr and qs are integers, $\dfrac{\boxed{}}{\boxed{}}$ is a rational number. So the set of rational numbers is closed under multiplication.

5. Prove that the product of an irrational number and a nonzero rational number is irrational. (Explore Activity 3)

Let a be an irrational number and let b be a nonzero rational number.

Then $b = \frac{r}{s}$, where r and s are integers and

r and s are not _____. The product $a \times b$ must be either rational or irrational. Assume

that _____

Then $a \times b = \dfrac{\boxed{}}{\boxed{}}$, where p and q are integers and q is not 0.

$a \times b = \dfrac{\boxed{}}{\boxed{}}$

$a \times b \cdot \frac{1}{b} = \dfrac{\boxed{}}{\boxed{}} \cdot \frac{1}{b} \; (b \neq 0)$

$a = \dfrac{\boxed{}}{\boxed{}} \div \boxed{} \quad (b \neq 0)$

$a = \dfrac{\boxed{}}{\boxed{}} \div \dfrac{\boxed{}}{\boxed{}} \quad (s \neq 0)$

$a = \dfrac{\boxed{}}{\boxed{}} \times \dfrac{\boxed{}}{\boxed{}} \quad (r \neq 0)$

$a = \dfrac{\boxed{}}{\boxed{}}$

The final statement shows that a is a _____ number. But a is given as an irrational number.

Therefore the assumption _____

_____ is incorrect. So the product of an irrational number and a nonzero

rational number is _____.

 ESSENTIAL QUESTION CHECK-IN

6. How do you show that a set of numbers is not closed under a given operation?

_____

2.2 Independent Practice

COMMON CORE   N.RN.3

Personal Math Trainer

my.hrw.com   Online Practice and Help

Write two numbers that fit each description. If there is no such number, write *none*.

7. negative integer

_____

8. negative rational number that is not an integer

_____

9. irrational integer

_____

10. negative irrational number

_____

Using *whole*, *integer*, *rational*, and *irrational*, name all the subsets of the real numbers to which each number belongs.

11. 15

_____

12. $\frac{\pi}{2}$

_____

13. $-\frac{\sqrt[3]{8}}{2}$

_____

14. $\frac{\sqrt{36}}{\sqrt{9}}$

_____

15. $\frac{0}{\sqrt{7}}$

_____

Tell whether the set is closed under the operation. If it is not closed, justify your answer using an example.

16. negative integers; subtraction

_____

17. negative integers; addition

_____

18. rational numbers; division

_____

19. {−2, 0, 2}; multiplication

_____

20. negative integers; multiplication

_____

21. negative rational numbers; multiplication

_____

22. positive irrational numbers; addition

_____

23. positive irrational numbers; multiplication

_____

24. {0, 1, 10}; multiplication

_____

25. even integers; subtraction

_____

Work Area

26. Make a Conjecture Consider any subset of the real numbers that consists only of negative numbers. What can you conclude about whether the set is closed under multiplication? Explain.

_____

_____

_____

_____

27. Communicate Mathematical Ideas Explain why any real number must be either a rational number or an irrational number.

_____

_____

_____

_____

_____

28. Explain the Error Drew wanted to determine whether the set of rational numbers is closed under division. He concluded that the set is not closed because $\frac{3}{4} \div \frac{1}{4} = 3$, and 3 is an integer. Explain Drew's error.

_____

_____

29. Draw Conclusions Consider a set of numbers that is closed under addition and subtraction. What number must be in such a set? Explain.

_____

_____

_____

30. Draw Conclusions Consider a set of numbers that is closed under multiplication and division. What number must be in such a set? Explain.

_____

_____

_____

Ready to Go On?

2.1 Radicals and Rational Exponents

Simplify each expression.

1. $36^{\frac{1}{2}} - 81^{\frac{1}{4}}$ _____

2. $64^{\frac{2}{3}} \div 32^{\frac{2}{5}}$ _____

3. $1^{\frac{5}{3}} \div 16^{\frac{3}{2}}$ _____

4. $125^{\frac{2}{3}} - 64^{\frac{1}{2}} - 8^{\frac{2}{3}}$ _____

Write the name of the property that is demonstrated by each equation.

5. $4^3 \cdot 5^3 = 20^3$

6. $4^3 \cdot 4^5 = 4^8$

_____

_____

7. Use the equation $t = \frac{1}{2}a^{\frac{3}{2}}$ to find the value of t when $a = 16$.

_____

2.2 Real Numbers

Using *whole*, *integer*, *rational*, and *irrational*, name all the subsets of the real numbers to which each number belongs.

8. $\sqrt{5}$ _____

9. $\sqrt{9}$ _____

_____

_____

10. -6 _____

11. $\sqrt[3]{\frac{1}{8}}$ _____

_____

_____

Tell whether the set is closed under the operation. If it is not closed, justify your answer using an example.

12. irrational numbers; addition

13. rational numbers; multiplication

_____

_____

? ESSENTIAL QUESTION

14. What sets of numbers are included in the real numbers?

_____

_____

_____

_____

MODULE 2
MIXED REVIEW

Assessment Readiness

Personal Math Trainer

Online Practice and Help

my.hrw.com

1. Evaluate each expression. Is the expression equal to 4?

   Select Yes or No for expressions A–C.

   A. $8^{\frac{2}{3}}$ ○ Yes   ○ No

   B. $16^{\frac{1}{2}}$ ○ Yes   ○ No

   C. $2^{\frac{1}{3}} \cdot 2^6$ ○ Yes   ○ No

2. Consider the set of real numbers.

   Choose True or False for each statement.

   A. The product of a nonzero rational number and an irrational number is always irrational.   ○ True   ○ False

   B. The product of two rational numbers is always rational.   ○ True   ○ False

   C. The product of two irrational numbers is always irrational.   ○ True   ○ False

3. Simplify the expression $\dfrac{3^{\frac{1}{3}}}{-3^{\frac{1}{3}}}$. Explain how the expression and its simplified form

   show that the set of irrational numbers is not closed under division.

4. A recipe calls for 150 grams of cheddar cheese. Dylan has 4.0 ounces of cheddar cheese. How many more ounces will he need for the recipe? Explain how you solved this problem. Use 1 kilogram ≈ 2.2 pounds.

Equations in Two Variables and Functions

ESSENTIAL QUESTION

What is a function and how can a function be represented?

Real-World Video

A function can be thought of as an industrial machine: only accepting of certain predefined inputs, performing a series of operations on what it's been fed, and delivering an output dependent on the initial input.

 my.hrw.com

GO DIGITAL
my.hrw.com

 my.hrw.com
Go digital with your write-in student edition, accessible on any device.

 Math On the Spot
Scan with your smart phone to jump directly to the online edition, video tutor, and more.

 Animated Math
Interactively explore key concepts to see how math works.

Personal Math Trainer
Get immediate feedback and help as you work through practice sets.

Are YOU Ready?

Complete these exercises to review skills you will need for this module.

Ordered Pairs

EXAMPLE (−3, 1)
Start at (0, 0).
Move 3 units to the left.   *The x-coordinate is −3.*
Move 1 unit up.   *The y-coordinate is 1.*

Graph each point on the coordinate plane.

1. (−2, 4)

2. (0, −5)

3. (1, −3)

4. (4, 2)

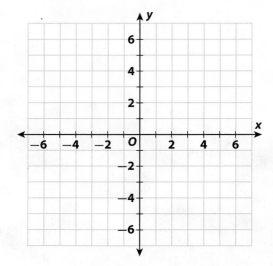

Evaluate Expressions

EXAMPLE Evaluate $4x$ for $x = 3$
$4x = 4(3)$ *Substitute 3 for x.*
$\quad = 12$ *Simplify.*

Evaluate each expression for $x = -2, -1, 0, 1,$ and 2.

5. $-2x - 1$

6. $x - 1$

7. $x^2 - 1$

8. $3(x + 2)$

9. $15 - 5x$

10. $2x^2 - 5x + 2$

11. $\frac{1}{2}x + \frac{3}{2}$

12. $0.05x - 0.1$

13. $(x + 1)^3 - x$

Reading Start-Up

Visualize Vocabulary

Complete the graphic using each review word.

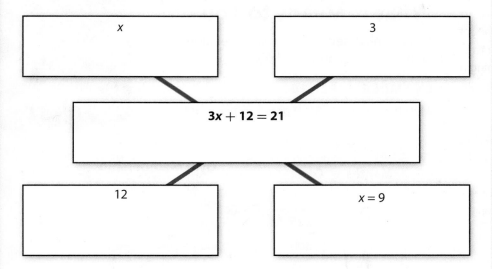

Understand Vocabulary

To become familiar with some of the vocabulary in the module, answer each question. You may refer to the module or the glossary.

1. You've learned what a solution of an equation in one variable is. What do you think the **solution of an equation in two variables** is?

   _____

   _____

2. Have you heard the term **sequence** before? What do you think it may mean mathematically?

   _____

   _____

© Houghton Mifflin Harcourt Publishing Company

Active Reading

Key-Term Fold Before beginning the module, create a Key-Term Fold Note to help you organize what you learn. Write a vocabulary term on each tab of the key-term fold. Under each tab, write the definition of the term and an example of the term.

Vocabulary

Review Words

coefficient (*coeficiente*)

constant (*constante*)

equation in one variable (*ecuación en una variable*)

solution of an equation in one variable (*solución de una ecuación en una variable*)

variable (*variable*)

Preview Words

equation in two variables

solution of an equation in two variables

function

domain

range

function notation

sequence

term

explicit rule

recursive rule

Equations in Two Variables and Functions

Understanding the standards and the vocabulary terms in the standards will help you know exactly what you are expected to learn in this module.

 **A.REI.10**

Understand that the graph of an equation in two variables is the set of all its solutions plotted in the coordinate plane, often forming a curve (which could be a line).

Key Vocabulary

solution of an equation in two variables *(solución de una ecuación en dos variables)*
An ordered pair of values for the variables making the equation true.

What It Means to You

You can represent mathematical relationships with words, equations, tables, and graphs.

EXAMPLE A.REI.10

Membership costs $150 plus $75 per month.

$$y = 75x + 150$$

Months	Cost ($)
0	150
1	225
2	300
3	375
4	450

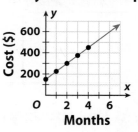

Gym Membership

COMMON CORE F.IF.1

Understand that a function from one set (called the domain) to another set (called the range) assigns to each element of the domain exactly one element of the range. If f is a function and x is an element of its domain, then $f(x)$ denotes the output of f corresponding to the input x. The graph of f is the graph of the equation $y = f(x)$.

Key Vocabulary

domain *(dominio)*
The set of all possible input values of a function.

range *(recorrido o rango)*
The set of all possible output values of a function.

What It Means to You

A function model guarantees that for any input value, you will get a unique output value.

EXAMPLE F.IF.1

Categorize each of the following as a function or not a function.

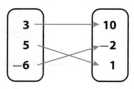

A function: each input number in the left box is matched with exactly one output number in the right box.

$\{(0, 3), (2, -1), (0, 0)\}$

Not a function: the input 0 is matched to two outputs (3 and 0).

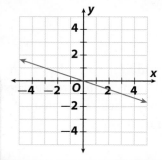

A function: each input (x-value) is matched with exactly one output (y-value).

Equations in Two Variables

COMMON CORE **A.REI.10**
Understand that the graph of an equation in two variables is the set of all its solutions plotted in the coordinate plane, often forming a curve (which could be a line).

Math On the Spot
⏻ my.hrw.com

? ESSENTIAL QUESTION

What is the relationship between the solutions of an equation in two variables and its graph?

Solutions of Equations in Two Variables

Equations in one variable usually have one solution. **Equations in two variables** usually have infinitely many solutions.

A **solution of an equation in two variables** x and y is any ordered pair (x, y) that makes the equation true. To determine whether an ordered pair (x, y) is a solution of an equation, substitute the values of x and y into the equation.

EXAMPLE 1

COMMON CORE **A.REI.10**

Tell whether each ordered pair is a solution of the given equation.

A $3x + 5y = 15$; $(8, 1)$

$$3(8) + 5(1) \overset{?}{=} 15 \qquad \text{Substitute.}$$
$$24 + 5 \overset{?}{=} 15 \qquad \text{Simplify.}$$
$$29 \neq 15$$

$(8, 1)$ is NOT a solution of $3x + 5y = 15$.

> **Math Talk**
> Mathematical Practices
>
> What do you know about the point $(0, 3)$ and its relationship to the graph of $3x + 5y = 15$?

B $3x + 5y = 15$; $(0, 3)$

$$3(0) + 5(3) \overset{?}{=} 15 \qquad \text{Substitute.}$$
$$0 + 15 \overset{?}{=} 15 \qquad \text{Simplify.}$$
$$15 = 15$$

$(0, 3)$ is a solution of $3x + 5y = 15$.

My Notes

C $x^2 - y = 23$; $(-5, 2)$

$$(-5)^2 - 2 \overset{?}{=} 23 \qquad \text{Substitute.}$$
$$25 - 2 \overset{?}{=} 23 \qquad \text{Simplify.}$$
$$23 = 23$$

> Remember that squaring a negative number results in a positive number: $(-5)^2$ means $(-5)(-5)$, which is positive 25.

$(-5, 2)$ is a solution of $x^2 - y = 23$.

D $x^2 - y = 23$; $(5, 2)$

$$(5)^2 - 2 \overset{?}{=} 23 \qquad \text{Substitute.}$$
$$25 - 2 \overset{?}{=} 23 \qquad \text{Simplify.}$$
$$23 = 23$$

$(5, 2)$ is a solution of $x^2 - y = 23$.

YOUR TURN

Tell whether each ordered pair is a solution of the given equation.

1. $x - 2y = 3$; $(5, 2)$ _____

2. $x - 2y = 3$; $(9, 3)$ _____

3. $2(x + 1)^2 + 3y = 15$; $(0, 5)$ _____

4. $2(x + 1)^2 + 3y = 15$; $(1, -1)$ _____

EXPLORE ACTIVITY   **COMMON CORE** A.REI.10

Exploring the Graph of an Equation

A Complete the table of values to find solutions of the equation $x + y = 5$.

x	y	(x, y)
−2		
0		
1		
3		
5		
7		

B Plot the ordered pairs on a coordinate grid.

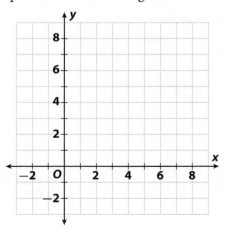

REFLECT

5. **Look for a Pattern** The plotted points are some of the solutions of the equation. What appears to be true about them?

_____

_____

Graphing Solutions of a Two-Variable Equation

An equation and a graph of its solutions can model a real-world situation. By reasoning about the quantities in the situation, you can determine the real-world meaning of each ordered pair.

Math On the Spot
⏻ my.hrw.com

EXAMPLE 2 COMMON CORE A.REI.10

The equation $y = 25{,}000x$ describes the average number of species y that become extinct in x years. Graph the solutions of the equation.

STEP 1 Create a table of values for the equation $y = 25{,}000x$. Choose several nonnegative values of x to find the corresponding values of y.

> *x* represents years, so the values must be nonnegative.

x	y = 25,000x	(x, y)
0	y = 25,000(0)	(0, 0)
2	y = 25,000(2)	(2, 50,000)
4	y = 25,000(4)	(4, 100,000)
6	y = 25,000(6)	(6, 150,000)

STEP 2 Plot the ordered pairs on a graph. Draw the line that passes through the points and contains all the solutions of the equation.

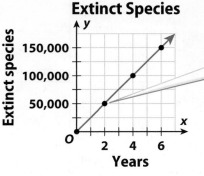

Extinct Species

> The x-value 2 represents 2 years. The y-value 50,000 represents the number of species that have become extinct in that amount of time.

My Notes

YOUR TURN

6. Mark wants to have a laser tag party. The cost of the party, y, can be modeled by the equation $y = 20x + 15$, where x is the number of guests. Complete the table and graph the equation.

x	y = 20x + 15	(x, y)
3	y = 20(3) + 15	(3, 75)
5	y = 20( ) + 15	( )
7	y =	( )
8	y =	( )

Cost of Party

Personal Math Trainer
Online Practice and Help
⏻ my.hrw.com

Tell whether each ordered pair is a solution of $6x - 3y = 24$. (Example 1)

1. (5, 1)

$6(\boxed{}) - 3(\boxed{}) \overset{?}{=} 24$

$\boxed{} - \boxed{} \overset{?}{=} 24$

$\boxed{} \overset{?}{=} 24$

(5, 1) | is / is not | a solution.

2. (0, −8)

$6(\boxed{}) - 3(\boxed{}) \overset{?}{=} 24$

$\boxed{} - \boxed{} \overset{?}{=} 24$

$\boxed{} \overset{?}{=} 24$

(0, −8) | is / is not | a solution.

Tell whether the ordered pair is a solution of the equation. (Example 1)

3. $2x + y^2 = 10$; (3, 2)

_____

4. $\frac{1}{2}x - 4y = 4$; $(10, \frac{1}{2})$

_____

5. $x^2 + y^2 = 2$; (0, 1)

_____

6. Complete the table of values and graph the ordered pairs to find solutions of the equation $4x - 6 = y$. (Explore Activity and Example 2)

x	4x − 6 = y	(x, y)
	4( ) − 6 = y	
	4( ) − 6 = y	
	4( ) − 6 = y	
	4( ) − 6 = y	
	4( ) − 6 = y	

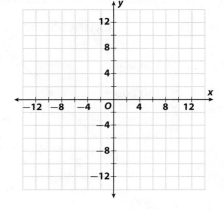

7. Kelly is saving money to buy a concert ticket. Her savings y for x days can be represented by the equation $y = x + 10$. Graph the solutions of the equation. (Example 2)

Savings

ESSENTIAL QUESTION CHECK-IN

8. How does a graph show solutions of a linear equation?

_____

_____

5.1 Independent Practice

 COMMON CORE **A.REI.10**

Tell whether each ordered pair is a solution of the equation. Justify your answers.

9. $-5x + 2y = 4$; $(4, 8)$

_____

_____

10. $2x - 7y = 1$; $(11, 3)$

_____

_____

11. $\frac{1}{3}x - 2y = 7$; $(9, -2)$

_____

_____

12. a. Complete the table for the equation $-2x + y = 3$. Then draw the graph.

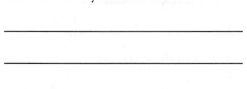

x	y

b. Using the graph, locate another solution of the equation. Explain how you can check to see if you are correct.

_____

_____

_____

13. Multiple Representations Trish can run the 200-meter dash in 25 seconds. The equation $8x + y = 200$ gives the distance y that Trish has left to run x seconds after the start of the race. The graph of this relationship is shown.

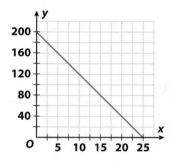

a. Identify three points on the graph and write their coordinates below.

_____

_____

b. Choose one of the ordered pairs and explain what the values mean.

_____

_____

_____

c. Select one ordered pair. Show that the ordered pair is a solution of $8x + y = 200$.

_____

_____

d. Select a point not on the line. Show that the ordered pair represented by this point is not a solution of the equation $8x + y = 200$.

_____

_____

14. Alex is making a rectangular wall hanging from fabric scraps. He has 36 inches of trim to go around the outside border, and he wants to use all of the trim. Let x represent the width of the wall hanging and let y represent the length. The solutions of the equation $2x + 2y = 36$ give the possible dimensions of Alex's wall hanging. Complete the table and graph the solutions.

x	y	(x, y)
2		
4		
6		
8		
10		

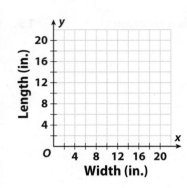

15. Represent Real-World Problems A family swimming pool holds 60 m³ of water. It loses 0.18 m³ of water to evaporation each day. This situation can be represented by the equation $y + 0.18x = 60$. Find an ordered pair solution of the equation and explain its real-world meaning.

_____

_____

 **FOCUS ON HIGHER ORDER THINKING**

Work Area

16. Justify Reasoning Jackie wants to earn $250 this summer by babysitting and dog walking. She earns $20 each time she babysits and $15 each time she walks dogs. This situation can be represented by the equation $20x + 15y = 250$. Use the equation to determine whether or not Jackie will earn $250 if she babysits 8 times and walks dogs 6 times. Justify your answer.

_____

_____

17. Critique Reasoning Max is asked to find 15 solutions of a linear equation. How could Max use a graph to help him find these solutions?

_____

_____

_____

18. Explain the Error Chanasia thinks that (3, 2) is a solution of the equation $5y + 10x = 35$ because $5(3) + 10(2) = 35$. Explain her error.

_____

_____

Representing Functions

COMMON CORE **F.IF.1**
Understand that a function from one set (called the domain) to another set (called the range) assigns to each element of the domain exactly one element of the range. If *f* is a function and *x* is an element of its domain, then *f(x)* denotes the output of *f* corresponding to the input *x*. The graph of *f* is the graph of the equation $y = f(x)$. Also *F.IF.2, F.IF.5, A.REI.11*

? ESSENTIAL QUESTION

How do you represent functions?

Understanding Functions

A **function** is a set of ordered pairs in which each value in the *domain* is paired with exactly one value in the *range*. The *x*-values are the **domain** of the function and the *y*-values are the **range** of the function. Functions can be expressed as tables, ordered pairs, graphs, equations, and mapping diagrams.

Math On the Spot
⊙ my.hrw.com

EXAMPLE 1   COMMON CORE   F.IF.1, F.IF.2, F.IF.5, A.REI.11

A fund-raising program awards $30 for first place, $20 for second place, $10 for third place, and $5 for fourth place. This function can be written as ordered pairs: $\{(1, 30), (2, 20), (3, 10), (4, 5)\}$. Express this function as a table, a graph, and a mapping diagram.

Table	Ranking	Prize in dollars	Write each *x*-value under "Ranking" and the corresponding *y*-value next to it, under "Prize, in Dollars".
	1	30	
	2	20	
	3	10	
	4	5	

Graph	**Fund Raising Prizes**	Plot each ordered pair represented in the table on the graph.

| Mapping diagram | Ranking → Prize, in Dollars: 1 → 30, 2 → 20, 3 → 10, 4 → 5 | Write each *x*-value in the region labeled "Ranking" and every *y*-value in the region labeled "Prize, in Dollars". Use arrows to connect each *x*-value to the corresponding *y*-value. |

© Houghton Mifflin Harcourt Publishing Company

REFLECT

1. The domain of the function in Example 1 is {1, 2, 3, 4}. What is the range?

YOUR TURN

2. Suppose each prize for the fundraiser was doubled. Complete the table, graph, and mapping diagram to show the new prize system.

Ranking	Prize, in Dollars
	60
	40
3	
4	

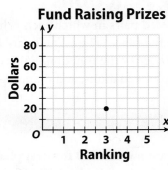

Fund Raising Prizes

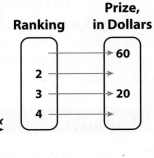

Ranking → **Prize, in Dollars**

Representing Functions with Equations

Another way to represent a function is with an equation in two variables, like $y = 2x + 8$. The x-value is the input for the function, and after performing one or more operations to the x-value, the output is the y-value.

Since not every equation in two variables is a function, we use function notation to describe functions. To write an equation in two variables using function notation, replace y with $f(x)$, which is read "f of x". In function notation, the equation $y = 2x + 8$ is written as $f(x) = 2x + 8$.

EXAMPLE 2 *Real World*   COMMON CORE A.REI.10

The number of dollars Julio earns for working x hours can be represented by the function $f(x) = 9x$. Graph this function.

STEP 1 Make a table of values. Choose values for x, and substitute them into the function to find the corresponding y-values.

x	$f(x) = 9x$	(x, y)
0	$f(0) = 9(0)$ $= 0$	$(0, 0)$
1	$f(1) = 9(1)$ $= 9$	$(1, 9)$
2	$f(2) = 9(2)$ $= 18$	$(2, 18)$
3	$f(3) = 9(3)$ $= 27$	$(3, 27)$

Remember that $y = f(x)$.

STEP 2 Graph the function by plotting the ordered pairs. Draw a line through the points to represent all the *x*-values you could have chosen and their corresponding *y*-values.

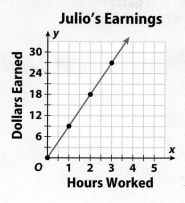

Julio's Earnings

REFLECT

3. **Explain the Error** Julio looks at the graph in Example 2 and concludes that the domain for the function is {0, 1, 2, 3}. Explain his error.

_____

_____

_____

YOUR TURN

4. The cost for *x* gallons of heating oil can be represented by the function $f(x) = 4x + 6$. Graph this function.

x	f(x) = 4x + 6	(x, y)
0	f(0) =	
2	f(2) =	
3	f(3) =	
5	f(5) =	

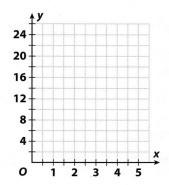

Personal Math Trainer

Online Practice and Help

⊙ my.hrw.com

Math On the Spot

⏻ my.hrw.com

Equality of Functions

When dealing with two different functions, you can use letters other than *f* to name the function, like the two functions $f(x) = 3x + 2$ and $g(x) = -x + 10$. The function $g(x)$ is read "*g* of *x*". You can find values that satisfy both functions by using properties of equality or by graphing.

EXAMPLE 3

COMMON CORE   A.REI.11

Given the functions $f(x) = 3x + 2$ and $g(x) = -x + 10$, find the value of *x* for which $f(x) = g(x)$.

Method 1   Set the function rules equal to each other. Then solve the equation.

> Solving this equation will give you the value of *x* when the *y*-values are equal to each other.

$3x + 2 = -x + 10$

$\dfrac{+x \qquad +x}{4x + 2 = \qquad 10}$ Add *x* to both sides.

$4x + 2 = 10$

$\dfrac{-2 \quad -2}{4x \quad = 8}$ Subtract 2 from both sides.

$4x = 8$

$\dfrac{4x}{4} = \dfrac{8}{4}$ Divide both sides by 4.

$x = 2$

So $f(x) = g(x)$ when $x = 2$.

Math Talk

Mathematical Practices

In this example, can there be more than one value of *x* such that $f(x) = g(x)$?

Method 2   Create tables to find a set of ordered pairs for each function. Then compare the ordered pairs to determine the value of *x* where the two functions have the same value.

x	$f(x) = 3x + 2$	(x, y)
0	$f(0) = 2$	$(0, 2)$
1	$f(1) = 5$	$(1, 5)$
2	$f(2) = 8$	$(2, 8)$
3	$f(3) = 11$	$(3, 11)$

> If the solution of the equation is not an integer, it may not be in your table. In that case, you can use the tables to find an approximate answer.

x	$g(x) = -x + 10$	(x, y)
0	$g(0) = 10$	$(0, 10)$
1	$g(1) = 9$	$(1, 9)$
2	$g(2) = 8$	$(2, 8)$
3	$g(3) = 7$	$(3, 7)$

$f(x)$ and $g(x)$ have the same value when $x = 2$.

Method 3 Generate ordered pairs for each function. Then use the ordered pairs to graph the functions and identify where the lines intersect. You can use the ordered pairs from the tables in Method 2.

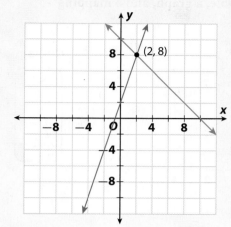

$f(x) = 3x + 2$

$g(x) = -x + 10$

> You can check your answer by substituting 2 for x in both function rules. If $f(x)$ and $g(x)$ are equal, the answer is correct.

The x-coordinate at the point of intersection is 2, so $f(x) = g(x)$ when $x = 2$.

REFLECT

5. In Example 3, $f(x) = g(x)$ when $x = 2$. Describe two ways to find the y-coordinate when $f(x) = g(x)$.

_____

_____

_____

6. **Analyze Relationships** What does the y-coordinate of the point of intersection represent?

_____

_____

7. **What If?** Given two functions m and n, is it possible for there to be no value of x that makes $m(x) = n(x)$? Can all real numbers make $m(x) = n(x)$? Explain.

_____

_____

_____

My Notes

YOUR TURN

8. Given the functions $f(x) = 4x - 2$ and $g(x) = 2x + 4$, find the value of x for which $f(x) = g(x)$. _____

Personal Math Trainer

Online Practice and Help

⊙ my.hrw.com

Express the function $\{(0, -1), (1, 1), (3, 5)\}$ as a table, a graph, and a mapping diagram. (Example 1)

1.

Domain	Range

2.

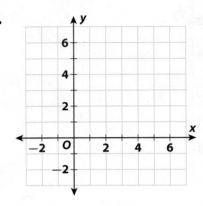

3.

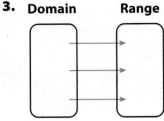

4. Complete the table for the function $f(x) = 2x - 4$. Then draw the graph. (Example 2)

x	$f(x) = 2x - 4$	(x, y)
−2	$f(-2) = 2(-2) - 4 =$	$(-2, -8)$
0	$f(0) = 2(\quad) - 4 =$	$(0, \quad)$
2	$f(2) = 2(\quad) - 4 =$	$(\quad, \quad)$
4	$f(4) = 2(\quad) - 4 =$	$(\quad, \quad)$

Given the functions $f(x) = -2x + 4$ and $g(x) = 2x - 8$, find the value of x for which $f(x) = g(x)$. (Example 3)

5. Set the function rules equal to each other.

Step 1:

$-2x + 4 = 2x - 8$

$+2x \qquad \boxed{}$

$\overline{\qquad\qquad}$

$4 = 4x - 8$

Step 2:

$4 = 4x - 8$

$+8 = \quad + 8$

$\overline{\qquad\qquad}$

$12 = \boxed{}$

Step 3:

$\dfrac{12}{\boxed{}} = \dfrac{4x}{\boxed{}}$

$\boxed{} = x$

The x-coordinate at the point of intersection is _____.

So $f(x) = g(x)$ when $x =$ _____.

6. Graph the functions.

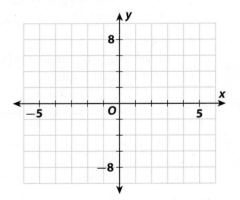

? ESSENTIAL QUESTION CHECK-IN

7. How do you represent functions? _____

_____

5.2 Independent Practice

Personal Math Trainer

Online Practice and Help

my.hrw.com

COMMON CORE F.IF.1, F.IF.2, F.IF.5, A.REI.11

For 8–10, tell whether each pairing of numbers describes a function. If so, identify the domain and the range. If not, explain why.

8. Each whole number from 0 to 9 is paired with its opposite.

_____

_____

_____

9. $(36, 6)$, $(49, 7)$, $(64, 8)$, $(36, -6)$, $(49, -7)$, $(64, -8)$ _____

_____

10. Each even number from 2 to 10 is paired with half the number.

_____

_____

11. **Multiple Representations** Neal has a $5 gift card for music downloads. Each song costs $1 to download. The amount of money left on the card, in dollars, can be represented by the function $f(x) = 5 - x$, where x is the number of downloaded songs.

a. Use the function to complete the table.

x	0				5
f(x)					

b. Graph the function.

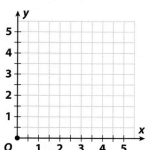

c. Identify the domain and range of the function.

_____

_____

d. **Explain the Error** Neal decided to connect the points on his graph. Explain Neal's error.

_____

_____

_____

_____

_____

_____

12. Sam is trying to lose weight, and George is trying to gain weight. Sam's weight in pounds can be represented by the function $f(x) = 240 - 2x$, where x is the number of weeks since Sam started losing weight. George's weight in pounds can be represented by the function $g(x) = 180 + 4x$, where x is the number of weeks since George starting gaining weight.

a. What is the x-value when $f(x) = g(x)$?

_____

b. When $f(x) = g(x)$, what does the x-value represent?

_____

_____

_____

c. When Sam and George weigh the same, what will their weight be?

_____

13. Represent Real-World Problems Jasmine has $15 dollars and saves $2.50 every month. Radha has $0 and saves $3.50 every month. Jasmine's savings after x months can be represented by the function $f(x) = 2.5x + 15$. Radha's savings after x months can be represented by the function $g(x) = 3.5x$.

a. After how many months will they both have the same amount in savings? Find the values of x for which $f(x) = g(x)$.

_____

b. Explain how to check your work.

_____

c. Explain what the graph of the two functions would look like.

_____

_____

H.O.T. FOCUS ON HIGHER ORDER THINKING

14. Critical Thinking Can a linear function be continuous but *not* have a domain and range of all real numbers? Justify your answer.

_____

_____

15. Justify Reasoning Fred's weekly earnings for mowing lawns can be represented by the function $f(x) = 45x - 40$, and George's weekly earnings for delivering papers can be represented by the function $g(x) = 85x - 110$. Fred says that after 3 weeks they will have earned the same amount. Determine whether Fred is correct. Explain.

_____

_____

_____

16. Communicate Mathematical Ideas The whole numbers from 10 to 12 are paired with their factors. Explain why this pairing of numbers does *not* describe a function.

_____

_____

_____

_____

COMMON CORE F.IF.3
Recognize that sequences are functions, sometimes defined recursively, whose domain is a subset of the integers. *Also* *F.BF.1, F.BF.1a, F.BF.2*

ESSENTIAL QUESTION

How are sequences and functions related?

EXPLORE ACTIVITY COMMON CORE F.IF.3

Understanding Sequences

A go-cart racing track charges $7 for a go-cart license and $2 per lap. If you list the charges for 1 lap, 2 laps, 3 laps, and so on, in order, the list forms a sequence of numbers:

9, 11, 13, 15, …

A **sequence** is a list of numbers in a specific order. Each element in a sequence is called a **term**. In a sequence, each term has a position number. In the sequence 9, 11, 13, 15, …, the second term is 11, so its position number is 2.

A The total cost (term) of riding a go-cart for different numbers of laps (position) is shown below. Complete the table.

Position number, n	1	2		4		6		8	Domain
Term of the sequence, $f(n)$	9	11	13		17				Range

B You can use the term and position number of a sequence to write a function. Using function notation, $f(2) = 11$ indicates that the second term is 11. Use the table to complete the following statements:

$f(1) =$ _____, $f(4) =$ _____

$f(8) =$ _____, $f($_____$) = 13$

REFLECT

1. Explain how to find the missing values in the table in the Explore Activity.

_____

_____

2. Describe the domain of the function in the Explore Activity.

_____

3. The go-cart racing track records the number of gallons of gas they have at the beginning of each day. The numbers form the following sequence: 25, 21, 17... Predict the next term in the sequence. Justify your answer.

_____

Using an Explicit Rule to Generate a Sequence

An **explicit rule** for a sequence defines the *n*th term as a function of *n*. Explicit rules can be used to find any specific term in a sequence without finding any of the previous terms.

EXAMPLE 1

COMMON CORE F.IF.3

My Notes

A Find the first four terms of the sequence defined by the explicit rule $f(n) = n^2 + 1$. Assume that the domain of the function is the set of whole numbers greater than 0.

Make a table and substitute values for *n*.

n	$f(n) = n^2 + 1$	f(n)
1	$f(1) = (1)^2 + 1 = 1 + 1 = 2$	2
2	$f(2) = (2)^2 + 1 = 4 + 1 = 5$	5
3	$f(3) = (3)^2 + 1 = 9 + 1 = 10$	10
4	$f(4) = (4)^2 + 1 = 16 + 1 = 17$	17

The first four terms are 2, 5, 10, 17.

B Find the 20th term of the sequence defined by the explicit rule $f(n) = n^2 + 1$. Assume that the domain of the function is the set of whole numbers greater than 0.

$$f(20) = (20)^2 + 1 \qquad \text{Substitute 20 for } n.$$

$$= 400 + 1$$

$$= 401$$

The 20th term in the sequence is 401.

REFLECT

4. Explain how to find the 6th term of the sequence defined by the explicit rule $f(n) = 3n - 2$. Assume that the domain of the function is the set of whole numbers greater than 0.

_____

_____

5. The number 121 is a term of the sequence defined by the explicit rule $f(n) = 3n - 2$. Assume that the domain of the function is the set of whole numbers greater than 0. Which term in the sequence is 121? Justify your answer.

_____

_____

6. Write the first 4 terms of the sequence defined by the explicit rule $f(n) = 3n + 1$. Assume that the domain of the function is the set of whole numbers greater than 0.

n	$f(n) = 3n + 1$	$f(n)$
1	$f(1) = 3(1) + 1$	
2		
3		
4		

The first four terms of the sequence are _____

7. What is the 15th term of the sequence defined by the explicit rule $f(n) = n^2 + n$? Assume that the domain of the function is the set of whole

numbers greater than 0. _____

8. What is the 8th term of the sequence defined by the explicit rule $f(n) = 2n^2 + 6$? Assume that the domain of the function is the set of whole

numbers greater than 0. _____

Using a Recursive Rule to Generate a Sequence

A **recursive rule** for a sequence defines the nth term by relating it to one or more previous terms. Unlike an explicit rule, a recursive rule cannot be used to find a specific term directly. To find a specific term's value, you need to know the value of one or more of the previous terms. The following is an example of a recursive rule:

$f(1) = 4$

$f(n) = f(n - 1) + 10$ for each whole number n greater than 1.

This rule means that after the first term of the sequence, every term $f(n)$ is the sum of the previous term $f(n - 1)$ and 10. The function table below shows the first 4 terms of the sequence.

Math On the Spot

my.hrw.com

n		$f(n)$
1	1st term	4
2	1st term + 10	$4 + 10 = 14$
3	2nd term + 10	$14 + 10 = 24$
4	3rd term + 10	$24 + 10 = 34$

EXAMPLE 2

COMMON CORE   F.IF.3

Write the first 4 terms of the sequence defined by the recursive rule below.

$$f(1) = 3$$

$$f(n) = f(n-1) + 2 \text{ for each whole number } n \text{ greater than 1.}$$

My Notes

STEP 1   Identify the domain of the function and the first term of the sequence. Describe the recursive rule.

The domain of the function is the set of whole numbers greater than 0.

The first term of the sequence is 3, and the recursive rule is adding 2 to each term to find the next term.

STEP 2   Create a table to find the first 4 terms in the sequence. Use 2, 3, and 4 as values for n.

n	$f(n) = f(n-1) + 2$	$f(n)$
1	1st term	3
2	$f(2) = f(2-1) + 2$ $= f(1) + 2$ $= 3 + 2$	5
3	$f(3) = f(3-1) + 2$ $= f(2) + 2$ $= 5 + 2$	7
4	$f(4) = f(4-1) + 2$ $= f(3) + 2$ $= 7 + 2$	9

Math Talk

Mathematical Practices

Describe how to find the 12th term of the sequence.

The first four terms of the sequence are 3, 5, 7, 9.

REFLECT

9. Suppose you want to find the 50th term of a sequence. Would you rather use a recursive rule or an explicit rule? Explain your reasoning.

_____

_____

_____

Personal Math Trainer

Online Practice and Help

⏻ my.hrw.com

YOUR TURN

10. Write the first 8 terms of the sequence with $f(1) = 37$ and $f(n) = f(n-1) - 3$ for each whole number greater than 1.

_____

Use the table to complete the statements. (Explore Activity)

1. $f(4) =$ _____

2. $f(7) =$ _____

n	1	2	3	4	...	7
$f(n)$	5	8	11	?	...	?

Write the first four terms of each sequence. Assume that the domain of the function is the set of whole numbers greater than 0. (Example 1)

3. $f(n) = (n-1)^2$

n	$f(n) = (n-1)^2$	$f(n)$
1	$(1-1)^2$	0
2	$(2-1)^2$	
3	$(\quad -1)^2$	
4	$(\quad -1)^2$	

4. $f(n) = 2n - 2$

n	$f(n) = 2n-2$	$f(n)$
1	$2(\quad) - 2$	
2		
3		
4		

5. $f(n) = \frac{1}{2}n + 3$

n	$f(n)$
1	
2	
3	
4	

Use the explicit rule to find the 25th term of each sequence. Assume that the domain of each function is the set of whole numbers greater than 0. (Example 1)

6. $f(n) = \frac{1}{2}n + 3$

$f(25) = \frac{1}{2} \boxed{} + 3 = \boxed{}$

7. $f(n) = \frac{n-3}{11}$

$f(25) = \dfrac{\boxed{} - 3}{11} = \boxed{}$

8. Complete the table to find the first 4 terms of the sequence with $f(1) = 2$ and $f(n) = f(n-1) + 6$ for each whole number greater than 1. (Example 2)

The first 4 terms of the sequence are

_____

n	$f(n) = f(n-1) + 6$	$f(n)$
1	1st term	2
2	$f(2-1) + 6 = f(1) + 6$ $+ 6 =$	
3		
4		

? ESSENTIAL QUESTION CHECK-IN

9. Why is a sequence a function?

_____

_____

_____

5.3 Independent Practice

Personal Math Trainer

Online Practice and Help

my.hrw.com

 COMMON CORE F.IF.3

For 10–19, assume that the domain of each function is the set of whole numbers greater than 0. Write the first four terms of each sequence.

10. $f(n) = \sqrt{n-1}$

_____

11. $f(n) = 2n(n+1)$

_____

12. $f(1) = 16$ and $f(n) = \frac{1}{2} \cdot f(n-1)$ for each whole number greater than 1

_____

13. $f(1) = 1$ and $f(n) = 2 \cdot f(n-1) + 1$ for each whole number greater than 1

_____

14. $f(n) = 1.5n + 6$

_____

15. $f(1) = 6.2$ and $f(n) = 20 - 2 \cdot f(n-1)$ for each whole number greater than 1

_____

Write the 12th term of each sequence.

16. $f(n) = \frac{5}{n}$

_____

17. $f(1) = 181$ and $f(n) = f(n-1) - 17$ for each whole number greater than 1

_____

18. $f(1) = 3.5$ and $f(n) = f(n-1) + 1.5$ for each whole number greater than 1

_____

19. $f(1) = 1$ and $f(n) = 2 \cdot f(n-1)$ for each whole number greater than 1

_____

20. Represent Real-World Problems A movie rental club charges $4.95 for membership and $18.95 for each month of subscription.

a. Complete the table to represent the fees paid over the first three months.

n	$f(n) = 18.95n + 4.95$

b. What would $f(0) = 4.95$ represent?

_____

c. What would the cost be for a year's membership? _____

d. If the first month were free, what would be the total cost of a yearly membership?

_____

e. Determine an explicit rule for the total fees paid to the movie rental club if the first month were free.

_____

21. Jessica had $150 in her savings account on the first Sunday of November. Beginning that week, she saved $35 each week.

a. Write a recursive rule that describes how much money Jessika had in her savings account at the end of n weeks.

_____

_____

b. How much money will Jessika have in her savings account at the end of 6 weeks? _____

22. Copper Creek Pizza is having a special. If you order a large pizza for the regular price of $17, you can order any number of additional large pizzas for $8.50 each.

a. Complete the table to show the cost of ordering up to 4 large pizzas.

Number of Large Pizzas	1	2	3	4
Total Cost				

b. Write an explicit and a recursive rule for the cost of placing an order for n large pizzas. _____

_____

c. What is the cost of placing an order for 20 large pizzas? _____

d. Five people each make an order for 3 large pizzas. How much money would they have saved if they placed one order for 15 pizzas? Explain.

_____

_____

23. The 5th term in a sequence is 25, and each term is 3 less than the previous term. Write an explicit rule and a recursive rule to describe the sequence.

_____

_____

24. An amusement park charges $12 for one round of mini-golf and a reduced fee for each additional round played. Tom paid $47 for 6 rounds of mini-golf.

a. What is the price per round for additional rounds of mini-golf?

_____

b. Write an explicit and a recursive rule for the cost of playing n rounds of mini-golf. _____

_____

c. What is the cost of playing 9 rounds of mini-golf? _____

25. **Represent Real-World Problems** Carrie borrowed money interest-free to pay for a car repair. She is repaying the loan in equal monthly payments. The table shows the loan balance at the end of each month, after she makes the payment.

Monthly payment number	n	1	2	3	4
Loan balance ($)	$f(n)$	840	720	600	480

a. After 6 months, how much will Carrie have left to repay? _____

b. How many months will it take Carrie to pay off the loan? _____

26. Kendall is stacking boxes that are 7.5 inches tall.

    a. Explain how to find the height (in inches) of the stack of boxes after Kendall adds the nth box.

    _____

    b. A sequence is defined by the rule $f(n) =$ the height (in inches) of n boxes.

    What is the fourth term of the sequence? _____

H.O.T.   **FOCUS ON HIGHER ORDER THINKING**

27. The explicit rule for a sequence is $f(n) = 1.25(n - 1) + 6.25$. Determine the recursive rule for the same sequence.

_____

28. The recursive rule for a sequence is $f(1) = 8\frac{1}{2}$, $f(n) = f(n - 1) - \frac{1}{2}$. Determine the explicit rule for the same sequence.

_____

29. **Analyze Relationships** Determine an explicit rule and a recursive rule to describe the following sequence.

2, 4, 6, 8, ...

_____

_____

_____

30. **Explain the Error** Shane is trying to find the 5th term of a sequence where $f(1) = 4$ and $f(n) = 2 \cdot f(n - 1) + 1$ for each whole number greater than 1. He reasons that he can find the 5th term by calculating $(4 \times 2 \times 2 \times 2 \times 2) + 1$. Explain Shane's error.

_____

_____

_____

_____

31. Write a recursive rule for a sequence where every term is the same.

_____

_____

_____

Ready to Go On?

Personal
Math Trainer

Online Practice
and Help

my.hrw.com

141

5.1 Equations in Two Variables

Complete the table of values to find solutions of the equation
$-x + y = 5$. Then graph the ordered pairs.

1.

x	y
−2	
−1	
0	
1	
2	

2.

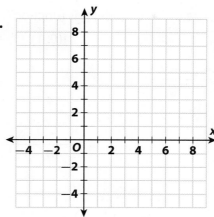

5.2 Representing Functions

3. Marco owed his father $150 and began paying him back $20 at the end of each week, beginning November 1. Joni owed her father $130 and began paying him back $15 at the end of each week, beginning on the same day. What Marco owed his father in dollars at the end of n weeks can be represented by $f(n) = 150 - 20n$. What Joni owed her father in dollars at the end of n weeks can be represented by $g(n) = 130 - 15n$.

Find the value of n for which $f(n) = g(n)$. What does that value mean in this situation?

_____

_____

5.3 Sequences

4. Write the first 4 terms of the sequence defined by the rule $f(n) = 2n^2 + 1$. Use the domain in the table.

n	1	2	3	4
f(n)				

? ESSENTIAL QUESTION

5. What is a function and how can it be represented?

_____

_____

_____

COMMON CORE

MODULE 5
MIXED REVIEW

Assessment Readiness

Personal Math Trainer

Online Practice and Help

⟳ my.hrw.com

1. Consider the function $f(x) = -3x + 1$ for the domain {0, 1, 2}.
   Which representation(s) below also model this function? Select all that apply.

   ○
x	0	1	2
f(x)	1	−4	−7

   ○ {(0, 1), (1, −2), (2, −5)}

   ○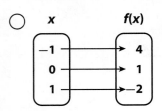

   ○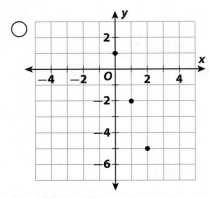

2. A grocery clerk is making a display of oranges. The numbers of oranges in the layers of the display form a sequence, with the top layer counting as layer 1. The explicit rule $f(n) = (n + 1)^2$ describes this sequence, where n is a whole number greater than 0. Will 50 oranges be enough to complete the top 4 layers of the display? Explain your reasoning.

3. Jonathon's suitcase can weigh no more than 50 pounds or he will have to pay an extra fee at the airport. His suitcase already weighs $44\frac{1}{2}$ pounds. Each pair of his jeans weighs about $\frac{7}{8}$ pound. How many more pairs of jeans can Jonathon pack without having to pay an extra fee? Explain your reasoning by writing and solving an inequality.

Study Guide Review

Equations and Inequalities in One Variable

? ESSENTIAL QUESTION

How can you solve an equation or inequality in one variable?

EXAMPLE 1

Francine opens a savings account with $150. At the end of every week, she adds $35 to her account. After how many weeks will Francine have $360 in her saving account?

Let w represent the number of weeks Francine has been saving.

$$150 + 35w = 360$$
$$\underline{-150 \qquad\qquad -150}$$
$$35w = 210$$

$$\frac{35w}{35} = \frac{210}{35}$$

$$w = 6$$

EXAMPLE 2

A test car has a velocity of 280 miles per hour minus five times the gear setting. The track has a speed limit of 150 miles per hour. What are the gear settings that can be used for the car in this trial?

Let x equal the gear setting.

$$280 - 5x \le 150$$
$$\underline{-280 \qquad\qquad -280}$$
$$-5x \le -130$$

$$\frac{-5x}{-5} \ge \frac{-130}{-5}$$

$$x \ge 26$$

EXERCISES

1. Megan has $25 to buy groceries. She has $15 worth of groceries in her cart, and would like to buy some melons that cost $1.25 each. Write an equation that describes the situation, and determine how many melons Megan can afford. (Lesson 4.1)

_____

2. Is 20 a solution for $2x - 5 > 30$? Explain your answer. (Lesson 4.2)

_____

Equations in Two Variables and Functions

Key Vocabulary

equation in two variables
(ecuación en dos variables)

solution of an equation in two variables (solución de una ecuación en dos variables)

function (función)

domain (dominio)

range (rango)

function notation (notación de función)

sequence (sucesión)

term (término)

? **ESSENTIAL QUESTION**

What is a function and how can a function be represented?

EXAMPLE 1

Graph the solutions of the equation $y = 2x + 4$.

Make a table.

x	y
−4	−4
−3	−2
−2	0
−1	2
0	4
1	6

Graph the ordered pairs.

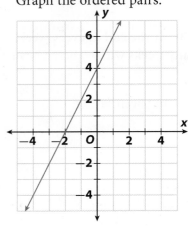

EXAMPLE 2

The functions $f(x)$ and $g(x)$ are defined by the explicit rules $f(x) = 5x + 1$ and $g(x) = 49 - 3x$. Find the value of x for which $f(x) = g(x)$.

Set the functions equal to each other, then solve.

$$f(x) = g(x)$$
$$5x + 1 = 49 - 3x$$
$$\underline{+3x \qquad\qquad +3x} \qquad \text{Add 3x to both sides.}$$
$$8x + 1 = 49$$

$$8x + 1 = 49$$
$$\underline{\quad -1 \quad -1} \qquad \text{Subtract 1 from both sides.}$$
$$8x \quad = 48$$

$$\frac{8x}{8} = \frac{48}{8} \qquad \text{Divide both sides by 8.}$$

$$x = 6$$

So, $f(x) = g(x)$ when $x = 6$.

EXAMPLE 3

Find the first 5 terms of the sequence defined by the explicit rule
$f(n) = 8n + 6$. **Assume that the domain of each function is the set of whole numbers greater than 0.**

Use the explicit rule and substitute the values 1 through 5 for n.

$f(1) = 8(1) + 6 = 14$

$f(2) = 8(2) + 6 = 22$

$f(3) = 8(3) + 6 = 30$

$f(4) = 8(4) + 6 = 38$

$f(5) = 8(5) + 6 = 46$

The first five terms are 14, 22, 30, 38, 46.

EXERCISES

3. Does $y = 6x + 5$ represent a function? Explain your answer.
(Lesson 5.2)

_____

_____

4. Given the functions $f(x) = 7x - 2$ and $g(x) = 3x + 6$, find the value of x for which $f(x) = g(x)$. (Lesson 5.2)

_____

Consider the function $y = 2x + 8$. **Determine if each ordered pair is a solution.** (Lesson 5.1)

5. (1, 10) _____ **6.** (3, 16) _____

7. (4, 16) _____ **8.** (5, 20) _____

Write the first four terms of the sequence. The domain of the function is the set of consecutive integers starting with 1. (Lesson 5.3)

9. $f(n) = 3n(n + 3)$ _____

10. $f(n) = 2(n + 3)$ _____

11. $f(1) = 3$ and $f(n) = f(n - 1) - 5$ _____

12. $f(1) = 4$ and $f(n) = 2 * f(n - 1) + 3$ _____

Round Trip

Joe rode his bike along Wheeler Road from home to the bike shop. After leaving his bike for a tune-up, he caught a ride home with a friend, a distance one-half mile less than the distance he rode to the shop. Joe spent a total of 30 minutes travelling to and from his house. The table gives his rates on both sections of the trip.

Part of Trip	Rate
Bicycling	15 miles/hour
Riding	30 miles/hour

For this project, create a presentation representing Joe's trip. Your presentation should include the following:

- A map including the bike shop, home, and both routes he took bicycling and riding. Give a scale for the map.
- An equation for the total distance x that Joe rode his bike
- The solution of the equation.

Use the space below to write down any questions you have or important information from your teacher.

MATH IN CAREERS | ACTIVITY

Astronomer Astronomers must sometimes predict the future position of an object. An astronomer discovers an object moving 2,000 kilometers per minute toward Earth. The object was spotted at 2,500,000 kilometers from Earth. Assuming constant speed, how long will it take for the object to reach the Moon's orbit, which is 160,000 kilometers away from Earth? Write and solve an equation.

Assessment Readiness

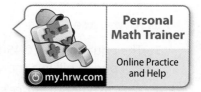

1. Consider each equation. Does it have infinitely many solutions?

Select Yes or No.

A. $4(n - 1) + 3 = 6n - 2n - 1$ ◯ Yes   ◯ No

B. $y - 4 = 6(y - 8)$ ◯ Yes   ◯ No

C. $-2(t + 1) = 5t - 30$ ◯ Yes   ◯ No

2. Consider the inequality $-5(x + 1) < 3x + 11$.

Choose True or False for each statement.

A. The graph of the inequality has an open circle at -2.   ◯ True   ◯ False

B. The graph of the inequality is shaded to include all values to the left of the endpoint.   ◯ True   ◯ False

C. The number 0 is included in the solution set.   ◯ True   ◯ False

3. The students in a college marching band are arranged in rows. The recursive rule $f(n) = f(n - 1) + 8$ and $f(1) = 13$, gives the number of students in each row, where n is the row number. All of the clarinet players are in row 1, and all of the trumpet players are in row 4. How many more trumpet players than clarinet players are there? Explain your reasoning.

4. A rancher is planning the goat pen shown in the diagram. Determine the value of x, given that the rancher plans to use 100 feet of fencing to enclose the pen. Explain how you solved this problem.

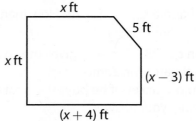

Performance Tasks

★ 5. The equation $a = 0.45(m - 450) + 39.99$ gives the amount a in dollars of Bruce's cell phone bill in a month when he uses m minutes of talk time.

    a. Last month, Bruce's bill was $53.49. How many minutes of talk time did he use?

    b. This month, Bruce promises to use no more than half the number of minutes he used last month. He has already used 225 minutes. How many more talk minutes can he use this month without breaking his promise? Use an inequality to explain your reasoning.

★★ 6. Mattie sells lotion for $10 per bottle. Mattie spends $4 to make each bottle and $100 for booth rental. The function $f(x) = 10x - 4x - 100$ models Mattie's profit in dollars when she sells x bottles.

    a. Make a table of values for the function, including Mattie's profit for selling 0, 10, 20, 30, and 40 bottles.

    b. Explain what negative values of $f(x)$ represent in this situation.

    c. Graph the function. Be sure to label the axes.

    d. Mattie wants to earn a profit of at least $250. How many bottles will she need to sell? Explain how you determined your answer.

★★★ 7. The numbers of seats in the rows of a theater form a sequence. The explicit rule $f(n) = 2n + 4$ defines this sequence, where n is the row number.

    a. The theater has a total of 66 seats. How many rows of seats does the theater have? Explain your reasoning.

    b. The equation $c = 28 - 3(n - 1)$ gives the cost in dollars of a ticket for a seat in row n of the theater. Mr. Zamora can spend up to $100 on tickets. Will he be able to buy more tickets if he buys them for the last row of the theater or the first row? Justify your answer.

Linear Relationships

MODULE 6

Linear Functions

COMMON CORE F.IF.4, F.IF.6, F.IF.7, F.IF.7a, F.IF.9, F.BF.3, F.LE.2

MODULE 7

Building Linear Functions

COMMON CORE F.BF.1a, F.LE.2, F.BF.4a, A.REI.12

MODULE 8

Modeling with Linear Functions

COMMON CORE S.ID.6, S.ID.6b, S.ID.6c, S.ID.7, S.ID.8

MODULE 9

Systems of Equations and Inequalities

COMMON CORE A.REI.5, A.REI.6, A.REI.12, A.CED.3

MATH IN CAREERS

Environmental Scientist An environmental scientist uses math to make models to analyze data and understand the effects of human activity on nature.

If you're interested in a career as an environmental scientist, you should study these subjects of math:
- Algebra
- Calculus
- Statistics

Research other careers that involve modeling data with mathematical functions.

ACTIVITY At the end of the unit, check out how an **environmental scientist** uses math.

© Houghton Mifflin Harcourt Publishing Company•Image Credits: © Photo Researchers/Getty Images

Unit Project Preview

Changing Flights

The Unit Project at the end of this unit involves designing a new flight of stairs. You will consider the space available and California safety regulations. To successfully complete the Unit Project you'll need to master these skills:

- Take accurate measurements and collect data.
- Represent real-world data with linear equations.
- Graph linear equations on a coordinate plane.

1. A California safety regulation for stairs states that the rise of each step in a stairway cannot be less than 4 inches or greater than $7\frac{1}{2}$ inches. The run cannot be less than 10 inches. Describe in your own words what this regulation means.

_____

_____

2. According to the safety regulation, what values of rise and run would give the steepest flight of stairs allowed? Explain.

_____

_____

_____

Tracking Your Learning Progression

This unit addresses important California Common Core Standards in the Critical Areas of working with functions, equations, and inequalities.

Domain **F.IF** Interpreting Functions

    Cluster Understand the concept of a function and use function notation.

The unit also supports additional standards.

Domain **F.BF** Building Functions

    Cluster Build a function that models a relationship between two quantities.

Domain **A.REI** Reasoning with Equations and Inequalities

    Cluster Solve equations and inequalities in one variable.

Linear Functions

ESSENTIAL QUESTION

How do equations, graphs, tables, and word descriptions related to linear functions?

Real-World Video

Cyclists adjust their gears to climb up a steep grade or through rocky terrain. Check out how gear ratios, rates of speed, and slope ratios can be used to solve problems involving speed, distance, and time when mountain biking.

my.hrw.com

© Houghton Mifflin Harcourt Publishing Company • Image Credits: © George Doyle/Getty Images

GO DIGITAL
my.hrw.com

my.hrw.com

Go digital with your write-in student edition, accessible on any device.

Math On the Spot

Scan with your smart phone to jump directly to the online edition, video tutor, and more.

Animated Math

Interactively explore key concepts to see how math works.

Personal Math Trainer

Get immediate feedback and help as you work through practice sets.

Are YOU Ready?

Complete these exercises to review skills you will need for this chapter.

Personal Math Trainer

Online Practice and Help

my.hrw.com

Solve Multi-Step Equations

EXAMPLE Solve $3x + 4 = 28$.

$$3x + 4 - 4 = 28 - 4 \quad \text{Subtract 4 from both sides.}$$
$$3x = 24$$
$$3x \cdot \frac{1}{3} = 24 \cdot \frac{1}{3} \quad \text{Multiply both sides by } \frac{1}{3}.$$
$$x = 8$$

Solve each equation.

1. $2x + 7 = 19$ **2.** $0.4y + 8 = -1$ **3.** $0 = 3z - 6$

_____   _____   _____

Ordered Pairs

EXAMPLE Graph (2, 4) on the coordinate plane.

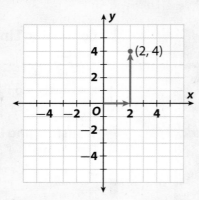

$(2, 4) \rightarrow (x, y)$
The x-coordinate or horizontal coordinate is 2.
Move *right* 2 units.
The y-coordinate or vertical coordinate is 4.
Move *up* 4 units.
Negative coordinates indicate movement to the *left* and *down*.

Graph each point on the coordinate plane provided.

4. $(-1, 3)$

5. $(4, -2)$

6. $(0, 1)$

7. $(-2, -3)$

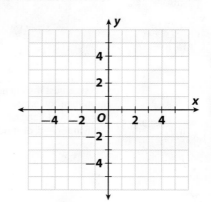

Reading Start-Up

Visualize Vocabulary

Use the Review Words to complete the chart.

Representation	Uses
	To show two expressions are equivalent
	To represent a relationship that has exactly one output for each input
	To visually represent a function on a coordinate plane
	To locate a single point on a coordinate plane

Understand Vocabulary

Complete the sentences using the preview words.

1. An equation written as $Ax + By = C$, where A, B, and C are real numbers is said to be in the

   _____

2. An equation written as $y = mx + b$, where m is the slope and b is the y-intercept is said to be in the

   _____

3. The _____ is the y-coordinate of the point where the graph of a line crosses the y-axis.

4. The _____ is the x-coordinate of the point where the graph of a line crosses the x-axis.

Active Reading

Key-Term Fold Before beginning the module, create a Key-Term Fold for taking notes as you read the module. Each tab can contain a key term on one side and its definition on the other. As you study each lesson, write important vocabulary and definitions under the appropriate tab.

Vocabulary

Review Words
✔ equation *(ecuación)*
✔ function *(función)*
✔ graph of a function *(gráfica de una función)*
  ordered pair *(línea)*
✔ ordered pair *(par ordenado)*

Preview Words
  family of functions
  linear function
  linear equation
  parent function
  parameter
  rate of change
  rise
  run
  slope
  slope formula
  slope-intercept form
  standard form of a linear equation
  x-intercept
  y-intercept

Linear Functions

Understanding the standards and the vocabulary terms in the standards will help you know exactly what you are expected to learn in this module.

COMMON CORE F.IF.4

For a function that models a relationship between two quantities, interpret key features of graphs and tables in terms of the quantities, and sketch graphs showing key features given a verbal description of the relationship.

Key Vocabulary

slope *(pendiente)*
The slope of a line is the ratio of rise to run for any two points on the line.

What It Means to You

Learning to interpret a graph enables a deep visual understanding of all sorts of relationships.

EXAMPLE F.IF.4

A group of friends walked to the town market, did some shopping there, then returned home.

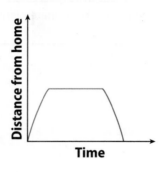

COMMON CORE F.IF.6

Calculate and interpret the average rate of change of a function (presented symbolically or as a table) over a specified interval. Estimate the rate of change from a graph.

Key Vocabulary

rate of change *(tasa de cambio)*
A ratio that compares the amount of change in a dependent variable to the amount of change in an independent variable.

What It Means to You

Average rate of change measures the change in the dependent variable over the change in the independent variable. This helps you understand how quickly the values in a function change.

EXAMPLE F.IF.6

$$\text{Average rate of change} = \frac{180 - 60}{3 - 1} = 60 \text{ mi/h}$$

Time (hours)	1	2	3	4
Distance (miles)	60	120	180	240

Visit **my.hrw.com** to see all **Common Core Standards** unpacked.

🕐 my.hrw.com

COMMON CORE   **F.IF.7**

Graph functions expressed symbolically and show key features of the graph, by hand in simple cases and using technology for more complicated cases. *Also F.IF.7a, F.IF.5*

? **ESSENTIAL QUESTION**

How can you use graphs and equations to identify linear functions?

EXPLORE ACTIVITY COMMON CORE   **F.IF.5, F.IF.7, F.IF.7a**

Exploring Linear Functions

You get a job planning birthday parties. You are paid a flat fee of $80 and then $15 for each hour you work. The function defined by $f(x) = 15x + 80$ represents your earnings in dollars when you work x hours. Assume you get paid for fractions of hours.

A Complete the table to represent the total wages for 0–4 hours worked.

Number of hours, x	Earnings in dollars, $f(x)$
0	
1	
2	
3	
4	

B Graph the function from Part A.

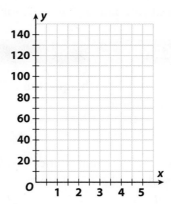

C How do you know that this is a function?

_____

REFLECT

1. Identify the domain and range for the function $f(x) = 15x + 80$.

Domain: _____

Range: _____

2. **Look for a Pattern** Describe the pattern formed by the points in the graph that are from the table.

_____

_____

Math On the Spot

my.hrw.com

Identifying Linear Functions

A **linear function** is a function whose graph forms a line that is not vertical.

The graph at the right is the graph of a linear function.

Both the domain and the range of the function are the set of all real numbers

If a function is linear, then it can be represented by a *linear equation*. A **linear equation** is any equation that can be written in the *standard form* below.

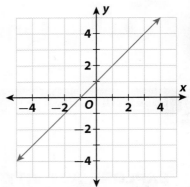

Standard Form of a Linear Equation

$Ax + By = C$ where A, B, and C are real numbers and A and B are not both 0.

Notice that when a linear equation is written in standard form the following are true.

- x and y both have exponents of 1.
- x and y are not multiplied together.
- x and y do not appear in denominators, exponents, or radicands.

EXAMPLE 1   COMMON CORE   F.IF.7, F.IF.7a

Tell whether each equation is linear. If so, graph the function represented by the equation.

A $-12x + y = -4$

The equation is linear because it is in the standard form of a linear equation: $A = -12$, $B = 1$, and $C = -4$.

To graph the function, first solve the equation for y.

$$-12x + y = -4$$

$$\underline{+12x \qquad\qquad +12x}$$ Subtraction Property of Equality

$$y = -4 + 12x$$

Make a table and plot the points. Then connect the points.

x	−2	0	2	4
y	−28	−4	20	44

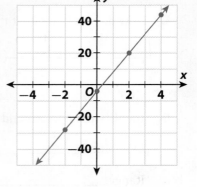

B $y = 12x^2 - 4$

The exponent on x in this equation is not 1, so the function is not linear.

C $xy - 4 = 12$

$$xy - 4 = 12$$

Since x and y are multiplied together, this function is not linear.

REFLECT

3. Communicate Mathematical Ideas Use the bulleted list above Example 1 to write at least two more equations that are not linear. Explain why they are not linear.

_____

_____

_____

_____

4. Make a Conjecture Why do you think the graph of a linear function has to be a non-vertical line?

_____

_____

_____

_____

_____

_____

YOUR TURN

Tell whether each equation is linear. If so, graph the function represented by the equation.

5. $y - 3 = 2x$

6. $y = \frac{2}{x}$

_____   _____

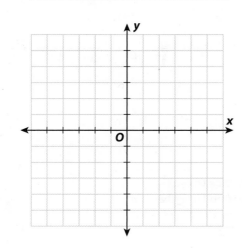   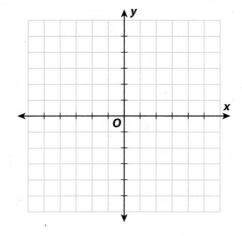

Personal Math Trainer

Online Practice and Help

my.hrw.com

© Houghton Mifflin Harcourt Publishing Company

Horizontal and Vertical Lines

As stated earlier in this lesson, a linear equation is in standard form if it is in the form $Ax + Bx = C$, where A, B, and C are real numbers and A and B are not both 0. Notice that in this definition, A and B cannot both be 0, but one or the other can be 0.

EXAMPLE 2

COMMON CORE   F.IF.7, F.IF.7a

Graph each line.

A $y = 8$

$0x + 1y = 8$ This is a linear equation in standard form $A = 0, B = 1, C = 8$.

x	y
0	8
1	8
2	8
3	8
4	8

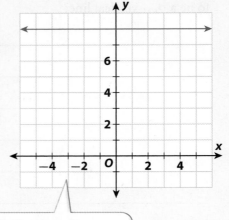

Notice that all ordered pairs have a y-coordinate of 8.

B $x = -1$

$1x + 0y = -1$ This is a linear equation in standard form $A = 1, B = 0, C = -1$.

x	y
-1	0
-1	1
-1	2
-1	3
-1	4

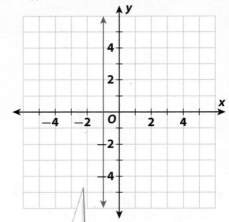

Notice that all ordered pairs have an x-coordinate of -1.

REFLECT

7. Communicate Mathematical Ideas When the equation of the graph of a horizontal line is written in standard form, the coefficient of x must be 0. Explain why.

_____

_____

_____

YOUR TURN

Tell whether the equation represents a horizontal line, vertical line, or neither. Graph the equation.

8. $y = 2x$ _____

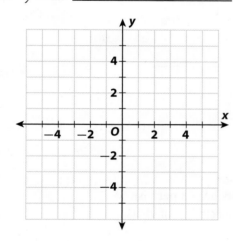

9. $y = -4$ _____

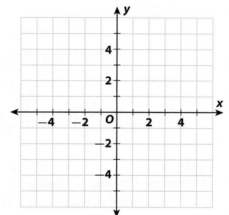

10. $3y = -4$ _____

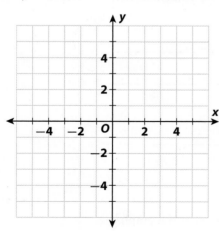

11. $x + 3 = 0$ _____

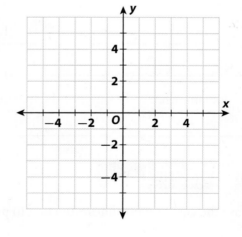

Personal Math Trainer

Online Practice and Help

my.hrw.com

Write a linear equation in the form $Ax + By = C$ for the given values of A, B, and C. Then simplify the equation. Tell whether the equation represents a horizontal line, vertical line, or neither. (Examples 1 and 2)

1. $A = 0, B = 3, C = 1$

$3y = 1$

_____

2. $A = 5, B = 0.1, C = 4$

$5x + 0y = 4$

_____

3. $A = -\frac{1}{2}, B = 0, C = 14$

$-\frac{1}{2}x = 14$

_____

Create a table of values for the function $y = 3x - 4$. Then graph the function, making sure to label the axes to show the scale. (Example 1)

4. $y = 3x - 4$

x	y
0	−4
1	−1
2	2

5. Andrea receives a $40 gift card to use at a town pool. It costs her $8 per visit to swim. A function relating the value of the gift card, v, to the number of visits, n, is $v(n) = 40 - 8n$. (Explore Activity)

a. Identify a reasonable domain of the function. Explain why you chose that domain.

$y = 40 - 8n$ 3, it is reasonable to go to the pool 3 times.

b. Given that domain, what is the range of the function.

$16 left in the card

? **ESSENTIAL QUESTION CHECK-IN**

6. How can you use the equation of a linear function to predict what the graph will look like?

you can write it in slope intercept form so you can see how it will look

6.1 Independent Practice

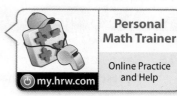
COMMON CORE F.IF.7, F.IF.7a

7. Two friends work at the same company. Friend A gets paid $50,000 for the year, no matter how many hours she works. Friend B gets paid $20 an hour. Write an equation for each person that shows the relationship between the annual salary y and the number of hours x that friend works. Fill in each table of values and graph each function.

a. Function for Friend A

_____

x	y
0	
1,000	
2,000	

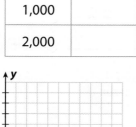

b. Function for Friend B

_____

x	y
0	
1,000	
2,000	

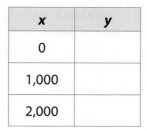

Tell whether each of the following equations represents a linear function.

8. $y = x^2 + 3$ _____

9. $3x = 4$ _____

10. $y = 1$ _____

11. $0.3x + y = 2$ _____

12. $x^2\left(\frac{1}{y}\right) = 3$ _____

13. $y = x$ _____

14. Select a linear equation from Questions 8–13 and create a graph for it.

_____

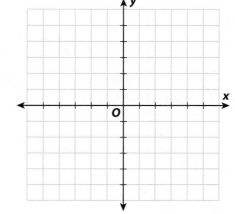

15. **Represent Real-World Problems** Write a real-world problem that could represent a function that has a range that includes negative numbers.

_____

_____

_____

_____

_____

16. **Communicate Mathematical Ideas** Recall that the standard form of a linear equation is $Ax + By = C$ where A, B, and C are real numbers and A and B are not both 0. Why do you think that A and B cannot both be zero?

_____

_____

17. **Explain the Error** A student was using a table of values to create a graph of a function. The table and graph are shown below. Explain the student's error.

x	y
0	0
1	3
−1	−3

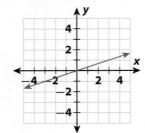

_____

_____

_____

18. **Communicate Mathematical Ideas** Consider the following graphs. They are for the same line. How is this possible?

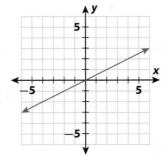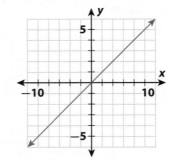

_____

COMMON CORE **F.IF.7a**
Graph liner and quadratic functions and show intercepts, maxima, and minima. *Also F.IF.4, F.IF.7*

ESSENTIAL QUESTION

How can you identify and use intercepts in linear relationships?

EXPLORE ACTIVITY COMMON CORE **F.IF.4, F.IF.7, F.IF.7a**

Identifying Intercepts

A diver explored the ocean floor at 120 feet below the surface. The diver then ascended at a constant rate over a period of 4 minutes until he reached the surface.

In the coordinate grid below, the horizontal axis represents the time in minutes from when the diver started ascending and the vertical axis represents the diver's elevation in feet.

A What point represents the diver's elevation at the beginning

of the ascent? Graph this point. _____

B What point represents the diver's elevation at the end of the

ascent? Graph this point. _____

C Connect the points with a line segment. The graph now shows the diver's elevation below sea level during the 4-minute ascent.

Look at points $(4, 0)$ and $(0, -120)$. Notice that these are points where the graph intersects the axes. These points are known as *intercepts*.

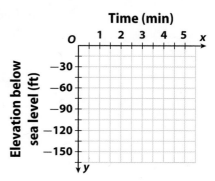

REFLECT

1. Communicate Mathematical Ideas The diver begins his ascent at the depth represented by the point where a graph intersects the y-axis of the graph. Will the point where a graph intersects the y-axis always be the lowest point of a linear graph? Explain.

_____

_____

_____

_____

_____

Finding Intercepts of Linear Equations

In the previous Explore Activity, the graph intersected the axes at $(0, -120)$ and $(4, 0)$.

The **y-intercept** is the y-coordinate of the point where the graph intersects the y-axis. The x-coordinate of this point is always 0. This was point $(0, -120)$ in the Explore Activity.

The **x-intercept** is the x-coordinate of the point where the graph intersects the x-axis. The y-coordinate of this point is always 0. This was point $(4, 0)$ in the Explore Activity.

EXAMPLE 1
COMMON CORE   F.IF.7, F.IF.7a

Find the x- and y-intercepts.

My Notes

A

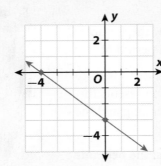

The graph crosses the x-axis at $(-4, 0)$.

The x-intercept is -4.

The graph crosses the y-axis at $(0, -3)$.

The y-intercept is -3.

B $3x - 2y = 12$

To find the x-intercept, replace y with 0 and solve for x.

$$3x - 2y = 12$$
$$3x - 2(0) = 12$$
$$3x - 0 = 12$$
$$3x = 12$$
$$\frac{3x}{3} = \frac{12}{3}$$
$$x = 4$$

The x-intercept is 4.

To find the y-intercept, replace x with 0 and solve for y.

$$3x - 2y = 12$$
$$3(0) - 2y = 12$$
$$0 - 2y = 12$$
$$-2y = 12$$
$$\frac{-2y}{-2} = \frac{12}{-2}$$
$$y = -6$$

The y-intercept is -6.

YOUR TURN

Find the x- and y-intercepts.

2.

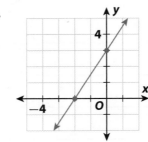

3. $-3x + 5y = 30$

_____

_____

Personal Math Trainer

Online Practice and Help

⏻ my.hrw.com

Interpreting Intercepts of Linear Equations

EXAMPLE 2 Real World

Math On the Spot
⏱ my.hrw.com

The Sandia Peak Tramway in Albuquerque, New Mexico, travels a distance of about 4500 meters to the top of Sandia Peak. Its speed is 300 meters per minute. The function $f(x) = 4500 - 300x$ gives the tram's distance in meters from the top of the peak after x minutes.

Graph this function and find the intercepts. What does each intercept represent?

x	f(x) = 4500 − 300x
0	4500
2	3900
5	3000

Neither time nor distance can be negative, so choose several nonnegative values for x. Use the function to generate ordered pairs.

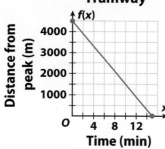

Sandia Peak Tramway

y-intercept: 4500

In the real world, the y-intercept represents the distance from the top at the start (time = 0).

x-intercept: 15

In the real world, the x-intercept represents the time it takes for the tram to reach the top (distance from peak = 0).

Math Talk
Mathematical Practices

A student says that the graph shows the path of the tram. Why is the student incorrect?

YOUR TURN

4. The temperature in an experiment is reduced at a constant rate over a period of time until the temperature reaches 0°C. The equation $y = 20 - \frac{2}{3}x$ gives the temperature y in degrees Celsius x hours after the beginning of the experiment.

a. Graph this function and find the x- and y-intercepts.

_____

b. What does each intercept represent?

_____

_____

_____

_____

_____

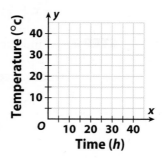

Personal Math Trainer

Online Practice and Help

⏱ my.hrw.com

Using Intercepts to Graph Linear Equations

EXAMPLE 3

COMMON CORE F.IF.7, F.IF.7a

My Notes

Use intercepts to graph the line described by each equation.

A $2x - 4y = 8$

STEP 1 Find the intercepts.

x-intercept:

$$2x - 4y = 8$$
$$2x - 4(0) = 8$$
$$2x = 8$$
$$\frac{2x}{2} = \frac{8}{2}$$
$$x = 4$$

y-intercept:

$$2x - 4y = 8$$
$$2(0) - 4y = 8$$
$$-4y = 8$$
$$\frac{-4y}{-4} = \frac{8}{-4}$$
$$y = -2$$

STEP 2 Graph the line.

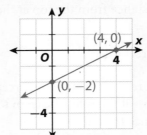

Plot $(4, 0)$ and $(0, -2)$.

Connect the points with a straight line.

B $\frac{2}{3}y = 4 - \frac{1}{2}x$

STEP 1 Write the equation in standard form.

$$\frac{1}{2}x + \frac{2}{3}y = 4 - \frac{1}{2}x + \frac{1}{2}x$$
$$\frac{1}{2}x + \frac{2}{3}y = 4$$

Add $\frac{1}{2}x$ to both sides so both variables are on the same side.

STEP 2 Find the intercepts.

x-intercept:

$$\frac{1}{2}x + \frac{2}{3}y = 4$$
$$\frac{1}{2}x + \frac{2}{3}(0) = 4$$
$$\frac{1}{2}x = 4$$
$$2\left(\frac{1}{2}x\right) = 2(4)$$
$$x = 8$$

y-intercept:

$$\frac{1}{2}x + \frac{2}{3}y = 4$$
$$\frac{1}{2}(0) + \frac{2}{3}y = 4$$
$$\frac{2}{3}y = 4$$
$$\frac{3}{2}\left(\frac{2}{3}y\right) = \frac{3}{2}(4)$$
$$y = 6$$

STEP 3 Graph the line.

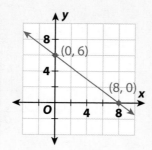

Plot (8, 0) and (0, 6).

Connect the points with a straight line.

REFLECT

5. Draw Conclusions Find the intercepts for a linear equation of the form $Ax = C$, where A and C are real numbers and A is not 0.

_____

_____

_____

_____

Use intercepts to graph the line described by each equation.

6. $-3x + 4y = -12$

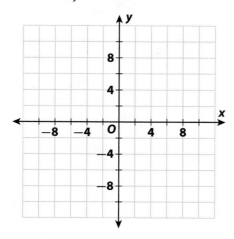

7. $y = \frac{1}{3}x - 2$

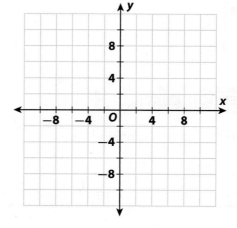

8. A function has x-intercept 4 and y-intercept 2. Name two other points on the graph of this function.

_____

Personal Math Trainer

Online Practice and Help

my.hrw.com

Find the *x*- and *y*-intercepts. (Example 1)

1.

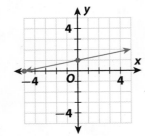

_____

2.

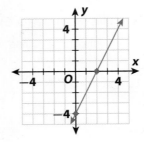

_____

3.

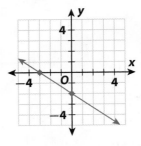

_____

4. $2x - 4y = 4$

_____

5. $-2y = 3x - 6$

_____

6. $4y + 5x = 2y - 3x + 16$

_____

Use intercepts to graph the line described by each equation. (Example 3)

7. $4x - 5y = 20$

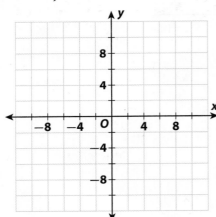

8. $y = \frac{1}{2}x - 4$

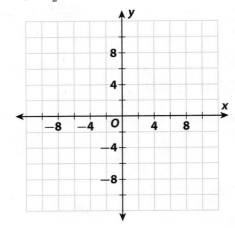

9. What are intercepts and how can they be used?

_____

_____

_____

_____

_____

6.2 Independent Practice

Personal Math Trainer

Online Practice and Help

my.hrw.com

COMMON CORE F-IF.4, F.IF.7, F.IF.7a

10. To thaw a specimen stored at −25 °C, the temperature of a refrigeration tank is raised 5 °C every hour. The temperature in the tank after x hours can be described by the function $f(x) = -25 + 5x$.

a. Graph the function and find its intercepts.

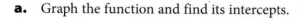

b. What does each intercept represent?

_____

_____

_____

_____

_____

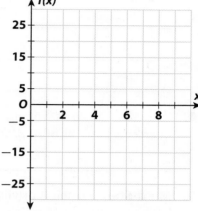

11. A fishing lake was stocked with 300 bass. Each year, the population decreases by 25. The population of bass in the lake after x years is represented by the function $f(x) = 300 - 25x$.

a. Graph the function and find its intercepts.

_____

b. What does each intercept represent?

_____

_____

_____

_____

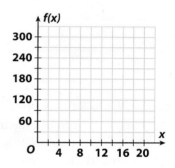

12. A bamboo plant is growing 1 foot per day. When first measured, it is 4 feet tall.

a. Write an equation to describe the height, y, in feet, of the bamboo plant

x days after you measure it. _____

b. What is the y-intercept? What does the y-intercept represent?

_____

_____

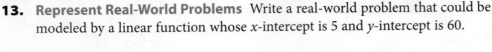
13. **Represent Real-World Problems** Write a real-world problem that could be modeled by a linear function whose *x*-intercept is 5 and *y*-intercept is 60.

_____

_____

_____

_____

14. **Draw Conclusions** For any linear equation $Ax + By = C$, what are the intercepts in terms of A, B, and C?

_____

15. **Multi-Step** Kirsten is driving to a city that is 400 miles away. When Kirsten left home, she had 15 gallons of gas in her car. Assume that her car gets 25 miles per gallon of gas. Define a function f so that $f(x)$ is the amount of gas left in her car after she has driven x miles from home. What are the intercepts for that function? What do they represent?

_____

_____

_____

_____

16. **Multiple Representations** Find the intercepts of $3x + 40y = 1200$. Explain how to use the intercepts to determine appropriate scales for the graph and then create a graph.

_____

_____

_____

_____

_____

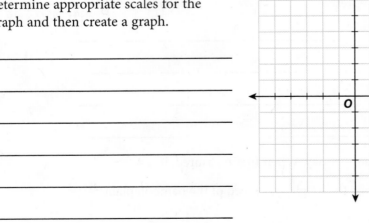

_____

_____

_____

COMMON CORE F.IF.6

Calculate and interpret the average rate of change of a function (presented symbolically or as a table) over a specified interval. Estimate the rate of change from a graph. *Also F.IF.4, F.IF.7, F.LE.1b*

? ESSENTIAL QUESTION

How can you relate rate of change and slope in linear relationships?

EXPLORE ACTIVITY 1   COMMON CORE F.IF.6

Finding Rates of Change

For a function defined in terms of x and y, the **rate of change** over a part of the domain of the function is a ratio that compares the change in y to the change in x in that part of the domain.

$$\text{rate of change} = \frac{\text{change in } y}{\text{change in } x}$$

A In 2004, the cost of sending a 1-ounce letter was 37 cents. In 2008, the cost was 42 cents. Find the rate of change in cost for this time period.

$$\text{rate of change} = \frac{\text{change in } y}{\text{change in } x} = \frac{\boxed{} - \boxed{}}{2008 - 2004} = \frac{\boxed{}}{\boxed{}} = \boxed{}$$

The rate of change was $\boxed{}$ cents per year.

B Find the rate of change for each time period.

Year (x)	1988	1990	1991	2004	2008
Cost in cents (y)	25	25	29	37	42

$$1988 \text{ to } 1990 = \frac{\boxed{} - \boxed{}}{1990 - 1988} = \boxed{} \text{ cents per year}$$

$$1990 \text{ to } 1991 = \frac{\boxed{} - \boxed{}}{1991 - 1990} = \boxed{} \text{ cents per year}$$

Round to the nearest hundredth of a cent.

$$1991 \text{ to } 2004 = \frac{\boxed{} - \boxed{}}{2004 - 1991} = \boxed{} = \boxed{} \text{ cents per year}$$

$$2004 \text{ to } 2008 = \frac{\boxed{} - \boxed{}}{2008 - 2004} = \boxed{} = \boxed{} \text{ cents per year}$$

REFLECT

1. **Interpret the Answer** The rate of change for 2004 to 2008 was 1.25 cents per year. Does this mean the actual change in cost each year was 1.25 cents? Explain.

_____

_____

_____

_____

Math On the Spot

my.hrw.com

Finding Slope of a Line

In the previous Explore Activity, the rate of change was not constant. It varied from 0 to 4 cents per year. However, for linear functions, the rate of change is constant.

The rate of change for a linear function can be calculated using the rise and run of the graph of the function. The **rise** is the difference in the y-values of two points on a line. The **run** is the difference in the x-values of two points on a line.

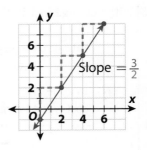

Slope $= \frac{3}{2}$

The **slope** of a line is the ratio of rise to run for any two points on the line.

$$\text{slope} = \frac{\text{rise}}{\text{run}} = \frac{\text{difference in } y\text{-values}}{\text{difference in } x\text{-values}}$$

EXAMPLE 1

COMMON CORE F.IF.6

Find the slope of each line.

A

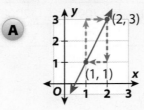

(2, 3)

(1, 1)

Use (2, 3) as the starting point. Subtract y-values to find the change in y or rise. Then subtract x-values to find the change in x or run.

$\text{slope} = \frac{1-3}{1-2} = \frac{-2}{-1} = 2$

It doesn't matter which point you start with as long as you are consistent. If you start with (1, 1), then $\text{slope} = \frac{3-1}{2-1} = \frac{2}{1} = 2$.

B

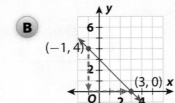

(−1, 4)

(3, 0)

Use (−1, 4) as the starting point. Subtract y-values to find the change in y or rise. Then subtract x-values to find the change in x or run.

$\text{slope} = \frac{0-4}{3-(-1)} = \frac{-4}{4} = -1$

My Notes

2. Find the slope of the line in the graph.

_____

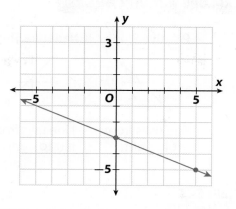

Personal Math Trainer

Online Practice and Help

my.hrw.com

EXPLORE ACTIVITY 2   **F.IF.6**

Classifying Slopes

As shown in the previous example, slope can be positive or negative. What about the slope of horizontal and vertical lines?

Find the slope of each line.

A

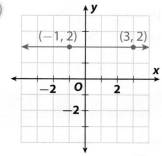

$$\text{slope} = \frac{\text{rise}}{\text{run}} = \frac{\boxed{}}{\boxed{}} = \frac{\boxed{}}{\boxed{}} = \boxed{}$$

B

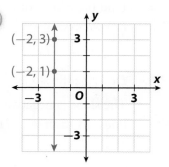

$$\text{slope} = \frac{\text{rise}}{\text{run}} = \frac{\boxed{}}{\boxed{}} = \frac{\boxed{}}{0}$$

Since you cannot divide by 0, the slope is undefined.

Positive Slope	Negative Slope	Zero Slope	Undefined Slope

Line rises from left to right.	Line falls from left to right.	Horizontal line	Vertical line

REFLECT

3. **Communicate Mathematical Ideas** Explain why the slope of a vertical line is undefined.

_____

_____

_____

Math On the Spot

my.hrw.com

Using the Slope Formula

The **slope formula** for the slope of a line is the ratio of the difference in y-values to the difference in x-values between any two different points on the line.

This means if (x_1, y_1) and (x_2, y_2) are any two points on a line, the slope is $m = \dfrac{y_2 - y_1}{x_2 - x_1}$.

EXAMPLE 2

COMMON CORE F.IF.6

Find the slope of the line passing through the points (5, 3) and (−1, 15). Describe the slope as positive, negative, zero, or undefined.

Animated Math

my.hrw.com

STEP 1 Find the rise or difference in y-values.

$$y_2 - y_1 = 15 - 3 = 12$$

STEP 2 Find the run or difference in x-values.

$$x_2 - x_1 = -1 - 5 = -6$$

STEP 3 Find the slope.

$$\text{slope} = \frac{\text{rise}}{\text{run}} = \frac{12}{-6} = -2$$

STEP 4 Describe the slope.

The slope is negative. The line falls from left to right.

Personal Math Trainer

Online Practice and Help

my.hrw.com

YOUR TURN

4. Find the slope of the line passing through the points (9, 1) and (−1, −4). Describe the slope as positive, negative, zero, or undefined.

_____

Interpreting Slope

Math On the Spot

🔵 my.hrw.com

EXAMPLE 3 Real World

COMMON CORE   F.IF.4, F.IF.6, F.IF.7, F.LE.1b

The graph shows the relationship between a person's age and his or her estimated maximum heart rate.

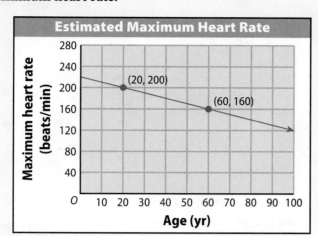

A Find the slope.

Use the two points that are labeled on the graph.

$$\text{slope} = \frac{\text{rise}}{\text{run}} = \frac{160 - 200}{60 - 20} = \frac{-40}{40} = -1$$

B Interpret the slope.

The slope of -1 means that for every year a person's age increases, his or her maximum heart rate decreases by 1 beat per minute.

REFLECT

5. Multi-Step Tara and Jade are hiking up a hill together. Each has a different stride. The run for Tara's stride is 32 inches, and the rise is 8 inches. The run for Jade's stride is 36 inches. What is the rise of Jade's stride? What is the slope and what does it mean in this problem?

_____

_____

Math Talk
Mathematical Practices

Why is it important to know both the formula and the description of what slope is?

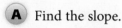

YOUR TURN

6. In an experiment, a car began traveling at a constant speed at 1:00 PM. Over a period of 5 hours, the car traveled a total 160 miles A graph shows the relationship between the length of time that the car had been traveling since 1:00 PM and the number of miles that it had traveled. What is the slope of the line? What does the slope mean?

_____

_____

Personal Math Trainer

Online Practice and Help

🔵 my.hrw.com

Given the linear relationship, find the slope. (Examples 1 and 2)

1. Line passing through the points (2, −1) and (0, 5)

_____

2.

x	y
0	1
1	3
2	5

_____

3.

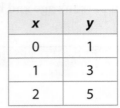

_____

4. The table shows the volume of gasoline in a gas tank at different times. (Examples 1 and 3)

Time (h)	Volume (gal)
0	12
1	9
3	5

a. Find the rate of change for each time interval.

_____

b. What does the difference in the rates of change mean in this situation?

_____

_____

_____

Tell whether the slope is positive, negative, zero, or undefined. (Explore Activity 2)

5.

_____

6.

_____

7.

_____

8.

_____

? ESSENTIAL QUESTION CHECK-IN

9. How are rate of change and slope related for a linear relationship?

_____

_____

_____

_____

© Houghton Mifflin Harcourt Publishing Company

6.3 Independent Practice

COMMON CORE F.IF.4, F.IF.6, F.IF.7, F.LE.1b

Personal Math Trainer

Online Practice and Help

my.hrw.com

10. At a particular college, a full-time student must take at least 12 credit hours per semester and may take at most 18 credit hours per semester. Tuition costs $200 per credit hour.

Credit Hours	Cost ($)
12	
13	
14	
15	
16	
17	
18	

a. Complete the table by using the information above.

b. What number is added to the cost in each row to get the cost in the next row?

_____

c. What does your answer to part b represent?

_____

_____

d. Graph the ordered pairs from the table.

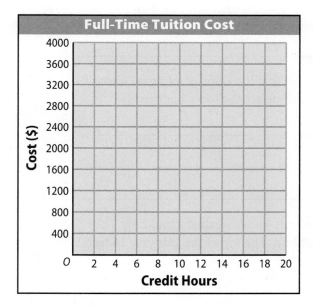

Full-Time Tuition Cost

Cost ($) / Credit Hours

e. Describe how the points in the graph are related.

_____

_____

_____

_____

11. **Draw Conclusions** The graph shows the number of files scanned by a computer virus detection program over time. Use estimation to find the rate of change between points A and B.

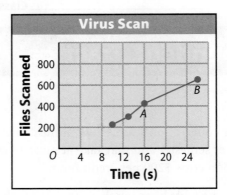

Virus Scan

_____

_____

H.O.T. **FOCUS ON HIGHER ORDER THINKING**

12. **Explain the Error** A student is asked to find the slope of a line containing the points $(4, 1)$ and $(-1, 11)$. He finds the slope the following way:
$\text{slope} = \frac{\text{rise}}{\text{run}} = \frac{4 - (-1)}{1 - 11} = \frac{5}{-10} = -\frac{1}{2}$. Explain the error.

_____

_____

_____

13. **Critical Thinking** In this lesson, you learned that the slope of a line is constant. Does this mean that all lines with the same slope are the same line? Explain.

_____

_____

_____

14. **Represent Real-World Problems** A ladder is leaned against a building. The bottom of the ladder is 9 feet from the building. The top of the ladder is 16 feet above the ground.

a. What is the slope of the ladder? _____

b. What does the slope of the ladder mean in the real world?

_____

_____

c. If the ladder were set closer to the building, would it be harder or easier to climb? Explain in terms of the slope of the ladder.

_____

_____

Slope-Intercept Form

COMMON CORE **F.IF.4**

For a function that models a relationship between two quantities, interpret key features of graphs and tables in terms of the quantities, and sketch graphs showing key features given a verbal description of the relationship. *Also A.CED.2, F.IF.6, F.IF.7, F.IF.7a, F.LE.1b*

? ESSENTIAL QUESTION

How can you use the slope-intercept form of a linear equation to model real-world linear relationships?

Using Slopes and Intercepts

If you know the equation that describes a line, you can find its slope by using any two ordered pairs of numbers that are solutions of the equation. It is often easiest to use the ordered pairs that contain the intercepts.

Math On the Spot
⏻ my.hrw.com

EXAMPLE 1
COMMON CORE **F.IF.6**

Find the slope of the line described by $6x - 5y = 30$.

STEP 1   Find the x-intercept.

Substitute 0 for y in the equation and solve for x.

$$6x - 5y = 30$$

$6x - 5(0) = 30$ Substitute.

$6x - 0 = 30$ Simplify.

$6x = 30$

$x = 5$ Divide both sides by 6.

STEP 2   Find the y-intercept.

Substitute 0 for x in the equation and solve for y.

$$6x - 5y = 30$$

$6(0) - 5y = 30$ Substitute.

$0 - 5y = 30$ Simplify.

$-5y = 30$

$y = -6$ Divide both sides by -5.

STEP 3   The line contains $(5, 0)$ and $(0, -6)$. Use the slope formula.

$$m = \frac{\text{change in } y\text{-coordinates}}{\text{change in } x\text{-coordinates}}$$

$$= \frac{-6 - 0}{0 - 5}$$

$$= \frac{-6}{-5}$$

$$= \frac{6}{5}$$

The slope of the line is $\frac{6}{5}$.

Math Talk
Mathematical Practices

How can you check if the slope you calculated is correct?

© Houghton Mifflin Harcourt Publishing Company

Personal Math Trainer

Online Practice and Help

🔵 my.hrw.com

1. Find the slope of the line described by $3x + 4y = 12$. _____

My Notes

Exploring the Slope Formula

If you know the slope of a line and the y-intercept, you can write an equation that describes the line.

EXPLORE ACTIVITY   COMMON CORE   A.CED.2

Write an equation for the line that has slope 2 and y-intercept 3.

STEP 1 The line has a slope of ⬜ and a y-intercept of ⬜.

Since ⬜ is the y-intercept, (⬜, ⬜) is a point on the line.

Substitute these values into the slope formula. Since you don't know the coordinates of any other point on the line, use a generic ordered pair (x, y).

$$m = \frac{\text{change in } y\text{-coordinates}}{\text{change in } x\text{-coordinates}} \qquad \boxed{} = \frac{y - \boxed{}}{x - \boxed{}}$$

STEP 2 Solve for y.

$$\boxed{} = \frac{y - \boxed{}}{x - \boxed{}}$$

$$\boxed{} = \frac{y - \boxed{}}{\boxed{}}$$

$$\boxed{} = y - \boxed{}$$

$$\boxed{} + \boxed{} = y$$

In this equation, the coefficient of x is equal to the _____,

and the constant is equal to the _____.

If a line has slope m and the y-intercept is b, then the line is described by the equation $y = mx + b$. This equation is called the **slope-intercept form** of a linear equation. A linear equation can be written in slope-intercept form by solving for y and simplifying.

© Houghton Mifflin Harcourt Publishing Company

2. Why can it be helpful to solve a linear equation for *y*?

_____

_____

Graphing a Linear Function
Using the Slope and *y*-intercept

You can graph the linear function $f(x) = mx + b$ using only the slope *m* and *y*-intercept *b*. First, locate the point $(0, b)$ on the *y*-axis. Next, use the rise and run of the slope to locate another point on the line. Draw a line through the two points.

EXAMPLE 2
COMMON CORE   F.IF.7a

Graph the function $f(x) = -\frac{2}{3}x + 4$ and determine its domain and range.

STEP 1   The *y*-intercept is 4.
Plot the point $(0, 4)$.

STEP 2   The slope is $-\frac{2}{3}$. If you
use -2 as the rise, then
the run is 3.

Use the slope to move
from the *y*-intercept to
a second point. Begin
by moving down 2
units, because the rise
is negative. Then move
right 3 units because
the run is positive. Plot the second point, $(3, 2)$.

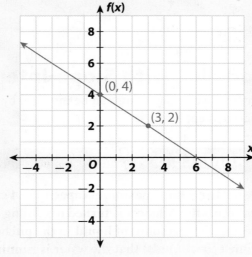

STEP 3   Draw a line through the two points.

STEP 4   The domain is the set of real numbers.
The range is the set of real numbers.

REFLECT

3. **Multiple Representations** How does the graph of the linear function
show that the domain is the set of real numbers and the range is the set of
real numbers?

_____

_____

_____

Graph each function.

4. $f(x) = -\frac{1}{2}x + 3$

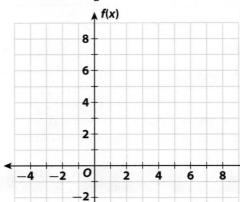

5. $f(x) = 2x - 1$

Modeling with Slope-Intercept Form

Many real-world situations can be modeled by linear equations in slope-intercept form.

EXAMPLE 3 *Real World*   COMMON CORE   F.IF.4, F.LE.1b

A pitcher with a maximum capacity of 4 cups contains 1 cup of apple juice concentrate. A faucet is turned on, filling the pitcher at a rate of 0.25 cup per second. The amount of liquid in the pitcher, $A(t)$, (in cups), is a function of the time t (in seconds) that the water is running. Graph the function $A(t)$, write the rule for the function, and state its domain and range.

STEP 1   The *y*-intercept is 1 because there is 1 cup in the pitcher at time 0. Plot the point that corresponds to the *y*-intercept, (0, 1).

STEP 2   The slope is the rate of change: 0.25 cup per second, or 1 cup in 4 seconds. So the rise is 1 and the run is 4.

STEP 3   Use the rise and run to move from the first point to a second point on the line by moving up 1 unit and right 4 units. Plot the second point, (4, 2).

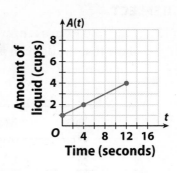

STEP 4   Connect the points and extend the line segment to the maximum value of the function, where $A(t) = 4$ cups.

STEP 5 Use $m = \frac{1}{4}$ and $b = 1$ to write the rule for the function: $A(t) = \frac{1}{4}t + 1$.

STEP 6 The domain is the set of all real numbers t such that $0 \leq t \leq 12$.

The range is the set of all real numbers $A(t)$ such that $1 \leq A(t) \leq 4$.

REFLECT

6. Critical Thinking Why are the domain and range restricted in Example 3, rather than each being the set of all real numbers?

_____

_____

_____

_____

_____

YOUR TURN

7. A pump is set to dispense chlorine from a full 5-gallon container into a swimming pool to sanitize the water. The pump will dispense the chlorine at a rate of 0.5 gallon per minute and will shut off when the container is empty. The amount of chlorine in the container, $A(t)$, (in gallons), is a function of the time t (in minutes) that the pump is running. Graph the function $A(t)$, write the rule for the function, and state its domain and range.

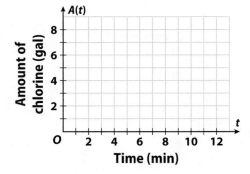

$A(t) =$ _____

Domain: _____

Range: _____

_____

Personal Math Trainer

Online Practice and Help

my.hrw.com

Find the slope of the line described by each equation. (Example 1)

1. $5x - 2y = 10$

$m =$ _____

2. $3y = 4$

$m =$ _____

3. $x - 3y = 6$

$m =$ _____

4. $4x + 2y = 12$

$m =$ _____

5. Graph the function $f(x) = -2x + 3$ and determine its domain and range. (Example 2)

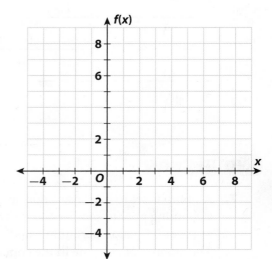

STEP 1 The y-intercept is ☐ .

Plot the point (☐ , ☐).

STEP 2 The slope is ☐ .

Use ☐ as the rise; then the run is ☐ .

Use the slope to move from the y-intercept to a second point. Begin by moving _____ unit(s). Then move _____ unit(s).

Plot the second point, (☐ , ☐).

STEP 3 Draw a line through the two points.

STEP 4 The domain is the set of _____ numbers.

The range is the set of _____ numbers.

? ESSENTIAL QUESTION CHECK-IN

6. How is the rate of change in a real-world linear relationship related to the slope-intercept form of the equation that represents the relationship?

_____

_____

_____

_____

6.4 Independent Practice

Personal Math Trainer

Online Practice and Help

my.hrw.com

COMMON CORE   F.IF.4, F.IF.6, F.IF.7, F.IF.7a, F.LE.1b, A.CED.2

Find the slope of the line described by each equation.

7. $5x + 3y = 0$

$m = $ _____

8. $3y = 6$

$m = $ _____

9. $6x - 12y = 36$

$m = $ _____

10. When graphing a linear function in slope-intercept form, why do you have to plot the y-intercept first? Why can't you use the slope first?

_____

_____

_____

_____

Graph each linear function.

11. $f(x) = \frac{1}{4}x - 3$

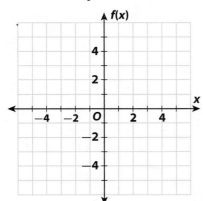

12. $f(x) = -5x + 1$

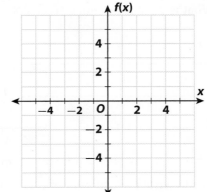

13. $f(x) = -1$

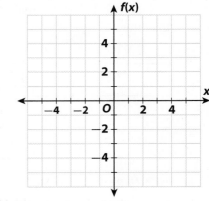

14. A company rents moving vans for a charge of $30 plus $0.50 per mile. The company only allows its vans to be used for "in-town" moves, with total mileage limited to 100 miles. The total rental cost, $C(m)$, (in dollars) is a function of the distance m (in miles) that the van is driven. State a rule for the function, graph the function, and state its domain and range.

$C(m) = $ _____

Domain: _____

_____

Range: _____

_____

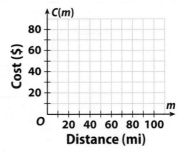

Work Area

15. Draw Conclusions The standard form of a linear equation is $Ax + By = C$. Rewrite this equation in slope-intercept form. What is the slope? What is the y-intercept?

_____

_____

16. What If? What if the person filling the pitcher in Example 3 gets distracted by a phone call and does not get to turn the faucet off as soon as the pitcher is full? How does this affect the domain and range of the function? How does it affect the graph?

_____

_____

_____

_____

_____

17. Find the Error Alyssa correctly determines that the graph of a linear equation intersects the x-axis at $(6, 0)$ and intersects the y-axis at $(0, 2)$. She calculates the slope and then writes the slope-intercept equation for the line as $y = -\frac{1}{3}x + 6$. What error did Alyssa make? What is the correct slope-intercept equation for this line?

_____

_____

_____

_____

18. Justify Reasoning Is it possible to write the equation of every line in slope-intercept form? Explain your reasoning.

_____

_____

_____

_____

_____

_____

Comparing Linear Functions

COMMON CORE **F.IF.9**
Compare properties of two functions each represented in a different way (algebraically, graphically, numerically in tables, or by verbal descriptions). *Also F.IF.1, F.IF.2, F.IF.5, F.LE.5, N.Q.1*

ESSENTIAL QUESTION

How can you compare linear functions that are represented in different ways?

EXPLORE ACTIVITY   COMMON CORE F.IF.9

Comparing Linear Relationships

Comparing linear relationships sometimes involves comparing relationships that are expressed in different ways.

Joe's Plumbing and Mark's Plumbing have different ways of charging their customers. The function defined by $J(t) = 40t$ represents the total amount in dollars that Joe's Plumbing charges for t hours of work. Mark's Plumbing Service charges $40 per hour plus a $25 trip charge.

A Define a function $M(t)$ that represents the total amount Mark's Plumbing Service charges for t hours of work and then complete the charts below.

$M(t) = 40t + 25$ represents the total amount in dollars that Mark's Plumbing Service charges for t hours of work.

Cost for Joe's Plumbing		
t	$J(t) = 40t$	$(t, J(t))$
0	0	$(0, 0)$
1		
2		
3		

Cost for Mark's Plumbing Service		
t	$M(t) = 40t + 25$	$(t, M(t))$
0	0	$(0, 25)$
1		
2		
3		

B What domain values for the functions $J(t)$ and for $M(t)$ are reasonable in this context? Explain.

_____

_____

C Graph the two cost functions for all appropriate domain values.

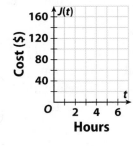

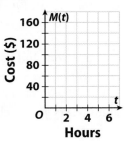

D Compare the graphs. How are they alike? How are they different?

_____

_____

REFLECT

1. Describe the range for $J(t)$ and $M(t)$.

_____

_____

_____

Math On the Spot

⏻ my.hrw.com

Comparing Linear Functions Given a Table and a Rule

A table and a rule are two ways that a linear relationship may be expressed. Sometimes it may be helpful to convert one representation to the other when comparing two relationships. Other times, making comparisons may be possible without converting either representation.

EXAMPLE 1

COMMON CORE · F.IF.9

The functions $f(x)$ and $g(x)$ are linear functions. The domain of each function is the set of all real numbers x such that $4 \le x \le 7$. The table shows some ordered pairs belonging to $f(x)$. The function $g(x)$ is defined by the rule $g(x) = 2x + 3$. Find the initial value and the range of each function.

x	f(x)
4	8
5	10
6	12
7	14

The initial value is the output that is paired with the least input.

The initial value of $f(x)$ is $f(4) = 8$ *The least input for f(x) is 4.*

The initial value of $g(x)$ is $g(4) = 2(4) + 3 = 11$.   *The least input for g(x) is 4.*

Since $f(x)$ is a linear function, and its domain is the set of all real numbers from 4 to 7, its range will be the set of all real numbers from $f(4)$ to $f(7)$. $f(4) = 8$ and $f(7) = 14$. Therefore, the range of $f(x)$ is the set of all real numbers $f(x)$ such that $8 \le f(x) \le 14$.

Since $g(x)$ is a linear function, and its domain is the set of all real numbers from 4 to 7, its range will be the set of all real numbers from $g(4)$ to $g(7)$. $g(4) = 2(4) + 3 = 11$ and $g(7) = 2(7) + 3 = 17$. Therefore, the range of $g(x)$ is the set of all real numbers $g(x)$ such that $11 \le g(x) \le 17$.

© Houghton Mifflin Harcourt Publishing Company

2. The rule for $f(x)$ is $f(x) = 2x$. If the domains were extended to all real numbers, how would the slopes and y-intercepts of $f(x)$ and $g(x)$ compare?

_____

_____

_____

Personal Math Trainer

Online Practice and Help

⏱ my.hrw.com

Comparing Linear Functions Given a Description and a Graph

Information about a relationship may have to be inferred from the context given in the problem.

Math On the Spot

⏱ my.hrw.com

EXAMPLE 2

COMMON CORE F.IF.9

Compare the following functions.

- A rainstorm in Atlanta lasted for 2.5 hours, during which time it rained at a steady rate of 0.5 inch per hour. The function $A(t)$ represents the amount of rain that fell in t hours.

- The graph at the right shows the amount of rain that fell during a rainstorm in Knoxville, $K(t)$ (in inches), as a function of time t (in hours).

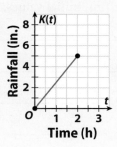

STEP 1 Write a rule for each function.

$A(t) = 0.5t$ for $0 \leq t \leq 2.5$

Since $(0, 0)$ and $(2, 5)$ are the coordinates of points on the line representing $K(t)$, the slope of the line is $\frac{5-0}{2-0} = \frac{5}{2} = 2.5$. The y-intercept is 0, so substituting 2.5 for m and 0 for b in $y = mx + b$ produces $y = 2.5t$, which yields $K(t) = 2.5t$ for $0 \leq t \leq 2$.

STEP 2 Compare the y-intercepts of the graphs of $A(t)$ and $K(t)$.

They are both 0.

Math Talk
Mathematical Practices

What is the meaning of the y-intercepts for the functions $A(t)$ and $K(t)$?

3. How do the slopes of the graphs of the functions $A(t)$ and $K(t)$ compare?

_____

_____

Personal Math Trainer

Online Practice and Help

⏱ my.hrw.com

The linear function $f(x)$ is defined by the table below. The linear function $g(x)$ is defined by the graph below. Assume that the domain of $f(x)$ includes all real numbers between the least and greatest values shown in the table. (Examples 1–2)

x	f(x)
0	−2
1	1
2	4
3	7
4	10
5	13

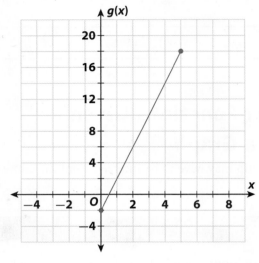

1. Compare the domains, initial values, and ranges of the functions.

Domain of $f(x)$: _____

Domain of $g(x)$: _____

Initial value of $f(x)$: _____

Initial value of $g(x)$: _____

Range of $f(x)$: _____

Range of $g(x)$: _____

2. Calculate how many inches of rain fell per hour during the Knoxville storm in Example 2. How many more inches per hour is this than in the Atlanta storm? (Example 2)

_____

3. How can you compare a linear function represented in a table to one represented as a graph?

_____

_____

_____

Transforming Linear Functions

COMMON CORE F.BF.3

Identify the effect on the graph of replacing $f(x)$ by $f(x) + k$, $k\,f(x)$, $f(kx)$, and $f(x + k)$ for specific values of k (both positive and negative); find the value of k given the graphs. Experiment with cases and illustrate an explanation of the effects on the graph using technology. *Also F.IF.4, F.LE.5*

? ESSENTIAL QUESTION

How are changes to the parameters of a linear function reflected in its graph?

EXPLORE ACTIVITY 1   COMMON CORE F.BF.3

Changing the Parameter b in $f(x) = mx + b$

Changing the value of m or b in $f(x) = mx + b$ causes a change in the graph of that function.

Investigate what happens to the graph of $f(x) = x + b$ when you change the value of b.

A Use a graphing calculator. Start with the standard viewing window, which you can obtain by pressing ZOOM and selecting ZStandard. If the distances between consecutive tick marks on the x-axis and y-axis are not equal, you can make them equal by pressing ZOOM again and selecting ZSquare.

What interval on each axis does the viewing window now show? (Press WINDOW to find out.)

_____

B Graph the function $f(x) = x$ by pressing Y= and entering the function's rule next to $Y_1 =$. As shown, the graph of the function is a line that makes a 45° angle with each axis.

What are the slope and y-intercept of the graph of $f(x) = x$?

_____

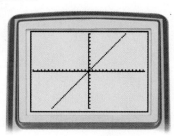

C Graph other functions of the form $f(x) = x + b$ by entering their rules next to $Y_2 =$, $Y_3 =$, and so on. Be sure to choose both positive and negative values of b. For instance, graph $f(x) = x + 2$ and $f(x) = x - 3$.

What do the graphs have in common? How are they different?

_____

REFLECT

1. A *vertical translation* moves all points on a figure the same distance either up or down. Use the idea of a vertical translation to describe what happens to the graph of $f(x) = x + b$ when you increase the value of b and decrease the value of b.

_____

_____

Changing the Parameter m in $f(x) = mx + b$

Investigate what happens to the graph of $f(x) = mx$ when you change the value of m.

A Use a graphing calculator. Press [Y=] and clear out all but the function $f(x) = x$ from Explore Activity 1. Then graph other functions of the form $f(x) = mx$ by entering their rules next to $Y_2=$, $Y_3=$, and so on. Use only values of m that are greater than 1. For instance, graph $f(x) = 2x$ and $f(x) = 6x$.

What do the graphs have in common? How are they different?

_____

_____

As the value of m increases from 1, does the graph become steeper or less

steep? _____

B Again, press [Y=] and clear out all but the function $f(x) = x$. Then graph other functions of the form $f(x) = mx$ by entering their rules next to $Y_2=$, $Y_3=$, and so on. This time use only values of m that are less than 1 but greater than 0. For instance, graph $f(x) = 0.5x$ and $f(x) = 0.2x$.

As the value of m decreases from 1 to 0, does the graph become steeper or

less steep? _____

C Again, press [Y=] and clear out all but the function $f(x) = x$. Then graph the function $f(x) = -x$ by entering its rule next to $Y_2=$.

What are the slope and y-intercept of the graph of $f(x) = -x$?

_____

How are the graphs of $f(x) = x$ and $f(x) = -x$ geometrically related?

_____

_____

D Again, press [Y=] and clear out all the functions. Graph $f(x) = -x$ by entering its rule next to $Y_1=$. Then graph other functions of the form $f(x) = mx$ where $m < 0$ by entering their rules next to $Y_2=$, $Y_3=$, and so on. Be sure to choose values of m that are less than -1 as well as values of m between -1 and 0.

Describe what happens to the graph of $f(x) = mx$ as the value of m decreases from -1 and as it increases from -1 to 0.

_____

_____

_____

My Notes

REFLECT

2. A function $f(x)$ is called an *increasing function* when the value of $f(x)$ always increases as the value of x increases. For what values of m is the function $f(x) = mx$ an increasing function? How can you tell from the graph of a linear function that it is an increasing function?

_____

3. A function $f(x)$ is called a *decreasing function* when the value of $f(x)$ always decreases as the value of x increases. For what values of m is the function $f(x) = mx$ a decreasing function? How can you tell from the graph of a linear function that it is a decreasing function?

_____

4. When $m > 0$, increasing the value of m results in an increasing linear function that increases *faster*. What effect does increasing m have on the graph of the function?

_____

5. When $m > 0$, decreasing the value of m toward 0 results in an increasing linear function that increases *slower*. What effect does decreasing m have on the graph of the function?

_____

6. When $m < 0$, decreasing the value of m results in a decreasing linear function that decreases *faster*. What effect does decreasing m have on the graph of the function?

_____

7. When $m < 0$, increasing the value of m toward 0 results in a decreasing linear function that decreases *slower*. What effect does increasing m have on the graph of the function?

_____

8. The *steepness* of a line refers to the absolute value of its slope. The greater the absolute value of the slope, the steeper the line. Complete the table to summarize, in terms of steepness, the effect of changing the value of m on the graph of $f(x) = mx$.

How the Value of m Changes	Effect on the Graph of $f(x) = mx$
Increase m when $m > 0$.	
Decrease m toward 0 when $m > 0$.	
Decrease m when $m < 0$.	
Increase m toward 0 when $m < 0$.	

COMMON CORE   F.BF.3

Families of Linear Functions

A A **family of functions** is a set of functions whose graphs have basic characteristics in common. What do all these variations on the original function $f(x) = x$ have in common?

_____

B The most basic function of a family of functions is called the **parent function**. What is the parent function of the family of functions explored in the first two Explore Activities?

_____

C A **parameter** is one of the constants in a function or equation that determines which variation of the parent function one is considering. For functions of the form $f(x) = mx + b$, what are the two parameters?

_____

For the family of all linear functions, the parent function is $f(x) = x$, where the parameters are $m = 1$ and $b = 0$. Other examples of families of linear functions are shown below. The example on the left shows a family with the same parameter m and differing parameters b. The example on the right shows a family with the same parameter b and differing parameters m.

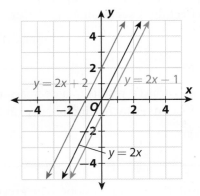
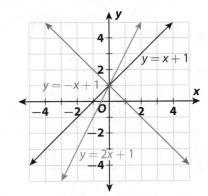

REFLECT

9. Describe the parameter that is left unchanged in the equations of the lines in the graph on the left above.

_____

_____

Math On the Spot
my.hrw.com

Modeling with Parameter Changes

Real-world scenarios can often be modeled by linear functions. Changes in a particular scenario can be analyzed by making changes in the corresponding parameter of the linear function.

EXAMPLE 1 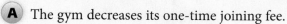 Real World

A gym charges a one-time joining fee of $50 and then a monthly membership fee of $25. The total cost C of being a member of the gym is given by the function $C(t) = 25t + 50$, where t is the time (in months) since joining the gym. For each situation described below, sketch a graph using the given graph of $C(t) = 25t + 50$ as a reference. Describe the impact of the changes on the domain and range of the function.

A The gym decreases its one-time joining fee.

Rather than graphing a specific function for this situation, sketch a representative graph of a function related to the function $C(t) = 25t + 50$ with the appropriate parameter changed.

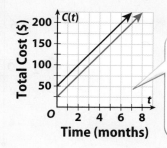

To sketch a graph that represents the new situation, make the y-intercept of the graph lower, but leave the slope the same.

The one-time joining fee is represented by the constant in the equation; the constant represents the y-intercept of the graph.

There is no change in the domain, but the bottom number of the range decreases from $C(t) = 50$ to $C(t)$ equals the new joining fee.

B The gym increases its monthly membership fee.

Rather than graphing a specific function for this situation, sketch a representative graph of a function related to the function $C(t) = 25t + 50$ with the appropriate parameter changed.

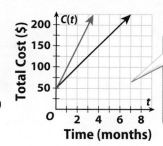

To sketch a graph that represents the new situation, increase the slope of the graph but leave the y-intercept the same.

The monthly membership fee is represented by the coefficient of t in the equation; the coefficient of t represents the slope of the graph.

There is no change in the domain or the range.

Animated Math
⏻ my.hrw.com

Math Talk
Mathematical Practices

Why is the graph of the function only in the first quadrant?

YOUR TURN

10. Once a year the gym offers a special in which the one-time joining fee is waived for new members. What impact does this special offer have on the graph of the original function $C(t) = 25t + 50$?

_____

_____

Personal Math Trainer

Online Practice and Help

⏻ my.hrw.com

1. The graph of the function $f(x) = x + 3$ is shown below. Graph two more functions in the same family for which the parameter being changed is the y-intercept. (Example 1)

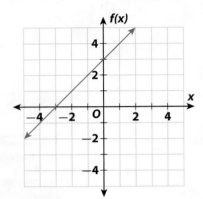

2. The graph of the function $f(x) = x + 3$ is shown below. Graph two more functions in the same family for which the parameter being changed is the slope. (Example 1)

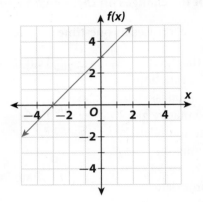

3. For the family of linear functions of the form $f(x) = mx + b$, the parameter

   that causes the steepness of the graph of the line to change is _____.
   (Explore Activities 1 and 2)

4. The graph of the parent linear function $f(x) = x$ is shown in black on the coordinate grid. Write the color of the line that represents this function with the indicated parameter changes. (Explore Activities 1 and 2)

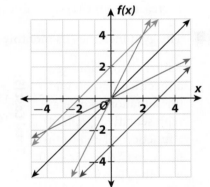

   a. m increased, b unchanged _____

   b. m decreased, b unchanged _____

   c. m unchanged, b increased _____

   d. m unchanged, b decreased _____

? ESSENTIAL QUESTION CHECK-IN

5. How do changes in m and b in the equation $y = mx + b$ affect the graph of the equation?

   _____

   _____

   _____

   _____

   _____

6.6 Independent Practice

COMMON CORE F.BF.3, F.IF.4, F.LE.5

Personal Math Trainer

Online Practice and Help

my.hrw.com

6. A salesperson earns a base monthly salary of \$2000 plus a 10% commission on sales. The salesperson's monthly income I (in dollars) is given by the function $I(s) = 0.1s + 2000$, where s is the sales (in dollars) that the salesperson makes. Sketch a graph to illustrate each situation using the graph of $I(s) = 0.1s + 2000$ as a reference.

a. The salesperson's base salary is increased.

b. The salesperson's commission rate is decreased.

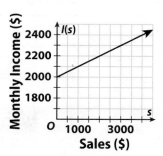

7. Mr. Resnick is driving at a speed of 40 miles per hour to visit relatives who live 100 miles away from his home. His distance d (in miles) from his destination is given by the function $d(t) = 100 - 40t$, where t is the time (in hours) since his trip began. Sketch a graph to illustrate each situation. The graphs shown already represent the function $d(t)$.

a. He increases his speed to get to his destination sooner.

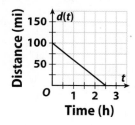

b. He encounters a detour that increases the driving distance.

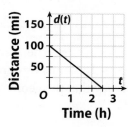

c. Give an example of another linear function within the same family of functions as $d(t) = 100 - 40t$. Explain the meaning of each parameter in your example.

_____

_____

8. Use the graph of $d(t) = 100 - 40t$ in Exercise 7 to identify the domain and range of the function. Then tell whether the domain, the range, neither, or both are affected by the changes described in each part.

_____

_____

9. For each linear function graphed on the coordinate grid, state the value of m and the value of b.

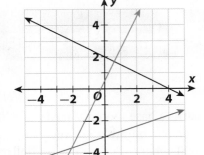

   a. black line: $m =$ _____, $b =$ _____

   b. blue line: $m =$ _____, $b =$ _____

   c. green line: $m =$ _____, $b =$ _____

10. Suppose the gym in Example 1 increases its one-time joining fee and decreases its monthly membership fee. Describe how you would alter the graph of $C(t) = 25t + 50$ to illustrate the new cost function.

_____

_____

_____

 **FOCUS ON HIGHER ORDER THINKING**

Work Area

11. Critique Reasoning Geoff says that changing the value of m while leaving b unchanged in $f(x) = mx + b$ has no impact on the intercepts of the graph. Marcus disagrees with this statement. Who is correct? Explain your reasoning.

_____

_____

_____

_____

12. Multiple Representations The graph of $y = x + 3$ is a vertical translation of the graph of $y = x + 1$, 2 units upward. Examine the intercepts of both lines and state another way that the geometric relationship between the two graphs can be described.

_____

_____

13. Critique Reasoning Stephanie says that the graphs of $y = 3x + 2$ and $y = 3x - 2$ are parallel. Isabella says that the graphs are perpendicular. Who is correct? Explain your reasoning.

_____

_____

_____

Writing Linear Functions

COMMON CORE **F.LE.2**
Construct liner and exponential functions, including arithmetic and geometric sequences, given a graph, a description of a relationship, or two input-output pairs (include reading these from a table). *Also A.CED.2, F.IF.6, F.BF.1*

? **ESSENTIAL QUESTION**

How can you represent a function symbolically from a graph, verbal description, or table of values?

Using Slope to Write a Linear Function

The information needed to write the equation of a linear function can be provided in different ways, including presented as a graph, given as a description of a relationship, or as input-output pairs. If you know the slope and the y-intercept of a linear function, you can find an equation representing the function.

Math On the Spot
my.hrw.com

EXAMPLE 1
COMMON CORE **A.CED.2, F.LE.2**

Write an equation for the linear function $f(x)$ whose graph has a slope of 3 and a y-intercept of -1.

A linear function has the form $f(x) = mx + b$ where m is the slope and b is the y-intercept.

$$f(x) = mx + b$$

$$f(x) = 3x + (-1)$$ The slope was given as 3, so substitute 3 for m.
The y-intercept was given as -1, so substitute -1 for b.

$$f(x) = 3x - 1$$

An equation for the function is $f(x) = 3x - 1$.

Math Talk
Mathematical Practices
If you graph the function $f(x)$, how can you use the graph to find more ordered pairs that satisfy the equation $f(x) = 3x - 1$?

REFLECT

1. How can you use the equation $f(x) = 3x - 1$ to find more ordered pairs that are part of the function?

_____

_____

YOUR TURN

Write an equation for the linear function $f(x)$ whose graph has the given slope and y-intercept.

2. slope of 4, y-intercept of -2

3. slope of -3, y-intercept of 5

_____

_____

4. slope of 6, y-intercept of 0

5. slope of 0, y-intercept of 6

_____

_____

Personal Math Trainer
Online Practice and Help
my.hrw.com

My Notes

EXAMPLE 2

COMMON CORE   A.CED.2, F.IF.6, F.LE.2

The table shows several ordered pairs for the linear function $f(x)$. Write an equation for $f(x)$.

x	f(x)
−1	5
3	−3
7	−11

STEP 1   Calculate the slope using any two ordered pairs from the table. Choose $(−1, 5)$ as the first point and $(3, −3)$ as the second point.

$$\text{slope} = \frac{y_2 - y_1}{x_2 - x_1}$$ Slope Formula

$$m = \frac{-3 - 5}{3 - (-1)}$$ Substitute values.

$$= \frac{-8}{4}$$ Simplify numerator and denominator.

$$= -2$$ Simplify fraction.

STEP 2   Find the value of b using the fact that $m = -2$ and $f(-1) = 5$.

$$f(x) = -2x + b$$ Write the function with the known value of m.

$$5 = -2(-1) + b$$ Substitute −1 for x and 5 for f(x).

$$5 = 2 + b$$ Simplify the right side of the equation.

$$3 = b$$ Solve for b.

So, the function is $f(x) = -2x + 3$.

REFLECT

6. How can you check that the equation is correct?

_____

_____

YOUR TURN

Write an equation of the linear function represented by each table of values.

7.

x	f(x)
−1	−4
1	6
3	16

8.

x	f(x)
−1	1
2	−5
4	−9

© Houghton Mifflin Harcourt Publishing Company

Writing a Linear Function from a Graph

Writing a linear function from a graph requires the same information and steps as writing a linear function from a table of values. The difference is that the ordered pairs must be determined from the graph. The ordered pairs may or may not be explicitly labeled.

Math On the Spot
⏱ my.hrw.com

EXAMPLE 3   COMMON CORE F.LE.2, F.IF.6, F.BF.1

The graph below shows the increase in pressure (measured in pounds per square inch) as a scuba diver descends from a depth of 10 feet to a depth of 30 feet. Pressure is a linear function of depth. At the water's surface, the pressure on the diver is a result of the pressure of the air in the atmosphere. What is the pressure on the diver at the water's surface?

STEP 1 Interpret the question.

Let $P(d)$ represent the pressure in pounds per square inch on the diver at a depth of d feet. At the water's surface, $d = 0$. If the graph below is extended to meet the vertical axis, the value $P(0)$ would represent the pressure on the diver at the water's surface.

STEP 2 Find the value of m in $P(d) = md + b$. Use the fact that $P(10) = 19.1$ and $P(30) = 28.0$.

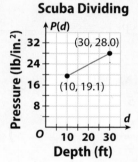

Scuba Dividing

$\text{slope} = \dfrac{\text{rise}}{\text{run}}$ Definition of slope

$m = \dfrac{P(30) - P(10)}{30 - 10}$ Write the slope formula.

$= \dfrac{28.0 - 19.1}{30 - 10}$ Substitute values.

$= \dfrac{8.9}{20}$ Simplify numerator and denominator.

$= 0.445$ Write in decimal form.

STEP 3 Now that you know the slope, you can find the value of b in $P(d) = md + b$. Use the value of m from Step 2 as well as the fact that $P(10) = 19.1$.

$P(d) = 0.445d + b$ Write the function with the known value of m.

$19.1 = 0.445(10) + b$ Substitute 10 for d and 19.1 for $P(d)$.

$19.1 = 4.45 + b$ Simplify the right side of the equation.

$14.7 \approx b$ Solve for b. Round to the nearest tenth.

An equation for the function is $P(d) = 0.445d + 14.7$.

STEP 4 Find the pressure at the water's surface, where $d = 0$.

$P(0) = 0.445(0) + 14.7$

$= 14.7$

The pressure on the diver at the water's surface is 14.7 pounds per square inch.

YOUR TURN

9. The graph of the linear function $f(x)$ is shown. Write an equation for the function. Then find $f(0)$.

_____

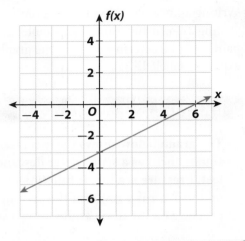

Guided Practice

Write an equation for the linear function $f(x)$ using the given information. (Examples 1–3)

1. slope $-\frac{3}{2}$, y-intercept 1 _____

2.

x	$f(x)$
-4	5
-2	6
4	9

_____

3.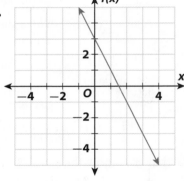

_____

? ESSENTIAL QUESTION CHECK-IN

4. What information can you use from the graph of a linear function to write the function?

_____

_____

_____

_____

6.7 Independent Practice

COMMON CORE F.LE.2, A.CED.2, F.IF.6, F.BF.1

Write an equation for the linear function $f(x)$ using the given information.

5. The graph of the function has a slope of $-\frac{2}{3}$ and a y-intercept of 5.

_____

6. The graph of the function has a slope of $\frac{7}{4}$ and a y-intercept of 0.

_____

7.

x	f(x)
0	−3
2	0
4	3

_____

8.

x	f(x)
5	−2
10	−6
15	−10

_____

9.

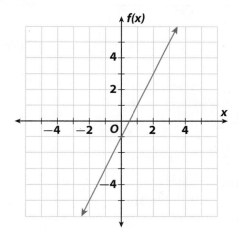

_____

10.

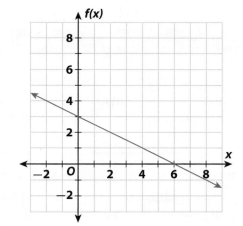

_____

11. Represent Real-World Problems Javier begins to save for a new bicycle that costs $415. He already has $140 and plans to save $25 per week. Let w represent the number of weeks he has been saving and $s(w)$ represent the total amount in dollars that he has saved. How long does he have to save to buy the bicycle?

a. Give the slope and the y-intercept of the function.

_____

b. Write a linear function using the given information. _____

c. Describe how to use the function to answer the question, and then answer the question.

_____

12. The graph shows the amount of gas remaining in the gas tank of Mrs. Liu's car as she drives at a steady speed for 2 hours. How long can she drive before her car runs out of gas?

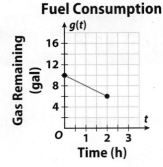

Fuel Consumption

a. Interpret the question by describing what aspect of the graph would answer the question.

_____

_____

b. Write a linear function whose graph includes the segment shown.

_____

c. Describe how to use the function to answer the question, and then answer the question.

_____

_____

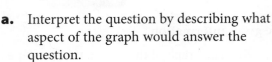 **FOCUS ON HIGHER ORDER THINKING**

Work Area

13. Draw Conclusions Maria and Sam are asked to write an equation representing a linear function with a slope of 2 and y-intercept of -3. Maria writes $y = 2x - 3$. Sam writes $2x - y = 3$. Who is correct? Explain.

_____

14. Communicate Mathematical Ideas You are given a table of values that represent a function, but you are not told whether the function is linear. How could you use the table to determine whether the function is linear?

_____

_____

_____

_____

15. Explain the Error Andrew was told that a linear function had a slope of 3 and that $(-2, 0)$ was on the graph. He wrote the function as $f(x) = 3x - 2$. What error did Andrew make? Write the function correctly.

_____

_____

_____

6.1–6.2 Linear Functions/Using Intercepts

Tell whether each equation is a linear function. If so, give the intercepts.

1. $12x + 3y = 6$

2. $-x^2 + 6y = 24$

3. $6x - \frac{1}{2}y = 3$

_____   _____   _____

6.3–6.4 Using Slope/Slope-Intercept Form

Rewrite in slope-intercept form. Find the slope and y-intercept.

4. $2x + 2y = 8$

5. $8x - 4y = 24$

6. $9 = 3y$

_____   _____   _____

_____   _____   _____

6.5–6.6 Comparing/Transforming Linear Functions

7. Graph each linear function. Compare their domains and ranges. Describe the effect of the parameters on each graph compared to the graph of $y = x$.

a. $f(x) = 3x - 2$

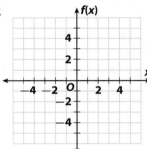

b. $f(x) = \frac{1}{3}x + 2$

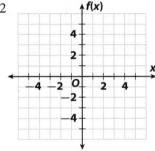

_____

_____

_____

6.7 Writing Linear Functions

8. The graph of the linear function $f(x)$ has a slope of $-\frac{3}{2}$ and a y-intercept

of -1. Write an equation for the function. _____

? ESSENTIAL QUESTION

9. What are some ways that linear functions can be represented? Give an example of how different representations are related.

_____

_____

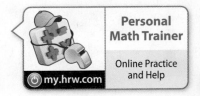
1. Is the graph of each linear function steeper than the one shown at the right?

   Select Yes or No for functions A–C.

   A. $f(x) = 0.5(x + 2)$ ○ Yes ○ No

   B. $f(x) = 1 + 2x$ ○ Yes ○ No

   C. $f(x) = \frac{3}{4}x + 1$ ○ Yes ○ No

2. Consider the linear function shown in the graph at the right.

   Choose True or False for each statement.

   A. The slope is $-\frac{1}{3}$. ○ True ○ False

   B. The function has no x-intercept. ○ True ○ False

   C. The y-intercept is 2. ○ True ○ False

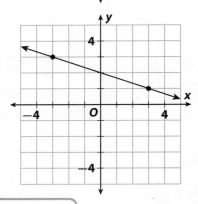

3. The function $f(x) = 16x + 12$ gives the number of pages Gwen has read in *The War of the Worlds* after x days, and the function $g(x) = 18x$ gives the number of pages Owen has read after x days. After how many days will Gwen and Owen have read the same number of pages? Explain how you solved this problem.

4. A truck driver is traveling from Sacramento to Reno. After 1 hour, the driver is 84 miles from Reno. After 2 hours, the driver is 36 miles from Reno. Write the linear function that relates the time x in hours since leaving Sacramento to the driver's distance y in miles from Reno. Explain the meaning of the slope and y-intercept in this situation.

Building Linear Functions

? ESSENTIAL QUESTION

How are mathematical operations related to solving linear equations and inequalities and creating new functions?

my.hrw.com

Real-World Video

Periodic comets have orbital periods of less than 200 years. Halley's comet is the only short-period comet that is visible to the naked eye. It returns every 76 years. You can build functions to represent and model predictable occurrences, such the recurrence of Halley's comet.

GO DIGITAL
my.hrw.com

my.hrw.com

Go digital with your write-in student edition, accessible on any device.

Math On the Spot

Scan with your smart phone to jump directly to the online edition, video tutor, and more.

X^2

Animated Math

Interactively explore key concepts to see how math works.

Personal Math Trainer

Get immediate feedback and help as you work through practice sets.

Are YOU Ready?

Complete these exercises to review skills you will need for this module.

Personal Math Trainer

my.hrw.com

Online Practice and Help

Evaluate Expressions

EXAMPLE   Evaluate $3x - 1$ for $x = 2$.

$3(2) - 1$ *Substitute 2 for x.*

$6 - 1$ *Simplify.*

5

Evaluate each expression for $x = -3$, 0, and 3.

1. $2x - 3$

2. $\frac{2}{3}x + 1$

3. $-2x + 4$

_____

4. $-x$

5. $x - 5$

6. $\frac{x}{2}$

_____

Solve for a Variable

EXAMPLE   Solve $4x - 2y = 10$ for y.

$4x - 2y = 10$

$-2y = -4x + 10$ *Subtract 4x from both sides.*

$y = 2x - 5$ *Divide both sides by −2.*

Solve each equation for y.

7. $y + 2 = 3x$

8. $2x - \frac{3}{4}y = -6$

9. $14 = x + (-2y)$

_____

Solve and Graph Inequalities

EXAMPLE   Solve and graph $x - 9 > -10$.

$x - 9 > -10$

$\underline{+9 > +9}$ *Add 9 to both sides.*

$x \quad > \quad -1$

Use an open circle for $>$.

Solve and graph each inequality.

10. $1 > x - 3$

11. $-5x \le -15$

_____

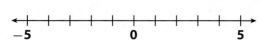

Reading Start-Up

Visualize Vocabulary

Use the Review words to complete the bubble map. You may put more than one word in each bubble. Some words may not be used.

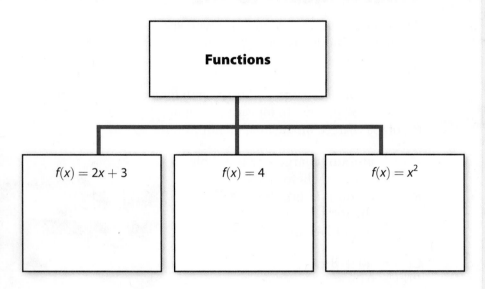

Functions

$f(x) = 2x + 3$

$f(x) = 4$

$f(x) = x^2$

Vocabulary

Review Words

constant function *(función constante)*

function *(función)*

function rule *(fórmula de función)*

inequality *(desigualdad)*

linear function *(función lineal)*

nonlinear function *(función no lineal)*

rate of change *(tasa de cambio)*

Preview Words

arithmetic sequence

boundary line

common difference

function of *x*

half-plane

inverse function

linear inequality

one-to-one function

solution of an inequality

Understand Vocabulary

To become familiar with some of the vocabulary terms in the module, consider the following. You may refer to the module, the glossary, or a dictionary.

1. Functions in which each *y*-value corresponds to only one *x*-value

   are called _____.

2. The term **boundary line** refers to part of the graph of a linear inequality. What part of the graph do you think **boundary line** refers to?

   _____

Active Reading

Four-Corner Fold Before beginning the module, create a four-corner fold to help you organize what you learn. As you study this module, note important ideas, vocabulary, properties, and formulas on the flaps. Use one flap for each lesson in the module. You can use your FoldNote later to study for tests and complete assignments.

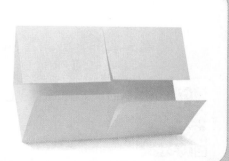

COMMON CORE

GETTING READY FOR
Building Linear Functions

Understanding the standards and the vocabulary terms in the standards will help you know exactly what you are expected to learn in this module.

 F.BF.1

Write a function that describes a relationship between two quantities.

Key Vocabulary

function *(función)*
A type of relation that pairs each element in the domain with exactly one element in the range.

What It Means to You

You can add, subtract, or multiply with linear functions to model real-world situations.

EXAMPLE F.BF.1

A cable company charges \$40 per month for basic cable plus an additional \$8 per month for each premium cable channel. There is a tax of 9% charged on the total monthly bill.

$C(c)$ = amount charged by the cable company before taxes
$R(c)$ = amount of tax charged
$T(c)$ = the total amount of the monthly cable bill

$C(c) = 40 + 8c$
$R(c) = 0.09$
$T(c) = C(c) \times R(c) = 3.6 + 0.72c$

COMMON CORE **F.BF.4a**

Solve an equation of the form $f(x) = c$ for a simple function f that has an inverse and write an expression for the inverse.

Key Vocabulary

inverse function *(función inversa)*
The function that results from exchanging the input and output values of a one-to-one function.

What It Means to You

You can find the inverse of a function by using inverse operations to solve for one variable and then switching the variables.

EXAMPLE F.BF.4A

To find the inverse of $f(x) = 3x - 12$, replace $f(x)$ with y.

$$y = 3x - 12$$

Then, solve the equation for x.

$$y + 12 = 3x$$
$$\tfrac{1}{3}y + 4 = x$$

Switch x and y in the equation.

$$\tfrac{1}{3}x + 4 = y$$

Replace y with the inverse function notation.

$$f^{-1}(x) = \tfrac{1}{3}x + 4$$

Visit **my.hrw.com** to see all **Common Core Standards** unpacked.

my.hrw.com

LESSON
7.1 Arithmetic Sequences

COMMON CORE F.BF.2

Write arithmetic and geometric sequences both recursively and with an explicit formula, use them to model situations, and translate between the two forms. *Also F.LE.2, F.IF.3, F.BF.1a*

ESSENTIAL QUESTION

How are rules for arithmetic sequences and linear functions alike, and how are they different?

EXPLORE ACTIVITY   **COMMON CORE** F.IF.3

Exploring Arithmetic Sequences

Avocados cost $1.50 each at the local market. The total cost, in dollars, of a avocados can be found using $C(a) = 1.5a$.

A Complete the table of values for $C(a) = 1.5a$.

Avocados	1	2	3	4
Total Cost ($)				

B List the consecutive elements of the range. _____

C What is the difference between any two consecutive elements of the range? _____

Math Talk
Mathematical Practices

How is the domain limited for this situation?

Writing Rules for an Arithmetic Sequence

In an **arithmetic sequence**, the difference between consecutive terms is always the same. The constant difference is called the **common difference**, often written as d.

Rules for arithmetic sequences can be *recursive* or *explicit*. A **recursive rule** gives the first term and defines the nth term by relating it to the previous term. An **explicit rule** defines the nth term as a function of n.

Math On the Spot
my.hrw.com

EXAMPLE 1   **COMMON CORE** F.IF.3, F.BF.1a, F.BF.2

This table shows the end-of-month balances in a bank account that does not earn interest. Write a recursive rule and an explicit rule for the arithmetic sequence described by the table.

Month	n	1	2	3	4	5
Account Balance ($)	$f(n)$	60	80	100	120	140

Write the recursive rule.

$f(1) = 60$ $f(1)$ is the first term.

$f(n) = 20 + f(n-1)$ for $n \geq 2$ All other terms are the sum of the previous term and the common difference.

Write the explicit rule.

n	$f(n)$	$f(1) + d \cdot x = f(n)$
1	60	$60 + 20(0) = 60$
2	80	$60 + 20(1) = 80$
3	100	$60 + 20(2) = 100$

Remember, d is the difference between two consecutive terms.

Since d is always multiplied by a number equal to $(n-1)$, we can generalize the results from the table: $f(n) = 60 + 20(n-1)$.

Personal Math Trainer

Online Practice and Help

⏻ my.hrw.com

YOUR TURN

1. The table shows the number of members in a theater group after n weeks. Write a recursive rule and an explicit rule for the arithmetic sequence.

Week	n	1	2	3	4	5
Members	$f(n)$	35	47	59	71	83

_____

_____

Math On the Spot

⏻ my.hrw.com

General Rules for Arithmetic Sequences

Arithmetic sequences can be described by general rules. You can substitute values into the general rules to find the recursive rule and explicit rule for a given sequence.

General Recursive Rule	General Explicit Rule
Given $f(1)$, $f(n) = f(n-1) + d$ for $n \geq 2$	$f(n) = f(1) + d(n-1)$

EXAMPLE 2

COMMON CORE   F.BF.1a, F.BF.2

Write a recursive rule and an explicit rule for the sequence 6, 9, 12, 15, 18…

Write the recursive rule.

Given $f(1)$, $f(n) = f(n-1) + d$ for $n \geq 2$ *Write the general form.*

$f(1) = 6$, $f(n) = f(n-1) + 3$ for $n \geq 2$ *Use $f(1) = 6$. Substitute 3 for d.*

The recursive rule is $f(1) = 6$, $f(n) = f(n-1) + 3$ for $n \geq 2$.

Write the explicit rule.

$$f(n) = f(1) + d(n - 1)$$ *Write the general form.*

$$f(n) = 6 + 3(n - 1)$$ *Substitute 6 for f(1) and 3 for d.*

The explicit rule is $f(n) = 6 + 3(n - 1)$.

YOUR TURN

2. Write a recursive rule and an explicit rule for the arithmetic sequence 20, 25, 30, 35, . . .

_____

_____

Personal Math Trainer

Online Practice and Help

⏻ my.hrw.com

Relating Arithmetic Sequences and Linear Functions

The explicit rule for an arithmetic sequence can be expressed as a linear function. You can use the graph of a linear function to help you write an explicit rule.

Math On the Spot

⏻ my.hrw.com

EXAMPLE 3   COMMON CORE   F.BF.2, F.LE.2

The graph shows how the cost of a whitewater rafting trip depends on the number of passengers. Write an explicit rule for the sequence of costs.

STEP 1   Represent the sequence in a table.

n	1	2	3	4
$f(n)$	75	100	125	150

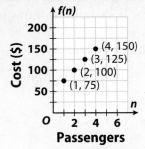

Whitewater Rafting

STEP 2   Find the common difference.

$$100 - 75 = 25$$ *Find the difference between two*
$$125 - 100 = 25$$ *consecutive terms.*
$$150 - 125 = 25$$ *d = 25*

STEP 3   Write an explicit rule for the sequence.

$$f(n) = f(1) + d(n - 1)$$ *Start with the general rule, then substitute values to find the explicit rule.*
$$f(n) = 75 + 25(n - 1)$$

3. Ed collects autographs. The graph shows the number of autographs that Ed has collected over time. Determine the explicit rule for the sequence.

_____

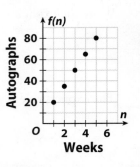

Guided Practice

Write a recursive rule and an explicit rule for the sequence. (Examples 1 and 2)

1.

n	1	2	3	4	5
$f(n)$	6	7	8	9	10

$f(1) = 6,$

$f(n) = f(\boxed{}) + \boxed{}$ for $n \geq 2;$

$f(n) = \boxed{} + \boxed{}$

2. 3, 7, 11, 15, . . .

_____

_____

Write an explicit rule for the sequence. (Example 3)

3. The graph shows the lengths of the rows formed by various numbers of grocery carts when they are nested together. Write an explicit rule for the sequence of row lengths.

_____

Nested Grocery Carts

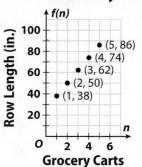

? ESSENTIAL QUESTION CHECK-IN

4. What two values do you need to know in order to write a recursive rule and an explicit rule for an arithmetic sequence?

_____

_____

7.1 Independent Practice

Personal Math Trainer

Online Practice and Help

my.hrw.com

5. Write a recursive rule and an explicit rule for each sequence.

n	1	2	3	4	5
$f(n)$	27	24	21	18	15

_____

_____

_____

6.

n	1	2	3	4	5
$f(n)$	3	6	9	12	15

_____

_____

_____

7. Write a recursive rule and an explicit rule for the arithmetic sequence 9, 24, 39, 54, . . .

_____

_____

_____

8. Write a recursive rule and an explicit rule for the arithmetic sequence 19, 9, −1, −11, . . .

_____

_____

_____

9. Write a recursive rule and an explicit rule for the arithmetic sequence 1, 2.5, 4, 5.5, . . .

_____

_____

_____

10. The explicit rule for an arithmetic sequence is $f(n) = 6 + 5(n - 1)$. What are the first three terms? _____

11. The explicit rule for an arithmetic sequence is $f(n) = 1 + 3(n - 1)$. What are the fourth and fortieth terms? _____

12. Indicate whether the sequence is arithmetic. If it is, list the common difference. −21, −18, −15, −12, . . .

_____

13. The first term of an arithmetic sequence is 4, and the common difference is 10. How can you find the sixth term of the sequence?

_____

_____

_____

_____

_____

14. Carrie borrowed money interest-free to pay for a car repair. The table shows how much money remains for Carrie to pay back after making n monthly payments.

Monthly Payment Number	n	1	2	3	4	5
Loan Balance ($)	$f(n)$	840	720	600	480	360

a. Explain how you know that the sequence of loan balances is arithmetic.

_____

_____

b. Write recursive and explicit rules for the sequence of loan balances.

c. How many months will it take Carrie to pay off the loan? Explain.

d. How much money did Carrie borrow? Explain.

H.O.T. FOCUS ON HIGHER ORDER THINKING

Work Area

15. Explain the Error The cost of postage for a 1-ounce letter is \$0.46. Each additional ounce costs \$0.20. Cindy wrote this explicit rule to describe the sequence of costs: $f(n) = 0.20 + 0.46(n - 1)$. She then determined the cost of postage for a 6-ounce letter to be \$2.46. Is she correct? If not, identify her error.

16. Communicate Mathematical Ideas What do all arithmetic sequences have in common?

17. Critical Thinking Trevor knows that the 5th term in a sequence is 32, and the 7th term in the same sequence is 48. Explain how he can find the common difference for this sequence.

18. Represent Real-World Problems Describe a situation whose sequence could be represented by the explicit rule $f(n) = 8 + 3(n - 1)$.

Operations with Linear Functions

COMMON CORE **F.BF.1b**

Combine standard function types using arithmetic operations. *Also F.BF.1, F.LE.2*

? ESSENTIAL QUESTION

How can you use operations with linear functions to model real-world situations?

Adding and Subtracting Linear Functions

You can add and subtract linear functions just as you would add and subtract any two expressions. When adding and subtracting functions, be sure to use a different letter to name each function, like $h(x) = f(x) + g(x)$.

Math On the Spot
my.hrw.com

EXAMPLE 1
COMMON CORE   F.BF.1b

Given the linear functions $f(x) = 2x + 9$ and $g(x) = 6x - 1$, find each new function.

A $h(x) = f(x) + g(x)$

$h(x) = (2x + 9) + (6x - 1)$ Substitute for $f(x)$ and $g(x)$.

$h(x) = (2x + 6x) + (9 - 1)$ Combine like terms.

$h(x) = 8x + 8$ Simplify.

B $j(x) = f(x) - g(x)$

$j(x) = (2x + 9) - (6x - 1)$ Substitute for $f(x)$ and $g(x)$.

$j(x) = (2x + 9) - 6x + 1$ Multiply by -1.

$j(x) = (2x - 6x) + (9 + 1)$ Combine like terms.

$j(x) = -4x + 10$ Simplify.

REFLECT

1. **Critical Thinking** James thinks that $f(x) - g(x)$ and $g(x) - f(x)$ are equal when $f(x) = 3x + 6$ and $g(x) = 5x + 2$. Is he correct? Explain.

_____

_____

YOUR TURN

2. Given $f(x) = 3x + 4$ and $g(x) = -x + 2$, find the sum $h(x) = f(x) + g(x)$ and the difference $j(x) = f(x) - g(x)$.

_____

Personal Math Trainer

Online Practice and Help

my.hrw.com

Multiplying Linear and Constant Functions

Multiplying a linear function by a constant function is similar to using the Distributive Property. When you multiply a linear function by a constant, the result is also a linear function.

My Notes

EXAMPLE 2

COMMON CORE   F.BF.1b

Given the linear functions $f(x) = 4$ and $g(x) = -3x + 2$, find the linear function $h(x) = f(x) \times g(x)$.

$h(x) = f(x) \times g(x)$

$h(x) = (4)(-3x + 2)$ Substitute for $f(x)$ and $g(x)$.

$h(x) = -12x + 8$ Multiply using the Distributive Property.

REFLECT

3. **Critical Thinking** Enrique knows that $f(x)$ is a constant function and that $g(x) = 5x + 6$. If $f(x) \times g(x) = 0$, determine $f(x)$.

   _____

4. **Explain the Error** Kelly thinks that the product of $f(x) = 6$ and $g(x) = 4x + 8$ is $24x + 8$. Is she correct? If not, explain her error.

   _____

   _____

   _____

YOUR TURN

Given the constant function $f(x)$ and the linear function $g(x)$, find the linear function $h(x) = f(x) \times g(x)$.

5. $f(x) = 7, g(x) = 4x - 2$

   _____

6. $f(x) = -3, g(x) = 2x - 11$

   _____

7. $f(x) = \frac{1}{2}, g(x) = 14x - 8$

   _____

Adding Linear Models

Real-world problems can often be solved by writing linear functions to model the situations, then adding the linear functions as you did in Example 1.

Math On the Spot
my.hrw.com

EXAMPLE 3 Real World   COMMON CORE   F.BF.1b, F.LE.2

Harriet rides from her house to her job using Friendly Taxi Company, which charges $5 plus $1.35 per mile. After work, Harriet uses the Great Taxi company to go home. They charge $2 plus $1.85 per mile. Find the total amount that Harriet spent on cab rides as a function of x, the distance in miles between her house and her job.

STEP 1   Write $f(x)$, the cost of the Friendly Taxi cab ride, as a function of x.

$$f(x) = 5 + 1.35x$$

STEP 2   Write $g(x)$, the cost of the Great Taxi cab ride, as a function of x.

$$g(x) = 2 + 1.85x$$

STEP 3   Write $t(x)$, the total cost of both cab rides, as a function of x. Find the sum of the costs of each taxi ride.

$$t(x) = f(x) + g(x)$$
$$t(x) = (5 + 1.35x) + (2 + 1.85x) \qquad \text{Substitute for } f(x) \text{ and } g(x).$$
$$t(x) = (1.35x + 1.85x) + (5 + 2) \qquad \text{Combine like terms.}$$
$$t(x) = 3.2x + 7 \qquad \text{Simplify.}$$

The cost of Harriet's rides can be represented by $t(x) = 3.2x + 7$.

Math Talk
Mathematical Practices

What does the number 7 represent in this situation?

REFLECT

8. What If? Describe the change to $t(x)$ if Harriet used Friendly Taxi to travel to and from her job.

_____

YOUR TURN

9. A tennis club is formed for boys and girls. In the first year, 4 boys and 5 girls join the club. Each year after, 2 more boys and 1 more girl join the club. Let t be the number of years since the club was formed. Find a rule for the function $f(t)$, representing the total number of club members.

_____

Personal Math Trainer

Online Practice and Help

my.hrw.com

Multiplying Linear and Constant Models

Some real-world situations are modeled by constant functions. To multiply these functions, use the same steps as in Example 2.

EXAMPLE 4 *Real World*   COMMON CORE F.BF.1b, F.LE.2

My Notes

A phone company charges $20 a month for service plus $0.05 per minute for calls. Tax is added to the total charge, and the tax rate is 8%. Find the amount of tax on a monthly bill for t minutes of calls.

STEP 1 Write $f(t)$, the amount charged by the phone company before taxes for service and t minutes of calls.

$f(t) = 20 + 0.05t$

STEP 2 Write $g(t)$, the tax rate applied to phone company charges.

$g(t) = 0.08$

STEP 3 Write $h(t)$, the tax charged for a monthly bill with t minutes of calls. Find the product of the amount charged by the phone company $f(t)$ and the constant tax rate $g(t)$.

$h(t) = f(t) \times g(t)$

$h(t) = (20 + 0.05t)(0.08)$ Substitute for $f(t)$ and $g(t)$.

$h(t) = 1.6 + 0.004t$ Multiply using the distributive property.

The amount of tax on a monthly bill for t minutes of calls is $h(t) = 1.6 + 0.004t$.

REFLECT

10. **Interpret the Answer** Interpret the number 1.6 in the simplified form of $h(t)$ in Example 4.

_____

_____

YOUR TURN

11. Sunshine Coffee Shop has 8 employees working, each of whom buy a large coffee. During the day, they sell x large coffees to customers. Each large coffee costs $1.75. Write a function $c(x)$ that represents the amount of money Sunshine Coffee Shop made selling large coffees.

_____

Given the functions $f(x) = 3x + 9$ and $g(x) = -2x + 5$, find each new function. (Example 1)

1. $h(x) = f(x) + g(x)$

$h(x) = (3x + 9) + ($ ⬚ $)$

$h(x) = (3x + $ ⬚ $) + $

$(9 + $ ⬚ $)$

$h(x) = $ ⬚

2. $j(x) = f(x) - g(x)$

$j(x) = ($ ⬚ $) - (-2x + 5)$

$j(x) = ($ ⬚ $ + 2x)$

$+ ($ ⬚ $- 5)$

$j(x) = $ ⬚

Given a constant function $f(x)$ and a linear function $g(x)$, find the function $h(x) = f(x) \times g(x)$. (Example 2)

3. $f(x) = 4, g(x) = 2x + 3$

$h(x) = f(x) \times g(x)$

$h(x) = 4($ ⬚ $)$

$h(x) = $ ⬚

4. $f(x) = -2, g(x) = 4x - 1$

$h(x) = f(x) \times g(x)$

$h(x) = $ ⬚ $(4x - 1)$

$h(x) = $ ⬚

5. Colton is making gift bags. He has 120 small prizes, and puts 3 in each gift bag. He also has 75 larger prizes, and puts 2 in each gift bag. Write the function $f(x)$ that represents how many prizes Colton has left after making x gift bags. (Example 3)

_____

6. Brenda is buying 6 concert tickets online. Each ticket costs $15, plus a service fee of x dollars. Write the function $g(x)$ that shows the total amount that Brenda will pay for the tickets. (Example 4)

_____

? **ESSENTIAL QUESTION CHECK-IN**

7. How is the sum or difference of linear functions related to the equations for the functions?

_____

_____

7.2 Independent Practice

COMMON CORE F.BF.1, F.BF.1b, F.LE.2

Given the functions $f(x)$ and $g(x)$, find the function $h(x) = f(x) + g(x)$.

8. $f(x) = 2x + 9, g(x) = 8x - 3$

_____

9. $f(x) = 17x - 1, g(x) = 5x + 5$

_____

10. $f(x) = -x - 2, g(x) = 4x - 3$

_____

Given the functions $f(x)$ and $g(x)$, find the function $h(x) = f(x) - g(x)$.

11. $f(x) = 4x + 10, g(x) = -2x + 8$

_____

12. $f(x) = 3x - 1, g(x) = 12x + 2$

_____

13. $f(x) = 6x + 7, g(x) = x + 6$

_____

Given the functions $f(x)$ and $g(x)$, find the function $h(x) = f(x) \times g(x)$.

14. $f(x) = 3, g(x) = 7x + 1$

_____

15. $f(x) = -2, g(x) = 4x - 6$

_____

16. $f(x) = \frac{1}{3}, g(x) = 9x - 6$

_____

17. A school is raising money for new desks. They have collected $400 in donations, and are hosting a dinner, which costs $10 to attend. Every person at the dinner buys a $2 raffle ticket, and the winner of the raffle gets $500.

a. Write a rule for the function $R(t)$, the profit the school makes on the raffle.

_____

b. Write a rule for the function $D(t)$, the earnings made from the donations and dinner.

_____

c. Describe how the function $T(t)$, the total amount of money raised by the school for new desks, is related to $R(t)$ and $D(t)$. Then, write a rule for $T(t)$.

_____

18. A birthday party is being planned for 20 people at an arcade. It costs $5 a person to provide food for everyone, and each game costs $1 per play. Assume that each person at the party plays the same number of games, x.

a. Write a rule for the function $C(x)$, the total cost per person.

_____

b. Write a rule for the function $n(x)$, the number of people who attend.

_____

c. Describe how the function $T(x)$, the total cost of the party, can be obtained from the functions $C(x)$ and $n(x)$. Then, write a rule for $T(x)$.

_____

19. Randy and Heloise both open savings accounts. Randy opens his savings account with $7 and deposits $10 every week. Heloise opens her savings account with $82 and withdraws $5 every week.

a. Write a function $r(x)$ to represent the amount of money Randy has in his savings account after x weeks.

_____

b. Write a function $h(x)$ to represent the amount of money Heloise has in her savings account after x weeks.

_____

c. Write a function $b(x)$ to represent the combined total in both savings accounts after x weeks.

_____

d. When Randy has $47 in his savings account, what is the combined total in both accounts?

_____

e. When Heloise has $47 in her savings account, what is the combined total in both accounts?

_____

20. A police department issues speeding tickets for $50 plus an additional dollar for each mile per hour over the speed limit the driver was going. Half of the money from speeding tickets goes toward buying new equipment for the police officers. Write a rule for the function $E(x)$, the amount of money for new equipment generated by a ticket for driving x miles per hour over the speed limit.

_____

21. Use the information in the table below to answer the following questions.

x	f(x)	g(x)
0	3	−2
2	−1	4
5	−7	13

a. Use the table to write rules for the functions $f(x)$ and $g(x)$.

_____

_____

b. Find the sum $h(x) = f(x) + g(x)$ and the difference $j(x) = f(x) - g(x)$.

_____

_____

c. Compare the functions $h(x)$ and $j(x)$ when $x = 3$.

_____

22. A new computer is valued at $1,000, and its value depreciates by $150 per year. A new printer is valued at $100, and its value depreciates by $5 per year.

a. Write a rule for the combined value of the computer and printer in terms of t, the time in years since the equipment was purchased.

_____

b. When will the computer and the printer have a combined value of $480?

_____

c. When the computer is worth $100, how much will the combined value of the computer and the printer be?

_____

H.O.T. FOCUS ON HIGHER ORDER THINKING

Work Area

23. Persevere in Problem Solving Let $f(x) = 3$, $g(x) = -2x + 5$, and $h(x) = x - 4$.

a. Find the function $j(x) = f(x) \times [g(x) + h(x)]$.

b. Find the function $k(x) = [f(x) \times g(x)] + [f(x) \times h(x)]$.

c. Find the function $l(x) = j(x) - k(x)$.

d. Explain how you could find $l(x)$ without finding $j(x)$ or $k(x)$.

24. Interpret the Answer Suppose $B(t)$ is a linear function representing the number of boys who attend a school in year t, and $G(t)$ is a linear function representing the number of girls who attend the same school in year t. What does the function $T(t) = G(t) + B(t)$ represent?

25. Analyze Relationships The function $f(x) = 3x + 3$. Find the function $g(x)$ such that $f(x) + g(x) = 0$ and $f(x) - g(x) = 2 \times f(x)$. What is the relationship between $f(x)$ and $g(x)$? Explain.

26. Analyze Relationships Is it possible for $f(x) - g(x)$ to equal $g(x) - f(x)$? If so, explain how.

Linear Functions and Their Inverses

COMMON CORE F.BF.4a

Solve an equation of the form $f(x) = c$ for a simple function f that has an inverse and write an expression for the inverse. *Also F.BF.4, F.IF.7a*

? ESSENTIAL QUESTION

How can you find the inverse of a linear function?

EXPLORE ACTIVITY

COMMON CORE F.BF.4a

Using Inverse Operations to Find an Inverse Function

The *inverse of a function* "undoes" every operation performed in the original function. Use inverse operations to find the inverse of the function $f(x) = 2x + 6$.

A Use the function $f(x) = 2x + 6$ to complete the table.

x	−2	1	3	6
y = 2x + 6				

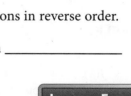

Function Machine

Input $x = 2$

$y = f(x) = x - 5$

Output $y = -3$

B To complete the table, you must first _____ each x-value by 2, and then _____ 6 to the result.

C Identify the inverse operations. The inverse of multiplying by 2 is _____ . The inverse of adding 6 is _____.

D To find the inverse function, use the inverse operations in reverse order.

First, _____ 6 from each x-value, then _____ the result by 2.

Math Talk
Mathematical Practices

How are the input and output values of a function and its inverse related?

E The inverse of $f(x) = 2x + 6$, denoted by $f^{-1}(x)$, is

$$f^{-1}(x) = (x \bigcirc 6) \bigcirc 2.$$

F Use the inverse function to complete the table.

x	2	8	12	18
y = (x 6) 2				

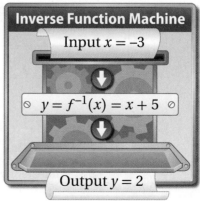

Inverse Function Machine

Input $x = -3$

$y = f^{-1}(x) = x + 5$

Output $y = 2$

REFLECT

1. Analyze Relationships Compare the x- and y-values in the two completed tables. How are they related?

_____

Solving for *x* to Find an Inverse Function

The **inverse of a function** interchanges the input and output values of the function. Thus, another method for finding an inverse involves rewriting the original function so that *x* is isolated on one side.

My Notes

EXAMPLE 1

COMMON CORE F.BF.4a

Find the inverse of $f(x) = \frac{1}{2}x + 3$.

STEP 1   Replace $f(x)$ with y in the function.

$$y = \tfrac{1}{2}x + 3$$

STEP 2   Solve the equation for *x*.

$$y = \tfrac{1}{2}x + 3$$

$$y - 3 = \tfrac{1}{2}x \qquad \text{Subtract 3 from both sides.}$$

$$2(y - 3) = x \qquad \text{Multiply both sides by 2.}$$

$$2y - 6 = x \qquad \text{Distribute to simplify.}$$

STEP 3   Switch *x* and *y* in the equation.

$$2x - 6 = y$$

STEP 4   Replace *y* with the inverse function notation, $f^{-1}(x)$.

$$f^{-1}(x) = 2x - 6$$

REFLECT

2. **Critique Reasoning** Jodie thinks that the inverse of the function $f(x) = 5x + 2$ is $f^{-1}(x) = -5x - 2$, because $(5x + 2) + (-5x - 2) = 0$. Has Jodie found the correct inverse function? Explain.

_____

_____

Personal Math Trainer

Online Practice and Help

my.hrw.com

YOUR TURN

3. Find the inverse of $f(x) = \frac{1}{3}x - 6$.

_____

Graphing the Inverse of a Linear Function

You graph the inverse of a linear function in the same manner as you graph the function.

Math On the Spot
my.hrw.com

EXAMPLE 2

COMMON CORE F.IF.7a, F.BF.4a

The function $f(x) = 3x - 12$ is shown on the graph. Find and graph the inverse function $f^{-1}(x)$.

STEP 1 Find the inverse of $f(x) = 3x - 12$.

$y = 3x - 12$	Substitute y for $f(x)$.
$y + 12 = 3x$	Add 12 to both sides.
$\frac{1}{3}(y + 12) = x$	Multiply both sides by $\frac{1}{3}$.
$\frac{1}{3}y + 4 = x$	Simplify.
$\frac{1}{3}x + 4 = y$	Switch x and y.
$f^{-1}(x) = \frac{1}{3}x + 4$	Substitute $f^{-1}(x)$ for y.

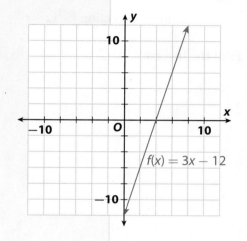

$f(x) = 3x - 12$

STEP 2 Make a table of ordered pairs for the inverse function.

x	$f^{-1}(x) = \frac{1}{3}x + 4$
−6	$f^{-1}(-6) = \frac{1}{3}(-6) + 4 = 2$
0	$f^{-1}(0) = \frac{1}{3}(0) + 4 = 4$
3	$f^{-1}(3) = \frac{1}{3}(3) + 4 = 5$

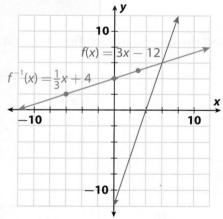

$f(x) = 3x - 12$

$f^{-1}(x) = \frac{1}{3}x + 4$

STEP 3 Plot the ordered pairs, and connect them with a line.

YOUR TURN

4. The graph of $f(x) = \frac{1}{2}x - 1$ is shown. Find the inverse function $f^{-1}(x)$ and graph it.

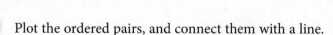

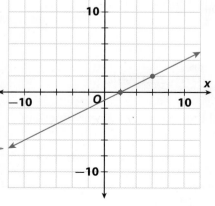

$f(x) = \frac{1}{2}x - 1$

Personal Math Trainer

Online Practice and Help

my.hrw.com

1. Use inverse operations to find the inverse of $f(x) = \frac{x}{2} - 3$. (Explore Activity)

To find values for $f(x)$, first you _____ x by 2, then you _____ 3 from the result.

The inverse operations in reverse order are _____.

The inverse function $f^{-1}(x) = $ _____.

Find the inverse of each function. (Example 1)

2. $f(x) = x - 1$

$$\boxed{} = x - 1$$

$$y + \boxed{} = x$$

$$\boxed{} + 1 = \boxed{}$$

$$f^{-1}(x) = \boxed{} + \boxed{}$$

3. $f(x) = x + 8$

$$\boxed{} = x + 8$$

$$y - \boxed{} = x$$

$$\boxed{} - 8 = \boxed{}$$

$$f^{-1}(x) = \boxed{} - \boxed{}$$

Find the inverse of each function and graph $f^{-1}(x)$. (Example 2)

4. _____

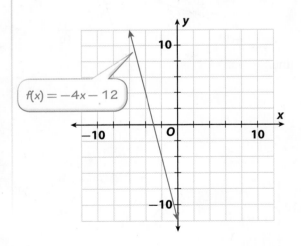

$f(x) = -4x - 12$

5. _____

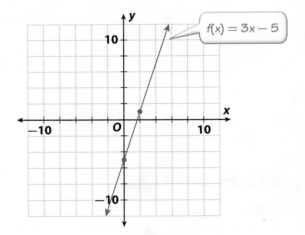

$f(x) = 3x - 5$

6. How can you find the inverse of a linear function?

_____

_____

_____

7.3 Independent Practice

COMMON CORE   F.IF.7a, F.BF.4, F.BF.4a

Personal Math Trainer

Online Practice and Help

my.hrw.com

7. Carla is ordering pizzas for delivery. Each pizza costs $8, and there is a $6 delivery charge per order.

a. Write the function $f(x)$ that Carla can use to determine the amount she will pay for having x pizzas delivered.

_____

b. Find the inverse of function $f(x)$.

_____

c. What does x represent in the inverse function $f^{-1}(x)$ in Part b?

_____

_____

8. Henry is a painter. He uses the function $h(x) = 50x - 20$ to determine the amount he charges for a painting that took him x hours to make.

a. Find the inverse of function $h(x)$.

_____

b. What can the inverse function $h^{-1}(x)$ be used to determine?

_____

_____

_____

9. The function $f(x) = \frac{5}{9}(x - 32)$ can be used to determine the temperature in °C when the temperature is x °F. Find the inverse function that can be used to determine the temperature in °F when the temperature is x °C.

_____

10. Is the function $f(x) = -x$ its own inverse? Justify your answer.

_____

_____

_____

_____

_____

_____

11. The graph shows the function $f(x) = -3x - 6$. Find the inverse function $f^{-1}(x)$ and graph it.

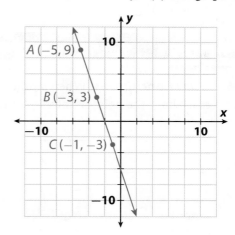

_____

12. The general form of a linear function is $f(x) = mx + b$, where m and b and constants.

a. Find $f^{-1}(x)$. _____

b. Will $f^{-1}(x)$ always be a linear function? Explain.

_____

_____

_____

13. Analyze Relationships The functions $f(x)$ and $g(x)$ intersect at the point $(0, 1)$. Is $g(x)$ the inverse of $f(x)$? Explain.

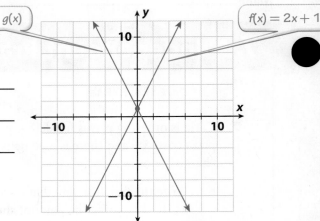

_____

_____

_____

14. Counterexample Keshawn thinks that the graph of a function $f(x)$ and its inverse $f^{-1}(x)$ will always intersect. Give a counterexample to disprove his statement.

_____

15. For the functions $f(x) = 3x + 2$ and $g(x) = -2x - 7$, $h(x) = f(x) + g(x)$, $j(x) = f(x) - g(x)$, and $k(x) = g(x) - f(x)$.

a. Find the inverse of function $h(x)$. _____

b. Find the inverse of function $j(x)$. _____

c. Find the inverse of function $k(x)$. _____

H.O.T. **FOCUS ON HIGHER ORDER THINKING**

Work Area

16. Draw Conclusions When a function and its inverse intersect, what must be true about the point of intersection?

_____

_____

17. Analyze Relationships If f^{-1} is the inverse of f, then is it reasonable to describe f as an inverse of f^{-1}?

_____

_____

_____

18. Critical Thinking Micah is running a sports trivia contest. The entrance fee is $20, and the winner will get $500. Micah will keep what is left over after paying the winner. The function $f(x) = 20x - 500$ describes how much money Micah earns if x people enter the contest. What does the inverse function $f^{-1}(x)$ describe?

_____

_____

_____

Linear Inequalities in Two Variables

COMMON CORE A.REI.12

Graph the solutions to a linear inequality in two variables as a half-plane (excluding the boundary in the case of a strict inequality), and graph the solution set to a system of linear inequalities in two variables as the intersection of the corresponding half-planes.

? ESSENTIAL QUESTION

How do you graph a linear inequality in two variables?

Graphing a Linear Inequality

A **linear inequality** results when you replace the = sign in a linear equation by $<, >, \leq,$ or $\geq$. For example, $7x + 14 \leq 28y$ is a linear inequality. A **solution of an inequality** is any ordered pair (x, y) that makes the inequality true.

Math On the Spot
⏻ my.hrw.com

EXAMPLE 1

COMMON CORE A.REI.12

Graph the solution set for $2x - 3y \geq 6$.

STEP 1 First solve the inequality for y.

$$2x - 3y \geq 6$$

$$-3y \geq 6 - 2x \qquad \text{Subtract } 2x \text{ from both sides.}$$

$$y \leq \frac{6 - 2x}{-3} \qquad \text{Divide both sides by } -3.$$

$$y \leq -2 + \frac{2}{3}x \qquad \text{Simplify.}$$

$$y \leq \frac{2}{3}x - 2 \qquad \text{Write in standard form.}$$

> Reverse the inequality sign when dividing both sides of an equation by a negative number.

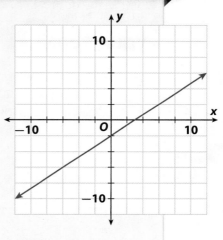

Consider the line where the inequality is replaced by an equal sign: $y = \frac{2}{3}x - 2$. The line is called the **boundary line** of the solution set.

STEP 2 Graph the boundary line. The inequality $y \leq \frac{2}{3}x - 2$ uses the symbol $\leq$, so the line will be solid, to show that the points on the line are part of the solution.

STEP 3 Shade the appropriate part of the graph. The inequality $y \leq \frac{2}{3}x - 2$ uses the symbol $\leq$, so shade below the boundary line.

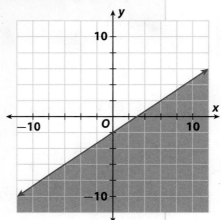

STEP 4 To check your work, choose one point above the boundary line and one point below the boundary line. Substitute both points into the original inequality, and verify that the point below the boundary line makes the inequality true.

Point	Above or Below Line	Inequality	True or False?
$(0, 0)$	Above	$2(0) - 3(0) \geq 6$	False
$(0, -4)$	Below	$2(0) - 3(-4) \geq 6$	True

The point below the line makes the inequality true, so the shaded graph is correct.

REFLECT

1. The set of solutions to an inequality is represented on a graph by a shaded region and boundary line. This area is called a **half-plane**. Why is half-plane a good name for this region?

_____

_____

YOUR TURN

2. Graph the solution set for $4x - 8y \geq 32$.

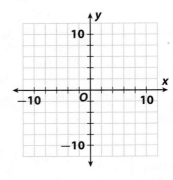

Graphing a Linear Inequality in Two Variables

EXAMPLE 2

COMMON CORE A.REI.12

Graph the solution set for the inequality $26 + 2y > 14x$.

STEP 1

$26 + 2y > 14x$

$2y > 14x - 26$ Subtract 26 from both sides.

$y > \frac{14x - 26}{2}$ Divide both sides by 2.

$y > 7x - 13$ Simplify.

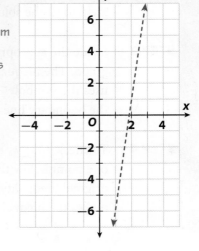

STEP 2 Graph the boundary line. The inequality $y > 7x - 13$ uses the symbol $>$, so use a dashed line to show that points on the line are not part of the solution.

STEP 3 Shade the appropriate part of the graph. The inequality $y > 7x - 13$ uses the symbol $>$, so shade above the boundary line.

STEP 4 To check your work, choose one point above the boundary line and one point below the boundary line. Substitute both points into the original inequality, and verify that the point above the boundary line makes the inequality true.

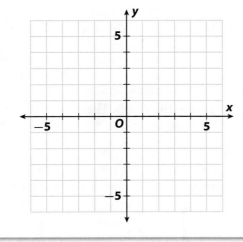

Math Talk
Mathematical Practices

How would the shaded region change if the inequality were $26 + 2y < 14x$?

Point	Above or Below Line	Inequality	True or False?
$(0, 0)$	Above	$26 + 2(0) > 14(0)$	True
$(4, 0)$	Below	$26 + 2(0) > 14(4)$	False

REFLECT

3. For the linear inequality, $6x - 3y < 24$, which of the following is a solution: $(0, -9)$, $(6, 4)$, or $(4, 1)$?

_____

_____

4. Is $(4, 0)$ a solution for the inequality $6x - 3y < 24$? Explain.

_____

_____

_____

YOUR TURN

5. Graph $6x + 3y < -12$.

Personal Math Trainer

Online Practice and Help

my.hrw.com

Writing and Solving Linear Inequalities

When writing a linear inequality for a situation, make sure to use the appropriate inequality symbol.

EXAMPLE 3   COMMON CORE   **A.REI.12**

Francesca can spend at most $6.75 on healthy snacks for a party. Veggie chips cost $1.00 per package and grapes cost $0.75 per bunch. Find two combinations of veggie chips and grapes that Francesca can buy.

STEP 1   Write a linear inequality to describe the situation.

Let x represent the number of packages of veggie chips and let y represent the number of bunches of grapes.

Write an inequality. Use $\leq$ for "at most."

Total cost of veggie chips	plus	Total cost of grapes	is at most	$6.75
$1.00x$	$+$	$0.75y$	$\leq$	6.75

Solve the inequality for y.

$$1.00x + 0.75y \leq 6.75$$

$$(100)(1.00x + 0.75y) \leq 100(6.75)$$ Multiply both sides of the equation by 100 to eliminate the decimals.

$$100x + 75y \leq 675$$

$$75y \leq 675 - 100x$$ Subtract 100x from both sides.

$$y \leq \frac{675 - 100x}{75}$$ Divide both sides by 75.

$$y \leq 9 - \frac{4}{3}x$$ Simplify.

STEP 2   Graph the boundary line. The inequality $y \leq 9 - \frac{4}{3}x$ uses the symbol $\leq$, so the line will be solid to show that the points on the line are part of the solution.

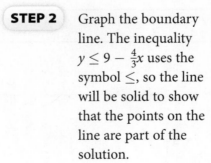

STEP 3   Shade the appropriate part of the graph. The inequality $y \leq 9 - \frac{4}{3}x$ uses the symbol $\leq$, so shade below the boundary line. Since the number of snacks cannot be negative, only shade in Quadrant 1.

STEP 4 Since the line is solid, any point on or underneath the line (in Quadrant 1) will be a solution. Choose two points, and make sure they make the inequality true.

$$1.00(3) + 0.75(5) \leq 6.75$$
$$1.00(2) + 0.75(3) \leq 6.75$$

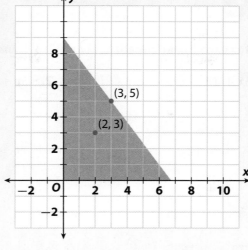

Two different combinations that Francesca could buy for $6.75 or less are 3 packages of veggie chips and 5 bunches of grapes, or 2 packages of veggie chips and 3 bunches of grapes.

REFLECT

6. What if? How would the graph of solutions change if grapes were sold at $0.25 per bunch?

_____

YOUR TURN

7. Lamar has $15.00 that he can spend on food for his cat. Dry cat food costs $4.50 per small bag and wet cat food costs $1.50 per tin can. Write a linear inequality that describes how many bags and cans of cat food Lamar can buy.

_____

_____

8. Graph the solution set of your linear inequality for Lamar.

9. Identify two combinations of dry and wet cat food that Lamar can afford.

_____

_____

_____

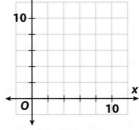

Personal Math Trainer

Online Practice and Help

my.hrw.com

Graph the solution set for each linear equality. (Examples 1 and 2)

1. $4y + 3x - y > -6x + 12$

$$- \boxed{} \qquad - \boxed{}$$

$$4y - y > \boxed{}\, x + 12$$

$$\boxed{} > \boxed{}\, x + 12$$

$$y > \boxed{}\, x + \boxed{}$$

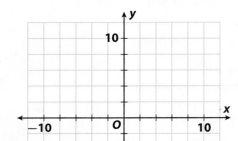

2. $5y + 3 < 2x$

$$\boxed{} \qquad \boxed{}$$

$$5y < \boxed{} - 3$$

$$y < \tfrac{2}{5}x - \tfrac{3}{5}$$

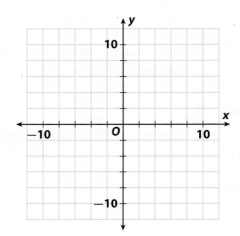

**Sam is buying chairs that cost \$15 and tables that cost \$20.
He wants to spend no more than \$140.** (Example 3)

3. Write a linear inequality to represent the amount Sam can pay for x

chairs and y tables. _____

4. Solve the inequality for y.

_____

5. Graph the inequality.

6. What are two combinations of chairs
and tables that Sam could buy?

_____

© Houghton Mifflin Harcourt Publishing Company

? ESSENTIAL QUESTION CHECK-IN

7. How do you graph a linear inequality in two variables?

_____

_____

7.4 Independent Practice

Personal
Math Trainer

Online Practice
and Help

my.hrw.com

COMMON
CORE   A.REI.12

Graph the inequality.

8. $y \leq 5$

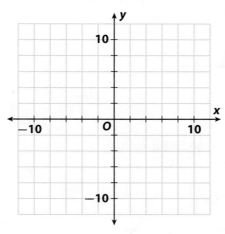

9. $x + 5y < 30$

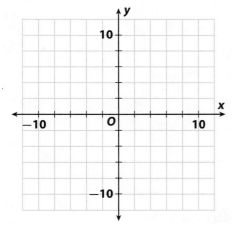

10. $3x - 3y \geq 21$

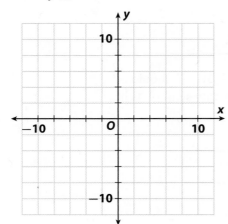

11. Represent Real World Problems Sandra was given a $60.00 gift card to an online music store. She can buy single songs for $1.00 and albums for $12.00.

a. Write the linear inequality that represents how many songs, x, and albums, y, that Sandra can buy with her gift card.

_____

b. Explain the steps you would take to solve the linear inequality for y, the number of albums Sandra buys.

_____

_____

_____

c. Complete the table to verify which points make the inequality true.

Point	Inequality	True or False?
(6, 4)		
(8, 5)		

d. Explain the meaning of the point in the table that makes the inequality true.

_____

_____

e. If you were to shade a graph of this linear inequality, would you shade the point $(-3, 4)$? Explain.

_____

_____

_____

12. Communicate Mathematical Ideas How is graphing a linear inequality on a coordinate plane similar to graphing an inequality on a number line?

_____

_____

_____

_____

_____

H.O.T. FOCUS ON HIGHER ORDER THINKING

13. Multi-step The fare for a taxi cab is $2.25 per passenger and $0.75 for each mile. A group of friends has $16.00 for cab fare.

a. Write a linear inequality to represent how many miles, y, the group can travel if there are x people in the group. _____

b. If there are 3 people in the group, how far can they travel by taxi? Explain.

_____

_____

c. If the group wants to travel 10 miles, what is the greatest number of passengers that can travel by taxi? Explain.

_____

_____

_____

14. Analyze Relationships For the graph of $x \geq 5$, the boundary line is the vertical line $x = 5$. Would you shade to the left or right of the boundary? Explain.

_____

_____

15. Critique Reasoning Baxter thinks that the inequality $2x - 3y \geq 6$ should be shaded above the boundary line because it uses the $\geq$ inequality symbol. Is he correct? Explain.

_____

_____

_____

Ready to Go On?

7.1 Arithmetic Sequences

Indicate whether each sequence is arithmetic. If so, write an explicit rule for the sequence.

1. 1, 3, 5, 7, …

2. 3, 6, 9, 14, …

3. 25, 20, 15, 10, …

7.2 Operations with Linear Functions

For $f(x) = 5x - 3$ and $g(x) = 2 - x$, compute the following functions.

4. $h(x) = f(x) + g(x)$

5. $j(x) = f(x) - g(x)$

6. $k(x) = 6 \cdot f(x)$

7.3 Linear Functions and Their Inverses

Find the inverse function for the following linear functions.

7. $f(x) = 4x + 2$

8. $g(x) = \frac{x + 5}{7}$

9. $h(x) = \frac{1}{2}x + \frac{2}{3}$

7.4 Linear Inequalities in Two Variables

Graph the following linear inequalities.

10. $3x + 2y \le 12$

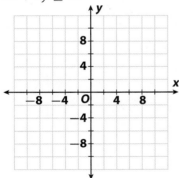

11. $5x - y \ge 10$

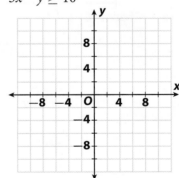

? ESSENTIAL QUESTION

12. How are arithmetic sequences similar to linear functions? How are they different?

MODULE 7

MIXED REVIEW

Assessment Readiness

COMMON CORE

Personal
Math Trainer

my.hrw.com

Online Practice
and Help

1. The first term of an arithmetic sequence is 7, and the common difference of the sequence is −4.

   Select Yes or No if the representation models the sequence.

   A. $f(n) = 7 - 4n$ ⚪ Yes ⚪ No

   B. 7, −4, −15, −26, . . . ⚪ Yes ⚪ No

   C. $f(1) = 7, f(n) = f(n - 1) - 4$, for $n \geq 2$ ⚪ Yes ⚪ No

   D.

n	1	2	3	4	. . .
f(n)	7	3	−1	−5	. . .

   ⚪ Yes ⚪ No

2. Consider the graph of the linear inequality $x - 4y < 8$.

   Choose True or False for each statement.

   A. The boundary line of the graph is given by $y = \frac{1}{4}x - 2$. ⚪ True ⚪ False

   B. The boundary line is graphed with a dashed line. ⚪ True ⚪ False

   C. The half-plane below the boundary line is shaded. ⚪ True ⚪ False

3. The table shows how the cost of judo lessons depends on the number of lessons taken. Write the linear function represented in the table. Explain how you determined your answer.

Number of Lessons	1	5	8	10
Cost Including Uniform ($)	48	96	132	156

4. A drill team is raising money by holding a car wash. The team earns $6.00 for each car washed. The team's expenses include $50.00 for advertising plus $0.50 in materials for each car washed. Let $f(x)$ represent the team's total earnings for washing x cars and $g(x)$ represent the team's total expenses for washing x cars. Describe how you can use $f(x)$ and $g(x)$ to obtain a function $p(x)$ that gives the team's profit for washing x cars. Then write a rule for $p(x)$.

Modeling with Linear Functions

? ESSENTIAL QUESTION

How can you use statistical methods to find relationships between sets of data?

Real-World Video

A fossil is a remnant or trace of an organism of a past geologic age that has been preserved in the earth's crust. Fossils are often dated by using interpolation, a type of calculation that uses an observed pattern to estimate a value between two known values.

 my.hrw.com

GO DIGITAL
my.hrw.com

my.hrw.com

Go digital with your write-in student edition, accessible on any device.

Math On the Spot

Scan with your smart phone to jump directly to the online edition, video tutor, and more.

Animated Math

Interactively explore key concepts to see how math works.

Personal Math Trainer

Get immediate feedback and help as you work through practice sets.

Are YOU Ready?

Complete these exercises to review skills you will need for this module.

Ordered Pairs

EXAMPLE Graph the ordered pairs
$A(2, 2)$, $B(-2, 0)$, and $C(-1, -3)$.

The first coordinate refers to position on the x-axis, and the second coordinate refers to position on the y-axis.

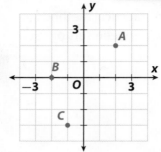

Graph each point on the coordinate plane provided.

1. $A(4, 0)$

2. $B(3, -4)$

3. $C(-1, -2)$

4. $D(-1, 3.5)$

5. $E(0, 5)$

6. $F(4.5, -3)$

7. $G(-2.5, 0.5)$

8. $H(-4, -2.5)$

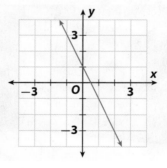

Graph Linear Functions

EXAMPLE Graph $y = -2x + 1$.

Find two points that satisfy the equation. Then connect the points with a straight line.

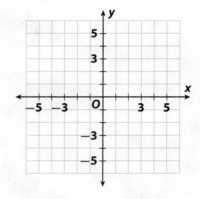

Graph each function.

9. $y = x - 2$

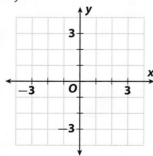

10. $y = -\frac{2}{3}x + 2$

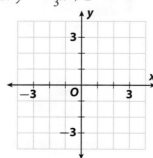

11. $y = \frac{5}{2}x - \frac{1}{2}$

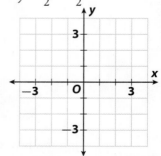

Reading Start-Up

Visualize Vocabulary

Use the review words to complete the sequence diagram.
Complete the blanks in each box.

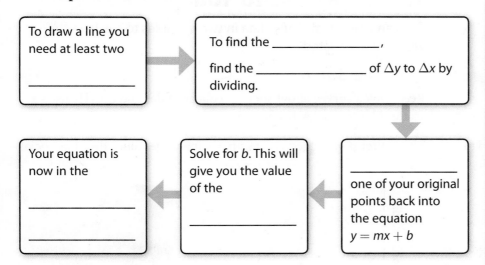

To draw a line you need at least two _____

To find the _____, find the _____ of Δy to Δx by dividing.

_____ one of your original points back into the equation $y = mx + b$

Solve for b. This will give you the value of the _____

Your equation is now in the _____ _____

Vocabulary

Review Words
- ✔ point *(punto)*
- ✔ ratio *(razón)*
- ✔ slope *(pendiente)*
- ✔ slope-intercept form *(forma de pendiente-intersección)*
- ✔ *y*-intercept *(intersección con el eje y)*

Preview Words
- causation
- correlation
- correlation coefficient
- interpolation
- linear regression
- least squares regression line
- line of best fit
- residual
- residual plot
- scatter plot

Understand Vocabulary

To become familiar with some of the vocabulary terms in the module, consider the following. You may refer to the module, the glossary, or a dictionary.

1. The word *regress* is used when you want to return to a less well-developed state. What do you think an **linear regression** might be?

_____

2. The word *residual* refers to what is left over. What do you think a **residual plot** might be?

_____

_____

Active Reading

Three-Panel Flip Chart Before beginning the module, create a three-panel flip chart to help you organize what you learn. Label each flap with one of the lesson titles from this module. As you study each lesson, write important ideas like vocabulary under the appropriate flap.

GETTING READY FOR
Modeling with Linear Functions

Understanding the standards and the vocabulary terms in the standards will help you know exactly what you are expected to learn in this module.

COMMON CORE S.ID.6

Represent data on two quantitative variables on a scatter plot, and describe how the variables are related.

Key Vocabulary

scatter plot *(diagrama de dispersión)*
A graph with points plotted to show a possible relationship between two variables.

What It Means to You

You can graph real-world data in two variables to see how the variables are related.

EXAMPLE S.ID.6

Reed took a survey about social media attitudes and age. He used a scatter plot to display his data.

The scatter plot suggests that as participants get older they like social media less.

COMMON CORE S.ID.6c

Fit a linear function for a scatter plot that suggests a linear association.

Key Vocabulary

linear function *(función lineal)*
A function whose graph is a straight line.

What It Means to You

In a linear relationship one quantity is directly proportional to another. For example, the greater the altitude, the thinner the air is in the atmosphere.

EXAMPLE S.ID.6C

Reed drew a line in his scatter plot, suggesting a linear correlation between age and how much people like social media.

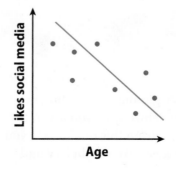

Visit **my.hrw.com** to see all **Common Core Standards** unpacked.

ⓑ my.hrw.com

COMMON CORE   S.ID.6

Represent data on two quantitative variables on a scatter plot, and describe how the variables are related. *Also S.ID.8, S.ID.9*

 ESSENTIAL QUESTION

How can you describe the relationship between two variables?

EXPLORE ACTIVITY   Real World   COMMON CORE   S.ID.6

Graphing Bivariate Data

Bivariate data is data that involves two variables. A **scatter plot** graphs bivariate data as a set of points whose coordinates correspond to the two variables. Scatter plots can help you see relationships between two variables. We say there is a **correlation** between two variables if their values are linked, as shown below.

   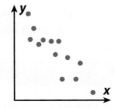   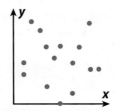

Positive Correlation	Negative Correlation	No Correlation
As the value of one variable increases, the value of the other variable also increases.	As the value of one variable decreases, the value of the other variable increases.	There is no relationship between the two variables.

The table below shows the number of species of mammals on the International Union for the Conservation of Nature's "Red List" of endangered species during the years 2004 to 2012.

IUCN Red List, Number of Endangered Mammal Species							
2004	2006	2007	2008	2009	2010	2011	2012
352	348	349	448	449	450	447	446

Source: *IUCN Red List version 2012*

A Make a scatter plot, using the data in the table as the coordinates of points on the graph. Use the calendar year as the *x*-value and the number of species as the *y*-value. One point is plotted for you.

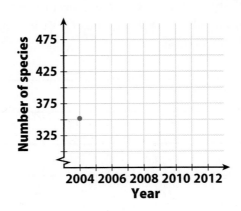

REFLECT

1. **Conjecture** Look at the pattern of points. Is there a positive correlation, negative correlation, or no correlation between the number of endangered mammal species and the year? What is the trend? Is the number of endangered species increasing or decreasing over time?

_____

_____

_____

_____

Math On the Spot

my.hrw.com

Describing Correlations from Scatter Plots

Scatter plots can help to visualize whether the correlation between variables is positive or negative—or if there is no correlation between the variables.

EXAMPLE 1 COMMON CORE S.ID.6

Describe the correlation illustrated by the scatter plot.

TV Watching and Test Scores

Test Score

TV-Watching time (h/day)

As the number of hours spent watching TV increased, test scores decreased. There is a negative correlation between the two data variables.

My Notes

REFLECT

2. **What if?** What would you expect to be true of a person from this survey who watches very few hours of TV? Is it possible for that person to have low test scores?

_____

_____

_____

_____

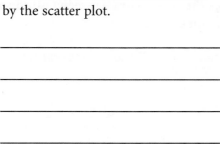

YOUR TURN

3. Describe the correlation illustrated by the scatter plot.

_____

_____

_____

_____

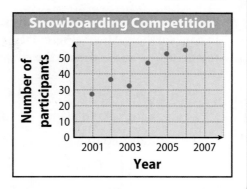

Snowboarding Competition

Personal Math Trainer

Online Practice and Help

⏱ my.hrw.com

Correlation Coefficients

One measure of the strength and direction of a correlation is the **correlation coefficient**, denoted by r. The value of r ranges from -1 to 1. Although r can be precisely calculated, in this lesson we examine qualitatively how its value describes a correlation.

A positive r value indicates a positive correlation, and a negative r value indicates a negative correlation. The stronger the correlation, the closer the correlation coefficient will be to -1 or 1. The weaker the correlation, the closer r will be to zero.

Math On the Spot

⏱ my.hrw.com

	Negative	**Positive**
Strong	Strong negative correlation points lie close to a line with negative slope. *r* is close to −1.	Strong positive correlation points lie close to a line with positive slope. *r* is close to 1.
Weak	Weak negative correlation points loosely follow a line with negative slope. *r* is between 0 and −1.	Weak positive correlation points loosely follow a line with positive slope. *r* is between 0 and 1.

If there is no correlation between the two variables in a data set, the points in a scatter plot do not lie along a line, and r is close to zero.

EXAMPLE 2 *Real World*

COMMON CORE S.ID.8

The table lists the latitude and average annual temperature for various cities in the Northern Hemisphere. Describe the correlation between latitude and temperature, and estimate the correlation coefficient.

City	Latitude	Avg. Annual Temperature
Bangkok, Thailand	13.7°N	82.6°F
Cairo, Egypt	30.1°N	71.4°F
London, England	51.5°N	51.8°F
Moscow, Russia	55.8°N	39.4°F
New Delhi, India	28.6°N	77.0°F
Tokyo, Japan	35.7°N	58.1°F
Vancouver, Canada	49.2°N	49.6°F

STEP 1   Make a scatter plot.

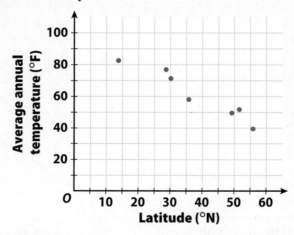

STEP 2   Describe the correlation, and estimate the correlation coefficient. Because the plotted points appear to lie very close to a line with a negative slope, the scatter plot shows a strong negative correlation. So the correlation coefficient is close to −1.

Math Talk
Mathematical Practices

If the point (19.4, 60.8) for Mexico City was added to the scatter plot, how would the correlation coefficient change?

YOUR TURN

4. Examine the scatter plot titled Snowboarding Competition in the previous Your Turn. Is the correlation coefficient for the data closer to −1, −0.5, 0, 0.5, or 1? Explain.

_____

_____

_____

Personal Math Trainer

Online Practice and Help

⏻ my.hrw.com

Distinguishing Causation from Correlation

A common error when interpreting paired data is confusing correlation and *causation*. If a correlation exists between two variables, this does not necessarily mean that one variable causes the other. When one variable increases, the other variable may increase (or decrease) as a result of other variables that are not being considered. Such variables are sometimes called *lurking variables*.

Math On the Spot

my.hrw.com

EXAMPLE 3

COMMON CORE   S.ID.9

Read the article. Does it describe a positive or negative correlation? Explain whether the correlation is a result of causation.

STEP 1 Identify the two variables.

- size of amygdala
- size of social network

STEP 2 Determine the correlation.

A larger amygdala corresponds to a larger social network, so there is a positive correlation.

STEP 3 Explain whether the correlation is a result of causation.

Causation is possible, but it's unknown which variable causes the other. Having a larger amygdala might cause a person to develop a larger social network, or having a large social network might cause a person's amygdala to grow. And it's possible that neither factor causes the other, but that a lurking third variable causes the amygdala to grow and causes the person to develop a large social network.

Brain's Amygdala Connected To Social Behavior

An almond-shaped part of the brain called the amygdala has long been known to play a role in people's emotional states. Now scientists studying the amygdala have discovered a connection between its size and the size of a person's social network. The scientists used a brain scanner to determine the size of the amygdala in the brains of 58 adults. They also gave each person a survey that measured the size of a person's social network. After analyzing the data, they found that people with larger amygdalas tend to have larger social networks.

YOUR TURN

5. A survey found that students who spent more time doing Algebra homework also spent more time doing Biology homework. Identify the two variables, indicate whether they have a positive or negative correlation, and discuss whether the correlation is a result of causation.

_____

_____

_____

_____

Personal Math Trainer

Online Practice and Help

my.hrw.com

A marine biologist kept a record of the length in inches and mass in kilograms of a newborn dolphin as it grew older. The results are shown in the table below.
(Explore Activity and Example 1)

Length (in.)	30	60	90	120	150	180	210
Mass (kg)	28	58	87	117	148	178	205

1. Make a scatter plot for this set of data.
What does the *x* value represent?
What does the *y* value represent?

_____

_____

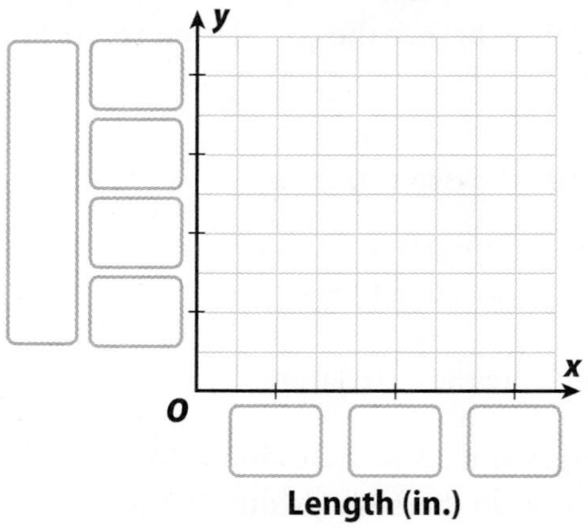

2. Describe the correlation. Explain.

_____

_____

_____

Length (in.)

3. Is the correlation coefficient for the data likely to be closest to -1, -0.5, 0,

0.5, or 1? (Example 2) _____

4. Suppose the biologist also kept track of the amount of food the dolphin ate and found that the amount of food was positively correlated with the length of the dolphin. Is this correlation due to causation? Explain. (Example 3)

_____

_____

_____

ESSENTIAL QUESTION CHECK-IN

5. How can you describe the relationship between two variables?

_____

_____

_____

_____

Name ______________________ Class ______________ Date ______________

8.1 Independent Practice

COMMON CORE S.ID.8, S.ID.6, S.ID.9

Personal Math Trainer
my.hrw.com
Online Practice and Help

The table lists the heights and weights of the six wide receivers that played for a college football team during last year's football season.

Wide Receiver	Height (inches)	Weight (pounds)
Jones	75	192
Walker	76	225
Edwards	71	200
Jefferson	74	210
Tory	69	190
Farmer	72	189

6. Make a scatter plot.

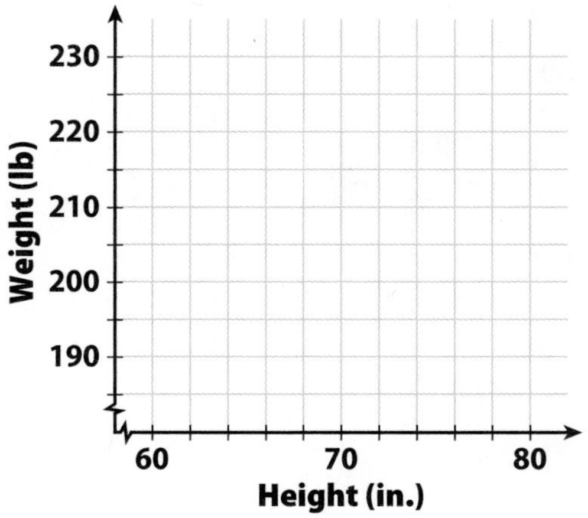

7. Describe the correlation. Is the correlation coefficient likely to be closest to −1, −0.5, 0, 0.5, or 1?.

____

8. Researchers studying senior citizens discovered that an elderly person's walking speed was correlated to that person's chance of living longer. The fastest walkers were more likely to live another 10 years than were the slowest walkers. Describe the correlation, and discuss whether it is due to causation.

____

____

____

____

Identify the correlation you would expect to see between each pair of variables. State whether the correlation coefficient is likely to be closer to −1, 0, or 1.

9. The temperature in Houston and the number of cars sold in Boston.

____

10. The number of members in a family and the size of the family's weekly grocery bill.

____

11. The number of times you sharpen your pencil and the length of the pencil.

_____

Work Area

12. Justify Reasoning Choose the scatter plot that best represents the relationship between the number of days since a sunflower seed was planted and the height of the plant. Explain.

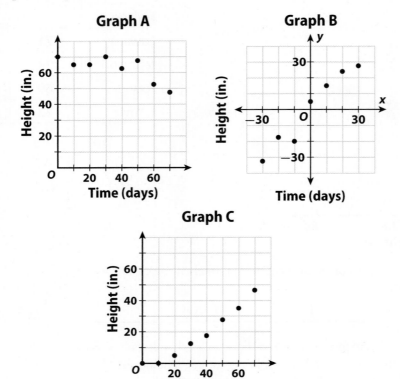

Graph A

Graph B

Graph C

_____

_____

_____

_____

_____

_____

13. Make a Prediction The scatter plot shows the average ocelot population in Laguna Atascosa National Wildlife Refuge near Brownsville, Texas. Based on this information, predict the number of ocelots living at the wildlife refuge in 2014 if conditions do not change.

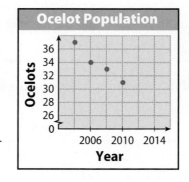

Ocelot Population

_____

LESSON
8.2 Fitting Lines to Data

COMMON CORE **S.ID.6c**

Fit a linear function for a scatter plot that suggests a linear association. *Also S.ID.6, S.ID.6a, S.ID.6b, and S.ID.7*

 ESSENTIAL QUESTION

How do you find a linear model for a bivariate data set, and how do you evaluate the quality of fit?

EXPLORE ACTIVITY COMMON CORE **S.ID.6c**

Finding a Line of Fit for Data

When the two variables in a bivariate data set have a strong positive or negative correlation, you can find a linear model for the data. The process is called fitting a line to the data or finding a **line of fit** for the data.

The table lists the median age of females living in the United States, based on the results of the U.S. Census over the past few decades. Determine whether a linear model is reasonable for the data. If so, find a linear model for the data.

Year	Median age of females
1970	29.2
1980	31.3
1990	34.0
2000	36.5
2010	38.2

A To simplify calculations with the data, let x represent time in years after 1970.

Let y represent the median age of females.

Make a table of paired values of x and y.

x					
y					

B Make a scatter plot of the data.

If the points fall close to a straight line, then a linear model may provide a good description of the data. Do the points appear to form a line?

_____

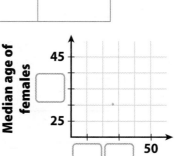

Time (years since 1970)

C Using a ruler, draw a line of fit that passes as close as possible to the plotted points. Your line does not necessarily have to pass through any of the points, but you should try to have about the same number of points above and below the line.

D Find the equation of the line of fit.

We will do the calculation for a line that passes through the points (20, 34) and (40, 38.2).

STEP 1 Find the slope.

$$m = \frac{38.2 - 34}{40 - 20}$$

$$m = \boxed{}$$

STEP 2 Find the y-intercept using (20, 34).

$$y = mx + b$$

$$\boxed{} = \boxed{} \left(\boxed{} \right) + b$$

$$\boxed{} = \boxed{} + b$$

$$\boxed{} = b$$

So, in terms of the variables x and y, the equation of the line of fit is

_____

REFLECT

1. What does the slope of the line of fit tell you about the data?

_____

_____

_____

2. What does the y-intercept of the line of fit tell you about the data?

_____

_____

_____

3. **Communicate Mathematical Ideas** How does the slope of the line of fit relate to the type of correlation in the data?

_____

_____

_____

Creating a Residual Plot

Some lines will fit a data set better than others. One way to evaluate how well a line fits a data set is to use *residuals*. A **residual** is the signed vertical distance between a data point and a line of fit.

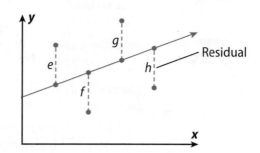

Residual

After calculating residuals, you can draw a **residual plot**, which is a graph of points whose *x*-coordinates are the values of the independent variable and whose *y*-coordinates are the corresponding residuals.

Looking at the distribution of residuals can help you determine how well a line of fit actually describes the data. The plots below illustrate how the residuals might be distributed for three different data sets and lines of fit.

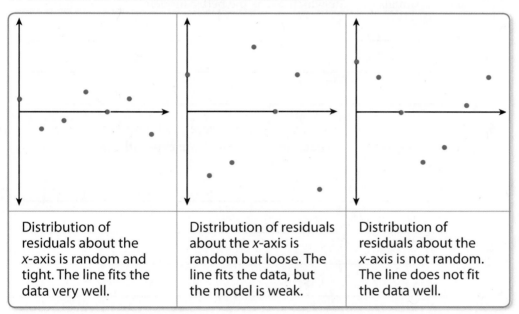

Distribution of residuals about the *x*-axis is random and tight. The line fits the data very well.	Distribution of residuals about the *x*-axis is random but loose. The line fits the data, but the model is weak.	Distribution of residuals about the *x*-axis is not random. The line does not fit the data well.

EXAMPLE 1

COMMON CORE S.ID.6b

Consider the data from the Explore Activity on median ages of females over time. Use residuals to evaluate the quality of fit for the line $y = 0.25x + 29$, where *x* is years since 1970, and *y* is median age.

STEP 1 Calculate the residuals.

x	actual *y*	predicted *y*, based on $y = 0.25x + 29$	residual Subtract predicted from actual to find the residual
0	29.2	29.0	0.2
10	31.3	31.5	−0.2
20	34.0	34.0	0
30	36.5	36.5	0
40	38.2	39.0	−0.8

STEP 2   Plot the residuals.

STEP 3   Evaluate the quality of fit to the data for the line $y = 0.25x + 29$.

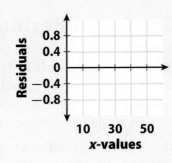

- The residuals are all small, so the points on the residual plot are tightly distributed around the x-axis.
- Therefore, the line given by $y = 0.25x + 29$ is an appropriate model.

REFLECT

4. If you are comparing two lines of fit for the same data set, how does the size of the residuals indicate which one is the better model?

_____

_____

_____

5. **Communicate Mathematical Ideas** Suppose you know that a linear model is a good fit for a data set. How would you expect the residual plot to look?

_____

_____

_____

_____

Math Talk

Mathematical Practices

How did changing the slope of the line of fit affect the residuals in this example?

YOUR TURN

6. Consider the data used in the Explore Activity and in Example 1 on median ages of females over time. Graph the residuals and evaluate the quality of fit for the line $y = 0.2x + 29.2$.

_____

_____

_____

_____

_____

_____

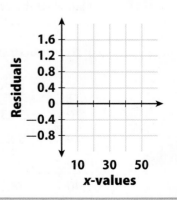

Using a Line of Fit to Make Predictions

Finding a linear model for a data set establishes one variable as a linear function of another variable. The domain of the function is determined by the least and greatest values of the *x*-values in the actual data.

A linear model can be used to make predictions. Making a prediction based on a value *within* the model's domain is called **interpolation**. Basing a prediction on a value *outside* the domain is called **extrapolation**.

Math On the Spot

⏱ my.hrw.com

EXAMPLE 2   COMMON CORE   S.ID.6a

Suppose you used the data table in the Explore Activity to derive the model $y = 0.25x + 29$, where *x* is the number of years since 1970 and *y* is the median age of females in the United States. Use this model to predict the median age of females for the years 1995 and 2015. State whether each prediction is an interpolation or an extrapolation.

My Notes

A Let $x = 25$ because $1995 - 1970 = 25$.

The predicted value of *y* is $0.25(25) + 29 \approx 35.3$ years old.
The *x*-values in the data go from 0 to 40.
The *x*-value 25 is between 0 and 40, so this prediction is an interpolation.

B Let $x = 45$ because $2015 - 1970 = 45$.

The predicted value of *y* is $0.25(45) + 29 \approx 40.3$ years old.
The *x*-values in the data go from 0 to 40.
The *x*-value 45 is greater than 40, so this prediction is an extrapolation.

REFLECT

7. The Census Bureau used interpolation to estimate the median age of females in 1995 and used extrapolation to predict the median age for 2033. They used only the data in the table at the start of this lesson. Which of their predictions is more likely to be accurate? Explain.

_____

_____

_____

_____

YOUR TURN

Use the linear model $y = 0.25x + 29$, where *x* is the number of years since 1970 and *y* is the median age of females, to predict the median age of females in the years below. State whether each prediction is an interpolation or an extrapolation.

8. 1989 _____

9. 2022 _____

_____   _____

Personal Math Trainer

Online Practice and Help

⏱ my.hrw.com

The table lists the median age of males based on the results of the U.S. Census.
(Explore Activity)

Year	1970	1980	1990	2000	2010
Median age of males	26.8	28.8	31.6	34.0	35.5

1. Let x represent time in years after 1970 and let y represent median age. Make a table of paired values of x and y.

x	0		20	30	
y		28.8			35.5

2. Draw a scatter plot and line of fit.

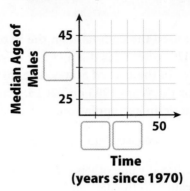

3. Find an equation of the line of fit. (Explore Activity)

_____

A student fit the line $y = 0.23x + 27$ to the data above. Use this model for Exercises 4–6.

4. Calculate the residuals. Evaluate the quality of fit. (Example 1)

x	y actual	y predicted	Residual
0		27	
	28.8		−0.5
20			
30		33.9	
	35.5		−0.7

_____

_____

_____

_____

_____

5. Predict the median age of males in 1995. (Example 2)

$y + 0.23 \left(\boxed{} \right) + 27 \approx \boxed{}$

6. Is the prediction for 1995 an interpolation or extrapolation? (Example 2)

_____

7. How do you find a linear model for bivariate data, and how do you evaluate the quality of fit?

_____

_____

8.2 Independent Practice

COMMON CORE   S.ID.6, S.ID.6a, S.ID.6b, S.ID.6c

Personal Math Trainer

Online Practice and Help

my.hrw.com

The table lists the length (in centimeters) and median weight (in kilograms) of male and female infants in the United States.

Length (cm)	50	60	70	80	90	100
Median weight (kg) of male infants	3.4	5.9	8.4	10.8	13.0	15.5
Median weight (kg) of female infants	3.4	5.8	8.3	10.6	12.8	15.2

8. Let *l* represent an infant's length in excess of 50 centimeters (for instance, for an infant whose length is 60 cm, *l* = 10) and let *w* represent the median weight of female infants. Make a table of paired values of *l* and *w*.

l						
w						

9. Draw a scatter plot of the data for female infants, and draw a line of fit.

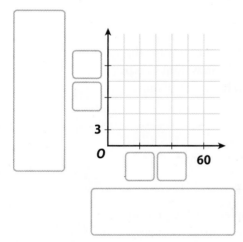

3

0   60

10. Critical Thinking Find an equation for the line of fit you drew on the scatter plot. According to your model, at what rate does the weight change as length increases?

_____

_____

_____

_____

11. Calculate the residuals, and make a residual plot.

l	*w* actual	*w* predicted	Residual
0	3.4		
10	5.8		
20	8.3		
30	10.6		
40	12.8		
50	15.2		

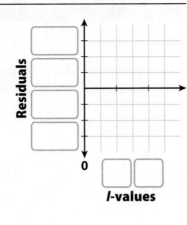

12. Evaluate the suitability of a linear fit and the quality of the fit.

_____

_____

_____

Work Area

13. Critique Reasoning Hector found a linear model based on the data for the length and weight of male infants, and he used it to predict the weight of a boy who is 150 centimeters tall. Is his prediction likely to be reliable? Explain.

_____

_____

_____

14. Analyze Relationships Suppose the line of fit in Example 1 with equation $w = 0.25l + 29$ is changed to $w = 0.25l + 28.8$. What effect does this change have on the residuals? On the residual plot?

_____

_____

15. What If? If the median weight of male infants is 0.2 kg above the median weight of female infants at the same length, how would the line of fit on a scatter plot for male infants' length and weight compare to the one for female infants?

_____

_____

Linear Regression

COMMON CORE **S.ID.6b**

Informally assess the fit of a function by plotting and analyzing residuals. *Also S.ID.6, S.ID.6a, S.ID.6c, S.ID.7, S.ID.8*

? ESSENTIAL QUESTION

How can you use the linear regression function on a graphing calculator to find the line of best fit for a bivariate data set?

EXPLORE ACTIVITY **S.ID.6**

Calculating Squared Residuals

In a previous lesson, you fit a line to data for the median age of females over time. Because each person in your class fit a line by eye, any two students are likely to have chosen slightly different lines of fit. Suppose one student came up with the equation $y = 0.25x + 29.0$ while another came up with $y = 0.25x + 28.8$ where in each case, x is the time in years since 1970 and y is the median age of females.

A Complete each table below in order to calculate the squares of the residuals for each line of fit.

$y = 0.25x + 29.0$				
x	y (actual)	y (predicted)	Residual	Square of residual
0	29.2	29.0	0.2	0.04
10	31.3			
20	34.0			
30	36.5			
40	38.2			

$y = 0.25x + 28.8$				
x	y (actual)	y (predicted)	Residual	Square of residual
0	29.2	28.8	0.4	0.16
10	31.3			
20	34.0			
30	36.5			
40	38.2			

B Find the sum of squared residuals for each line of fit.

Sum of squared residuals for $y = 0.25x + 29.0$: _____

Sum of squared residuals for $y = 0.25x + 28.8$: _____

C Which line has the smaller sum of squared residuals? _____

REFLECT

1. Analyze Relationships How does squaring a residual affect its value?

_____

_____

_____

_____

2. Suppose the residuals for a line of fit for a data set are 2.6, 2.3, −2.3, and −2.5, and the residuals for a second line of fit are 0.6, 0.2, −0.2, and −0.4.

a. Which line fits the data better? How can you tell?

_____

b. Would the sum of the residuals or the sum of the squared residuals be a better measure of the quality of fit? Explain.

_____

_____

_____

_____

_____

_____

Comparing Squared Residuals

The quality of a line of fit can be evaluated by finding the sum of the squared residuals. The closer the sum of the squared residuals is to 0, the better the line fits the data.

EXAMPLE 1 COMMON CORE S.ID.6b

The data in the table below are graphed at right along with two possible lines of fit. For each line, find the sum of the squares of the residuals. Which line is a better fit?

x	2	4	6	8
y	6	3	7	5

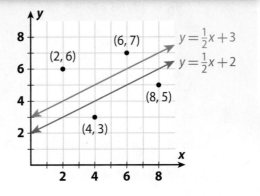

STEP 1 Find the residuals of each line.

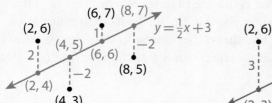

x	y (actual)	y predicted by $y = \frac{1}{2}x + 3$	residual for $y = \frac{1}{2}x + 3$	y predicted by $y = \frac{1}{2}x + 2$	residual for $y = \frac{1}{2}x + 2$
2	6	4	2	3	3
4	3	5	-2	4	-1
6	7	6	1	5	2
8	5	7	-2	6	-1

STEP 2 Square the residuals and find their sum.

$$y = \frac{1}{2}x + 3: (2)^2 + (-2)^2 + (1)^2 + (-2)^2 = 4 + 4 + 1 + 4 = 13$$

$$y = \frac{1}{2}x + 2: (3)^2 + (-1)^2 + (2)^2 + (-1)^2 = 9 + 1 + 4 + 1 = 15$$

The sum of the squares for $y = \frac{1}{2}x + 3$ is smaller, so it provides the better fit for the data.

REFLECT

3. **What If?** Suppose the data pair (5, 4) was added to the data set. Which of the two lines would fit the data better now?

_____

_____

_____

YOUR TURN

4. Find the sum of the squares of the residuals for the data above using the line $y = \frac{1}{2}x + 4$. How good is this fit?

_____

_____

_____

_____

Personal
Math Trainer

Online Practice
and Help

my.hrw.com

Performing Linear Regression

The **least-squares line** for a data set is the line of fit for which the sum of the squares of the residuals is as small as possible. So, the least-squares line is a *line of best fit*. A **line of best fit** is the line that comes closest to all of the points in the data set, using a given process. **Linear regression** is a method for finding the least-squares line.

EXAMPLE 2   COMMON CORE   S.ID.6, S.ID.8

The table shows latitudes and average temperatures for several cities. Use a calculator to estimate the average temperature in Vancouver, Canada at 49.1°N

City	Latitude	Average temperature (°C)
Barrow, Alaska	71.2° N	−12.7
Yakutsk, Russia	62.1° N	−10.1
London, England	51.3° N	10.4
Chicago, Illinois	41.9° N	10.3
San Francisco, California	37.5° N	13.8
Yuma, Arizona	32.7° N	22.8
Tindouf, Algeria	27.7° N	22.8
Dakar, Senegal	14.0° N	24.5
Mangalore, India	12.5° N	27.1

Use your calculator to find an equation for a line of best fit.

STEP 1   Press the [STAT] key and select **1:Edit**. Enter the latitudes in column **L1** and the average temperatures in column **L2**.

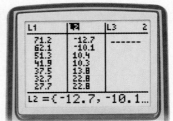

STEP 2   Press [STAT] [PLOT] to create a scatter plot of the data.

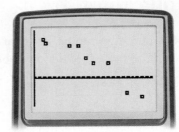

STEP 3 Press **STAT** again and choose **CALC**. From the menu choose **4:LinReg($ax + b$)**. The calculator will display the slope, a, and the y-intercept, b, of the line of best fit. The screen also displays values for the correlation coefficient r and r^2.

STEP 4 Round the values for a and b and write the equation for the best fit line: $y \approx -0.693x + 39.11$.

STEP 5 Press **Y=**, then enter the best fit equation you found in Step 4, then press **GRAPH**. The calculator graphs the line.

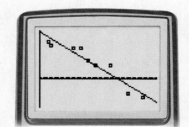

Use the equation to estimate the average temperature in Vancouver, Canada at 49.1° N.

$$y \approx -0.693x + 39.11$$

$$\approx -0.693(49.1) + 39.11 \qquad \textit{Substitute the given value for x.}$$

$$\approx 5.1 \qquad \textit{Solve.}$$

The average temperature in Vancouver should be near 5.1° C.

Math Talk

Mathematical Practices

Nashville is 5.7° south of Chicago. What estimate would you give for its average temperature?

REFLECT

5. Interpret the slope and y-intercept of the equation from the calculator. For each degree of latitude, how does the temperature change?

_____

_____

_____

_____

_____

YOUR TURN

6. Use the equation from Example 2 to estimate the average temperature in Munich, Germany at 48.1° N.

_____

Personal Math Trainer

Online Practice and Help

my.hrw.com

Follow the steps to evaluate lines of fit for the data set given in the table.
(Explore Activity)

x	1	2	3	6
y (actual)	3	6	4	5
y predicted by $y = \frac{3}{4}x + 3$				
Residual				
Squared residual				

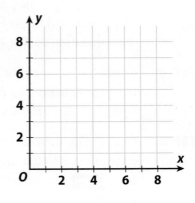

1. Make a scatter plot of the data in the table.

2. Graph the line of fit $y = \frac{3}{4}x + 3$ on the scatter plot.

3. Calculate the y-values predicted by $y = \frac{3}{4}x + 3$, and write them in the table.

4. Calculate the residuals and squared residuals, and write them in the table.

5. What is the sum of the squares of the residuals for the line

   $y = \frac{3}{4}x + 3$? _____

6. Draw the line of fit $y = \frac{3}{4}x + 4$ and calculate the sum of squared residuals for this line. Which line is a better fit? Explain. (Example 1)

   _____

   _____

   _____

7. Use your calculator to find an equation for a line of best fit. (Example 2)

   _____

? ESSENTIAL QUESTION CHECK-IN

8. How can you use a graphing calculator to find the line of best fit for a bivariate data set?

   _____

   _____

   _____

8.3 Independent Practice

Personal Math Trainer

Online Practice and Help

my.hrw.com

COMMON CORE S.ID.6, S.ID.6a, S.ID.6b, S.ID.6c, S.ID.7, S.ID.8

9. The table gives the distance in meters of the gold medal-winning discus throw between 1920 and 1964. When appropriate, use a graphing calculator to solve the problems below.

Olympic Games year	Gold medal discus throw distance (m)
1920	44.685
1924	46.155
1928	47.32
1932	49.49
1936	50.48
1940	No Olympics
1944	No Olympics
1948	52.78
1952	55.03
1956	56.36
1960	59.18
1964	61.00

a. What are the independent variable and dependent variable in this data set?

_____

_____

b. In which column on the graphing calculator will you represent: years? distance? Write the first 3 entries for each column.

_____

_____

c. Enter your data. What values does the calculator give for the slope, intercept, and correlation coefficient? Write the best fit equation for the data set.

_____

_____

_____

d. **Draw a Conclusion** How good was the fit of the equation you wrote for this data? Explain.

_____

_____

e. Suppose the Olympics had been held in 1940 and 1944. What distance

would you predict for each year? _____

f. **Make a Prediction** In the 2012 London Olympics, Robert Harting of Germany took the Gold Medal with a throw of 68.27 m. Was this distance greater or less than the best fit equation would predict? Explain.

_____

_____

_____

H.O.T. FOCUS ON HIGHER ORDER THINKING

Work Area

10. Represent Real-World Problems The table lists the median heights (in centimeters) of girls and boys from age 2 to age 10.

Age (years)	Median Height (cm) of Girls	Median Height (cm) of Boys
2	84.98	86.45
3	93.92	94.96
4	100.75	102.22
5	107.66	108.90
6	114.71	115.39
7	121.49	121.77
8	127.59	128.88
9	132.92	133.51
10	137.99	138.62

a. Identify the real-world variables that x and y will represent.

b. Find the equation of each line of best fit.

c. Find each correlation coefficient.

d. Evaluate the quality of fit for each line.

e. **Analyze Relationships** Which line is the better line of best fit for its data? Explain.

Ready to Go On?

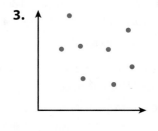
8.1 Correlation

Estimate the correlation coefficient for each scatter plot.

1.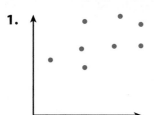

2.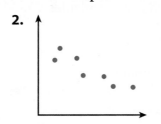

3.

_____ _____ _____

8.2 Fitting Lines to Data

The table gives data for the average salary, in millions of dollars, of players on baseball teams and the number of wins each team had last year.

4. Make a scatter plot of the data.

Average Salary	Number of Wins
$2.6	81
$2.7	73
$3.8	83
$4.6	88
$4.6	93
$5.3	89
$6.2	95

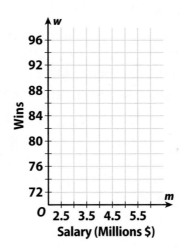

8.3 Linear Regression

5. Use your calculator to find the line of best fit for the data.

Graph the line on the scatter plot. _____

? ESSENTIAL QUESTION

6. How can you use statistical methods to find relationships between variables?

_____

_____

_____

1. Consider the relationship between each pair of variables. Would a scatter plot of the relationship likely show a positive correlation?

Select Yes or No for A–C.

A. the distance a car travels and the amount of gas the car uses ○ Yes ○ No

B. the average speed of a car and the time to travel between Houston and Dallas ○ Yes ○ No

C. the age of a car and the number of oil changes the car has had ○ Yes ○ No

2. The table shows the number of first downs and the number of points scored by a football team during its first 4 games. A student wrote the equation $y = 0.3x + 13$ to model the data.

First Downs, x	44	23	9	31
Points, y	26	23	15	19

Choose True or False for each statement.

A. The model predicts that the team will score 15.7 points when it makes 9 first downs. ○ True ○ False

B. The residual for the data point (44, 26) is 5.2. ○ True ○ False

C. The sum of the squares of the residuals is 21.03. ○ True ○ False

3. The graph shows how Ivy's time to run a mile has changed since March 1. Write the equation of a line of fit for the data. Explain what the slope and y-intercept represent in this situation.

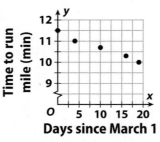

4. The function $f(x) = 250x$ models the maximum number of songs that can be stored on an MP3 player with a capacity of x gigabytes. Find the inverse function $f^{-1}(x)$, and explain what it represents in this situation.

Systems of Equations and Inequalities

? **ESSENTIAL QUESTION**

How are the graphs of systems of linear equations and inequalities related to their solutions?

Real-World Video

A Mars rover is sent into space to land on Mars. This requires planning the trajectory of the rover to intersect with the orbit of Mars. Systems of equations are used to find the intersection of graphs.

my.hrw.com

G0 DIGITAL
my.hrw.com

my.hrw.com

Go digital with your write-in student edition, accessible on any device.

Math On the Spot

Scan with your smart phone to jump directly to the online edition, video tutor, and more.

Animated Math

Interactively explore key concepts to see how math works.

Personal Math Trainer

Get immediate feedback and help as you work through practice sets.

Are YOU Ready?

Complete these exercises to review skills you will need for this module.

Graph Functions

EXAMPLE Graph $y = 2x - 4$.
1. Make a table of values.
2. Plot the ordered pairs.
3. Draw a line through the points.

x	y
0	−4
2	0
−2	−8

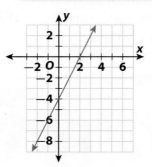

Graph each function.

1. $y = 3x + 6$

2. $y = -x + 5$

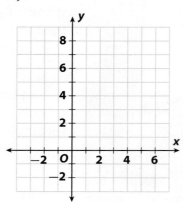

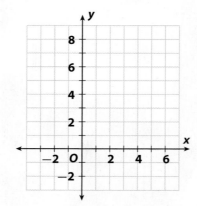

Combine Like Terms

EXAMPLE Simplify $2x + 3 + 3x$.
$2x + 3x + 3$ *Combine like terms.*
$5x + 3$

Simplify each expression.

3. $-4y + (-2y) + 6 - 4$

4. $12x - (-4) - 3x$

5. $9 - 10c + 4c$

6. $9t + (-12t) - 6s + 3s$

7. $-7x - 5y - (-7x) + 2y$

8. $4a + 5b + 3 - (6a + 5b + 8)$

Reading Start-Up

Visualize Vocabulary

Use the ✔ words to complete the chart.

Word	Example
	$y = 2x - 5$
	$y < 2x - 5$
	(x, y)
	$(0, y)$
	$(x, 0)$

Understand Vocabulary

To become familiar with some of the vocabulary terms in the module, read the description and write the term described. You may refer to the module, the glossary, or a dictionary.

1. The word *system* means "a group." How do you think a system of linear equations is different from a linear equation?

_____

_____

2. What does the word eliminate mean? What might the *elimination* method refer to when solving mathematical equations?

_____

_____

3. A solution of a linear equation was the ordered pair that made the equation true. Modify this to define solution of a linear inequality.

_____

Vocabulary

Review Words

Distributive Property *(Propiedad distributiva)*

✔ linear equation *(ecuación lineal)*

✔ linear inequality *(desigualdad lineal)*

✔ ordered pair *(par ordenado)*

solution of a linear equation in two variables *(solución de una ecuación lineal en dos variables)*

✔ x-intercept *(intersección con el eje x)*

✔ y-intercept *(intersección con el eje y)*

Preview Words

elimination method

solution of a system of linear equations

solution of a system of linear inequalities

substitution method

system of linear equations

Active Reading

Tri-Fold Before beginning the module, create a tri-fold to help you learn the concepts and vocabulary in this module. Fold the paper into three sections. Label the columns "What I Know," "What I Want to Know," and "What I Learned." Complete the first two columns before you read. After studying the module, complete the third column.

GETTING READY FOR
Systems of Equations and Inequalities

Understanding the standards and the vocabulary terms in the standards will help you know exactly what you are expected to learn in this module.

 A.REI.6

Solve systems of linear equations exactly and approximately (e.g., with graphs), focusing on pairs of linear equations in two variables.

Key Vocabulary

system of linear equations (*sistema de ecuaciones lineales*)
A system of equations in which all of the equations are linear.

What It Means to You

You can solve systems of equations to find out when two relationships involving the same variables are true at the same time.

EXAMPLE A.REI.6

Find the solution of the system of equations.

$$\begin{cases} y = 2x - 3 \\ y = -\frac{1}{2}x + 2 \end{cases}$$

The solution of the system is the point (x, y) that satisfies both equations simultaneously. On a graph, it is the point at which the lines intersect, $(2, 1)$.

COMMON CORE A.CED.3

Represent constraints by equations or inequalities, and by systems of equations and/or inequalities, and interpret solutions as viable or nonviable options in a modeling context.

Key Vocabulary

inequality (*desigualdad*)
A statement that compares two expressions by using one of the following signs: $<$, $>$, $\leq$, $\geq$, or $\neq$.

solution of an inequality in one variable (*solución de una desigualdad en una variable*)
A value or values that make the inequality true.

What It Means to You

You can use inequalities to represent limits on the values in a situation so that the solutions make sense in a real-world context.

EXAMPLE A.CED.3

Anyone riding the large water slide at the park must be at least 40 inches tall.

Let h represent the heights that are allowed.

Height is at least **40 inches.**
$$h \qquad \geq \qquad 40$$

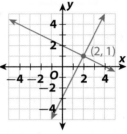

Visit **my.hrw.com** to see all **Common Core Standards** unpacked.

my.hrw.com

Solving Linear Systems by Graphing

COMMON CORE   A.REI.6
Solve systems of linear equations exactly and approximately (e.g., with graphs), focusing on pairs of linear equations in two variables. *Also A.CED.3*

? **ESSENTIAL QUESTION**

How can you find the solution of a system of linear equations by graphing?

Solving a Linear System by Graphing

A **system of linear equations,** also called a *linear system*, consists of two or more linear equations that have the same variables. A **solution of a system of linear equations** with two variables is an ordered pair that satisfies all of the equations in the system. The values of the variables in the ordered pair make each equation in the system true.

Systems of linear equations can be solved by graphing and by using algebraic methods. In this lesson you will learn to solve linear systems by graphing the equations in the system and analyzing how those graphs are related.

EXAMPLE 1

COMMON CORE   A.REI.6

Solve the system of linear equations below by graphing. Check your answer.

$$\begin{cases} -x + y = 3 \\ 2x + y = 6 \end{cases}$$

STEP 1   Find the intercepts for each equation, plus a third point for a check. Graph each line.

$-x + y = 3$	$2x + y = 6$
x-intercept: -3	x-intercept: 3
y-intercept: 3	y-intercept: 6
third point: $(3, 6)$	third point: $(-1, 8)$

STEP 2   Find the point of intersection.

The two lines appear to intersect at $(1, 4)$.

STEP 3   Check to see if $(1, 4)$ makes both equations true.

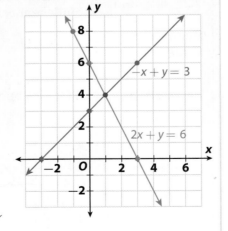

$$-x + y = 3 \qquad 2x + y = 6$$

$$-(1) + 4 \overset{?}{=} 3 \qquad 2(1) + 4 \overset{?}{=} 6$$

$$3 = 3 \checkmark \qquad\qquad 6 = 6 \checkmark$$

The solution is $(1, 4)$.

YOUR TURN

1. Solve the system of linear equations below by graphing. Check your answer.

$$\begin{cases} x + y = 8 \\ x - y = 2 \end{cases}$$

Solution: _____

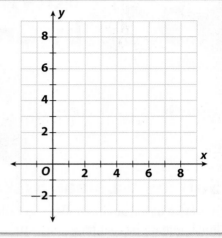

Special Systems of Linear Equations

When a system of equations consists of two lines that intersect in one point, as shown in Figure 1 below, there is exactly one solution to the system.

If two linear equations in a system have the same graph, as shown in Figure 2, the graphs are coincident lines, or the same line. There are infinitely many solutions of the system because every point on the line represents a solution of both equations.

A system with at least one solution is a **consistent system**. Consistent systems can either be independent or dependent.

- An **independent system** has exactly one solution. The graph of an independent system consists of two intersecting lines.
- A **dependent system** has infinitely many solutions. The graph of a dependent system consists of two coincident lines.

When the two lines in a system do not intersect, as shown in Figure 3, they are parallel lines. There are no ordered pairs that satisfy both equations, so there is no solution. A system that has no solution is an **inconsistent system**.

The table below summarizes how systems of linear equations can be classified.

Classification of Systems of Linear Equations			
Classification	**Consistent and Independent**	**Consistent and Dependent**	**Inconsistent**
Number of Solutions	Exactly one	Infinitely many	None
Description	Different slopes	Same slope, same y-intercept	Same slope, different y-intercepts
Graph	Figure 1	Figure 2	Figure 3

EXAMPLE 2   COMMON CORE A.REI.6

Use the graph to solve each system of linear equations. Classify each system.

A $\begin{cases} x + y = 7 \\ 2x + 2y = 6 \end{cases}$

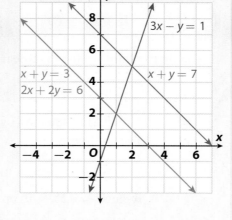

The lines do not intersect and appear to be parallel lines.

This system has no solution. The system is inconsistent.

B $\begin{cases} 2x + 2y = 6 \\ x + y = 3 \end{cases}$

The equations have the same graph, so the graphs are coincident lines.

This system has infinitely many solutions. The system is consistent and dependent.

REFLECT

2. Use the graph above to identify two lines that represent a linear system that is consistent and independent. What are the equations of the lines? Explain your reasoning.

_____

_____

Math Talk
Mathematical Practices

What is the possible number of solutions for a system of linear equations whose graph shows two distinct lines? Explain.

YOUR TURN

Graph each system of linear equations. Classify each system.

3. $\begin{cases} 2x + 2y = 8 \\ x - y = 4 \end{cases}$

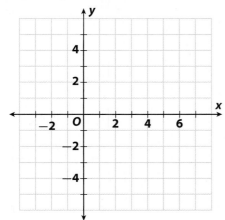

4. $\begin{cases} y = 2x - 4 \\ y = 2x + 6 \end{cases}$

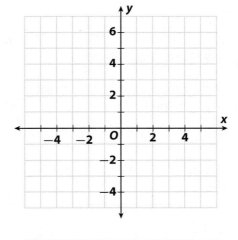

_____   _____

_____   _____

Personal Math Trainer

Online Practice and Help

⏻ my.hrw.com

Estimating a Solution by Graphing

You can estimate a solution for a linear system by graphing and then check your estimate to determine if it is an approximate solution.

EXAMPLE 3

COMMON CORE A.REI.6

Estimate the solution for the linear system by graphing.

$$\begin{cases} x + 2y = 2 \\ 2x - 3y = 12 \end{cases}$$

STEP 1 Graph each equation by finding intercepts.

$x + 2y = 2$	$2x - 3y = 12$
x-intercept: 2	x-intercept: 6
y-intercept: 1	y-intercept: -4

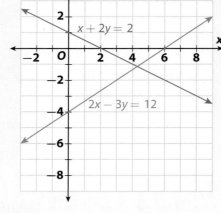

STEP 2 Find the point of intersection.

The two lines appear to intersect at about $\left(4\frac{1}{4}, -1\frac{1}{8}\right)$.

STEP 3 Check if $\left(4\frac{1}{4}, -1\frac{1}{8}\right)$ is an approximate solution.

$$x + 2y = 2 \qquad\qquad 2x - 3y = 12$$

$$4\frac{1}{4} + 2\left(-1\frac{1}{8}\right) \overset{?}{=} 2 \qquad 2\left(4\frac{1}{4}\right) - 3\left(-1\frac{1}{8}\right) \overset{?}{=} 12$$

$$4\frac{1}{4} + \left(-2\frac{1}{4}\right) \overset{?}{=} 2 \qquad\qquad 8\frac{1}{2} - \left(-3\frac{3}{8}\right) \overset{?}{=} 12$$

$$2 = 2 \checkmark \qquad\qquad\qquad 11\frac{7}{8} \approx 12 \checkmark$$

The point $\left(4\frac{1}{4}, -1\frac{1}{8}\right)$ does not make both equations true, but it is acceptable since $11\frac{7}{8}$ is close to 12. So, $\left(4\frac{1}{4}, -1\frac{1}{8}\right)$ is an approximate solution.

YOUR TURN

5. Estimate the solution for the linear system by graphing.

$$\begin{cases} x - y = 3 \\ x + 2y = 4 \end{cases}$$

Approximate solution:

_____

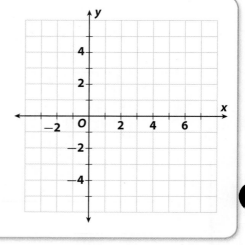

Guided Practice

Solve the system of linear equations by graphing. Check your answer. (Example 1)

1. $\begin{cases} x - y = 7 \\ 2x + y = 2 \end{cases}$

$x - y = 7$

x-intercept: _____

y-intercept: _____

$2x + y = 2$

x-intercept: _____

y-intercept: _____

The solution of the system is _____.

Does your solution check in both original equations? _____

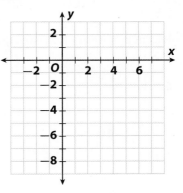

Use the graph to solve and classify each system of linear equations. (Example 2)

2. $\begin{cases} x + y = -1 \\ -2x + 2y = -2 \end{cases}$

Is the system consistent?

_____

Is the system independent?

_____

Solution: _____

3. $\begin{cases} -x + y = 3 \\ -2x + 2y = -2 \end{cases}$

Is the system consistent?

_____

Solution: _____

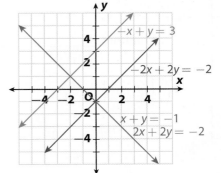

Estimate the solution for the system of linear equations by graphing. (Example 3)

4. $\begin{cases} x + y = -1 \\ 2x - y = 5 \end{cases}$

$x + y = -1$

x-intercept: _____

y-intercept: _____

$2x - y = 5$

x-intercept: _____

y-intercept: _____

The two lines appear to intersect at

_____.

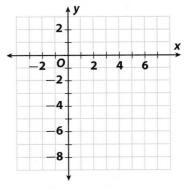

? ESSENTIAL QUESTION CHECK-IN

5. How does graphing help you solve a system of linear equations?

_____

_____

_____

9.1 Independent Practice

Personal Math Trainer

my.hrw.com   Online Practice and Help

A.REI.6, A.CED.3

Solve each system of linear equations by graphing.

6. $\begin{cases} x - y = -2 \\ 2x + y = 8 \end{cases}$

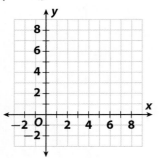

Solution: _____

7. $\begin{cases} x - y = -5 \\ 2x + 4y = -4 \end{cases}$

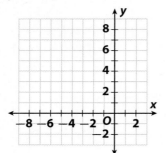

Solution: _____

8. $\begin{cases} x + 2y = -8 \\ -2x - 4y = 4 \end{cases}$

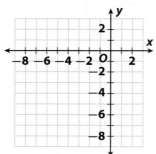

Solution: _____

Estimate the solution for the linear system by graphing.

9. $\begin{cases} x + y = 5 \\ x - 3y = 3 \end{cases}$

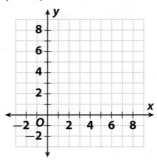

Approximate solution: _____

Graph each system. Then classify it as *consistent and independent*, *consistent and dependent*, or *inconsistent*.

10. $\begin{cases} x + 2y = 6 \\ x = 2 \end{cases}$

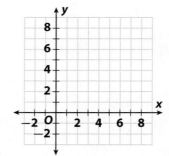

_____

11. $\begin{cases} 2x - y = -6 \\ 4x - 2y = -12 \end{cases}$

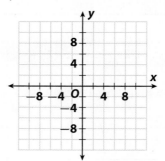

_____

12. Use the graphed system below to find an approximate solution. Then write a system of equations that represents the system.

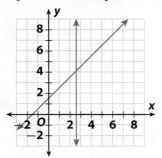

_____

_____

13. **Communicate Mathematical Ideas** When a system of linear equations is graphed, how is the graph of each equation related to the solutions of that equation?

_____

_____

_____

_____

_____

_____

14. **Critical Thinking** Write *sometimes, always,* or *never* to complete the following statement:

If the equations in a system of linear equations have the same slope, there are _____ infinitely many solutions for the system.

_____

15. Suppose you use the graph of a system of linear equations to estimate the solution. Explain how you would check your estimate to determine if it is an approximate solution.

_____

_____

_____

_____

_____

_____

_____

16. Without graphing, describe the graph of this linear system of equations.

$$\begin{cases} x = 3 \\ y = 4 \end{cases}$$

What is the solution of the linear system?

_____

_____

_____

_____

_____

17. How can you recognize a dependent system of equations by analyzing the equations in the system? _____

_____

_____

18. How would you classify a system of equations whose graph is composed of two lines with different slopes and the same *y*-intercepts? What is the solution to the system?

_____

_____

_____

19. Sophie and Marcos are each saving for new bicycles. So far, Sophie has $10 saved and can earn $5 per hour walking dogs. Marcos has $4 saved and can earn $8 per hour at his family's plant nursery. After how many hours of work will Sophie and Marcos have saved the same amount? What will that amount be? Use the system of equations below to complete the graph.

Sophie: $y = 5x + 10$
Marcos: $y = 8x + 4$

_____

20. **Represent Real-World Problems** Cora ran 1 mile last week and will run 7 miles per week from now on. Hana ran 2 miles last week and will run 4 miles per week from now on. The system of linear equations $\begin{cases} y = 7x + 1 \\ y = 4x + 2 \end{cases}$ can be used to represent this situation. Explain what x and y represent in the equations.

_____

_____

_____

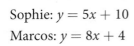 **FOCUS ON HIGHER ORDER THINKING**

21. **Explain the Error** Jake was asked to give an example of an inconsistent system of linear equations. He wrote the system shown below. Explain Jake's error.

$$\begin{cases} y = 2x - 4 \\ y = x - 4 \end{cases}$$

_____

_____

_____

22. **Draw Conclusions** The equations in a system of linear equations have different slopes and the same y-intercept. Can you find the solution without graphing? Explain.

_____

_____

_____

_____

LESSON 9.2
Solving Linear Systems by Substitution

COMMON CORE A.REI.6

Solve systems of linear equations exactly and approximately (e.g., with graphs), focusing on pairs of linear equations in two variables. *Also A.CED.3*

? ESSENTIAL QUESTION

How can you solve a system of linear equations by using substitution?

EXPLORE ACTIVITY

COMMON CORE A.REI.6

Solve by Substituting

In the system of linear equations shown below, the value of y is given. You can use this value of y to find the value of x and the solution of the system.

$$\begin{cases} y = 3 \\ x + y = 5 \end{cases}$$

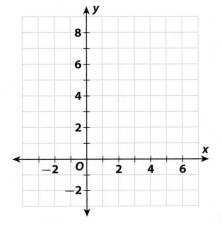

A Substitute the value for y in the second equation and solve for x.

$$x + y = 5$$

$$x + \boxed{} = 5$$

$$x = \boxed{}$$

B You know the values of x and y. What is the solution of the system?

Solution: ($\boxed{}$, $\boxed{}$)

C Graph the system of linear equations. How do your solutions compare?

_____

D Use substitution to find the values of x and y in this system of linear equations. Once you find the value for x, substitute it either original equation to find the value for y.

$$\begin{cases} y = 3x \\ 2x + 3y = 55 \end{cases}$$

Solution: ($\boxed{}$, $\boxed{}$)

REFLECT

1. For the system in part D, what equation did you get after substituting $3x$ for y in $2x + 3y = 55$ and simplifying?

_____

2. How could you check your solution in part D?

_____

_____

Solve a Linear System by Substitution

The **substitution method** is used to solve systems of linear equations by solving an equation for one variable and then substituting the resulting expression for that variable into the other equation. The steps for this method are as follows:

1. Solve one of the equations for one of its variables.

2. Substitute the expression from Step 1 into the other equation and solve for the other variable.

3. Substitute the value from Step 2 into either original equation and solve to find the value of the variable in Step 1.

EXAMPLE 1

COMMON CORE   A.REI.6

Solve the system of linear equations by substitution. Check your answer.

$$\begin{cases} -3x + y = 1 \\ 4x + y = 8 \end{cases}$$

My Notes

STEP 1   Solve an equation for one variable.

$-3x + y = 1$ *Select one of the equations.*
$y = 3x + 1$ *Solve for the variable y. Isolate y on one side.*

STEP 2   Substitute the expression for y in the other equation and solve.

$4x + 3x + 1 = 8$ *Substitute the expression for the variable y.*
$7x + 1 = 8$ *Combine like terms.*
$7x = 7$ *Subtract 1 from each side.*
$x = 1$ *Divide each side by 7.*

STEP 3   Substitute the value of x you found into one of the equations and solve for the other variable, y.

$-3(1) + y = 1$ *Substitute the value of x into the first equation.*
$-3 + y = 1$ *Simplify.*
$y = 4$ *Add 3 to each side.*

So, (1, 4) is the solution of the system.

STEP 4   Check the solution by graphing.

$-3x + y = 1$ $4x + y = 8$
x-intercept: $-\frac{1}{3}$ x-intercept: 2
y-intercept: 1 y-intercept: 8

The point of intersection is (1, 4).

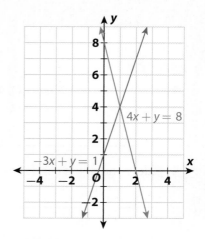

REFLECT

3. Justify Reasoning Is it more efficient to solve $-3x + y = 1$ for x? Why or why not?

_____

_____

4. What is another way to check your solution?

_____

_____

YOUR TURN

Solve each system of linear equations by substitution. Check your answer.

5. $\begin{cases} 2x + y = 5 \\ \quad\ y = x - 4 \end{cases}$

6. $\begin{cases} \ x + 3y = 4 \\ -x + 2y = 6 \end{cases}$

Solution: _____

Solution: _____

Personal Math Trainer

Online Practice and Help

⏻ my.hrw.com

Solving Special Systems by Substitution

You can use the substitution method for systems of linear equations that have infinitely many solutions and for systems that have no solutions.

Math On the Spot

⏻ my.hrw.com

EXAMPLE 2   COMMON CORE A.REI.6

Solve each system of linear equations by substitution.

A $\begin{cases} \ x - y = -2 \\ -x + y = 4 \end{cases}$

STEP 1 Solve $x - y = -2$ for x: $x = y - 2$

STEP 2 Substitute the resulting expression into the other equation and solve.

$-(y - 2) + y = 4$ Substitute.

$2 = 4$ Simplify.

The resulting equation is false, so the system has no solutions.

STEP 3 Graph the equations to provide more information.

The graph shows that the lines are parallel and do not intersect.

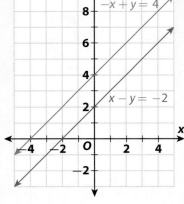

B $\begin{cases} 2x + y = -2 \\ 4x + 2y = -4 \end{cases}$

STEP 1 Solve $2x + y = -2$ for y: $\qquad y = -2x - 2$

STEP 2 Substitute the resulting expression into the other equation and solve.

$4x + 2(-2x - 2) = -4$ Substitute.

$\qquad 4x - 4x - 4 = -4$ Use the Distributive Property.

$\qquad\qquad\qquad -4 = -4$ Simplify.

The resulting equation is true so the system has infinitely many solutions.

STEP 3 Graph the equations to provide more information.

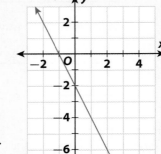

The graphs are the same line, so the system has infinitely many solutions.

REFLECT

7. In part B of Example 2, why is it more efficient to solve and substitute for y than to solve and substitute for x?

_____

_____

_____

8. Give two possible solutions of the system in part B of Example 2. How are all the solutions of this system related to one another?

_____

_____

_____

Personal Math Trainer

Online Practice and Help

🔘 my.hrw.com

YOUR TURN

Solve each system of linear equations by substitution.

9. $\begin{cases} x + 3y = 6 \\ 2x + 6y = 12 \end{cases}$

Solution: _____

_____

10. $\begin{cases} 2x - y = -1 \\ 2x - y = -4 \end{cases}$

Solution: _____

_____

Modeling with Linear Systems

You can use a system of linear equations and its graph to model many real-world situations.

EXAMPLE 3   COMMON CORE   A.REI.6, A.CED.3

One family fitness center has a $50 enrollment fee and costs $30 per month. Another center has no enrollment fee and costs $40 per month. Write an equation for each option. Let t represent the total amount paid and m represent the number of months. In how many months will both fitness centers cost the same? What will that cost be?

	Total cost	is	**enrollment fee**	plus	cost per month	times	months.
Option 1	t	$=$	50	$+$	30	$\cdot$	m
Option 2	t	$=$	0	$+$	40	$\cdot$	m

STEP 1
$t = 50 + 30m$
$t = 40m$

Write the system of equations.

STEP 2
$50 + 30m = 40m$

Substitute $50 + 30m$ for t in the second equation.

$\dfrac{-30m \quad -30m}{50 = 10m}$

Subtract $30m$ from each side.

$\dfrac{50}{10} = \dfrac{10m}{10}$

Divide each side by 10.

$5 = m$

STEP 3
$t = 40m$
$\quad = 40(5)$
$\quad = 200$

Write one of the original equations.
Substitute 5 for m.

STEP 4
$(5, 200)$

Write the solution as an ordered pair.

In 5 months, the total cost for each option will be the same, $200.

Math Talk
Mathematical Practices

In a graph of the system of equations, why must the values of the variables be greater than or equal to zero?

YOUR TURN

11. One high-speed Internet provider has a $30 setup fee and charges $40 per month. Another provider has a $60 setup fee and charges $30 per month. In how many months will the cost be the same?

_____

Guided Practice

Solve each system of linear equations by substitution. Check your answer. (Examples 1 and 2)

1. $\begin{cases} y = x + 5 \\ 4x + y = 20 \end{cases}$

STEP 1 Find the value of x.

$$4x + y = 20$$

$$4x + \boxed{} = 20$$

$$\boxed{}\, x = \boxed{}$$

$$x = \boxed{}$$

STEP 2 Find the value of y.

$$y = x + 5$$

$$y = \boxed{} + 5$$

$$y = \boxed{}$$

Solution: _____

2. $\begin{cases} x + 2y = 6 \\ 2x + 4y = 12 \end{cases}$

STEP 1 Solve $x + 2y = 6$ for x.

$$x = \boxed{}$$

STEP 2 Substitute that expression for x into $2x + 4y = 12$.

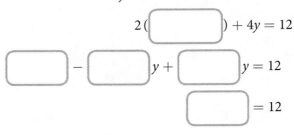

$$2\left(\boxed{}\right) + 4y = 12$$

$$\boxed{} - \boxed{}\,y + \boxed{}\,y = 12$$

$$\boxed{} = 12$$

Solution: _____

_____

Solve each system of linear equations by substitution. Check your answer. (Examples 1 and 2)

3. $\begin{cases} x + 2y = 7 \\ 4x + 3y = 3 \end{cases}$

Solution: _____

4. $\begin{cases} 2x - y = -4 \\ 2x - 2y = -10 \end{cases}$

Solution: _____

5. $\begin{cases} 2x - 4y = 8 \\ 2y - x = -6 \end{cases}$

Solution: _____

6. The Blanco family is deciding between two lawn-care services. Evergreen charges a $49 startup fee, plus $29 per month. Great Grass charges a $25 startup fee, plus $37 per month. In how many months will both lawn-care services cost the same? What will that cost be? (Example 3)

_____

© Houghton Mifflin Harcourt Publishing Company

? ESSENTIAL QUESTION CHECK-IN

7. Explain how you can solve a system of linear equations by substitution.

_____

_____

_____

_____

9.2 Independent Practice

Personal Math Trainer

Online Practice and Help

my.hrw.com

For each linear system, tell whether it is more efficient to solve for *x* and then substitute for *x* or to solve for *y* and then substitute for *y*. Explain your reasoning. Then solve the system.

8. $\begin{cases} 6x - 3y = 15 \\ x + 3y = -8 \end{cases}$

_____

_____

_____

_____

_____

Solution: _____

9. $\begin{cases} 3x - y = -1 \\ 5x - y = 3 \end{cases}$

_____

_____

_____

_____

Solution: _____

For each system of linear equations, write the expression you could substitute for *x*. Then solve the system.

10. $\begin{cases} 2x - y = 6 \\ x + y = -3 \end{cases}$

_____

Solution: _____

11. $\begin{cases} x - 2y = 0 \\ 4x - 3y = 15 \end{cases}$

_____

Solution: _____

12. **Communicate Mathematical Ideas** The solution of a system of two linear equations yields the equation $0 = 3$. Describe what the graph of the system looks like.

_____

_____

_____

13. Use *one solution, no solutions,* or *infinitely many solutions* to complete this statement.

When the solution of a system of linear equations yields the equation $4 = 6$, the system has _____.

_____

14. **Represent Real-World Problems** Ella buys a book and a pen for $14. The cost of the book is $2 more than twice the cost of the pen. Write a system of linear equations for the situation. Then find the cost of each item. Let *x* represent the cost of the pen, and let *y* represent the cost of the book.

_____

_____

_____

15. **Interpret the Answer** The perimeter of a rectangular picture frame is 66 inches. The length is 3 inches greater than the width. The system of linear equations used to represent the situation is shown below.

$\begin{cases} 2x + 2y = 66 \\ x + 3 = y \end{cases}$

Solve the system. Name the dimension represented by each variable.

_____

_____

16. Kim and Leon exercise a total of 20 hours each week. Leon exercises 2 hours less than 3 times the number of hours Kim exercises. How many hours does each exercise?

_____

17. Use the receipts below to write and solve a system of linear equations to find the cost of a large fruit bucket and the cost of a small drink.

_____

_____

Work Area

18. **Multiple Representations** For the first equation in the system of linear equations below, write an equivalent equation without denominators. Then solve the system.

$$\begin{cases} \dfrac{x}{2} + \dfrac{y}{3} = 6 \\ x - y = 2 \end{cases}$$

_____

19. **Critical Thinking** Is it possible for a system of three linear equations to have one solution? If so, give an example.

_____

_____

_____

_____

20. **Draw Conclusions** Is it possible to use substitution to solve a system of linear equations if one equation represents a horizontal line and the other equation represents a vertical line? Explain.

_____

_____

_____

Solving Linear Systems by Adding or Subtracting

COMMON CORE A.REI.6

Solve systems of linear equations exactly and approximately (e.g., with graphs), focusing on pairs of linear equations in two variables. Also *A.CED.3*

ESSENTIAL QUESTION

How can you solve a system of linear equations by using addition and subtraction?

EXPLORE ACTIVITY   A.REI.6

Exploring the Effects: Adding Equations

Remember that the sum of a number and its opposite is zero. You can use that fact to help you solve some systems of linear equations.

A Look at the system of linear equations below.

$$\begin{cases} x - 3y = -15 \\ 5x + 3y = -3 \end{cases}$$

What do you notice about the coefficients of the y-terms.

_____

B What is the sum of $-3y$ and $3y$? How do you know?

_____

C Find the sum of the two equations by combining like terms.

$$\begin{array}{rrl} x & -3y & = -15 \\ +5x & +3y & = \underline{-3} \end{array}$$

$$\boxed{} + \boxed{} = \boxed{}$$

D Use the resulting equation from part C to find the value of x.

$$x = \boxed{}$$

E Use the value of x to find the value of y. What is the solution of the system?

$$y = \boxed{}$$ Solution: _____

REFLECT

1. When you add $5x + 3y$ to $x - 3y$ and add -3 to -15, how do you know that the resulting sums are equal?

_____

_____

_____

2. How could you check your solution in part E?

_____

_____

Solving a Linear System by Adding or Subtracting

The **elimination method** is another method used to solve a system of linear equations. In this method, one variable is *eliminated* by adding or subtracting the two equations of the system to obtain a single equation in one variable. The steps for this method are as follows:

1. Add or subtract the equations to eliminate one variable, and then solve for the other variable.

2. Substitute the value into either original equation to find the value of the eliminated variable.

3. Write the solution as an ordered pair.

EXAMPLE 1 — COMMON CORE A.REI.6

Solve each system of linear equations using the indicated method. Check your answer.

A Solve the system of linear equations below by adding.
$$\begin{cases} 4x - 2y = 12 \\ x + 2y = 8 \end{cases}$$

STEP 1 Add the equations.

$$4x - 2y = 12 \qquad \text{Write the equations so that like terms are aligned.}$$
$$\underline{+\ x + 2y = 8} \qquad \text{Notice that the terms } -2y \text{ and } 2y \text{ are opposites.}$$
$$5x + 0 = 20 \qquad \text{Add to eliminate the variable } y.$$
$$5x = 20 \qquad \text{Simplify.}$$
$$x = 4 \qquad \text{Divide each side by 5.}$$

STEP 2 Substitute the value of x into one of the equations and solve for y.

$$x + 2y = 8 \qquad \text{Use the second equation.}$$
$$4 + 2y = 8 \qquad \text{Substitute 4 for the variable } x.$$
$$2y = 4 \qquad \text{Subtract 4 from each side.}$$
$$y = 2 \qquad \text{Divide each side by 2.}$$

STEP 3 Write the solution as an ordered pair.

(4, 2) is the solution of the system.

STEP 4 Check the solution by graphing.

$4x - 2y = 12$ $x + 2y = 8$

x-intercept: 3 x-intercept: 8

y-intercept: -6 y-intercept: 4

The point of intersection is (4, 2).

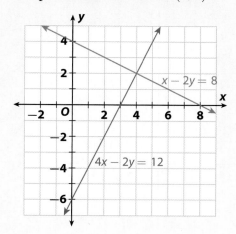

B Solve the system of linear equations below by subtracting.

$$\begin{cases} 2x + 6y = 6 \\ 2x - y = -8 \end{cases}$$

STEP 1 Subtract the equations.

$2x + 6y = 6$ — Write the equations so that like terms are aligned.

$-(2x - y = -8)$ — Notice that both equations contain the term $2x$.

$0 + 7y = 14$ — Subtract to eliminate the variable x.

$7y = 14$ — Simplify.

$\dfrac{7y}{7} = \dfrac{14}{7}$ — Divide each side by 7.

$y = 2$ — Simplify.

STEP 2 Substitute the value of y into one of the equations and solve for x.

$2x - y = -8$ — Use the second equation.

$2x - 2 = -8$ — Substitute 2 for the variable y.

$2x = -6$ — Add 2 to each side.

$x = -3$ — Divide each side by 2.

STEP 3 Write the solution as an ordered pair.

$(-3, 2)$ is the solution of the system.

STEP 4 Check the solution by graphing.

$2x + 6y = 6$ $2x - y = -8$

x-intercept: 3 x-intercept: -4

y-intercept: 1 y-intercept: 8

The point of intersection is $(-3, 2)$.

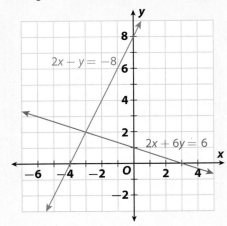

REFLECT

3. Draw Conclusions Can the system in part A be solved by subtracting one of the original equations from the other? Why or why not?

_____

_____

4. What If? In part B, what would happen if you added the original equations instead of subtracted?

_____

_____

_____

5. Justify Reasoning How can you decide whether to add or subtract to eliminate a variable in a linear system? Explain your reasoning.

_____

_____

_____

_____

Solve each system of linear equations by adding or subtracting.

6. $\begin{cases} 2x + 5y = -24 \\ 3x - 5y = 14 \end{cases}$

7. $\begin{cases} 3x + 2y = 10 \\ 3x - y = 22 \end{cases}$

Solution: _____

Solution: _____

8. $\begin{cases} 3x + 2y = 5 \\ x + 2y = -1 \end{cases}$

9. $\begin{cases} 3x - y = -2 \\ -2x + y = 3 \end{cases}$

Solution: _____

Solution: _____

Personal Math Trainer

Online Practice and Help

⏻ my.hrw.com

Solving Special Systems

You can use the elimination method for systems of linear equations that have infinitely many solutions and for systems that have no solutions.

Math On the Spot

⏻ my.hrw.com

EXAMPLE 2 COMMON CORE A.REI.6

Solve each system of linear equations by adding or subtracting.

A $\begin{cases} -4x - 2y = 4 \\ 4x + 2y = -4 \end{cases}$

STEP 1 Add the equations.

$$\begin{array}{r} -4x - 2y = 4 \\ +4x + 2y = -4 \\ \hline 0 + 0 = 0 \\ 0 = 0 \end{array}$$

Notice that the terms $-4x$ and $4x$ and $-2y$ and $2y$ are opposites.

Add to eliminate the variables.

Simplify.

The resulting equation is true so the system has infinitely many solutions.

STEP 2 Graph the equations to provide more information.

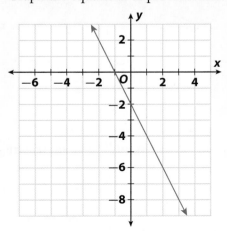

The graphs are the same line, so the system has infinitely many solutions.

B $\begin{cases} x + y = -2 \\ x + y = 4 \end{cases}$

STEP 1 Subtract the equations.

$$x + y = -2$$ Write the equations so that like terms are aligned.

$$\underline{-(x + y) = -(4)}$$ Notice that both equations contain the terms x and y.

$$0 + 0 = -6$$ Subtract to eliminate the variables.

$$0 = -6$$ Simplify.

The resulting equation is false, so the system has no solutions.

STEP 2 Graph the equations to provide more information.

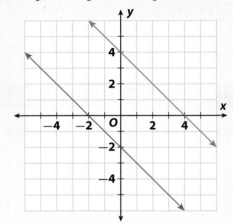

The graph shows that the lines are parallel and do not intersect.

Math Talk

Mathematical Practices

When a linear system has no solution, what happens when you try to solve the system by adding or subtracting?

REFLECT

10. Communicate Mathematical Ideas Suppose you solve a system of linear equations in which both variables are eliminated by subtraction. What is the solution of your system?

_____

_____

_____

Personal Math Trainer

Online Practice and Help

⏻ my.hrw.com

YOUR TURN

Solve each system of linear equations by adding or subtracting.

11. $\begin{cases} 4x - y = 3 \\ 4x - y = -2 \end{cases}$

Solution: _____

_____

12. $\begin{cases} x - 6y = 7 \\ -x + 6y = -7 \end{cases}$

Solution: _____

_____

Modeling with Linear Systems

Some real-world situations can be modeled with systems of equations that can be solved by the elimination method.

Math On the Spot
my.hrw.com

EXAMPLE 3   COMMON CORE   A.REI.6, A.CED.3

Best Backyards is building a rectangular deck for a customer. The customer wants the perimeter to be 40 meters and the difference between twice the length and twice the width to be 4 meters. What will be the length and width of the deck?

Write an equation for each requirement.

Let l represent the length and w represent the width.

Perimeter:	Twice the length	plus	twice the width	is	40
	$2l$	$+$	$2w$	$=$	40

Difference:	Twice the length	minus	twice the width	is	4
	$2l$	$-$	$2w$	$=$	4

STEP 1   Add the equations.

$$2l + 2w = 40$$ Align like terms. Notice that the terms $2w$ and $-2w$ are opposites.

$$\underline{2l - 2w = 4}$$

$$4l + 0 \ = 44$$ Add to eliminate the variable w.

$$4l = 44$$ Simplify.

$$l = 11$$ Divide each side by 4.

STEP 2   Substitute the value of l into one of the equations and solve for w.

$$2l + 2w = 40$$ Use the first equation.

$$2(11) + 2w = 40$$ Substitute 11 for the variable l.

$$22 + 2w = 40$$ Simplify.

$$2w = 18$$ Subtract 22 from each side.

$$w = 9$$ Divide each side by 2.

STEP 3   Write the solution as an ordered pair.

$(l, w) = (11, 9)$ is the solution of the system.

The length of the deck will be 11 meters, and the width will be 9 meters.

Personal Math Trainer

Online Practice and Help

⏻ my.hrw.com

YOUR TURN

13. Movies and More is having a one-day sale on certain movie DVDs and video games. You can buy 3 DVDs and 2 video games for $74. Or you can buy 5 DVDs and 2 video games for $98. Write and solve a system of equations to find the cost of one DVD and the cost of one video game.

_____

Guided Practice

Solve each system of linear equations by adding or subtracting. Check your answer. (Examples 1 and 2)

1. $\begin{cases} -5x + y = -3 \\ 5x - 3y = -1 \end{cases}$

STEP 1 Add the equations. Find the value of y.

$$-5x + y = -3$$
$$\underline{+5x - 3y = -1}$$

$\boxed{} + \boxed{} = \boxed{}$

$y = \boxed{}$

STEP 2 Find the value of x.

$$-5x + y = -3$$

$-5x + \boxed{} = -3$

$-5x = \boxed{}$

$x = \boxed{}$

Solution: _____

2. $\begin{cases} 2x + y = -6 \\ -5x + y = 8 \end{cases}$

Solution: _____

3. $\begin{cases} 6x - 3y = 15 \\ 4x - 3y = -5 \end{cases}$

Solution: _____

4. $\begin{cases} -5x - y = -3 \\ -5x - y = -2 \end{cases}$

Solution: _____

5. A picture frame has a perimeter of 62 inches. The difference between the length and twice the width is 1 inch. What are the length and width of the frame? (Example 3)

_____

?

ESSENTIAL QUESTION CHECK-IN

6. When you solve a system of linear equations by adding or subtracting, what needs to be true about the variable terms in the equations?

_____

_____

9.3 Independent Practice

 COMMON CORE A.REI.6, A.CED.3

Personal Math Trainer

Online Practice and Help

my.hrw.com

7. The sum of two numbers is 65. The difference of the two numbers is 27. Write and solve a system of linear equations to find the two numbers. Let x represent the greater number, and let y represent the lesser number.

System: _____

Greater number: _____

Lesser number: _____

8. The sum of the digits in a two-digit number is 12. The tens digit is 2 more than the ones digit. Write and solve a system of linear equations to find the number. Let x represent the tens digit, and let y represent the ones digit.

System: _____

Number: _____

9. Justify Reasoning Solve the system of equations below by substitution and by elimination.

$$\begin{cases} x + y = -4 \\ 2x + y = -3 \end{cases}$$

Which method do you prefer? Explain your reasoning.

Solution: _____

_____

_____

10. Can you solve this system of linear equations by adding or subtracting? Why or why not?

$$\begin{cases} x + 2y = 7 \\ 4x + 3y = 3 \end{cases}$$

_____

_____

11. Draw Conclusions Use addition or subtraction to find the solution of the system below. What does the solution tell you about the graph of the solution of this system?

$$\begin{cases} x + y = 5 \\ x - 3y = 3 \end{cases}$$

Solution: _____

_____

_____

_____

12. A garden has a perimeter of 120 feet. The difference between the length and twice the width is 24 feet. Write a system of linear equations that represents this situation. Then solve the system to find the length and width of the garden.

System: _____

Length: _____

Width: _____

13. The sum of two angles is 90°. The difference between twice the larger angle and the smaller angle is 105°. Write a system of linear equations that represents this situation. Then solve the system to find the measures of the two angles.

System: _____

Larger angle: _____

Smaller angle: _____

14. Use *one solution, no solutions,* or *infinitely many solutions* to complete this statement.

When the solution of a system of linear equations yields the equation 4 = 4, the

system has _____.

15. Represent Real-World Problems For a school play, Ricco bought 3 adult tickets and 5 child tickets for $40. Sasha bought 1 adult ticket and 5 child tickets for $25. Find the cost of an adult ticket and the cost of a child ticket. Then find how much Julia will pay for 5 adult tickets and 3 child tickets.

_____

_____

16. Bright Pools is building a rectangular pool at a new house. The perimeter of the pool has to be 94 feet, and the length has to be 2 feet more than twice the width. What will be the length and width of the pool?

_____

 **FOCUS ON HIGHER ORDER THINKING**

Work Area

17. Multiple Representations You can use subtraction to solve the system of linear equations shown below.

$$\begin{cases} 2x + 4y = -4 \\ 2x - 2y = -10 \end{cases}$$

Instead of subtracting $2x - 2y = -10$ from $2x + 4y = -4$, what equation can you add to get the same result? Explain.

_____

_____

18. Explain the Error Liang's solution of a system of linear equations is shown below.

$$\begin{cases} 3x - 2y = 12 \\ -x - 2y = -20 \end{cases}$$

$$
\begin{aligned}
3x - 2y &= 12 \\
+ -x - 2y &= -20 \\
\hline
2x \quad\quad &= -8 \\
x \quad\quad &= -4 \\
3x + 2y &= 12 \\
3(-4) + 2y &= 12 \\
2y &= 24 \\
y &= 12
\end{aligned}
$$

Solution: $(-4, 12)$

Explain Liang's error and give the correct solution.

_____

_____

_____

Solving Linear Systems by Multiplying

COMMON CORE · A.REI.5
Prove that, given a system of two equations in two variables, replacing one equation by the sum of that equation and a multiple of the other produces a system with the same solutions.
Also A.CED.3, A.REI.6

? ESSENTIAL QUESTION

How can you solve a system of linear equations by using multiplication and elimination?

EXPLORE ACTIVITY 1   COMMON CORE   A.REI.5, A.REI.6

Understanding Linear Systems and Multiplication

A Graph this system of linear equations. Label each equation and find the solution.

$$\begin{cases} 2x - y = 1 \\ x + y = 2 \end{cases}$$

The solution of the system is _____.

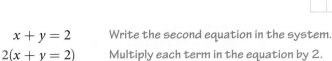

B Use one of the equations in the system to write a new equation.

$x + y = 2$	*Write the second equation in the system.*
$2(x + y = 2)$	*Multiply each term in the equation by 2.*
$2x + 2y = 4$	*Simplify.*

C Graph the new equation. How is the graph of this equation related to the graphs of the original two equations?

_____

_____

REFLECT

1. Draw Conclusions What is true about the equations $x + y = 2$ and $2x + 2y = 4$?

_____

2. Could you solve the original system by using the elimination method? Explain. Could you solve a new system that contained the new equation and the first equation in the original system? Explain.

_____

_____

_____

Proving the Elimination Method with Multiplication

If you add the new equation you found in Explore Activity 1 and the first equation in the original system, you get a third equation. The graph of this new equation is shown at the right.

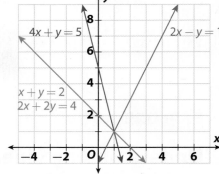

$$2x + 2y = 4$$
$$\underline{+\ 2x - \ y = 1}$$
$$4x + \ y = 5$$

A Is the solution of the original system also a solution of the system formed by the equation $2x - y = 1$ and the third equation? Explain. _____

_____

B If the original system is $Ax + By = C$ and $Dx + Ey = F$, where A, B, C, D, E, and F are constants, then multiply the second equation by a nonzero constant k to get $kDx + kEy = kF$. Then add this equation to the first equation to get the third equation.

$$Ax + \qquad By = C$$
$$\underline{+\ kDx + \qquad kEy = \qquad kF}$$
$$(A + kD)x + (B + kE)y = C + kF$$

C Complete the following proof to show that if (x_1, y_1) is a solution of the original system, then it is also a solution of the new system below.

$$\begin{cases} Ax + By = C \\ (A + kD)x + (B + kE)y = C + kF \end{cases}$$

$Ax_1 + By_1 = C$	(x_1, y_1) is a solution of $Ax + By = C$.
$Dx_1 + Ey_1 = F$	(x_1, y_1) is a solution of $Dx + Ey = F$.
$\boxed{}(Dx_1 + Ey_1) = kF$	Multiplication Property of Equality
$kDx_1 + kEy_1 = kF$	Distributive Property
$C + kDx_1 + kEy_1 = \boxed{} + kF$	Addition Property of Equality
$Ax_1 + \boxed{} + kDx_1 + kEy_1 = C + kF$	Substitute $Ax_1 + By_1$ for C on left.
$Ax_1 + kDx_1 + \boxed{} + kEy_1 = C + kF$	Commutative Property of Addition
$(Ax_1 + kDx_1) + (By_1 + kEy_1) = C + kF$	Associative Property of Addition
$(A + kD)x_1 + (\boxed{} + kE)y_1 = C + kF$	Distributive Property

Because $(A + kD)x_1 + (B + kE)y_1 = C + kF$, (x_1, y_1) is a solution of the new system.

Solving a Linear System by Multiplying One Equation

Math On the Spot
my.hrw.com

In some linear systems, neither variable can be eliminated by adding or subtracting the equations directly. In systems like these, you need to multiply one or both of the equations by a constant so that adding or subtracting the equations will eliminate one or more of the variables. The steps for this method are as follows:

1. Decide which variable to eliminate.

2. Multiply one or both equations by a constant so that adding or subtracting will eliminate that variable.

3. Solve the system using the elimination method.

EXAMPLE 1   COMMON CORE   A.REI.6

Solve the system of linear equations by multiplying. Check your answer.

$$\begin{cases} 3x + 8y = 7 \\ 2x - 2y = -10 \end{cases}$$

STEP 1   Multiply the second equation by a constant and then add the equations.

$4(2x - 2y = -10)$ *Multiply each term in the second equation by 4 to get opposite y-coefficients.*

$8x - 8y = -40$

$\underline{+ \; 3x + 8y = \quad 7}$ *Add the first equation to the new equation.*

$11x + 0y = -33$ *Add the two equations.*

$11x = -33$ *Simplify.*

$x = -3$ *Divide each side by 11.*

STEP 2   Substitute the value of x into one of the original equations and solve for y.

$3x + 8y = 7$ *Use the first equation.*

$3(-3) + 8y = 7$ *Substitute −3 for the variable x.*

$-9 + 8y = 7$ *Simplify.*

$8y = 16$ *Add 9 to each side.*

$y = 2$ *Divide each side by 8.*

STEP 3   Write the solution as an ordered pair: $(-3, 2)$.

My Notes

STEP 4 Check the solution by graphing.

$$3x + 8y = 7 \qquad 2x - 2y = -10$$

x-intercept: $2\frac{1}{3}$ x-intercept: -5

y-intercept: $\frac{7}{8}$ y-intercept: 5

The point of intersection is $(-3, 2)$.

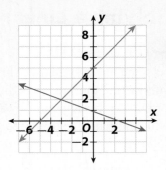

The solution of the system is $(-3, 2)$.

Personal Math Trainer

Online Practice and Help

⏻ my.hrw.com

YOUR TURN

3. Solve the system of linear equations by multiplying. Check your answer.

$$\begin{cases} -3x + 4y = 12 \\ 2x + y = -8 \end{cases} \quad \text{Solution: _____}$$

Math On the Spot

⏻ my.hrw.com

Solving a Linear System by Multiplying Both Equations

You may need to multiply both equations in a system before you can add or subtract.

EXAMPLE 2   **COMMON CORE**   **A.REI.6**

Solve the system of linear equations by multiplying.

$$\begin{cases} -3x + 9y = -3 \\ 4x - 13y = 5 \end{cases}$$

STEP 1 Multiply the first equation by 4 and the second equation by 3 to get opposite x-coefficients.

$4(-3x + 9y = -3)$	Multiply the first equation by 4.
$3(4x - 13y = 5)$	Multiply the second equation by 3.
$-12x + 36y = -12$	Simplify the first equation.
$+12x - 39y = 15$	Simplify the second equation.
$-3y = 3$	Add the two equations.
$\dfrac{-3y}{-3} = \dfrac{3}{-3}$	Divide each side by -3.
$y = -1$	Simplify.

STEP 2   Substitute the value of y into one of the equations and solve for x.

$$4x - 13y = 5$$ Use the second equation.

$$4x - 13(-1) = 5$$ Substitute -1 for the variable y.

$$4x + 13 = 5$$ Simplify.

$$4x = -8$$ Subtract 13 from both sides.

$$x = -2$$ Divide each side by 4.

STEP 3   Write the solution as an ordered pair: $(-2, -1)$.

Math Talk
Mathematical Practices

Describe how to find the numbers by which you would multiply both equations to eliminate a variable.

YOUR TURN

Solve each system of linear equations by multiplying. Check your answer.

4. $\begin{cases} 2x + 3y = -1 \\ 5x - 2y = -12 \end{cases}$

5. $\begin{cases} 5x - 2y = 11 \\ 3x + 5y = 19 \end{cases}$

Solution: _____

Solution: _____

Personal Math Trainer

Online Practice and Help

⏻ my.hrw.com

Applying Linear Systems

EXAMPLE 3   *Real World*   COMMON CORE   A.REI.6, A.CED.3

Math On the Spot
⏻ my.hrw.com

Jessica spent \$14.85 to buy 13 flowers. The bouquet contained daisies, which cost \$1.25 each, and tulips, which cost \$0.90 each. How many of each type of flower did Jessica buy?

Total Number:	Number of daisies	plus	number of tulips	is	13
	d	$+$	t	$=$	13
Total Cost:	Cost of daisies	plus	cost of tulips	is	14.85
	$1.25d$	$+$	$0.90t$	$=$	14.85

STEP 1   Multiply the first equation by a constant and then subtract the equations.

$$0.90d + 0.90t = 11.70$$ Multiply the first equation by 0.90.

$$-(1.25d + 0.90t) = -(14.85)$$ Subtract the second equation.
$$\overline{}$$
$$-0.35d = -3.15$$

$$\frac{-0.35d}{-0.35} = \frac{-3.15}{-0.35}$$ Divide each side by −0.35.

$$d = 9$$ Simplify

STEP 2 Substitute the value of d into one of the equations and solve for t.

$$d + t = 13 \quad \text{Use the first equation.}$$

$$(9) + t = 13 \quad \text{Substitute 9 for the variable } d.$$

$$t = 4 \quad \text{Simplify.}$$

Jessica bought 9 daisies and 4 tulips.

YOUR TURN

6. Roses are \$2.50 each and lilies are \$1.75 each. Ellis spent \$24.75 for 12 of the flowers. How many of each type of flower did he buy?

_____

Guided Practice

1. Solve the system of linear equations by multiplying. Check your answer. (Example 1)

$$\begin{cases} -2x + 2y = 2 \\ 5x - 6y = -9 \end{cases}$$

$$\boxed{}\,x + \boxed{}\,y = 6$$

$$\underline{+5x - 6y = -9}$$

$$-x = \boxed{}$$

Solution: _____

Solve each system of linear equations by multiplying. Check your answer. (Examples 1 and 2)

2. $$\begin{cases} 3x + 3y = 12 \\ 6x + 11y = 14 \end{cases}$$

   Solution: _____

3. $$\begin{cases} 4x + 3y = 11 \\ 2x - 2y = -12 \end{cases}$$

   Solution: _____

4. $$\begin{cases} 3x + 8y = 17 \\ -2x + 9y = 3 \end{cases}$$

   Solution: _____

5. The length of a rectangle is 8 inches more than the width. The perimeter of the rectangle is 56 inches. Write and solve a system of linear equations to find the length and width of the rectangle. (Example 3)

_____

 ESSENTIAL QUESTION CHECK-IN

6. Explain how you can solve a system of linear equations by using multiplication and elimination.

_____

_____

_____

9.4 Independent Practice

COMMON CORE A.REI.6, A.CED.3

Personal Math Trainer

Online Practice and Help

my.hrw.com

For each linear system, tell whether you would multiply the terms in the first or second equation in order to eliminate one of the variables. Give the number by which you could multiply. Then solve the system.

7. $\begin{cases} x + 3y = -14 \\ 2x + y = -3 \end{cases}$

Equation: _____

Number: _____

Solution: _____

8. $\begin{cases} 9x - 3y = 3 \\ -3x - 8y = 17 \end{cases}$

Equation: _____

Number: _____

Solution: _____

For each linear system, give the number by which you would multiply the terms in each equation in order to eliminate one of the variables. Then solve the system.

9. $\begin{cases} -3x + 2y = 4 \\ 5x - 3y = 1 \end{cases}$

First equation number: _____

Second equation number:

_____

Solution: _____

10. $\begin{cases} 5x + 2y = -1 \\ 3x + 7y = 11 \end{cases}$

First equation number: _____

Second equation number:

_____

Solution: _____

11. Critical Thinking Suppose you want to eliminate y in this system.

$\begin{cases} 2x + 11y = -3 \\ 3x + 4y = 8 \end{cases}$

What numbers would you need to multiply the two equations by to eliminate y? Why might you choose to eliminate x instead?

_____

_____

_____

_____

_____

_____

12. Represent Real-World Problems The Tran family is bringing 12 packages of cheese to the neighborhood picnic. Sliced cheese cost $2.00 per package. Chunk cheese cost $1.50 per package. They spent $20 for the cheese. Write and solve a system of equations that can be used to find the number of packages of each type of cheese they purchased.

System: _____

Sliced cheese: _____

Chunk cheese: _____

13. Conrad drew 2 angles. Three times the measure of angle 1 is 30° more than 5 times the measure of angle 2. The sum of twice the measure of angle 1 and twice the measure of angle 2 is 180°. Find the measure of each angle.

Angle 1: _____

Angle 2: _____

14. Represent Real-World Problems The school store is running a promotion on school supplies. Different supplies are placed on two shelves. You can purchase 3 items from shelf A and 2 from shelf B for $16. Or you can purchase 2 items from shelf A and 3 from shelf B for $14. How much more does one item on shelf A cost than an item on shelf B? Explain.

_____

_____

15. A local boys club sold 176 bags of mulch and made a total of $520. They did not sell any of the expensive cocoa mulch. Use the table to determine how many bags of each type of mulch they sold.

	Mulch Prices		
Type of mulch	Cocoa	Hardwood	Pine Bark
Price	$4.75	$3.50	$2.75

_____

 **FOCUS ON HIGHER ORDER THINKING**

Work Area

16. Explain the Error A linear system has two equations, $Ax + By = C$ and $Dx + Ey = F$. A student multiplies the x- and y-coefficients in the second equation by a constant k to get $kDx + kEy = F$. The student then adds the result to $Ax + By = C$ to write a new equation.

a. What is the new equation that the student wrote?

_____

b. If the ordered pair (x_1, y_1) is a solution of the original system and not $(0, 0)$, will it also be a solution of the new equation? Why or why not?

_____

_____

_____

17. Critical Thinking Would you prefer to solve the system in Exercise 7 by using substitution? Explain your reasoning.

_____

_____

_____

_____

_____

Solving Systems of Linear Inequalities

Graph the solutions to a linear inequality in two variables as a half-plane (excluding the boundary in the case of a strict inequality), and graph the solution set to a system of linear inequalities in two variables as the intersection of the corresponding half-planes. *Also A.CED.3*

? **ESSENTIAL QUESTION**

How do you solve a system of linear inequalities?

EXPLORE ACTIVITY · COMMON CORE · A.REI.12

Graphing Linear Inequalities on the Same Coordinate Plane

A Graph the inequality $x + y \leq 4$.

Did you shade above or below the boundary line?

_____

B Graph the inequality $x - y \geq 2$.

Did you shade above or below the boundary line?

_____

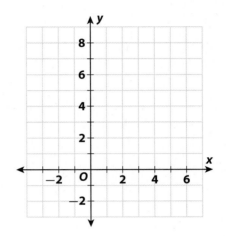

C Look at the region of your graph where the graphs of the two inequalities overlap. Choose three ordered pairs from that region. Test each pair in each inequality.

_____

Ordered pair	Satisfies $x + y \leq 4$?	Satisfies $x - y \geq 2$?

REFLECT

1. If you test another ordered pair in the region where the graphs overlap, do you think it will satisfy one, both, or neither of the inequalities? Explain your reasoning.

_____

_____

_____

2. **Draw Conclusions** An ordered pair that makes a linear inequality true is a solution of that linear inequality. What can you conclude about the ordered pairs in the region where the graphs overlap?

_____

_____

_____

Solving a System of Linear Inequalities by Graphing

A **system of linear inequalities** consists of two or more linear inequalities that have the same variables. The **solutions of a system of linear inequalities** are all the ordered pairs that make all the inequalities in the system true.

My Notes

EXAMPLE 1

COMMON CORE A.REI.12

Solve the system of inequalities by graphing. Check your answer.

$$\begin{cases} x + 2y > 2 \\ -x + y \le 4 \end{cases}$$

STEP 1 Graph $x + 2y > 2$.

The equation of the boundary line is $x + 2y = 2$.

x-intercept: 2 y-intercept: 1

The inequality symbol is $>$, so use a dashed line.

Shade above the boundary line because $(0, 0)$ is *not* a solution of the inequality.

STEP 2 Graph $-x + y \le 4$.

The equation of the boundary line is $-x + y = 4$.

x-intercept: -4 y-intercept: 4

The inequality symbol is $\le$, so use a solid line.

Shade below the boundary line because $(0, 0)$ *is* a solution of the inequality.

STEP 3 Identify the solutions.

The solutions are the points in the region where the graphs overlap.

STEP 4 Check your answer by testing a point from each region.

Ordered pair	Satisfies $x + 2y > 2$?	Satisfies $-x + y \le 4$?	In the region where the graphs overlap?
$(0, 0)$			
$(2, 3)$			
$(-4, 2)$			
$(-2, 4)$			

REFLECT

3. Draw Conclusions How does testing specific ordered pairs tell you that the solution you graphed is correct?

_____

_____

4. Is $(-2, 2)$ a solution of the system of inequalities? Why or why not?

_____

_____

_____

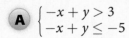 **YOUR TURN**

5. Solve the system of inequalities by graphing. Check your answer.

$$\begin{cases} x - y \geq -1 \\ y > 2 \end{cases}$$

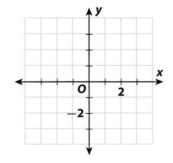

Personal Math Trainer
Online Practice and Help
⏻ my.hrw.com

Solving Systems of Inequalities Whose Graphs Have Parallel Boundary Lines

The graphs of linear inequalities in a system can have parallel boundary lines. Unlike in systems of *equations* containing parallel lines, this does not always mean the system of inequalities has no solution.

Math On the Spot
⏻ my.hrw.com

EXAMPLE 2   COMMON CORE A.REI.12

Graph each system of linear inequalities. Describe the solutions.

A $\begin{cases} -x + y > 3 \\ -x + y \leq -5 \end{cases}$

The two regions do not overlap.

The system has no solution.

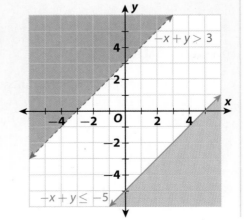

B $\begin{cases} x + y > -4 \\ x + y > -1 \end{cases}$

The solutions are all the points in the region where the graphs overlap. They are all the solutions of $x + y > -1$.

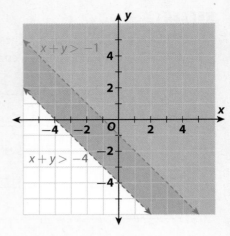

C $\begin{cases} -x + 3y \leq 3 \\ -x + 3y \geq -3 \end{cases}$

The solutions are all the points in the regions between the boundary lines and on the boundary lines.

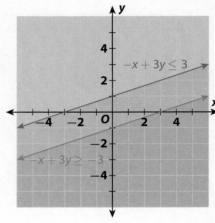

REFLECT

6. Can the solution of a system of linear inequalities be a line? If so, give an example.

_____

_____

7. Does the system $3x - 2y < 4$ and $3x - 2y > 4$ have a solution? Explain.

_____

_____

_____

YOUR TURN

8. Graph the system of linear inequalities. Describe the solutions.

$\begin{cases} x - y < -1 \\ x - y \geq 3 \end{cases}$

Description: _____

_____

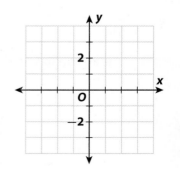

Modeling with Systems of Linear Inequalities

You can use a system of linear inequalities and its graph to model many real-world situations.

Math On the Spot
⏻ my.hrw.com

EXAMPLE 3 Real World

COMMON CORE A.REI.12, A.CED.3

Rosa is buying T-shirts and shorts. T-shirts cost \$12 and shorts cost \$20. She plans to spend no more than \$120 and buy at least 4 items. Show and describe all possible combinations of the number of T-shirts and shorts she could buy. List two possible combinations.

STEP 1 Write a system of linear inequalities. Let t represent the number of T-shirts and s represent the number of shorts.

Total items: $t + s \geq 4$ — She wants to buy at least 4 items.

Total spent: $12t + 20s \leq 120$ — She wants to spend no more than \$120.

STEP 2 Graph the system. The graph should be in only the first quadrant because the numbers of T-shirts and shorts are not negative.

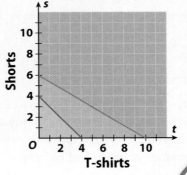

Rosa's Options

STEP 3 Describe all of the possible combinations. Rosa could buy any combination of T-shirts and shorts represented by a point in the region where the graphs overlap. Answers must be whole numbers because she cannot buy part of a T-shirt or pair of shorts.

STEP 4 List two possible combinations. Two possible combinations: 2 T-shirts and 3 shorts or (2, 3), 1 T-shirt and 5 shorts or (1, 5)

Math Talk
Mathematical Practices

How do you choose which region to select the combinations from?

YOUR TURN

9. Sergio is building a garden. He wants the length to be at least 30 feet and the perimeter to be no more than 100 feet. Graph all possible dimensions of the garden. Is a length of 35 feet and a width of 10 feet a possible combination?

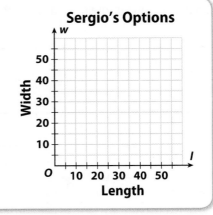

Sergio's Options

_____

Personal Math Trainer
Online Practice and Help
⏻ my.hrw.com

Solve each system of linear inequalities by graphing. Describe the solutions. (Examples 1 and 2)

1. $\begin{cases} x - y \leq -3 \\ x - y > 3 \end{cases}$

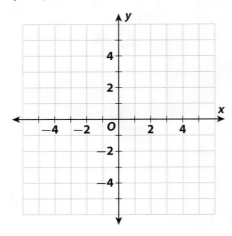

2. $\begin{cases} x + y \leq -2 \\ -x + y > 1 \end{cases}$

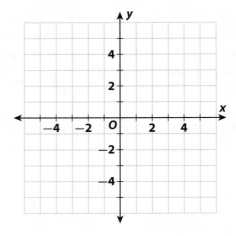

_____

_____

_____

_____

3. Jason is buying grapes for a picnic. Green grapes cost $2 a pound and red grapes cost $3 a pound. He plans to buy at least 4 pounds of grapes and spend no more than $20. List two possible combinations of the number of pounds of green and red grapes he could buy. (Example 3)

Jason's Options

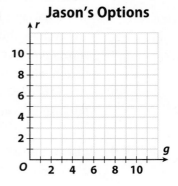

_____

_____

? **ESSENTIAL QUESTION CHECK-IN**

4. How do you solve a system of linear inequalities?

_____

_____

_____

_____

9.5 Independent Practice

Personal Math Trainer

Online Practice and Help

my.hrw.com

A.REI.12, A.CED.3

Solve each system of linear inequalities by graphing. Name two ordered pairs that are solutions of the system.

5. $\begin{cases} y \geq -2 \\ 4x + y \geq 2 \end{cases}$

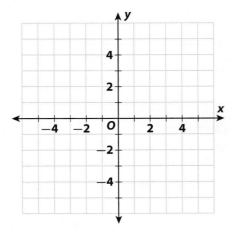

6. $\begin{cases} x < 1 \\ 2x + y > 1 \end{cases}$

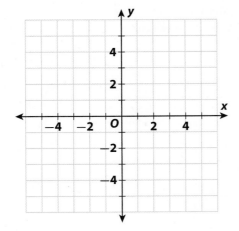

7. $\begin{cases} 4x + y \geq 4 \\ 4x + y \geq -4 \end{cases}$

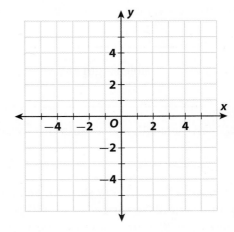

8. The system of inequalities below defines the boundaries of a region in the plane. What inequality symbol or symbols could replace "?" to make the solution a triangular region?

$$\begin{cases} y \leq -x + 1 \\ y \geq \frac{1}{3}x - 3 \\ x \underline{\ ?\ } -4 \end{cases}$$

_____

9. Describe the solutions of this system of linear inequalities. Then write a possible system for the graphed inequalities.

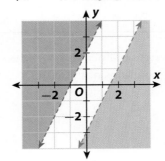

_____

_____

10. Critical Thinking Without graphing, describe the solution of $\begin{cases} x \geq 3 \\ y \leq 4 \end{cases}$.

_____

_____

11. Natalia is drawing a rectangle. She wants the width to be at least 10 inches and the perimeter to be no more than 72 inches.

   a. Write a system of inequalities that can be used to solve this problem.

   _____

   b. Give a possible length and width for the rectangle.

   _____

   c. Give a length and a width that cannot be used for the rectangle.

   _____

12. Leon works at a grocery store for $8 an hour. He also mows lawns for $10 an hour. He needs to earn at least $120 per week, but he does not want to work more than 20 hours per week. Use a system of inequalities to find a possible combination of hours he can work at the grocery store and mowing lawns in order to meet his goal.

_____

 **FOCUS ON HIGHER ORDER THINKING**

Work Area

13. Communicate Mathematical Ideas Is it possible for a system of two linear inequalities to have every point in the plane as a solution? Why or why not?

_____

_____

_____

_____

14. Graph the system of linear inequalities. Describe the solutions of the system.
$$\begin{cases} x + 4y > -4 \\ x + y \leq 2 \\ x - y \geq 2 \end{cases}$$

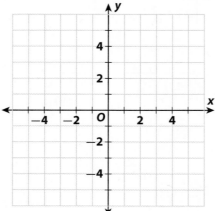

_____

_____

_____

_____

Ready to Go On?

9.1 Solving Linear Systems by Graphing

Solve each system of linear equations by graphing.

1. $\begin{cases} x - y = 5 \\ x + y = 3 \end{cases}$ Solution: _____

2. $\begin{cases} -x + y = 3 \\ -2x + y = 6 \end{cases}$ Solution: _____

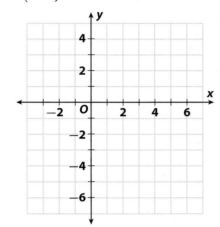

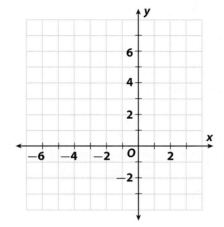

9.2 Solving Linear Systems by Substitution

Solve each system of linear equations by substitution.

3. $\begin{cases} x + y = -2 \\ 2x - 2y = 8 \end{cases}$ Solution: _____

4. $\begin{cases} x - 2y = -7 \\ 2x - 3y = -10 \end{cases}$ Solution: _____

9.3, 9.4 Solving Linear Systems by Elimination

Solve each system of linear equations by elimination.

5. $\begin{cases} x + 3y = 5 \\ 2x + 3y = 7 \end{cases}$ Solution: _____

6. $\begin{cases} 2x + 5y = 4 \\ 4x + 7y = 2 \end{cases}$ Solution: _____

9.5 Solving Systems of Linear Inequalities

7. Solve the system of linear inequalities by graphing.

$\begin{cases} 2x + y \leq 8 \\ 3x - y < 2 \end{cases}$

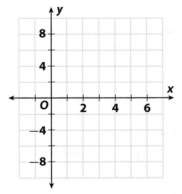

? ESSENTIAL QUESTION

8. How are the graphs of systems of linear equations and inequalities related to their solutions?

_____

_____

MODULE 9

MIXED REVIEW

Assessment Readiness

Personal Math Trainer

my.hrw.com

Online Practice and Help

1. Consider the system of inequalities $\begin{cases} 3x + 2y < 8 \\ x - 2y > -4 \end{cases}$.
   Which ordered pair(s) below are solutions of the system? Select all that apply.

   ○ $(-2, -1)$ ○ $(0, 2)$ ○ $(1, 1)$ ○ $(4, -2)$

2. Look at each set of steps. Could the steps be used to eliminate a variable from the system $\begin{cases} 6x + 3y = -3 \\ 2x - 6y = 20 \end{cases}$?
   Select Yes or No for A–C.

   A. Multiply the first equation by 2,
   and then add the equations.   ○ Yes   ○ No

   B. Multiply the second equation by 3,
   and then subtract the equations.   ○ Yes   ○ No

   C. Multiply the second equation by 6,
   and then add the equations.   ○ Yes   ○ No

3. The table shows data about largemouth bass. Use a calculator to find the equation of the line of best fit for the data. Then predict the weight of a largemouth bass with a length of 12 inches. Explain your reasoning.

Length (in.), x	10.0	14.5	17.0	20.0	23.5
Weight (lb), y	0.48	1.63	2.74	4.68	7.95

4. The Larsen family bought 3 jumbo burritos and 2 regular burritos for $13.65. The Russo family bought 5 jumbo burritos and 2 regular burritos for $20.23. Does a jumbo burrito cost more than $3.00? Write and solve a system of equations to justify your answer.

Study Guide Review

MODULE 6 **Linear Functions**

Key Vocabulary

linear function *(función lineal)*

linear equation *(ecuación lineal)*

standard form of a linear equation *(forma estándar de una ecuación lineal)*

x-intercept *(intersección con el eje x)*

y-intercept *(intersección con el eje y)*

rate of change *(tasa de cambio)*

rise *(distancia vertical)*

run *(distancia horizontal)*

slope *(pendiente)*

slope formula *(formula de pendiente)*

slope-intercept form *(forma de pendiente-intersección)*

family of functions *(familia de funciones)*

parent function *(función madre)*

parameter *(parámetro)*

ESSENTIAL QUESTION

How do equations, graphs, tables, and word descriptions relate to linear functions?

EXAMPLE 1

Find the slope and the *y*-intercept of the line that is graphed below. Then, write the equation of the line in slope-intercept form.

The *y*-intercept is at 2. Since the line goes through the points $(0, 2)$ and $(4, 4)$, the slope is $m = \frac{(4 - 2)}{(4 - 0)} = \frac{1}{2}$. So, the equation for the line in slope-intercept form is $y = \frac{1}{2}x + 2$.

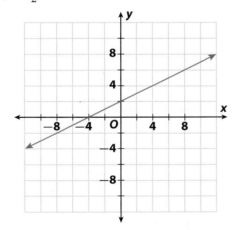

EXAMPLE 2

Find the slope of the line that has its *x*-intercept at 3 and its *y*-intercept at 4.

The intercepts give two points on the line, $(3, 0)$ and $(0, 4)$. The slope can be found using these two points in the slope formula: $m = \frac{(4 - 0)}{(0 - 3)} = -\frac{4}{3}$.

EXERCISES

1. Tell whether the function given by $y - 3 = 2x$ is linear. Compare it to the linear function represented by the table below. Describe how the functions are alike and how they are different. (Lessons 6.1, 6.5)

x	1	2	3	4
y	1	3	5	7

_____

_____

2. Find the slope and the intercepts of the line from the graph. Then, write the equation of the line in slope-intercept form. (Lessons 6.2, 6.3, 6.7)

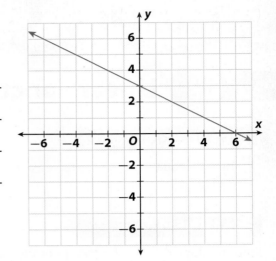

_____

_____

_____

_____

3. Find the slope of the line that has its x-intercept at -2 and its y-intercept at 7. (Lesson 6.4)

_____

4. Brandon's cell phone bill can be represented by $y = 0.15x + 5$ and Lisa's cell phone bill is given by $y = 0.20x + 25$, where x is the number of text messages each sends in a month. Interpret the meaning of 0.15 and 0.20 in these equations, and describe the difference between the graphs of the functions. (Lesson 6.6)

_____

_____

_____

_____

_____

Building Linear Functions

© Houghton Mifflin Harcourt Publishing Company

Key Vocabulary

arithmetic sequence
   (sucesión aritmética)
common difference
   (diferencia común)
inverse of a function
   (función inversa)
linear inequality in two
   variables *(desigualdad
   lineal en dos variables)*
solution of an inequality
   *(solución de
   una desigualdad)*
boundary line *(linea de limite)*
half-plane *(semiplano)*

? ESSENTIAL QUESTION

How are mathematical operations related to solving linear equations and inequalities and creating new functions?

EXAMPLE 1

Add the linear functions $f(x) = 2x - 7$ and $g(x) = 4x + 3$ to get the linear function $h(x) = f(x) + g(x)$.

$f(x) + g(x) = (2x - 7) + (4x + 3)$ Substitute for $f(x)$ and $g(x)$.

$\quad\quad\quad = (2x + 4x) + (-7 + 3)$ Combine like terms.

$\quad\quad\quad = 6x - 4$ Simplify.

EXAMPLE 2

The amount of money, A, that a tour guide earns in a day is given by $A = 20x + 40$, where x is the number of tours given by the guide. Find the number of tours given as a function of A.

$A = 20x + 40$ *Start with A as a function of x.*

$A - 40 = 20x$ *Subtract.*

$\frac{A}{20} - 2 = x$ *Divide.*

$x = \frac{A}{20} - 2$ *Solve for x.*

EXERCISES

Write a recursive rule and an explicit rule for each arithmetic sequence. (Lesson 7.1)

5. 8, 11, 14, 17, … _____

6. 10, 5, 0, −5, … _____

7. An employee earns a base salary of $30,000 plus an additional $2,000 for each project completed in a year. Her income tax rate is 20%. Write a function $S(x)$ for the salary earned for completing x projects in a year. Then write a function $T(x)$ for the tax owed by the employee for completing x projects in a year. (Lesson 7.2)

_____

_____

8. Find the sum, $h(x)$, of the function $f(x) = 3x + 7$ and the function

$g(x) = -2x - 5$. (Lesson 7.2) _____

9. Subtract the function $f(x) = 6x - 5$ from the function $g(x) = -2x + 9$.

Denote the difference by $h(x)$. (Lesson 7.2) _____

10. Find the product, $h(x)$, of the function $f(x) = -5x + 7$ and the function $g(x) = 3$. (Lesson 7.2)

_____

11. Find the inverse of the linear function $y = 7x + 3$. (Lesson 7.3)

_____

12. Find the inverse of the linear function $f(x) = 3x - 5$. (Lesson 7.3)

_____

13. Find the inverse of the linear function $g(x) = \frac{1}{2}x + 9$. (Lesson 7.3)

_____

14. Graph the solution set for $4x + 2y > 5$. (Lesson 7.4)

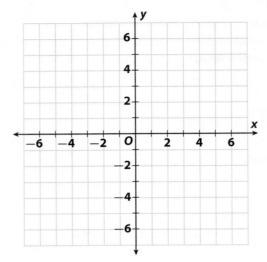

Modeling with Linear Functions

Key Vocabulary
bivariate data
scatter plot (*diagrama de dispersión*)
correlation (*correlación*)
correlation coefficient (*coeficiente de correlación*)
line of fit (*línea de ajuste*)
residual (*residual*)
residual plot (*parcela residual*)
interpolation (*interpolación*)
extrapolation
linear regression (*regresión lineal*)
least squares regression line (*mínimos cuadrados línea de regresión*)
line of best fit (*línea de major ajuste*)

? ESSENTIAL QUESTION

How can you use statistical methods to find relationships between sets of data?

EXAMPLE

Describe the correlation in the scatter plot below, and estimate the correlation coefficient.

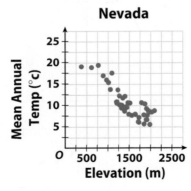

The scatter plot shows a strong negative correlation. Points lie close to a line with a negative slope. The correlation coefficient is close to -1.

EXERCISES

15. The scatter plot shows a relationship between years of experience at a job and income earned. The line of best fit is $I = 1.32x + 25$, where I is income in thousands of dollars per year and x is years of experience. Estimate the correlation coefficient. Then, predict the income earned by someone with 40 years of experience. (Lessons 8.1, 8.2)

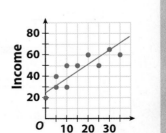

16. The table below gives the ages, t, of boys on a middle-school basketball team and their shoe sizes, s. One student estimates that the line of best fit is given by $S_F = 0.8t + 0.5$. Use the table to compute the squares of the residuals for this line. *(Lesson 8.3)*

s = 0.8t + 0.5				
t	s (actual)	s (predicted)	Residuals	Square of Residuals
10	9	8.5	0.5	0.25
11	7			
12	10			
13	12			
13	9.5			

MODULE 9

Systems of Equations and Inequalities

? ESSENTIAL QUESTION

How are the graphs of systems of linear equations and inequalities related to their solutions?

EXAMPLE

Solve the system of linear equations.

$$\begin{cases} y = 3x + 1 \\ 2y - 3 = 4x \end{cases}$$

$2(3x + 1) - 3 = 4x$ *Substitute the first equation into the second.*

$6x - 1 = 4x$ *Distribute.*

$2x = 1$ *Combine like terms.*

$x = \dfrac{1}{2}$ *Solve for x.*

$y = 3\left(\dfrac{1}{2}\right) + 1$ *Substitute $\dfrac{1}{2}$ into the first equation to find y.*

$y = \dfrac{5}{2}$

The solution is $\left(\dfrac{1}{2}, \dfrac{5}{2}\right)$.

Key Vocabulary

system of linear equations *(sistema de ecuaciones lineales)*

solution of a system of linear equations *(solución de un sistema de ecuaciones lineales)*

substitution method *(sustitución)*

elimination method *(eliminación)*

system of linear inequalities *(sistema de desigualdades lineales)*

solution of a system of linear inequalities *(solución de un sistema de desigualdades lineales)*

EXERCISES

17. Solve the system of equations by substitution. (Lesson 9.2)

$$\begin{cases} y - 2 = 4x \\ 5y - 2x = 1 \end{cases}$$

_____

Solve each system of equations by elimination. (Lessons 9.3, 9.4)

18. $\begin{cases} 4x + 6y = 38 \\ 4x - 2y = 14 \end{cases}$ **19.** $\begin{cases} 3x - 2y = 9 \\ 5x + \ y = 2 \end{cases}$

_____   _____

Solve each system of equations or inequalities by graphing.
(Lessons 9.1, 9.5)

20. $\begin{cases} y = 4x + 9 \\ y = 2x - 1 \end{cases}$ _____

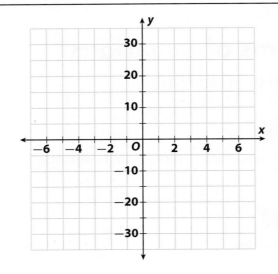

21. $\begin{cases} y = 5x - 6 \\ y = 2x + 3 \end{cases}$ _____

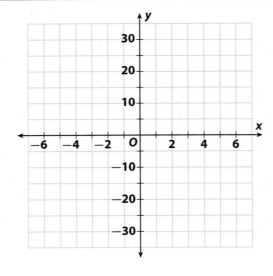

22. $\begin{cases} 3x - y = -4 \\ y = 3x - 5 \end{cases}$ _____

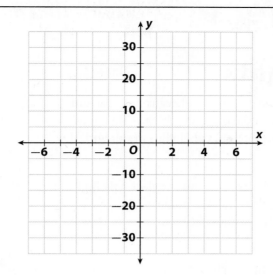

23. $\begin{cases} 2x - y = -5 \\ 3y = 6x + 15 \end{cases}$ _____

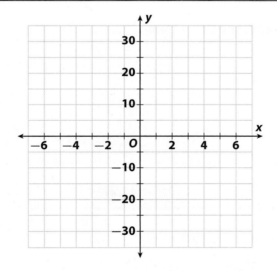

24. $\begin{cases} 4y \leq 15x + 40 \\ 2y + 50 \geq 25x \end{cases}$

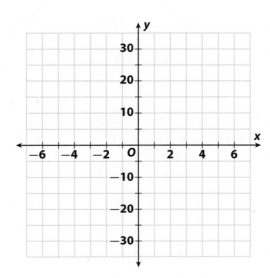

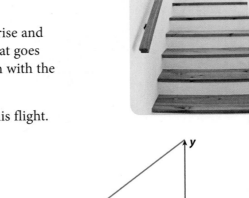

Changing Flights

Choose a flight of stairs at home or school. Measure the rise and run of a step. Write and graph an equation for the line that goes from the bottom of the stairs to the top. Label your graph with the number of steps of the flight.

Design two different flights of stairs that could replace this flight. For each plan, include the rise and run of a single step. Be sure to consider the California safety regulation from the Unit Project Preview.

Graph and label equations for the alternate flights of stairs on the same coordinate plane as the original flight. Write a paragraph that describes which flight you think is best and why.

Use the space below to write down any questions you have or important information from your teacher.

MATH IN CAREERS   ACTIVITY

Environmental Scientist To rate the fuel efficiency of a car, the following data were collected comparing the distance traveled to the amount of gasoline used on the trip.

fuel (gal)	1.3	7.5	3.9	2.1	10.8	3.3	6.7
dist. (mi)	42	223	109	58	330	97	188

Draw a scatter plot representing this data, and then use linear regression to find the equation of the line of best fit. What does the slope of the line represent in this situation?

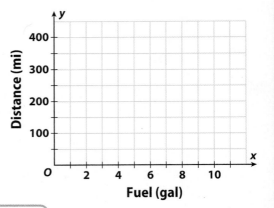

1. Consider each linear function. Does the function have a greater *y*-intercept than the linear function represented in the table?

   Select Yes or No.

   A. $g(x) = 2x + 3$ ○ Yes ○ No

   B. $g(x) = 1 + 5x$ ○ Yes ○ No

   C. $g(x) = -4(x - 1)$ ○ Yes ○ No

x	f(x)
2	10
4	18
6	26
8	34

2. The table shows how the price of apples at a store has changed over the past 6 months.

   Choose True or False for each statement.

   A. A scatter plot of the data shows a negative correlation.   ○ True ○ False

   B. The correlation coefficient for the data is closer to 1 than to 0.   ○ True ○ False

   C. The *y*-intercept of the best line of fit is greater than 1.50.   ○ True ○ False

Month, x	Price per pound ($), y
1	1.69
2	1.79
3	1.50
4	1.38
5	1.32
6	1.36

3. Adult tickets to a play cost $20.50, and student tickets cost $16.00. Ms. Powers can spend no more than $120.00 on tickets. If she buys 3 student tickets, how many adult tickets is she able to buy? Use a linear inequality in two variables to explain your reasoning.

4. A hobby pack of baseball cards contains 9 cards, and a jumbo pack contains 35 cards. Ethan bought 7 packs for a total of 141 cards. Write and solve a system of equations to find the number of each type of pack that he bought. State and justify your solution method.

Performance Tasks

★ **5.** A store rents backpacks and sleeping bags. Backpack rental costs $0.88 per day, plus an initial fee of $24.84. Sleeping bag rental costs are shown in the table. Write the function $f(x)$ to represent the cost of renting both a backpack and a sleeping bag for x days. Explain how you determined your answer.

Sleeping Bag Rental	
Time (days)	Cost ($)
3	18.28
6	20.65
9	23.02
12	25.39

★★ **6.** The table shows data for 6 gas-engine cars.

   a. Make a scatter plot of the data in the table.

   b. Write an equation of a line of fit for the data, and tell what the slope represents.

   c. What is the inverse of the linear function you wrote in part b?

   d. Predict the weight of a gas-engine car that gets 35 mi/gal. Justify your reasoning.

Weight (lb), x	Gas Mileage (mi/gal), y
3192	28
3427	26
2716	31
3108	31
2907	30
3295	27

★★★ **7.** Rita and Chris are making patterns out of tiles. The first 4 figures in each of their patterns is shown. Continuing these patterns, is there a figure for which the number of tiles in Rita's figure will be the same as the number of tiles in Chris's figure? If so, what is the figure number, and how many tiles will be in each figure? Explain.

Rita's Pattern

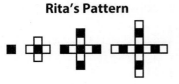

Chris's Pattern

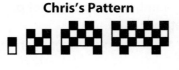

Exponential Relationships

MATH IN CAREERS

Statistician   A statistician collects, analyzes, and interprets numerical data of all types. He or she also helps design surveys and experiments. A solid science background is beneficial when helping others design and interpret experiments; for example, monitoring the rise and decline of animal populations. If you're interested in a career as a statistician, you should study these mathematical subjects:

- Algebra
- Trigonometry
- Calculus

Research other careers that require the use of statistics to analyze and interpret data.

ACTIVITY   At the end of the unit, check out how **statisticians** use math.

Unit Project Preview

Bank on It

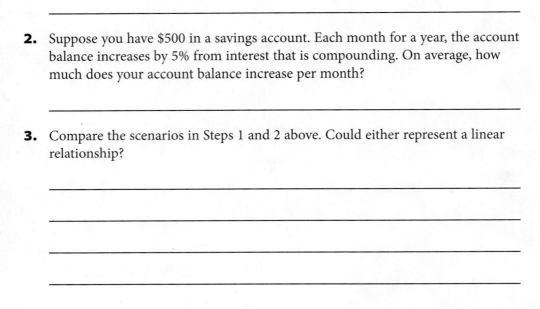

The Unit Project at the end of this unit involves determining the best investment. You will calculate interest rates and create a presentation to a potential investor. To successfully complete the Unit Project you'll need to master these skills:

- Calculate with exponential expressions.
- Determine exponential models for given data.
- Graph exponential functions.

1. Suppose you have $500 in a savings account. You deposit a total of $300 in equal monthly payments over the next year. By how much does your account balance increase per month?

_____

2. Suppose you have $500 in a savings account. Each month for a year, the account balance increases by 5% from interest that is compounding. On average, how much does your account balance increase per month?

_____

3. Compare the scenarios in Steps 1 and 2 above. Could either represent a linear relationship?

_____

_____

_____

_____

_____

Tracking Your Learning Progression

This unit addresses important Common Core Standards in the Critical Areas of understanding and modeling linear, quadratic, and exponential functions

Domain F.LE Linear, Quadratic, and Exponential Models

Cluster Construct and compare linear, quadratic, and exponential models and solve problems.

Exponential Functions and Equations

ESSENTIAL QUESTION

How can exponential functions be used to represent real-world situations?

Real-World Video

Scientists have found many ways to use radioactive elements that decay exponentially over time. Uranium-235 is used to power nuclear reactors, and scientists use Carbon-14 dating to calculate how long ago an organism lived.

my.hrw.com

GO DIGITAL
my.hrw.com

my.hrw.com

Go digital with your write-in student edition, accessible on any device.

Math On the Spot

Scan with your smart phone to jump directly to the online edition, video tutor, and more.

Animated Math

Interactively explore key concepts to see how math works.

Personal Math Trainer

Get immediate feedback and help as you work through practice sets.

Are YOU Ready?

Complete these exercises to review skills you will need for this module.

Exponents

EXAMPLE Write 10^4 as a multiplication of factors.

$10^4 = 10 \times 10 \times 10 \times 10$

10 is the base. It tells you the factor to multiply.
4 is the exponent. It tells you how many times the base is used as a factor. If the exponent is 0, remember that the product is 1.

Write each expression as a multiplication of factors.

1. 5^1 _____

2. 9^0 _____

3. 3^5 _____

4. 2^4 _____

5. 6^3 _____

6. a^2 _____

Evaluate Powers

EXAMPLE Evaluate 4^3.

$4^3 = 4 \times 4 \times 4$ *Rewrite as repeated multiplication.*

$= 64$ *Evaluate.*

Evaluate each power.

7. 8^2 _____

8. 5^4 _____

9. 6^0 _____

Properties of Exponents

EXAMPLE Simplify $x^4 x^5$.

$x^4 x^5 = x^{4+5} = x^9$ *When multiplying numbers with the same base, add exponents.*

Simplify.

10. $x^3 x$ _____

11. $x^3 y^4 \cdot y^3$ _____

12. $5a^2 b \cdot 6a^3 b$ _____

Reading Start-Up

Visualize Vocabulary

Use the ✔ Review Words to complete the bubble map.

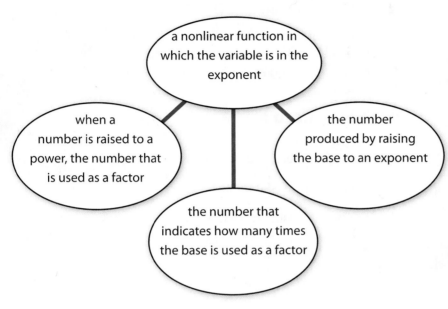

a nonlinear function in which the variable is in the exponent

when a number is raised to a power, the number that is used as a factor

the number produced by raising the base to an exponent

the number that indicates how many times the base is used as a factor

Understand Vocabulary

To become familiar with some of the vocabulary terms in the module, consider the following. You may refer to the module, the glossary, or a dictionary.

1. Occurs in an exponential function when the output gets smaller as the input gets larger.

_____

2. Occurs in an exponential function when the output gets larger as the input gets larger.

_____

Active Reading

Booklet Before beginning the module, create a booklet to help you learn the concepts in this module. Write the main idea of each lesson on each page of the booklet. As you study each lesson, write important details that support the main idea, such as vocabulary and formulas. Refer to your finished booklet as you work on assignments and study for tests.

Vocabulary

Review Words
- ✔ base (base)
- explicit rule (fórmula explícita)
- ✔ exponential function (función exponencial)
- ✔ exponent (exponente)
- family of functions (familia de funciones)
- parameter (parámetro)
- parent function (función madre)
- ✔ power (potencia)
- ratio (razón)
- recursive rule (fórmula recurrente)
- sequence (sucesión)
- term (término)

Preview Words
- common ratio
- decreasing function
- exponential growth
- exponential decay
- exponential function
- geometric sequence
- increasing function

Exponential Functions and Equations

Understanding the standards and the vocabulary terms in the standards will help you know exactly what you are expected to learn in this module.

COMMON CORE · A.CED.2

Create equations in two or more variables to represent relationships between quantities; graph equations on coordinate axes with labels and scales.

Key Vocabulary

equation *(ecuación)*
A mathematical statement that two expressions are equivalent.

COMMON CORE · F.IF.7e

Graph exponential and logarithmic functions, showing intercepts and end behavior, and trigonometric functions, showing period, midline, and amplitude.

Key Vocabulary

exponential function *(función exponencial)*
A function that can be written in the form $f(x) = ab^x$.

What It Means to You

Creating equations in two variables to describe relationships gives you access to the tools of graphing and algebra to solve the equations.

EXAMPLE A.CED.2

A customer spent $29 on a bouquet of roses and daisies. Roses cost $2.50 each and daisies cost $1.75 each.

r = number of roses in bouquet

d = number of daisies in bouquet

$$2.5r + 1.75d = 29$$

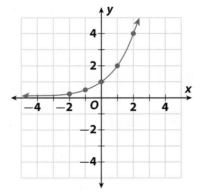

What It Means to You

You will learn to graph a new type of function, called an exponential function, in which successive output values have a constant ratio for each unit increase in the input values.

EXAMPLE F.IF.7E

Graph the function $f(x) = 2^x$.

Find points on the graph using a table, then graph the points and connect them with a smooth curve.

x	f(x)
−2	0.25
−1	0.5
0	1
1	2
2	4

Visit my.hrw.com to see all **Common Core Standards** unpacked.

ⓘ my.hrw.com

LESSON
10.1 Exponential Functions

COMMON CORE **F.LE.2**

Construct linear and exponential functions, including arithmetic and geometric sequences, given a graph, a description of a relationship, or two input-output pairs (include reading these from a table). *Also F.IF.5, F.IF.7e, A.CED.2, A.SSE.3c*

? ESSENTIAL QUESTION

How can you identify and represent an exponential function?

EXPLORE ACTIVITY   COMMON CORE   **A.SSE.3c**

Zero and Negative Exponents

Complete the table, and examine the patterns.

Power	5^5	5^4	5^3	5^2	5^1	5^0	5^{-1}	5^{-2}
Values	3125	625	125	25	5			

$\div 5 \quad \div 5 \quad \div 5 \quad \div 5$

A What happens to the value of the power with each decrease of 1 in the exponent?

_____

B Show the pattern that you used to find the value for 5^0, 5^{-1}, and 5^{-2}.

_____

REFLECT

1. Communicating Mathematics Describe how to find the value of 5^{-2} without dividing the value of 5^{-1} by 5.

_____

_____

The properties of zero and negative exponents are given below.

Zero and Negative Exponents		
Words	**Algebra**	**Example**
Any nonzero number raised to the zero power is 1.	$c^0 = 1, c \neq 0$	$12^0 = 1$
Any nonzero number raised to a negative power is equal to 1 divided by the number raised to the opposite power.	$c^{-n} = \frac{1}{c^n}, c \neq 0$	$2^{-3} = \frac{1}{2^3} = \frac{1}{8}$

Representing an Exponential Function

In an **exponential function**, as the input values increase by 1, the successive output values are related by a constant ratio. An *exponential function* can be represented by an equation of the form $f(x) = ab^x$, where a, b, and x are real numbers, $a \neq 0$, $b > 0$, and $b \neq 1$. The constant ratio is the base b. When evaluating exponential functions, you will need to use the properties of exponents.

EXAMPLE 1

COMMON CORE F.IF.7e

My Notes

Make a table for the function $f(x) = 2\left(\frac{2}{3}\right)^x$ using the input values $x = -2, -1,$ 0, 1, 2, 3. Then graph the function using the ordered pairs from the table as a guide.

STEP 1 Make a table of values by calculating the function values for the given values of x.

x	$f(x) = 2\left(\frac{2}{3}\right)^x$	$(x, f(x))$
-2	$2\left(\frac{2}{3}\right)^{-2} = 2\left(\frac{1}{\left(\frac{2}{3}\right)^2}\right) = 2\left(\frac{1}{\frac{4}{9}}\right) = 2\left(\frac{9}{4}\right) = \frac{9}{2}$	$\left(-2, \frac{9}{2}\right)$
-1	$2\left(\frac{2}{3}\right)^{-1} = 2\left(\frac{1}{\left(\frac{2}{3}\right)^1}\right) = 2\left(\frac{1}{\frac{2}{3}}\right) = 2\left(\frac{3}{2}\right) = 3$	$(-1, 3)$
0	$2\left(\frac{2}{3}\right)^0 = 2(1) = 2$	$(0, 2)$
1	$2\left(\frac{2}{3}\right)^1 = 2\left(\frac{2}{3}\right) = \frac{4}{3}$	$\left(1, \frac{4}{3}\right)$
2	$2\left(\frac{2}{3}\right)^2 = 2\left(\frac{4}{9}\right) = \frac{8}{9}$	$\left(2, \frac{8}{9}\right)$
3	$2\left(\frac{2}{3}\right)^3 = 2\left(\frac{8}{27}\right) = \frac{16}{27}$	$\left(3, \frac{16}{27}\right)$

Math Talk
Mathematical Practices

Explain why $f(x)$ is called a decreasing function.

STEP 2 Graph the function.

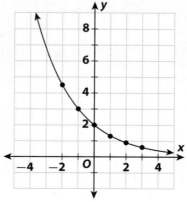

YOUR TURN

2. Find the value of the function $f(x) = 2\left(\frac{2}{3}\right)^x$ when $x = -3$. Graph the corresponding point on the coordinate grid in the example.

_____

Writing an Equation from a Verbal Description

You can model a real-world exponential relationship by identifying the values of a and b in the function $f(x) = ab^x$.

EXAMPLE 2   COMMON CORE F.LE.2

When a piece of paper is folded in half, the total thickness doubles. Suppose an unfolded piece of paper is 0.1 millimeter thick. Write an equation for the total thickness $t(n)$ as a function of the number of folds n. Then use the function to determine the thickness of the paper after 5 folds and 8 folds.

STEP 1   Identify the values of a and b, and write the equation in the form $t(n) = ab^n$.

- The value of a is the original thickness of the paper before any folds are made, or 0.1 millimeter.
- Because the thickness doubles with each fold, the value of b (the constant ratio) is 2.
- The equation for the function is $t(n) = 0.1(2)^n$.

STEP 2   To find the thickness after 5 and 8 folds, evaluate the function for $n = 5$ and $n = 8$.

$t(5) = 0.1(2)^5 = 0.1(32) = 3.2$

$t(8) = 0.1(2)^8 = 0.1(256) = 25.6$

After 5 folds the paper is 3.2 millimeters thick.

After 8 folds, the paper is 25.6 millimeters thick.

Math Talk
Mathematical Practices

How can you tell that the function described in the example is an exponential function?

YOUR TURN

3. Write a function for the thickness of folding a piece of paper that is 0.2 millimeters thick, and determine the thickness after 3 and 7 folds.

_____

© Houghton Mifflin Harcourt Publishing Company

Math On the Spot

my.hrw.com

Writing an Equation from Input-Output Pairs

Many real-world situations can be modeled by exponential functions. Some of these situations can be easily observed and data from the observations can be used to write the corresponding exponential function.

EXAMPLE 3   COMMON CORE F.LE.2

The height $h(n)$ of a dropped ball is an exponential function of the number of bounces n. On its first bounce, a certain ball reached a height of 15 inches. On its second bounce, the ball reached a height of 7.5 inches. Write an equation for the height of the ball, in inches, as a function of the number of bounces.

STEP 1   Divide successive function values, or heights, to find the constant ratio b. $b = 7.5 \div 15 = 0.5$

STEP 2   Use the value of b and a known ordered pair to find the value of a.

$h(n) = ab^n$ *Write the general form.*

$h(n) = a(0.5)^n$ *Substitute the value for b.*

$15 = a(0.5)^1$ *Substitute the input and output values (1, 15) for the first bounce.*

$15 = 0.5a$ *Simplify.*

$30 = a$ *Solve for a.*

STEP 3   Write an equation for the function: $h(n) = 30(0.5)^n$.

REFLECT

4. **Justify Reasoning** Use unit analysis to explain why b has no unit of measurement.

_____

_____

5. **What If?** Show that using the values for the second bounce will give the same result for a.

_____

YOUR TURN

Personal Math Trainer

Online Practice and Help

my.hrw.com

6. A pharmaceutical company is testing a new antibiotic. The number of bacteria present in a sample 1 hour after application of the antibiotic is 50,000. After another hour, the number of bacteria present in the sample is 25,000. The number of bacteria remaining $r(n)$ is an exponential function of the number of hours since the antibiotic was applied n. Write an equation

for the number of bacteria remaining after n hours. _____

1. Make a table of values for the function $f(x) = 2^x$ and graph the function. (Example 1)

x	$f(x) = 2^x$	$(x, f(x))$
−3	$f(\quad) = 2 \quad =$	
−2	$f(\quad) = 2 \quad =$	
−1	$f(\quad) = 2 \quad =$	
0	$f(\quad) = 2 \quad =$	
1	$f(\quad) = 2 \quad =$	
2	$f(\quad) = 2 \quad =$	
3	$f(\quad) = 2 \quad =$	

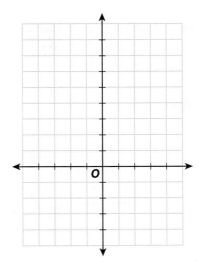

Use two points to write an equation for each function. (Examples 2 and 3)

2.

x	−3	−2	−1	0
$f(x)$	8	4	2	1

$\dfrac{f(-1)}{f(-2)} = \boxed{}$, so $b = \boxed{}$

$a = f\left(\boxed{}\right) = \boxed{}$

$f(x) = \boxed{}$

3.

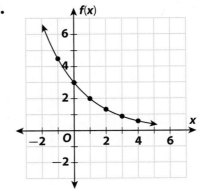

$f(x) = \underline{\hspace{4cm}}$

4. How can you determine the values of a and b from a description of an exponential function of the form $f(x) = ab^x$?

_____

_____

10.1 Independent Practice

COMMON CORE   F.LE.2, A.CED.2, A.SSE.3c, F.IF.5, F.IF.7e

Personal Math Trainer

Online Practice and Help

my.hrw.com

Make a table of values and a graph for each function.

5. $f(x) = 2\left(\frac{3}{4}\right)^x$

x	f(x)
−3	
−2	
−1	
0	
1	
2	
3	

6. $f(x) = 0.9(0.6)^x$

x	f(x)
−3	
−2	
−1	
0	
1	
2	
3	

Use two points to write an equation for each function.

7.

x	1	2	3	4
f(x)	8	6.4	5.12	4.096

_____

8.

x	−1	0	1	2
f(x)	0.75	3	12	48

_____

9.

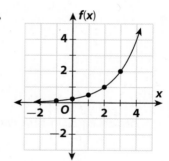

_____

10.

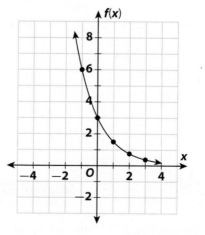

_____

11. Look for a Pattern As the x-values of an exponential function increase by a constant amount, the values of the function are multiplied by the constant ratio, b. What is the value of b in the function below?

x	f(x)
−1	1.5
0	3
1	6
2	12

_____

12. The area of the top surface of an 8.5-inch by 11-inch piece of paper is a function of the number of times it is folded in half.

a. Identify the value of a. What does it represent in this situation?

_____

_____

_____

b. Write an equation for the function that models this situation. Explain why this is an exponential function.

_____

_____

_____

c. What is the area of the top surface after 4 folds? Round to the nearest tenth of a square inch.

_____

d. What if? What would the equation be if the original piece of paper had dimensions 11 inches by 17 inches? Compare this with the equation in Part b.

_____

_____

_____

13. Suppose you do a favor for 3 people. Then you ask each of them to do a favor for 3 more people, passing along the request that each person who receives a favor does a favor for 3 more people. Suppose you do 3 favors on day 1, each recipient does 3 favors on day 2, and so on.

a. Complete the table for the first five days.

Day (n)	Favors f(n)
1	3
2	9
3	
4	
5	

b. Write an equation for the exponential function that models this situation.

_____

c. According to the model, how many favors will be done on day 10? Explain your reasoning.

_____

_____

_____

_____

_____

d. What would the equation be if everyone did a favor for 4 people rather than 3 people?

_____

14. Write an equation for the function whose graph is shown at the right.

_____

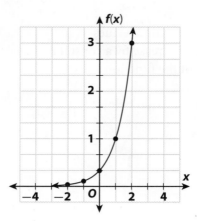

Work Area

15. **Draw Conclusions** Assume that the domain of the function $f(x) = 3(2)^x$ is the set of all real numbers. What is the range of the function? Explain.

_____

_____

_____

16. **Find the Error** Kaylee needed to write the equation of an exponential function from points on the graph of the function. To determine the value of b, Kaylee chose the ordered pairs $(1, 6)$ and $(3, 54)$ and divided 54 by 6. She determined that the value of b was 9. What error did Kaylee make?

_____

_____

_____

17. **What If?** An exponential function can be represented by the equation $f(x) = ab^x$, where a, b, and x are real numbers, $a \neq 0$, $b > 0$, and $b \neq 1$. Why must it be specified that $b \neq 1$? What would the graph of the function look like if $b = 1$?

_____

_____

_____

_____

18. Use properties of exponents to compare the functions $f(x) = 3(4)^{\frac{t}{2}}$ and $g(x) = 3(2)^t$.

_____

Exponential Growth and Decay

COMMON CORE F.LE.1c

Recognize situations in which a quantity grows or decays by a constant percent rate per unit interval relative to another. Also *A.SSE.3c, F.IF.4, F.IF.5, F.IF.7, F.IF.7e, F.IF.8b, F.LE.2, F.LE.5*

? ESSENTIAL QUESTION

How can exponential functions model the increase or decrease of a quantity over time?

Exponential Growth

Exponential growth occurs when a quantity increases by the same rate r in each unit of time t. When this happens, the value of the quantity at any given time can be calculated as a function of the rate and the original amount. Because the function value increases as time increases, exponential growth functions are examples of increasing functions.

Math On the Spot
⟳ my.hrw.com

Exponential Growth

An exponential growth function has the form $y = a(1 + r)^t$, where $a > 0$.

y represents the final amount.

a represents the original amount.

r represents the rate of growth expressed as a decimal.

t represents time.

The exponential growth form $y = a(1 + r)^t$ is equivalent to the form $y = ab^x$, with $b = 1 + r$, $b > 1$, and $x = t$.

EXAMPLE 1

COMMON CORE F.LE.1c, F.IF.5

A painting is sold for \$1400, and its value increases by 9% each year after it is sold. Write an exponential growth function to model this situation. Then find the value of the painting in 25 years. Graph the function. State the domain and range of the function. What does the y-intercept represent in the context of the problem?

STEP 1 Write the exponential growth function for this situation.

$y = a(1 + r)^t$ Write the formula.

$= 1400(1 + 0.09)^t$ Substitute 1400 for *a* and 0.09 for *r*.

$= 1400(1.09)^t$ Simplify.

STEP 2 Find the value in 25 years.

$y = 1400(1.09)^t$

$= 1400(1.09)^{25}$ Substitute 25 for *t*.

$\approx 12{,}072.31$ Use a calculator and round to the nearest hundredth.

After 25 years, the painting will be worth approximately \$12,072.31.

© Houghton Mifflin Harcourt Publishing Company

STEP 3 Create a table of values to graph the function.

t	y	(t, y)
0	1400	(0, 1400)
1	1526	(1, 1526)
2	1663.34	(2, 1663.34)
3	1813.04	(3, 1813.04)
4	1976.21	(4, 1976.21)
5	2154.07	(5, 2154.07)
25	12072.31	(25, 12072.31)

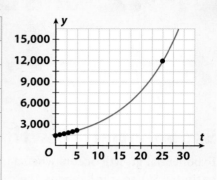

STEP 4 Determine the domain and the range of the function.

The input values represent years after a painting was sold for the first time. The values cannot be negative.

The domain is the set of real numbers t such that $t \geq 0$.

The output values represent the value of the painting in dollars. These values cannot be negative. Also, since this is an increasing function, the values cannot be less than the initial value of the painting.

The range is the set of real numbers y such that $y \geq 1400$.

STEP 5 The y-intercept is the value of y when $t = 0$. In the context of this problem, $t = 0$ is the time when the painting first sold. Therefore, the y-intercept represents the value of the painting when it was first sold.

Math Talk

Mathematical Practices

What is the constant ratio between successive function values when t increases by 1?

YOUR TURN

1. A sculpture is increasing in value at a rate of 8% per year, and its value in 2008 was $1200. Write an exponential growth function to model this situation. Then find the sculpture's value in 2014. Graph the function.

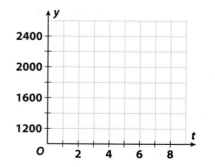

_____

_____

Personal Math Trainer

Online Practice and Help

⟳ my.hrw.com

Exponential Decay

Exponential decay occurs when a quantity decreases by the same rate r in each unit of time t. Just like exponential growth, the value of the quantity at any given time can be calculated as a function of the rate and the original amount. Because the function value decreases as time increases, exponential decay functions are examples of decreasing functions.

Math On the Spot

my.hrw.com

> ### Exponential Decay
>
> An exponential decay function has the form $y = a(1 - r)^t$, where $a > 0$.
>
> y represents the final amount.
>
> a represents the original amount.
>
> r represents the rate of decay as a decimal.
>
> t represents time.

Notice an important difference between exponential growth functions and exponential decay functions. For exponential growth, the value inside the parentheses will be greater than 1 because r is added to 1 and $r > 0$. For exponential decay, the value inside the parentheses will be less than 1 because r is subtracted from 1 and $r > 0$.

The exponential decay form $y = a(1 - r)^t$ is equivalent to the form $y = ab^x$, with $b = 1 - r$, $0 < b < 1$, and $x = t$.

EXAMPLE 2

F.LE.1c, F.IF.5

The population of a town is decreasing at a rate of 1% per year. In 2005 there were 1300 people. Write an exponential decay function to model this situation. Then find the population in 2013. Graph the function. State the domain and range of the function. What does the y-intercept represent in the context of the problem?

STEP 1   Write the exponential decay function.

$$y = a(1 - r)^t$$
$$= 1300(1 - 0.01)^t \qquad \text{Substitute 1300 for } a \text{ and 0.01 for } r.$$
$$= 1300(0.99)^t \qquad \text{Simplify.}$$

STEP 2   Find the population in 2013.

2013 is 8 years after 2005, the year for which the initial value of the population is given. So $t = 8$.

$$y = 1300(0.99)^t$$
$$= 1300(0.99)^8 \qquad \text{Substitute 8 for } t.$$
$$\approx 1200 \qquad \text{Use a calculator.}$$

The population in 2013 is approximately 1200 people.

STEP 3 Create a table of values to graph the function.

t	y	(t, y)
0	1300	(0, 1300)
1	1287	(1, 1287)
2	1274	(2, 1274)
3	1261	(3, 1261)
4	1249	(4, 1249)
5	1236	(5, 1236)
8	1200	(8, 1200)

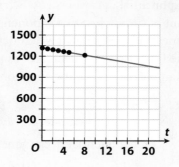

Note that while the graph may appear to be linear, it is not. The graph has this appearance because the population is declining at a slow rate.

STEP 4 Determine the domain and the range of the function.

The input values represent years after the initial population was given. The values cannot be negative.

The domain is the set of real numbers t such that $t \geq 0$.

The output values represent the population of the town. These values cannot be negative. Also, since this is a decreasing function, the values cannot be more than the initial population.

The range is the set of real numbers y such that $0 \leq y \leq 1300$.

STEP 5 The y-intercept is the value of y when $t = 0$. In the context of this problem, $t = 0$ is the year 2005. Therefore, the y-intercept represents the population of the town in 2005.

Math Talk
Mathematical Practices

What would a negative value of t represent in this context?

YOUR TURN

2. The fish population in a local stream is decreasing at a rate of 3% per year. The original population was 48,000. Write an exponential decay function to model this situation. Then find the population after 7 years. Graph the function.

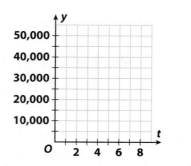

Personal Math Trainer
Online Practice and Help
my.hrw.com

Comparing Exponential Growth and Exponential Decay

You can use graphs to describe and compare exponential growth and exponential decay models over time.

EXAMPLE 3

COMMON CORE F.LE.1c

The graph shows the value of two different shares of stock over the period of four years since they were purchased. The values have been changing exponentially. For each stock write the equation of the function that represents the value of the stock. Describe and compare the behaviors of the two stocks.

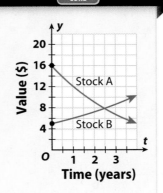

STEP 1 The graph for Stock A shows that the value of the stock is decreasing as time increases.

The initial value, when $t = 0$, is 16. The value when $t = 1$ is 12. Since $12 \div 16 = 0.75$, the function that represents the value of Stock A after t years is $A(t) = 16(0.75)^t$. $A(t)$ is an exponential decay function.

STEP 2 The graph for Stock B shows that the value of the stock is increasing as time increases.

The initial value, when $t = 0$, is 5. The value when $t = 1$ is 6. Since $6 \div 5 = 1.2$, the function that represents the value of Stock B after t years is $B(t) = 5(1.2)^t$. $B(t)$ is an exponential growth function.

STEP 3 The value of Stock A is going down over time. The value of Stock B is going up over time. The initial value of Stock A is greater than the initial value of Stock B. However, after about 2.5 years, the value of Stock B becomes greater than the value of Stock A.

Math Talk
Mathematical Practices

Is it likely that the function representing the value of Stock B can be used to predict its value for 30 years? Explain.

YOUR TURN

3. Two shares of two different stocks changed exponentially over a period of 3 years. For each stock, write the equation and function that represents the value of the stock. For Stock A, the initial value when $t = 0$ is 12. The value when $t = 1$ is 6. For stock B, the initial value when $t = 0$ is 4. The value when $t = 1$ is 6. Describe and compare the two stocks.

_____

_____

_____

_____

Personal Math Trainer

Online Practice and Help

⏱ my.hrw.com

© Houghton Mifflin Harcourt Publishing Company

Write an exponential growth or decay function to model each situation. Graph each function. Then find the value of the function after the given amount of time.

1. The cost of tuition at a college is $12,000 and is increasing at a rate of 6% per year; 4 years. (Example 1)

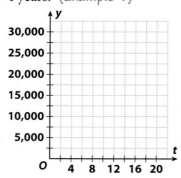

_____

2. The value of a car is $18,000 and is depreciating at a rate of 12% per year; 10 years. (Example 2)

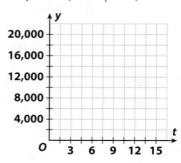

_____

3. The value of two parcels of land have been changing exponentially since they were purchased, as shown in the graph. Describe and compare the values of the two parcels of land. (Example 3)

_____

_____

_____

_____

_____

_____

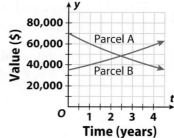

4. How can you tell from its graph whether a function represents exponential growth or exponential decay?

_____

_____

_____

_____

_____

10.2 Independent Practice

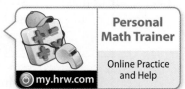

Personal
Math Trainer

Online Practice
and Help

my.hrw.com

Write an exponential growth or decay function to model each situation. Graph each function. Then find the value of the function after the given amount of time.

5. The amount (to the nearest hundredth) of a 10-mg dose of a certain antibiotic decreases in your bloodstream at a rate of 16% per hour; 4 hours.

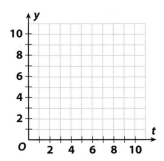

_____

6. The number of student-athletes at a local high school is 300 and is increasing at a rate of 8% per year; 5 years.

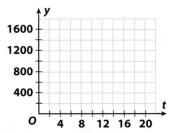

_____

Write an exponential growth or decay function to model each situation. Then find the value of the function after the given amount of time.

7. Annual sales for a company are $149,000 and are increasing at a rate of 6% per year; 7 years. _____

8. The population of a town is 18,000 and is decreasing at a rate of 2% per year; 6 years. _____

9. The population of a small town is 1600 and is increasing at a rate of 3% per year; 10 years. _____

10. The value of a book is $58 and decreases at a rate of 10% per year; 8 years.

_____

11. A new savings account starts at $700 and increases at 1.2% yearly; 7 years.

_____

12. Mr. Nevin buys a car for $18,500. The value of the car depreciates 9% per year; 7 years. _____

13. If the domain consists of the set of all nonnegative real numbers, then for the graph of an exponential growth function, the *y*-intercept represents the

_____ value of the function. For the graph of an exponential

decay function, the *y*-intercept represents the _____ value of the function. Even though the graph of an exponential decay function is decreasing, if the initial value of the function is positive, the function will never

reach the _____.

H.O.T. FOCUS ON HIGHER ORDER THINKING

14. Explain the Error Two students were asked to find the value of a $1000 item after 3 years. The item was depreciating at a rate of 40% per year. Which is incorrect? Explain the error.

$1000(0.6)^3$

$216

Student A

$1000(0.4)^3$

$64

Student B

_____

_____

15. Make a Conjecture The value of a certain car can be modeled by the function $y = 20{,}000(0.84)^t$, where *t* is time in years. Will the value ever be zero? Explain.

_____

_____

_____

16. Communicate Mathematical Ideas Lynn says that it is always possible to look at a graph of an exponential function and determine whether it represents growth or decay. Nigel says he thinks it might not be. Who is correct? Explain.

_____

_____

_____

_____

_____

COMMON CORE **F.LE.2**

Construct linear and exponential functions, including arithmetic and geometric sequences, given a graph, a description of a relationship, or two input-output pairs (include reading these from a table). *Also, A.SSE.3c, F.BF.1, F.BF.1a, F.BF.2, F.IF.3, F.IF.8b, F.LE.1a*

? ESSENTIAL QUESTION

How can a geometric sequence be described?

Writing General Rules for Geometric Sequences

In a **geometric sequence**, the ratio of consecutive terms is constant. The constant ratio is called the **common ratio**, often represented by r.

EXAMPLE 1

COMMON CORE **F.BF.2**

Math On the Spot
⏻ my.hrw.com

Makers of Japanese swords in the 1400s repeatedly folded and hammered the metal to form layers. The folding process increased the strength of the sword.

The table shows how the number of layers depends on the number of folds. Write a recursive rule and an explicit rule for the geometric sequence represented by the table.

Number of Folds	n	1	2	3	4	5
Number of Layers	$f(n)$	2	4	8	16	32

STEP 1 Find the common ratio by calculating the ratios of consecutive terms.

$$\frac{4}{2} = 2 \qquad\qquad \frac{8}{4} = 2$$

$$\frac{16}{8} = 2 \qquad\qquad \frac{32}{16} = 2$$

The common ratio r is 2.

STEP 2 Write a recursive rule for the sequence.

The first term is 2, so $f(1) = 2$.

All terms after the first term are the product of the previous term and the common ratio: $f(2) = f(1) \cdot 2, f(3) = f(2) \cdot 2, f(4) = f(3) \cdot 2, \ldots$

The recursive rule is stated by providing the first term and the rule for successive terms.

$$f(1) = 2$$

$$f(n) = f(n-1) \cdot 2 \text{ for } n \geq 2$$

This can be read as "each term in the sequence after the first term is equal to the previous term times two."

STEP 3 Write an explicit rule for the sequence by writing each term as the product of the first term and a power of the common ratio.

n	f(n)
1	$2(2)^0 = 2$
2	$2(2)^1 = 4$
3	$2(2)^2 = 8$
4	$2(2)^3 = 16$
5	$2(2)^4 = 32$

Generalize the results from the table: $f(n) = 2 \cdot 2^{n-1}$.

REFLECT

1. Draw Conclusions How can you use properties of exponents to simplify the explicit rule found in Example 1?

_____

_____

_____

2. Justify Reasoning Explain why the sequence 4, 12, 36, 108, 324, … appears to be a geometric sequence.

_____

_____

_____

3. What If? A geometric sequence has a common ratio of 5. The 6th term of the sequence is 30. What is the 7th term? What is the 5th term? Explain.

_____

_____

_____

4. Communicate Mathematical Ideas The first term of a geometric sequence is 81 and the common ratio is $\frac{1}{3}$. Explain how you could find the 4th term of the sequence.

_____

_____

5. What is the recursive rule for the sequence $f(n) = 5(4)^{n-1}$?

_____

6. Write a recursive rule and an explicit rule for the geometric sequence represented by the table.

n	1	2	3	4	5
$f(n)$	2	6	18	54	162

_____

_____

7. Write a recursive rule and an explicit rule for the geometric sequence 128, 32, 8, 2, 0.5, … .

_____

_____

EXPLORE ACTIVITY   COMMON CORE   F.BF.2

General Rules for Geometric Sequences

Use the geometric sequence 6, 24, 96, 384, 1536, … to help you write a recursive rule and an explicit rule for any geometric sequence. For the general rules, the values of n are consecutive integers starting with 1.

A Find the common ratio.

Numbers

6, 24, 96, 384, 1536, …

Common ratio = 4

Algebra

$f(1), f(2), f(3), f(4), f(5), …$

Common ratio = r

B Write a recursive rule.

Numbers

$f(1) = 6$ and

$f(n) = f(n - 1) \cdot 4$ for $n \geq 2$

Algebra

Given $f(1)$,

$f(n) = f(n - 1) \cdot r$ for $n \geq 2$

C Write an explicit rule.

Numbers

$f(n) = 6 \cdot 4^{n - 1}$

Algebra

$f(n) = f(1) \cdot r^{n - 1}$

Writing a Geometric Sequence Given Two Terms

The explicit and recursive rules for a geometric sequence can also be written in *subscript notation*. In subscript notation, the subscript indicates the position of the term in the sequence. a_1, a_2, and a_3 are the first, second, and third terms of a sequence, respectively. In general, a_n is the *n*th term of a sequence.

EXAMPLE 2 Real World

COMMON CORE F.LE.2

The shutter speed settings on a camera form a geometric sequence where a_n is the shutter speed in seconds and *n* is the setting number. The fifth setting on the camera is $\frac{1}{60}$ second, and the seventh setting on the camera is $\frac{1}{15}$ second. Write an explicit rule for the sequence using subscript notation.

STEP 1 Identify the given terms in the sequence.

$a_5 = \frac{1}{60}$ The fifth term of the sequence is $\frac{1}{60}$.

$a_7 = \frac{1}{15}$ The seventh term of the sequence is $\frac{1}{15}$.

STEP 2 Find the common ratio.

Math Talk
Mathematical Practices

When finding the common ratio, why can you ignore the negative square root of 4 when solving $4 = r^2$?

$a_7 = a_6 \cdot r$ Write the recursive rule for a_7.

$a_6 = a_5 \cdot r$ Write the recursive rule for a_6.

$a_7 = a_5 \cdot r \cdot r$ Substitute the expression for a_6 into the rule for a_7.

$\frac{1}{15} = \frac{1}{60} \cdot r^2$ Substitute $\frac{1}{15}$ for a_7 and $\frac{1}{60}$ for a_5.

$4 = r^2$ Multiply both sides by 60.

$2 = r$ Definition of positive square root

STEP 3 Find the first term of the sequence.

$a_n = a_1 \cdot r^{n-1}$ Write the general explicit rule.

$\frac{1}{60} = a_1 \cdot 2^{5-1}$ Substitute $\frac{1}{60}$ for a_n, 2 for *r*, and 5 for *n*.

$\frac{1}{60} = a_1 \cdot 16$ Simplify.

$\frac{1}{960} = a_1$ Divide both sides by 16.

STEP 4 Write the explicit rule.

$a_n = a_1 \cdot r^{n-1}$ Write the general explicit rule.

$a_n = \frac{1}{960} \cdot 2^{n-1}$ Substitute $\frac{1}{960}$ for a_1 and 2 for *r*.

Therefore, $a_n = \frac{1}{960} \cdot 2^{n-1}$.

YOUR TURN

8. The third term of a geometric sequence is $\frac{1}{54}$. The fifth term of the sequence is $\frac{1}{6}$. All terms of the sequence are positive numbers. Write an explicit rule for the sequence using subscript notation. _____

Relating Geometric Sequences and Exponential Functions

A geometric sequence is equivalent to an exponential function with a domain that is restricted to the positive integers. For an exponential function of the form $f(n) = ab^n$, recall that a represents the initial value and b is the common ratio. Compare this to $f(n) = f(1) \cdot r^{n-1}$, where $f(1)$ represents the initial value and r is the common ratio.

Math On the Spot

my.hrw.com

EXAMPLE 3 **COMMON CORE** **F.LE.2**

The graph shows the heights to which a ball bounces after it is dropped. Write an explicit rule for the sequence of bounce heights.

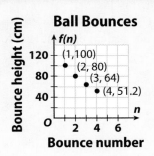

Ball Bounces

Bounce height (cm)

$f(n)$

(1, 100)
(2, 80)
(3, 64)
(4, 51.2)

Bounce number

STEP 1 Represent the sequence in a table.

n	1	2	3	4
$f(n)$	100	80	64	51.2

STEP 2 Examine the sequence to determine whether it is geometric. The sequence is geometric because each term is the product of 0.8 and the previous term. The common ratio is 0.8.

STEP 3 Write an explicit rule for the sequence.

$f(n) = f(1) \cdot r^{n-1}$ *Write the general rule.*

$f(n) = 100 \cdot 0.8^{n-1}$ *Substitute 100 for $f(1)$ and 0.8 for r.*

The sequence has the rule $f(n) = 100 \cdot 0.8^{n-1}$, where n is the bounce number and $f(n)$ is the bounce height.

YOUR TURN

9. The number of customers $f(n)$ projected to come into a new store in month number n is represented by the following table.

n	1	2	3	4
$f(n)$	1000	1500	2250	3375

Write an explicit rule for the sequence. _____

1. The table shows the beginning-of-month balances, rounded to the nearest cent, in Marla's saving account for the first few months after she made an initial deposit in the account. (Example 1)

Month	n	1	2	3	4
Account balance ($)	$f(n)$	2000	2010.00	2020.05	2030.15

a. Explain how you know that the sequence of account balances is a geometric sequence.

_____

b. Write recursive and explicit rules for the sequences of account balances.

Recursive rule: $f(1) =$ ⬚ , $f(n) =$ ⬚ $\cdot$ ⬚
for $n \geq 2$

Explicit rule: $f(n) =$ ⬚ $\cdot$ ⬚

2. Write a recursive rule and an explicit rule for the geometric sequence 9, 27, 81, 243. (Example 1)

$\dfrac{27}{9} =$ ⬚ $\dfrac{81}{27} =$ ⬚ $\dfrac{243}{81} =$ ⬚

Recursive rule: _____

Explicit rule: _____

3. Write an explicit rule for the geometric sequence with terms $a_2 = 12$ and $a_4 = 192$. Assume that the common ratio r is positive. (Example 2)

_____

4. Write an explicit rule for the geometric sequence with terms $a_3 = 1600$ and $a_5 = 256$. Assume that the common ratio is positive. (Example 2)

_____

? ESSENTIAL QUESTION CHECK-IN

5. How can you write the explicit rule for a geometric sequence if you know the recursive rule for the sequence?

_____

_____

_____

10.3 Independent Practice

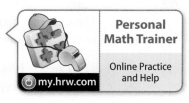

COMMON CORE   A.SSE.3c, F.BF.1, F.BF.1a, F.BF.2, F.IF.3, F.IF.8b, F.LE.1a, F.LE.2

6. The graph shows the number of players in the first four rounds of the U.S Open women's singles tennis tournament.

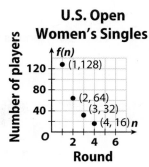

U.S. Open Women's Singles

  a. Write an explicit rule for the sequence of players in each round.

  _____

  b. How many rounds are there in the tournament? (*Hint:* In the last round, only two players are left.)

  _____

7. Write a recursive rule and an explicit rule for the geometric sequence $12, 3, \frac{3}{4}, \frac{3}{16}, \ldots$

  Recursive rule: _____

  Explicit rule: _____

Each rule represents a geometric sequence. If the given rule is recursive, write it as an explicit rule. If the rule is explicit, write it as a recursive rule. Assume that $f(1)$ is the first term of the sequence.

8. $f(n) = 6(3)^{n-1}$

_____

_____

9. $f(1) = 10; f(n) = f(n-1) \cdot 8$ for $n \geq 2$

_____

_____

Write an explicit rule for each geometric sequence based on the given terms from the sequence. Assume that the common ratio r is positive.

10. $a_2 = 50$ and $a_4 = 12.5$

_____

11. $a_3 = 24$ and $a_5 = 384$

_____

12. An economist predicts that the cost of food will increase by 4% per year for the next several years.

  a. Use the economist's prediction to write an explicit rule for a geometric sequence that gives the cost in dollars of a box of cereal in year n that costs $3.20 in year 1.

  _____

  b. What is the fourth term of the sequence, and what does it represent in this situation?

  _____

  _____

13. The numbers of points that a player must accumulate to reach the next level of a video game form a geometric sequence, where $f(n)$ is the number of points needed to complete level n.

a. A player needs 1000 points to complete level 2 and 8,000,000 to complete level 5. Write an explicit rule for the sequence.

_____

b. How many points are needed for level 7?

_____

 **FOCUS ON HIGHER ORDER THINKING**

14. Justify Reasoning If a geometric sequence has a common ratio r that is negative, describe the terms of the sequence. Explain.

_____

_____

_____

_____

15. Communicate Mathematical Ideas If you are given the seventh term of a geometric sequence and the common ratio, how can you determine the second term of the sequence without writing an explicit rule or recursive rule? Explain.

_____

_____

_____

_____

_____

16. Critique Reasoning Miguel writes the following: 5, ___, 5, ___, ...

He tells Alicia that what he has written represents a geometric sequence and asks Alicia to fill in the missing terms. Alicia says that the missing terms must both be 5. Miguel says that Alicia is incorrect. Who is right? Explain.

_____

_____

_____

_____

_____

Transforming Exponential Functions

COMMON CORE   F.BF.3

Identify the effect on the graph of replacing $f(x)$ by $f(x) + k$, $kf(x)$, $f(kx)$, and $f(x + k)$ for specific values of k (both positive and negative); find the value of k given the graphs. Experiment with cases and illustrate an explanation of the effects on the graph using technology.

? ESSENTIAL QUESTION

How does the graph of $f(x) = ab^x$ change when a and b are changed?

EXPLORE ACTIVITY 1   COMMON CORE   F.BF.3

Changing the Value of a in $f(x) = ab^x$

Recall that a family of functions is a set of functions whose graphs have basic characteristics in common. The most basic function of a family of functions is called the parent function. For exponential functions, every different base determines a different parent function for its own family of functions.

You can explore the behavior of an exponential function of the form $f(x) = ab^x$ by examining *parameters* a and b.

A Graph parent function $Y_1 = (1.5)^x$ and functions $Y_2 = 2(1.5)^x$ and $Y_3 = 3(1.5)^x$ on a graphing calculator. Use a viewing window from -5 to 5 for x and from -1 to 6 for y, using a scale of 1. Sketch the curves.

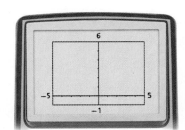

B Use the CALC feature while viewing the graphs to calculate the value of Y_1 when $x = -2$. Then use the up and down arrow keys to jump to the other curves and calculate their values when $x = -2$. Round to the nearest thousandth if necessary. Repeat this process until you have completed the table.

A **vertical stretch** of a graph is the result of pulling the graph away from the x-axis. Each y-value of an (x, y) pair is multiplied by a factor a such that $a > 1$.

A **vertical compression** of a graph is the result of pushing the graph toward the x-axis. Each y-value of an (x, y) pair is multiplied by a factor a such that $0 < a < 1$.

x	Y_1	Y_2	Y_3
-2			
-1			
0			
1			
2			

REFLECT

1. **Communicate Mathematical Ideas** Is the graph of Y_2 a vertical stretch or a vertical compression of the graph of Y_1? By what factor is it multiplied? In the same way, describe the graph of Y_1 compared to the graph of Y_2.

_____

_____

_____

COMMON CORE   F.BF.3

Changing the Value of b in $f(x) = b^x$

A Graph the functions $Y_1 = 1.2^x$ and $Y_2 = 1.5^x$ on a graphing calculator. Use a viewing window from -5 to 5 for x and from -2 to 5 for y, with a scale of 1 for both. Sketch the curves.

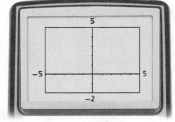

B Use the TBLSET and TABLE features to make a table of values starting at -2 with an increment of 1. Then complete the table. Round to the nearest thousandth if necessary.

C Which graph rises more quickly as x increases to the right of 0? Which graph falls, or approaches 0, more quickly as x decreases to the left of 0?

_____

_____

_____

_____

x	Y_1	Y_2
-2	0.694	
-1		0.667
0		
1	1.2	1.5
2		

D Identify the y-intercepts of the graphs of Y_1 and Y_2.

_____

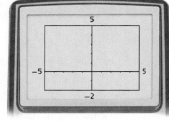

E Using the same window as above, graph the functions $Y_3 = 0.6^x$ and $Y_4 = 0.9^x$. Sketch the curves.

F Make a table of values starting at -2 with an increment of 1. Then complete the table.

X	Y_3	Y_4
-2	2.778	
-1		1.111
0		
1	0.6	0.9
2		

Math Talk
Mathematical Practices

For the graphs of Y_3 and Y_4, which graph rises more quickly as x decreases to the left of 0? Which graph falls more quickly as x increases to the right of 0?

REFLECT

2. **What If?** Consider the function $Y_5 = 1.3^x$. How will its graph compare with the graphs of Y_1 and Y_2? Discuss end behavior and the y-intercept.

_____

_____

_____

_____

_____

Adding a Constant to an Exponential Function

Adding a constant to an exponential function causes the graph of the function to translate up or down, depending on the constant.

EXAMPLE 1

COMMON CORE   F.BF.3

Describe the effect of transforming the function $f(x) = 1.5^x$ into $g(x) = 1.5^x + 2$.

Make a table of values for the functions and graph them. Round values in the table to the nearest thousandth.

x	f(x)	g(x)
−2	0.444	2.444
−1	0.667	2.667
0	1	3
1	1.5	3.5
2	2.25	4.25

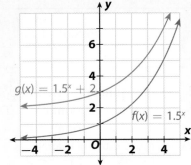

$g(x)$ is a vertical translation of $f(x)$ up 2 units.

Animated Math
my.hrw.com

YOUR TURN

3. Describe the effect of transforming the function $f(x) = 2^x$ into $g(x) = 2^x - 5$.

_____

Personal Math Trainer

Online Practice and Help

my.hrw.com

In general, the constant that is added to an exponential function $f(x)$ determines the size and direction of the translation. For example, if $f(x) = 0.75^x$ and $h(x) = 0.75^x - 3$, then $h(x)$ is a vertical translation of $f(x)$ down 3 units.

The table below summarizes the general shapes of exponential function graphs.

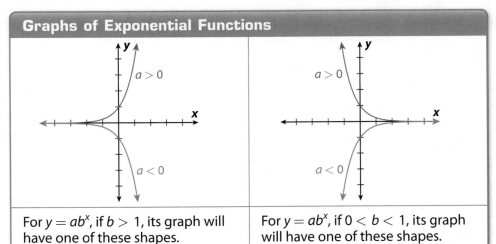

Graphs of Exponential Functions	
For $y = ab^x$, if $b > 1$, its graph will have one of these shapes.	For $y = ab^x$, if $0 < b < 1$, its graph will have one of these shapes.

Guided Practice

The graphs of the parent function $Y_1 = (0.5)^x$ and the function $Y_2 = 2(0.5)^x$ are shown. Use the graphs for Exercises 1–4. (Explore Activity 1)

1. If Y_1 is written in the form $Y_1(x) = ab^x$, what is a? _____

2. If Y_2 is written in the form $Y_2(x) = ab^x$, what is a? _____

3. Look at the graphs. Are the values of Y_2 greater than or less than the values of Y_1?

   _____

4. Is Y_2 a *vertical stretch* or a *vertical compression* of Y_1?

   _____

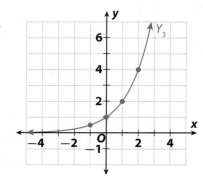

5. The function Y_3 is an exponential function. Use two points from the graph of the function to write an equation for Y_3. Then use a different value for b to write an equation for a function in the same family of functions that rises more quickly than Y_3 as x increases to the right of 0. (Explore Activity 2)

   _____

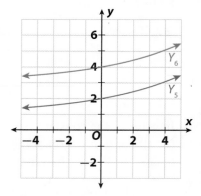

The graphs of the function $Y_5 = 1.2^x + 1$ and the function $Y_6 = 1.2^x + 3$ are shown. Use the graphs for Exercises 6–7. (Example 1)

6. Which graph rises more quickly as x increases to the right of 0? Which graph falls, or approaches 0, more quickly as x decreases to the left of 0?

   _____

7. Y_6 is a vertical translation of Y_5. Tell the number of units Y_5 was translated and the direction of the translation.

   _____

? **ESSENTIAL QUESTION CHECK-IN**

8. If a and b are positive real numbers and $b \neq 1$, how does the graph of $f(x) = ab^x$ change when b is changed?

   _____

   _____

   _____

   _____

   _____

10.4 Independent Practice

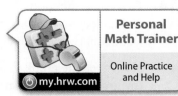

Personal Math Trainer

Online Practice and Help

⏻ my.hrw.com

COMMON CORE **F.BF.3**

A parent function and a function in the same family are given. Tell whether the value of *a* or the value of *b* was changed in $f(x) = ab^x$.

9. $f(x) = (0.2)^x$ $f(x) = 2(0.2)^x$ _____

10. $f(x) = 3^x$ $f(x) = 3.5^x$ _____

11. $f(x) = 3^x$ $f(x) = 1.5(3)^x$ _____

Values of the function $Y_1 = (2.5)^x$ and the function $Y_2 = 0.5(2.5)^x$ are shown in the table.

x	Y_1	Y_2
−2	0.16	0.08
−1	0.4	0.2
0	1	0.5
1	2.5	1.25
2	6.25	3.125

12. How do the values in the table for Y_2 compare with the values for Y_1?

_____

_____

_____

_____

13. Is Y_2 a *vertical stretch* or a *vertical compression* of Y_1? Explain how you know.

_____

_____

_____

_____

_____

Values of a parent function are shown below.

x	−2	−1	0	1	2
f(x)	4	2	1	0.5	0.25

14. Write an equation for the parent function.

_____

15. Write an equation for a function in the same family of functions whose graph will rise more quickly than the parent function as x decreases to the left of 0.

_____

The graphs of the function $Y_3 = 2^x + 4$ and the function $Y_4 = 2^x + 2$ are shown.

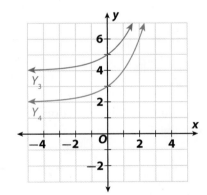

16. Identify the *y*-intercepts of Y_3 and Y_4.

_____

17. **Justify Reasoning** Was Y_4 translated up or down from the graph of Y_3 by the change in the constant? Explain.

_____

_____

_____

_____

18. Graph the functions $Y_1 = 0.6^x$ and $Y_2 = 0.3^x$ on a graphing calculator. Use a viewing window from -5 to 5 for x and from -2 to 8 for y, with a scale of 1 for both. Sketch the curves.

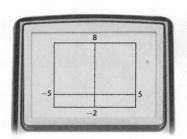

How does the graph of Y_1 compare with the graph of Y_2? Discuss how the graphs rise or fall and the y-intercepts.

_____

_____

_____

_____

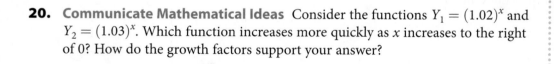

FOCUS ON HIGHER ORDER THINKING

Work Area

19. Critical Thinking Describe how the graph of $f(x) = ab^x$ changes for a given positive value of a as you increase the value of b when $b > 1$. Discuss the rise and fall of the graph and the y-intercept.

_____

_____

_____

_____

_____

20. Communicate Mathematical Ideas Consider the functions $Y_1 = (1.02)^x$ and $Y_2 = (1.03)^x$. Which function increases more quickly as x increases to the right of 0? How do the growth factors support your answer?

_____

_____

_____

_____

21. Communicate Mathematical Ideas Consider the functions $Y_1 = (0.94)^x$ and $Y_2 = (0.98)^x$. Which function decreases more quickly as x increases to the right of 0? How do the decay factors support your answer?

_____

_____

_____

_____

LESSON
10.5

Equations Involving Exponents

COMMON CORE   A.CED.1

Create equations and inequalities in one variable and use them to solve problems. Include equations arising from linear and quadratic functions, and simple rational and exponential functions. *Also A.CED.2, F.BF.1, F.BF.1a, F.LE.2*

? **ESSENTIAL QUESTION**

How can you solve equations involving variable exponents?

EXPLORE ACTIVITY   COMMON CORE   A.CED.1

Exploring Equations Containing Exponents

Some equations have an exponent that is a variable. You can use what you know about powers to find the value of the variable.

A $2^x = 8$

Write 8 as a power of 2.

$$2^x = 8$$

$$2^x = \boxed{} \cdot \boxed{} \cdot \boxed{}$$

$$2^x = \boxed{}^{\boxed{}}$$

B $2^{\boxed{}} = 8 = 2^x$, so $x = \boxed{}$

C $3^x = 81$

Write 81 as a power of 3.

$$3^x = 81$$

$$3^x = \boxed{} \cdot \boxed{} \cdot \boxed{} \cdot \boxed{}$$

$$3^x = \boxed{}^{\boxed{}}$$

D $3^{\boxed{}} = 81 = 3^x$, so $x = \boxed{}$

REFLECT

1. **Communicating Mathematical Ideas** What do you notice about the bases

of the expressions 2^x and 2^3? _____

Equality of Bases Property		
Words	**Algebra**	**Example**
Two powers with the same positive base other than 1 are equal if and only if the exponents are equal.	If $b > 0$ and $b \neq 1$, then $b^x = b^y$ if and only if $x = y$.	If $2^x = 2^9$, then $x = 9$. If $x = 9$, then $2^x = 2^9$.

Solving Equations by Equating Exponents

You can apply the properties of equations you already know and the Equality of Bases Property to solve equations involving exponents.

EXAMPLE 1   COMMON CORE A.CED.1

Solve each equation.

A $\dfrac{5}{2}(2)^x = 80$

$$\dfrac{2}{5} \cdot \dfrac{5}{2}(2)^x = \dfrac{2}{5} \cdot 80$$ Multiply by the reciprocal to isolate the power $(2)^x$.

$$(2)^x = 32$$ Simplify.

$$(2)^x = 2^5$$ Write 32 as a power of 2.

$$x = 5$$ $b^x = b^y$ if and only if $x = y$.

B $4\left(\dfrac{5}{3}\right)^x = \dfrac{500}{27}$

$$\dfrac{1}{4} \cdot 4\left(\dfrac{5}{3}\right)^x = \dfrac{1}{4} \cdot \dfrac{500}{27}$$ Multiply by the reciprocal to isolate the power.

$$\left(\dfrac{5}{3}\right)^x = \dfrac{125}{27}$$ Simplify.

$$\left(\dfrac{5}{3}\right)^x = \left(\dfrac{5}{3}\right)^3$$ Write the fraction as a power of $\dfrac{5}{3}$.

$$x = 3$$ $b^x = b^y$ if and only if $x = y$.

REFLECT

2. How can you check a solution?

_____

_____

3. Communicate Mathematical Ideas How can you work backward to write $\dfrac{125}{27}$ as a power of $\dfrac{5}{3}$?

_____

_____

4. Justify Reasoning Is it possible to solve the equation $2^x = 96$ using the method in Example 1? Why or why not?

_____

_____

_____

My Notes

YOUR TURN

Solve each equation.

5. $\frac{2}{3}(3)^x = 54$

$x =$ _____

6. $6\left(\frac{5}{4}\right)^x = \frac{75}{8}$

$x =$ _____

7. $\frac{1}{2}(4)^x = 32$

$x =$ _____

8. $5(3)^x = 405$

$x =$ _____

Personal Math Trainer

Online Practice and Help

my.hrw.com

Writing an Equation and Solving by Graphing

Some equations cannot be solved using the method in Example 1 because it isn't possible to write both sides of the equation as a whole number power of the same base. Instead, you can consider the expressions on either side of the equation as the rules for two different functions. You can then solve the original equation in one variable by graphing the two functions. The solution is the input value for the point where the two graphs intersect.

Math On the Spot

my.hrw.com

EXAMPLE 2 Real World

COMMON CORE F.BF.1, F.LE.2

A town has 78,918 residents. The population is increasing at a rate of 6% per year. The town council is offering a prize for the best prediction of how long it will take for the population to reach 100,000. Make a prediction.

STEP 1 Write an exponential model to represent the situation.

Let y represent the population and x represent time (in years).

$y = 78{,}918(1 + 0.06)^x$

STEP 2 Write an equation in one variable to represent the time, x, when the population reaches 100,000.

$100{,}000 = 78{,}918(1.06)^x$

STEP 3 Write functions for the expressions on either side of the equation.

$f(x) = 100{,}000$ *f(x) is a constant function.*

$g(x) = 78{,}918(1.06)^x$ *g(x) is an exponential growth function.*

STEP 4 Graph the functions on a graphing calculator. Let $Y_1 = f(x)$ and $Y_2 = g(x)$. Use a viewing window from -2 to 8 for x, using a scale of 1, and a viewing window from $-20,000$ to $200,000$ for y, using a scale of $20,000$. Sketch the graphs.

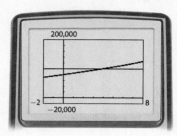

STEP 5 Use the intersect feature on the CALC menu to find the input value where the graphs intersect. (Do not round more than the calculator has already done.)

The input value where the graphs intersect is 4.063245.

STEP 6 Use the input value to make a prediction as to the number of years until the population reaches 100,000.

The population will reach 100,000 in just over 4 years.

REFLECT

9. Communicate Mathematical Ideas Why is the input value of the intersection point of $f(x)$ and $g(x)$ the solution?

_____

_____

_____

_____

Math Talk

Mathematical Practices

Suppose the contest is announced on January 1. Explain how to predict the date on which the population will be 100,000.

YOUR TURN

There are 250 bass in a lake. The population is increasing at the rate of 20% per year. You want to make a prediction for how long it will take the population to reach 400.

10. Write an equation in one variable to represent the time x when the population reaches 400.

_____

11. Make a prediction for how long will it take for the bass population to reach

400. Round the answer to the nearest tenth of a year. _____

Personal Math Trainer

Online Practice and Help

⏻ my.hrw.com

Solve each equation without graphing. (Example 1)

1. $\frac{3}{4}(6)^x = 162$

$(6)^x = \boxed{}$

$(6)^x = 6^{\boxed{}}$

$x = \boxed{}$

2. $3\left(\frac{5}{6}\right)^x = \frac{75}{36}$

$\left(\frac{5}{6}\right)^x = \boxed{}$

$\left(\frac{5}{6}\right)^x = \left(\frac{5}{6}\right)^{\boxed{}}$

$x = \boxed{}$

3. $7\left(\frac{1}{2}\right)^x = \frac{7}{8}$

$x = $ _____

4. $\frac{1}{5}(5)^x = 125$

$x = $ _____

5. $10(4)^x = 640$

$x = $ _____

Solve each equation by graphing. Round to the nearest hundredth. (Example 2)

6. $6^x = 100$

$x \approx $ _____

7. $7^x = 400$

$x \approx $ _____

8. $(2.5)^x = 100$

$x \approx $ _____

There are 225 wolves in a state park. The population is increasing at the rate of 15% per year. You want to make a prediction for how long it will take the population to reach 500. (Example 2)

9. Write an equation in one variable to represent the time, x, when the population

reaches 500. _____

10. Make a prediction for how long will it take for the wolf population to reach 500.

Round the answer to the nearest tenth of a year. _____

? ESSENTIAL QUESTION CHECK-IN

11. How can you solve equations involving variable exponents?

_____

_____

_____

_____

_____

_____

10.5 Independent Practice

 A.CED.1, A.CED.2, F.BF.1, F.BF.1a, F.LE.2

Personal Math Trainer

Online Practice and Help

my.hrw.com

Solve each equation without graphing.

12. $8(3)^x = 648$

$x =$ _____

13. $\frac{1}{5}(5)^x = 5$

$x =$ _____

14. $3\left(\frac{3}{10}\right)^x = \frac{27}{100}$

$x =$ _____

15. $6(5)^x = 750$

$x =$ _____

16. $\frac{3}{4}\left(\frac{2}{3}\right)^x = \frac{4}{27}$

$x =$ _____

17. $\frac{1}{2}\left(\frac{1}{5}\right)^x = \frac{1}{50}$

$x =$ _____

18. What would you do first to solve the equation $\frac{1}{25}(5)^x = 5$?

_____

For Exercises 19–22, solve each equation by graphing. Round to the nearest hundredth.

19. $6^x = 150$

$x \approx$ _____

20. $5^x = 20$

$x \approx$ _____

21. $3^x = 100$

$x \approx$ _____

22. $(5.5)^x = 40$

$x \approx$ _____

23. Write the constant function and the exponential function you would graph in order to solve the equation $4^x = 20$.

constant function: $f(x) =$ _____

exponential function: $g(x) =$ _____

24. Can you solve the equation $30 = (1.5)^x$ using the method shown in Example 1? Explain.

_____

_____

Use the equation $2^x = 16$ for Exercises 25–27.

25. Solve the equation using properties of equations and the Equality of Bases Property.

$x =$ _____

26. Solve the equation by graphing a constant function and an exponential function on the coordinate plane below.

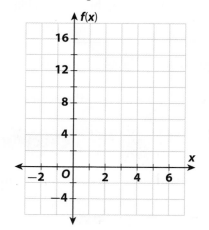

$x =$ _____

27. How do your solutions in Exercises 26 and 25 compare?

_____

_____

28. **Justify Reasoning** Which method do you prefer for solving the equation $2^x = 16$? Explain.

_____

_____

_____

_____

29. Which method would be better for solving the equation $2^x = 20$? Explain.

_____

_____

_____

Use the following information for 30–34. There are 175 deer in a state park. The population is increasing at the rate of 12% per year. You want to make a prediction for how long it will take the population to reach 300.

30. Write an equation in one variable to represent the time x when the population reaches 300.

_____

_____

31. Write the constant function and the exponential function you will graph to find the time x when the population reaches 300.

constant function: $f(x) =$ _____

exponential function: $g(x) =$ _____

32. Graph the functions from Exercise 31 on a graphing calculator. Sketch the graphs.

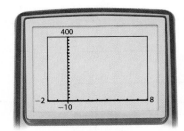

33. Explain how you can use the graphs to find the time when the population reaches 300.

_____

_____

_____

_____

34. Make a prediction for how long it will take for the deer population to reach 300. Round the answer to the nearest tenth of a year.

_____

Use the following information for 35–37. A city has 175,000 residents. The population is increasing at the rate of 10% per year. You want to make a prediction for how long it will take the population to reach 300,000.

35. Write an equation in one variable to represent the time, x, when the population reaches 300,000.

_____

_____

36. Make a prediction for how long will it take for the population to reach 300,000. Round the answer to the nearest tenth of a

year. _____

37. **What If?** Suppose there are 350,000 residents of another city. The population of this city is decreasing at a rate of 3% per year. Which city's population will reach 300,000 sooner? Explain.

_____

_____

_____

_____

_____

38. Last year a debate club sold 972 fundraiser tickets on their most successful day. This year the 4 club officers plan to match that number on a particular day of ticket sales.

To start off, on Day 0, each of the 4 officers will sell 3 tickets and ask each buyer to sell 3 more tickets the next day. Every time a ticket is sold, the buyer of the ticket will be asked to sell 3 more tickets the next day.

If the plan works, on what day will the number of tickets sold be 972?

a. Write an equation in one variable to model the situation. _____

b. If the plan works, on what day will the number sold be 972? _____

 **FOCUS ON HIGHER ORDER THINKING**

39. Explain the Error Jean and Marco each solved the equation $9(3)^x = 729$. Which is incorrect? Explain your reasoning.

Jean
$9(3)^x = 729$
$\frac{1}{9} \cdot 9(3)^x = \frac{1}{9} \cdot 729$
$3^x = 81$
$3^x = 3^4$
$x = 4$

Marco
$9(3)^x = 729$
$(3)^x = 9 \cdot 729$
$3^x = 6,561$
$3^x = 3^8$
$x = 8$

_____

_____

_____

_____

_____

40. Critical Thinking Without solving, determine which of the following equations has a greater solution. Explain your reasoning.

$$\frac{1}{3}(3)^x = 243 \qquad\qquad \frac{1}{3}(9)^x = 243$$

_____

_____

_____

_____

_____

Ready to Go On?

10.1 Exponential Functions

Use two points to write an equation for each function shown.

1.

x	−2	−1	0	1	2
f(x)	2.5	5	10	20	40

_____

2.

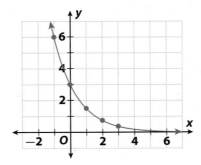

_____

10.2–10.3 Exponential Growth and Decay/Geometric Sequences

Write an exponential growth or decay function to model each situation. Then find the value of the function after the given amount of time.

3. An antique car is worth $35,000, and its value grows by 6% per year; 8 years.

_____

4. The student enrollment is 980 students and decreases by 1.3% per year; 7 years.

_____

If the given rule is recursive, write it as an explicit rule. If the rule is explicit, write it as a recursive rule. Assume that $f(1)$ is the first term of the sequence.

5. $f(1) = 4.5; f(n) = f(n − 1) \cdot 6$ for $n \geq 2$

_____

6. $f(n) = 0.6(7)^{n − 1}$

_____

10.4–10.5 Transforming Exponential Functions/Equations Involving Exponents

7. Describe the effect of replacing $f(x) = 4^x$ by $g(x) = 4^x + 1$.

_____

8. Solve $5\left(\frac{1}{3}\right)^x = \frac{5}{27}$ without using a calculator.

_____

ESSENTIAL QUESTION

9. How can exponential functions be used to represent real-world situations?

_____

_____

_____

1. Look at each system of equations. Does the system have exactly one solution? Select Yes or No for systems A–C.

   A. $\begin{cases} x + y = 16 \\ 3x - 5y = 16 \end{cases}$

   B. $\begin{cases} 2x + 3y = 4 \\ 6x + 9y = -21 \end{cases}$

   C. $\begin{cases} 3x - y = 5 \\ 2x - y = 0 \end{cases}$

   ○ Yes ○ No   ○ Yes ○ No   ○ Yes ○ No

2. Consider the exponential functions $f(x) = 3^x$ and $g(x) = 2(3)^x$.
   Choose True or False for each statement.

   A. The graph of $g(x)$ is a vertical translation of the graph of $f(x)$.   ○ True ○ False

   B. The y-intercept of $g(x)$ is greater than the y-intercept of $f(x)$.   ○ True ○ False

   C. For any value of x, the value of $g(x)$ is greater than the value of $f(x)$.   ○ True ○ False

3. The table shows how a population of gray seals has changed over time. Write an explicit rule for the geometric sequence represented by the table. In what year will the population first exceed 25,000? Explain your reasoning.

Time (years), n	Population, $f(n)$
1	3000
2	3300
3	3630
4	3993

4. The Kramer family bought a house for $164,000. The value of the house is expected to increase at a rate of 2.3% per year. Is the house expected to be worth more than $200,000 after 10 years? Use an exponential function to justify your answer.

Modeling with Exponential Functions

MODULE

11

COMMON CORE

? ESSENTIAL QUESTION

When do you use exponential functions to model real-world data?

Real-World Video

Pythons originally kept as pets but later released into the Florida ecosystem find themselves in an environment with no natural predators and prey ill-equipped to evade or defend itself. As a result, the python population can grow exponentially, causing havoc among local wildlife and pets.

my.hrw.com

GO DIGITAL
my.hrw.com

my.hrw.com

Go digital with your write-in student edition, accessible on any device.

Math On the Spot

Scan with your smart phone to jump directly to the online edition, video tutor, and more.

Animated Math

Interactively explore key concepts to see how math works.

Personal Math Trainer

Get immediate feedback and help as you work through practice sets.

© Houghton Mifflin Harcourt Publishing Company • Image Credits: © R.Hambley/Shutterstock

Are YOU Ready?

Complete these exercises to review the skills you will need for this module.

Percent Problems

EXAMPLE What is 108% of $500?

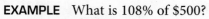

$x = 1.08 \times 500$ Translate.

$x = (1.08)(500)$ Simplify.

$x = 540$

Simplify each expression.

1. What is 103% of $800?

_____

2. What is 95% of 15,000 people?

_____

3. What is 84% of 200 milligrams?

_____

4. What is 105% of 105% of $30,000?

_____

Function Tables

EXAMPLE Generate ordered pairs for the function $y = 3x + 2$ for $x = 0, 1, 2, 3$.

x	y = 3x + 2	y
0	$y = 3(0) + 2 = 2$	2
1	$y = 3(1) + 2 = 5$	5
2	$y = 3(2) + 2 = 8$	8
3	$y = 3(3) + 2 = 11$	11

Generate ordered pairs for each function for $x = 0, 1, 2, 3, 4$.

5. $y = 25,000 + 1050x$

x	y
0	
1	
2	
3	
4	

6. $y = 25,000(1.04)^x$

x	y
0	
1	
2	
3	
4	

Reading Start-Up

Visualize Vocabulary

Use the Review Words with a check next to them to complete the Venn diagram.

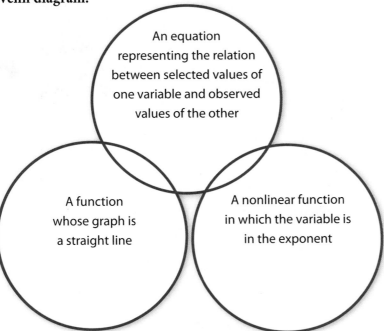

An equation representing the relation between selected values of one variable and observed values of the other

A function whose graph is a straight line

A nonlinear function in which the variable is in the exponent

Vocabulary

Review Words

correlation coefficient *(coeficiente de correlación)*

✔ exponential function *(función exponencial)*

✔ linear function *(función lineal)*

✔ regression equation *(ecuación de regresión)*

residual *(residuo)*

scatter plot *(diagrama de dispersión)*

Understand Vocabulary

Use some of the vocabulary terms in this module to answer the following questions. You may refer to the module, the glossary, or a dictionary.

1. The _____ provides an indication of how well the regression model fits the data.

2. The term scatter plot refers to a type of graph. What do you think a *scatter plot* looks like?

_____

Active Reading

Double-Door Fold Create a double-door fold to help you understand the concepts in this module. Label one flap "Exponential Model" and the other flap "Comparing Linear and Exponential Models." As you study the lessons, write important ideas under the appropriate flap.

COMMON CORE

GETTING READY FOR
Modeling with Exponential Functions
Understanding the standards and the vocabulary terms in the standards
will help you know exactly what you are expected to learn in this module.

COMMON CORE S.ID.6a

Fit a function to the data; use functions fitted to data to solve problems in the context of the data.

Key Vocabulary

function *(función)*
An input-output relationship that has exactly one output for each input.

What It Means to You

You can use a function to approximate the relationship between two variables.

EXAMPLE S.ID.6A

This table shows the number of Blu-ray discs Clarissa has sold each year since she opened her video store in 2006.

Years since 2006	0	1	2	3	4	5	6
Number of Blu-rays sold	27	117	252	313	395	423	573

Enter the data from the table on a graphing calculator. Use the calculator's linear regression feature to find the model of the data. This data can be represented by the linear function $f(x) = 85.46x + 43.61$.

COMMON CORE F.LE.1

Distinguish between situations that can be modeled with linear functions and with exponential functions.

Key Vocabulary

exponential function *(función exponencial)*
A non-linear function in which the variable is in the exponent.

linear function *(función lineal)*
A function that has a graph that is a straight line.

What It Means to You

You can determine whether a linear or exponential function is best to model a set of real-world data.

EXAMPLE F.LE.1

The value of a $15,000 car decreases by $1000 each year.

The amount of decrease, $1000, remains constant. The value of the car for the first 3 years is: $15,000, $15,000 − $1000 = $14,000, and $14,000 − $1000 = $13,000, respectively. This shows a linear function.

The value of a $15,000 car decreases by 10% each year.

The percent of decrease, 10%, remains constant. But the amount of decrease changes each year based on the value of the car that year. The value of the car for the first 3 years is: $15,000, $15,000 × 0.90 = $13,500, and $13,500 × 0.9 = $12,150, respectively. This shows an exponential function.

Visit **my.hrw.com**
to see all
**Common Core
Standards**
unpacked.

⏱ my.hrw.com

© Houghton Mifflin Harcourt Publishing Company • Image Credits: © Nick Koudis/Photodisc/Getty Images; © Guo ZhongHua/Shutterstock

LESSON
11.1 Exponential Regression

COMMON CORE S.ID.6a

Fit a function to the data; use functions fitted to data to solve problems in the context of the data.

COMMON CORE S.ID.6b

Informally assess the fit of a function by plotting and analyzing residuals. *Also A.CED.2, F.LE.5*

? **ESSENTIAL QUESTION**

How can you use exponential regression to model data?

Fitting an Exponential Function to Data

This lesson will explore data that is best approximated by an exponential function of the form $y = f(x) = ab^x$.

Math On the Spot
⏱ my.hrw.com

EXAMPLE 1   **COMMON CORE** S.ID.6a

Use a calculator to find an exponential function that models the data.

Number of Internet hosts						
Years since 2001	0	1	2	3	4	5	6
Number (millions)	110	147	172	233	318	395	433

STEP 1 Enter the data from the table on a graphing calculator, with years since 2001 (the *x*-value) in List 1 and the number of Internet hosts (the *y*-value) in List 2. Then, graph the data as a scatter plot.

Choose scatter plot with no line

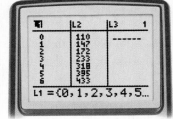  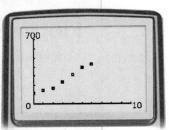

The points in the scatter plot follow an upward curve. An exponential function might fit the data better than a linear model.

STEP 2 Use the exponential regression feature.

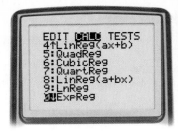 

Math Talk
Mathematical Practices

What is the growth rate for the exponential model?

Round the values of *a* and *b* to write the function $y = 113(1.27)^x$. Because the *r* value is close to 1, the model is a good fit.

REFLECT

1. **Communicate Mathematical Ideas** Which parameter, a or b, represents the initial value of y? Explain how you know.

_____

_____

_____

YOUR TURN

2. Use your calculator to find an exponential function that models the average number of text messages a month shown in the table.

Average Number of Monthly Text Messages							
	2006 (Q4)	2007 (Q1)	2007 (Q2)	2007 (Q3)	2007 (Q4)	2008 (Q1)	2008 (Q2)
Quarter Years	0	1	2	3	4	5	6
Average Number	108	129	172	193	218	288	357

EXPLORE ACTIVITY

COMMON CORE S.ID.6b

Plotting and Analyzing Residuals

Recall that a residual is the difference between the actual y-value in the data set and the predicted y-value. Residuals can be used to assess how well a model fits a data set. If a model fits the data well, then:

- The numbers of positive and negative residuals are roughly equal.
- The residuals are randomly distributed about the x-axis on a residual plot.
- The absolute value of the residuals is small relative to the data values.

Analyze the residuals of the exponential model found in Example 1.

A The portion of the regression model and scatter plot corresponding to the second data point of the Internet host data is shown. Name the actual y-value from the data y_d, and name the y-value predicted by the model y_m. Find the difference between these values $(y_d - y_m)$, and then place the result in the residual column for $x = 1$ in the chart in the next step.

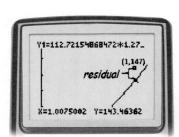

B On your calculator, enter the regression equation as the rule for equation Y_1. Then view the table to find the y-values predicted by model (y_m). Record the results in the table.

C Now complete the residuals column by subtracting the predicted values from the actual values.

D Set up a residual scatter plot of the data and graph it. (The residuals data will automatically be saved as Plot 2. Adjust the viewing window as needed.) Plot the points on the graph provided.

	Number of Internet hosts (millions)		
x	Actual value y_d	Predicted value y_m	Residual $y_d - y_m$
0	110	113	−3
1	147	143	
2	172		
3	233		
4	318		
5	395		
6	433		

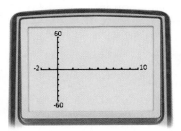

REFLECT

3. Multiple Representations What does the residual plot reveal about the fit of the model? Does this agree with the correlation coefficient?

_____

_____

_____

_____

_____

4. Look for Patterns What can you infer about the accuracy of the model as it moves further away from the initial value? Explain.

_____

_____

_____

_____

_____

The first two columns of the table show the population of Arizona (in thousands) in each census from 1900–2000. (Example 1 and Explore Activity)

1. Find an exponential function that models the data. Plot the remaining data points on the screen and sketch the regression line.

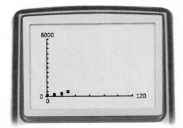

2. Round the parameters a and b to four significant digits. The regression equation is:

$y = f(x) = \boxed{} \times \boxed{}^x$

The regression equation approximates the Arizona population in 1900 to

be _____ people and the growth rate

to be _____, meaning the population

increases by _____% each year.

Arizona population in thousands (y)			
Years since 1900 (x)	Actual y_d	Predicted y_m	Residual $y_d - y_m$
0	123		
10	204		8
20	334	283	
30	436		
40	499		−88
50	750	847	
60	1302		
70	1771		
80	2718		178
90	3665		
100	5131	5281	

3. Round the value of the correlation coefficient to three significant digits.

$r = \boxed{}$, suggesting the model is / is not a good approximation

of the population data.

4. Complete the Arizona population table by filling in the remaining y_m and $y_d - y_m$ values. Use the regression model stored in your calculator to obtain the y_m values. Round to the nearest whole number.

5. Complete the residual plot in which five of the residuals have already been plotted.

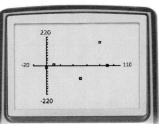

? ESSENTIAL QUESTION CHECK-IN

6. How can you use exponential regression to model data?

_____

_____

_____

11.1 Independent Practice

COMMON CORE S.ID.6a, S.ID.6b, A.CED.2, F.LE.5

Personal
Math Trainer

Online Practice
and Help

my.hrw.com

7. **Multistep** In 2012, the number of Internet hosts was reported to be 888 million.

a. Based on the model found in Example 1, predict the number of Internet hosts for 2012.

_____

_____

_____

_____

b. Does the residual for 2012 meet the good-fit requirement of being small relative to the data? Explain.

_____

_____

_____

_____

c. Discuss the likely accuracy of the number of Internet hosts predicted for 2025. Explain your answer.

_____

_____

_____

_____

_____

_____

8. **What if?** Use a graphing calculator to model the Arizona population data in Guided Practice through **linear** regression.

a. Describe the shape of the residual plot and explain what this suggests about the fit of the model.

_____

_____

_____

_____

_____

b. Would the correlation coefficient lead you to draw the same conclusion regarding how well the model approximates the data? Explain.

_____

_____

_____

_____

9. **Make a Prediction** Use the exponential regression model of the Arizona population data to predict the year in which the state's population will first exceed 15,000. Explain how you arrived at your answer.

_____

_____

_____

_____

_____

10. Interpret the Answer The concentration of ibuprofen in a person's blood was plotted each hour. An exponential model fit the data with $a = 400$ and $b = 0.71$. Interpret these parameters.

_____

_____

_____

H.O.T. FOCUS ON HIGHER ORDER THINKING

Work Area

11. Critique Reasoning The absolute values of the residuals in Mark's regression model are less than 20. Working on a different data set, Sandy obtained residuals in the hundreds. This led Mark to conclude his data is a better fit than Sandy's. Explain why Mark is wrong to base his critique of their regression models on the values of the residuals.

_____

_____

_____

_____

12. Make a Conjecture When Chris used exponential regression on the Arizona population data in Guided Practice, he obtained the following results: $a = 186$, $b = 1.026$, $r = 0.813$. When he reviewed the data in his lists, he found he had entered a number incorrectly. Is it more likely that his error was in entering the last population value too high or too low? Justify your reasoning.

_____

_____

_____

_____

_____

13. Draw Conclusions Madelyn has recorded the number of bacteria on her growth plate every hour for three hours. She finds that a linear model fits her data better than the expected exponential model. What should she do to improve her model?

_____

_____

_____

_____

Comparing Linear and Exponential Models

F.LE.1

Distinguish between situations that can be modeled with linear functions and with exponential functions. *Also F.LE.1a, F.LE.1b, F.LE.1c, F.LE.3*

 ESSENTIAL QUESTION

How can you recognize when to use a linear or exponential model?

EXPLORE ACTIVITY 1

COMMON CORE   F.LE.1b, F.LE.1c

Comparing Constant Change and Constant Percent Change

Suppose that you are offered a job that pays $1000 the first month with a raise every month after that. You can choose a $100 raise or a 10% raise. Which option would you choose? What if the raise were 8%, 6%, or 4%?

A Find the monthly salaries for the first three months. Record the results in the table, rounded to the nearest dollar.

- For the $100 raise, enter 1000 into your graphing calculator, press Enter, enter +100, press ENTER, and then press ENTER repeatedly.
- For the 10% raise, enter 1000, press ENTER, enter × 1.10, press ENTER, and then press ENTER repeatedly.
- For the other raises, multiply by 1.08, 1.06, or 1.04.

Monthly Salary After Indicated Monthly Raise					
Month	$100	10%	8%	6%	4%
0	$1000	$1000	$1000	$1000	$1000
1	$1100	$1100	$1080	$1060	$1040
2					
3					

B For each option, find how much the salary changes each month, both in dollars and as a percent of the previous month's salary. Record the values in the table.

Change in Salary per Month for Indicated Monthly Raise										
Interval	$100		10%		8%		6%		4%	
	$	%	$	%	$	%	$	%	$	%
0 – 1	$100	10%	$100	10%	$80	8%	$60	6%	$40	4%
1 – 2	$100			10%		8%		6%		4%
2 – 3	$100			10%		8%		6%		4%

C Continue the calculations you did in Part A until you find the number of months it takes for each salary with a percent raise to exceed the salary with the $100 raise. Record the number of months in the table below.

Number of Months Until Salary with Percent Raise Exceeds Salary with $100 Raise			
10%	8%	6%	4%
2			

REFLECT

1. **Analyze Relationships** Compare and contrast the salary changes per month for the raise options. Explain the source of any differences.

   _____

   _____

   _____

2. **Justify Reasoning** Which raise option would you choose? What would you consider when deciding? Explain your reasoning.

   _____

   _____

   _____

Math On the Spot

my.hrw.com

Comparing Linear and Exponential Functions

When comparing raises, a fixed dollar increase can be modeled by a linear function and a fixed percent increase can be modeled by an exponential function. Using a calculator to graph these functions can help you compare them.

EXAMPLE 1 COMMON CORE F.LE.1, F.LE.3

Compare the two salary plans listed. Will Job B ever have a higher monthly salary than Job A? If so, after how many months will this occur?

- Job A: $1000 for the first month with $100 raise every month thereafter
- Job B: $1000 for the first month with a 1% raise every month thereafter

STEP 1 Write functions that represent the monthly salaries.

   Let t represent the number of elapsed months.

   Job A: $S_A(t) = 1000 + 100t$ *linear function*

   Job B: $S_B(t) = 1000 \times 1.01^t$ *exponential function*

STEP 2   Graph the functions on a calculator using Y_1 for Job A and Y_2 for Job B.

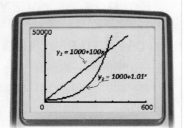

Animated Math

⏵ my.hrw.com

STEP 3   Estimate the number of months it takes for the salaries to become equal using the intersect feature of the calculator.

At $x \approx 364$ months, the salaries are equal.

STEP 4   Go to the estimated intersection point in the table feature. Find the first x-value at which Y_2 exceeds Y_1.

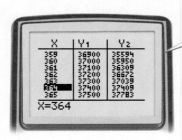

At $x = 364$, $Y_2 > Y_1$

Job B will have a higher monthly salary than Job A at 364 months.

REFLECT

3. Draw Conclusions Which job offers a monthly salary that reflects a constant change, and which offers a monthly salary that reflects a constant percent change?

_____

_____

_____

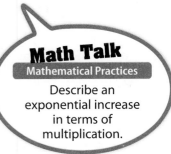

Math Talk

Mathematical Practices

Describe an exponential increase in terms of multiplication.

YOUR TURN

4.   Companies A and B each have 50 employees. If Company A increases its workforce by 2 employees per month, and Company B increases its workforce by an average of 2% per month, will Company B ever have more employees than company A? If so, when?

_____

_____

Personal Math Trainer

Online Practice and Help

⏵ my.hrw.com

How Linear and Exponential Functions Grow

Linear functions undergo a constant change (change by equal differences) while exponential functions undergo a constant percent change (change by equal factors). Now you will explore the proofs of these statements. $x_2 - x_1$ and $x_4 - x_3$ represent two intervals in the x-values of a function.

A Complete the proof that linear functions grow by equal differences over equal intervals.

Given: $x_2 - x_1 = x_4 - x_3$

   f is a linear function of the form $f(x) = mx + b$

Prove: $f(x_2) - f(x_1) = f(x_4) - f(x_3)$

Proof:

1. $x_2 - x_1 = x_4 - x_3$ ⸻ *Given*

2. $m(x_2 - x_1) = \boxed{}(x_4 - x_3)$ ⸻ *Mult. Prop. of Equality*

3. $mx_2 - \boxed{} = mx_4 - \boxed{}$ ⸻ *Distributive Property*

4. $mx_2 + b - mx_1 - b =$ ⸻ *Add. & Sub. Prop. of Equality*

   $mx_4 + \boxed{} - mx_3 - \boxed{}$

5. $mx_2 + b - (mx_1 + b) =$ ⸻ *Distributive Property*

   $mx_4 + b - \boxed{}$

6. $f(x_2) - f(x_1) = $ _____ ⸻ *Definition of f(x)*

B Complete the proof that exponential functions grow by equal factors over equal intervals.

Given: $x_2 - x_1 = x_4 - x_3$

   g is an exponential function of the form $g(x) = ab^x$

Prove: $\dfrac{g(x_2)}{g(x_1)} = \dfrac{g(x_4)}{g(x_3)}$

Proof:

1. $x_2 - x_1 = x_4 - x_3$ ⸻ *Given*

2. $b^{(x_2 - x_1)} = b^{(x_4 - x_3)}$ ⸻ *If x = y, then $b^x = b^y$.*

3. $\dfrac{b^{x_2}}{b^{x_1}} = \dfrac{b^{x_4}}{b^{\boxed{}}}$ ⸻ *Quotient of Powers Prop.*

4. $\dfrac{ab^{x_2}}{ab^{x_1}} = \dfrac{ab^{x_4}}{\boxed{}}$ ⸻ *Mult. Prop. of Equality*

5. $\dfrac{g(x_2)}{g(x_1)} = \dfrac{g(x_4)}{\boxed{}}$ ⸻ *Definition of g(x)*

Choosing a Modeling Function

Both linear equations and exponential equations and their graphs can model real-world situations. Determine whether the dependent variable appears to change by a common difference or a common ratio to select the correct model.

EXAMPLE 2 　　　　　　　　　 COMMON CORE **F.LE.1, F.LE.3**

A gas had an initial pressure of 150 torr. Its pressure was then measured every 5 seconds for 25 seconds. Determine whether the change in pressure over time is best described by an increasing or decreasing function, and whether it is a linear or exponential function. Find a regression equation.

STEP 1 Determine whether the dependent variable changes by increasing or decreasing.

Pressure decreases over time.

STEP 2 Determine if the dependent

Pressure over time		Change per interval	
time (s)	pressure (torr)	difference $P(t_n) - P(t_{n-1})$	$P(t_n)$ factor $\dfrac{P(t_n)}{P(t_{n-1})}$
0	150	—	—
5	117	−33	0.78
10	90	−27	0.77
15	70	−20	0.78
20	56	−14	0.80
25	41	−15	0.73

The factor changes are close to equal while the difference changes are not, suggesting an exponential regression model should be used.

variable appears to change by equal differences or by equal factors over equal intervals.

STEP 3 Perform the exponential regression analysis, and evaluate the fit.

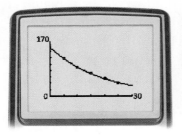  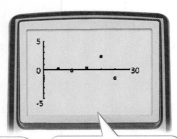

r-value suggests a good fit.

Analysis of residuals suggests a good fit.

A regression equation is $P(t) = 151(0.950)^t$.

YOUR TURN

5. The volume of a gas was measured as the temperature was increased from 173 K to 423 K in 50 K intervals. The gas volumes recorded, starting at 173 K, were 16, 21, 26, 30, 36, and 40 cm³. Determine whether the data is best described by an increasing or decreasing function, and whether it is linear or exponential. Find a regression equation.

Personal Math Trainer

Online Practice and Help

⊙ my.hrw.com

1. Centerville has 2500 residents and Easton has 2000 residents. Centerville's population decreases by 80 people per year and Easton's population decreases by 3% per year. Will Easton ever have a greater population than Centerville? If so, when? (Example 1)

If t is time in years from now, Centerville's population is given by the equation

$$P_C(t) = \boxed{} - \boxed{}\, t$$

and Easton's population is given by the equation

$$P_E(t) = \boxed{} \times \boxed{}^{\,t}$$

Graph both functions on your calculator. The functions intersect at $t \approx$ _____.

Using the table feature on your calculator, find the first x-value at which Easton's population is greater than Centerville's.

Easton's population will exceed Centerville's after _____ years. At this time,

Centerville will have _____ residents, and Easton will have _____ residents.

Complete each statement with the correct function from the table.
(Explore Activity 1, Example 2)

2. _____ decreases by a constant amount per interval, so it is

a(n) _____ function.

3. _____ decreases by a constant percent per interval, so it is

a(n) _____ function.

4. An equation for the linear function is:

_____

5. An equation for the exponential function is:

_____

x	$f(x)$ height of ball after each bounce	$g(x)$ number of cookies remaining each day
0	200	300
1	150	288
2	113	276
3	84	264
4	63	252
5	47	240

? ESSENTIAL QUESTION CHECK-IN

6. How can you recognize when to use a linear or exponential model?

_____

_____

_____

11.2 Independent Practice

Personal Math Trainer

Online Practice and Help

my.hrw.com

COMMON CORE   F.LE.1, F.LE.1a, F.LE.1b, F.LE.1c, F.LE.3

For 7–9, without graphing, tell whether the situation involves a quantity that is changing at a constant rate per unit of time, at a constant percent rate per unit of time, or neither. Justify your reasoning.

7. Amy received a $15,000 interest-free loan from her parents and agreed to make monthly payments of $150.

_____

_____

8. Carla's salary is $50,000 in her first year on a job plus a 1% commission on sales.

_____

_____

_____

9. Enrollment at school is 976 students initially and then increases 2.5% each year thereafter.

_____

_____

_____

_____

10. **Draw Conclusions** Maria would like to put $500 in savings for a 5-year period. Should she choose a simple interest account that pays an interest rate of 10% of the principal (initial amount) each year or a compounded interest account that pays 3% of the total account value each month?

_____

_____

_____

_____

11. **Critical Thinking** Will an exponential growth function always eventually exceed a linear growth function? Explain.

_____

_____

_____

_____

12. **Interpret the Answer** Westward and Middleton each have 40,000 residents. Westward's population decreases by 900 people per year and Middleton's population decreases by 2% per year.

a. Write a function for each town's population.

_____

_____

b. Sketch the functions on the screen provided. Label the functions and include the scale.

c. Will Westward ever have a greater population than Middleton? If so, when? Explain your reasoning.

_____

_____

_____

_____

_____

13. Critique Reasoning Jordan analyzed the following data showing the number of cells in a bacteria culture over time.

Time (min)	0	6.9	10.8	13.5	15.7	17.4
Cells	8	16	24	32	40	48

He concluded that since the number of cells showed a constant change and the time did not, neither a linear function nor an exponential function modeled the number of cells over time well. Was he correct? Explain how you know.

_____

_____

_____

_____

_____

14. Check for Reasonableness In Example 2, an exponential function was chosen to model the pressure data even though the dependent variable did not change by exactly the same factor in every interval.

a. Do you think this was the best model for the real-world data? Justify your reasoning.

_____

_____

_____

_____

_____

b. Another parameter of the data to consider is the average rate of change (AROC), which is the slope of the line that passes through any two consecutive data points. How does the AROC change for the data in Example 2? Is this more consistent with an exponential or linear function? Explain.

_____

_____

_____

_____

_____

Ready to Go On?

Personal Math Trainer

Online Practice and Help

my.hrw.com

11.1 Exponential Regression

The first two columns of the table show the population of box turtles in a Tennessee zoo over a period of 5 years.

1. Use a graphing calculator to find an exponential function model for the data. Round to the nearest thousandth.

_____

2. Use the model to predict the number of box turtles in the sixth year.

_____

_____

_____

Population of box turtles			
Year (x)	Actual (y_d)	Predicted (y_m)	Residual ($y_d - y_m$)
1	21	22	−1
2	27		
3	33		
4	41		
5	48		

3. Complete the chart using the observed and predicted values for the number of box turtles. Round to the nearest whole number.

11.2 Comparing Linear and Exponential Models

4. Julio is offered jobs with two different companies.

Company A is offering $2000 a month for the first month with a $50 raise every month after. Company B is offering $2000 a month for the first month with a 2% raise every month after.

Write functions that represent the monthly salary at each company, and use the functions to determine which company will have a higher monthly salary after 2 years.

Company A _____

Company B _____

_____

? ESSENTIAL QUESTION

5. When do you use exponential functions to model real-world data?

_____

_____

MODULE 11

MIXED REVIEW

COMMON CORE

Assessment Readiness

Personal Math Trainer

Online Practice and Help

my.hrw.com

1. The recursive rule $f(1) = 20$ and $f(n) = f(n-1) - 6$ for $n \geq 2$ represents an arithmetic sequence.

Which model(s) below could represent this sequence? Select all that apply.

- ○ $f(n) = 20 - 6(n-1)$ for $n \geq 1$
- ○ $20, 14, 8, 2, -4, \ldots$
- ○ The first term of the sequence is 20, and the common difference is 6.

○

n	1	2	3	4
f(n)	20	26	32	38

2. A dog receives a dose of an antibiotic. The table shows the amount of antibiotic remaining in the dog's bloodstream over time. A student wrote the equation $y = 212(0.39)^x$ to model the data.

Time (h), x	Amount (mg), y
0	200
1	82
2	39
3	11

Choose True or False for each statement.

A. The model predicts that less than 1 milligram of the antibiotic will remain after 5 hours.

○ True ○ False

B. The residual for the data point (1, 82) is −0.68.

○ True ○ False

C. The model predicts that the amount of antibiotic remaining decreases by 61% each hour.

○ True ○ False

3. Maya and Jordan both start blogs in the same month. In the initial month, Maya has 30 page hits, and her number of page hits increases by about 10 per month. Jordan has 18 page hits in the initial month, and his number of page hits increases by about 10% per month. Based on these patterns, how many months after the initial month will Jordan's blog get more page hits than Maya's blog? Explain.

Study Guide Review

Exponential Functions and Equations

Key Vocabulary
common ratio
(razón común)
exponential growth
(crecimiento exponencial)
exponential decay
(disminución exponencial)
exponential function
(función exponencial)
geometric sequence
(sucesión geométrica)

? ESSENTIAL QUESTION

How can exponential functions be used to represent real-world situations?

EXAMPLE 1

James bought several shares of two different stocks. The graph below shows the value of Stock A and Stock B over time.

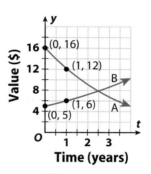

A Write the exponential decay function, $f(t)$, for the price of Stock A.

STEP 1 $b = 12 \div 16 = 0.75$

STEP 2 $f(n) = ab^n$

$f(n) = a(0.75)^n$

$12 = a(0.75)^1$

$12 = 0.75a$

$a = 16$

STEP 3 $f(t) = ab^t$

$f(t) = 16(0.75)^t$

B Write the exponential growth function, $g(t)$, for the price of Stock B.

STEP 1 $b = 6 \div 5 = 1.2$

STEP 2 $g(n) = ab^n$

$g(n) = a(1.2)^n$

$6 = a(1.2)^1$

$6 = 1.2a$

$a = 5$

STEP 3 $f(t) = ab^t$

$f(t) = 5(1.2)^t$

EXAMPLE 2

Write a recursive rule and an explicit rule for the geometric sequence 6, −24, 96, −384.... Determine the sixth term in the sequence.

Identify the first term: 6

Calculate the common ratio: $-24 \div 6 = -4$

Recursive rule: $f(1) = 6, f(n) = f(n - 1) \times (-4)$ for $n \geq 2$

Explicit rule: $f(n) = 6 \times (-4)^{n-1}$

Use the explicit rule to find the sixth term: $f(6) = 6 \times (-4)^{6-1} = -6144$

EXAMPLE 3

The graphs of three exponential functions, Y_1, Y_2, and Y_3, are provided. Based on the graphs, identify the parameter changes relative to Y_1 and write the equations of all three functions.

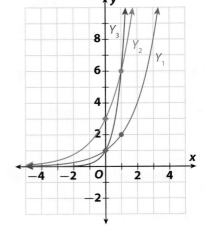

First find the common ratio b for each function.

Y_1	Y_2	Y_3
$(0, 1)$ and $(1, 2)$	$(0, 3)$ and $(1, 6)$	$(0, 1)$ and $(1, 6)$
$2 \div 1 = 2$	$6 \div 3 = 2$	$6 \div 1 = 6$

Use the value of b and a known point to find the value of a.

$Y_1 = ab^x$	$Y_2 = ab^x$	$Y_3 = ab^x$
$Y_1 = a(2)^x$	$Y_2 = a(2)^x$	$Y_3 = a(6)^x$
$2 = a(2)^1$	$6 = a(2)^1$	$6 = a(6)^1$
$2 = 2a$	$6 = 2a$	$6 = 6a$
$1 = a$	$3 = a$	$1 = a$

Write an equation for the function.

$$Y_1 = 1(2)^x = 2^x \qquad Y_2 = 3(2)^x = 3(2)^x \qquad Y_3 = 1(6)^x = 6^x$$

Y_2 is a vertical stretch of Y_1. Y_1 and Y_2 increase at the same rate. Y_3 increases more quickly than Y_1.

EXERCISES

An invasive plant species was introduced into a lake in 2002. Two years later, the invasive plant population was recorded at 42 plants; 3 years after the introduction, the plants numbered 55; and after 4 years, their population totaled 72 plants. (Lesson 10.1, 10.2)

1. Determine the common ratio to the nearest tenth and the initial invasive plant population in 2002 to the nearest tenth. Write the function corresponding to the data described. [Let 2002 correspond to $x = 0$.]

_____

2. Construct a scatter plot of the data for the first five years, including the initial population value, on the graph provided.

3. Is the data represented by an exponential growth or exponential decay function? What is the percent rate of change? Explain.

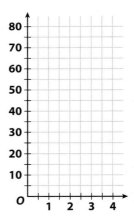

_____

_____

_____

_____

4. Based on the model, find the invasive plant population in 2012. Explain.

_____

_____

The number of players after each round of an online video game tournament is shown in the table. (Lesson 10.3)

Round	Number of Players
1	3840
2	2573
3	1724
4	1155

5. Write the recursive and explicit rules for the geometric sequence.

_____

_____

6. Determine how many players remain after the 11th round.

_____

The graphs of three exponential functions, Y_1, Y_2, and Y_3, are provided. (Lessons 10.4, 10.1)

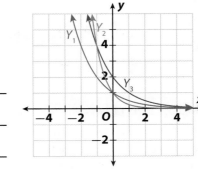

7. Which two functions have the same constant ratio b? Compare the value of a in those two functions.

_____

_____

_____

_____

_____

_____

8. Which two functions have the same y-intercept (value of a)? Compare the value of b in those two functions.

_____

_____

_____

_____

9. Write the equation of each function.

_____

The equation $10 \times 4^x = 640$ can be solved by equating exponents or by graphing each side of the equation as the rule for a function. (Lesson 10.5)

10. Solve by equating exponents. Explain your process.

_____

_____

_____

11. Solve by graphing on a graphing calculator. Sketch your functions on the graph provided and indicate how the value of the exponent is determined from this information.

_____

_____

_____

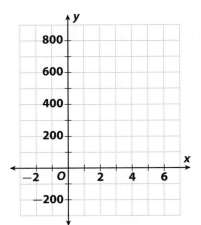

Modeling with Exponential Functions

When do you use exponential functions to model real-world data?

EXAMPLE 1

Job A has a salary plan beginning at $1000 for the first month with a $50 raise every month thereafter. The salary plan of Job B also starts at $750 the first month but includes a 1% raise every month thereafter. Determine if a linear or exponential growth function applies to each salary plan and write the corresponding function. Determine how many months it will take for Job B to have a higher monthly salary than Job A.

Let t represent the number of elapsed months.

Job A: The salary increases by a constant amount each month, so the function is linear: $S_A(t) = 1000 + 50t$.

Job B: The salary increases by a constant percent change, so the function is exponential: $S_B(t) = 750 \times 1.01^t$.

Graph the functions as Y_1 and Y_2. The point of intersection gives an estimate of the month in which the salaries are equal. This information is then used to search the table for a more precise value of x. When $x = 311$, the salary of Job B ($16558) first exceeds the salary of Job A ($16550).

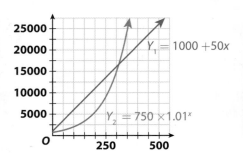

EXERCISES

12. Jan has $1200 to start an investment account. Investment plan A will pay 1.3% of the monthly principal. Investment plan B will pay $24 per month. Write the functions that represent the monthly account balances; let t represent the number of elapsed months. Graph the functions using a calculator. Sketch the functions on the graph provided; include axis labels and the coordinates of intersection. Compare and contrast the benefits of each plan. (Lesson 11.2)

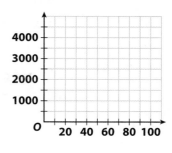

_____

_____

_____

_____

_____

The table shows the temperature of a pizza over three-minute intervals after taking it out of the oven. (Lessons 11.1, 11.2)

Time (min)	0	3	6	9	12	15	18	21
Temperature (°F)	450	350	290	230	190	150	130	110

13. Based on the data, explain why an exponential model is predicted to be a better fit than a linear model.

_____

_____

_____

14. Use technology to find an exponential function model for the data. Report the parameters in the equation to two significant digits. Assess the fit of the model based on the correlation coefficient and the residual plot. Using the regression model, predict how long it will take the pizza to cool down to a room temperature of 70°F.

_____

_____

_____

_____

_____

_____

Bank On It

An investor has $5000 to invest for 10 years in one of the banks listed below. Each bank offers an interest rate that is compounded annually.

Bank	Principal	Years	Balance
Super Save	$1000	6	$1173.34
Star Financial	$2500	3	$2684.35
Better Bank	$4000	5	$4525.63

The investor chooses Better Bank because it earned over $100 per year, which is much more than the other banks earned per year.

Create a presentation to the investor explaining which bank is the best choice, based on the given information. Include for each bank

1. a graph showing how the investment would grow over a 10-year period, and

2. the interest rate, including how you found it.

Use the space below to write down any questions you have or important information from your teacher.

MATH IN CAREERS | ACTIVITY

Statistician When researching data concerning caribou populations in the Arctic, Lee uncovered some archives of old caribou populations, shown in the first two columns of the table. Use a graphing calculator to find an exponential function that models the data. Complete the table and use the data to make an inference about the accuracy of the model.

Years Since 1972	Actual y_d	Predicted y_m	Residual $y_d - y_m$
0	2812		
1	2880		
2	2970		
3	3130		
4	3281		
5	3437		

UNIT 2B

MIXED REVIEW

Assessment Readiness

Personal Math Trainer

Online Practice and Help

my.hrw.com

1. Consider each ordered pair. Is the ordered pair a solution of the equation $4x - 3y = 12$?

   Select Yes or No.

   A. $(-3, -8)$ ○ Yes ○ No
   B. $(3, 4)$ ○ Yes ○ No
   C. $(9, 8)$ ○ Yes ○ No

2. The graph shows two exponential functions.

   Choose True or False for each statement.

   A. The parameter a is greater for $f(x)$ than for $g(x)$. ○ True ○ False

   B. The parameter b is greater for $f(x)$ than for $g(x)$. ○ True ○ False

   C. For both functions, b is greater than 1. ○ True ○ False

   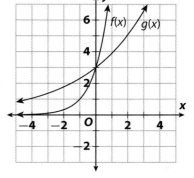

3. A test tube initially holds 25 bacteria. The population of bacteria in the test tube doubles each hour. Without making a graph, determine how many hours it will take for the population of bacteria in the test tube to reach 800. Explain how you solved this problem.

4. The table shows how the price of an item that cost $10.00 in 1913 has changed over time. Use a calculator to find the exponential function that models the data. Then predict how much an item that cost $10.00 in 1913 will cost in 2025. Explain how you made your prediction.

Years since 1913 (x)	Cost of item ($)
0	10.00
20	13.13
40	26.97
60	44.85
80	145.96
100	234.51

Performance Tasks

★ **5.** The number of matches played in each round of a doubles tennis tournament forms a geometric sequence. In the third round, there are 8 matches, and in the fourth round, there are 4 matches.

   a. Write an explicit rule for the geometric sequence.

   b. How many matches will there be in this tournament? Explain.

★★ **6.** The number of members over time in an online music sharing club can be modeled by an exponential function. The club started with 2100 members. After 1 month, the club had 2142 members.

   a. Write an equation for the number of members as a function of time in months since the club started.

   b. Graph the function, and label the axes.

   c. What is the parameter b in the equation, and what does it represent in this situation?

   d. Will the club have more than 5000 members during its first year? Justify your reasoning.

★★★ **7.** The table shows how the number of college degrees earned in the United States has changed over time.

   a. Is a linear function or an exponential function a better model for the data? Justify your answer.

   b. Predict the number of college degrees earned in the United States in 2050. Is this more likely to be an underestimate or an overestimate? Explain.

Year	College degrees (thousands)
1910	37
1930	122
1950	432
1970	792
1990	1051
2010	1650

Statistics and Data

MATH IN CAREERS

Sports Recruiter Sports recruiters find athletes from all over the world. They use statistics to find the best athletes based on their workouts and games.

If you're interested in a career as a sports recruiter, you should study these subjects of math:

- Statistics
- Algebra
- Calculus

Research other careers that require the use of statistics to make decisions.

ACTIVITY At the end of the unit, check out how a **sports recruiter** uses math.

Unit Project Preview

True Story?

The Unit Project at the end of this unit involves analyzing a claim in a current event or advertisement. To successfully complete the Unit Project you'll need to master these skills:

- Research the statistical data behind claims made in a recent news item or advertisement.
- Interpret the statistical data, and consider if the data shows correlation or causation.
- Represent the data using a data display.

Researchers from the Australian National University and the British Antarctic Survey found data taken from an ice core also shows the summer ice melt has been 10 times more intense over the past 50 years compared with 600 years ago.

1. Amy is reading a magazine article about Antarctic ice melt, which begins with the sentence shown above. What statistical or numerical information is given in the statement? What descriptive words require further definition?

   _____

   _____

   _____

   _____

   _____

2. What sources would you use to further research this article?

   _____

Tracking Your Learning Progression

This unit addresses important Common Core Standards in the Critical Area of working with categorical and quantitative data.

Domain S.ID Interpreting Categorical and Quantitative Data

   Cluster Summarize, represent, and interpret data on a single count or measurement variable.

Descriptive Statistics

MODULE

COMMON CORE

12

COMMON CORE STANDARDS

LESSON 12.1
Two-Way Frequency Tables
COMMON CORE S.ID.5

LESSON 12.2
Relative Frequency
COMMON CORE S.ID.5

ESSENTIAL QUESTION

How can you summarize two categories of categorical data and recognize associations and trends between two categories of categorical data?

Real-World Video

With emotions riding high, it can be difficult to evaluate popular opinion concerning personal preferences such as favorite sports teams. Polls and surveys use a methodical, mathematical approach to reduce or eliminate bias.

my.hrw.com

GO DIGITAL
my.hrw.com

my.hrw.com

Go digital with your write-in student edition, accessible on any device.

 Math On the Spot

Scan with your smart phone to jump directly to the online edition, video tutor, and more.

 Animated Math

Interactively explore key concepts to see how math works.

 Personal Math Trainer

Get immediate feedback and help as you work through practice sets.

Are YOU Ready?

Complete these exercises to review skills you will need for this module.

Fractions, Decimals, and Percents

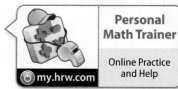

Personal Math Trainer

Online Practice and Help

my.hrw.com

EXAMPLE Write $\frac{5}{40}$ as a decimal.

$5 \div 40 = 0.125$ *Divide 5 by 40.*

$\frac{5}{40} = 0.125$

Write each fraction as a decimal.

1. $\frac{12}{48}$ **2.** $\frac{9}{30}$ **3.** $\frac{25}{40}$ **4.** $\frac{6}{16}$

_____   _____   _____   _____

Write each decimal as a percent.

5. 0.65   **6.** 0.07   **7.** 0.092   **8.** 0.122

_____   _____   _____   _____

Write each fraction as a percent.

9. $\frac{7}{20}$ **10.** $\frac{15}{80}$ **11.** $\frac{2}{25}$ **12.** $\frac{65}{125}$

_____   _____   _____   _____

Tables and Charts

EXAMPLE Use the table below to find the number of marbles that are blue or red.

$15 + 12 = 27$ *Add the number of blue marbles to the number of red marbles.*

The table shows the colors of all the marbles Arturo owns.

13. How many of Arturo's marbles are white, orange, or blue?

_____

14. How many marbles does Arturo own in all?

_____

15. What percent of Arturo's marbles are white, orange, or blue?

_____

Color	Number of Marbles
Red	15
Blue	12
White	6
Orange	2
Green	10
Purple	5

Reading Start-Up

Vocabulary

Review Words

✔ correlation *(correlación)*
✔ scatter plot *(diagrama de dispersión)*
✔ two-variable data *(data de dos variables)*

Preview Words

categorical data
conditional relative frequency
frequency table
joint relative frequency
marginal relative frequency
quantitative data
relative frequency
two-way frequency table

Visualize Vocabulary

Complete the concept map using the Review Words.

Data that involves two variables describing the same set of items.	→	A group of plotted points that shows the relationship between two variables.	→	The amount of relationship existing between two variables.
_____ _____		_____ _____		_____ _____

Understand Vocabulary

Draw a line to match the Preview Word with its definition.

Preview Words	Definitions
1. frequency table	• A relative frequency that is found by dividing a frequency that is not in the Total row or the Total column by the grand total
2. joint relative frequency	• Data that can be expressed with categories such as male/female, analog/digital, citizen/alien and so on
3. relative frequency	• A table that lists the number of times, or frequency, that each data value occurs
	• For a category in a frequency table, the frequency of the category divided by the total of the frequencies

Active Reading

Two-Panel Flip Chart Create a Two-Panel Flip Chart to help you understand the concepts in this module. Label each flap with the title of one of the lessons in the module. As you study each lesson, write important ideas under the appropriate flap. Include any examples that will help you remember the concepts later when you look back at your notes.

GETTING READY FOR

Descriptive Statistics

Understanding the standards and the vocabulary terms in the standards will help you know exactly what you are expected to learn in this module.

COMMON CORE S.ID.5

Summarize categorical data for two categories in two-way frequency tables. Interpret relative frequencies in the context of the data (including joint, marginal, and conditional relative frequencies). Recognize associations and trends in the data.

Key Vocabulary

frequency table *(tabla de frecuencia)*
A table that lists the number of times, or frequency, that each data value occurs

joint relative frequency *(frecuencia relativa conjunta)*
A relative frequency that is found by dividing a frequency that is not in the Total row or the Total column by the grand total

marginal relative frequency *(frecuencia relativa marginal)*
A relative frequency that is found by dividing a row total or column total by the grand total

conditional relative frequency *(frecuencia relativa condicional)*
A relative frequency that is found by dividing a frequency that is not in the Total row or the Total column by the frequency's row total or column total

Visit **my.hrw.com** to see all **Common Core Standards** unpacked.

○ my.hrw.com

What It Means to You

Two-way frequency tables give you a visual way to organize data categorized by two different variables so that you can more easily identify relationships.

EXAMPLE S.ID.5

The two-way frequency table below shows the numbers of households in a study that own a dog, a cat, or both.

| | **Owns a Cat** | | |
Owns a Dog	**Yes**	**No**	**Total**
Yes	15	24	39
No	18	43	61
Total	33	67	100

Here are a few conclusions you can draw from the table.

- $\frac{39}{100}$, or 39%, of households own a dog; $\frac{33}{100}$, or 33%, own a cat.

- $\frac{15}{100}$, or 15%, own a dog and a cat; $\frac{43}{100}$, or 43%, own neither.

- Of dog owners, $\frac{15}{39}$, or about 38.5%, also own a cat.

- Of cat owners, $\frac{15}{33}$, or about 45.5%, also own a dog.

You can also show the data in a two-way *relative* frequency table by dividing each number by the grand total and expressing the answer as a percent.

joint relative frequency

| | **Owns a Cat** | | |
Owns a Dog	**Yes**	**No**	**Total**
Yes	15%	24%	39%
No	18%	43%	61%
Total	33%	67%	100%

This cell should always be 100% in a two-way relative frequency table.

marginal relative frequencies

Two-Way Frequency Tables

COMMON CORE S.ID.5

Summarize categorical data for two categories in two-way frequency tables. Interpret relative frequencies in the context of the data (including joint, marginal, and conditional relative frequencies). Recognize possible associations and trends in the data.

? ESSENTIAL QUESTION

How can categorical data for two categories be summarized?

EXPLORE ACTIVITY **S.ID.5**

Categorical Data and Frequencies

Data that can be expressed with numerical measurements is **quantitative data**. In this lesson you will examine *qualitative data*, or **categorical data**, which cannot be expressed using numbers. Data describing animal type, model of car, or favorite song are examples of categorical data.

A Circle the categorical data variable. Justify your choice.

temperature   weight   height   color

_____

_____

B Identify whether the given data is categorical or quantitative.

large, medium, small _____

120 ft^2, 130 ft^2, 140 ft^2 _____

C A **frequency table** shows how often each item occurs in a set of categorical data. Use the categorical data listed on the left to complete the frequency table.

Ways Students Get to School
bus car walk car car car bus walk walk walk bus bus car bus bus walk bus car bus car

Way	Frequency
bus	
car	
walk	

REFLECT

1. How did you determine the numbers for each category in the frequency column? _____

_____

2. What must be true about the sum of the frequencies in a frequency table?

_____

Constructing a Two-Way Frequency Table

If a data set has two categorical variables, you can list the frequencies of the paired values in a **two-way frequency table**.

EXAMPLE 1

COMMON CORE S.ID.5

Jenna asked 40 randomly selected students whether they preferred dogs, cats, or other pets. She also recorded the gender of each student. The results are shown in the two-way frequency table below. Each entry is the frequency of students who prefer a certain pet and are a certain gender. For instance, 8 girls prefer dogs as pets. Complete the table.

Animated Math

ⓞ my.hrw.com

STEP 1   Find the row totals.

Girl: $8 + 7 + 1 = 16$

Boy: $10 + 5 + 9 = 24$

Gender	Preferred Pet			
	Dog	Cat	Other	Total
Girl	8	7	1	16
Boy	10	5	9	24
Total	18	12	10	40

STEP 2   Find the column totals.

Dog: $8 + 10 = 18$

Cat: $7 + 5 = 12$

Other: $1 + 9 = 10$

My Notes

STEP 3   Find the grand total.

Sum of row totals = $16 + 24 = 40$

Sum of column totals = $18 + 12 + 10 = 40$

Both sums are equal to the grand total. So grand total = 40

REFLECT

3. Look at the totals for each row. Was Jenna's survey evenly distributed among boys and girls? _____

4. Look at the totals for each column. Which pet is preferred most? Justify your answer. _____

_____

YOUR TURN

5. Complete the two-way frequency table.

Grade	Preferred Fruit			
	Apple	Orange	Banana	Total
9th grade	19	12	23	
10th grade	22	9	15	
Total				

Reading a Two-Way Frequency Table

You can extract information about paired categorical variables by reading a two-way frequency table.

Math On the Spot

⏻ my.hrw.com

EXAMPLE 2   COMMON CORE S.ID.5

One hundred students were surveyed about which beverage they chose at lunch. The results are shown in the two-way frequency table below. Fill in the missing information.

Gender	Lunch Beverage			
	Juice	Milk	Water	Total
Girl	10		17	
Boy	15	24	21	60
Total				

STEP 1   Find the total number of girls.

$100 - 60 = 40$ *Subtract the number of boys from 100.*

There are 40 girls in total.

STEP 2   Find the number of girls who chose milk.

$40 - 10 - 17 = 13$ *Subtract the number of girls who chose juice and the number who chose water from the total number of girls, 40.*

The number of girls who chose milk is 13.

STEP 3   Find the totals for each beverage and check that the grand total equals the total number of students surveyed (100). Complete the table.

Gender	Lunch Beverage			
	Juice	Milk	Water	Total
Girl	10	13	17	40
Boy	15	24	21	60
Total	25	37	38	100

Math Talk
Mathematical Practices

Which lunch beverage is the least preferred? How do you know?

YOUR TURN

6. One hundred students were surveyed about whether they played video games. The results are shown in the two-way frequency table. Complete the table.

Gender	Play Video Games		
	Yes	No	Total
Girl	34	19	53
Boy		9	
Total			

Personal Math Trainer

Online Practice and Help

⏻ my.hrw.com

In Exercises 1 and 2, identify whether the data is categorical or quantitative. (Explore Activity)

1. gold medal, silver medal, bronze medal _____

2. 100 m, 200 m, 400 m _____

3. A theater company asked its members to bring in canned food for a food drive. Use the categorical data to complete the frequency table. (Explore Activity)

Cans Donated to Food Drive
peas corn peas soup corn
corn soup soup corn peas
peas corn soup peas corn
peas corn peas corn soup
corn peas soup corn corn

Cans	Frequency
soup	
peas	
corn	

4. Antonio surveyed 60 of his classmates about their participation in school activities and whether they have a part-time job. The results are shown in the two-way frequency table below. Complete the table. (Example 1)

	Activities				
Have a Job	**Clubs only**	**Sports only**	**Both**	**Neither**	**Total**
Yes	12	13	16	4	
No	3	5	5	2	
Total					

5. Marta surveyed 100 students about whether they like swimming or bicycling. Complete the two-way frequency table. (Example 2)

	Like Swimming		
Like Bicycling	**Yes**	**No**	**Total**
Yes	65	16	81
No		6	
Total			

How many of the students surveyed

like swimming but not bicycling? _____

? ESSENTIAL QUESTION CHECK-IN

6. How can categorical data for two categories be summarized?

_____

12.1 Independent Practice

COMMON CORE S.ID.5

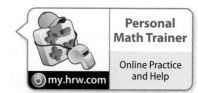

Personal Math Trainer

Online Practice and Help

my.hrw.com

Identify whether the given data is categorical or quantitative.

7. 75°, 79°, 82° _____

8. juice, soda, water _____

Two hundred students were asked to name their favorite science class. The results are shown in the two-way frequency table. Use the table for Exercises 9 and 10.

Gender	Favorite Science Class			
	Biology	Chemistry	Physics	Total
Girl	42	39	23	104
Boy		45	32	
Total				

9. How many boys were surveyed? Explain how you found your answer.

_____

_____

10. Complete the table. How many more girls than boys chose Biology as their favorite science class? Explain how you found your answer.

_____

_____

_____

The results of a survey of 150 students about whether they own an electronic tablet or a laptop are shown in the two-way frequency table. Use the table for Exercises 11 and 12.

Gender	Device				
	Electronic tablet	Laptop	Both	Neither	Total
Girl	15	54		9	88
Boy		35	8	5	
Total					

11. Complete the table. Do the surveyed students own more laptops or more

electronic tablets? _____

12. Which group had more people answer the survey: boys, or students who own an electronic tablet only? Explain.

_____

_____

13. **Critical Thinking** Teresa surveyed 100 students about whether they like pop music or country music. Out of the 100 students surveyed, 42 like pop only, 34 like country only, 15 like both pop and country, and 9 do not like either pop or country. Use this data to complete the two-way frequency table below.

Like Country	Like Pop		
	Yes	No	Total
Yes			
No			
Total			

14. The table shows the results of a survey about students' preferred frozen yogurt flavor. Complete the table and use it to complete the statement below.

Gender	Preferred Flavor			
	Vanilla	Chocolate	Strawberry	Total
Girl		15	18	45
Boy	17	25		
Total				100

Students preferred _____ the most and _____ the least.

Work Area

15. **Multiple Representations** Use the data in Exercise 13 to complete the Venn diagram below.

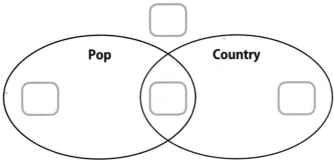

16. **Justify Reasoning** Charles surveyed 100 boys about their favorite color. Of the 100 boys surveyed, 44 preferred blue, 25 preferred green, and 31 preferred red. Can you make a two-way frequency table from the survey results? Explain your reasoning.

_____

_____

_____

COMMON
CORE S.ID.5

Summarize categorical data for two categories in two-way frequency tables. Interpret relative frequencies in the context of the data (including joint, marginal, and conditional relative frequencies). Recognize possible associations and trends in the data.

? ESSENTIAL QUESTION

How can you recognize possible associations and trends between two categories of categorical data?

EXPLORE ACTIVITY COMMON CORE S.ID.5

Relative Frequencies

To show what portion of a data set each category in a frequency table makes up, you can convert the data to *relative frequencies*. The **relative frequency** of a category is the frequency of the category divided by the total of all the frequencies.

The frequency table below shows the results of a survey Kenesha took at school. She asked 80 randomly selected students whether they preferred basketball, football, or soccer.

Preferred Sport	Basketball	Football	Soccer	Total
Frequency	20	32	28	80

A Use the frequencies to make a relative frequency table that uses decimals. Divide each number in the frequency table by the total to obtain the corresponding relative frequency as a decimal. Record the results in the table below.

Preferred Sport	Basketball	Football	Soccer	Total
Relative Frequency	$\frac{20}{80} = 0.25$			

B Make a relative frequency table that uses percents.

Preferred Sport	Basketball	Football	Soccer	Total
Relative Frequency	25%			

REFLECT

1. Explain what the numerator and denominator of the ratio $\frac{20}{80}$ refer to in part A.

_____

_____

_____

2. What types of numbers can you use to write relative frequencies?

_____

Math On the Spot
my.hrw.com

Two-Way Relative Frequency Tables

You can obtain the following relative frequencies from a two-way frequency table:

- A **marginal relative frequency** is found by dividing a row total or a column total by the grand total. It tells what portion of the total has a specified characteristic.
- A **joint relative frequency** is found by dividing a frequency that is not in the Total row or the Total column by the grand total. It tells what portion of the total has both of two specified characteristics.

EXAMPLE 1

COMMON CORE S.ID.5

For her survey about sports preferences, Kenesha also recorded the gender of each student. The results are shown in the two-way frequency table below. Create a two-way relative frequency table for Kenesha's data.

My Notes

Gender	Preferred Sport			
	Basketball	Football	Soccer	Total
Girl	6	12	18	36
Boy	14	20	10	44
Total	20	32	28	80

To find the joint relative frequencies and marginal relative frequencies, divide each number in the two-way frequency table by the grand total. Write the quotients as decimals.

joint relative frequency:
7.5% of students surveyed are girls who prefer basketball.

marginal relative frequency:
45% of students surveyed are girls.

Gender	Preferred Sport			
	Basketball	Football	Soccer	Total
Girl	$\frac{6}{80} = 0.075$	$\frac{12}{80} = 0.15$	$\frac{18}{80} = 0.225$	$\frac{36}{80} = 0.45$
Boy	$\frac{14}{80} = 0.175$	$\frac{20}{80} = 0.25$	$\frac{10}{80} = 0.125$	$\frac{44}{80} = 0.55$
Total	$\frac{20}{80} = 0.25$	$\frac{32}{80} = 0.4$	$\frac{28}{80} = 0.35$	$\frac{80}{80} = 1$

To check your work, add the joint relative frequencies in each row or column. Verify that the sum equals the row or column's marginal relative frequency.

Girl row:	$0.075 + 0.15 + 0.225 = 0.45$
Boy row:	$0.175 + 0.25 + 0.125 = 0.55$
Basketball column:	$0.075 + 0.175 = 0.25$
Football column:	$0.15 + 0.25 = 0.4$
Soccer column:	$0.225 + 0.125 = 0.35$

3. Find the joint relative frequency of students surveyed who like jogging and like aerobics. Express your answer as a decimal and as a percent.

_____

	Like Aerobics		
Like Jogging	**Yes**	**No**	**Total**
Yes	7	14	21
No	12	7	19
Total	19	21	40

Personal Math Trainer
Online Practice and Help
⏱ my.hrw.com

Conditional Relative Frequencies

Conditional relative frequency describes what portion of a group with a given characteristic also has another specified characteristic. A conditional relative frequency is found by dividing a frequency that is not in the Total row or the Total column by the total for that row or column.

Math On the Spot
⏱ my.hrw.com

EXAMPLE 2　　　　　　　　　　COMMON CORE　S.ID.5

From Kenesha's two-way frequency table about preferred sports, you know that 36 students surveyed were girls and 28 students surveyed prefer soccer. You also know that 18 students surveyed are girls who prefer soccer. Use this information to find each conditional relative frequency.

A Find the conditional relative frequency that a student surveyed prefers soccer, given that the student is a girl. Express your answer as a decimal and as a percent.

$\frac{18}{36} = 0.5$, or 50%　　*Divide the number of girls who prefer soccer by the total number of girls.*

The conditional relative frequency is 0.5, or 50%. This means that 50% of girls surveyed prefer soccer.

B Find the conditional relative frequency that a student surveyed is a girl, given that the student prefers soccer. Express your answer as a decimal and as a percent.

$\frac{18}{28} \approx 0.643$, or about 64.3%　　*Divide the number of girls who prefer soccer by the number of students who prefer soccer.*

The conditional relative frequency is about 0.643, or 64.3%. This means that about 64.3% of students who prefer soccer are girls.

REFLECT

4. **Communicate Mathematical Ideas** In part A, why was the number of girls who prefer soccer not divided by 80, the grand total?

_____

_____

_____

5. From Kenesha's table, you know that 44 students surveyed were boys, 20 students preferred basketball, and 14 students were boys who prefer basketball. Find the conditional relative frequency that a student surveyed is a boy, given that the student prefers basketball. Express your answer as a decimal and as a percent. _____

Finding Possible Associations

Two-way frequency tables can be analyzed to locate possible associations or patterns in the data.

EXAMPLE 3   COMMON CORE S.ID.5

Kenesha is interested in the question, "Does gender influence what type of sport people prefer?" If there is no influence, then the distribution of gender within each sport preference will roughly equal the distribution of gender within the whole group. Analyze the results of Kenesha's survey from Example 1. Determine which sport each gender is more likely to prefer.

A Analyze the data about the girls that were surveyed.

STEP 1 Identify the percent of all students surveyed who are girls.

$$\frac{36}{80} = 0.45 = 45\%$$

STEP 2 Determine each conditional relative frequency.

Basketball: Of the 20 students who prefer basketball, 6 are girls. Percent who are girls, given a preference for basketball:

$$\frac{6}{20} = 0.3 = 30\%$$

Football: Of the 32 students who prefer football, 12 are girls. Percent who are girls, given a preference for football:

$$\frac{12}{32} = 0.375 = 37.5\%$$

Soccer: Of the 28 students who prefer soccer, 18 are girls. Percent who are girls, given a preference for soccer:

$$\frac{18}{28} \approx 0.643 = 64.3\%$$

My Notes

STEP 3 Interpret the results by comparing each conditional relative frequency to the percent of all students surveyed who are girls.

Basketball: 30% is less than 45%
Girls are less likely than boys to prefer basketball.

Football: 37.5% is less than 45%
Girls are less likely than boys to prefer football.

Soccer: 64.3% is greater than 45%
Girls are more likely than boys to prefer soccer.

B Analyze the data about boys that were surveyed.

STEP 1 Identify the percent of all students surveyed who are boys. Subtract the percent for girls from 100%.

$$100\% - 45\% = 55\%$$

STEP 2 Determine each conditional relative frequency for boys. Subtract each percent for girls from 100%.

Basketball: 100% − 30% = **70%**
70% of students who prefer basketball are boys.

Football: 100% − 37.5% = **62.5%**
62.5% of students who prefer football are boys.

Soccer: 100% − 64.3% = **35.7%**
35.7% of students who prefer soccer are boys.

STEP 3 Interpret the results by comparing each conditional relative frequency to the percent of all students surveyed who are boys.

Basketball: 70% is more than 55%
Boys are more likely than girls to prefer basketball.

Football: 62.5% is more than 55%
Boys are more likely than girls to prefer football.

Soccer: 35.7% is less than 55%
Boys are less likely than girls to prefer soccer.

Math Talk
Mathematical Practices

If sport preference were completely uninfluenced by gender, about how many girls would prefer each sport? Explain.

YOUR TURN

6. Steven asks 40 students whether they regularly eat breakfast. Of the 25 students who regularly eat breakfast, 9 are boys. Of the 15 who do not regularly eat breakfast, 10 are boys. Which gender is more likely to eat breakfast?

_____

_____

Personal Math Trainer

Online Practice and Help

my.hrw.com

The results of a survey of 40 students and the foreign language they are studying are shown in the two-way frequency table. Use the data for Exercises 1 and 2.

Gender	Foreign Language			
	Chinese	French	Spanish	Total
Girl	2	8	12	22
Boy	4	1	13	18
Total	6	9	25	40

1. Complete the two-way relative frequency table below using decimals. (Explore Activity and Example 1)

Gender	Foreign Language			
	Chinese	French	Spanish	Total
Girl	$\frac{2}{40} = 0.05$	$\frac{8}{40} =$		
Boy				$\frac{18}{40} = 0.45$
Total		$\frac{9}{40} = 0.225$		

2. Give each conditional relative frequency as a percent. (Example 2)

   a. The conditional relative frequency that a student surveyed is studying Chinese, given that the student is a boy:

   $$\frac{\text{number of boys studying Chinese}}{\text{total number of boys surveyed}} = \frac{4}{18} \approx \boxed{} \underline{}$$

   b. The conditional relative frequency that a student surveyed is a girl, given

   that the student is studying Spanish: _____

3. Determine which gender is more likely to study each foreign language. (Example 3)

   _____

   _____

4. How can you recognize possible associations and trends between two categories in categorical data?

   _____

   _____

   _____

12.2 Independent Practice

 S.ID.5

Personal Math Trainer

my.hrw.com Online Practice and Help

Jasmine surveyed 80 students about their after-school activities. She recorded her results in the two-way frequency table below. Use the data for Exercises 5–12.

Gender	Activity			
	Sports	Clubs	Other	Total
Girl	9	21	8	38
Boy	22	8	12	42
Total	31	29	20	80

5. Create a two-way relative frequency table for the data using decimals.

Gender	Activity			
	Sports	Clubs	Other	Total
Girl				
Boy				
Total				

6. Find the relative frequency, expressed as a percent, of surveyed students who have clubs as their activity.

_____

7. Is the relative frequency of surveyed girls that have sports as their activity a joint relative frequency or a marginal relative frequency? Explain.

_____

_____

_____

_____

_____

8. Find the joint relative frequency of surveyed students who are boys and have clubs as their activity. _____

9. Find the marginal relative frequency of surveyed students who have sports as their activity. _____

10. What If? Jasmine surveys 10 more students. Of these, 6 are boys and all 6 boys have sports as their activity. None of the new girls have sports as their activity. How does this new data change the marginal relative frequency of surveyed students who have sports as their activity?

_____

11. Find the conditional relative frequency that a surveyed student has clubs as their activity, given that the student is a girl. Express your answer as a decimal and a percent. Explain how you found your answer.

_____

_____

_____

12. Find the conditional relative frequency that a surveyed student is a boy, given that the student has an activity other than sports or clubs. Express your answer as a decimal and a percent. Explain how you found your answer.

_____

_____

_____

In some states, a driver of a vehicle may not use a handheld cell phone while driving. In one state with this law, 250 randomly selected drivers were surveyed to determine the association between drivers who know the law and drivers who obey the law. The results are shown in the table below.

Obeys Law	Knows Law		
	Yes	No	Total
Yes	160	45	205
No	25	20	45
Total	185	65	250

13. Give each conditional relative frequency as a percent.

a. The conditional relative frequency that a driver surveyed obeys the handheld cell phone law, given that the driver knows the law:

_____

b. The conditional relative frequency that a driver surveyed knows the handheld cell phone law, given that the driver obeys the law:

_____

c. The conditional relative frequency that a driver surveyed obeys the law, given that the driver does not know the law:

_____

14. Is there any association between the drivers who know the handheld cell phone law and drivers who obey the handheld cell phone law? Explain.

_____

_____

H.O.T. **FOCUS ON HIGHER ORDER THINKING**

Work Area

15. **Analyze Relationships** Explain the difference between a relative frequency and a conditional relative frequency in a two-way frequency table.

_____

_____

_____

16. **Explain the Error** For the data about handheld cell phone laws above, Chelsea found the conditional frequency that a driver surveyed does not know the law, given that the driver obeys the law, by dividing 45 by 250. Explain Chelsea's error.

_____

_____

Ready to Go On?

Personal Math Trainer

my.hrw.com

Online Practice and Help

12.1 Two-Way Frequency Tables

The results of a survey of 150 students about the type of movie they prefer are shown in the two-way frequency table. Use the table for Exercises 1 and 2.

1. Complete the table. How many boys were surveyed? _____

2. How many girls like science fiction movies? _____

Gender	Preferred Movie Type			
	Comedy	Drama	Science fiction	Total
Girl	24	33		72
Boy		12	36	
Total				

12.2 Relative Frequency

Use the data in the two-way frequency table above for Exercises 3 and 4.

3. Complete the two-way relative frequency table for the data using decimals.

4. Find the conditional relative frequency that a student surveyed is a boy, given that the student prefers comedy.

_____

Gender	Preferred Movie Type			
	Comedy	Drama	Science fiction	Total
Girl				
Boy				
Total				

5. Use the data to identify which gender is more likely to prefer comedy. Explain.

_____

_____

_____

ESSENTIAL QUESTION

6. How can you recognize possible associations between two categories of categorical data?

_____

_____

_____

MODULE 12
MIXED REVIEW

Assessment Readiness

Personal Math Trainer

Online Practice and Help

my.hrw.com

1. In a survey, 150 randomly selected students were asked whether they are right- or left-handed. The two-way frequency table shows the results. Look at each number below. Does the number belong in the cell that matches the letter?

   Select Yes or No for A–C.

   A. 135 ⃝ Yes ⃝ No
   B. 6 ⃝ Yes ⃝ No
   C. 73 ⃝ Yes ⃝ No

	Hand used		
Gender	**Right**	**Left**	**Total**
Boy	78	9	87
Girl	57	B	C
Total	A	15	150

2. A two-way relative frequency table for the data in Item 1 has been partially completed.

   Choose True or False for each statement.

   A. The joint relative frequency of girls who use their right hands is 0.38.

   ⃝ True ⃝ False

   B. The marginal relative frequency of girls in the survey is 0.5.

   ⃝ True ⃝ False

	Hand used		
Gender	**Right**	**Left**	**Total**
Boy	0.52	0.06	
Girl			
Total			1

3. Use the data from Item 1. Based on the survey, which gender is more likely to be left-handed? Justify your answer.

4. Fatima earns $8 per hour for the first 40 hours she works in a week and $12 per hour for each additional hour she works. Fatima always puts 10% of her earnings into her savings account. Write an expression for the amount of money Fatima will put in her savings account for a week in which she works h hours, where $h > 40$. Simplify the expression, and tell which properties you used.

Data Displays

ESSENTIAL QUESTION

How can data sets be displayed and compared, and what statistics can be gathered using the display?

Real-World Video

In baseball, there are many options for how a team executes a given play. The use of statistics for in-game decision making sometimes reveals surprising strategies that run counter to the common wisdom.

my.hrw.com

GO DIGITAL
my.hrw.com

my.hrw.com

Go digital with your write-in student edition, accessible on any device.

Math On the Spot

Scan with your smart phone to jump directly to the online edition, video tutor, and more.

Animated Math

Interactively explore key concepts to see how math works.

Personal Math Trainer

Get immediate feedback and help as you work through practice sets.

© Houghton Mifflin Harcourt Publishing Company • Image Credits: © Duane Osborn/Somos Images/Corbis

Are YOU Ready?

Complete these exercises to review skills you will need for this module.

Solve Proportions

EXAMPLE

$$\frac{3}{4} = \frac{x}{12}$$

$4x = 36$ *Cross-multiply.*

$x = 9$ *Solve for the unknown.*

Solve each proportion.

1. $\frac{15}{9} = \frac{3}{x}$

2. $\frac{10}{20} = \frac{x}{100}$

3. $\frac{250}{1500} = \frac{x}{100}$

4. $\frac{32}{10} = \frac{4}{x}$

5. $\frac{3}{4} = \frac{x}{200}$

6. $\frac{15}{18} = \frac{x}{42}$

Compare and Order Real Numbers

EXAMPLE Compare. Write $<$, $>$, or $=$.

20 ◯ 13   *20 is greater than 13.*

Compare. Write $<$, $>$, or $=$.

7. -18 ◯ -17

8. $\frac{2}{3}$ ◯ $\frac{1}{2}$

9. 0.75 ◯ $\frac{9}{12}$

10. 0.16 ◯ 0.8

Fractions, Decimals, and Percents

EXAMPLE Write the equivalent decimal.

$\frac{1}{2} = 0.5$ *Divide the numerator by the denominator.*

$45\% = 0.45$ *Write the percent over 100 and convert to a decimal.*

Write the equivalent percent.

$\frac{1}{4} = 0.25 \times 100 = 25\%$ *Convert to a decimal and then multiply by 100.*

Write the equivalent decimal.

11. $\frac{3}{5} =$ _____

12. $8\% =$ _____

13. $\frac{3}{4} =$ _____

Write the equivalent percent.

14. $0.2 =$ _____

15. $\frac{1}{10} =$ _____

16. $0.36 =$ _____

Reading Start-Up

Visualize Vocabulary

Use the Review Words to complete the chart.

Word	Definition	Example
	The number of times a data value occurs in a set of data	Henry's goals in each game: 0, 1, 1, 3, 2, 0, 1, 0, 2, 1, 1 Goals | Frequency 0 | 3 1 | 5 2 | 2 3 | 1
	Numerical measurements gathered from a survey or experiment	Quiz grades: 78, 82, 85, 90, 88, 79
	Data that is qualitative in nature	"liberal," "moderate," or "conservative"

Understand Vocabulary

To become familiar with some of the vocabulary terms in the module, consider the following. You may refer to the module, the glossary, or a dictionary.

1. In a _____ distribution, a vertical line can be drawn and the result is a graph divided in two parts that are approximate mirror images of each other.

2. A _____ is a bar graph used to display the frequency of data divided into equal intervals.

3. A _____ is a data representation that uses a number line and x's or dots to show frequency. A _____ displays a five-number summary of a data set.

Active Reading

Layered Book Before beginning the module, create a Layered Book to help you organize what you learn. Write a vocabulary term or new concept on each page as you proceed. Under each tab, write the definition of the term and an example of the term or concept. See how the concepts build on one another.

GETTING READY FOR
Data Displays
Understanding the standards and the vocabulary terms in the standards will help you know exactly what you are expected to learn in this module.

COMMON CORE **S.ID.2**

Use statistics appropriate to the shape of the data distribution to compare center (median, mean) and spread (interquartile range, standard deviation) of two or more different data sets.

Key Vocabulary

mean *(media)*
The average of the data values.

median *(mediana)*
The middle value when values are listed in numerical order.

interquartile range *(rango intercuartil)*
A measure of the spread of a data set, obtained by subtracting the first quartile from the third quartile.

What It Means to You

You can use the mean and median of data sets to compare the centers of the data sets. You can use the range, interquartile range, or standard deviation to compare the spreads of the data sets.

EXAMPLE S.ID.2

The lengths in feet of the alligators at a zoo are 9, 7, 12, 6, and 10. The lengths in feet of the crocodiles at the zoo are 13, 10, 8, 19, 18, and 16.

What is the difference between the mean length of the crocodiles and the mean length of the alligators?

$$\text{Alligators: } \frac{9 + 7 + 12 + 6 + 10}{5} = 8.8$$

$$\text{Crocodiles: } \frac{13 + 10 + 8 + 19 + 18 + 16}{6} = 14$$

$$14 - 8.8 = 5.2 \text{ ft}$$

COMMON CORE **S.ID.1**

Represent data with plots on the real number line (dot plots, histograms, and box plots).

Key Vocabulary

dot plot *(diagrama de puntos)*
A data representation that uses a number line and x's or dots to show frequency.

What It Means to You

You can represent data sets using various models and use those models to interpret the information.

EXAMPLE S.ID.1

Class Scores on First Test (top) and Second Test (bottom)

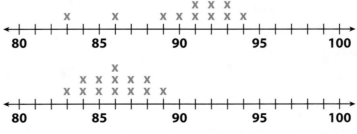

How do the medians of the two sets of test scores compare?

Look at each dot plot and locate the median. The median for the first test (92) is higher than the median for the second test (86).

LESSON 13.1 Measures of Center and Spread

COMMON CORE **S.ID.2**
Use statistics appropriate to the shape of the data distribution to compare center (median, mean) and spread (interquartile range, standard deviation) of two or more different data sets.

ESSENTIAL QUESTION

How can you describe and compare data sets?

EXPLORE ACTIVITY   COMMON CORE **S.ID.2**

Exploring Data Sets

Caleb and Kim have bowled three games. Their scores are shown in the chart below.

Name	Game 1	Game 2	Game 3	Average score
Caleb	151	153	146	
Kim	122	139	189	

A Complete the table by finding each player's average score. How do the average scores compare?

_____

B Whose game is more consistent? Explain why.

_____

_____

C Suppose that in a fourth game, Caleb scores 150 and Kim scores 175. How would that affect your conclusions about the average and consistency of their scores?

_____

_____

REFLECT

1. Draw Conclusions Do you think the average is an accurate representation of the three games that Caleb and Kim played? Why or why not?

_____

_____

_____

_____

Measures of Center: Mean and Median

Two commonly used *measures of center* for a set of numerical data are the mean and median. Measures of center represent a central or typical value of a data set.

- The **mean** is the sum of the values in the set divided by the number of values in the set.
- The **median** is the middle value in a set when the values are arranged in numerical order.

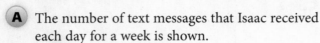

EXAMPLE 1

COMMON CORE S.ID.2

Find the mean and the median for each set of values.

A The number of text messages that Isaac received each day for a week is shown.

$$47, 49, 54, 50, 48, 47, 55$$

Mean:

$47 + 49 + 54 + 50 + 48 + 47 + 55 = 350$ Find the sum.

$$\frac{350}{7} = 50$$ Divide the sum by the number of data values.

Median:

$$47, 47, 48, \textbf{49}, 50, 54, 55$$ Order values, then find the middle value.

Mean: 50 text messages a day;
Median: 49 text messages a day

B The amount of money Elise earns in tips per day for six days is listed below.

$$\$75, \$97, \$360, \$84, \$119, \$100$$

Mean:

$75 + 97 + 360 + 84 + 119 + 100 = 835$ Find the sum of the data values.

$$\frac{835}{6} = 139.1\overline{66}$$ Divide the sum by the number of data values.

$$\approx \$139.17$$

Median:

$$75, 84, \textbf{97}, \textbf{100}, 119, 360$$ Order values, then find the mean of the two middle numbers.

$$\frac{97 + 100}{2} = 98.5$$

Mean: $139.17 a day; Median: $98.50 a day

Math Talk

Mathematical Practices

For part B, which measure of center better describes Elise's tips? Explain.

YOUR TURN

2. Niles scored 70, 74, 72, 71, 73, and 96 on his six geography tests. Find the mean and median of his scores.

_____

Measures of Spread: Range and IQR

Measures of spread describe how data values are spread out from the center. Two commonly used *measures of spread* for a set of numerical data are the range and interquartile range.

- The **range** is the difference between the greatest and the least data values.
- **Quartiles** are values that divide a data set into four equal parts. The **first quartile (Q_1)** is the median of the lower half of the set, the second quartile is the median of the whole set, and the **third quartile (Q_3)** is the median of the upper half of the set.
- The **interquartile range (IQR)** of a data set is the difference between the third and first quartiles. It represents the range of the middle half of the data.

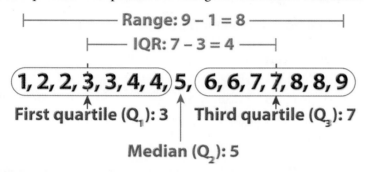

Range: 9 − 1 = 8

IQR: 7 − 3 = 4

1, 2, 2, 3, 3, 4, 4, 5, 6, 6, 7, 7, 8, 8, 9

First quartile (Q_1): 3   Third quartile (Q_3): 7

Median (Q_2): 5

EXAMPLE 2

COMMON CORE S.ID.2

The April high temperatures for five years in Boston are 77 °F, 86 °F, 84 °F, 93 °F, and 90 °F. Find the median, range, and IQR for the set.

Find the median.

77, 84, 86, 90, 93   *Order the values and identify the middle value.*

The median is 86.

Find the range.

Range = 93 − 77 = 16

Find the interquartile range. When finding the quartiles, do not include the median as part of either the lower half or the upper half of the data.

This is the lower half.

77, 84, 86, 90, 93

This is the median.

This is the upper half.

$Q_1 = \frac{77 + 84}{2} = 80.5$ and $Q_3 = \frac{90 + 93}{2} = 91.5$

Find the difference between Q_3 and Q_1: IQR = 91.5 − 80.5 = 11

Math Talk
Mathematical Practices
Why is the IQR less than the range?

YOUR TURN

3. Find the median, range, and interquartile range for this data set.

   21, 31, 26, 24, 28, 26 _____

Measures of Spread: Standard Deviation

Standard deviation, another measure of spread, represents the average of the distances between individual data values and the mean.

The formula for finding the standard deviation of the data set $x_1, x_2, \ldots, x_n$ is:

$$\text{standard deviation} = \sqrt{\frac{(x_1 - \bar{x})^2 + (x_2 - \bar{x})^2 + \ldots + (x_n - \bar{x})^2}{n}}$$

where $\bar{x}$ is the mean of the set of data, and n is the number of data values.

EXAMPLE 3   COMMON CORE   S.ID.2

Calculate the standard deviation for the temperature data from Example 2.

The April high temperatures were 77, 86, 84, 93, 90.

STEP 1   Find the mean.   Mean $= \dfrac{77 + 86 + 84 + 93 + 90}{5} = \dfrac{430}{5} = 86$

STEP 2   Complete the table.

Data value, x	Deviation from mean, $x - \bar{x}$	Squared deviation, $(x - \bar{x})^2$
77	$77 - 86 = -9$	$(-9)^2 = 81$
86	$86 - 86 = 0$	$0^2 = 0$
84	$84 - 86 = -2$	$(-2)^2 = 4$
93	$93 - 86 = 7$	$7^2 = 49$
90	$90 - 86 = 4$	$4^2 = 16$

STEP 3   Find the mean of the squared deviations.

Mean $= \dfrac{81 + 0 + 4 + 49 + 16}{5} = \dfrac{150}{5} = 30$

STEP 4   Take the square root of the mean of the squared deviations. Use a calculator, and round to the nearest tenth.

Square root of mean $= \sqrt{30} \approx 5.5$

The standard deviation is approximately 5.5.

Math Talk

Mathematical Practices

In terms of the data values used, what makes calculating the standard deviation different from calculating the range?

Personal Math Trainer

Online Practice and Help

⏱ my.hrw.com

YOUR TURN

4. Find the standard deviation to the nearest tenth for a data set with the following values: 122, 139, 189.

_____

© Houghton Mifflin Harcourt Publishing Company

Comparing Data Sets

Numbers that characterize a data set, such as measures of center and spread, are called **statistics**. They are useful when comparing large sets of data.

Math On the Spot
⏻ my.hrw.com

EXAMPLE 4 COMMON CORE S.ID.2

The tables list the average ages of players on 15 teams randomly selected from the 2010 teams in the National Football League (NFL) and Major League Baseball (MLB). Calculate the mean, median, interquartile range, and standard deviation for each data set, and describe how the average ages of NFL players compare to those of MLB players.

NFL Players' Average Ages, by Team
25.8, 26.0, 26.3, 25.7, 25.1, 25.2, 26.1, 26.4, 25.9, 26.6, 26.3, 26.2, 26.8, 25.6, 25.7

MLB Players' Average Ages, by Team
28.5, 29.0, 28.0, 27.8, 29.5, 29.1, 26.9, 28.9, 28.6, 28.7, 26.9, 30.5, 28.7, 28.9, 29.3

STEP 1 On a graphing calculator, enter the two sets of data into two lists, L_1 and L_2.

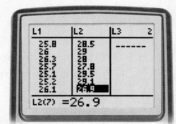

STEP 2 Use the "1-Var Stats" feature to find statistics for the data in lists L_1 and L_2. Your calculator may use the following notations:

Mean: $\bar{x}$

Standard deviation: σx

Scroll down to see the median (Med), Q1, and Q3. Calculate the interquartile range by subtracting Q_1 from Q_3.

	Mean	Median	IQR $(Q_3 - Q_1)$	Standard Deviation
NFL	25.98	26.00	0.60	0.46
MLB	28.62	28.70	1.10	0.91

STEP 3 Compare the corresponding statistics for the NFL data and the MLB data. The mean and median are lower for the NFL than for the MLB; so we can conclude that NFL players tend to be younger than MLB players.

The IQR and standard deviation are smaller for the NFL; so we know that the ages of NFL players are closer together than those of MLB players.

YOUR TURN

5. a. The average member ages for every gym in Newman County are: 21, 23, 28, 28, 31, 32, 32, 35, 37, 39, 41, 41, 44, 45. Calculate the mean, median, interquartile range, and standard deviation for the data set.

_____

b. The following statistics describe the average member ages at gyms in Oldport County: mean = 39, median = 39, IQR = 9, and standard deviation = 6.2. Describe how the ages of gym members in Oldport County compare to those of gym members in Newman County.

_____

_____

_____

Guided Practice

There are 28, 30, 29, 26, 31, and 30 students in a school's six Algebra 1 classes. There are 34, 31, 39, 31, 35, and 34 students in the school's six Spanish classes. (Explore Activity and Examples 1–2)

1. Find the mean, median, range and interquartile range for the number of students in an Algebra 1 class.

mean: _____   median: _____

range: _____   IQR: _____

2. Find the standard deviation to the nearest tenth for the number of students in an Algebra 1 class, and find the standard deviation to the nearest tenth for the number of students in a Spanish class. (Example 3)

Algebra class: _____   Spanish class: _____

3. Draw a conclusion about the typical size of an Algebra 1 class and the typical size of a Spanish class. (Example 4)

_____

_____

? ESSENTIAL QUESTION CHECK-IN

4. How can you describe and compare data sets?

_____

_____

13.1 Independent Practice

Personal
Math Trainer

Online Practice
and Help

my.hrw.com

COMMON CORE S.ID.2

Find the mean, median, and range of each data set.

5. 75, 63, 89, 91

_____

6. 19, 25, 31, 19, 34, 22, 31, 34

_____

Find the mean, median, range, and interquartile range for this data set.

13, 14, 18, 13, 12, 17, 15, 12, 13,
19, 11, 14, 14, 18, 22, 23

7. Mean: _____

8. Median: _____

9. Range: _____

10. Interquartile range: _____

The numbers of members in six yoga clubs are: 80, 74, 77, 71, 75, 91. Use this data set for questions 11–13.

11. Explain the steps for finding the standard deviation of the set of membership numbers.

_____

_____

_____

_____

_____

_____

_____

12. Find the standard deviation of the number

of members to the nearest tenth. _____

13. **Explain the Error** Suppose a person in the club with 91 members transfers to the club with 71 members. A student claims that the measures of center and the measures of spread will all change. Correct the student's error.

_____

_____

_____

_____

_____

14. **Represent Real-World Problems** Lamont's bowling scores were 153, 145, 148, and 166 in four games. For each question, choose the mean, median, or range, and give its value.

a. Which measure gives Lamont's average

score? _____

b. Which measure should Lamont use to convince his parents that he's skilled enough to join a bowling league? Explain.

_____

_____

_____

_____

c. Lamont bowls one more game. Give an example of a score that would convince Lamont to use a different measure of center to persuade his parents. Explain.

_____

_____

_____

15. **Represent Real-World Problems** The table lists the heights (in centimeters) of 8 males and 8 females on the U.S. Olympic swim team, all randomly selected from the team that participated in the 2008 Olympic Games in Beijing, China.

Heights of Olympic male swimmers	196	188	196	185	203	183	183	196
Heights of Olympic female swimmers	173	170	178	175	173	180	180	175

a. Use a graphing calculator to complete the table below.

	Center		Spread	
	Mean	**Median**	**IQR** $(Q_3 - Q_1)$	**Standard deviation**
Olympic male swimmers				
Olympic female swimmers				

b. What can you conclude about the heights of Olympic male swimmers and Olympic female swimmers?

_____

_____

_____

16. **What If?** If all the values in a set are increased by 10, does the range also increase by 10? Explain.

_____

_____

17. **Communicate Mathematical Ideas** Jorge has a data set with the following values: 92, 80, 88, 95, and x. If the median value for this set is 88, what must be true about x? Explain.

_____

_____

18. **Critical Thinking** If the value for the median of a set is not found in the data set, what must be true about the data set? Explain.

_____

_____

_____

COMMON CORE S.ID.3

Interpret differences in shape, center, and spread in the context of the data sets, accounting for possible effects of extreme data points (outliers). *Also S.ID.1, S.ID.2*

? ESSENTIAL QUESTION Which statistics are most affected by outliers, and what shapes can data distributions have?

Using Dot Plots to Display Data

A **dot plot** is a data representation that uses a number line and x's, dots, or other symbols to show frequency. Dot plots are sometimes called line plots.

EXAMPLE 1 COMMON CORE S.ID.1

Math On the Spot
⏻ my.hrw.com

Twelve employees at a small company make the following annual salaries (in thousands of dollars):

25, 30, 35, 35, 35, 40, 40, 40, 45, 45, 50, 60

Choose an appropriate scale for the number line. Create a dot plot of the data by putting an X above the number line for each time that value appears in the data set.

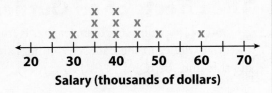

Salary (thousands of dollars)

REFLECT

1. Recall that quantitative data can be expressed as a numerical measurement. Categorical, qualitative data is expressed in categories, such as attributes or preferences. Is it appropriate to use a dot plot for displaying quantitative data, qualitative data, or both? Explain.

_____

_____

2. Analyze Relationships How can you use a dot plot to find the median value? What is the median salary at the company?

_____

_____

_____

3. When you examine the dot plot above, which data value appears most unlike the other values? Explain.

_____

_____

YOUR TURN

4. A cafeteria offers items at seven different prices. John counted how many items were offered at each price one week. Make a dot plot of the data.

Price ($)	1.50	2.00	2.50	3.00	3.50	4.00	4.50
Items	3	3	5	8	6	5	3

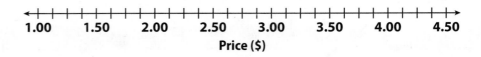

1.00   1.50   2.00   2.50   3.00   3.50   4.00   4.50

Price ($)

EXPLORE ACTIVITY   **COMMON CORE**   S.ID.1

The Effects of an Outlier in a Data Set

An **outlier** is a value in a data set that is much greater or much less than most of the other values in the data set. Outliers are determined using the first or third quartile and the IQR.

How to Identify an Outlier
A data value x is an outlier if $x < Q_1 - 1.5(IQR)$ or if $x > Q_3 + 1.5(IQR)$.

Suppose the list of salaries in Example 1 is expanded to include the owner's salary, which is $150,000. Now the list of salaries is: 25, 30, 35, 35, 35, 40, 40, 40, 45, 45, 50, 60, 150.

A Create a dot plot for the revised data set. Choose an appropriate scale for the number line.

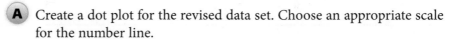

20 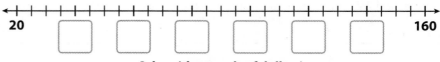 160

Salary (thousands of dollars)

B Is the owner's salary an outlier? Determine if $150 > Q_3 + (1.5)IQR$.

$Q_3 =$ _____ $Q_1 =$ _____

$IQR =$ _____

$Q_3 + (1.5)IQR =$ _____

Is 150 an outlier? _____

EXPLORE ACTIVITY *(cont'd)*

C Complete the table to see how the owner's salary changes the data set. Use a calculator and round to the nearest hundredth, if necessary.

	Mean	Median	Range	IQR	Standard deviation
Set without 150					
Set with 150					

D Complete each sentence by stating whether the statistic increased, decreased, or stayed the same when the data value 150 was added to the original data set. If the statistic increased or decreased, say by what amount.

The mean _____.

The median _____.

The range _____.

The IQR _____.

The standard deviation _____.

Math Talk

Mathematical Practices

How does an outlier affect measures of center?

REFLECT

5. Critical Thinking Explain why the median was unaffected by the outlier 150.

_____

_____

_____

_____

6. Is the value 60 an outlier of the data set including 150? Justify your answer.

_____

_____

YOUR TURN

Use the following data set to solve each problem: 21, 24, 3, 27, 30, 24

7. Is there an outlier? If so, identify the outlier. _____

8. Determine how the outlier affects the mean, median, and range of the data.

_____

_____

Personal Math Trainer

Online Practice and Help

my.hrw.com

Math On the Spot
my.hrw.com

Comparing Data Distributions

A data distribution can be described as symmetric, skewed to the left, or skewed to the right, depending on the general shape of the distribution in a dot plot or other data display.

Skewed to the Left	Symmetric	Skewed to the Right
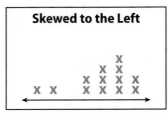	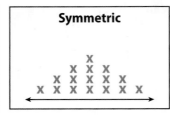	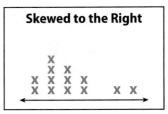

EXAMPLE 2

COMMON CORE S.ID.1

The data table shows the number of miles run by members of two track teams during one day. Make a dot plot and determine the type of distribution for each team. Explain what the distribution means for each.

Miles	3	3.5	4	4.5	5	5.5	6
Members of Team A	2	3	4	4	3	2	0
Members of Team B	1	2	2	3	4	6	5

Make dot plots of the data.

Team A

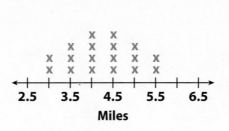

Team B

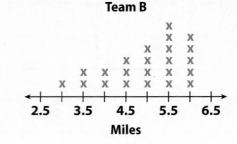

The data for team A show a symmetric distribution. The distances run are evenly distributed about the mean.

The data for team B show a distribution skewed to the left. More than half of the team members ran a distance greater than the mean.

REFLECT

9. Will the mean and median in a symmetric distribution always be approximately equal? Explain.

_____

_____

10. Will the mean and median in a skewed distribution always be approximately equal? Explain.

_____

_____

My Notes

YOUR TURN

11. Create a dot plot for the data. Describe the distribution as skewed to the left, skewed to the right, or symmetric.

Miles	3	3.5	4	4.5	5	5.5	6
Members of Team C	2	2	3	3	3	2	2

Team C

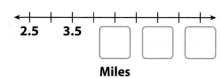

Miles

2.5   3.5

This distribution is _____.

Guided Practice

The list gives the grade level for each member of the marching band at JFK High. (Example 1)

9, 10, 9, 12, 11, 12, 10, 10, 11, 10, 10, 9, 11, 9, 11, 10, 12, 9, 11

1. Make a dot plot of the data.

JFK High Marching Band Member Grade Levels

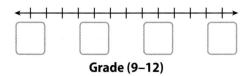

Grade (9–12)

2. Show that the data set {7, 10, 54, 9, 12, 8, 5} has an outlier. Then determine the effect of the outlier. (Explore Activity)

a. Determine if $54 > Q_3 + (1.5)IQR$.

$Q_3 =$ _____ $Q_1 =$ _____

$IQR =$ _____

$Q_3 + (1.5)IQR =$ _____

Is 54 an outlier? _____

b. Complete the table.

	Mean	Median	Range
Set without 54			
Set with 54			

c. How does the outlier affect the mean, the median, and the range?

_____

_____

Use the dot plots below to answer Exercises 3–6. (Example 2)

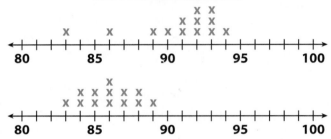

**Class Scores on First Test (top)
and Second Test (bottom)**

3. How do the medians of the two sets of test scores compare?

_____

_____

4. For which test is the distribution of scores symmetric? _____

5. For which test is the median greater than the mean? _____

6. Which measure of center is appropriate for comparing the two sets

of test scores? _____

? ESSENTIAL QUESTION CHECK-IN

7. Which statistics are most affected by outliers, and what shapes can data distributions have?

_____

_____

_____

_____

13.2 Independent Practice

COMMON CORE S.ID.1, S.ID.2, S.ID.3

Personal
Math Trainer

Online Practice
and Help

my.hrw.com

Rounded to the nearest $50,000, the values (in thousands of dollars) of homes sold by a realtor are listed below. Use the data set for Exercises 8–12.

300   250   200   250   350
400   300   250   400   300

8. Use the number line to create a dot plot for the data set.

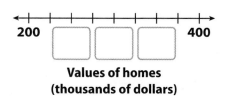

**Values of homes
(thousands of dollars)**

9. Suppose the realtor sells a home with a value of $650,000. Which statistics are affected when 650 is included in the data set?

_____

_____

10. Would 650 be considered an outlier? Explain.

_____

_____

_____

11. Find the mean and median for the data set with and without the data value 650.

_____

_____

12. If 650 is included in the data set, why might the realtor want to use the mean instead of the median when advertising the typical value of homes sold?

_____

_____

13. Represent Real-World Problems The table shows Chloe's scores on math tests in each quarter of the school year.

Chloe's Scores			
I	II	III	IV
74	77	79	74
78	75	76	77
82	80	74	76
76	75	77	78
85	77	87	85

a. Use the number line below to create a dot plot for all of Chloe's scores.

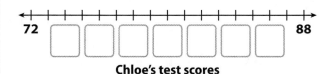

Chloe's test scores

b. Complete the table below for the data set.

Mean	Median	Range	IQR	Standard deviation

c. Identify any outliers in the data set.

_____

d. Which of the statistics from the table above would change if the outliers were removed?

_____

_____

_____

e. Describe the shape of the distribution.

_____

14. Critical Thinking Magdalene and Peter conducted the same experiment. Both of their data sets had the same mean. Both made dot plots of their data that showed symmetric distributions, but Peter's dot plot shows a greater IQR than Magdalene's dot plot. Identify which plot below belongs to Peter and which belongs to Magdalene.

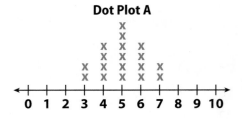

Dot Plot A

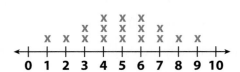

Dot Plot B

_____

15. Justify Reasoning Why will outliers always have an effect on the range?

_____

_____

_____

_____

16. Explain the Error Chuck and Brenda are discussing the distribution of the dot plot shown. Brenda says that if you add some families with 5 or 6 siblings then there will be a symmetric distribution. Explain her error.

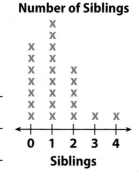

_____

_____

_____

_____

_____

17. Critique Reasoning Victor thinks that only the greatest and the least values in a data set can be outliers, since an outlier must be much greater or much less than the other values. Is he correct? Explain.

_____

_____

_____

_____

13.3 Histograms

COMMON CORE **S.ID.1**

Represent data with plots on the real number line (dot plots, histograms, and box plots).

? **ESSENTIAL QUESTION**

How can you estimate statistics from data displayed in a histogram?

EXPLORE ACTIVITY   **S.ID.1**

Understanding Histograms

A **histogram** is a bar graph that is used to display the frequency of data divided into equal intervals. The bars must be of equal width and should touch but not overlap. The heights of the bars indicate the frequency of data values within each interval.

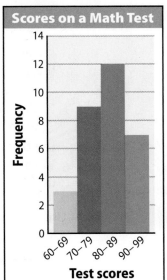

A Look at the histogram of "Scores on a Math Test." Which axis indicates the frequency?

_____

_____

B What does the horizontal axis indicate, and how is it organized?

_____

_____

_____

C How many students had test scores in the

interval 60–69? _____ between 70 and 79? _____

REFLECT

1. What statistical information can you tell about a data set by looking at a histogram? What statistical information cannot be determined by looking at a histogram?

_____

_____

2. How many test scores were collected? How do you know?

_____

_____

Creating a Histogram

When creating a histogram, make sure that the bars are of equal width and that they touch without overlapping. Create a frequency table to help organize the data before constructing the histogram.

EXAMPLE 1   COMMON CORE **S.ID.1**

Listed below are the ages of the 100 U.S. senators at the start of the 112th Congress on January 3, 2011. Create a histogram for this data set.

39, 39, 42, 44, 46, 47, 47, 47, 48, 49, 49, 49, 50, 50, 51, 51, 52, 52, 53, 53, 54, 54, 55, 55, 55, 55, 55, 55, 56, 56, 57, 57, 57, 58, 58, 58, 58, 58, 59, 59, 59, 59, 60, 60, 60, 60, 60, 60, 60, 61, 61, 62, 62, 62, 63, 63, 63, 63, 64, 64, 64, 64, 66, 66, 66, 67, 67, 67, 67, 67, 67, 67, 68, 68, 68, 68, 69, 69, 69, 70, 70, 70, 71, 71, 73, 73, 74, 74, 74, 75, 76, 76, 76, 76, 77, 77, 78, 86, 86, 86

STEP 1 Create a frequency table.

- It may be helpful to organize the data by listing from least to greatest.
- Decide the interval width and where to start the first interval.
- Use the data to complete the table. When done, check that the sum of the frequencies is 100.

> The data values range from 39 to 86, so use an interval width of 10 and start the first interval at 30.

Age interval	Frequency
30–39	2
40–49	10
50–59	30
60–69	37
70–79	18
80–89	3

STEP 2 Use the frequency table to create a histogram.

> Remember to give the graph a title and label both axes.

Ages of U.S. Senators at the Start of the 112th Congress

(histogram with Frequency on the y-axis from 0 to 40 and Ages on the x-axis with intervals 30–39, 40–49, 50–59, 60–69, 70–79, 80–89)

REFLECT

3. Describe the shape of the distribution of senators' ages. Explain.

_____

_____

_____

_____

_____

YOUR TURN

4. Listed below are the scores from a golf tournament.

68, 78, 76, 71, 69, 73, 72, 74, 76, 70, 77, 74, 75, 76, 71

a. Complete the frequency table.

Golf scores	Frequency
68 – 70	
71 – 73	
74 – 76	
77 – 79	

b. Complete the histogram.

Personal Math Trainer

Online Practice and Help

my.hrw.com

Estimating Statistics from a Histogram

You can estimate statistics by studying a histogram. Reasonable estimates of the mean, median, IQR, and standard deviation can be based on information provided by a histogram.

EXAMPLE 2

COMMON CORE   S.ID.1

Look at the histogram from Example 1. Estimate the mean and the median ages from the histogram.

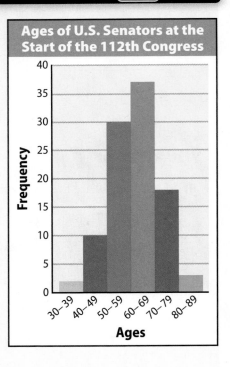

Ages of U.S. Senators at the Start of the 112th Congress

A To estimate the mean, first find the midpoint of each interval and multiply by the frequency. Add the results and divide by the total number of values.

1st interval: 2nd interval:
$(34.5)(2) = 69$ $(44.5)(10) = 445$

3rd interval: 4th interval:
$(54.5)(30) = 1635$ $(64.5)(37) = 2386.5$

5th interval: 6th interval:
$(74.5)(18) = 1341$ $(84.5)(3) = 253.5$

Mean: $\dfrac{69 + 445 + 1635 + 2386.5 + 1341 + 253.5}{100}$

$= \dfrac{6130}{100} = 61.3$

A good estimate for the mean of this set is 61.3.

Math Talk

Mathematical Practices

What is represented by the product of the midpoint of an interval and the frequency of that interval?

B To estimate the median, you need to estimate the average of the 50th and 51st numbers in the ordered set.

First, use the histogram to find which interval contains these values. There are 42 values in the first 3 intervals, so the 50th and 51st values will be in the interval 60−69.

The median is the average of the 8th and 9th values in this interval. This interval has 37 values. To estimate how far into this interval the median is located, find $\frac{8.5}{37} \approx 0.23$, or 23%, of the interval width, 10. Then add the result to the interval's least value, 60.

$(0.23)10 + 60 \approx 62$

A good estimate for the median of this set is 62.

REFLECT

5. Are these estimates of the mean and median reasonable? Explain.

_____

_____

_____

6. The histogram shows the ages of teachers at Plainsville High School. Estimate the teachers' mean and median ages from the histogram.

_____

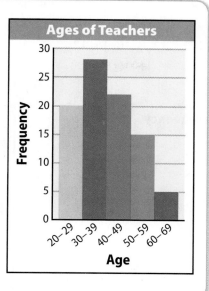

Ages of Teachers

Guided Practice

The histogram shows the 2004 Olympic results for women's weightlifting. Medals were awarded to the three athletes who lifted the most weight. (Explore Activity)

1. How many women lifted between 160 and 169.9 kg?

   _____

2. How many women lifted between 170 and 209.9 kg?

   _____

3. Tara Cunningham from the United States lifted 172.5 kg. Did she win a medal for this lift? Explain.

   _____

   _____

   _____

   _____

4. Can you determine which weight earned the silver medal? Explain.

   _____

   _____

   _____

   _____

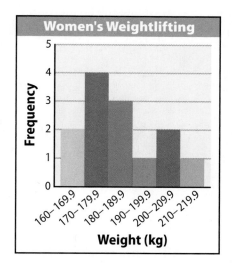

Women's Weightlifting

The length (in days) of Maria's last 15 vacations are given.
(Examples 1 and 2)

4, 8, 6, 7, 5, 4, 10, 6, 7, 14, 12, 8, 10, 15, 12

5. Make a frequency table.

Days	Frequency
4–6	
7–9	
10–12	
13–15	

6. Create a histogram using the frequency table.

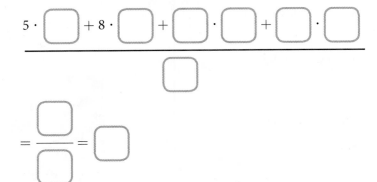

Maria's Vacations

Frequency / Length (in days)

7. Estimate the mean from the histogram.

$$5 \cdot \boxed{} + 8 \cdot \boxed{} + \boxed{} \cdot \boxed{} + \boxed{} \cdot \boxed{}$$
$$\overline{\boxed{}}$$

$$= \frac{\boxed{}}{\boxed{}} = \boxed{}$$

Multiply the midpoint value of each interval by its frequency. Divide the sum of those numbers by the total number of values.

The mean calculated from the data set is about _____,

so the estimate is ⌜ **very close / not very close** ⌝.

Calculate the mean from the data set and compare the results to your estimate.

? **ESSENTIAL QUESTION CHECK-IN**

8. How can you estimate statistics from data displayed in a histogram?

_____

_____

_____

_____

13.3 Independent Practice

COMMON CORE **S.ID.1**

Use the histogram for Exercises 9 and 10.

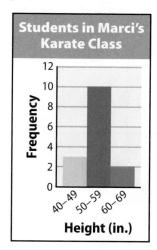

Students in Marci's Karate Class

Height (in.)

9. How many students are in the class? _____

10. Describe the shape of the distribution.

_____

11. The breathing intervals of gray whales are shown. Make a histogram for the data.

Breathing Intervals (min)

Interval	Frequency
5–7	4
8–10	7
11–13	7
14–16	8

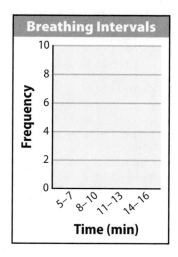

Breathing Intervals

Time (min)

The ages of the first 44 U.S. presidents on the date of their first inauguration are shown in the histogram. Use the histogram for Exercises 12 and 13.

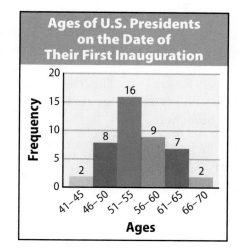

Ages of U.S. Presidents on the Date of Their First Inauguration

Ages

12. Communicate Mathematical Ideas Describe the shape of the distribution by telling whether it is approximately symmetric, skewed to the right, or skewed to the left. Explain.

_____

_____

_____

_____

_____

13. Use the histogram to estimate the mean and median age of presidents at their first inauguration.

a. Mean presidential age at first

inauguration: _____

b. Median presidential age at first

inauguration: _____

14. Communicate Mathematical Ideas Describe how you could estimate the IQR of a data set from a histogram.

_____

_____

_____

_____

_____

Work Area

15. Justify Reasoning The frequencies of starting salary ranges for college graduates are shown in the histogram.

Bobby says the mean is found in the following way:

$$\frac{24.5 + 34.5 + 44.5 + 54.5}{4} = \frac{158}{4} = 39.5$$

What is his error?

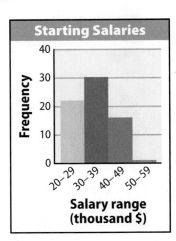

Starting Salaries

Frequency

Salary range
(thousand $)

_____

_____

_____

_____

_____

_____

16. Critical Thinking Margo's assignment is to make a data display of some data she finds in a newspaper. She found a frequency table with the intervals shown at the right.

Explain why Margo must be careful when drawing the bars of the histogram.

Age
Under 18
18–30
31–54
55 and older

_____

_____

_____

_____

_____

LESSON
13.4 Box Plots

COMMON CORE   **S.ID.1**
Represent data with plots on the real number line (dot plots, histograms, and box plots).
Also S.ID.2

? ESSENTIAL QUESTION

How can you compare data sets using box plots?

Constructing a Box Plot

A **box plot** can be used to show how the values in a data set are distributed. You need five values to make a box plot: the minimum (or least value), first quartile, median, third quartile, and maximum (or greatest value).

Math On the Spot
my.hrw.com

EXAMPLE 1 Real World

COMMON CORE   **S.ID.1**

The numbers of runs scored by a softball team in 20 games are given. Use the data to make a box plot.

3, 4, 8, 12, 7, 5, 4, 12, 3, 9, 11, 4, 14, 8, 2, 10, 3, 10, 9, 7

STEP 1 Order the data from least to greatest.

2, 3, 3, 3, 4, 4, 4, 5, 7, 7, 8, 8, 9, 9, 10, 10, 11, 12, 12, 14

STEP 2 Identify the five needed values. Those values are the minimum, first quartile, median, third quartile, and maximum.

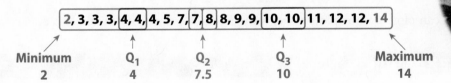

Minimum	Q_1	Q_2	Q_3	Maximum
2	4	7.5	10	14

STEP 3 Draw a number line and plot a point above each of the five needed values. Draw a box whose ends go through the first and third quartiles, and draw a vertical line through the median. Draw horizontal lines from the box to the minimum and maximum.

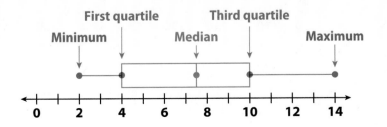

Animated Math
my.hrw.com

© Houghton Mifflin Harcourt Publishing Company • Image Credits: ©Sportlibrary/Shutterstock

REFLECT

1. The lines that extend from the box in a box plot are sometimes called "whiskers." What part (lower, middle, or upper) and about what percent of the data does the box represent? What part and about what percent does each "whisker" represent?

_____

_____

2. Which measures of spread can be determined from the box plot, and how are they found? Calculate each measure.

_____

_____

YOUR TURN

3. Use the data to make a box plot.

13, 14, 18, 13, 12, 17, 15, 12, 13, 19, 11, 14, 14, 18, 22, 23

Comparing Data Using Box Plots

You can plot two box plots above a single number line to compare two data sets.

EXAMPLE 2 Real World

COMMON CORE S.ID.1

The box plots show the ticket sales, in millions of dollars, for the top 25 movies of 2000 and 2007. Use the box plots to compare the data sets.

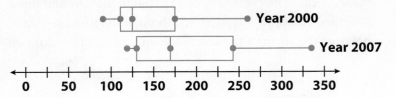

(A) Identify the set with the greater median.

The median for 2000 is about 125. The median for 2007 is about 170. The data set for 2007 has the greater median.

B Identify the set with the greater interquartile range.

The length of the box for 2007 is greater than the length of the box for 2000. The data set for 2007 has a greater interquartile range.

C About how much greater were the ticket sales for the top movie in 2007 than for the top movie in 2000?

2007 maximum: about $335 million   *Read the maximum values from the box plots.*

2000 maximum: about $260 million

$335 - 260 = 75$ *Find the difference between the maximum values.*

The ticket sales for the top movie in 2007 were about $75 million more than for the top movie in 2000.

Math Talk

Mathematical Practices

Explain how to find which data set has a smaller range.

REFLECT

4. **Analyze Relationships** Use the box plots to compare the shape of the two data distributions.

_____

_____

_____

_____

_____

YOUR TURN

The box plots show the scores, in thousands of points, of two players of a video game.

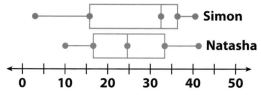

5. Which data set has a greater median? _____

6. Which data set has the greater interquartile range? _____

7. Which player had a higher top score? About how much higher was it than

the other player's top score? _____

_____

Personal
Math Trainer

Online Practice
and Help

⏻ my.hrw.com

Use the data to make a box plot. (Example 1)

1. 25, 28, 26, 16, 18, 15, 25, 28, 26, 16

   a. Order the data from least to greatest.

   _____

   b. Identify the median and the first and third quartiles.

   Median = _____

   First quartile = _____

   Third quartile = _____

   c. Identify the minimum and maximum.

   Minimum = _____

   Maximum = _____

   d. Construct the box plot.

The box plots show the prices, in dollars, of athletic shoes at two sports apparel stores. Use the box plots for Exercises 2 and 3. (Example 2)

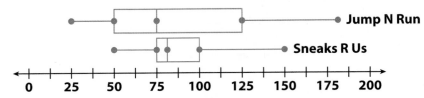

2. Which store has the greater median price? About how much greater?

_____

3. Which store has the smaller interquartile range? What does this tell you about the data sets?

_____

_____

4. How can you compare data sets using box plots?

_____

_____

_____

_____

13.4 Independent Practice

Personal Math Trainer

Online Practice and Help

my.hrw.com

 S.ID.1, S.ID.2

The finishing times of two runners for several one-mile races, in minutes, are shown below. Use the box plots for Exercises 5–7.

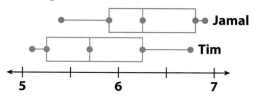

5. Who has the faster median time?

_____

6. Who has the slowest time?

_____

7. Overall, who is the faster runner? Explain.

_____

_____

The table below shows the scores that Gabrielle and Marcus each earned the last 15 times they played a board game together. Use the table to complete Exercises 8–10.

Gabrielle	150, 195, 180, 225, 120, 135, 115, 220, 190, 185, 230, 170, 160, 200, 120
Marcus	170, 155, 175, 200, 190, 165, 170, 180, 160, 175, 155, 170, 160, 180, 175

8. Create a box plot for each data set on the number line below.

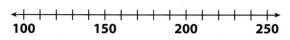

9. Which set has the higher median?

_____

10. Which set has more scores that are close to the median? Explain.

_____

_____

_____

_____

_____

The number of traffic citations given daily by two police departments over a two-week period is shown. Use the box plots for Exercises 11–13.

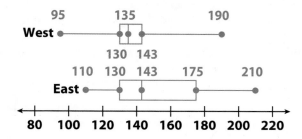

11. Which department gave the greatest number of citations in a day? How much higher was that number than the greatest number given by the other

department? _____

12. What is the difference in the median number of citations given by the two

departments? _____

13. Detective Costello says that it looks like the mean numbers of citations per day given by the two departments are about the same because the range looks similar. Is she correct? Explain.

_____

_____

The box plots show the prices of vehicles at a used-car dealership.

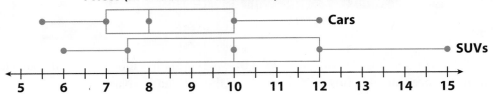

Prices (in Thousands of Dollars) of Cars and SUVs

14. Suppose the dealership acquires a used car that it intends to sell for $15,000. Would the price of the car be an outlier? Explain.

_____

15. Compare the distribution of SUV prices with the distribution of car prices.

_____

_____

_____

 **FOCUS ON HIGHER ORDER THINKING**

Work Area

Dolly and Willie's scores are shown. Use the box plots for Exercises 16 and 17.

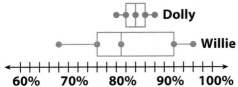

First Quarter Assignments

16. Dolly claims that she is the better student. What statistics make Dolly seem like the better student? Explain.

_____

_____

17. Willie claims that he is the better student. What statistics make Willie seem like the better student? Explain.

_____

_____

18. **Critical Thinking** Suppose the minimum in a data set is the same as the first quartile. How would this affect a box plot of the data? Explain.

_____

_____

COMMON CORE S.ID.2

Use statistics appropriate to the shape of the data distribution to compare center (median, mean) and spread (interquartile range, standard deviation) of two or more different data sets.
Also S.ID.1

? **ESSENTIAL QUESTION**

How can you use characteristics of a normal distribution to make estimates and probability predictions about the population that the data represents?

EXPLORE ACTIVITY 1   COMMON CORE   S.ID.2

Investigating Symmetric Distributions

A bell-shaped, symmetric distribution with a tail on each end is called a **normal distribution.**

Use a graphing calculator and the infant birth mass data in the table below to determine if the set represents a normal distribution.

Birth Mass (kg)				
3.3	3.6	3.5	3.4	3.7
3.6	3.5	3.4	3.7	3.5
3.4	3.5	3.2	3.6	3.4
3.8	3.5	3.6	3.3	3.5

A Enter the data into a graphing calculator as a list. Calculate the "1-Variable Statistics" for the distribution of data.

Mean, $\bar{x} \approx$ _____

Standard deviation, $\sigma x \approx$ _____

Median = _____

IQR $= Q_3 - Q_1 =$ _____

B Plot a histogram.

- Turn on a statistics plot, select the histogram option, and choose your data for Xlist.
- Set the viewing window to display one bar per data value. Use the values shown.
- Use the calculator to generate the histogram by pressing GRAPH. You can obtain the heights of the bars by pressing TRACE and using the arrow keys.

WINDOW
Xmin=3.15
Xmax=3.85
Xscl=.1
Ymin=0
Ymax=8
Yscl=1
↓Xres=1

C Sketch the histogram. Always include labels for the axes and the bar intervals.

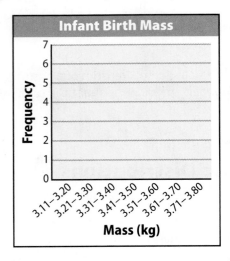

Infant Birth Mass

D Could this data be described by a normal distribution? Explain.

_____

REFLECT

1. Which intervals on the histogram had the fewest values? Which interval had the greatest number of values?

_____

_____

_____

2. **Make a Conjecture** For this normal distribution, the mean and the median are the same. Is this true for every normal distribution? Explain.

_____

_____

_____

_____

3. **Counterexamples** Allison thinks that every symmetric distribution must be bell-shaped. Provide a counterexample to show that she is incorrect.

_____

_____

_____

_____

Investigating a Symmetric Relative Frequency Histogram

The table gives the frequency of each mass from the data set used in Explore Activity 1.

Mass (kg)	3.2	3.3	3.4	3.5	3.6	3.7	3.8
Frequency	1	2	4	6	4	2	1

A Use the frequency table to make a relative frequency table. Notice that there are 20 data values.

Mass (kg)	3.2	3.3	3.4	3.5	3.6	3.7	3.8
Relative frequency	$\frac{1}{20} = 0.05$						

What is the sum of the relative frequencies? _____

B Sketch a relative frequency histogram. The heights of the bars now indicate relative frequencies.

C Recall from Explore Activity 1 that the mean of this data set is 3.5 and the standard deviation is 0.14. By how many standard deviations does a birth mass of 3.2 kg differ from the mean? Justify your answer.

_____

_____

_____

_____

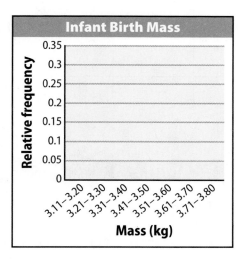

Infant Birth Mass

REFLECT

4. Identify the interval of values that are within one standard deviation of the mean. Use the frequency table to determine what percent of the values in the set are in this interval.

_____

_____

5. Identify the interval of values that are within two standard deviations of the mean. Use the frequency table to determine what percent of the values in the set are in this interval.

_____

_____

Finding Areas Under a Normal Curve

The smaller the intervals are in a symmetric, bell-shaped relative frequency histogram, the closer the shape of the histogram is to a curve called a *normal curve*.

> ### Properties of Normal Curves
>
> A **normal curve** has the following properties:
>
> - 68% of the data fall within 1 standard deviation of the mean.
> - 95% of the data fall within 2 standard deviations of the mean.
> - 99.7% of the data fall within 3 standard deviations of the mean.

The symmetry of a normal curve allows you to separate the area under the curve into eight parts and know what percent of the data is contained in each part.

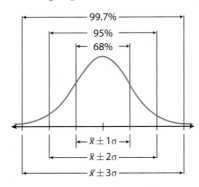

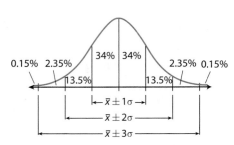

EXAMPLE 1

COMMON CORE S.ID.2

Animated Math

my.hrw.com

The masses (in grams) of pennies minted in the United States after 1982 are normally distributed with a mean of 2.50 g and a standard deviation of 0.02 g. Find the percent of pennies that have a mass between 2.46 g and 2.54 g.

Find the distance between 2.46 and the mean. $2.50 - 2.46 = 0.04$ g; 0.04 g is twice the standard deviation of 0.02 g, so 2.46 g is 2 standard deviations below the mean.

Find the distance between 2.54 and the mean. $2.54 - 2.50 = 0.04$ g; so 2.54 g is 2 standard deviations above the mean.

95% of the data in a normal distribution fall within 2 standard deviations of the mean.

95% of pennies have a mass between 2.46 g and 2.54 g.

Personal Math Trainer

Online Practice and Help

my.hrw.com

YOUR TURN

6. Find the percent of pennies that have a mass between 2.48 g and 2.52 g.

Using a Normal Curve to Find Probabilities

Knowing the percentages of data under sections of a normal curve allows you to make predictions about the larger population that a normally distributed sample of data represents.

Math On the Spot

my.hrw.com

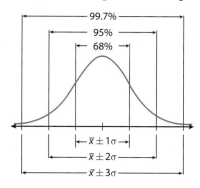

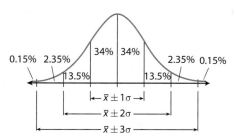

EXAMPLE 2

COMMON CORE   S.ID.2

The masses of pennies minted in the United States after 1982 are normally distributed with a mean of 2.50 g and a standard deviation of 0.02 g. Find the probability that a randomly chosen penny has a mass greater than 2.52 g.

STEP 1   Determine the distance between 2.52 and the mean.
The mean is 2.50; $2.52 - 2.50 = 0.02$.

Determine how many standard deviations this distance is.
The distance of 0.02 equals the standard deviation, so 2.52 is 1 standard deviation above the mean.

STEP 2   Look at the parts of the curve that are more than 1 standard deviation above the mean. Identify what percent of the data is contained in the area under each part.

13.5%, 2.35%, 0.15%

STEP 3   The total probability is the sum of the probabilities for each part of the curve. Express the probability as a percent and as a decimal.

$13.5\% + 2.35\% + 0.15\% = 16\%$

The probability is 16%, or 0.16.

YOUR TURN

7. Find the probability that a randomly chosen penny has a mass less than or equal to 2.50 g.

_____

Personal Math Trainer

Online Practice and Help

my.hrw.com

Suppose the scores on a test given to all juniors in a school district are normally distributed with a mean of 74 and a standard deviation of 8. Find the following.
(Examples 1 and 2)

1. The percent of juniors whose score is no more than 90

_____

2. The percent of juniors whose score is between 58 and 74

_____

3. The percent of juniors whose score is at least 74

_____

4. The percent of juniors whose score is below 66

_____

5. The probability that a randomly chosen junior has a score above 82

_____

6. The probability that a randomly chosen junior has a score between 66 and 90

_____

7. The probability that a randomly chosen junior has a score below 74

_____

8. The probability that a randomly chosen junior has a score above 98

_____

? ESSENTIAL QUESTION CHECK-IN

9. How do you find percents of data and probabilities of events associated with normal distributions?

_____

_____

_____

_____

_____

13.5 Independent Practice

 COMMON CORE S.ID.2, S.ID.1

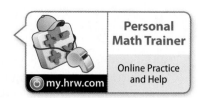

Personal Math Trainer

Online Practice and Help

my.hrw.com

10. A normal distribution has a mean of 10 and a standard deviation of 1.5.

 a. Between which two values do 95% of the data fall?

 _____

 b. Between which two values do 68% of the data fall?

 _____

Suppose the heights (in inches) of adult males in the United States are normally distributed with a mean of 72 inches and a standard deviation of 2 inches. Find each of the following.

11. The percent of men who are no more than 68 inches tall

 _____

12. The percent of men who are between 70 and 72 inches tall

 _____

13. The percent of men who are at least 76 inches tall

 _____

14. The probability that a randomly chosen man is more than 72 inches tall

 _____

15. The probability that a randomly chosen man is between 68 and 76 inches tall

 _____

16. The probability that a randomly chosen man is less than 76 inches tall

 _____

17. Ten customers at Fielden Grocery were surveyed about how long they waited in line to check out. Their wait times, in minutes, are shown.

16	15	10	7	5
5	4	3	3	2

 a. What is the mean of the data set?

 _____

 b. How many data points are below the mean, and how many are above the mean?

 _____

 _____

 _____

 c. Do the data appear to be normally distributed? Explain.

 _____

 _____

 _____

 _____

 _____

 _____

18. Kori is analyzing a normal data distribution, but the data provided is incomplete. Kori knows that the mean of the data is 120, and that 84% of the data values are less than 130. Find the standard deviation for this data set.

 _____

19. Critical Thinking The calculator screen on the left shows the probability distribution for the number of "heads" that come up when six coins are flipped. The screen on the right shows the probability distribution for the number of 1s that come up when six dice are rolled. For which distribution is it reasonable to use a normal curve as an approximation? Why?

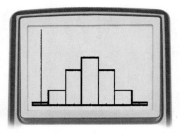 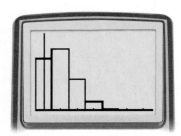

_____

_____

_____

Suppose the upper arm length (in centimeters) of adult males in the United States is normally distributed with a mean of 39.4 cm and a standard deviation of 2.3 cm.

20. Justify Reasoning What percent of adult males have an upper arm length between 34.8 and 41.7 cm? Explain how you got your answer.

_____

_____

_____

_____

_____

21. Communicate Mathematical Ideas Explain how you can determine whether a set of data is normally distributed.

_____

_____

_____

_____

_____

_____

Ready to Go On?

13.1 Measures of Center and Spread

1. The high temperatures in degrees Fahrenheit on 11 days were 68, 71, 75, 74, 75, 71, 73, 71, 72, 74, and 79. Find the mean, median, and range.

_____

13.2 Data Distributions and Outliers

2. Describe the shape of the distribution. If a data point with a value of 3.0 inches is added, how will the median change?

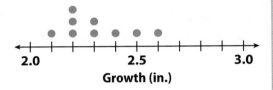

_____

13.3–13.4 Histograms/Box Plots

3. Use the table showing the average number of hours of sleep for people at different ages to create a histogram.

Age	3–9	10–13	14–18	19–30	31–45	46–50
Sleep (h)	11	10	9	8	7.5	6

4. Find the range and the IQR of the data in the box plot.

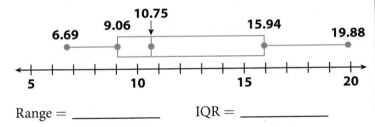

Range = _____   IQR = _____

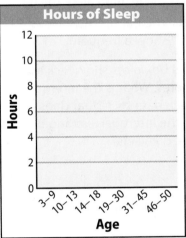

13.5 Normal Distributions

5. Suppose compact fluorescent light bulbs last, on average, 10,000 hours. The standard deviation is 500 hours. What percent of light bulbs burn out within 11,000 hours? _____

ESSENTIAL QUESTION

6. How can data sets be displayed and compared, and what statistics can be gathered using the display? _____

_____

MODULE 13
MIXED REVIEW

Assessment Readiness

Personal Math Trainer

Online Practice and Help

my.hrw.com

1. Consider each measurement below. Should the measurement be given to 3 significant digits? Select Yes or No for A–C.

   A. The perimeter of a rectangle with a length of 3.6 m and a width of 2.25 m
   ○ Yes   ○ No

   B. The area of a rectangle with a length of 4.8 m and a width of 2.2 m
   ○ Yes   ○ No

   C. The volume of a rectangular prism with a base area of 10.8 m^2 and a height of 3.45 m
   ○ Yes   ○ No

2. Freya plans to make a histogram of the data set shown in the table.

   Choose True or False for each statement.

   A. The intervals 71–80, 81–90, and 91–100 will include all of the data values.
   ○ True   ○ False

   B. The bar for the interval 91–100 should show a frequency of 3.
   ○ True   ○ False

Biology Quiz Scores
82, 93, 74, 85, 88, 70
94, 76, 84, 85, 97, 86

3. The box plots show Rick and Jin's archery scores. What is the interquartile range of each data set? What does the difference in the interquartile ranges indicate about the data sets?

   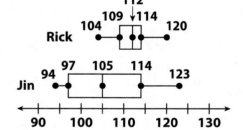

4. The numbers of raisins per box in a certain brand of cereal are normally distributed with a mean of 339 raisins and a standard deviation of 9 raisins. Find the percent of boxes of this brand of cereal that have fewer than 330 raisins. Explain how you solved this problem.

   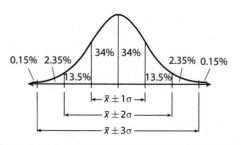

Study Guide Review

MODULE **12** **Descriptive Statistics**

Key Vocabulary

categorical data *(datos categóricos)*

conditional relative frequency *(frecuencia relativa condicional)*

frequency table *(tabla de frecuencia)*

joint relative frequency *(frecuencia relativa conjunta)*

marginal relative frequency *(frecuencia relativa marginal)*

quantitative data *(datos cuantitativos)*

relative frequency *(frecuencia relativa)*

ESSENTIAL QUESTION

How can you summarize two categories of categorical data and recognize associations and trends between two categories of categorical data?

EXAMPLE 1

Quan asked 100 randomly selected students whether they preferred winter, spring, summer, or fall. He also recorded the gender of each student. The results are shown in the two-way frequency table below. Complete the table.

	Preferred Season				
Gender	**Winter**	**Spring**	**Summer**	**Fall**	**Total**
Girl	8	12	25	5	?
Boy	9	5	30	6	?
Total	?	?	?	?	?

Find the total for each gender by adding the frequencies in each row. Write the row totals in the Total column.

Find the total for each preferred season by adding the frequencies in each column. Write the column totals in the Total row.

Find the grand total, which is the sum of the row totals as well as the sum of the column totals. Write the grand total in the lower-right corner of the table (the intersection of the Total column and the Total row.)

	Preferred Season				
Gender	**Winter**	**Spring**	**Summer**	**Fall**	**Total**
Girl	8	12	25	5	50
Boy	9	5	30	6	50
Total	17	17	55	11	100

EXAMPLE 2

Does gender influence a student's preference for a particular season?

Use the data from Quan's survey to create a two-way relative frequency table. Find the joint relative frequencies and marginal relative frequencies by dividing each number in the frequency table by the grand total. Write the quotients as decimals.

Gender	Preferred Season				
	Winter	Spring	Summer	Fall	Total
Girl	$\frac{8}{100} = 0.08$	$\frac{12}{100} = 0.12$	$\frac{25}{100} = 0.25$	$\frac{5}{100} = 0.05$	$\frac{50}{100} = 0.5$
Boy	$\frac{9}{100} = 0.09$	$\frac{5}{100} = 0.05$	$\frac{30}{100} = 0.3$	$\frac{6}{100} = 0.06$	$\frac{50}{100} = 0.5$
Total	$\frac{17}{100} = 0.17$	$\frac{17}{100} = 0.17$	$\frac{55}{100} = 0.55$	$\frac{11}{100} = 0.11$	$\frac{100}{100} = 1$

Determine each conditional relative frequency to find what percent of the students who prefer each season are girls. Compare each percentage to the percent of surveyed students who are girls (50%).

Winter: $\frac{8}{17} \approx 0.47 = 47\%$ 8 out of 17 people who prefer winter are girls.

Spring: $\frac{12}{17} \approx 0.71 = 71\%$ 12 out of 17 people who prefer spring are girls.

Summer: $\frac{25}{55} \approx 0.45 = 45\%$ 25 out of 55 people who prefer Summer are girls.

Fall: $\frac{5}{11} \approx 0.45 = 45\%$ 5 out of 11 people who prefer Fall are girls.

All of the percentages are close to 50% except spring. According to the survey, girls are more likely than boys to prefer spring.

EXERCISES

The results of a survey asking 40 students the number of siblings they have are shown in the two-way relative frequency table below. (Lessons 16.1, 16.2)

1. Complete the table.

Gender	Siblings				
	0	1	2	3+	Total
Freshman	$\frac{6}{40} = $ _____	$\frac{7}{40} = $ _____	$\frac{6}{40} = $ _____	$\frac{3}{40} = $ _____	$\frac{}{40} = $ _____
Seniors	$\frac{4}{40} = $ _____	$\frac{8}{40} = $ _____	$\frac{4}{40} = $ _____	$\frac{2}{40} = $ _____	$\frac{}{40} = $ _____
Total	$\frac{}{40} = $ _____	$\frac{}{40} = $ _____	$\frac{}{40} = $ _____	$\frac{}{40} = $ _____	$\frac{}{40} = $ _____

2. Analyze the data to decide if freshman are more likely or less likely than seniors to have zero siblings. Explain.

_____

_____

_____

_____

_____

? **ESSENTIAL QUESTION**

How can data sets be displayed and compared, and what statistics can be gathered using the display?

EXAMPLE 1

Estimate the mean, median, and standard deviation of the heights from the histogram.

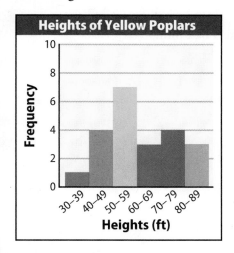

Find the estimated mean.

30–39: 34.5; 1   Find the midpoint of each range.

40–49: 44.5; 4   Find the frequency of each range.

50–59: 54.5; 7

60–69: 64.5; 3

70–79: 74.5; 4

80–89: 84.5; 3

$$\frac{34.5 \times 1 + 44.5 \times 4 + 54.5 \times 7 + 64.5 \times 3 + 74.5 \times 4 + 84.5 \times 3}{22} \approx 61$$

Multiply each midpoint by the frequency for that interval, and then find the mean of those values.

Find the estimated standard deviation.

30–39: $(34.5 - 61)^2 = 702.25$ Subtract the estimated mean from the midpoint of each range and square it.

40–49: $(44.5 - 61)^2 = 272.25$

50–59: $(54.5 - 61)^2 = 42.25$

60–69: $(64.5 - 61)^2 = 12.25$

70–79: $(74.5 - 61)^2 = 182.25$

80–89: $(84.5 - 61)^2 = 552.25$

$$\sqrt{\frac{702.25 \times 1 + 272.25 \times 4 + 42.25 \times 7 + 12.25 \times 3 + 182.25 \times 4 + 552.25 \times 3}{22}} \approx 14$$

Multiply each square by the frequency for the corresponding interval, and then find the mean of the products. Take the square root of the result.

Find the estimated median.

The median value will be the mean of the 11th value and the 12th value in the ordered set. This falls in the 50–59 range.

This interval has seven values. Since the previous intervals together contain five values, the median will be the mean of the 6th and 7th values in the interval 50–59. Estimate the median as the sum of the interval's least value, 50, and $\frac{1}{7}$ of the interval width, 10, multiplied by the mean of 6 and 7

$50 + \left(\frac{1}{7} \times 10 \times \frac{6 + 7}{2} \right) \approx 59.3$, so 59 is a good estimate for the median.

EXAMPLE 2

The heights of pine trees in a forest are given. Use the data to make a box plot.
18, 13, 22, 25, 27, 32, 35, 60, 36, 16, 26, 24, 31, 46, 38, 29, 23, 19, 42, 34

Order the data from least to greatest.
13, 16, 18, 19, 22, 23, 24, 25, 26, 27, 29, 31, 32, 34, 35, 36, 38, 42, 46, 60

Find the **minimum**, **first quartile**, **median**, **third quartile**, and **maximum**.

Remember, you may have to calculate the mean of two numbers when finding the median and the first and third quartiles.

$\text{median} = \dfrac{27 + 29}{2} = 28$

$\text{first quartile} = \dfrac{22 + 23}{2} = 22.5$

$\text{third quartile} = \dfrac{35 + 36}{2} = 35.5$

Plot these points above a number line and draw the box plot.

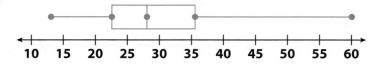

EXAMPLE 3

Suppose the heights of professional basketball players in the United States are distributed normally, with a mean of 79 inches and a standard deviation of 4 inches. Find the percent of players that have a height between 71 and 75 inches.

How far below the mean is 71 inches?
$79 - 71 = 8$ inches

How many standard deviations is this?
The standard deviation is 4 inches, so 8 inches is 2 standard deviations.

How far below the mean is 75 inches?
$79 - 75 = 4$ inches

How many standard deviations is this?
The standard deviation is 4 inches, so 4 inches is 1 standard deviation.

Look at the following graph to find what percent of the data distribution falls under the curve between 1 and 2 standard deviations below the mean.

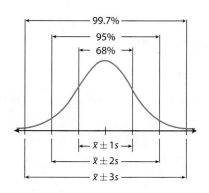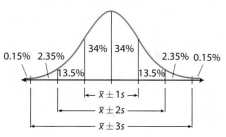

This is the third section of the second graph, which includes 13.5% of the data values.

EXERCISES

The histogram represents the test scores in two different math classes. (Lesson 17.3)

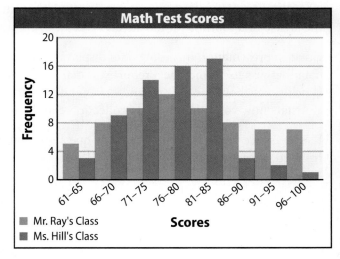

Math Test Scores

■ Mr. Ray's Class
■ Ms. Hill's Class

1. Which class has a greater median?

   _____

2. Which class has a greater standard deviation?

   _____

The following box plot represents the amount people spend at two different movie theaters. (Lessons 17.1, 17.2, 17.4)

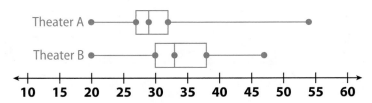

3. Which set has a greater median? _____

4. Which set has a greater interquartile range? _____

5. Is the maximum value for Theater A, 54, an outlier? Explain.

   _____

   _____

6. Suppose the mean 40-yard dash time of professional football players is 4.41 seconds with a standard deviation of 0.15 seconds. Assume normal distribution. What is the percent of players who run the 40-yard dash in between 4.11 and 4.41 seconds? (Lesson 17.5)

   _____

True Story?

Statistical information floods our news stream every day. In this project, you will research claims made in a recent article or advertisement.

Find a statistical claim based on surveys or experiments. To verify the claim you may have to perform additional research beyond that noted in the article or advertisement. Look for a source listed toward the end of the article or a footnote in the advertisement.

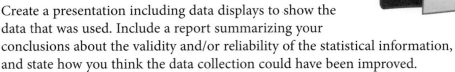

Create a presentation including data displays to show the data that was used. Include a report summarizing your conclusions about the validity and/or reliability of the statistical information, and state how you think the data collection could have been improved.

Use the space below to write down any questions you have or important information from your teacher.

MATH IN CAREERS | ACTIVITY

Sports Recruiter The data table shows the 40-yard dash times of two running backs over a week. Find the mean, median, range, and standard deviation for both athletes' times. Which athlete would you choose to be your team's running back? Explain.

	1	2	3	4	5	6	7
Athlete A	4.21	4.18	4.28	4.15	4.19	4.18	4.25
Athlete B	4.15	4.31	4.24	4.41	4.26	4.24	4.31

COMMON CORE

UNIT 3

MIXED REVIEW

Assessment Readiness

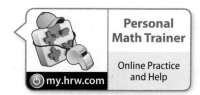

Personal
Math Trainer

Online Practice
and Help

my.hrw.com

1. Consider each function. Is it an exponential growth function?

   Select Yes or No.

   A. $y = 0.3(1 + 0.5)^t$ ◯ Yes ◯ No

   B. $y = 28(0.85)^t$ ◯ Yes ◯ No

   C. $y = \frac{1}{2}(2)^t$ ◯ Yes ◯ No

2. The two-way frequency table shows the results of a survey of a group of randomly selected students about whether they own a cat or a dog.

	Has a Dog		
Has a Cat	Yes	No	Total
Yes	10	16	26
No	21	33	54
Total	31	49	80

   Choose True or False for each statement.

   A. Ten students in the survey own both pets. ◯ True ◯ False

   B. The marginal relative frequency of students surveyed who own a cat is 32.5%. ◯ True ◯ False

   C. The joint relative frequency of students surveyed who own a dog but not a cat is about 67.7%. ◯ True ◯ False

3. The weights of 5 lion cubs in pounds are 19, 22, 21, 23, and 21. Is the standard deviation of the weights more than 1 lb? Explain.

4. A machine produces bolts with a mean thread diameter of 0.250 inch and a standard deviation of 0.002 inch. Any bolts with a thread diameter greater than 0.250 inch or less than 0.244 inch must be rejected. What is the probability that a bolt produced by the machine will be rejected? Explain how you know.

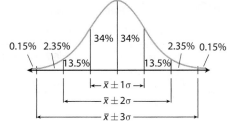

Performance Tasks

★ **5.** The dot plot shows the number of actors in each scene of an episode of a television show. Identify the outlier in the data and determine how it affects the mean and median of the data.

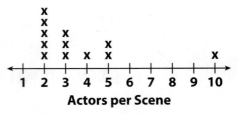

Actors per Scene

★★ **6.** Last month, a car dealership sold 96 cars. Of the 2-door cars, 2 were hybrids and 21 were not hybrids. Of the 4-door cars, 5 were hybrids, and 68 were not hybrids.

Doors	Hybrid		
	Yes	No	Total
2			
4			
Total			

   a. Complete the two-way frequency table for the data.

   b. Create a two-way relative frequency table for the data.

   c. For the cars sold at the dealership, is there any association between the number of car doors and whether the car is a hybrid? Justify your reasoning.

★★★ **7.** A college baseball coach is deciding between two pitchers to add to the team. In general, a better pitcher throws more strikes. The table shows the percent of strikes thrown per game by the two pitchers in their last high school baseball season. Which pitcher should the coach add to the team? Justify your answer by using both data displays and statistics.

Acevedo	59, 62, 71, 67, 64, 58, 68, 63, 65, 64, 59, 69
Forbes	54, 67, 51, 61, 52, 54, 52, 60, 64, 51, 60, 62

Polynomial Expressions and Equations

MATH IN CAREERS

Investigator An investigator is called upon to evaluate and determine the cause of traffic accidents. Investigators use math to calculate a vehicle's stopping distance, which allows them to determine how fast the vehicle was traveling at the time of the accident.

If you're interested in a career as an investigator, you should study these mathematical subjects:
- Algebra
- Geometry
- Trigonometry
- Calculus

Research other careers that require the use of mathematical formulas to understand real-world scenarios.

ACTIVITY At the end of the unit, check out how an **Investigator** uses math.

Going Down?

For the Unit Project at the end of this unit you will conduct an experiment and collect data to estimate g, the acceleration due to gravity. To successfully complete the Unit Project you'll need to master these skills:

- Collect, organize, and represent data.
- Apply the quadratic formula to a real-world situation.
- Fit a quadratic function to data observations.

1. In the equation $d = \frac{1}{4}gt^2$, d represents distance in feet, t represents time in seconds, and g represents acceleration due to gravity. What are the units for g? Explain how you know.

_____

_____

2. When rolling a ball down a ramp, what are some parameters to consider when collecting results?

_____

_____

_____

Tracking Your Learning Progression

This unit addresses important Common Core Standards in the Critical Areas of operating on polynomials arithmetically and solving one-variable equations and inequalities.

Domain A.APR Arithmetic with Polynomials and Rational Expressions

    Cluster Perform arithmetic operations on polynomials.

The unit also supports additional standards.

Domain A.REI Reasoning with Equations and Inequalities

    Cluster Solve equations and inequalities in one variable.

Domain A.SSE Seeing Structure in Expressions

    Cluster Interpret the structure of expressions

Polynomials and Operations

? ESSENTIAL QUESTION

How are polynomials like other number systems, such as whole numbers and integers?

Real-World Video

Vehicles, such as planes and cars, are aerodynamically tested in a wind tunnel. The complex factors involved in wind tunnel testing can be modeled with polynomial functions.

⏻ my.hrw.com

GO DIGITAL
my.hrw.com

my.hrw.com

Go digital with your write-in student edition, accessible on any device.

Math On the Spot

Scan with your smart phone to jump directly to the online edition, video tutor, and more.

Animated Math

Interactively explore key concepts to see how math works.

Personal Math Trainer

Get immediate feedback and help as you work through practice sets.

Are YOU Ready?

Complete these exercises to review skills you will need for this module.

Personal Math Trainer

Online Practice and Help

my.hrw.com

Distributive Property

EXAMPLE
$$4(5 - 2) = 4(5) + 4(-2)$$
$$= 20 - 8$$
$$= 12$$

Apply $a(b + c) = ab + ac$.
Simplify.

$$-2(3 + x) = (-2)(3) + (-2)(x)$$
$$= -6 - 2x$$

Apply $a(b + c) = ab + ac$.
Simplify.

Simplify each expression.

1. $3(x + 2)$

2. $7(y - 5)$

3. $(3 - 2x)8$

4. $2(-x - 3)$

_____

_____

_____

_____

5. $-6(-4x + 1)$

6. $(8 - 5x)(-4)$

7. $-3(x - 5)$

8. $-8(-6x - 9)$

_____

_____

_____

_____

Combine Like Terms

EXAMPLE
$$18 + 7y - 8 - 5y$$
$$18 - 8 + 7y - 5y$$
$$18 - 8 = 10$$
$$7y - 5y = (7 - 5)y = 2y$$
$$10 + 2y$$

Reorder.
Subtract.
Add.
Simplify.

Simplify each expression by combining like terms.

9. $5x + 15 + 2x$

10. $6a + 9 - 4a - 11$

11. $-5 + c - 10 + 3d$

_____

_____

_____

12. $22y - 15y + y - 15z$

13. $45 - 12 + 15x - 12y + 3x$

14. $-n + 15 + 4m - 18o - 1$

_____

_____

_____

15. $-8a - 4b + 18a - 5c + 2c - 12d + e - 45d + 4c$

_____

Reading Start-Up

Visualize Vocabulary

Use the Reviews Words with a check next to them to complete the chart.

The property that states the sum or product of any two real numbers will equal another real number.	The property that states that numbers can be added in any order without changing the sum.
Properties	
The property that states that for all real numbers, the sum is always the same, regardless of their grouping.	The property that states if you multiply a sum by a number, you will get the same result if you multiply each addend by that number and then add the products.

Vocabulary

Review Words

✔ Associative Property
  (*Propiedad asociativa*)

✔ Commutative Property
  (*Propiedad conmutativa*)

✔ Closure Property
  (*Propiedad cerradura*)

✔ Distributive Property
  (*Propiedad distributiva*)

  like terms
  (*términos similares*)

  properties of exponents
  (*propiedades de exponentes*)

  terms (*términos*)

Preview Words

  binomial
  degree of a polynomial
  FOIL method
  monomial
  polynomial
  trinomial

Understand Vocabulary

To become familiar with some of the vocabulary terms in the module, consider the following. You may refer to the module, the glossary, or a dictionary.

1. The prefix *tri-* is used to identify an item that has three parts, such as a *triangle* or a *tricycle*. What do you think a **trinomial** might be?

_____

2. The prefix *poly-* is used to identify an item with many elements, such as a *polygon*. What do you think a **polynomial** might be?

_____

Active Reading

Layered Book Before beginning the module, create a layered book to help you learn the concepts in this module. Label each flap with lesson titles from this module. As you study each lesson, write important ideas, such as vocabulary and formulas under the appropriate flap. Refer to your finished layered book as you work on exercises from this module.

GETTING READY FOR
Polynomials and Operations

Understanding the standards and the vocabulary terms in the standards will help you know exactly what you are expected to learn in this module.

Understand that polynomials form a system analogous to the integers, namely, they are closed under the operations of addition, subtraction, and multiplication; add, subtract, and multiply polynomials.

Key Vocabulary

monomial *(monomio)*
A number or product of numbers and variables with whole-number exponents, or a polynomial with one term.

What It Means to You

You will learn how to perform addition, subtraction, and multiplication on monomials and polynomials.

EXAMPLE A.APR.1

What is the sum, difference, and product of the polynomials $-4x^2$ and $3x^2 + 7x - 8$?

Sum	Difference	Product
$\begin{array}{r} -4x^2 \\ +3x^2 + 7x - 8 \\ \hline -x^2 + 7x - 8 \end{array}$	$\begin{array}{r} -4x^2 \\ -(3x^2 + 7x - 8) \\ \hline -7x^2 - 7x + 8 \end{array}$	$\begin{aligned} &-4x^2\,(3x^2 + 7x - 8) \\ &= (-4x^2)(3x^2) + \\ &\quad (-4x^2)(7x) - (-4x^2)8 \\ &= -12x^4 - 28x^3 + 32x^2 \end{aligned}$

Use the structure of an expression to identify ways to rewrite it. For example, see $x^4 - y^4$ as $(x^2)^2 - (y^2)^2$, thus recognizing it as a difference of squares that can be factored as $(x^2 - y^2)(x^2 + y^2)$.

Key Vocabulary

polynomial *(polynomio)*
A monomial or a sum or difference of monomials.

What It Means to You

Expressions can be written many different ways.

EXAMPLE A.SSE.2

Pam wrote the polynomial $k^2 - 9$ while Sam wrote $(k - 3)^2$. Pam claimed that the two expressions were equivalent. Sam disagreed. Who was right?

Expand Sam's expression:

$$(k - 3)^2 = (k - 3)(k - 3)$$

Using the FOIL method:

$$(k - 3)(k - 3) = k^2 - 3k - 3k + 9$$

$$= k^2 - 6k + 9$$

Sam was right. The two expressions are not equivalent.

LESSON 14.1 Understanding Polynomials

COMMON CORE A.SSE.1a
Interpret parts of an expression, such as terms, factors, and coefficients. *Also A.CED.1, A.APR.1*

? ESSENTIAL QUESTION

What are polynomial expressions, and how do you simplify them?

EXPLORE ACTIVITY **A.SSE.1a**

Identifying Monomials

A **monomial** is a number, variable, or product of numbers and variables that have whole number exponents. A monomial cannot have more than one term, and it cannot have a variable in its denominator.

Monomials				Not Monomial		
5	x	$-7xy$	$0.5x^4$	$-0.3x^{-2}$	$4x - y$	$\frac{2}{x^3}$

Complete the table to identify which terms are monomials.

Term	Is this a monomial?	Explain your reasoning.
$3bc$	yes	$3bc$ is the product of a number, 3, and the variables b and c.
x^3		x^3 is the product of the variable x, three times.
$\sqrt{Z}$	no	
2^5		
$\frac{6}{k^2}$	no	
$4x + 7$		

REFLECT

1. **Communicate Mathematical Ideas** Explain why $16^{\frac{1}{2}}$ is a monomial, but $x^{\frac{1}{2}}$ is not a monomial.

_____

_____

_____

Lesson 14.1 **485**

Classifying Polynomials

A **polynomial** can be one monomial, or the sum of more than one monomial. Polynomials are classified by the number of terms: a monomial has one term, a **binomial** has two terms, and a **trinomial** has three terms. Polynomials are also classified by the **degree of a polynomial**, which is the greatest sum of the exponents on the variables in each term.

EXAMPLE 1   COMMON CORE   A.SSE.1a

Classify each polynomial by its degree and the number of terms.

A $6x^3 - 5x^2y^2$

Degree: 4 $6x^3$ has degree 3, and   *Find the degree of*
            $5x^2y^2$ has degree 4.   *each term by adding*
                                           the exponents of
Binomial   *There are 2 terms.*   *the variables in that*
                                           term. The greatest
$6x^3 - 5x^2y^2$ is a 4th degree binomial. *degree is the degree*
                                           of the polynomial.

B $3^5 + 2n^2 + 8n$

Degree: 2 3^5 has degree 0, $2n^2$ has degree 2 and $8n$ has degree 1.

Trinomial   *There are 3 terms.*

$3^5 + 2n^2 + 8n$ is a 2nd degree trinomial.

REFLECT

2. Is $x^3y^2 + x^{0.5}$ a polynomial? Justify your answer.

_____

_____

_____

_____

 **YOUR TURN**

Classify each polynomial by its degree and the number of terms.

3. $4xy^2 + 3x^2y^2 + 5xy$ **4.** $8ab^2 - 4a^2b$

_____   _____

5. $15g^2h + 3g^2$ **6.** $4p^2q^2 + 3q^5 + 5pq$

_____   _____

Personal Math Trainer

Online Practice and Help

my.hrw.com

Simplifying Polynomials

You can simplify polynomials by combining the like terms. *Like terms* are monomials that have the same variables that are raised to the same powers.

Math On the Spot
my.hrw.com

Like terms:
- Same variable
- Same power

$r^2 + 2r^3 + 3r^2$

Unlike terms:
- Different power

EXAMPLE 2
COMMON CORE A.APR.1

Combine like terms to simplify each polynomial.

A $3r^3 - 2r^2 + 5r^2 - 4r^3$

My Notes

$3r^3 - 4r^3 - 2r^2 + 5r^2$ Rearrange in descending order of exponents.

$3r^3 - 4r^3 - 2r^2 + 5r^2$ Identify like terms.

$r^3(3-4) + r^2(-2+5)$ Combine using the Distributive Property.

$-1r^3 + 3r^2$ Simplify.

$-r^3 + 3r^2$

B $p^2q^5 - 4p^5q^4 - 4p^2q^5 + 3p^5q^4$

$-4p^5q^4 + 3p^5q^4 + p^2q^5 - 4p^2q^5$ Rearrange in descending order of exponents.

$-4p^5q^4 + 3p^5q^4 + p^2q^5 - 4p^2q^5$ Identify like terms.

$p^5q^4(-4+3) + p^2q^5(1-4)$ Combine using the Distributive Property.

$(-1)p^5q^4 + (-3)p^2q^5$ Simplify.

$-p^5q^4 - 3p^2q^5$

REFLECT

7. Can you combine like terms without formally showing the Distributive Property? Explain.

_____

_____

_____

_____

YOUR TURN

8. Simplify $5r^3 - r^2s + 6 - 3r^2s - 1r^3 + 2^5$

_____

9. Simplify $7a^2 - ab - 75 - 5ab + 1a^2 + 5^3$

_____

Evaluating Polynomials

You can evaluate polynomials by substituting values for variables.

EXAMPLE 3   Real World   COMMON CORE   A.CED.1

A skyrocket is launched from a 6-foot-high platform with initial speed 200 ft/s. The polynomial $-16t^2 + 200t + 6$ gives the height in feet that the skyrocket will rise in t seconds. How high will the rocket rise if it has a 5-second fuse?

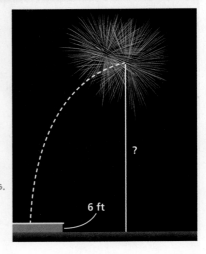

$-16t^2 + 200t + 6$ *Write the expression.*

$-16(5)^2 + 200(5) + 6$ *The time is 5 seconds.*

$-16(25) + 200(5) + 6$ *Use order of operations.*

$-400 + 1000 + 6 = 606$

The rocket will rise 606 feet.

Math Talk
Mathematical Practices

What would be the expression in Example 3 if the rocket was launched from the ground? Explain.

REFLECT

10. **Critical Thinking** Kaylynn says that the expression $-16t^2 + 200t + 50$ can be used to model the height after t seconds of a rocket that starts 100 feet off the ground. Is she correct? Explain.

_____

_____

YOUR TURN

11. A skyrocket is launched from a 20-foot-high platform, with initial speed 200 ft/s. If the polynomial $-16t^2 + 200t + 20$ gives the height that the rocket will rise in t seconds, how high will a rocket with a 4-second fuse rise?

_____

Determine whether each term is a monomial. Give justification for your answer. (Explore Activity)

1. Is $3x^2y$ a monomial? _____ Justify your answer.

_____

_____

2. Is $2xy + 7x$ a monomial? _____ Justify your answer.

_____

Classify each polynomial by its degree and the number of terms. (Example 1)

3. $8x^2 - 3y + 7$

_____

4. $2x^6y - 8x^3y^3$

_____

Simplify each polynomial. (Example 2)

5. $2y^3 - y^2 + 2y^4 + 7y^3$

_____

6. $2mn^3 - 11n^3 + 5mn^3 + 2n^3$

_____

7. $6d^3 - 5d^2 + 2d - 5d^3 - 8d^2$

_____

8. $j^3k^2 + 10j^2k^3 + 5j^3k^2 - 7j^2k^3$

_____

Solve the problem by evaluating the polynomial. (Example 3)

9. Nate's architectural client said she wanted the width of every room in her house increased by 2 feet and the length decreased by 5 feet. The polynomial $2w^2 - w - 10$ gives the area of any room in the house with w representing the room's width. The width of the kitchen is 16 feet. What is the area of the kitchen?

_____

ESSENTIAL QUESTION CHECK-IN

10. What are polynomial expressions, and how do you simplify them?

_____

_____

_____

_____

14.1 Independent Practice

Personal
Math Trainer

Online Practice
and Help

my.hrw.com

Identify each expression as a monomial, a binomial, trinomial, or none of the above. Write the degree of each expression.

11. $2z^2 - 5z - 10$

_____

12. $24x^2y$

_____

13. $5a^2b^3 - 4a^2b^3 + 2a^4b^3$

_____

14. $9q + \frac{4q}{5p} - 3p^2$

_____

Simplify each expression.

15. $3q^2 + 20 - 6q^2 - 17$

_____

16. $4k + 9k^2 - 13 - 6k - 4k^2$

_____

17. $6(x^2 + 2x - 3xy) + 8xy$

_____

18. $5t^2s^4 - 4ts^3 + 4ts + 2ts^3 + 7t^2s^4$

_____

19. $(3r^2 + 4)(2r - 1) - 8r^3 + 6r^2$

_____

20. $3p^2q + 3p(2p^2 + 2pq - 4) + 5p^3$

_____

21. Make a Prediction The number of cells in a bacteria colony increases according to the expression $t^2 + 4t + 4$ with t representing the time in seconds that the colony is allowed to grow at 20°C and $t^2 + 3t + 4$ when the colony grows at 30°C.

a. After 1 minute, which will be greater in number, a colony at 20°C or 30°C? Explain.

_____

_____

_____

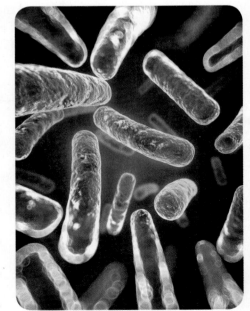

b. After 10 minutes, how will the colonies compare in size? Explain.

_____

_____

_____

_____

c. Which colony will have one million cells first? To the nearest minute, how long would it take to reach this size? Explain how you got your answer.

_____

_____

_____

_____

22. The polynomial $s^3 - \left(\frac{4}{3}\right)(3.14)\left(\frac{s}{2}\right)^3$ describes how much waste is made from carving a cube with side length s into the largest possible sphere.

a. How much waste is made from carving a cube into a sphere when $s = 6$ ft?

_____

b. How much waste is made from carving a cube into a sphere when $s = 12$ ft?

_____

Determine the polynomial that has the greater value for the given value of x.

23. $5x^2 - 2x + 6$ or $5x^2 - 6x + 2$, for $x = 8$

_____

24. $9x^3 - 3x^2 + 8$ or $3x^3 - 8x^2 + 9$, for $x = 2$

_____

25. $3x^3 - 8x^2 + x$ or $2x^3 + 17$, for $x = 3$

_____

26. A book store has a Valued Customer Club which gives its members discounts. The table shows the polynomials that are used to determine the total cost of an online order, including shipping, for people who belong to the Valued Customer Club and people who do not.

Valued Customer Club members	Non-members
$10.95x + 2.50$, where x is the number of books ordered	$12.50x + 4.50$, where x is the number of books ordered

a. How much do members pay for an online order of 8 books? _____

b. How much do non-members pay for an online order of 6 books? _____

c. Do members and non-members ever pay the same amount for an order of x books? Explain.

_____

_____

_____

27. Explain the Error Enrique thinks that the polynomial $4x^3 - 8x^2 + 9x$ has a degree of 16, since $4 \times 3 = 12$, $8 \times 2 = 16$, and $9 \times 1 = 9$. Explain his error, and determine the correct degree.

_____

_____

28. Multi-step Claire and Richard are both artists who use square canvases. Claire uses the polynomial $50x^2 + 250$ to decide how much to charge for her paintings and Richard uses the polynomial $40x^2 + 350$ to decide how much to charge for his paintings. In each polynomial, x is the height of the painting in feet.

a. How much does Claire charge for a 6-foot-tall painting? _____

b. How much does Richard charge for a 5-foot-tall painting? _____

c. To the nearest tenth, for what height will both Claire and Richard charge the same amount for a painting? Explain how to find the answer.

_____

d. When both Claire and Richard charge the same amount for a painting,

how much does each charge? _____

 **FOCUS ON HIGHER ORDER THINKING**

Work Area

29. Justify Reasoning Carson says that the lowest degree a polynomial can have is 1. Gillian says that the lowest degree a polynomial can have is 0. Who is correct? Explain.

_____

_____

_____

30. Analyze Relationships A right triangle has height h and base $h + 4$. Write an expression that represents the area of the triangle. Then calculate the area of a triangle with a height of 12 cm.

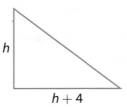

_____

31. Explain the Error Sewell says that the expression $(x + 1)^2$ will be greater than $(x - 1)^2$ for all values of x because $x + 1$ will always be greater than $x - 1$. Explain why Sewell is wrong. Give an example to show his error.

_____

_____

_____

LESSON
14.2

COMMON CORE A.APR.1
Understand that polynomials form a system analogous to the integers, namely, they are closed under the operations of addition, subtraction, and multiplication; add, subtract, and multiply polynomials.
Also A.SSE.2, A.CED.1

Adding and Subtracting Polynomials

ESSENTIAL QUESTION

How do you add and subtract polynomials?

EXPLORE ACTIVITY 1   COMMON CORE   A.APR.1

Properties of Polynomial Addition

The Commutative Property of addition states that changing the order in which terms are added will not affect the answer. For example,

$5x + 4 = 4 + 5x$, and $-2 + 6x = 6x + (-2)$.

The Associative Property of addition states that changing the way in which terms are grouped will not affect the answer. For example,

$3 + (7 + 2x) = (3 + 7) + 2x$, and $(5 - 2x) + 6x = 5 + (-2x + 6x)$.

Identify the property being used to change the expression at each step.

A $45x + (8 + 15x)$ This step changes the _____ of the
    $45x + (15x + 8)$

terms, so the _____ Property of
addition is used.

$(45x + 15x) + 8$ This step changes the _____ of the

terms, so the _____ Property of
$60x + 8$ addition is used.

B $(4h + 30) + (8 + 6h)$ This step changes the _____ of the
    $4h + (30 + 8) + 6h$

terms, so the _____ Property of
addition is used.

$(30 + 8) + 4h + 6h$ This step changes the _____ of the

terms, so the _____ Property of
$38 + 10h$ addition is used.

REFLECT

1. Why isn't there a Commutative Property for subtraction as well as for addition? Explain using an example.

_____

_____

_____

Adding Polynomials

The Commutative and Associative properties are useful when adding polynomials. Remember, when adding terms, the order in which they are added and the way in which they are grouped does not affect the answer.

My Notes

EXAMPLE 1

A.APR.1

Add.

A $(6x^2 + 5x + 2) + (-4x^2 + 3x - 7)$

$$
\begin{array}{r}
(6x^2 + 5x + 2) \\
+(-4x^2 + 3x - 7) \\
\hline
2x^2 + 8x - 5
\end{array}
$$

Rewrite the problem vertically.

Add like terms.

B $(3a^3 - 2a + 4a^2 - 14) + (5a + 6 - 5a^3)$

$(3a^3 + 4a^2 - 2a - 14) + (-5a^3 + 5a + 6)$

Reorder using the Commutative Property. Write terms in order of degree.

$(3a^3 - 5a^3) + 4a^2 + (-2a + 5a) + (-14 + 6)$

Group like terms using the Associative Property.

$(-2a^3) + 4a^2 + (3a) + (-8)$

Add like terms.

$-2a^3 + 4a^2 + 3a - 8$

REFLECT

2. Is the sum of two polynomials always another polynomial? Explain.

_____

_____

_____

_____

YOUR TURN

Find each sum.

3. $(-7x^2 + 3) + (-x^2)$

_____

4. $(5x^2 - 2x + 3) + (x^2 + x + 2)$

_____

5. $-6x^2 + (3x^2 + 5x)$

_____

6. $(x^2 - x - 1) + (6x - 3)$

_____

Finding Opposite Polynomials

The Distributive Property states that multiplying a number by a sum is the same as multiplying the number by each part of the sum, then adding the results. For example, $8(3x + 2) = (8)(3x) + (8)(2)$.

Use the Distributive Property to find the opposite of each polynomial.

A $3d^2 - 5d + 7$

$-1(3d^2 - 5d + 7)$ Multiply the polynomial by

_____ to find the opposite.

$(-1)(\boxed{}) + (\boxed{})(-5d)$ Use the Distributive Property

$+ (-1)(\boxed{})$ to multiply _____ by each
part of the sum.

$\boxed{}d^2 + \boxed{}d - \boxed{}$

B $-4g^3 + 5g^2 - 9$

$-1(-4g^3 + 5g^2 - 9)$ Multiply the polynomial by

_____ to find the opposite.

$(-1)(\boxed{}) + (-1)(5g^2) + (-1)(\boxed{})$ Use the Distributive Property

to multiply _____ by each
part of the sum.

$\boxed{}g^3 - \boxed{}g + \boxed{}$

REFLECT

7. Critical Thinking Describe how a polynomial and its opposite are alike, and how they are different.

_____

_____

_____

_____

8. Make a Conjecture Subtraction is defined as adding the opposite. Describe how you might subtract one polynomial from another.

_____

_____

_____

Subtracting Polynomials

When subtracting polynomials, remember to use the Distributive Property. A negative sign outside of a set of parentheses will change the sign of every term inside the parentheses.

EXAMPLE 2 A.APR.1

Subtract.

A $(5n^2 + 4n + 3) - (2n^2 - 6n + 8)$

$$\begin{array}{r}(5n^2 + 4n + 3) \\ -(2n^2 - 6n + 8) \\ \hline\end{array}$$ Rewrite the problem vertically, with terms in columns.

$$\begin{array}{r}(5n^2 + 4n + 3) \\ -2n^2 + 6n - 8 \\ \hline 3n^2 + 10n - 5\end{array}$$ Distribute the negative sign.

Combine like terms.

B $(-3b + 4b^3 + 9 - 7b^2) - (-6b^2 + 2 - b^3)$

$(4b^3 - 7b^2 - 3b + 9) - (-b^3 - 6b^2 + 2)$ Reorder using the Commutative Property. Write terms in order of degree.

$4b^3 - 7b^2 - 3b + 9 + b^3 + 6b^2 - 2$ Distribute the negative sign.

$(4b^3 + b^3) + (-7b^2 + 6b^2) - 3b + (9 - 2)$ Group the like terms.

$(5b^3) + (-1b^2) - 3b + (7)$

$5b^3 - b^2 - 3b + 7$

Math Talk
Mathematical Practices

Is it possible to add or subtract two polynomials that have no like terms? If so, give an example.

REFLECT

9. Is the difference of two polynomials always another polynomial? Explain.

_____

_____

_____

_____

_____

YOUR TURN

Find each difference.

10. $(4m^3 - m^2n + 6m^3) - (5m^2n - 1m^3 + 7mn^2)$ _____

11. $(2x^3y - 6y + 7x^3) - (6y + 2x^3 - 3x^3y)$ _____

Modeling with Polynomials

When solving problems by modeling, be sure to choose the correct operation for combining the polynomials.

Math On the Spot

⏻ my.hrw.com

EXAMPLE 3 | COMMON CORE | A.APR.1, A.CED.1

Suppose the cost in dollars of producing x toothbrushes is given by the polynomial $400,000 + 3x$ and the revenue generated from sales is given by the polynomial $20x - 0.00004x^2$.

STEP 1 Write a polynomial expression for the profit from making and selling x toothbrushes.

$(20x - 0.00004x^2) - (400,000 + 3x)$	Profit = Revenue − Cost
$20x - 0.00004x^2 + (-400,000 - 3x)$	Add the opposite.
$20x - 0.00004x^2 - 400,000 - 3x$	Associative Property.
$-0.00004x^2 + 17x - 400,000$	Combine like terms.

STEP 2 Find the profit for selling 200,000 toothbrushes.

$-0.00004x^2 + 17x - 400,000$

$-0.00004(200,000)^2 + 17(200,000) - 400,000$

$1,400,000$

The profit is $1,400,000 or $1.4 million.

REFLECT

12. If the toothbrush company sold 10,000 toothbrushes, how much would the company gain or lose?

_____

YOUR TURN

The profit from a company's factory in California is given by $n^2 - 15n + 23$. The company's profit from their factory in Florida is given by $n^2 - 20n - 14$. In both, n equals the number of goods produced in the factory.

13. Write a polynomial that represents the difference in profits between the California factory and the Florida factory.

_____

14. Write a polynomial that represents the total profits of the two factories.

_____

Personal Math Trainer

Online Practice and Help

⏻ my.hrw.com

Identify whether the Commutative or the Associative Property is being used for each step. (Explore Activity 1)

1. $(5d^2 + 2d) + 3d^2$

$(2d + 5d^2) + 3d^2$ _____ Property

$2d + (5d^2 + 3d^2)$ _____ Property

$2d + 8d^2$

Add or subtract using the vertical method. (Example 1 and Example 2)

2. $(5bc^2 + 3bc + 3b) - (4bc^2 - 8bc - 2b)$

$5bc^2 + 3bc + 3b$

$\underline{-4bc^2 + 8bc + 2b}$

3. $(9g^2 + 6g - 3) + (9g^2 - 6g + 3)$

$9g^2 + 6g - 3$

$\underline{+9g^2 - 6g + 3}$

Add or subtract using the horizontal method. (Example 1 and Example 2)

4. $(13m^2 - m + 1) - (-10m^2 - 7m + 2)$

$13m^2 - m + 1$ _____

5. $(-y^2 + 11y - 2) + (-6y^2 + 6y - 5)$

$-y^2 + 11y - 2$ _____

Use the Distributive Property to find the opposite of the polynomial $-13x^3 + 12 - 6x$. (Explore Activity 2)

6. $(-1)(-13x^3 + 12 - 6x)$

$(-1)(\boxed{}x^3) + (\boxed{})(12) + (-1)(\boxed{}x)$

$\boxed{}x^3 - \boxed{} + \boxed{}x$

7. The volume of a rectangular prism, in cubic inches, is given by the expression $x^3 + 3x^2 - 5x + 7$. The volume of a smaller rectangular prism is given by the expression $5x^3 - 6x^2 - 7x - 14$. How much greater is the volume of the larger rectangular prism? (Example 3)

large prism − small prism $= (x^3 + 3x^2 - 5x + 7) - (5x^3 - 6x^2 - 7x - 14)$

_____

? **ESSENTIAL QUESTION CHECK-IN**

8. How do you add and subtract polynomials?

_____

_____

_____

14.2 Independent Practice

 COMMON CORE A.APR.1, A.SSE.2, A.CED.1

Add or subtract.

9. $(6^2 - 51 + 2) + (-12^2 - 8 + 22)$

_____

10. $(-13^2 + 100 - 29) + (5^3 + 80 - 44)$

_____

11. $(10p^2 - 2p + 1) + (-5p^2 - 3p + 12)$

_____

12. $(-6x^2 + 11x - 2) + (-6x^2 + 6x - 4)$

_____

13. $(-d^2 + 19d - 8) - (-5d^2 - 6d + 12)$

_____

14. $(8r^3s^2 + 6rs^2 + 6r) - (4r^3s^2 - 2rs^2 - 5r)$

_____

15. $(-3z^2 + 16z - 8) + (-3z^2 - 6z + 13)$

_____

16. $(8w^3t^2 + 6wt^2 + 6w) - (4w^3t^2 - 2wt^2 - 3w)$

_____

17. $(6x^2 + 7x - 2) + (3x^2 - 4x - 7)$

_____

18. $(18n^2 + n + 1) - (15n^2 - 4n - 11)$

_____

19. $(-5a^2 + 15a - 8) - (-5a^2 - 7a + 12)$

_____

20. $(7q^3r^2 + 14qr^2 + 21q) - (14q^3r^2 - 3qr^2 - 5q)$

_____

21. **Multi-Step** The height of the water in a leaking pool is determined by $8g^2 + 3g - 4$, the rate that the water is filled, and $9g^2 - 2g - 5$, the rate that water leaks from the pool, where g represents the number of gallons entering or leaving the pool per minute.

a. Write an expression that determines the height of the water in the pool.

_____

b. What will be the height of the water if $g = 1, 2, 3,$ and 4?

_____

_____

c. To the nearest tenth, at which value for g will the water reach its greatest height? What is that height?

_____

22. In square inches, the area of the square is $4x^2 - 2x - 6$ and the area of the triangle $2x^2 + 4x - 5$. What polynomial represents the area of the shaded region?

_____

23. Analyze Relationships The area of the shaded triangle is $5x^2 + 3x - 4$. What is the area of the entire figure?

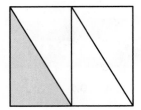

_____

Work Area

24. Communicate Mathematical Ideas Hallie subtracted a quantity from the polynomial $3y^2 + 8y - 16$ and produced the expression $(y + 2)(y - 2)$. What quantity did Hallie subtract? Explain how you got your answer.

_____

_____

25. Explain the Error Geoffrey thinks that the sum of $5x^2y^3 + 6x + 7y$ and $8y + 4x^3y^2 + 2x$ is $9x^2y^3 + 8x + 15y$. Explain Geoffrey's error, and find the correct sum.

_____

_____

26. Analyze Relationships Write a polynomial that represents the difference between the perimeter of a square and the circumference of a circle that have the same side length and diameter, represented by x. What is the difference when x is 9 inches? Use 3.14 for π.

_____

27. Critical Thinking A set is closed under an operation if performing that operation on two members of the set results in another member of the set. Is the set of polynomials closed under addition? under subtraction? Explain.

_____

_____

_____

28. Persevere in Problem Solving John has yellow and green cubes, each with side length c. Eight yellow cubes are glued together to make a larger cube. An even larger cube is made by gluing on green cubes until no yellow cubes can be seen. The large green cube has a side length of $4c$. Write an expression for the volume of the green cubes.

_____

_____

_____

Multiplying Polynomials by Monomials

COMMON CORE **A.APR.1**
Understand that polynomials form a system analogous to the integers, namely, they are closed under the operations of addition, subtraction, and multiplication; add, subtract, and multiply polynomials.
Also A.SSE.2, A.CED.1

? ESSENTIAL QUESTION

How can you multiply polynomials by monomials?

EXPLORE ACTIVITY COMMON CORE **A.APR.1**

Modeling Polynomial Multiplication

You can use algebra tiles to model the multiplication of a polynomial by a monomial.

> **Rules**
>
> 1. The first factor goes on the left side of the grid, the second factor on the top.
>
> 2. Fill in the grid with tiles that have the same height as tiles on the left and the same length as tiles on the top.
>
> 3. Follow the key on the right. The product of two tiles of the same color is positive; the product of two tiles of different colors is negative.

A Use algebra tiles to find $2(x + 1)$.

> **KEY**
>
>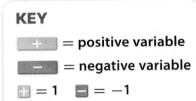

STEP 1 Fill in the factors.

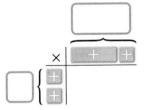

Place the factor 2 on the left.
Place the factor $x + 1$ on the top.

STEP 2 Fill in the grid.

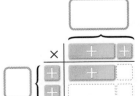

Fill in the grid according to Rule 2 above.
Draw the missing tiles.

STEP 3 Count the positive and negative tiles in the grid.

x tiles: _____

1 tiles: _____

Expression: _____

B Use algebra tiles to find $2x(x - 3)$.

STEP 1 Fill in the factors.

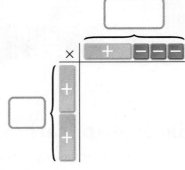

Remember, the first factor goes on the left side and the second factor goes on the top row.

STEP 2 Fill in the grid.

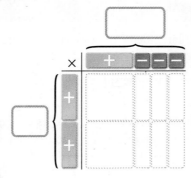

Fill in the grid according to Rule 2.
Draw the tiles.
Positives are yellow, negatives are red.

STEP 3 Count the positive and negative tiles in the grid.

x^2 tiles: _____

x tiles: _____

1 tiles: _____

expression: _____

REFLECT

1. How do the tiles illustrate the idea of x^2 geometrically?

_____

_____

2. How does the grid illustrate the Distributive Property? Explain.

_____

_____

_____

_____

Multiplying Monomials

When multiplying monomials, you may have to multiply variables with exponents. Recall the Product of Powers Property, which states that $a^m \times a^n = a^{(m+n)}$.

Math On the Spot

my.hrw.com

EXAMPLE 1
COMMON CORE A.APR.1

Multiply.

A $(2x^4)(-3x^5)$

$(2 \cdot -3)(x^4 \cdot x^5)$ *Group factors that use the same variable.*

$(2 \cdot -3)(x^{4+5})$ *Product of Powers Property*

$-6x^9$ *Simplify.*

B $(8g^2h^5)(6gh^3)$

$(8 \cdot 6)(g^2 \cdot g)(h^5 \cdot h^3)$ *Group factors that use the same variable.*

$(8 \cdot 6)(g^{2+1})(h^{5+3})$ *Product of Powers Property*

$48g^3h^8$ *Simplify.*

REFLECT

3. What can you conclude about the order of factors in multiplication?

_____

_____

Math Talk
Mathematical Practices

Is the product of two monomials always a monomial? Explain.

4. Explain the Error Felicity reasons that $g^2 \cdot g^{0.5} = g^1$, since $2 \cdot 0.5 = 1$. Explain her error and find the correct product for $g^2 \cdot g^{0.5}$.

_____

_____

5. Communicate Mathematical Ideas If $x^8 \cdot x^y = x$, what is the value of y? Explain.

_____

_____

YOUR TURN

Find the products.

6. $12x^5(5x^4)$ _____

7. $6a^4b(4a^3b^2)$ _____

8. $(6a^2b^5)(3ab)$ _____

9. $(4k^2d^5)(9d^3j^2)$ _____

Personal Math Trainer

Online Practice and Help

my.hrw.com

My Notes

Multiplying a Polynomial by a Monomial

Remember, the Distributive Property states that multiplying a term by a sum is the same thing as multiplying the term by each part of the sum, then adding the results.

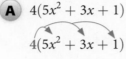

EXAMPLE 2 COMMON CORE A.APR.1

Find each product.

A $4(5x^2 + 3x + 1)$

$4(5x^2 + 3x + 1)$ Distribute 4.

$4(5x^2) + 4(3x) + 4(1)$ Regroup and multiply.

$20x^2 + 12x + 4$ Simplify.

B $2x\,(3x^2 + 2x - 4)$

$2x(3x^2 + 2x - 4)$ Distribute 2x. Remember, $2x = 2x^1$.

$2x^1(3x^2) + 2x^1(2x^1) - 2x^1(4)$ Regroup.

$6x^{1+2} + 4x^{1+1} - 8x^1$ Multiply and combine exponents.

$6x^3 + 4x^2 - 8x$ Simplify.

REFLECT

10. Is the product of a monomial and a polynomial always a polynomial? Explain. If so, how many terms does it have?

_____

_____

_____

_____

YOUR TURN

Find each product.

11. $(4m^3n^2)(5m^2n - 3mn - 2)$

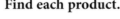

12. $2a^2(5b^2 + 3ab + 6a + 1)$

13. $3ab(2a^2b + 6ab^2 + 8b)$

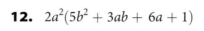

© Houghton Mifflin Harcourt Publishing Company

Application of Multiplying Polynomials and Monomials

Knowing how to multiply polynomials and monomials is useful when solving real-world problems.

EXAMPLE 3   COMMON CORE **A.APR.1, A.CED.1**

Chrystelle is making a planter box with a square base. She wants the height of the box to be 3 inches more than the length. If she needs the volume of the box to be as close as possible to 6,000 in³, what should the length of the box be to the nearest whole inch?

STEP 1 Define terms and write what you know.

$$\text{side length} = s$$
$$\text{height} = s + 3$$
$$\text{volume} = (\text{side length}) \cdot (\text{side length}) \cdot \text{height}$$
$$= (s \cdot s)(s + 3)$$
$$= s^2(s + 3) = s^3 + 3s^2$$

STEP 2 Make a plan.

Chrystelle wants the volume of the planter to be as close as possible to 6000 in³, so you need to find a value for s that gives a product that is close to 6000 in³.

s	$s^3 + 3s^2$
15	$15^3 + 3(15)^2 = 4050$
16	$16^3 + 3(16)^2 = 4864$
17	$17^3 + 3(17)^2 = 5780$
18	$18^3 + 3(18)^2 = 6804$

STEP 3 Select the best answer.

6,000 is closer to 5780 than it is to 6804, so the length of the planter to the nearest whole inch should be 17 inches.

REFLECT

14. What If? Explain how the answer would change if Chrystelle wanted the volume as close as possible to 4,400 in³.

_____

YOUR TURN

15. David needs a piece of paper where the length is 4 inches more than the width, and the area is as close as possible to 50 in². To the nearest whole inch, what should the measurements be for the piece of paper?

_____

Personal Math Trainer
Online Practice and Help
my.hrw.com

Guided Practice

Use the algebra tiles to find the product of polynomials. (Explore Activity)

1. What multiplication problem is being modeled? _____

2. Fill in the grid.

3. What is the product? _____

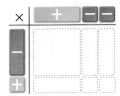

Find the product of the monomials. (Example 1)

4. $d^5f^2(16d^3e^4f^2)$

$$= (\boxed{} \cdot \boxed{})$$

$$(\boxed{} \cdot \boxed{})$$

$$= \underline{\hspace{3cm}}$$

5. $-13r^3s^5(-3rs^2)$

$$= \underline{\hspace{5cm}}$$

$$= \underline{\hspace{5cm}}$$

Find the product of each monomial and polynomial. (Example 2)

6. $5(2k^2 + k + 3)$

$5(\boxed{}) + 5(\boxed{}) + 5(\boxed{})$

_____

7. $8t(3t^2 + 5ts + 2s)$

$\boxed{}(\boxed{}) + \boxed{}(\boxed{}) + 8t(\boxed{})$

_____

8. A jeweler sells gems at a cost in dollars per centigram that is 4 more than 6 times the weight of the gem in centigrams. Thus, a gem that weighs w centigrams will be sold at a price of $6w + 4$ dollars per centigram — meaning that a larger, heavier gem will cost more per centigram than a smaller gem. If the jeweler sold a single gem for about $2500, what did the gem weigh to the nearest centigram? (Example 3)

_____

 ESSENTIAL QUESTION CHECK-IN

9. How can you multiply a polynomial by a monomial?

_____

_____

_____

_____

14.3 Independent Practice

COMMON CORE   A.APR.1, A.SSE.2, A.CED.1

Find each product.

10. $4x(3x^3y^4)$

_____

11. $-0.5m(-16m^4n^2)$

_____

12. $8a^2 b^4(-7a^3b^2)$

_____

13. $5(2k^2 + k + 4)$

_____

14. $9j(6k^2 - 2k + 13j)$

_____

15. $9a^2 b^2(-4a^3b^5)$

_____

16. $3i(3i^2 + 3ig + 3i^2g^2)$

_____

17. $-2t(3t^3 + 7ts + 5s)$

_____

18. $0.25de^2(-4d^2 + 12de^2 - 8d^2e)$

_____

19. $-6v^2w^3 (v^2 - 11v^2w^5 + 6w^4)$

_____

20. $7a^3b^4 (-3a^2 + 8ab^2 - 7a^2b)$

_____

21. $-10x^4y^4 (x^4 - 4x^4y^4 + 4y^3)$

_____

22. Interpret the Answer A construction engineer needs to make 25 square concrete slabs with sides of length x feet and height $x - 3$ feet. If the engineer can use at most 350,000 ft^3 of concrete, what should the dimensions of each slab be, to the nearest foot?

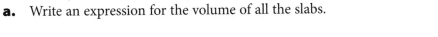

a. Write an expression for the volume of all the slabs.

_____

b. What should x equal, to the nearest foot?

_____

23. A fish market sells sushi-grade fish at a price of $4f - 2$ dollars per foot, meaning that the larger the fish is, the greater its price per foot will be. If the market sold a fish for $552, what was the length of the fish?

_____

24. Analyze Relationships The target heart rate for a fit person of age a exercising at p percent of his or her heart rate is determined by the expression $\frac{1}{2}p(418 - a)$ for women and $\frac{1}{2}p(400 - a)$ for men. What is the difference between the target heart rates for a fit woman and a fit man?

_____

Work Area

25. Represent Real World Problems The Reflecting Pool near the Washington Monument is a rectangle with a length that is 50 feet more than 15 times its width. The depth of the pool is $\frac{1}{50}$ of the width. Let w represent the width of the pool.

a. Write polynomial expressions for the length and depth of the pool in terms of w. Then write a polynomial expression for the volume of the pool in terms of w.

_____

_____

b. The depth of the pool is 3 feet. What is the volume of the pool?

_____

_____

26. Explain the Error Sandy says the product of x^2 and $x^3 + 5x^2 + 1$ is $x^6 + 5x^4 + x^2$. Explain the error that Sandy made and give the correct product.

_____

_____

_____

27. Critical Thinking You are finding the product of a monomial and a binomial. How is the degree of the product related to the degree of the monomial and the degree of the binomial? Give examples and explain your reasoning.

_____

_____

_____

_____

_____

_____

LESSON
14.4 Multiplying Polynomials

COMMON CORE **A.APR.1**

Understand that polynomials form a system analogous to the integers, namely, they are closed under the operations of addition, subtraction, and multiplication; add, subtract, and multiply polynomials. *Also A.SSE.2, A.CED.1*

? ESSENTIAL QUESTION

How can you multiply binomials and polynomials?

EXPLORE ACTIVITY COMMON CORE **A.APR.1**

Modeling Binomial Multiplication

Using algebra tiles to model the product of two binomials is very similar to using algebra tiles to model the product of a monomial and a polynomial.

Rules

1. The first factor goes on the left side of grid, the second factor on the top.

2. Fill in the grid with tiles that have the same height as tiles on the left and the same length as tiles on the top.

3. Follow the key on the right. The product of two tiles of the same color is positive; the product of two tiles of different colors is negative.

Use the tiles to find $(x + 1)(x - 2)$.

KEY

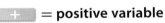 = **positive variable**

 = **negative variable**

 = **1** = **−1**

STEP 1 Fill in the factors, then fill in the grid.
Count the positive and negative tiles in the grid.

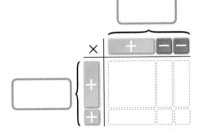

Fill in the grid according to Rule 2.

x^2 tiles: _____

x tiles: _____

1 tiles: _____

STEP 2 Remove any zero pairs.

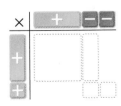

$x + (-x) = 0$, so these tiles represent a zero pair.

Remove one x tile and one $-x$ tile from the grid.

STEP 3 Recount the tiles in the grid and write the expression.

x^2 tiles: _____

x tiles: _____

1 tiles: _____

Expression: _____

REFLECT

1. Communicate Mathematical Ideas How can you tell when tiles form a zero pair?

_____

_____

2. Is it possible for more than one pair of tiles to form a zero pair? Explain.

_____

_____

Math On the Spot

my.hrw.com

Multiplying Binomials

You can use the Distributive Property to multiply two binomials.

$$(x + y)(x + z) = x(x + z) + y(x + z) = x^2 + xz + xy + yz$$

Another way to use the Distributive Property is the **FOIL** method. The FOIL method uses the Distributive Property to multiply terms of the binomials in this order: First terms, Outer terms, Inner terms, and Last terms.

$$(x + y)(x + z) = x^2 + xz + xy + yz$$

EXAMPLE 1

COMMON CORE A.APR.1

Multiply.

A $(x^2 + 3)(x + 2)$

Use the FOIL method.

$(x^2 + 3)(x + 2) = (x^2 + 3)(x + 2)$ F Multiply the first terms. Result: x^3

$= (x^2 + 3)(x + 2)$ O Multiply the outer terms. Result: $2x^2$

$= (x^2 + 3)(x + 2)$ I Multiply the inner terms. Result: $3x$

$= (x^2 + 3)(x + 2)$ L Multiply the last terms. Result: 6

Add the results.

$$(x^2 + 3)(x + 2) = x^3 + 2x^2 + 3x + 6$$

F   O   I   L

B $(3x^2 - 2x)(x + 5)$

Use the FOIL method.

$(3x^2 - 2x)(x + 5) = (3x^2 - 2x)(x + 5)$ F Multiply the **first** terms. Result: $3x^3$

$\qquad\qquad\qquad = (3x^2 - 2x)(x + 5)$ O Multiply the **outer** terms. Result: $15x^2$

$\qquad\qquad\qquad = (3x^2 - 2x)(x + 5)$ I Multiply the **inner** terms. Result: $-2x^2$

$\qquad\qquad\qquad = (3x^2 - 2x)(x + 5)$ L Multiply the **last** terms. Result: $-10x$

Add the results. Group like terms.

$$(3x^2 - 2x)(x + 5) = 3x^3 + 15x^2 - 2x^2 - 10x = 3x^3 + 13x^2 - 10x$$

F   O   I   L

My Notes

REFLECT

3. The FOIL method finds the sum of four partial products. Why does the result from part B only have three terms?

_____

_____

4. **Analyze Relationships** Would you use the FOIL method for numeric expressions like $(5 + 3)(7 + 2)$? Explain.

_____

_____

_____

YOUR TURN

Multiply.

5. $(x + 4)(x - 3)$

_____

6. $(2n + 6)(n + 3)$

_____

Personal Math Trainer

Online Practice and Help

my.hrw.com

Math On the Spot

my.hrw.com

Multiplying Polynomials

To multiply polynomials with more than two terms, you can use the Distributive Property several times.

EXAMPLE 2 COMMON CORE A.APR.1

Multiply.

A $(x + 2)(x^2 - 5x + 4)$

$(x + 2)(x^2 - 5x + 4) = x(x^2 - 5x + 4) + 2(x^2 - 5x + 4)$ Distribute.

$= x(x^2 - 5x + 4) + 2(x^2 - 5x + 4)$ Distribute again.

$= x(x^2) + x(-5x) + x(4) + 2(x^2)$ Write products
$+ 2(-5x) + 2(4)$ of terms.

$= x^3 - 5x^2 + 4x + 2x^2 - 10x + 8$ Simplify.

$= x^3 - 3x^2 - 6x + 8$ Combine like terms.

B $(3x - 4)(-2x^3 + 5x - 6)$

$(3x - 4)(-2x^3 + 5x - 6) = 3x(-2x^3 + 5x - 6) - 4(-2x^3 + 5x - 6)$ Distribute.

$= 3x(-2x^3) + 3x(5x) + 3x(-6)$ Write
$- 4(-2x^3) - 4(5x) - 4(-6)$ products of terms.

$= -6x^4 + 15x^2 - 18x + 8x^3$ Simplify.
$-20x + 24$

$= -6x^4 + 8x^3 + 15x^2 - 38x + 24$ Combine like terms.

> **Math Talk**
> Mathematical Practices
>
> Can you use the method shown here to multiply two trinomials? Explain.

REFLECT

7. Is the product of two polynomials always another polynomial? Explain.

_____

_____

_____

_____

Personal Math Trainer

Online Practice and Help

my.hrw.com

YOUR TURN

Multiply.

8. $(x - 5)(x^2 + 4x - 6)$

9. $(3x + 1)(x^3 + 4x^2 - 7)$

_____   _____

Special Products of Binomials

The binomial products $(a + b)^2$, $(a - b)^2$, and $(a + b)(a - b)$ are called *special products*. You can multiply these special products by using the FOIL method or by using the special product rules given in the table.

Math On the Spot
my.hrw.com

Special Product Rules	
Sum and difference	$(a + b)(a - b) = a^2 - b^2$
Square of a binomial	$(a + b)^2 = a^2 + 2ab + b^2$ $(a - b)^2 = a^2 - 2ab + b^2$

EXAMPLE 3

COMMON CORE   A.APR.1, A.SSE.2

Find each product.

A $(x - 3)^2$ **Using FOIL**

$(x - 3) \ (x - 3)$

$x^2 - 3x - 3x + 3^2$

$x^2 - 6x + 9$

$(x - 3)^2$ **Using Rules**

$(x - 3)^2$

$x^2 - 2(x)(3) + 3^2$

$x^2 - 6x + 9$

Animated Math
my.hrw.com

B $(2z + 5)^2$ **Using FOIL**

$(2z + 5) \ (2z + 5)$

$4z^2 + 2z(5) + 2z(5) + 5^2$

$4z^2 + 20z + 25$

$(2z + 5)^2$ **Using Rules**

$(2z + 5)^2$

$2z^2 + 2(2z)(5) + 5^2$

$2z^2 + 20z + 25$

C $(n + 3)(n - 3)$ **Using FOIL**

$(n + 3) \ (n - 3)$

$n^2 + 3n - 3n - 3^2$

$n^2 - 9$

$(n + 3)(n - 3)$ **Using Rules**

$(n + 3)(n - 3)$

$n^2 - 3^2$

$n^2 - 9$

YOUR TURN

Find each product.

10. $(x + 5)^2$

11. $(2p - 3)^2$

12. $(3s + 1)(3s - 1)$

_____

_____

_____

13. $(2x + 5)(2x - 5)$

14. $(3g + 6)^2$

15. $(4t - 8)^2$

_____

_____

_____

Personal Math Trainer
Online Practice and Help
my.hrw.com

Guided Practice

Use algebra tiles to find each product. (Explore Activity)

1. $(x - 2)(x + 3)$

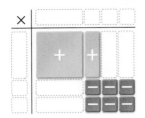

_____

2. $(2x - 1)(x + 3)$

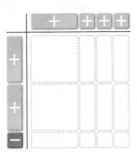

_____

Use the FOIL method to find each product. (Example 1)

3. $(x - 3)(x - 5)$

$\boxed{} - \boxed{}x - \boxed{}x + \boxed{}$

_____

4. $(y + 9)(y - 3)$

$\boxed{} - \boxed{}y + \boxed{}y - \boxed{}$

_____

5. $(4a - 4)(2a + 1)$

$\boxed{} + \boxed{}a - \boxed{}a - \boxed{}$

_____

6. $(3g + 2h)(-5g + 6h)$

$\boxed{} + \boxed{}gh - \boxed{}hg + 12\boxed{}$

_____

Find each product. (Example 2 and Example 3)

7. $(x + 3)(x^2 - 2x + 1)$

$(x^{\boxed{}} - \boxed{}x^2 + \boxed{}x)$

$+ (\boxed{}x^2 - \boxed{}x + 3)$

_____

8. $(4k - 3)(-k^3 + 6k - 4)$

$(\boxed{} + \boxed{}k^2 - \boxed{}k)$

$+ (\boxed{}k^3 - \boxed{}k + 12)$

_____

9. $(2b + 7)(2b - 7)$

_____

10. $(5x + 1)(5x + 1)$

_____

? ESSENTIAL QUESTION CHECK-IN

11. How can you multiply binomials and polynomials?

_____

Name _____ Class _____ Date _____

14.4 Independent Practice

 COMMON CORE A.APR.1, A.SSE.2, A.CED.1

Personal Math Trainer

Online Practice and Help

my.hrw.com

Use the Distributive Property or FOIL method to find the product.

12. $(m + 3)(m + 7)$

13. $(4r + 7)(r - 2)$

14. $(3x + 7)(2x + 5)$

15. $(k - 2)(k^2 - k + 1)$

16. $(x + 4)(x^2 + 6x - 5)$

17. $(-d + 7)(2d^2 - d - 9)$

18. $(2y + 5)^2$

19. $(2x + 1)(2x - 1)$

20. $(5n - 3)^2$

21. Trina has two brothers. One brother is 7 years older than Trina and the other brother is 7 years younger than Trina. The product of her brothers' ages is 95.

a. If x represents Trina's age, write an equation to describe the product of her brothers' ages. _____

b. Solve the equation for x. How old is Trina? _____

22. Ociel has designed a square mural that measures 10 feet on each side. Bill has also designed a square mural, but his measures y feet shorter on each side.

a. Write an expression to represent the area of Bill's mural. _____

b. How much smaller than Ociel's mural is Bill's mural? Explain.

_____

_____

_____

_____

23. **Explain the Error** Mika thinks that $(7x^2 - 12y^3)^2$ is equal to $49x^4 - 84x^2y^3 + 144y^6$. Explain her error, and find the correct product.

_____

_____

_____

© Houghton Mifflin Harcourt Publishing Company

24. Represent Real-World Problems Joanna, the line manager at Smedley Electronics, works 14 hours a week more than her line workers and gets paid $6.50 more per hour. Line workers work h hours per week and get paid d dollars per hour.

a. Write an expression for how much a line worker gets paid each week and how much Joanna gets paid each week.

_____

b. Write an expression for how much more Joanna gets paid each week than one of her line workers.

_____

_____

c. If line workers get paid $576 for a 36-hour week, how much does Joanna get paid per week?

_____

_____

H.O.T. **FOCUS ON HIGHER ORDER THINKING**

Work Area

25. Critical Thinking The product of 3 consecutive odd numbers is 2145. Write an expression for finding the numbers, then find the numbers.

_____

_____

26. Represent Real-World Problems The town swimming pool is d feet deep. The width of the pool is 10 feet greater than 5 times the depth. The length of the pool is 25 feet greater than the width.

a. Write and simplify an expression to represent the volume of the pool.

_____

_____

b. If the pool holds 51,000 ft^3 of water, what are the dimensions of the pool?

_____

27. Communicate Mathematical Ideas Explain how to find a general rule for the product $(a + b)^3$. Then use your reasoning to write a general rule for $(a - b)^3$.

_____

_____

_____

Ready to Go On?

14.1 Understanding Polynomials

Simplify each polynomial.

1. $a^2 + 12a - 7 - 3a^2 - 5a + 8$ _____

2. $7x^3y^2 + 3xy^2 + 6x - 9x^3y^2 + 2xy^2 + 5x - 1$ _____

14.2 Adding and Subtracting Polynomials

Add or subtract.

3. $(3x^2 - 6x + 2) - (8x + 6 - 5x^2)$

4. $(3a^2b - 6ab^2 + 2a) + (4ab^2 - 3b - 2a^2b)$

14.3 Multiplying Polynomials by Monomials

Multiply.

5. $4e(4e^2 + 5eg + 6e^2g^2)$

6. $-2u(4u^3 + 5u^2s^2 + 6s)$

14.4 Multiplying Polynomials

Multiply.

7. $(5c + 7)(5c - 7)$

8. $(6y^2 - 3y)^2$

9. $(9p^2 - 3q)(4p^3 - 5)$

10. $(4y - 3)(y^2 + 8y - 6)$

? ESSENTIAL QUESTION

11. How are polynomials like other number systems such as whole numbers and integers?

_____

_____

_____

_____

MODULE 14

MIXED REVIEW

Assessment Readiness

Personal Math Trainer

Online Practice and Help

my.hrw.com

1. Consider each expression. Is the expression a third-degree polynomial? Select Yes or No for expressions A–C.

   A. $8g^2h - 4gh^2$ ○ Yes ○ No

   B. $3x^2 + 5x + 6$ ○ Yes ○ No

   C. $8 + 4n - 5n^2 + n^3$ ○ Yes ○ No

2. Consider the polynomials $4x - 6$ and $2x^2 - 5x + 1$. Choose True or False for each statement.

   A. The sum of the polynomials is $2x^2 - x - 5$. ○ True ○ False

   B. The first polynomial minus the second polynomial is $-2x^2 + 9x - 7$. ○ True ○ False

   C. The product of the polynomials is $8x^3 - 20x^2 - 6$. ○ True ○ False

3. The width of a box of crackers is 10 centimeters less than the length, and the height is 5 centimeters more than the length, as shown at the right. Write and simplify an expression for the volume of the box in cubic centimeters in terms of x. How did the Distributive, Commutative, and Associative Properties help you solve this problem?

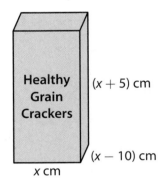

Healthy Grain Crackers

$(x + 5)$ cm

$(x - 10)$ cm

x cm

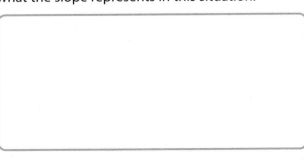

4. The graph shows how a plane's altitude is changing over time. Find the slope of the line, and then tell what the slope represents in this situation.

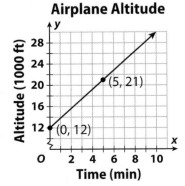

Airplane Altitude

Altitude (1000 ft)

(5, 21)

(0, 12)

Time (min)

Factoring Polynomials

? ESSENTIAL QUESTION

How can you factor expressions of the form $ax^2 + bx + c$?

Real-World Video

Ruling out common elements in a scientific experiment is similar to removing common factors in an equation: logically, whatever is common to two samples can't be the cause of differences between them.

○ my.hrw.com

GO DIGITAL
my.hrw.com

my.hrw.com

Go digital with your write-in student edition, accessible on any device.

Math On the Spot

Scan with your smart phone to jump directly to the online edition, video tutor, and more.

Animated Math

Interactively explore key concepts to see how math works.

Personal Math Trainer

Get immediate feedback and help as you work through practice sets.

Are YOU Ready?

Complete these exercises to review skills you will need for this module.

Factors

EXAMPLE List the factors of 12.

1, 12
3, 4
2, 6

Any whole number that can be multiplied by another whole number to get 12 is a factor of 12.

List the factors of each number.

1. 8

2. 10

3. 30

Multiply Monomials and Polynomials

EXAMPLE Multiply.

$6x(2x + 5)$ Apply the Distributive Property.
$6x(2x) + 6x(5) = 12x^2 + 30x$

Multiply.

4. $10(x - 5)$

5. $3h(h^2j + 2h^2)$

6. $y(7y^3 - 4y^2 - 1)$

Multiply Binomials

EXAMPLE Find the product.

$(x + 3)(x + 8)$

First: $x \cdot x = x^2$
Outer: $x \cdot 8 = 8x$
Inner: $3 \cdot x = 3x$
Last: $3 \cdot 8 = 24$
$x^2 + 8x + 3x + 24 = x^2 + 11x + 24$

Use FOIL to multiply each term in the first binomial by each term in the second binomial.

Find each product.

7. $(b - 7)(b + 1)$

8. $(2p - 5)(p - 1)$

9. $(3n + 4)(2n + 3)$

Reading Start-Up

Visualize Vocabulary

Fill in the missing information in the chart below.

Word	Definition	Examples
factor		$12 = 3 \cdot 4$ 3 and 4 are factors of 12. $xy = x \cdot y$ x and y are factors of xy.
binomial	a polynomial with ☐ terms	
	a polynomial with ☐ terms	
constant		$4, 0, \pi$

Understand Vocabulary

To become familiar with some of the vocabulary in the module, consider the following. You may refer to the module, the glossary, or a dictionary.

1. The largest common factor of two or more given numbers is the

_____.

2. The _____ of monomials is the product of the greatest integer and the greatest power of each variable that divide evenly into each monomial.

Active Reading

Four-Corner Fold Before beginning the module, create a Four-Corner Fold to help you organize what you learn. Use one flap for each lesson in the module. As you study the module, note important facts, examples, and formulas on the flaps. Look for similarities and differences between the lessons. Use your FoldNote to complete assignments and to study for tests.

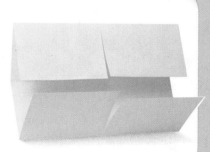

Vocabulary

Review Words
- ✔ binomial *(binomio)*
- ✔ constant *(constante)*
- ✔ factor *(factor)*
-   prime factor *(factor primo)*
- ✔ trinomial *(trinomio)*

Preview Words
- greatest common factor (GCF)

© Houghton Mifflin Harcourt Publishing Company

GETTING READY FOR
Factoring Polynomials
Understanding the standards and the vocabulary terms in the standards will help you know exactly what you are expected to learn in this module.

 A.SSE.2

Use the structure of an expression to identify ways to rewrite it. For example, see $x^4 - y^4$ as $(x^2)^2 - (y^2)^2$, thus recognizing it as a difference of squares that can be factored as $(x^2 - y^2)(x^2 + y^2)$.

Key Vocabulary

greatest common factor *(máximo común divisor de una expresión)*
Factors that are shared by two or more whole numbers are called common factors. The greatest of these common factors is the greatest common factor.

What It Means to You

You can rewrite expressions by factoring out common factors and working FOIL in reverse.

EXAMPLE A.SSE.2

Martown Park has an area of $(x^2 - 3x - 18)$ feet. If the width is $(x + 3)$ feet, what is the length?

$$lw = \text{area}$$

$$\boxed{\text{length?}}\,(x + 3) = (x^2 - 3x - 18)$$

think about FOIL in reverse:

$$\boxed{(x + \text{ or } - \,?)}(x + 3) = (x^2 - 3x - 18)$$

The missing value and 3 need to have a sum of -3, which means the binomial needs to be $(x - \mathbf{6})$.

The length is $(x - 6)$ feet.

A.SSE.3

Choose and produce an equivalent form of an expression to reveal and explain properties of the quantity represented by the expression.

What It Means to You

You can use patterns to recognize and rewrite expressions to reveal properties of the expression.

EXAMPLE A.SSE.3

Factor $25m^2 - 16n^2$.

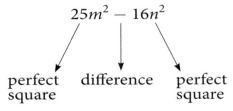

This binomial is the difference of two squares, so it factors as

$$(5m - 4n)(5m + 4n)$$

Visit **my.hrw.com** to see all **Common Core Standards** unpacked.

my.hrw.com

ESSENTIAL QUESTION

How can you use the greatest common factor to factor polynomials?

EXPLORE ACTIVITY   COMMON CORE   A.SSE.2

Factoring and Greatest Common Factor

Factors that are shared by two or more whole numbers are called *common factors*. The greatest of these common factors is called the **greatest common factor**, or GCF.

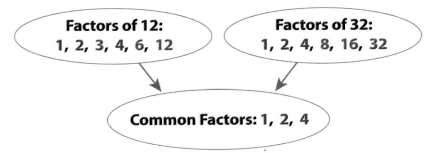

The greatest common factor is 4.

Use the greatest common factor (GCF) and the Distributive Property to factor the expression $30x + 18$.

A Write out the prime factors of each term.

$30x + 18 = 2 \cdot \underline{\hspace{1cm}} \cdot \underline{\hspace{1cm}} \cdot x + 2 \cdot \underline{\hspace{1cm}} \cdot \underline{\hspace{1cm}}$

B Circle the common factors.

$30x + 18 = 2 \cdot \underline{\hspace{1cm}} \cdot \underline{\hspace{1cm}} \cdot x + 2 \cdot \underline{\hspace{1cm}} \cdot \underline{\hspace{1cm}}$

C Write the expression as the product of the GCF and a sum.

$30x + 18 = (\underline{\hspace{1cm}}) (\underline{\hspace{1cm}} x + \underline{\hspace{1cm}})$

REFLECT

1. Will you get a completely factored expression if you factor out a common factor that is not the GCF? Explain.

_____

_____

2. Is the expression $2(3x - 4x)$ completely factored? Explain.

_____

_____

Greatest Common Factor of Monomials

To find the GCF of monomials, factor each coefficient and write all powers of variables as products. Then find the product of the common factors.

EXAMPLE 1 COMMON CORE A.SSE.2

Find the GCF of each pair of monomials.

A $3x^3$ and $6x^2$

$3x^3 = 3 \cdot x \cdot x \cdot x$ Factor each coefficient and write powers as products. Find the common factors.

$6x^2 = 2 \cdot 3 \cdot x \cdot x$

↓ ↓ ↓

$3 \cdot x \cdot x$ Find the product of the common factors.

The GCF of $3x^3$ and $6x^2$ is $3x^2$.

B $4x^2$ and $5y^3$

$4x^2 = 2 \cdot 2 \cdot x \cdot x$ Factor each coefficient and write powers as products.

$5y^3 = 5 \cdot y \cdot y \cdot y$

Since there are no common factors other than 1, the GCF of $4x^2$ and $5y^3$ is 1.

Math Talk
Mathematical Practices
Does factoring an expression change its value?

REFLECT

3. **Analyze Relationships** If two terms contain the same variable raised to different powers, to what power will the variable be raised in the GCF?

_____

4. Can the GCF of two positive numbers be greater than both numbers? Explain.

_____

_____

YOUR TURN

Find the GCF of each pair of monomials.

5. $18g^2$ and $27g^3$

_____

6. $16a^6$ and $9b$

_____

7. $15g^4$ and $45g^3$

_____

8. $9ab$ and $16bc$

_____

Factoring by Using the GCF

Remember that the Distributive Property states that $ab + ac = a(b + c)$.
Use the Distributive Property to factor out the GCF of the terms in a polynomial
to write the polynomial in factored form.

Math On the Spot
my.hrw.com

EXAMPLE 2

COMMON CORE   A.SSE.2

Factor each polynomial. Check your answer.

A $10y^3 + 20y^2 - 5y$

$2y^2(5y) + 4y(5y) - 1(5y)$ The GCF is 5y.

$5y(2y^2 + 4y - 1)$ Use the Distributive Property.

Check:

$5y(2y^2 + 4y - 1)$

$10y^3 + 20y^2 - 5y$ ✓   The product is the original polynomial.

B $-12x - 8x^2$ Both coefficients are negative.

$-1(12x + 8x^2)$ Factor out -1.

$1[3(4x) + 2x(4x)]$ The GCF of 12x and $8x^2$ is 4x.

$1[4x(3 + 2x)]$ Use the Distributive Property.

$1(4x)(3 + 2x)$ Use the Associative Property.

$-4x(3 + 2x)$

Check:

$-4x(3 + 2x) = -12x - 8x^2$ ✓   The product is the original polynomial.

My Notes

REFLECT

9. Can the polynomial $5x^2 + 7$ be factored? Explain.

_____

_____

YOUR TURN

Factor each polynomial. Check your answer.

10. $-28y^2 - 12y^5$ **11.** $8x^4 + 4x^3 - 2x^2$

_____   _____

**Personal
Math Trainer**

Online Practice
and Help

my.hrw.com

Factoring Out a Common Binomial Factor

Sometimes the GCF of the terms in an expression is a binomial. Such a GCF is called a *common binomial factor*. You factor out a common binomial factor the same way you factor out a monomial factor.

My Notes

EXAMPLE 3

Factor each expression.

A $7(x - 3) - 2x(x - 3)$

$7(x - 3) - 2x(x - 3)$ $(x - 3)$ is a common binomial factor.

$(x - 3)(7 - 2x)$ Factor out $(x - 3)$.

B $-t(t^2 + 4) + (t^2 + 4)$

$-t(t^2 + 4) + (t^2 + 4)$ $(t^2 + 4)$ is a common binomial factor.

$-t(t^2 + 4) + 1(t^2 + 4)$ $(t^2 + 4) = 1(t^2 + 4)$

$(t^2 + 4)(-t + 1)$ Factor out $(t^2 + 4)$.

C $5x(x + 3) - 4(3 + x)$

$5x(x + 3) - 4(3 + x)$ $(3 + x) = (x + 3)$, so $(x + 3)$ is a common binomial factor.

$5x(x + 3) - 4(x + 3)$

$(x + 3)(5x - 4)$ Factor out $(x + 3)$.

D $-3x^2(x + 2) + 4(x - 7)$

$-3x^2(x + 2) + 4(x - 7)$ There are no common factors.

The expression cannot be factored.

YOUR TURN

Factor each expression, if possible.

12. $7x(2x + 3) + (2x + 3)$

_____

13. $-4x(x + 2) + 9(x + 2)$

_____

14. $7(3t - 2) + 2t^2(2t - 3)$

_____

15. $5t(t + 6) - 8(6 + t)$

_____

Factoring by Grouping

Some polynomials can be factored by grouping. When a polynomial has four terms, you may be able to make two groups and factor the GCF from each.

Math On the Spot
my.hrw.com

EXAMPLE 4
COMMON CORE A.SSE.2

Factor each polynomial by grouping. Check your answer.

A $12a^3 - 9a^2 + 20a - 15$

$(12a^3 - 9a^2) + (20a - 15)$	Group terms that have a common number or variable as a factor.
$3a^2(4a - 3) + 5(4a - 3)$	Factor out the GCF of each group.
$3a^2(4a - 3) + 5(4a - 3)$	$(4a - 3)$ is a common factor.
$(4a - 3)(3a^2 + 5)$	Factor out $(4a - 3)$.

Check:

$(4a - 3)(3a^2 + 5)$	Multiply using FOIL.
$4a(3a^2) + 4a(5) - 3(3a^2) - 3(5)$	
$12a^3 + 20a - 9a^2 - 15$	
$12a^3 - 9a^2 + 20a - 15$ ✓	The product is the original polynomial.

B $2g^4 + 10g^3 + g + 5$

$(2g^4 + 10g^3) + (g + 5)$	Group terms.
$2g^3(g + 5) + 1(g + 5)$	Factor out the GCF of each group.
$2g^3(g + 5) + 1(g + 5)$	$(g + 5)$ is a common factor.
$(g + 5)(2g^3 + 1)$	Factor out $(g + 5)$.

Check:

$(g + 5)(2g^3 + 1)$	Multiply using FOIL.
$g(2g^3) + g(1) + 5(2g^3) + 5(1)$	
$2g^4 + g + 10g^3 + 5$	
$2g^4 + 10g^3 + g + 5$ ✓	The product is the original polynomial.

YOUR TURN

Factor each polynomial. Check your answer.

16. $6b^3 + 8b^2 + 9b + 12$

17. $4r^3 + 24r + r^2 + 6$

Personal Math Trainer

Online Practice and Help

my.hrw.com

Factoring with Opposites

Recognizing opposite binomials can help you factor polynomials. The binomials $(5 - x)$ and $(x - 5)$ are opposites, because $(5 - x) = -1(x - 5)$.

My Notes

EXAMPLE 5

COMMON CORE A.SSE.2

Factor the polynomial by grouping and using opposites. Check your answer.

$3x^3 - 15x^2 + 10 - 2x$	
$(3x^3 - 15x^2) + (10 - 2x)$	Group terms.
$3x^2(x - 5) + 2(5 - x)$	Factor out the GCF of each group.
$3x^2(x - 5) + 2(-1)(x - 5)$	Write $(5 - x)$ as $-1(x - 5)$.
$3x^2(x - 5) - 2(x - 5)$	Simplify.
$(x - 5)(3x^2 - 2)$	Factor out $(x - 5)$.

Check:

$(x - 5)(3x^2 - 2)$	Multiply using FOIL.
$x(3x^2) - x(2) - 5(3x^2) - 5(-2)$	
$3x^3 - 2x - 15x^2 + 10$	
$3x^3 - 15x^2 + 10 - 2x$ ✓	The product is the original polynomial.

REFLECT

18. Critique Reasoning Inara thinks that the opposite of $(a - b)$ is $(a + b)$, since addition and subtraction are opposites. Is she correct? Explain.

_____

_____

_____

YOUR TURN

Factor each polynomial. Check your answer.

19. $15x^2 - 10x^3 + 8x - 12$

20. $8y - 8 - x + xy$

_____

_____

21. $48n^6 - 18n^5 - 56n + 21$

22. $8t^4 - 48t^3 - 3t + 18$

_____

_____

Write the expression as a product of the greatest common factor and a sum. (Explore Activity)

1. $15y^3 + 20y$

   a. Write out the prime factors of each term.

$$15y^3 + 20y = 3 \cdot \underline{\hspace{1cm}} \cdot \underline{\hspace{1cm}} \cdot \underline{\hspace{1cm}} \cdot y + 2 \cdot \underline{\hspace{1cm}} \cdot \underline{\hspace{1cm}} \cdot y$$

   b. Circle the common factors.

$$15y^3 + 20y = 3 \cdot \underline{\hspace{1cm}} \cdot \underline{\hspace{1cm}} \cdot \underline{\hspace{1cm}} \cdot \textcircled{y} + 2 \cdot \underline{\hspace{1cm}} \cdot \underline{\hspace{1cm}} \cdot \textcircled{y}$$

   c. Write the product of the GCF and a sum.

$$15y^3 + 20y = (\underline{\hspace{1cm}})(\underline{\hspace{1cm}} y^2 + \underline{\hspace{1cm}})$$

Find the GCF of each pair of monomials. (Example 1)

2. $9s$ and $63s^3$

$$9s \ = 3 \cdot \boxed{} \cdot \boxed{}$$

$$63s^3 = 3 \cdot \boxed{} \cdot 7 \cdot \boxed{} \cdot \boxed{} \cdot \boxed{}$$

The GCF of $9s$ and $63s^3$ is _____.

3. $-14y^3 + 28y^2$

$$-14y^3 = \boxed{}$$

$$28y^2 = \boxed{}$$

The GCF of $-14y^3$ and $28y^2$ is _____.

Factor each polynomial. (Example 2)

4. $-18y^3 - 7y^2 - y$

$$-y(\boxed{} y^2 + \boxed{} + 1)$$

5. $9d^2 - 18$

$$\boxed{}(d^2 - \boxed{})$$

6. $6x^4 - 2x^3 + 10x^2$

_____

7. $36t^3 + 63$

_____

Factor each expression. (Example 3)

8. $4s(s + 6) - 5(s + 6)$

$$(\boxed{})(s + 6)$$

9. $-3(2 + b) + 4b(b + 2)$

$$(\boxed{})(\boxed{})$$

10. $(6z)(z + 8) + (z + 8)$

_____

11. $8w(5 - w) + 3(w - 5)$

_____

Factor each polynomial. (Example 4)

12. $9x^3 + 18x^2 + x + 2$

$(9x^3 + \boxed{}) + (\boxed{})$

$\boxed{}(x + \boxed{}) + \boxed{}(\boxed{})$

$(\boxed{})(\boxed{})$

13. $2m^3 + 4m^2 + 6m + 12$

$(\boxed{} + 4m^2) + (\boxed{})$

$\boxed{}(m + \boxed{}) + \boxed{}(m + \boxed{})$

$(m + \boxed{})(\boxed{})$

$2(m + \boxed{})(\boxed{})$

14. $10x^3 - 40x^2 + 14x - 56$

_____

15. $2n^5 - 2n^4 + 7n^2 - 7n$

_____

Factor each polynomial. (Example 5)

16. $2r^2 - 6r + 12 - 4r$

$(2r^2 - \boxed{}) + (\boxed{})$

$\boxed{}(\boxed{} - 3) + \boxed{}(\boxed{})$

$2r(r - 3) + 4\boxed{}(\boxed{})$

$(\boxed{})(\boxed{})$

$\boxed{}(\boxed{})(\boxed{})$

17. $14q^2 - 21q + 6 - 4q$

$(\boxed{}) + (\boxed{})$

$7q(\boxed{}) + 2(\boxed{})$

$7q(\boxed{}) + 2\boxed{}(\boxed{})$

$(\boxed{})(\boxed{})$

18. $6c - 48 + 40c^2 - 5c^3$

_____

19. $3x^3 - 27x^2 + 45 - 5x$

_____

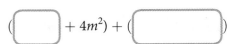

ESSENTIAL QUESTION CHECK-IN

20. How can you use the greatest common factor to factor polynomials?

_____

_____

_____

_____

15.1 Independent Practice

Personal Math Trainer

Online Practice and Help

my.hrw.com

COMMON CORE A.SSE.2, A.SSE.3

21. Find the GCF of $-64n^4$ and $24n^2$.

_____

Factor each expression or state if it cannot be factored.

22. $13q^4 + 2p^2$

_____

23. $14n^3 + 7n + 7n^2$

_____

24. $2b(b + 3) + 5(b + 3)$

_____

25. $4(x - 3) - x(y + 2)$

_____

26. $7r^3 - 35r^2 + 6r - 30$

_____

27. Explain how to check that a polynomial has been factored correctly.

_____

_____

_____

_____

28. **Explain the Error** Billie says the factored form of $18x^8 - 9x^4 - 6x^3$ is $3x(6x^7 - 3x^3 - 2x^2)$. Explain her error and give the correct factored form.

_____

_____

_____

_____

29. After t years, the amount of money in a savings account that earns simple interest is $P + Prt$, where P is the starting amount and r is the yearly interest rate. Factor this expression.

_____

30. **Communicate Mathematical Ideas** Explain how you can show that $(x - a)$ and $(a - x)$ are opposites.

_____

_____

_____

_____

_____

_____

31. The solar panel on Mandy's calculator has an area of $(7x^2 + x)$ cm^2. Factor this polynomial to find possible expressions for the dimensions of the solar panel.

_____

_____

_____

32. A model rocket is fired vertically into the air at 320 ft/s. The expression $-16t^2 + 320t$ gives the rocket's height after t seconds. Factor this expression.

_____

33. The area of a triangle is $\frac{1}{2}(x^3 - 2x + 2x^2 - 4)$. The height h is $x + 2$. Write an expression for the base b of the triangle. (*Hint*: Area of a triangle $= \frac{1}{2}bh$)

_____

34. Raspberries come in a container with a square bottom whose bottom side length is x. An expression for its volume is $x^3 - 2x^2$. Blueberries come in a container with a square bottom whose bottom side length is $(x - 2)$. An expression for its volume is $x^3 - 4x^2 + 4x$. Factor both expressions.

_____

_____

35. The area of a rectangle is represented by the polynomial $x^2 + 3x - 6x - 18$.

a. Find possible expressions for the length and width of the rectangle.

_____

b. Use your answers from part a to find the length, width, and area of the rectangle if $x = 12$.

_____

 **FOCUS ON HIGHER ORDER THINKING**

Work Area

36. Critical Thinking Show two methods of factoring the expression $ax - bx - ay + by$. Is the result the same?

_____

_____

_____

37. Explain the Error Audrey and Owen came up with two different answers when they factored the expression $3n^3 - n^2$. Who was correct? Explain the error.

Owen	Audrey
$3n^3 - n^2$	$3n^3 - n^2$
$n^2(3n) - n^2(0)$	$n^2(3n) - n^2(1)$
$n^2(3n - 0)$	$n^2(3n - 1)$

_____

38. Communicating Mathematical Ideas
Describe how to find the area of the figure. Show each step and write your answer in factored form.

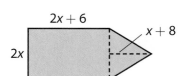

_____

_____

_____

_____

ESSENTIAL QUESTION

How can you factor expressions of the form $x^2 + bx + c$?

EXPLORE ACTIVITY 1   COMMON CORE A.SSE.2

Exploring Factors of $x^2 + bx + c$ when c is Positive

You know how to multiply binomials using FOIL. In this lesson, you will learn how to reverse this process and factor trinomials into two binomials.

Use algebra tiles to factor $x^2 + 7x + 6$.

A Identify the tiles you need to model the expression.

_____ x^2-tile(s), _____ x-tile(s), and _____ unit tile(s)

B Arrange the algebra tiles on the grid. Place the _____ x^2-tile in

the upper left corner, and arrange the _____ unit tiles in two rows and three columns in the lower right corner.

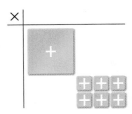

C Fill in the empty spaces on the grid with x-tiles. Only _____ x-tiles fit on the grid, so this arrangement is not correct.

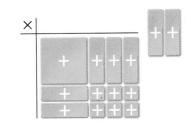

D Rearrange the unit tiles into a rectangle with different dimensions.

What is the length and width of the new rectangle? _____

E Fill in the empty spaces on the grid with x-tiles.

All _____ x-tiles were used, so this arrangement is correct.

$x^2 + 7x + 6 = (x + \boxed{})(x + \boxed{})$

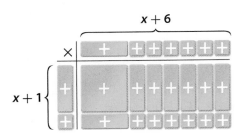

REFLECT

1. Finn checks the answer by multiplying and gets $x^2 + 1x + 6x + 6$. He believes he must have made a multiplication error. Is he correct? Explain.

_____

_____

2. What If? Suppose the second arrangement of unit tiles was a rectangle 1 tile high and 6 tiles wide. Could the arrangement have used a rectangle 6 tiles high and 1 tile wide? Explain.

_____

_____

3. Critical Thinking Are there any other ways to factor the polynomial $x^2 + 7x + 6$ besides $(x + 1)(x + 6)$? Explain.

_____

_____

EXPLORE ACTIVITY 2　　COMMON CORE　A.SSE.2

Exploring Factors of $x^2 + bx + c$ when c is Negative

When using algebra tiles to factor polynomials, you may have to use both negative and positive tiles.

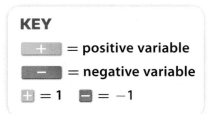

KEY

█ **+** ▐ = **positive variable**

█ **–** ▐ = **negative variable**

⊞ = **1**　　⊟ = **–1**

Use algebra tiles to factor $x^2 + x - 2$.

A Identify the tiles you need to model the expression.

_____ positive x^2-tile

_____ positive x-tile

_____ negative unit tiles

B The unit tiles will be placed on a grid to form a rectangle. List all the factor pairs for 2: _____

C Arrange the algebra tiles on the grid. Place the

_____ positive x^2-tile in the upper left

corner, and arrange the _____ negative
unit tiles in the lower right corner.

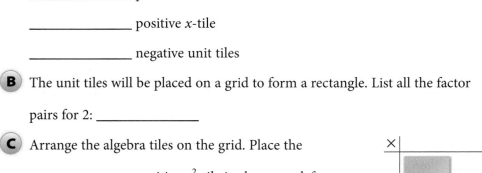

D Fill in the empty spaces on the grid with x-tiles. There is _____ positive x-tile to place on the grid, so there will be _____ empty places for x-tiles.

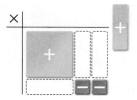

E Fill the empty places with zero pairs. A zero pair is two tiles that add to 0.

Add 1 positive _____ and

1 negative _____ to the grid.

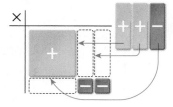

F The empty spaces on the grid were completely filled by zero pairs, so this arrangement is correct.

$$x^2 + x - 2 = (x + \boxed{})(x - \boxed{})$$

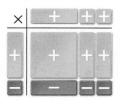

REFLECT

4. **Analyze Relationships** Why were the unit tiles not rearranged when the x-tile did not complete the grid?

_____

_____

_____

_____

5. Why were both positive x-tiles placed in the top row?

_____

_____

_____

_____

Factoring Trinomials

When factoring a polynomial in the form $x^2 + bx + c$, you are looking for two binomials in the form $(x + n)$ and $(x + m)$, where n and m are a pair of numbers whose product is c and whose sum is b.

The first step is to find factor pairs of c. Always pay attention to the sign of c. If c is positive, find factors of c that both have the same sign. If c is negative, find one positive factor and one negative factor.

Math On the Spot

my.hrw.com

EXAMPLE 1 COMMON CORE A.SSE.2

A Factor $x^2 - 7x + 12$.

STEP 1 List factor pairs of c and find the sum of each pair. Since $c = 12$, use factor pairs where both factors have the same sign.

Math Talk
Mathematical Practices

If c is positive, how can you use the sign of b to decide whether to choose positive or negative factors of c?

Factors of 12	Sum of Factors
1 and 12	$1 + 12 = 13$
2 and 6	$2 + 6 = 8$
3 and 4	$3 + 4 = 7$
-1 and -12	$(-1) + (-12) = -13$
-2 and -6	$(-2) + (-6) = -8$
-3 and -4	$(-3) + (-4) = -7$

-7 is the sum that you're looking for.

STEP 2 Use the factor pair whose sum equals b to factor the polynomial.

$$x^2 - 7x + 12 = (x - 3)(x - 4)$$

B Factor $x^2 + 4x - 45$.

STEP 1 List factor pairs of c and find the sum of each pair. Since $c = -45$, use factor pairs where one factor is positive and the other factor is negative.

Factors of -45	Sum of Factors
1 and -45	$1 + (-45) = -44$
3 and -15	$3 + (-15) = -12$
5 and -9	$5 + (-9) = -4$
9 and -5	$9 + (-5) = 4$

4 is the sum that you're looking for. You can stop here.

STEP 2 Use the factor pair whose sum equals b to factor the polynomial.

$$x^2 + 4x - 45 = (x + 9)(x - 5)$$

REFLECT

6. When factoring a trinomial of the form $x^2 + bx + c$ where c is negative, one binomial factor contains a positive factor of c and one contains a negative factor of c. How do you know which factor of c should be positive and which should be negative?

_____

_____

_____

YOUR TURN

Factor each trinomial.

7. $x^2 - 11x + 30$

_____

8. $x^2 + 5x + 4$

_____

9. $x^2 - 5x - 14$

_____

10. $x^2 - x - 6$

_____

11. $x^2 + 4x - 21$

_____

12. $x^2 + 2x - 15$

_____

Guided Practice

1. Use algebra tiles to factor $x^2 + 6x + 8$. (Explore Activity 1)

  a. Identify the tiles you will need to model the expression.

  _____ x^2-tile _____ x-tiles _____ unit tiles

  b. This arrangement does not model the correct factors

  because it needs _____ x-tiles to fill the grid.

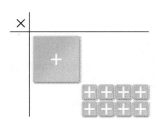

  c. This arrangement models the correct factors because it

  needs _____ x-tiles to fill the grid.

  d. $x^2 + 6x + 8 = (x + \boxed{})(x + \boxed{})$

2. Use algebra tiles to factor $x^2 - 4x - 5$. (Explore Activity 2)

  a. Identify the tiles you will need to model the expression.

  _____ positive x^2-tile _____ negative x-tiles _____
  negative unit tiles

  b. This arrangement has space for _____ x-tiles. You will

  have to add a _____ of x-tiles.

  c. $x^2 - 4x - 5 = (x - \boxed{})(x + \boxed{})$

3. Factor the polynomial $x^2 - 10x + 9$. (Example 1)

a. Complete the table with factor pairs of c.

Factors of 9	Sum of Factors
1 and _____	$1 + 9 = 10$
3 and _____	$3 + $_____$ = $_____
-1 and _____	$-1 + ($_____$) = $_____
_____ and _____	_____ $+$ _____ $= $_____

The factor pair whose sum equals b is _____ and _____.

b. $x^2 - 10x + 9 = (x - \boxed{})(x - \boxed{})$

Factor each trinomial. (Example 1)

4. $x^2 + 6x + 9$

$(x + \boxed{})(x + 3)$

5. $x^2 - 5x + 4$

$(x - 1)(x - \boxed{})$

6. $x^2 - 3x - 18$

$(x + 3)(\boxed{})$

7. $x^2 + 14x + 40$

$(x + 4)(\boxed{})$

8. $x^2 + 9x - 36$

_____

9. $x^2 - 2x - 35$

_____

10. $x^2 - 7x - 30$

_____

11. $x^2 + 2x - 8$

_____

12. The length of a rectangular porch is $(x + 7)$ feet. The area of the porch is $(x^2 + 9x + 14)$ square feet. Factor the expression for the area in order to find an expression for the width of the porch.

_____

? **ESSENTIAL QUESTION CHECK-IN**

13. How can you factor expressions of the form $x^2 + bx + c$?

_____

_____

_____

_____

15.2 Independent Practice

Personal Math Trainer

Online Practice and Help

my.hrw.com

COMMON CORE   A.SSE.2, A.SSE.3

Factor each trinomial.

14. $x^2 - 2x - 15$

_____

15. $x^2 + 9x + 18$

_____

16. $x^2 + 13x - 30$

_____

17. $x^2 + 11x + 28$

_____

18. $x^2 - 10x - 24$

_____

19. $x^2 - 12x + 32$

_____

20. Write the polynomial modeled and then factor it.

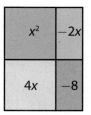

_____

_____

21. The area of a rectangle in square feet can be represented by $x^2 + 8x + 12$. The length is $(x + 6)$ ft. What is the width of the rectangle?

_____

_____

22. A homeowner wants to enlarge a rectangular closet that has an area of $(x^2 + 3x + 2)$ ft^2. The length is $(x + 2)$ ft. After construction, the area will be $(x^2 + 8x + 15)$ ft^2 with a length of $(x + 3)$ ft.

a. Find the dimensions of the closet before construction.

_____

_____

b. Find the dimensions of the closet after construction.

_____

_____

c. By how many feet will the length and width increase after construction?

_____

_____

23. Can all trinomials of the form $x^2 + bx + c$ be factored? Explain and defend your answer with an example.

_____

_____

_____

_____

_____

24. Give a value of b that would make $x^2 + bx - 36$ factorable. Show the factorization.

_____

_____

25. **Represent Real-World Problems** The area of a rectangular fountain is $(x^2 + 12x + 20)$ ft^2. The width is $(x + 2)$ ft.

a. Find the length of the fountain.

_____

b. A 2-foot wide walkway is built around the fountain. Find the dimensions of the outside border of the walkway.

_____

c. Find the total area covered by the fountain and walkway.

_____

26. Give a value of b that would **not** make $x^2 + bx - 36$ factorable. Show that it cannot be factored.

_____

_____

Work Area

27. **Justify Reasoning** The area of a rectangle is $x^2 + 6x + 8$. The length is $(x + 4)$. Find the width of the rectangle. Is the rectangle a square? Explain.

_____

_____

28. **Communicate Mathematical Ideas** Rico says the expression $x^2 + bx + c$ is factorable when $b = c = 4$. Are there any other values where $b = c$ that make the expression factorable? Explain.

_____

_____

_____

_____

29. **Critical Thinking** Explain how to find all the possible positive values of b such that $x^2 + bx + 6$ can be factored into binomial factors. Write the possible trinomials.

_____

_____

_____

_____

_____

15.3 Factoring $ax^2 + bx + c$

COMMON CORE A.SSE.2

Use the structure of an expression to identify ways to rewrite it. *Also A.SSE.3*

? ESSENTIAL QUESTION

How can you factor expressions of the form $ax^2 + bx + c$?

Factoring $ax^2 + bx + c$ where $c > 0$

When you factor a polynomial in the form $ax^2 + bx + c$, the result will be the product of two binomial factors, in the form $(\square x + \square)(\square x + \square)$. The product of the two coefficients of x will be a, and the product of the two constant terms will be c. The sum of the products of the inner and outer terms will be bx.

Math On the Spot

my.hrw.com

Product = a ⌐ ⌐ **Product = c**

$$(\square\; x + \square)(\square\; x + \square) = ax^2 + bx + c$$

Sum of outer and inner products = b

EXAMPLE 1

COMMON CORE A.SSE.2

A Factor $4x^2 + 26x + 42$.

STEP 1 Factor out any common factors of 4, 26, and 42.

$4x^2 + 26x + 42 = 2(2x^2 + 13x + 21)$

STEP 2 Make a table that lists the factor pairs for a and c. Find the value of b that results from each combination of factor pairs.

Factors of a $a = 2$	Factors of c $c = 21$	Outer Product + Inner Product
1 and 2	1 and 21	$(1)(21) + (2)(1) = 23$
1 and 2	3 and 7	$(1)(7) + (2)(3) = 13$
1 and 2	7 and 3	$(1)(3) + (2)(7) = 17$
1 and 2	21 and 1	$(1)(1) + (2)(21) = 43$

13 is the sum that you're looking for.

STEP 3 Use the combination of factor pairs that yields the correct value of b to factor the polynomial.

$(1x + 3)(2x + 7) = (x + 3)(2x + 7)$

$4x^2 + 26x + 42 = 2(x + 3)(2x + 7)$

B Factor $3x^2 - 26x + 35$.

STEP 1 Factor out any common factors of 3, −26, and 35.

3, −26, and 35 share no common factors other than 1.

STEP 2 Make a table that lists the factor pairs for a and c. Find the value of b that results from each combination of factor pairs.

Factors of a $a = 3$	Factors of c $c = 35$	Outer Product + Inner Product
1 and 3	−1 and −35	$(1)(-35) + (3)(-1) = -38$
1 and 3	−5 and −7	$(1)(-7) + (3)(-5) = -22$
1 and 3	−7 and −5	$(1)(-5) + (3)(-7) = -26$
1 and 3	−35 and −1	$(1)(-1) + (3)(-35) = -106$

STEP 3 Use the combination of factor pairs that yields the correct value of b to factor the polynomial.

> −26 is the sum that you're looking for.

$$3x^2 - 26x + 35 = (1x - 7)(3x - 5) = (x - 7)(3x - 5)$$

REFLECT

1. Critical Thinking When factoring $3x^2 - 26x + 35$, why should both factors of c be negative?

_____

_____

_____

_____

2. What If? If none of the factor pairs for a and c result in the correct value for b, what do you know about the polynomial?

_____

_____

YOUR TURN

Factor each polynomial.

3. $5x^2 - 14x + 8$

_____

4. $3x^2 + 11x + 6$

_____

5. $12x^2 - 48x + 45$

_____

6. $12x^2 + 62x + 70$

_____

7. $14x^2 + 33x + 18$

_____

8. $50x^2 - 165x + 135$

_____

Personal Math Trainer

Online Practice and Help

⏻ my.hrw.com

Factoring $ax^2 + bx + c$ where $c < 0$

When factoring $ax^2 + bx + c$, if the value of c is negative, you know that one of the factors of c must be negative and one must be positive. Apply what you already know about factoring trinomials to this new situation.

Math On the Spot

⏻ my.hrw.com

EXAMPLE 2

COMMON CORE **A.SSE.2**

  A **Factor** $6x^2 - 21x - 45$.

STEP 1 Factor out any common factors of 6, –21, and –45.

$$6x^2 - 21x - 45 = 3(2x^2 - 7x - 15)$$

STEP 2 Make a table that lists the factor pairs for a and c. Since c is negative, one factor will be positive and the other will be negative.

Factors of a $a = 2$	Factors of c $c = -15$	Outer Product + Inner Product
1 and 2	1 and −15	$(1)(-15) + (2)(1) = -13$
1 and 2	3 and −5	$(1)(-5) + (2)(3) = 1$
1 and 2	5 and −3	$(1)(-3) + (2)(5) = 7$
1 and 2	15 and −1	$(1)(-1) + (2)(15) = 29$
1 and 2	−1 and 15	$(1)(15) + (2)(-1) = 13$
1 and 2	−3 and 5	$(1)(5) + (2)(-3) = -1$
1 and 2	−5 and 3	$(1)(3) + (2)(-5) = -7$
1 and 2	−15 and 1	$(1)(1) + (2)(-15) = -29$

−7 is the sum that you're looking for.

STEP 3 Use the combination of factor pairs that yields the correct value of b to factor the polynomial.

$$(1x - 5)(2x + 3) = (x - 5)(2x + 3)$$

$$6x^2 - 21x - 45 = 3(x - 5)(2x + 3)$$

B **Factor** $4x^2 + 4x - 35$.

STEP 1 Factor out any common factors for 4, 4, and –35.

4, 4, and –35 share no common factors other than 1.

STEP 2 Make a table that lists the factor pairs for a and c. Since c is negative, one factor will be positive and the other will be negative.

Factors of a $a = 4$	Factors of c $c = -35$	Outer Product + Inner Product
1 and 4	1 and -35	$(1)(-35) + (4)(1) = -31$
1 and 4	5 and -7	$(1)(-7) + (4)(5) = 13$
1 and 4	7 and -5	$(1)(-5) + (4)(7) = 23$
1 and 4	35 and -1	$(1)(-1) + (4)(35) = 139$
1 and 4	-1 and 35	$(1)(35) + (4)(-1) = 31$
1 and 4	-5 and 7	$(1)(7) + (4)(-5) = -13$
1 and 4	-7 and 5	$(1)(5) + (4)(-7) = -23$
1 and 4	-35 and 1	$(1)(1) + (4)(-35) = -139$
2 and 2	1 and -35	$(2)(-35) + (2)(1) = -68$
2 and 2	5 and -7	$(2)(-7) + (2)(5) = -4$
2 and 2	7 and -5	$(2)(-5) + (2)(7) = 4$
2 and 2	35 and -1	$(2)(-1) + (2)(35) = 68$

Math Talk

Mathematical Practices

How does the sign of c help you choose the correct factor pair for c?

STEP 3 Use the combination of factor pairs that yields the correct value of b to factor the polynomial.

> 4 is the sum that you're looking for.

$$4x^2 + 4x - 35 = (2x + 7)(2x - 5)$$

REFLECT

9. **What If?** Suppose a is a negative number. What would be the first step in factoring $ax^2 + bx + c$? Explain.

_____

_____

_____

10. **Make a Conjecture** Using the information in the tables in Example 2, make a conjecture about what happens to b when you swap the positions of the plus and minus signs in the binomial factors.

_____

_____

Personal Math Trainer

Online Practice and Help

my.hrw.com

YOUR TURN

Factor each polynomial.

11. $24x^2 + 32x - 6$

12. $9x^2 + 21x - 8$

_____

_____

1. Factor $3x^2 + 13x + 12$. (Example 1)

Complete the table for all factors of a and c.

Factors of a $a = 3$	Factors of c $c = 12$	Outer Product + Inner Product
1 and 3	1 and 12	$(1)(12) + (3)(1) = $ _____
1 and 3	2 and _____	$(1)(\_\_\_) + (\_\_\_)(2) = 12$
1 and 3	_____ and _____	$(1)(___) + (3)(___) = $ _____
1 and 3	_____ and _____	$(1)(___) + (___)(4) = $ _____
1 and 3	_____ and _____	$(1)(___) + (___)(___) = $ _____
1 and 3	_____ and 1	$(1)(1) + (\_\_\_)(\_\_\_) = 37$

The factored form of $3x^2 + 13x + 12$ is $(x + \boxed{})(\boxed{}x + \boxed{})$.

2. Factor $8x^2 - 2x - 6$. (Example 2)

8, -2, and -6 have a common factor of _____, so $8x^2 - 2x - 6 = \boxed{}(4x^2 - x - 3)$

Complete the table for all factors of a and c.

Factors of a $a = 4$	Factors of c $c = -3$	Outer Product + Inner Product
1 and 4	1 and -3	$(1)(-3) + (4)(1) = 1$
1 and _____	3 and _____	$(1)(___) + (4)(___) = $ _____
1 and _____	_____ and _____	$(1)(___) + (___)(___) = $ _____
1 and _____	_____ and _____	$(1)(___) + (___)(___) = $ _____
2 and _____	_____ and _____	$(2)(___) + (___)(1) = $ _____
_____ and _____	3 and _____	$(2)(\_\_\_) + (2)(3) = 4$

The factored form of $8x^2 - 2x - 6$ is $\boxed{}(x - \boxed{})(4x + \boxed{})$.

ESSENTIAL QUESTION CHECK-IN

3. How can you factor expressions of the form $ax^2 + bx + c$?

_____

_____

15.3 Independent Practice

Personal Math Trainer

Online Practice and Help

my.hrw.com

COMMON CORE A.SSE.2, A.SSE.3

Factor each trinomial, if possible.

4. $30x^2 + 35x - 15$

_____

5. $6x^2 - 29x + 9$

_____

6. $30x^2 + 82x + 56$

_____

7. $5z^2 + 17z + 6$

_____

8. $30d^2 + 7d - 15$

_____

9. $2y^2 - 11y + 14$

_____

10. $-4g^2 + 11g + 20$

_____

11. $9n^2 + 3n + 1$

_____

12. How is factoring a trinomial in the form $ax^2 + bx + c$ similar to factoring a trinomial in the form $x^2 + bx + c$? How is it different?

_____

_____

_____

_____

13. The area of a soccer field is $(24x^2 + 100x + 100)$ m². The width of the field is $(4x + 10)$ m. What is the length?

_____

14. Find all the possible values of b such that $3x^2 + bx - 2$ can be factored.

_____

15. Write the polynomial modeled, and then factor it.

$12x^2$	$4x$
$-15x$	-5

_____

_____

16. **Representing Real-World Problems** The attendance at a team's basketball game can be approximated with the polynomial $5x^2 + 80x + 285$, where x is the number of wins the team had in the previous month.

a. Factor the polynomial completely.

_____

b. Estimate the attendance if the team won 4 games in the previous month.

_____

17. Kyle stood on a bridge and threw a rock up and over the side. The height of the rock, in meters, can be approximated by $-5t^2 + 5t + 24$, where t is the time in seconds after Kyle threw it. Completely factor the expression.

_____

18. A triangle has an area of $\frac{1}{2}(4x^2 + 29x + 30)$ ft². If the base of the triangle is $(x + 6)$ ft, find the height of the triangle.

_____

19. Draw Conclusions If a polynomial in the form $ax^2 + bx + c$ has $a = b = c = 1$, can the expression be factored? Explain.

_____

_____

_____

_____

20. Counterexamples Marc thinks the only time a polynomial in the form $ax^2 + bx + c$ cannot be factored is when at least one of the values for a, b, or c is a prime number. Find a counterexample to Marc's statement.

_____

_____

21. Shruti has a rectangular picture frame with an area of $30x^2 + 5x - 75$ cm².

   a. Find the width of the frame if the height is $(3x + 5)$ cm. _____

   b. Find the width of the frame if the height is $(2x - 3)$ cm. _____

   c. Find the width of the frame when the height is 5 cm. _____

22. Communicate Mathematical Ideas Has the expression $(3x + 7)(6x + 3)$ been factored completely? Explain.

_____

_____

_____

23. Explain the Error Luna performed the work shown below to factor the polynomial $24x^2 + 18x + 3$. Explain her error, and find the correctly factored form.

$$24x^2 + 18x + 3 = 3(8x^2 + 6x + 0)$$
$$= 3(8x^2 + 6x)$$
$$= 3(2x)(4x + 3)$$

_____

_____

_____

24. The length of Rebecca's rectangular garden was two times the width, w. Rebecca increased the length and width of the garden so that the area of the new garden is $(2w^2 + 7w + 6)$ square yards. By how much did Rebecca increase the length and the width?

_____

25. The height in feet above the ground of a football that has been thrown or kicked can be described by the expression $-16t^2 + vt + h$ where t is the time in seconds, v is the initial upward velocity in feet per second, and h is the initial height in feet.

a. Write an expression for the height of a football at time t when the initial upward velocity is 20 feet per second and the initial height is 6 feet.

_____

b. Factor your expression from part **a**.

_____

c. Find the height of the football after 1 second.

_____

 **FOCUS ON HIGHER ORDER THINKING**

Work Area

26. **Critical Thinking** Is there a value of m that will make $x^2 + mx + 80$ factorable? If so, how many? Explain and give all the possible values.

_____

_____

_____

_____

27. **Explain the Error** Frank has factored the polynomial $12x^2 + 5x - 2$ as $(3x - 1)(4x + 2)$. Explain his error. Give the correct factorization.

_____

_____

_____

28. **Communicate Mathematical Ideas** Can the polynomial $4x^2 + 0x - 25$ be factored? Explain.

_____

_____

_____

LESSON
15.4

Factoring Special Products

COMMON CORE A.SSE.2

Use the structure of an expression to identify ways to rewrite it. *Also A.SSE.3*

? ESSENTIAL QUESTION

How can you use special products to aid in factoring?

EXPLORE ACTIVITY COMMON CORE A.SSE.2

Factoring a Perfect-Square Trinomial

When you use algebra tiles to factor a polynomial, you must arrange the unit tiles on the grid in a rectangle. Sometimes, you can arrange the unit tiles to form a square. Trinomials of this type are called *perfect-square trinomials*.

Use algebra tiles to factor $x^2 + 6x + 9$.

A Identify the tiles you need to model the expression.

_____ x^2-tile; _____ x-tiles; _____ unit tiles

B The unit tiles will be placed on a grid to form a square. Which factor pair for 9 will arrange the tiles in a square? _____

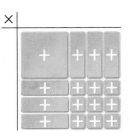

C Arrange the algebra tiles on the grid. Place the _____ x^2-tile in the upper left corner, and arrange the _____ unit tiles in the lower right corner.

D Fill in the empty spaces on the grid with x-tiles.

All _____ x-tiles were used, so this arrangement is correct.

$x^2 + 6x + 9 = (x + \boxed{})(x + \boxed{})$

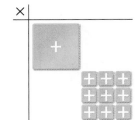

Now, use algebra tiles to factor $x^2 - 8x + 16$.

E Identify the tiles you need to model the expression.

_____ positive x^2-tile _____ negative x-tiles

_____ positive unit tiles

F The unit tiles will be placed on a grid to form a square. Which factor pair for 16 will arrange the tiles in a square? _____

G Arrange the algebra tiles on the grid.

Place the _____ positive x^2-tile in the upper left corner, and

arrange _____ positive unit tiles in the lower right corner.

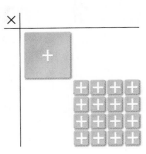

H Fill in the empty spaces on the grid

with x-tiles. All _____ negative x-tiles were used, so this arrangement is correct.

$x^2 - 8x + 16 =$

$(x - \boxed{})(x - \boxed{})$

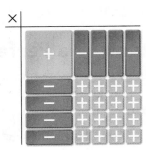

Math Talk

Mathematical Practices

How would the algebra tile grid change if the trinomial was $x^2 + 8x + 16$?

REFLECT

1. **What If?** Suppose that the middle term in $x^2 + 6x + 9$ was changed from $6x$ to $10x$. How would this affect the way you factor the polynomial?

_____

_____

_____

2. If the unit tiles are arranged in a square when factoring with algebra tiles, what will be true about the binomial factors?

_____

Factoring Perfect-Square Trinomials

A trinomial is a **perfect-square trinomial** if the first and last terms are perfect squares and the middle term is 2 times one factor of the first term times one factor of the last term. This can be represented algebraically in either the form $a^2 + 2ab + b^2$ or the form $a^2 - 2ab + b^2$. Factor perfect-square trinomials according to the rules below.

Math On the Spot

my.hrw.com

Perfect-Square Trinomials	
Perfect-Square Trinomial	**Example**
$a^2 + 2ab + b^2 = (a + b)(a + b)$ $= (a + b)^2$	$x^2 + 6x + 9 = (x + 3)(x + 3)$ $= (x + 3)^2$
$a^2 - 2ab + b^2 = (a - b)(a - b)$ $= (a - b)^2$	$x^2 - 2x + 1 = (x - 1)(x - 1)$ $= (x - 1)^2$

EXAMPLE 1

COMMON CORE A.SSE.2

Factor each perfect-square trinomial.

A $x^2 + 12x + 36$

$x^2 + 2(x)(6) + 6^2$	Rewrite in the form $a^2 + 2ab + b^2$.
$(x + 6)(x + 6)$	Rewrite in the form $(a + b)(a + b)$.

The factored form of $x^2 + 12x + 36$ is $(x + 6)(x + 6)$, or $(x + 6)^2$.

B $4x^2 - 12x + 9$

$(2x)^2 - 2(2x)(3) + 3^2$	Rewrite in the form $a^2 - 2ab + b^2$.
$(2x - 3)(2x - 3)$	Rewrite in the form $(a - b)(a - b)$.

The factored form of $4x^2 - 12x + 9$ is $(2x - 3)(2x - 3)$, or $(2x - 3)^2$.

C $36x^2 + 180x + 225$

$9(4x^2 + 20x + 25)$	Factor out the GCF of the terms.
$9[(2x)^2 + 2(2x)(5) + 5^2]$	Rewrite in the form $a^2 + 2ab + b^2$.
$9(2x + 5)(2x + 5)$	Rewrite in the form $(a + b)(a + b)$.

The factored form of $36x^2 + 180x + 225$ is $9(2x + 5)(2x + 5)$, or $9(2x + 5)^2$.

REFLECT

3. Lee says that the trinomial $4x^2 + 15x + 9$ is a perfect-square trinomial, because $4x^2$ and 9 are both perfect squares. Is Lee correct? Explain.

_____

_____

4. Wendy checked the answer to Example 1A. Her work is shown below. Explain her error.

$$(x + 6)^2 = x^2 + 6^2 = x^2 + 36$$

_____

_____

_____

5. Perfect-square trinomials can be in the form $a^2 + 2ab + b^2$ or $a^2 - 2ab + b^2$. Why is the b^2 term always positive?

_____

_____

My Notes

YOUR TURN

Factor each perfect-square trinomial.

6. $x^2 + 16x + 64$

_____

7. $25x^2 + 60x + 36$

_____

8. $36x^2 - 12x + 1$

_____

9. $16x^2 - 16x + 4$

_____

10. $9x^2 - 18x + 9$

_____

11. $4x^2 + 24x + 36$

_____

Math On the Spot

⟳ my.hrw.com

Factoring a Difference of Squares

What does "difference of two squares" mean?

$$x^2 - 100$$

square   difference   square

A polynomial is a **difference of two squares** if:
- It has two terms, one subtracted from the other.
- Both terms are perfect squares.

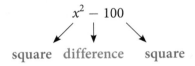

The difference of two squares can be written algebraically as $a^2 - b^2$ and factored as $(a + b)(a - b)$.

Difference of Two Squares	
Difference of Two Squares	**Example**
$a^2 - b^2 = (a + b)(a - b)$	$x^2 - 9 = (x + 3)(x - 3)$

EXAMPLE 2

Factor each difference of squares.

A $x^2 - 81$

$x^2 - 9^2$ Rewrite in the form $a^2 - b^2$.

$(x + 9)(x - 9)$ Rewrite in the form $(a + b)(a - b)$.

The factored form of $x^2 - 81$ is $(x + 9)(x - 9)$.

B $16q^2 - 9p^4$ Remember $(a^m)^n = a^{mn}$.

$(4q)^2 - (3p^2)^2$ Rewrite in the form $a^2 - b^2$.

$(4q + 3p^2)(4q - 3p^2)$ Rewrite in the form $(a + b)(a - b)$.

The factored form of $16q^2 - 9p^4$ is $(4q + 3p^2)(4q - 3p^2)$.

C $4y^4 - 25y^2$

$y^2(4y^2 - 25)$ Factor out the GCF of the terms.

$y^2[(2y)^2 - 5^2]$ Rewrite in the form $a^2 - b^2$.

$y^2(2y + 5)(2y - 5)$ Rewrite in the form $(a + b)(a - b)$.

The factored form of $4y^4 - 25y^2$ is $y^2(2y + 5)(2y - 5)$.

> **Math Talk**
> Mathematical Practices
>
> Why isn't there a b term in a difference of two squares?

REFLECT

12. Explain the Error Sam factored $9x^6 - 25x^4$ as $(3x^3 + 5x^2)(3x^3 - 5x^2)$. Explain his error.

_____

_____

YOUR TURN

Factor each difference of squares.

13. $1 - 4x^2$

_____

14. $16x^2 - 4y^6$

_____

15. $p^8 - 49q^6$

_____

Personal Math Trainer

Online Practice and Help

my.hrw.com

Guided Practice

For each trinomial, draw algebra tiles to show the factored form, then write the factored form. (Explore Activity)

1. $x^2 - 10x + 25$

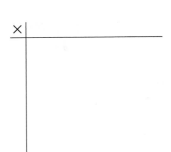

2. $x^2 + 8x + 16$

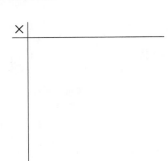

Factor each perfect-square trinomial. (Example 1)

3. $9x^2 + 18x + 9$

4. $25x^2 + 20x + 4$

5. $64x^2 - 12x + 1$

6. $4x^2 + 24x + 36$

7. $16x^4 - 24x^2 + 9$

8. $25x^2 + 10x + 1$

Factor each difference of two squares. (Example 2)

9. $s^2 - 16$

10. $81 - 144x^4$

11. $x^8 - 49$

12. $400x^4 - 484x^2$

13. $49x^6 - 36y^2$

14. $25t^2 - 64$

? ESSENTIAL QUESTION CHECK-IN

15. How can you use the rules for special products to aid in factoring?

15.4 Independent Practice

  A.SSE.2, A.SSE.3

Personal Math Trainer

Online Practice and Help

my.hrw.com

Determine whether each polynomial is a perfect-square trinomial or the difference of two squares. Then factor each expression.

16. $4x^2 - 20x + 25$

_____

17. $16b^2 - 169c^6$

_____

_____

18. $49x^2 + 140x + 100$

_____

19. $4x^2 - 36$

_____

_____

20. An architect is designing square windows with an area of $(x^2 + 20x + 100)$ ft². The dimensions of the windows are of the form $ax + b$, where a and b are whole numbers.

a. Find the dimensions of each square window. _____

b. Find an expression for the perimeter of a window. _____

c. Find the perimeter of a window when $x = 4$. _____

21. **Explain the Error** Ed factored $16x^2 - 8xy + y^2$ as $(4x + y)^2$. What was his error?

_____

_____

_____

22. **Represent Real-World Problems** You are given a sheet of paper and asked to cut out a square piece with an area of $(4x^2 - 44x + 121)$ mm². The dimensions of the square have the form $ax - b$, where a and b are whole numbers.

a. Find the length of one of the sides of the square you cut out.

_____

b. Find an expression for the perimeter of the square you cut out.

_____

c. Find the perimeter when $x = 41$.

_____

23. **Critique Reasoning** Michelle factored $x^2 - 6x + 9$ as follows:
$x^2 - 6x + 9 =$
$x^2 - 2(x \cdot 3) + 3^2 =$
$(x - 3)(x + 3)$
Is she correct? If not, explain and correct her error.

_____

_____

_____

_____

_____

_____

_____

24. A square poster has an area of $x^2 + 16x + 64$ square inches. Find the length of one side of the square.

_____

25. An artist framed a picture. The dimensions of the picture and frame are shown.

Completely factor the expression for the area of the frame.

_____

4x

2y

4x

2y

26. Explain how to find the value of z if you know that $100x^2 + 120x + z$ is a perfect square trinomial.

_____

_____

27. Multi-step The area of a square is $(36d^2 - 36d + 9)$ in^2.

   a. What expression represents the length of a side of the square?

   _____

   b. What expression represents the perimeter of the square? _____

   c. What are the length of a side, the perimeter, and the area of the square when $d = 2$?

   _____

H.O.T.   **FOCUS ON HIGHER ORDER THINKING**

Work Area

28. Critical Thinking Sinea thinks that the fully factored form of the expression $(x^4 - 1)$ is $(x^2 - 1)(x^2 + 1)$. Is she correct? Explain.

_____

_____

29. Explain the Error When Jeremy factored $144x^2 - 100$, he first got $(12x + 10)(12x - 10)$. Then he noticed a common factor, so he factored it further to get $2(6x + 5)(6x - 5)$. What was his error, and what is the correct factorization?

_____

_____

_____

30. Communicate Mathematical Ideas Explain how to fully factor the expression $x^4 - 2x^2y^2 + y^4$.

_____

_____

_____

Ready to Go On?

15.1 Factoring Polynomials

Factor each expression.

1. $-14x - 12x^2$

2. $3x(x + 6) - 5(6 + x)$

3. $2x^3 - 12x^2 + 18 - 3x$

15.2 Factoring $x^2 + bx + c$

Factor each trinomial.

4. $x^2 - 20x + 19$

5. $n^2 + 13n + 36$

6. $x^2 - 4x - 21$

15.3 Factoring $ax^2 + bx + c$

Factor each trinomial.

7. $3n^2 - 26n + 35$

8. $6y^2 + 11y + 4$

9. $-4x^2 - 10x - 6$

15.4 Factoring Special Products

Determine whether each polynomial is a perfect-square trinomial or the difference of two squares. Then factor each polynomial.

10. $4x^2 - 12x + 9$

11. $36n^2 + 24n + 4$

12. $4b^4 - 49b^2$

? ESSENTIAL QUESTION

13. How can you factor expressions of the form $ax^2 + bx + c$?

MODULE 15

MIXED REVIEW

COMMON CORE

Assessment Readiness

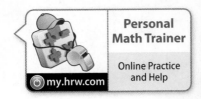

Personal Math Trainer

Online Practice and Help

my.hrw.com

1. Look at each polynomial below. Does the polynomial have a factor of $(x - 4)$? Select Yes or No for polynomials A–C.

   A. $6x - 10$ ◯ Yes   ◯ No

   B. $x^2 - x - 12$ ◯ Yes   ◯ No

   C. $2x^2 + 7x - 4$ ◯ Yes   ◯ No

2. Consider the polynomial $4x^2 + 40x + 36$.

   Choose True or False for each statement.

   A. The GCF of the terms is 4.   ◯ True   ◯ False

   B. The factored form has a factor of $(x + 1)$.   ◯ True   ◯ False

   C. The polynomial is a perfect-square trinomial.   ◯ True   ◯ False

3. A school plans to expand its rectangular vegetable garden. Both the length and the width will be increased by x feet. After the expansion, the garden will have an area of $(x^2 + 12x + 32)$ square feet. What are the original length and width of the garden? Explain how you used factoring to determine your answer.

4. Emily can spend no more than $40.00 on a raincoat. Sales tax is 8.25% of the marked price. Can Emily afford a raincoat priced at $37.95? Write and solve an inequality to support your answer.

Solving Quadratic Equations

ESSENTIAL QUESTION

How do you determine the best method for solving a quadratic equation or a system of equations?

Real-World Video

The designers of a fireworks display need to make precise timing calculations. An explosion too soon or too late could spell disaster!

⏻ my.hrw.com

GO DIGITAL
my.hrw.com

my.hrw.com
Go digital with your write-in student edition, accessible on any device.

Math On the Spot
Scan with your smart phone to jump directly to the online edition, video tutor, and more.

Animated Math
Interactively explore key concepts to see how math works.

Personal Math Trainer
Get immediate feedback and help as you work through practice sets.

Are YOU Ready?

Complete these exercises to review skills you will need for this module.

Personal Math Trainer

Online Practice and Help

my.hrw.com

Simplify Polynomial Expressions

EXAMPLE $4r - 3r^2 + 2(6r + 5)$
$4r - 3r^2 + 12r + 10$ Multiply by 2.
$-3r^2 + 16r + 10$ Collect like terms.

Simplify each expression.

1. $8g - 5 + 2g^2 + 5g^2$

2. $3x - 5(x^2 + 3) - 2x^2$

Solve Multi-Step Equations

EXAMPLE   Solve $2x - 5 = 17$
$2x = 22$ Add 5 to both sides
$x = 11$ Divide both sides by 2.

Solve the following equations.

3. $2x + 7 = 0$ _____

4. $14 - 3y = -7$ _____

Multiply Binomials

EXAMPLE   Distributive Property
$(x + 2)(x - 5)$
$= x(x - 5) + 2(x - 5)$
$= x^2 - 5x + 2x - 10$
$= x^2 - 3x - 10$

FOIL
$(x + 2)(x - 5)$
  F O I L
$= x^2 - 5x + 2x - 10$
$= x^2 - 3x - 10$

Find each product.

5. $(x + 2)(x + 5)$

6. $(x - 7)(x + 2)$

7. $(3x - 8)(3x + 6)$

Factor Trinomials

EXAMPLE $x^2 + 7x - 18$
$= (x + \boxed{})(x + \boxed{})$
$= (x + 9)(x - 2)$

Factors of -18	Sum
-1 and 18	17 ✗
-2 and 9	7 ✔

Factor each polynomial completely.

8. $x^2 - 2x + 1$

9. $3x^2 - 22x + 7$

10. $x^2 - 7x - 18$

Reading Start-Up

Visualize Vocabulary

Use the review words to complete the chart.

	a square of a whole number
	one of the two equal factors of a number
	a set of two or more equations that contain two or more variables
	an equation of the form $ax^2 + bx + c = 0$, where a is not 0
	a function where the y-value increases as the x-value increases

Vocabulary

Review Words

✔ increasing function
(*función de incremento*)

✔ perfect square
(*cuadrado perfecto*)

✔ quadratic equation
(*ecuación cuadrática*)

✔ square root
(*raíz cuadrada*)

✔ system of equations
(*sistema de ecuaciones*)

Preview Words

discriminant

completing the square

properties of radicals

quadratic formula

Understand Vocabulary

To become familiar with some of the vocabulary terms in the module, consider the following. You may refer to the module, the glossary, or a dictionary.

1. The _____ gives the solutions of a quadratic equation.

2. The _____ tells how many real solutions a quadratic equation will have.

3. _____ is a process that forms a perfect square trinomial.

Active Reading

Key-Term Fold Note Before beginning the module, create a key-term fold note to help you organize what you learn. Write a vocabulary term on each tab of the key-term fold. Under each tab, write the definition of the term.

GETTING READY FOR

Solving Quadratic Equations

Understanding the standards and the vocabulary terms in the standards will help you know exactly what you are expected to learn in this module.

COMMON CORE A.REI.4B

Solve quadratic equations by inspection, taking square roots, completing the square, the quadratic formula, and factoring, as appropriate, to the initial form of the equation. Recognize when the quadratic formula gives complex solutions and write them as $a \pm bi$ for real numbers a and b.

Key Vocabulary

quadratic equation *(ecuación cuadrática)*

    an equation of the form $ax^2 + bx + c = 0$, where $a \neq 0$

COMMON CORE A.REI.7

Solve a simple system consisting of a linear equation and a quadratic equation in two variables, algebraically and graphically.

Key Vocabulary

system of equations *(sistema de ecuaciones)*

    a set of two or more equations that contain two or more variables

---

What It Means to You

You can solve quadratic equations by various methods. The best method to use depends upon the initial form of the equation.

EXAMPLE A.REI.4B

The equation $x^2 + x - 12 = 0$ can best be solved by factoring.

$$x^2 + x - 12 = 0$$
$$(x + 4)(x - 3) = 0$$
$$x + 4 = 0 \quad \text{or} \quad x - 3 = 0$$
$$x = -4 \quad \text{or} \quad x = 3$$

What It Means to You

Given a linear equation and a quadratic equation, you can find 0, 1, or 2 ordered pairs that are solutions to both equations.

EXAMPLE A.REI.7

You can solve the system of equations algebraically.

$$y = x - 3 \text{ and } y = x^2 - 5x + 2$$

First, set the equations equal to each other and solve for x.

$$x - 3 = x^2 - 5x + 2$$
$$-3 = x^2 - 6x + 2$$
$$0 = x^2 - 6x + 5$$
$$0 = (x - 5)(x - 1)$$
$$x = 5 \text{ or } x = 1$$

Next, substitute the x values into one of the equations to find the y values.

$$y = 5 - 3 = 2 \text{ and } y = 1 - 3 = -2$$

So, the ordered pairs $(5, 2)$ and $(1, -2)$ are solutions of the system of equations.

Visit **my.hrw.com** to see all **Common Core Standards** unpacked.

my.hrw.com

COMMON
CORE   A.REI.4b

Solve quadratic equations by inspection, taking square roots, completing the square, the quadratic formula and factoring, as appropriate to the initial form of the equation. Recognize when the quadratic formula gives complex solutions and write them as $a \pm bi$ for real numbers a and b. Also A.CED.1

LESSON 16.1 Solving Quadratic Equations Using Square Roots

? ESSENTIAL QUESTION

How can you solve quadratic equations using square roots?

EXPLORE ACTIVITY A.REI.4b

Exploring Square Roots

Recall that the square root of a nonnegative number, a, is the real number, b, such that $b^2 = a$. Since $4^2 = 16$ and $(-4)^2 = 16$, the square roots of 16 are 4 and -4. Thus, every positive real number has two square roots, one positive and one negative. The positive square root is given by $\sqrt{a}$ and the negative square root by $-\sqrt{a}$. These can be combined as $\pm\sqrt{a}$.

The **Product Property of Radicals** states that for nonnegative a and b, $\sqrt{ab} = \sqrt{a} \cdot \sqrt{b}$. You can use this property to simplify $\sqrt{45}$.

$$\sqrt{45} = \sqrt{9 \cdot 5}$$ Rewrite 45 as a product using a perfect square.

$$= \sqrt{9} \cdot \sqrt{5}$$ Use the product property.

$$= 3 \cdot \sqrt{5}$$ The square root of 9 is 3.

The **Quotient Property of Radicals** states that for nonnegative a and positive b, $\sqrt{\frac{a}{b}} = \frac{\sqrt{a}}{\sqrt{b}}$. You can use this property to simplify $-\sqrt{0.07}$.

$$-\sqrt{0.07} = -\sqrt{\frac{7}{100}}$$ Rewrite the decimal as a fraction.

$$= -\frac{\sqrt{7}}{\sqrt{100}}$$ Use the quotient property.

$$= -\frac{\sqrt{7}}{10}$$ The square root of 100 is 10.

Simplify each square root.

A $\pm\sqrt{16}$ = _____ or _____

B $\pm\sqrt{25}$ = _____ or _____

C Use the Product Property of Radicals to evaluate:

$$\pm\sqrt{12} = \pm\sqrt{(4 \cdot 3)} = \pm\sqrt{\boxed{}} \cdot \sqrt{3} = \pm 2 \cdot \sqrt{3}$$

D Use the Quotient Property of Radicals to evaluate: $\pm\sqrt{\frac{16}{9}} = \pm\dfrac{\sqrt{16}}{\sqrt{\boxed{}}} = \pm\dfrac{4}{\boxed{}}$

E Use properties to evaluate:

$$\pm\sqrt{0.27} = \pm\sqrt{\frac{\boxed{}}{100}} = \pm\frac{\sqrt{27}}{\sqrt{100}} = \pm\frac{\sqrt{\boxed{} \cdot \boxed{}}}{\boxed{}} = \bigcirc\frac{\sqrt{9} \cdot \sqrt{\boxed{}}}{10} = \pm\frac{3 \cdot \sqrt{\boxed{}}}{\boxed{}}$$

REFLECT

1. **Analyze Relationships** Explain why $\sqrt{6^2}$ and $\sqrt{(-6)^2}$ have the same value.

_____

_____

2. **Communicate Mathematical Ideas** Explain why a must be nonnegative when you find $\sqrt{a}$.

_____

_____

_____

Math On the Spot

my.hrw.com

Solving $ax^2 - c = 0$ Using Square Roots

A **quadratic equation** is an equation that can be written in the standard form $ax^2 + bx + c = 0$, where a, b, and c are real numbers and $a \neq 0$. There are a number of methods that can be used to solve a quadratic equation. Simple quadratic equations of the form $ax^2 - c = 0$ can be solved by taking square roots.

EXAMPLE 1

COMMON CORE A.REI.4b

Solve $2x^2 - 8 = 0$.

$$2x^2 - 8 = 0$$

$$2x^2 = 8 \qquad \text{Add 8 to both sides.}$$

$$x^2 = 4 \qquad \text{Divide both sides by 2.}$$

$$x = \pm\sqrt{4} \qquad \text{Take the square root of both sides of the equation.}$$

$$x = \pm 2 \qquad \text{Simplify the square root.}$$

The solutions are 2 and -2.

Personal Math Trainer

Online Practice and Help

my.hrw.com

YOUR TURN

Solve.

3. $x^2 - 9 = 0$

_____

4. $2x^2 - 128 = 0$

_____

Solving $a(x + b)^2 = c$ Using Square Roots

When solving quadratic equations, the solutions may not be opposites, or they may be irrational numbers, or there may not be a real-number solution.

EXAMPLE 2

COMMON CORE   A.REI.4b

A Solve $(x + 5)^2 = 36$.

$$(x + 5)^2 = 36$$
$$x + 5 = \pm\sqrt{36} \qquad \text{Take the square root of both sides.}$$
$$x + 5 = \pm 6 \qquad \text{Simplify the square root.}$$
$$x = \pm 6 - 5 \qquad \text{Subtract 5 from both sides.}$$
$$x = -6 - 5 \text{ or } x = 6 - 5 \qquad \text{Solve for both cases.}$$
$$x = -11 \qquad x = 1$$

The solutions are -11 and 1.

My Notes

B Solve $2(x - 3)^2 = -32$.

$$2(x - 3)^2 = -32$$
$$(x - 3)^2 = -16 \qquad \text{Divide both sides by 2.}$$

Stop here. The square of a number is never negative, so this equation does not have real-number solutions.

C Solve $3(x - 5)^2 = 18$.

$$3(x - 5)^2 = 18$$
$$(x - 5)^2 = 6 \qquad \text{Divide both sides by 3.}$$
$$x - 5 = \pm\sqrt{6} \qquad \text{Take the square root of both sides.}$$
$$x = 5 \pm \sqrt{6} \qquad \text{Add 5 to both sides.}$$
$$x = 5 + \sqrt{6} \text{ or } x = 5 - \sqrt{6} \qquad \text{Solve for both cases.}$$

The solutions are $5 + \sqrt{6}$ and $5 - \sqrt{6}$.

Rounding to the nearest hundredth gives solutions of 7.45 and 2.55.

YOUR TURN

Solve.

5. $2(x - 2)^2 = 98$

6. $(x + 4)^2 = 30$

Personal Math Trainer

Online Practice and Help

⊙ my.hrw.com

Math On the Spot
my.hrw.com

Solving Real-World Problems

Real-world situations can sometimes be analyzed by solving a quadratic equation using square roots.

EXAMPLE 3 Real World

COMMON CORE A.CED.1, A.REI.4b

A contractor is building a fenced-in playground at a daycare. The playground will be rectangular with its width equal to half of its length. The total area will be 5000 square feet. Determine how many feet of fencing the contractor will use.

STEP 1 Remember a rectangle has two pairs of equal sides, and the equation for the area of a rectangle is $A = lw$.

STEP 2 Substitute what you know into the equation and solve it.

$5000 = \frac{1}{2} \cdot x \cdot x$ The width is half the length. Substitute $\frac{1}{2}x$ for w and x for l. Also substitute 5000 for A.

$5000 = \frac{1}{2} x^2$ Simplify.

$10,000 = x^2$ Multiply both sides by 2.

$x = \pm 100$ Take square roots of both sides.

STEP 3 Interpret the solution to the problem.

$x = 100$ and $x = -100$ are the solutions.

The answer must be positive, so ignore the negative result and obtain $x = 100$ feet of fence for the length.

Thus, the length of fencing used will be
$100 + 100 + 50 + 50 = 300$ feet.

Math Talk
Mathematical Practices

How can the negative solution found in Step 3 be interpreted?

Personal Math Trainer

Online Practice and Help
my.hrw.com

YOUR TURN

7. A rectangular picture has a width that is $\frac{1}{3}$ of the length. Find the length if the area of the picture is 300 cm². The formula for area of a rectangle is $A = lw$.

_____

Guided Practice

Simplify. (Explore Activity)

1. $\pm\sqrt{25}$ _____ 5,

2. $\pm\sqrt{100}$ _____ , −10

3. $\pm\sqrt{49}$ _____

4. $\pm\sqrt{63}$ _____

5. $\pm\sqrt{\dfrac{13}{25}}$ _____

6. $\pm\sqrt{\dfrac{36}{49}}$ _____

Solve each simple quadratic equation. (Example 1)

7. $2x^2 - 6 = 0$

$2x^2 = \boxed{}$

$x^2 = \boxed{}$

$\boxed{} = \boxed{}$

The solutions are $\boxed{}$ and $\boxed{}$.

8. $y^2 = 81$

$y = \boxed{}$

$y = \pm\,9$

The solutions are $\boxed{}$ and $\boxed{}$.

Solve each quadratic equation. (Example 2)

9. $(x + 2)^2 = 64$

$x + 2 = \boxed{}$

$x + 2 = \boxed{}$ or $x + 2 = \boxed{}$

$x + 2 = 8$

$x = \boxed{}$

$x + 2 = -8$

$x = \boxed{}$

The two solutions for this equation are

$\boxed{}$ and $\boxed{}$.

10. $(x - 3)^2 = 49$

$x - 3 = \pm\boxed{}$

$x - 3 = \boxed{}$ or $x - 3 = \boxed{}$

$x - 3 = 7$

$x = \boxed{}$

$x - 3 = -7$

$x = \boxed{}$

The two solutions for this equation are

$\boxed{}$ and $\boxed{}$.

Solve each quadratic equation. (Example 2)

11. $(x+4)^2 = 81$

$$x + 4 = \pm\sqrt{\boxed{}}$$

$$x + 4 = \boxed{} \quad \text{or } x + 4 = \boxed{}$$

$$x + 4 = 9 \qquad\qquad x + 4 = -9$$

$$x = \boxed{} \qquad\qquad x = \boxed{}$$

The two solutions for this equation are $\boxed{}$ and $\boxed{}$.

12. $4(x+1)^2 = -100$

$$(x+1)^2 = \boxed{}$$

There are _____ real number solutions for this equation.

13. A rectangular garden has a length that is $\frac{1}{4}$ of its width. Find the width of the garden if the area is 300 square meters. (Example 3)

Area of a rectangle $= \boxed{}$

$$300 = \frac{1}{4}w^2$$

$$w^2 = \boxed{}$$

$$w = +\boxed{} \quad \text{or } w = \boxed{}$$

Rounding to the nearest hundredth gives $\boxed{}$ and $\boxed{}$.

The only reasonable solution for this problem is $\boxed{}$.

? ESSENTIAL QUESTION CHECK-IN

14. How can you solve quadratic equations using square roots?

_____

_____

_____

_____

_____

_____

16.1 Independent Practice

Personal
Math Trainer

Online Practice
and Help

my.hrw.com

COMMON CORE A.CED.1, A.REI.4b

Simplify.

15. $\sqrt{144}$ _____

16. $\sqrt{400}$ _____

17. $\sqrt{4}$ _____

Choose either PP (Product Property) or QP (Quotient Property) to simplify. Then simplify.

18. $\sqrt{32}$ _____

19. $\sqrt{\dfrac{16}{25}}$ _____

20. $\sqrt{75}$ _____

21. $\sqrt{0.0025}$ _____

22. $\sqrt{\dfrac{17}{169}}$ _____

23. $\sqrt{54}$ _____

24. $\sqrt{\dfrac{144}{36}}$ _____

25. $\sqrt{48}$ _____

Solve the quadratic equations using square roots.

26. $x^2 - 20 = 0$ _____

27. $x^2 - 144 = 0$ _____

28. $x^2 - 35 = 0$ _____

29. $x^2 - 81 = 0$ _____

30. $x^2 - 100 = 0$ _____

Solve for x. Then check your answer.

31. $(x + 7)^2 = 49$

   a. Solve for x.

   _____

   b. Check your answer.

   _____

32. $(x - 3)^2 = 144$

   a. Solve for x.

   _____

   b. Check your answer.

   _____

   _____

33. $(x - 5)^2 = 81$

   a. Solve for x.

   _____

   b. Check your answer.

   _____

   _____

34. $(x + 3)^2 - 2 = 34$

   a. Solve for x.

   _____

   b. Check your answer.

   _____

   _____

35. A square field has an area of 2500 square meters. What is the length of the field?

_____

36. A rectangular prism has a volume of 100 cm^3. The base of the prism is a square, and the height is the product of the length and width of the prism. Find the exact dimensions of the prism.

_____

_____

37. You have to decorate a cardboard sign with colored construction paper. The width of the sign is $\frac{1}{5}$ times the length of the sign, and the total area is 200 square inches.

a. What is the length of the sign? _____

b. What is the width of the sign? _____

38. **Explain the Error** Bob is simplifying $\sqrt{150}$ and begins as shown.

$$\sqrt{150} = \sqrt{10 \cdot 15} = \sqrt{10} \cdot \sqrt{15}.$$

a. Explain the error that Bob made.

_____

b. Show the steps in the correct simplification of $\sqrt{150}$.

_____

 **FOCUS ON HIGHER ORDER THINKING**

39. **Critical Thinking** If $a = 2b$ and $2ab = 36$, find all possible values for a and b.

_____

40. **Justify Reasoning** For the equation $x^2 = a$, describe the values of a that will result in each of the following. Explain your reasoning.

a. two real solutions

_____

_____

b. one real solution

_____

_____

c. no real solution

_____

_____

41. **Communicate Mathematical Ideas** Explain why the quadratic equation $x^2 + b = 0$, where $b > 0$, has no real solutions, but the quadratic equation $x^2 - b = 0$, where $b > 0$, has two real solutions.

_____

_____

_____

_____

Solving $x^2 + bx + c = 0$ by Factoring

COMMON CORE A.REI.4b

Solve quadratic equations by inspection (e.g., for $x^2 = 49$), taking square roots, completing the square, the quadratic formula and factoring, as appropriate to the initial form of the equation. Recognize when the quadratic formula gives complex solutions and write them as $a \pm bi$ for real numbers a and b. Also A.CED.1, A.REI.4, A.SSE.3, A.SSE.3a, F.IF.8, F.IF.8a

? ESSENTIAL QUESTION

How can you use factoring to solve quadratic equations in standard form when $a = 1$?

EXPLORE ACTIVITY COMMON CORE A.REI.4b, A.SSE.3a

Zero Product Property

For all real numbers a and b, the following is true.

Words	Sample Numbers	Algebra
If the product of two quantities equals zero, at least one of the quantities equals zero.	$5(0) = 0$ $(0)6 = 0$	If $ab = 0$, then $a = 0$ or $b = 0$.

Consider the equation $x^2 - 25 = 0$.

A Factor the left side as $\left(\boxed{} + \boxed{}\right)\left(\boxed{} - \boxed{}\right)$.

B Apply the Zero Product Property to $(x + 5)(x - 5) = 0$

$$\boxed{} + \boxed{} = 0 \quad \text{or} \quad \boxed{} - \boxed{} = 0$$

$$x = \boxed{} \quad \text{or} \quad x = \boxed{}$$

The solutions of the equation $x^2 - 25 = 0$ are called the *zeros* of the related function $f(x) = x^2 - 25$ because they satisfy the equation $f(x) = 0$.

To see this, you can substitute 5 and -5 for x in $f(x) = x^2 - 25$.

The result is $f(5) = 0$ and $f(-5) = 0$.

REFLECT

1. **Analyze Relationships** Describe how to use the Zero Product Property to solve the equation $(x + 5)(x - 12) = 0$. Then identify the solutions.

_____

_____

_____

_____

_____

Applying the Zero Product Property to Functions

When given a function of the form $f(x) = (x + a)(x + b)$, you can use the Zero Product Property to find the zeros of the function.

EXAMPLE 1

COMMON CORE A.REI.4b, A.SSE.3a

Find the zeros of $f(x) = (x - 2)(x - 9)$.

My Notes

> **STEP 1**   Set $f(x)$ equal to zero.
>
> $(x - 2)(x - 9) = 0$

> **STEP 2**   Applying the Zero Product Property, either term can be equal to zero.
>
> $x - 2 = 0$ or $x - 9 = 0$

> **STEP 3**   Solve for x.
>
> $x = 2$ or $x = 9$
>
> The zeros are 2 and 9.

REFLECT

2. **Critique Reasoning** Jodie was given the function $f(x) = (x - 1)(x + 2)$ and asked to find the zeros. The answer she provided was $x = -1$ and $x = 2$. Do you agree or disagree? Why?

   _____

   _____

3. **What If?** How would you find the zeros of the function $f(x) = -3(x + 5)$?

   _____

   _____

4. **Communicate Mathematical Ideas** Can you use the Zero Product Property to find the zeros of the function $f(x) = (1 + x) + (1 - 2x)$? Explain.

   _____

Personal Math Trainer

Online Practice and Help

my.hrw.com

YOUR TURN

5.   Find the zeros of $f(x) = x(x + 8)$.

   _____

Solving Quadratic Equations by Factoring

You can use the Zero Product Property to solve any quadratic equation written in standard form, $ax^2 + bx + c = 0$, provided the quadratic expression is factorable.

EXAMPLE 2
COMMON CORE A.REI.4b

Solve $x^2 + 10x = -21$.

STEP 1 Write the equation in standard form.

$$x^2 + 10x + 21 = 0$$ Bring the constant term to the left hand side.

STEP 2 Find those factors of c whose sum equals b in the trinomial.

Factors of 21	Sum of Factors
1, 21	22
7, 3	10

10 is the sum that you're looking for.

STEP 3 Use the factor pair whose sum equals b to factor the quadratic expression.

$$x^2 + 10x + 21 = 0$$
$$(x + 3)(x + 7) = 0$$

Math Talk
Mathematical Practices

How can you check that the solutions are correct?

STEP 4 Apply the Zero Product Property to find x.

$$x + 3 = 0 \text{ or } x + 7 = 0$$ Equate each factor with zero.

$$x = -3 \text{ or } x = -7$$

The solutions are -3 and -7.

YOUR TURN

Solve each equation.

6. $x^2 + 14x + 49 = 0$

7. $x^2 + 12x = -36$

8. $x^2 + 7x + 10 = 0$

9. $x^2 + 2x = 8$

Solving Real-World Problems

You can write quadratic equations for given situations and solve them by factoring.

EXAMPLE 3 Real World
COMMON CORE · A.REI.4b, F.IF.8a

A golf ball is hit from a hill, and its height can be modeled by $h = -16t^2 + 32t + 48$, where h is height in feet and t is time in seconds. How long is the ball in the air?

STEP 1 Write the equation.
Substitute 0 for h for the height of the ball when it lands.

$h = -16t^2 + 32t + 48$
$0 = -16t^2 + 32t + 48$
$0 = -16(t^2 - 2t - 3)$ *Factor out the common factor -16.*
$0 = t^2 - 2t - 3$ *Divide both sides by -16.*

STEP 2 Find those factors of c whose sum equals b in the trinomial.

Factors of -3	Sum of Factors
$-3, 1$	-2
$3, -1$	2

-2 is the sum that you're looking for.

STEP 3 Use the factor pair whose sum equals b to factor the quadratic expression.

$t^2 - 2t - 3 = 0$
$(t + 1)(t - 3) = 0$

STEP 4 Apply the Zero Product Property to find t.

$t + 1 = 0$ or $t - 3 = 0$ *Equate each factor with zero.*
$t = -1$ or $t = 3$

Since time cannot be a negative number, the ball is in the air for 3 seconds.

> **Math Talk**
> **Mathematical Practices**
> If you were to graph the function $f(x) = x^2 - 4x - 12$, what points would be associated with the zeros of the function?

YOUR TURN

10. The height of a cliff diver above the water during a dive can be modeled by $h = -16t^2 + 16t + 96$, where h is the height in feet and t is the time in seconds. How long is the diver in the air?

_____

1. Find the zeros of the equation $x^2 - 49 = 0$. (Explore Activity)

   Factor the left side as $\boxed{}(x - 7) = 0$.

   Apply the Zero Product Property to $\boxed{} = 0$.

   $\boxed{} + \boxed{} = 0$ or $\boxed{} - \boxed{} = \boxed{}$

   $x = \boxed{}$ or $x = \boxed{}$

Find the zeros of each function. (Example 1)

2. $f(x) = (x + 1)(x - 1)$

   $-1,\boxed{}$

3. $f(x) = (x - 2)(x + 7)$

   $\boxed{},-7$

4. $f(x) = (x + 3)(x - 6)$

   $\boxed{},\boxed{}$

5. $\left(x + \frac{1}{2}\right)(x - 5) = 0$

   $\boxed{},\boxed{}$

6. Solve $x^2 - 6x + 8 = 0$. (Example 2)

   $$x^2 - 6x + 8 = 0$$

   $$\left(x - \boxed{}\right)\left(x - \boxed{}\right) = 0$$

   $$x = \boxed{} \text{ or } \boxed{}$$

7. Solve $x^2 - 2x = 15$. (Example 2)

   $$x^2 - 2x = 15$$

   $$x^2 - 2x - 15 = \boxed{}$$

   $$\left(x - \boxed{}\right)\left(x + \boxed{}\right) = 0$$

   $$x = \boxed{} \text{ or } x = \boxed{}$$

8. The perimeter of a rectangle is 22 centimeters and its area is 24 square centimeters. What is the measure of its shorter side? (Example 3)

$$\text{Area} = l \times w = \boxed{}$$

$$l = \frac{24}{w}$$

$$\text{Perimeter} = 2l + 2w = 22$$

$$2\left(\frac{24}{w}\right) + 2\,\boxed{} = 22$$

$$\boxed{} + 2w^2 = 22w$$

$$w^2 - \boxed{}\,w + 24 = 0$$

$$\left(\boxed{} - \boxed{}\right)\left(\boxed{} - \boxed{}\right) = 0$$

$$w = \boxed{} \quad \text{or} \quad w = \boxed{}$$

The measure of the shorter side is $\boxed{}$ cm.

9. The height of an arrow after being shot directly upwards can be modeled by $h = -16t^2 + 128t$, where h is the height in feet and t is the time in seconds. Find the time it takes the arrow to fall to the ground. (Example 3)

$$h = -16t^2 + 128t$$

$$-16t^2 + 128t = 0$$

$$t^2 - \boxed{} = 0$$

$$\boxed{}\left(\boxed{} - \boxed{}\right) = 0$$

$$t = \boxed{} \quad \text{or} \quad t = \boxed{}$$

The time is $\boxed{}$ seconds.

ESSENTIAL QUESTION CHECK-IN

10. How can you use factoring to solve quadratic equations in standard form when $a = 1$?

_____

_____

_____

_____

_____

16.2 Independent Practice

COMMON CORE A.CED.1, A.REI.4, A.REI.4b, A.SSE.3, A.SSE.3a, F.IF.8, F.IF.8a

Find the zeros of each function.

11. $f(x) = (x - 4)(x + 2)$

_____

12. $f(x) = (x + 3)(x + 1)$

_____

13. $f(x) = (4x - 3)(2x - 1)$

_____

14. $f(x) = (x - a)(x - b)$

_____

Find the zeros of each function by first factoring the polynomial.

15. $f(y) = y^2 + 3y - 4$

_____

16. $f(p) = p^2 - 2p - 24$

_____

17. $f(z) = z^2 - 7z + 12$

_____

18. $f(q) = q^2 + 25q + 100$

_____

Solve each equation.

19. $x^2 + 7x = -10$

_____

20. $x^2 + 2x = 8$

_____

21. $x^2 + 2x + 1 = 0$

_____

22. $-2x^2 = 18 - 12x$

_____

23. Find three consecutive positive integers such that the product of the larger two is equal to twice the second integer plus twice the sum of all three integers.

_____

24. The height of a flare fired from a 32-foot high platform can be modeled by the function $h = -16t^2 + 16t + 32$, where h is the height in feet above the ground and t is the time in seconds. Find the time it takes the flare to reach the ground.

_____

25. The height of a ball kicked into the air from the ground can be approximated by the function $h = -5t^2 + 15t$, where h is the height in meters and t is the time in seconds. Find the time it takes the ball to hit the ground.

_____

26. The length of a rectangle is 1 ft less than 3 times the width. The area is 310 ft^2. Find the dimensions of the rectangle.

_____

27. The height of a fireworks rocket in meters can be approximated by $h = -5t^2 + 30t$, where h is the height in meters and t is time in seconds. Find the time it takes the rocket to reach the ground after it has been launched.

_____

28. A tee box is 64 feet above its fairway. When a golf ball is hit from the tee box with an initial vertical velocity of 48 ft/s, the quadratic equation $0 = -16t^2 + 48t + 64$ gives the time, t, in seconds when a golf ball is at height 0 feet on the fairway.

a. Solve the quadratic equation by factoring to see how long the ball is in

the air. _____

b. What is the height of the ball at 1.5 seconds? _____

c. Is the ball at its maximum height at 1.5 seconds? Explain.

_____

_____

29. Write an equation that could be used to find two consecutive even integers whose product is 24. Let x represent the first integer. Solve the equation and give the two integers.

_____

30. **Draw Conclusions** A ball is kicked into the air from ground level. It follows a symmetric upside-down U-shaped curve given by the equation $h = -2d^2 + 8d$, where h is the height, in meters, the ball reaches at distance d. At what distance from the point at which it is kicked will the ball reach its maximum height? Explain.

_____

_____

_____

Work Area

31. **Analyze Relationships** The graph of a function of the form $f(x) = ax^2 + bx + c$ can have up to two x-intercepts. Describe the relationships among the solutions of $x^2 - 4x - 12 = 0$ and the zeros and x-intercepts of $f(x) = x^2 - 4x - 12$.

_____

_____

_____

32. **Justify Reasoning** Can you solve $(x - 2)(x + 3) = 5$ by solving $x - 2 = 5$ and $x + 3 = 5$? Why or why not?

_____

_____

_____

COMMON
CORE   A.REI.4b

Solve quadratic equations by inspection (e.g., for $x^2 = 49$), taking square roots, completing the square, the quadratic formula and factoring, as appropriate to the initial form of the equation. Recognize when the quadratic formula gives complex solutions and write them as $a \pm bi$ for real numbers a and b. Also A.CED.1, A.REI.4, A.SSE.3, F.IF.8

LESSON 16.3 Solving $ax^2 + bx + c = 0$ by Factoring

? ESSENTIAL QUESTION

How can you use factoring to solve the quadratic equation $ax^2 + bx + c = 0$?

EXPLORE ACTIVITY A.REI.4b

Using the Zero Product Property to Solve $(ax + b)(cx + d) = 0$

You have used the Zero Product Property to solve equations of the form $(x + a)(x + b) = 0$. The property also holds if the coefficients of x are not 1.

Solve $(3x + 5)(2x - 1) = 0$.

A Use the Zero Product Property to set each factor equal to zero.

$\boxed{} = 0$ $\boxed{} = 0$

B Solve the first equation for x.
$3x + 5 = 0$

$3x = \boxed{}$ Subtract _____ from both sides.

$x = \boxed{}$ Divide both sides by _____.

The first solution is $\boxed{}$.

C Solve the second equation for x.
$2x - 1 = 0$

$2x = \boxed{}$ Add _____ to both sides.

$x = \boxed{}$ Divide both sides by _____.

The second solution is $\boxed{}$.

D The solutions to $(3x + 5)(2x - 1) = 0$ are $\boxed{}$ and $\boxed{}$.

REFLECT

1. What are the general forms of the solutions to $(ax + b)(cx + d) = 0$? How did you find these?

_____

_____

Factoring and Using the Zero Product Property to Solve Quadratic Equations

You can use factoring and the Zero Product Property to solve quadratic equations of the form $ax^2 + bx + c = 0$ where a is a number other than 1. The method is the same as for equations whose leading coefficient is 1: write the equation in standard form, factor the quadratic expression, solve for the variable.

EXAMPLE 1

COMMON CORE A.REI.4b

Solve the quadratic equation $3x^2 + x = 6x + 2$ by factoring.

My Notes

STEP 1 Subtract $6x$ and 2 from both sides to make the right side of the equation equal 0.

$$3x^2 + x - 6x - 2 = 0$$

STEP 2 $3x^2 - 5x - 2 = 0$ *Combine like terms.*

STEP 3 $(3x + 1)(x - 2) = 0$ *Factor.*

STEP 4 $3x + 1 = 0$ or $x - 2 = 0$ *Use the Zero Product Property.*

STEP 5 $x = -\frac{1}{3}$ or $x = 2$ *Solve each equation.*

REFLECT

2. Describe the steps necessary to find the solution $x = -\frac{1}{3}$.

_____

_____

_____

3. **Communicate Mathematical Ideas** Why is it necessary to rewrite the equation so that one side equals 0 before factoring?

_____

_____

Personal Math Trainer

Online Practice and Help

⏱ my.hrw.com

YOUR TURN

Solve each quadratic equation by factoring.

4. $14x^2 + 3x = 2x + 3$

5. $8x^2 + 3 = 8x + 9$

_____ _____

Special Cases

Factoring can be made easier by first factoring out a common factor from every term, if there is one. Additionally, when possible, apply the factoring patterns.

Math On the Spot

⏻ my.hrw.com

Factoring Patterns	
Difference of Two Squares	$a^2 - b^2 = (a + b)(a - b)$
Perfect-Square Trinomial	$a^2 + 2ab + b^2 = (a + b)(a + b) = (a + b)^2$
	$a^2 - 2ab + b^2 = (a - b)(a - b) = (a - b)^2$

EXAMPLE 2

COMMON CORE   A.REI.4b

Solve each equation by factoring.

A

$4x^2 - 24x + 36 = 0$

$4(x^2 - 6x + 9) = 0$ Factor out a common factor.

$4(x - 3)(x - 3) = 0$ Factor a perfect-square trinomial.

$x = 3$ Solve using Zero Product Property.

B

$9x^2 - 36 = 0$

$9(x^2 - 4) = 0$ Factor out a common factor.

$9(x - 2)(x + 2) = 0$ Factor the difference of squares.

$x = 2 \text{ or } x = -2$ Solve using Zero Product Property.

C

$3x^2 + 6x + 3 = 0$

$3(x^2 + 2x + 1) = 0$ Factor out a common factor.

$3(x + 1)^2 = 0$ Factor a perfect-square trinomial.

$x = -1$ Solve using Zero Product Property.

YOUR TURN

Solve each equation by factoring.

6. $5x^2 - 20 = 0$

7. $2x^2 - 8x + 8 = 0$

_____   _____

Personal Math Trainer

Online Practice and Help

⏻ my.hrw.com

Solving Real-World Problems

Real-world situations can sometimes be modeled by quadratic equations.

EXAMPLE 3 **Real World**

COMMON CORE · A.CED.1, A.REI.4b

When a baseball player hits a pitch into the air, the height of the ball at time t is modeled by $h = -16t^2 + v_0t + h_0$, where v_0 is the initial upward velocity of the ball, and h_0 is the height at which the ball is hit. If a ball is 3 feet off the ground when it is hit with an initial upward velocity of 47 feet per second, how long will it be until the ball hits the ground?

STEP 1 Use the given information to write the equation.

$$-16t^2 + 47t + 3 = 0 \qquad \text{Substitute 0 for } h, 47 \text{ for } v_0 \text{ and 3 for } h_0.$$

$$-1(16t^2 - 47t - 3) = 0 \qquad \text{Factor out } -1.$$

$$-(16t + 1)(t - 3) = 0 \qquad \text{Factor.}$$

STEP 2 Solve the equation, and interpret the solution to the problem.

The solutions are $t = -\frac{1}{16}$ and $t = 3$.

The answer should be positive, so $t = 3$ seconds.

Math Talk

Mathematical Practices

Why must the negative solution found in step 2 be disregarded?

REFLECT

8. **Communicate Mathematical Ideas** How is solving for the number of seconds it takes for the ball to hit the ground related to finding the zeros of a quadratic function?

_____

_____

_____

YOUR TURN

9. The profit earned by an electronics company for selling printers is modeled by the function $P = -3x^2 + 33x - 72$, where x is the number of printers in hundreds, and P is measured in thousands of dollars. What two numbers of printers sold will result in zero profit?

_____

Solve each quadratic equation by factoring. (Example 1)

1. $7x^2 + 35x = 5x - 8$

$7x^2 + \boxed{}x + \boxed{} = 0$

$(7x + \boxed{})(x + \boxed{}) = 0$

$x = \boxed{}$ or $x = \boxed{}$

2. $6x^2 - 10x + 5 = 3x$

$6x^2 - \boxed{}x + 5 = 0$

$(\boxed{}x - 5)(\boxed{}x - 1) = 0$

$x = \boxed{}$ or $x = \boxed{}$

3. $4x^2 + 16x + 12 = 0$

$\boxed{}(x^2 + 4x + 3) = 0$

$\boxed{}(x + \boxed{})(x + \boxed{}) = 0$

$x = \boxed{}$ or $x = \boxed{}$

4. $18x^2 - 18x - 36 = 0$

$\boxed{}(x^2 - x - 2) = 0$

$\boxed{}(x + \boxed{})(x - \boxed{}) = 0$

$x = \boxed{}$ or $x = \boxed{}$

Solve each equation by factoring. (Example 2)

5. $11x^2 + 44x + 44 = 0$

$\boxed{}(x^2 + 4x + 4) = 0$

$\boxed{}(x + \boxed{})^2 = 0$

$x = \boxed{}$

6. $3x^2 - 30x + 75 = 0$

$\boxed{}(x^2 - 10x + 25) = 0$

$\boxed{}(x - \boxed{})^2 = 0$

$x = \boxed{}$

7. $12x^2 - 108 = 0$

$12(x^2 - \boxed{}) = 0$

$12(x + \boxed{})(x \bigcirc 3) = 0$

$x = \boxed{}$ or $x = \boxed{}$

8. $5x^2 - 30x + 45 = 0$

$5(x^2 - \boxed{}x + \boxed{}) = 0$

$5(x - \boxed{})(x \bigcirc 3) = 0$

$x = \boxed{}$

9. $7x^2 = 70x - 175$

$7x^2 - 70x + \boxed{} = 0$

$7(x^2 - \boxed{}x + \boxed{}) = 0$

$7(x - \boxed{})(x \bigcirc 5) = 0$

$x = \boxed{}$

10. $2x^2 + 128 = -32x$

$2x^2 + 32x + 128 = 0$

$2(x^2 + \boxed{}x + \boxed{}) = 0$

$2(x + \boxed{})(x \bigcirc 8) = 0$

$x = \boxed{}$

11. The height of a model rocket launched into the air from a rooftop is given by the quadratic equation $h = -16t^2 + 64t + 80$, where t is the time in seconds since launch, and h is measured in feet. At what time does the rocket land on the ground? (Example 3)

$$-16t^2 + 64t + 80 = 0$$

$$\boxed{}\,(t^2 - \boxed{}\,t - \boxed{}\,) = 0$$

$$\boxed{}\,(t + \boxed{}\,)(t - \boxed{}\,) = 0$$

$$t = \boxed{} \quad \text{or } t = \boxed{}$$

The rocket lands on the ground in _____ seconds.

12. A missile is fired with an initial upward velocity of 2320 feet per second. The height can be modeled by $h = -16t^2 + 2320t$, where h is the height in feet above the ground and t is the time in seconds. Find the time it takes the missile to reach a height of 40,000 feet. (Example 3)

$$-16t^2 + 2320t = 40{,}000$$

$$-16t^2 + 2320t - \boxed{} = 0$$

$$\boxed{}\,(t^2 - \boxed{}\,t + \boxed{}\,) = 0$$

$$-16\,(t - \boxed{}\,)(t - \boxed{}\,) = 0$$

$$t = \boxed{} \quad \text{or } t = \boxed{}$$

The missile will have a height of 40,000 feet at _____ seconds and

at _____ seconds.

ESSENTIAL QUESTION CHECK-IN

13. What extra step is involved in factoring $ax^2 + bx + c = 0$ when a is not equal to 1?

_____

_____

_____

_____

_____

_____

16.3 Independent Practice

COMMON CORE A.CED.1, A.REI.4, A.REI.4b, A.SSE.3

Personal
Math Trainer

Online Practice
and Help

my.hrw.com

Solve each quadratic equation by factoring.

14. $5x^2 - 10x = 9x + 4$

_____

15. $6x^2 - 8x = 2x - 4$

_____

16. $7x^2 - 1 = -50x - 8$

_____

17. $8x^2 - 4x = 2x + 9$

_____

18. $3x^2 - 48 = 0$

_____

19. $4x^2 = 16x$

_____

20. $2x^2 - 10x = -38x - 98$

_____

21. $9x^2 - 25x - 6 = 0$

_____

22. $11x^2 = 99$

_____

23. $25x^2 - 150x = -225$

_____

24. A model rocket is fired from the ground at time $t = 0$, and its height is given (in cm) by the formula $h = -490t^2 + 1470t$, where t is measured in seconds.

a. Write an equation to find when the height of the rocket is 980 cm.

_____

b. Solve the equation by factoring.

_____

c. Explain why there are two solutions to this problem.

_____

_____

_____

_____

25. As a satellite falls from outer space onto Mars, its distance in miles from the planet is given by the formula $d = -9t^2 + 776$, where t is the number of hours it has fallen.

a. Write an equation to find when the satellite will be 200 miles away from Mars.

_____

b. Solve the equation by factoring.

_____

c. Explain why only one of these solutions makes sense for this problem.

_____

_____

_____

_____

26. A volleyball player sets the ball in the air, and the height of the ball after t seconds is given in feet by $h = -2t^2 + 4t + 8$. A teammate wants to wait until the ball is 10 feet in the air before she spikes it.

a. Write an equation to find when the teammate should spike the ball.

_____

b. Solve the equation by factoring.

_____

c. Explain why there is only one possible solution to this problem.

_____

_____

H.O.T. FOCUS ON HIGHER ORDER THINKING

Work Area

27. Justify Reasoning You throw a ball into the air with an initial vertical velocity of 31 feet per second. The ball leaves your hand when it is 6 feet above the ground. You catch the ball at a height of 4 feet above the ground. The ball's height can be modeled by $h = -16t^2 + 31t + 6$, where t is the time in seconds since you threw the ball and h is the height in feet. After how many seconds did you catch the ball? Explain.

_____

_____

_____

_____

_____

28. Explain the Error In an attempt to solve the equation $3x^2 + 9x - 84 = 0$, a student factors to get $3(x + 7)(x - 4) = 0$. The student then reasons that, since there are three factors, by the Zero Product Property there will be three solutions, one for each factor. Explain the error in the student's reasoning.

_____

_____

29. Explain the Error To solve the equation $4x^2 = 4x$, a student first divides both sides by $4x$, and then claims the only solution is $x = 1$. Explain the mistake that the student made; what solution did he or she leave out?

_____

_____

_____

Solving $x^2 + bx + c = 0$ by Completing the Square

COMMON CORE A.REI.4a

Use the method of completing the square to transform any quadratic equation in x into an equation of the form $(x - p)^2 = q$ that has the same solutions. Derive the quadratic formula from this form. *Also A.REI.4, A.REI.4b, A.SSE.1, A.SSE.2, A.SSE.3b*

? ESSENTIAL QUESTION

How can you solve $x^2 + bx + c = 0$ without factoring?

EXPLORE ACTIVITY **A.SSE.2**

Visualizing Completing the Square

The diagram below represents the expression $x^2 + 6x + c$ with the constant term missing.

A Complete the diagram by filling the bottom-right corner with 1-tiles to form a square.

B How many 1-tiles did you add to the expression? _____

C Write the trinomial represented by the algebra tiles for the complete square.

$$x^2 + \boxed{}x + \boxed{}$$

D You should recognize this trinomial as an example of the special case $(a + b)^2 = a^2 + 2ab + b^2$. Recall that trinomials of this form are called perfect-square trinomials. Since the trinomial is a perfect square, you can factor it into two binomials that are the same.

$$x^2 + \boxed{}x + \boxed{} = (\boxed{} + \boxed{})^2$$

REFLECT

1. Look at the algebra tiles above. The x-tiles are divided equally, with three tiles on the right side and three tiles on the bottom side of the x^2-tile. How does the number 3 relate to the total number of x-tiles? How does the number 3 relate to the number of 1-tiles?

_____

_____

2. Communicate Mathematical Ideas Suppose you want to complete the square for the expression $x^2 - 10x + c$. What would be the sign of the x-tiles? How many 1-tiles would you have?

_____

Completing the Square

Finding the value of c needed to make an expression such as $x^2 + 6x + c$ into a perfect square trinomial is called **completing the square**.

To complete the square for the expression $x^2 + bx + c$, replace c with $\left(\frac{b}{2}\right)^2$. The perfect-square trinomial is $x^2 + bx + \left(\frac{b}{2}\right)^2$, and it factors as $\left(x + \frac{b}{2}\right)^2$.

Using algebra tiles, half of the x-tiles are placed along the right side and half along the bottom side of the x-tile. The number of 1-tiles added is the square of the number of x-tiles on either side of the x^2-tile.

My Notes

EXAMPLE 1

COMMON CORE A.SSE.2

Complete the square to form a perfect-square trinomial. Then factor the trinomial.

A $x^2 + 12x + c$

$b = 12$	Identify b.
$c = \left(\frac{b}{2}\right)^2 = \left(\frac{12}{2}\right)^2 = 36$	Find c.
$x^2 + 12x + 36$	Write the trinomial.
$(x + 6)^2$	Factor the trinomial.

B $z^2 - 26z + c$

$b = -26$	Identify b.
$c = \left(\frac{b}{2}\right)^2 = \left(\frac{-26}{2}\right)^2 = 169$	Find c.
$z^2 - 26z + 169$	Write the trinomial.
$(z - 13)^2$	Factor the trinomial.

REFLECT

3. Communicate Mathematical Ideas In part A, b is positive, and in part B, b is negative. Does this affect the sign of c? Why or why not?

_____

_____

_____

YOUR TURN

4. Complete the square for the expression $x^2 + 4x + c$, then factor the trinomial.

_____

Solving Quadratic Equations by Completing the Square

Math On the Spot
my.hrw.com

EXAMPLE 2

COMMON CORE A.REI.4a, A.REI.4b

Solve $x^2 + 14x = 15$.

$$x^2 + 14x = 15$$

$$\left(\frac{14}{2}\right)^2 = 7^2 = 49 \qquad \text{Find } \left(\frac{b}{2}\right)^2.$$

$$x^2 + 14x + 49 = 15 + 49 \qquad \text{Complete the square.}$$

$$(x + 7)^2 = 64 \qquad \text{Factor and simplify.}$$

$$x + 7 = \pm 8 \qquad \text{Take square root of both sides.}$$

$$x + 7 = 8 \text{ or } x + 7 = -8 \qquad \text{Write and solve two equations.}$$

$$x = 1 \text{ or } x = -15$$

> $(x + 7)(x + 7) = (x + 7)^2$. So the square root of $(x + 7)^2$ is $x + 7$.

Check

$x^2 + 14x =$	15
$(1)^2 + 14(1)$	15
$1 + 14$	15
15	15 ✓

$x^2 + 14x =$	15
$(-15)^2 + 14(-15)$	15
$225 - 210$	15
15	15 ✓

REFLECT

5. **Communicate Mathematical Ideas**

   a. What method would you use to solve the equation $x^2 + 3x - 4 = 0$? Explain why you would use this method.

   _____

   _____

   _____

   b. If you did solve $x^2 + 3x - 4 = 0$ by completing the square, what would be the first step?

   _____

YOUR TURN

6. Solve $x^2 - 2x - 1 = 0$.

   _____

Personal Math Trainer

Online Practice and Help

my.hrw.com

Solving Real-World Problems

EXAMPLE 3 *(Real World)*

COMMON CORE   A.REI.4a, A.REI.4b

Jenny's rectangular garden has an area of 2816 square feet. The length of the garden is 20 feet longer than the width. Using the formula for the area of a rectangle, find the dimensions of her garden.

STEP 1   The **solution** will be the length and width of the garden.

List the important information:

- The total area of the garden is 2816 square feet.
- One side of the garden is 20 feet longer than the other side.

STEP 2   Set the formula for the area of a rectangle equal to 2816, the area of the garden. Solve the equation.

STEP 3   Let x be the width and $(x + 20)$ be the length.

Use the formula for area of a rectangle (length · width = area) and substitute values.

$(x + 20) \cdot (x) = 2816$	Write the area equation.
$x^2 + 20x = 2816$	Simplify.
$\left(\frac{20}{2}\right)^2 = 10^2 = 100$	Find $\left(\frac{b}{2}\right)^2$.
$x^2 + 20x + 100 = 2816 + 100$	Add 100 to both sides.
$(x + 10)^2 = 2916$	Factor the perfect-square trinomial.
$x + 10 = \pm 54$	Take the square root of both sides.
$x + 10 = 54 \text{ or } x + 10 = -54$	Write and solve two equations.
$x = 44 \text{ or } x = -64$	

Math Talk
Mathematical Practices

Why is 100 added to each side of the equation $x^2 + 20x = 2{,}816$?

Since the width cannot be negative, the answer -64 can be discarded.

Therefore, the width is 44 feet, and the length is $44 + 20$, or 64 feet.

The length of the garden is 20 feet greater than the width. This checks because $44(64) = 2816$.

7. What If? Suppose the area of Jenny's garden is 3500 square feet and the length is still 20 feet longer than the width. What would the dimensions of the garden be?

_____

_____

8. Critical Thinking Suppose you want to double the area of Jenny's garden by increasing the length and width by the same amount. What would the approximate new dimensions of the garden be?

_____

_____

9. Communicate Mathematical Ideas Can you solve the equation in step 3 by factoring? If so, show the steps.

_____

_____

_____

YOUR TURN

10. A landscaper is designing a rectangular brick patio. She has enough bricks to cover 144 square feet. She wants the length of the patio to be 10 feet greater than the width. What dimensions should she use for the patio?

_____

Personal Math Trainer

Online Practice and Help

my.hrw.com

Guided Practice

Complete the square to form a perfect-square trinomial. (Example 1)

1. $x^2 + 14x +$ ⬜

2. $x^2 - 4x +$ ⬜

3. $x^2 - 3x +$ ⬜

4. $x^2 + 12x +$ ⬜

5. $x^2 - 14x +$ ⬜

6. $x^2 + 18x +$ ⬜

Solve each equation by completing the square. (Example 2)

7. $x^2 + 6x = -5$

$x^2 + 6x + \boxed{} = -5 + \boxed{}$

$(x + \boxed{})^2 = \boxed{}$

$x + \boxed{} = \pm \boxed{}$

$x = \boxed{}$ or $x = \boxed{}$

8. $x^2 - 8x = 9$

$x^2 - 8x + \boxed{} = 9 + \boxed{}$

$(x - \boxed{})^2 = \boxed{}$

$x - \boxed{} = \pm \boxed{}$

$x = \boxed{}$ or $x = \boxed{}$

9. $r^2 - 4r = 165$

$r^2 - 4r + \boxed{} = 165 + \boxed{}$

$(r - \boxed{})^2 = \boxed{}$

$r - \boxed{} = \pm \boxed{}$

$r = \boxed{}$ or $r = \boxed{}$

10. $t^2 + 2t = 224$

$t^2 + 2t + \boxed{} = 224 + \boxed{}$

$(t + \boxed{})^2 = \boxed{}$

$t + \boxed{} = \pm \boxed{}$

$t = \boxed{}$ or $t = \boxed{}$

11. $x^2 + 6x = 27$

_____

12. $x^2 + 4x = 6$

_____

13. **Multi-Step** The length of a rectangle is 4 meters longer than the width. The area of the rectangle is 80 square meters. Find the length and width. Round your answers to the nearest tenth of a meter. (Example 3)

_____

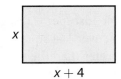

x

$x + 4$

? ESSENTIAL QUESTION CHECK-IN

14. How can you use completing the square to solve quadratic equations?

_____

_____

_____

_____

_____

_____

_____

16.4 Independent Practice

COMMON CORE A.REI.4, A.REI.4a, A.REI.4b, A.SSE.1, A.SSE.2, A.SSE.3b

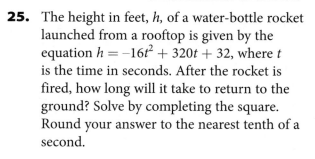

Personal Math Trainer

Online Practice and Help

my.hrw.com

Complete the square to form a perfect-square trinomial.

15. $w^2 - 11w +$ _____

16. $c^2 - 14c +$ _____

Solve by completing the square.

17. $x^2 + 4x = 12$

_____

18. $x^2 + 6x = 16$

_____

19. $x^2 + 12x = -11$

_____

20. $x^2 - 12x = -26$

_____

21. $-x^2 + 4x + 12 = 0$

_____

22. $x^2 + 4x + 6 = 0$

_____

23. $4x^2 = 16x - 12$

_____

24.

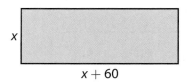

The length of Bill's backyard swimming pool is 60 feet longer than the width of the pool. The surface area of the water is 1600 square feet. What is the width and length of the pool?

_____

_____

25. The height in feet, h, of a water-bottle rocket launched from a rooftop is given by the equation $h = -16t^2 + 320t + 32$, where t is the time in seconds. After the rocket is fired, how long will it take to return to the ground? Solve by completing the square. Round your answer to the nearest tenth of a second.

_____

26.

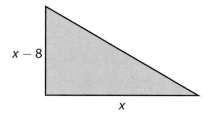

The height of a right triangle is 8 inches less than the length of its base. The area of the triangle is 90 square inches. What is the height and base of the triangle?

_____

_____

27.

Workmen created a roped-off border of width x around a 34-by-10-foot rectangular museum display to house Egyptian artifacts, as shown. The combined area of the display and the roped-off area is 640 square feet.

a. Write an equation for the combined area.

_____

b. Find the width of the roped-off area.

_____

28. The larger base of a trapezoid is three times as long as the shorter base, and the height of the trapezoid is 2 inches longer than the shorter base. The area of the trapezoid is 70 square inches. What is the length of the shorter base, x?

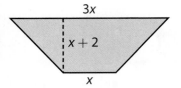

_____

Work Area

29. Explain the Error While attempting to solve the equation $x^2 + 4x = 77$, a student made an error. Explain the mistake, and provide the correct answer(s).

$$x^2 + 4x = 77$$
$$x^2 + 4x + 4 = 77 + 4$$
$$(x + 2)^2 = 81$$
$$x + 2 = 9$$
$$x = 7$$

_____

_____

_____

30. Communicate Mathematical Ideas Consider the right triangle shown at right. If the area is 96 square centimeters, briefly describe two separate methods you might use to find the length of the shorter leg, x.

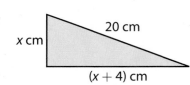

_____

_____

_____

_____

_____

31. Justify Reasoning Using the method of completing the square, Sal is working to find the solution of the equation $x^2 + 6x = -10$. If his work is accurate, will he produce an answer that is a _real_ number? Explain your reasoning.

_____

_____

_____

_____

Solving $ax^2 + bx + c = 0$ by Completing the Square

COMMON CORE A.REI.4a

Use the method of completing the square to transform any quadratic equation in x into an equation of the form $(x - p)^2 = q$ that has the same solutions. Derive the quadratic formula from this form. Also A.REI.4, A.REI.4b, A.SSE.1, A.SSE.2, A.SSE.3b

? ESSENTIAL QUESTION

How can you solve $ax^2 + bx + c = 0$ by completing the square when $a \neq 1$?

EXPLORE ACTIVITY   **A.SSE.2**

Exploring Completing the Square when $a \neq 1$

Recall that quadratic expressions can be modeled using algebra tiles representing variable expressions and units. Visualizing a square with algebra tiles can help you understand what is really meant by completing the square. Use the diagram to answer A and B below.

A What is the expression represented by the tiles in the

diagram? _____

Complete the square by filling in the bottom-right corner with 1-tiles. How many 1-tiles did you add to the

diagram? _____

B Write the trinomial represented by the algebra tiles, including the completed square.

$$\boxed{}x^2 + \boxed{}x + \boxed{}$$

Recall that a perfect-square trinomial is the square of a binomial. The binomial is represented by one "side" of the algebra tile square. Use the algebra tiles to write the trinomial as the square of a binomial.

$$\boxed{}x^2 + \boxed{}x + \boxed{} = (\boxed{}x + \boxed{})^2$$

REFLECT

1. **Analyze Relationships** The coefficient of x^2 in the trinomial is 4. What is it about the number 4 that makes it possible to arrange the x^2-tiles in such a way that you can complete the square? Does the coefficient of x^2 always have to be this type of number to complete the square? Explain.

_____

_____

_____

_____

Completing the Square When *a* Is a Perfect Square

When *a* is a perfect square, completing the square is simpler than in other cases. Consider the case involving the algebra tiles in the Explore Activity: The number of 1-tiles needed to complete the square is equal to the square of *b* divided by four times *a*, or $\frac{b^2}{4a}$. This relationship is always the case when *a* is a perfect square.

EXAMPLE 1 COMMON CORE A.REI.4a , A.REI.4b

Solve $4x^2 + 8x = 21$ by completing the square.

STEP 1   Add $\frac{b^2}{4a}$ to both sides of the equation.

$$4x^2 + 8x = 21$$
$$4x^2 + 8x + \frac{8^2}{4 \cdot 4} = 21 + \frac{8^2}{4 \cdot 4}$$
$$4x^2 + 8x + 4 = 21 + 4 = 25$$

STEP 2   Factor the left side of the equation as a perfect-square trinomial.

$$(2x + 2)^2 = 25$$

STEP 3   Apply the definition of a square root. Write two equations, and solve each equation to find the two solutions.

$$2x + 2 = \pm 5$$ *Take the square root of both sides of the equation.*

$$2x + 2 = 5 \text{ or } 2x + 2 = -5$$ *Rewrite as two equations.*

$$2x = 3 \text{ or } 2x = -7$$ *Solve for x.*

$$x = \frac{3}{2} \text{ or } x = -\frac{7}{2}$$

REFLECT

2. Why does *a* have to be a perfect square for this procedure to work?

_____

_____

_____

_____

YOUR TURN

3. Solve $36x^2 + 36x = 7$ by completing the square.

_____

My Notes

Completing the Square When *a* Is Not a Perfect Square

When the leading coefficient *a* is not a perfect square, you can transform the equation by multiplying both sides by a value such that *a* becomes a perfect square. Once *a* is a perfect square, proceed as in the previous example.

Math On the Spot
my.hrw.com

EXAMPLE 2

COMMON CORE   A.REI.4a, A.REI.4b

Solve $2x^2 - 6x = 5$ by completing the square.

STEP 1 Since the coefficient of x^2 is 2, which is not a perfect square, multiply both sides by a value so the coefficient will be a perfect square, such as 2.

$$2(2x^2 - 6x) = 2(5)$$
$$4x^2 - 12x = 10$$

Math Talk
Mathematical Practices

Why is 2 the best value by which to multiply both sides of the equation before completing the square?

STEP 2 Add $\frac{b^2}{4a}$ to both sides of the equation. In this case, $\frac{b^2}{4a} = \frac{-12^2}{4 \cdot 4} = \frac{144}{16} = 9$.

$$4x^2 - 12x + 9 = 10 + 9 = 19$$

STEP 3 Factor the left side of the equation as a perfect-square trinomial.

$$(2x - 3)^2 = 19$$

STEP 4 Apply the definition of a square root. Write two equations, and solve each equation to find the two solutions:

$$2x - 3 = \pm\sqrt{19} \qquad \text{Take the square root of both sides.}$$

$$2x - 3 = \sqrt{19} \text{ or } 2x - 3 = -\sqrt{19} \qquad \text{Rewrite as two equations.}$$

$$2x = 3 + \sqrt{19} \text{ or } 2x = 3 - \sqrt{19} \qquad \text{Solve for x.}$$

$$x = \frac{3 + \sqrt{19}}{2} \text{ or } x = \frac{3 - \sqrt{19}}{2}$$

REFLECT

4. Make a Conjecture Would you get the same result for Example 2 if you divide each side by 2 in Step 1 and then complete the square? Explain.

_____

_____

YOUR TURN

5. Solve $3x^2 + 4x = 9$ by completing the square.

_____

Personal Math Trainer

Online Practice and Help

my.hrw.com

Solving Real-World Problems

Many real-world phenomena can be modeled using quadratic equations, and solving those equations by completing the square can be an effective way to answer questions about these situations.

EXAMPLE 3   COMMON CORE   A.REI.4a, A.REI.4b

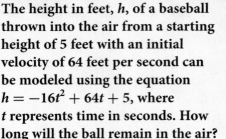

The height in feet, h, of a baseball thrown into the air from a starting height of 5 feet with an initial velocity of 64 feet per second can be modeled using the equation $h = -16t^2 + 64t + 5$, where t represents time in seconds. How long will the ball remain in the air?

STEP 1   Set the equation equal to 0, and subtract the constant term from both sides so the equation will be in $ax^2 + bx = c$ format.

$$-16t^2 + 64t + 5 = 0$$

$$-16t^2 + 64t = -5$$

STEP 2   To complete the square, a must be positive (since the square root of a it will be a real number). To make a positive, multiply all three terms by -1.

$$16t^2 - 64t = 5$$

STEP 3   Add $\frac{b^2}{4a}$ to both sides of the equation. In this case, $\frac{b^2}{4a} = \frac{(-64)^2}{4 \cdot 16} = 64$.

$$16t^2 - 64t + 64 = 5 + 64 = 69$$

STEP 4   Factor the left side of the equation as a perfect-square trinomial.

$$(4t - 8)^2 = 69$$

STEP 5   Apply the definition of a square root. Write two equations, and solve each equation to find the two solutions:

$$4t - 8 = \pm\sqrt{69}$$ *Take the square root of both sides.*

$$4t - 8 = \sqrt{69} \text{ or } 4t - 8 = -\sqrt{69}$$ *Rewrite as two equations.*

$$4t = 8 + \sqrt{69} \text{ or } 4t = 8 - \sqrt{69}$$ *Solve for t.*

$$t = \frac{8 + \sqrt{69}}{4} \text{ or } t = \frac{8 - \sqrt{69}}{4}$$

Rounded to the nearest hundredth, $t = 4.08$ or $t = -0.08$. The negative solution can be discarded. The ball will remain in the air approximately 4.08 seconds.

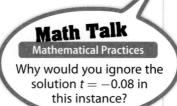

Math Talk

Mathematical Practices

Why would you ignore the solution $t = -0.08$ in this instance?

6. A baseball is thrown down from a 30-foot-high roof with an initial speed of 56 feet per second. The height in feet, h, of the baseball can be modeled by the equation $h = -16t^2 - 56t + 30$, where t represents time in seconds. How long will it be before the ball hits the ground? Round your answer to the nearest hundredth of a second.

Personal Math Trainer

Online Practice and Help

⊙ my.hrw.com

_____

Guided Practice

Solve by completing the square. (Example 1)

1. $9x^2 + 30x = 16$

$$9x^2 + 30x + \boxed{} = 16 + \boxed{}$$

$$\left(\boxed{}\, x + \boxed{}\right)^2 = \boxed{}$$

$$\boxed{}\, x + \boxed{} = \pm\sqrt{\boxed{}}$$

$$x = \boxed{} \quad \text{or} \quad x = \boxed{}$$

2. $25x^2 + 40x = 20$

$$25x^2 + 40x + \boxed{} = 20 + \boxed{}$$

$$\left(\boxed{}\, x + \boxed{}\right)^2 = \boxed{}$$

$$\boxed{}\, x + \boxed{} = \pm\sqrt{\boxed{}}$$

$$x = \boxed{} \quad \text{or} \quad x = \boxed{}$$

Solve by completing the square. (Example 2)

3. $5x^2 - 6x = 11$

$$\boxed{} \cdot [5x^2 - 6x = 11]$$

$$\boxed{}\, x^2 - \boxed{}\, x = \boxed{}$$

$$\boxed{}\, x^2 - \boxed{}\, x + \boxed{} = \boxed{} + \boxed{}$$

$$\left(\boxed{}\, x - \boxed{}\right)^2 = \boxed{}$$

$$\boxed{}\, x - \boxed{} = \pm\sqrt{\boxed{}}$$

$$x = \boxed{} \quad \text{or} \quad x = \boxed{}$$

4. $3x^2 + 8x = 5$

$$\boxed{} \cdot [3x^2 + 8x = 5]$$

$$\boxed{}\, x^2 + \boxed{}\, x = \boxed{}$$

$$\boxed{}\, x^2 + \boxed{}\, x + \boxed{} = \boxed{} + \boxed{}$$

$$\left(\boxed{}\, x + \boxed{}\right)^2 = \boxed{}$$

$$\boxed{}\, x + \boxed{} = \pm\sqrt{\boxed{}}$$

$$x = \boxed{} \quad \text{or} \quad x = \boxed{}$$

5. $2x^2 - 3x = 20$

$\boxed{} \cdot [2x^2 - 3x = 20]$

$\boxed{}\, x^2 - \boxed{}\, x = \boxed{}$

$\boxed{}\, x^2 - \boxed{}\, x + \boxed{} = \boxed{} + \boxed{}$

$\left(\boxed{}\, x - \boxed{}\right)^2 = \boxed{}$

$\boxed{}\, x - \boxed{} = \pm\sqrt{\boxed{}}$

$\boxed{}\, x - \boxed{} = \pm\, \boxed{}$

$x = \boxed{}$ or $x = \boxed{}$

6. $3x^2 + 7x = 3$

$\boxed{} \cdot [3x^2 + 7x = 3]$

$\boxed{}\, x^2 + \boxed{}\, x = \boxed{}$

$\boxed{}\, x^2 + \boxed{}\, x + \boxed{} = \boxed{} + \boxed{}$

$\left(\boxed{}\, x + \boxed{}\right)^2 = \boxed{}$

$\boxed{}\, x + \boxed{} = \pm\sqrt{\boxed{}}$

$\boxed{}\, x + \boxed{} = \pm\, \boxed{}$

$x = \boxed{}$ or $x = \boxed{}$

7. The height in feet, h, of a projectile launched from the top of a 50-foot hill, with an initial velocity of 24 feet per second can be modeled using the equation $h = -16t^2 + 24t + 50$, where t is the time in seconds. Complete the square to solve for t, and determine how long the projectile will be in the air. Round to the nearest hundredth. (Example 3)

$\boxed{}\, t^2 - \boxed{}\, t = \boxed{}$

$\boxed{}\, t^2 - \boxed{}\, t + \boxed{} = \boxed{}$

$\left(\boxed{}\, t - \boxed{}\right)^2 = \boxed{}$

$t = \dfrac{\boxed{} - \sqrt{\boxed{}}}{\boxed{}}$ or $t = \dfrac{\boxed{} + \sqrt{\boxed{}}}{\boxed{}}$

$t \approx \boxed{}$ sec. (The negative answer is not possible.)

? **ESSENTIAL QUESTION CHECK-IN**

8. When an equation is in the form $ax^2 + bx + c$, with $a \neq 1$, how can you solve for x without eliminating the coefficient of x^2?

_____

_____

16.5 Independent Practice

Personal Math Trainer

Online Practice and Help

my.hrw.com

COMMON CORE A.REI.4, A.REI.4a, A.REI.4b, A.SSE.1, A.SSE.2, A.SSE.3b

Solve by completing the square.

9. $-x^2 + x + 6 = 0$ _____

10. $3x^2 - 6x - 9 = 0$ _____

Use the expression $\frac{b^2}{4a}$ to determine the constant that should be added to the expression to create a perfect-square trinomial.

11. $25x^2 + 10x$ _____

12. $100x^2 - 40x$ _____

Solve the following quadratic equations by completing the square.

13. $49x^2 + 28x = -3$ _____

14. $9x^2 - 18x = 7$ _____

15. $18x^2 + x = 5$ _____

16. $64x^2 + 16x = 14$ _____

17. $121x^2 - 110x = 4$ _____

Complete each trinomial so that it is a perfect square.

18. $x^2 + 18x + c$ _____

19. $x^2 + bx + 4$ _____

20. $x^2 - 100x + c$ _____

21. $x^2 - bx + \frac{81}{4}$ _____

22. $9x^2 - 24x + c$ _____

23. $25x^2 + 10x + c$ _____

24. $4x^2 - 6x + c$ _____

25. $49x^2 - 7x + c$ _____

Solve the following quadratic equations by completing the square.

26. $2x^2 + 10x = 12$ _____

27. $3x^2 - 8x = 3$ _____

28. $20x^2 - 12x = 11$ _____

29. $27x^2 + 18x = 4$ _____

30. **Multi-Step** A roped-off area of width x is created around a 30- by 10-foot rectangular museum display of Native American artifacts. The combined area of the display and the roped-off area is 800 square feet.

a. Write an equation for the combined area. _____

b. Find the width of the roped-off area.

_____

31. A rocket is shot straight up from a 30-foot rooftop with an initial velocity of 128 feet per second. The height, h, of the rocket is given by the equation $h = -16t^2 + 128t + 30$, where t is the time elapsed in seconds and h is the height in feet.

a. How long will it take the rocket to return to the ground? Round your answer to the nearest tenth of a second.

_____

b. The maximum height that the rocket achieves is 286 feet. At what time does it reach that height? Round your answer to the nearest tenth of a second.

_____

32. During construction, a fuse is thrown straight down an elevator shaft from the thirty-seventh floor (370 feet above ground level) with an initial speed of 64 feet per second. The height, h, of the fuse is given by the equation $h = -16t^2 - 64t + 370$, where t is the time elapsed in seconds and h is the height in feet. How long will it take until the fuse hits the ground? Round your answer to the nearest tenth of a second.

_____

Work Area

33. Represent Real-World Problems The length of a rectangular garden is 2 meters less than twice its width. If the area of the garden is 35 square meters, what are the dimensions of the garden? Round answers to the nearest tenth.

_____

34. Draw Conclusions In the problems above, only one of two solutions is included as an answer. Why are certain solutions considered extraneous? Is one solution to a real-world problem involving a quadratic equation always extraneous?

_____

_____

_____

_____

_____

35. Find the Error Kendra was asked to solve $2x^2 + 14x = 27$ by completing the square. Her work is shown below. Where did she make her mistake?

$$2 \cdot [2x^2 - 14x = 27]$$

$$4x^2 - 28x = 54$$

$$4x^2 - 28x + 49 = 103$$

$$(2x - 7)^2 = 103$$

$$2x - 7 = \pm \sqrt{103}$$

$$2x = \sqrt{103} + 7 \text{ or } 2x = \sqrt{103} - 7$$

$$x = \frac{7 + \sqrt{103}}{2} \text{ or } x = \frac{-7 + \sqrt{103}}{2}$$

_____

_____

_____

16.6 The Quadratic Formula

COMMON CORE **A.REI.4b**

Solve quadratic equations by ... completing the square, the quadratic formula and factoring, as appropriate to the initial form of the equation. Recognize when the quadratic formula gives complex solutions and write them as $a \pm bi$ for real numbers a and b. *Also A.REI.4, A.REI.4a*

? ESSENTIAL QUESTION

What is the quadratic formula, and how can you use it to solve quadratic equations?

EXPLORE ACTIVITY   COMMON CORE   A.REI.4a

Deriving the Quadratic Formula

In this Explore Activity, you will derive the quadratic formula, a formula that can be used to solve any quadratic equation.

Solve the general form of a quadratic equation, $ax^2 + bx + c = 0$, $a \neq 0$, by completing the square to find the values of x in terms of a, b and c.

A Write the standard form of a quadratic equation.

$$ax^2 + bx + c = \boxed{}$$

Subtract c from both sides.

$$ax^2 + bx = \boxed{}$$

B Multiply both sides by $4a$ to make the coefficient of x^2 a perfect square.

$$4a^2x^2 + \boxed{} = \boxed{}$$

C Add b^2 to both sides of the equation to complete the square.

$$4a^2x^2 + 4abx + b^2 = -4ac + \boxed{}$$

D Factor the left side to write the trinomial as the square of a binomial. Simplify the right side.

$$\left(\boxed{} \right)^2 = b^2 - 4ac$$

E Take square roots of both sides.

$$\boxed{} = \pm \sqrt{\boxed{}}$$

F Subtract b from both sides.

$$2ax = \boxed{} \pm \sqrt{\boxed{}}$$

Divide both sides by $2a$ to solve for x, remembering to include both roots.

$$x = \frac{\boxed{} \pm \sqrt{\boxed{}}}{\boxed{}}$$

The formula you just derived, $x = \dfrac{-b \pm \sqrt{(b^2 - 4ac)}}{2a}$, is called the **quadratic formula**.

REFLECT

1. What if? If the derivation had begun by dividing each term by a, what would the resulting binomial have been? Does one derivation method appear to be simpler than the other? Explain.

_____

Solving Quadratic Equations Using the Quadratic Formula

The quadratic formula can be used to solve any quadratic equation written in standard form. To use the formula, check that the equation is in standard form. If not, rewrite it in standard form. Then substitute the values of a, b, and c into the formula.

EXAMPLE 1

COMMON CORE   A.REI.4b

Solve using the quadratic formula.

A $2x^2 + 3x - 5 = 0$

$a = 2, b = 3, c = -5$ — Identify a, b and c.

$x = \dfrac{-b \pm \sqrt{(b^2 - 4ac)}}{2a}$ — Use the quadratic formula.

$x = \dfrac{-3 \pm \sqrt{3^2 - 4(2)(-5)}}{2(2)}$ — Substitute the identified values into the quadratic formula.

$x = \dfrac{-3 \pm \sqrt{49}}{4}$ — Simplify the radicand and the denominator.

$x = \dfrac{-3 \pm 7}{4}$ — Evaluate the square root.

$x = \dfrac{-3 + 7}{4}$ or $x = \dfrac{-3 - 7}{4}$ — Write as two equations.

$x = 1$ or $x = \dfrac{-5}{2} = -\dfrac{5}{2}$ — Simplify both equations.

The solutions are 1 and $-\dfrac{5}{2}$.

B $2x = x^2 - 4$

$x^2 - 2x - 4 = 0$ — Write in standard form.

$a = 1, b = -2, c = -4$ — Identify a, b and c.

$x = \dfrac{-(-2) \pm \sqrt{(-2)^2 - 4(1)(-4)}}{2(1)}$ — Substitute the identified values into the quadratic formula.

$x = \dfrac{2 \pm \sqrt{20}}{2}$ — Simplify the radicand and the denominator.

$x = \dfrac{2 + \sqrt{20}}{2}$ or $x = \dfrac{2 - \sqrt{20}}{2}$ — Write as two equations.

$x = 1 + \sqrt{5}$ or $x = 1 - \sqrt{5}$ — Simplify each expression.

The solutions are $1 + \sqrt{5}$ and $1 - \sqrt{5}$.

Math Talk

Mathematical Practices

How can you use substitution to check your solutions?

YOUR TURN

Solve using the quadratic formula.

2. $5x + 2 = 3x^2$

3. $2x^2 - 8x + 1 = 0$

Finding the Number of Solutions

Recall that a quadratic equation can have two, one, or no real solutions. By evaluating the part of the quadratic formula under the radical sign, $b^2 - 4ac$, called the **discriminant**, you can determine the number of real solutions.

Math On the Spot

my.hrw.com

EXAMPLE 2

COMMON CORE   A.REI.4b

Find the number of real solutions of each equation using the discriminant.

A $x^2 - 4x + 3 = 0$

$a = 1, b = -4, c = 3$ Identify a, b and c.

$b^2 - 4ac$ Use the discriminant.

$(-4)^2 - 4(1)(3)$ Substitute the identified values into the discriminant.

$16 - 12 = 4$ Simplify.

Since $b^2 - 4ac > 0$, the equation has 2 real solutions.

B $x^2 + 2x + 1 = 0$

$a = 1, b = 2, c = 1$ Identify a, b and c.

$b^2 - 4ac$ Use the discriminant.

$(2)^2 - 4(1)(1)$ Substitute the identified values into the discriminant.

$4 - 4 = 0$ Simplify.

Since $b^2 - 4ac = 0$, the equation has 1 real solution.

C $x^2 - 2x + 2 = 0$

$a = 1, b = -2, c = 2$ Identify a, b and c.

$b^2 - 4ac$ Use the discriminant.

$(-2)^2 - 4(1)(2)$ Substitute the identified values into the discriminant.

$4 - 8 = -4$ Simplify.

Since $b^2 - 4ac < 0$, the equation has NO real solutions.

My Notes

YOUR TURN

Find the number of real solutions of each equation using the discriminant.

4. $9x^2 - 6x + 1 = 0$ **5.** $3x^2 + 10x + 2 = 0$ **6.** $x^2 + x + 1 = 0$

_____   _____   _____

Personal Math Trainer

Online Practice and Help

my.hrw.com

Solving Quadratic Equations Using Different Methods

There is no one correct way to solve a quadratic equation. The choice of method usually depends on the form of the equation, the coefficient values, and personal preference.

EXAMPLE 3 **A.REI.4b**

Solve $x^2 + 7x + 6 = 0$ using the method indicated.

My Notes

A Factoring

$$x^2 + 7x + 6 = 0$$

$$(x + 6)(x + 1) = 0 \qquad \text{Factor.}$$

$$x + 6 = 0 \text{ or } x + 1 = 0 \qquad \text{Use the Zero Product Property.}$$

$$x = -6 \text{ or } x = -1 \qquad \text{Solve each equation.}$$

B Completing the square

$$x^2 + 7x + 6 = 0$$

$$x^2 + 7x = -6 \qquad \text{Subtract the constant term from both sides.}$$

$$x^2 + 7x + \frac{49}{4} = -6 + \frac{49}{4} \qquad \text{Add } \left(\frac{b}{2}\right)^2 \text{ to both sides.}$$

$$\left(x + \frac{7}{2}\right)^2 = \frac{25}{4} \qquad \text{Factor the left. Simplify the right.}$$

$$x + \frac{7}{2} = \pm\frac{5}{2} \qquad \text{Take the square root of both sides.}$$

$$x + \frac{7}{2} = \frac{5}{2} \text{ or } x + \frac{7}{2} = -\frac{5}{2} \qquad \text{Write as two equations.}$$

$$x = -1 \text{ or } x = -6 \qquad \text{Solve each equation.}$$

C Using the quadratic formula

$$a = 1, b = 7, c = 6 \qquad \text{Identify } a, b, \text{ and } c.$$

$$x = \frac{-(7) \pm \sqrt{(7)^2 - 4(1)(6)}}{2(1)} \qquad \text{Substitute the identified values into the quadratic formula.}$$

$$x = \frac{-7 \pm \sqrt{25}}{2} \qquad \text{Simplify the discriminant and the denominator.}$$

$$x = \frac{-7 + 5}{2} \text{ or } x = \frac{-7 - 5}{2} \qquad \text{Evaluate the square root and write as two equations.}$$

$$x = -1 \text{ or } x = -6 \qquad \text{Simplify both equations.}$$

REFLECT

7. What are the disadvantages to solving a quadratic equation by factoring? What are the advantages?

_____

_____

_____

_____

_____

_____

8. What are the disadvantages of solving a quadratic equation by completing the square? What are the advantages?

_____

_____

_____

_____

_____

_____

9. What are the disadvantages to using the quadratic formula for solving a quadratic equation? What are the advantages?

_____

_____

_____

_____

_____

YOUR TURN

Choose a method to solve each quadratic equation. Give the solutions.

10. $x^2 + 4x = 9$

11. $2x^2 + 9x + 4 = 0$

12. $2x^2 + 3x - 11 = 0$

_____   _____   _____

Personal Math Trainer

Online Practice and Help

my.hrw.com

Solve using the quadratic formula, $x = \dfrac{-b \pm \sqrt{(b^2 - 4ac)}}{2a}$. (Example 1)

1. $6x^2 + 5x - 4 = 0$

$a = \boxed{}$, $b = \boxed{}$, $c = -4$

$x = \dfrac{-\boxed{} \pm \sqrt{5^2 - 4(\boxed{})(\boxed{})}}{2(\boxed{})}$

$x = \dfrac{-\boxed{} \pm \sqrt{\boxed{}}}{\boxed{}}$

$x = \dfrac{\boxed{} + \boxed{}}{\boxed{}}$, or $x = \dfrac{\boxed{} - \boxed{}}{\boxed{}}$

$x = \dfrac{\boxed{}}{2}$ or $x = \dfrac{\boxed{}}{3}$

2. $x^2 - 4x = -1$

$x^2 - 4x + \boxed{} = \boxed{}$

$a = 1,\ b = \boxed{}$, $c = \boxed{}$

$x = \dfrac{-\boxed{} \pm \sqrt{(\boxed{})^2 - 4(1)(\boxed{})}}{2(\boxed{})}$

$x = \dfrac{4 + \sqrt{\boxed{}}}{\boxed{}}$ or $x = \dfrac{\boxed{} - \sqrt{\boxed{}}}{2}$

Find the number of real solutions using the discriminant, $b^2 - 4ac$. (Example 2)

3. $2x^2 - 2x + 3 = 0$

There are ____ real solutions.

4. $x^2 + 4x + 4 = 0$

There is ____ real solution.

5. $x^2 - 9x - 4 = 0$

There are ____ real solutions.

6. Which method would you use to solve the equation $x^2 + 4x + 3 = 0$? Explain your choice and give your solutions. (Example 3)

_____

_____

_____

_____

7. What is the quadratic formula, and how can you use it to solve quadratic equations?

_____

_____

16.6 Independent Practice

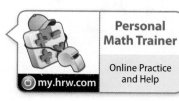
COMMON CORE A.REI.4, A.REI.4a, A.REI.4b

8. Critique Reasoning Dan said that if a quadratic equation does not have any real solutions, then it does not represent a function. Critique this reasoning.

_____

_____

_____

_____

_____

_____

_____

9. Interpret the Answer A diver jumps from a platform 10 meters above the surface of the water. The diver's height is given by the equation $h = -4.9t^2 + 3.5t + 10$, where t is the time in seconds after the diver jumps.

a. How many real solutions does the equation have when the diver's height is 1 m? What are they? Round to the hundredths place.

_____

_____

b. Do both solutions make sense in this situation? Explain.

_____

_____

_____

_____

_____

_____

10. Represent Real-World Problems The height in meters of a model rocket on a particular launch can be modeled by the equation $h = -4.9t^2 + 102t + 100$, where t is the time in seconds after its engine burns out 100 m above the ground.

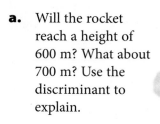

a. Will the rocket reach a height of 600 m? What about 700 m? Use the discriminant to explain.

_____

_____

_____

_____

_____

_____

b. How can the quadratic formula be used to determine how long the rocket stays in the air?

_____

_____

_____

_____

_____

c. How long does the rocket remain in the air? Round your answer to the nearest tenth.

_____

11. **Communicate Mathematical Ideas** Explain why a positive discriminant results in two real solutions.

_____

_____

_____

12. **Persevere in Problem Solving** A gymnast, who can stretch her arms up to reach 6 feet, jumps straight up on a trampoline. The height of her feet above the trampoline can be modeled by the equation $h = -16x^2 + 12x$, where x is the time in seconds after her jump.

a. Do the gymnast's hands reach a height of 10 feet above the trampoline? Use the discriminant to explain. (*Hint*: Since h = height of feet, you must use the difference between the heights of the hands and feet.)

_____

_____

_____

_____

_____

b. Use the discriminant to determine the maximum height the gymnast reaches. Explain your method.

_____

_____

_____

_____

c. Solve the equation to determine the amount of time it takes the gymnast to reach her maximum height. Explain your method.

_____

_____

_____

_____

Ready to Go On?

16.1–16.6 Solving Quadratic Equations

Solve each quadratic equation using the method stated.

1. $(x + 5)^2 - 4 = 12$; square roots

2. $3x^2 + 11x - 20 = 0$; factoring

3. $x^2 - 4x + 4 = 0$; completing the square

4. $5x^2 - 3x = 7$; quadratic formula

5. $3x^2 = 48$; square roots

6. $x^2 - 4x - 32 = 0$; factoring

7. $x^2 - 8 = -7x$; completing the square

8. $x^2 + 4x = 5$; quadratic formula

9. $x^2 + 1 + 5x = 0$; quadratic formula

10. $2x - 3 + x^2 = 0$; completing the square

11. $49x^2 + 64 = 0$; square roots

12. $-16x^2 + 8x + 24 = 0$; factoring

13. $x^2 - 14x - 11 = 0$; completing the square

14. $7x^2 - 5x - 1 = 0$; quadratic formula

? ESSENTIAL QUESTION

15. How do you determine the best method for solving a quadratic equation?

MODULE 16

MIXED REVIEW

Assessment Readiness

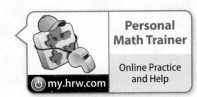

Personal Math Trainer

Online Practice and Help

my.hrw.com

1. Look at each equation. Does the equation have two distinct solutions?

   Select Yes or No for A–C.

   A. $0 = 2x^2 - 12x + 18$ ◯ Yes   ◯ No

   B. $0 = x^2 + 2x - 3$ ◯ Yes   ◯ No

   C. $0 = 4x^2 + 20x + 24$ ◯ Yes   ◯ No

2. Consider the quadratic equation $4x^2 - 8x = 96$.

   Choose True or False for each statement.

   A. To write the left side of the equation as a perfect-square trinomial, add 4 to both sides.   ◯ True   ◯ False

   B. To solve the equation by using the quadratic formula, use 4 for a, –8 for b, and 96 for c.   ◯ True   ◯ False

   C. The factored form of the equation is $4(x + 4)(x - 6) = 0$.   ◯ True   ◯ False

3. A soccer player heads a ball from a height of 6 feet with an initial vertical velocity of 20 feet per second. The height h in feet of the ball is given by $h = -16t^2 + 20t + 6$, where t is the time elapsed in seconds. How long will it take the ball to hit the ground if no other players touch it? State the method you used to solve this quadratic equation and why you chose that method.

4. Veterinarians sometimes need to know the body surface area of an animal in order to determine the proper dose of medicine. The expression $0.1m^{\frac{2}{3}}$ gives the approximate surface area in square meters of a cat with a mass of m kilograms. What is the approximate surface area of a cat with a mass of 8 kilograms? Explain how you determined your answer.

Study Guide Review

? ESSENTIAL QUESTION

How are polynomials like other number systems such as whole numbers and integers?

EXAMPLE 1

A new company is producing T-shirts for sale online. The cost, in dollars, to produce x T-shirts is modeled by the polynomial $350 + 2.5x$. The revenue the company generates from the sale of T-shirts can be modeled by the monomial $12x$. If 752 T-shirts have been sold, how much profit has the company generated?

$Profit = Revenue - Cost$ Difference of costs and income

$\qquad = (12x) - (350 + 2.5x)$ Substitute expressions.

$\qquad = (12x - 2.5x) - 350$ Group like terms.

$\qquad = 9.5x - 350$ Simplify.

$Profit = 9.5(752) - 350$ Substitute 752 for x.

$\qquad = 6{,}794$ Simplify.

EXAMPLE 2

Simplify the expression $(x + 3)(x^2 + 6x - 2) + (x^3 - 2x^2 - 5)$.

First simplify $(x + 3)(x^2 + 6x - 2)$.

$(x + 3)(x^2 + 6x - 2) = x(x^2 + 6x - 2) + 3(x^2 + 6x - 2)$

$\qquad\qquad = x(x^2) + x(6x) - x(2) + 3(x^2) + 3(6x) - 3(2)$

$\qquad\qquad = x^3 + 6x^2 - 2x + 3x^2 + 18x - 6$

$\qquad\qquad = x^3 + (6x^2 + 3x^2) + (18x - 2x) - 6$

$\qquad\qquad = x^3 + 9x^2 + 16x - 6$

Substitute $x^3 + 9x^2 + 16x - 6$ for $(x + 3)(x^2 + 6x - 2)$.

$(x + 3)(x^2 + 6x - 2) + (x^3 - 2x^2 - 5) = (x^3 + 9x^2 + 16x - 6) + (x^3 - 2x^2 - 5)$

$\qquad\qquad = x^3 + 9x^2 + 16x - 6 + x^3 - 2x^2 - 5$

$\qquad\qquad = (x^3 + x^3) + (9x^2 - 2x^2) + 16x - (6 + 5)$

$\qquad\qquad = 2x^3 + 7x^2 + 16x - 11$

1. The polynomial $0.5t^2 + 2t - 6$ represents the distance (in feet) a model car travels in t seconds. How far will the car travel in 5 seconds? (Lesson 14.1) _____

2. Add $(2x^2 + 3x - 4) + (5x^2 - 2x + 3)$. (Lesson 14.2) _____

3. Multiply $(3x + 7)(3x - 7)$. (Lesson 14.4) _____

4. Use the FOIL method to find the product $(x + 9)(x - 7)$.

   (Lesson 14.4) _____

MODULE 15 Factoring Polynomials

Key Vocabulary
greatest common factor
(maximo común factor)

? ESSENTIAL QUESTION

How can you factor expressions of the form $ax^2 + bx + c$?

EXAMPLE 1

A carpenter is building square tables with the top surface area represented by the trinomial $(x^2 + 8x + 16)$ ft². The side lengths of the tables are of the form $ax + b$, where a and b are whole numbers. Find an expression to represent the side lengths of the square tabletops.

Factor the trinomial $x^2 + 8x + 16$.

$$x^2 + 8x + 16 \text{ is a perfect square trinomial.}$$
$$x^2 + 8x + 16 = (x + 4)^2$$

Each side length is represented by the expression $(x + 4)$ ft.

EXAMPLE 2

Factor $8x^2 + 52x + 60$.

STEP 1 Factor out any common factors.
$$8x^2 + 52x + 60 = 4(2x^2 + 13x + 15)$$

STEP 2 List all factor pairs for $a = 2$, and $c = 15$.

Factors of a $a = 2$	Factors of c $c = 15$	Outer Product + Inner Product
1 and 2	1 and 15	$(1)(15) + (2)(1) = 17$
1 and 2	3 and 5	$(1)(5) + (2)(3) = 11$
1 and 2	5 and 3	$(1)(3) + (2)(5) = 13$
1 and 2	15 and 1	$(1)(1) + (2)(15) = 31$

STEP 3 Use the correct factors of a and c to write the factored form.

$$8x^2 + 52x + 60 = 4(x + 5)(2x + 3)$$

EXERCISES

Factor each polynomial. (Lesson 15.1)

5. $5x^2 + 10x$ _____

6. $3x^2 - 12x - 6$ _____

7. $8x^2 - 6x + 4$ _____

8. $12x^2 - 30x - 18$ _____

Factor each trinomial. (Lessons 15.2 and 15.3)

9. $x^2 + 12x + 35$ _____

10. $x^2 - 3x - 54$ _____

11. $6x^2 + 29x + 28$ _____

12. $2x^2 - 9x - 18$ _____

13. $6x^2 - x - 15$ _____

14. $6x^2 - 38x + 12$ _____

15. Determine whether the trinomial $16x^2 + 40x + 25$ is a perfect square. If so, factor. If not, explain. (Lesson 15.4)

_____

Use the special product factoring rules to factor each polynomial.

16. $x^2 - 10x + 25$ _____

17. $x^2 + 14x + 49$ _____

18. $x^2 - 36$ _____

19. $4x^2 + 12x + 9$ _____

20. $9x^2 - 24x + 16$ _____

21. $25x^2 - 4$ _____

Solving Quadratic Equations

Key Vocabulary

discriminant *(discriminante)*

end behavior
 (comportamiento extremo)

quadratic formula *(fórmula cuadrática)*

? ESSENTIAL QUESTION

How do you determine the best method for solving a quadratic equation or a system of equations?

EXAMPLE 1

Solve $(x - 3)^2 = 49$ using square roots.

$(x - 3)^2 = 49$

    $x - 3 = \pm\sqrt{49}$ Take the square root of both sides.

    $x - 3 = \pm 7$ Use $\pm$ to show both square roots.

      $x = \pm 7 + 3$

$x = 7 + 3$ and $x = -7 + 3$

$x = 10$ $x = -4$ Simplify each equation.

The solutions are -4 and 10.

EXAMPLE 2

Solve the quadratic equation $-x^2 - 3 = x^2 - 21$ by factoring.

   $-x^2 - 3 - x^2 + 21 = 0$ Move all terms to one side.

          $-2x^2 + 18 = 0$ Combine like terms.

        $-2(x^2 - 9) = 0$ Factor.

$-2(x + 3)\,(x - 3) = 0$

              $x = \pm 3$ Solve.

EXAMPLE 3

Solve $x^2 - 6x - 12 = 0$ by completing the square.

$x^2 - 6x - 12 = 0$

     $x^2 - 6x = 12$ Add 12 to both sides.

  $x^2 - 6x + 9 = 12 + 9$ Complete the square.

     $(x - 3)^2 = 21$ Factor left side.

    $x - 3 = \pm\sqrt{21}$ Take square roots.

       $x = 3 \pm \sqrt{21}$ Solve for x.

$x = 3 + \sqrt{21}$ or $x = 3 - \sqrt{21}$

EXAMPLE 4

Solve $3x^2 - 5x - 4 = 0$ by using the quadratic formula.

$3x^2 - 5x - 4 = 0$

$a = 3, b = -5, c = -4$ Find a, b, c.

$x = \dfrac{-(-5) \pm \sqrt{(-5)^2 - 4(3)(-4)}}{2(3)}$ Use quadratic formula.

$\quad = \dfrac{5 \pm \sqrt{25 - (-48)}}{6}$

$\quad = \dfrac{5 \pm \sqrt{73}}{6}$

$x = 5 + \dfrac{\sqrt{73}}{6}$ or $x = 5 - \dfrac{\sqrt{73}}{6}$

EXERCISES

Solve each quadratic equation by using square roots. (Lesson 16.1)

22. $(x - 7)^2 = 121$ _____

23. $(x + 5)^2 = 81$ _____

24. $(3x + 3)^2 = 81$ _____

Solve each quadratic equation by factoring. (Lessons 16.2, 16.3)

25. $x^2 - x - 20 = 0$ _____

26. $x^2 - 4x - 12 = 0$ _____

27. $3x^2 + 5x - 12 = 0$ _____

Solve each quadratic equation by completing the square. (Lessons 16.4, 16.5)

28. $x^2 - 8x - 20 = 0$ _____

29. $9x^2 - 12x - 45 = 0$ _____

Solve each quadratic equation by using the quadratic formula. (Lesson 16.6)

30. $5x^2 + 19x - 4 = 0$ _____

31. $3x^2 - 5x + 11 = 0$ _____

Unit Project

Going Down?

Construct a ramp that is at least 4 feet long. The angle the ramp makes with the ground should be 30°. Working with a partner, release a ball from various points on the ramp. Measure the distance the ball rolls and the time (using a stopwatch) that it rolls. You should perform several trials for various distances.

The quadratic equation $d = \frac{1}{4}gt^2$ models the distance d (in feet) that the ball rolls in t seconds. Use your data and the equation to estimate the value of g. Create a report that explains your approach, organizes all of the collected data in tables, and shows your calculations. You can use a graphing calculator to fit your data to a quadratic regression line.

Use the space below to write down any questions you have or important information from your teacher.

MATH IN CAREERS │ ACTIVITY

Investigator The reaction distance, r(ft), is the distance that a vehicle travels from the time the driver decides to stop until he or she applies the brakes. The braking distance, b(ft), is the distance the vehicle travels once the brake is applied until it reaches a complete stop. Both distances are influenced by the initial speed of the vehicle. The stopping distance, s(ft), is the sum of these.

$s = r + b$

$r = 1.47vt$, where $v =$ speed (mi/h) and $t =$ reaction time (s).

$b = 1.075\frac{v^2}{a}$, where $v =$ speed (mi/h) and $a =$ deceleration rate (ft/s²)

Transportation departments typically use a reaction time of 2.5 seconds and a deceleration rate of 11.2 ft/s² to calculate stopping distance. Find the reaction time, breaking distance, and stopping distance for a driver traveling at 60 miles per hour.

Assessment Readiness

Personal Math Trainer

Online Practice and Help

my.hrw.com

1. Look at the number of points scored by each team in its last 8 games. Is the median score for the team greater than 60 points?

   Select Yes or No for each team.

   A. Arrows: 79, 48, 84, 72, 55, 68, 64, 44   ○ Yes   ○ No

   B. Cobras: 54, 52, 65, 54, 67, 63, 73, 61   ○ Yes   ○ No

   C. Hornets: 82, 56, 63, 57, 48, 70, 50, 66   ○ Yes   ○ No

2. Consider the polynomial $6x^2 - 5x - 4$.

   Choose True or False for each statement.

   A. The polynomial is a trinomial.   ○ True   ○ False

   B. The factored form of the polynomial is $(3x + 4)(2x - 1)$.   ○ True   ○ False

   C. The polynomial is equal to the sum of $4x^2 - 2x + 3$ and $2x^2 - 3x - 7$.   ○ True   ○ False

3. A rectangular swimming pool is 50 meters long and 25 meters wide. A concrete walkway with a width of x meters will surround the pool. The combined area of the pool and the walkway will be 1736 square meters. Solve the equation $(50 + 2x)(25 + 2x) = 1736$ to find the width of the walkway. Justify that your answer is reasonable.

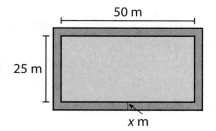

4. Wendy is pulling a bucket up from a well at the same time as Lucas drops a penny down the well. The equation $d = 16t^2$ gives the depth d in feet of the penny t seconds after it is dropped. The equation $d = 56 - 4t$ gives the depth d in feet of the bucket t seconds after the penny is dropped. After how many seconds will the penny hit the bucket? Explain how you solved this problem.

Performance Tasks

★ **5.** A baseball player hits a ball from a height of 5 feet with an initial vertical velocity of 54 feet per second. The function $h = -16t^2 + 54t + 5$ models the height h in feet of the ball t seconds after it is hit. Will the ball reach a height of 50 feet? Justify your answer.

★★ **6.** A rancher has a rectangular sheep pen that is 3 meters long and 2 meters wide. The rancher plans to increase both the length and the width of the pen by x feet so that the new area of the pen will be 20 square meters.

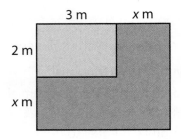

a. Write an equation that can be used to solve for x.

b. Write the equation from part a in standard form.

c. Solve the equation and interpret the solutions. Round to the nearest tenth if needed.

d. Which method did you use to solve the equation? Why did you choose this method?

★★★ **7.** Blair Jeans makes and sells blue jeans. The expression $40x$ represents the company's revenue in dollars in a month when it sells x pairs of jeans. The expression $32{,}000 + 26x - 0.001x^2$ represents the company's costs in dollars in a month when it makes x pairs of jeans. The company's monthly profit is equal to its revenue minus its costs. How many pairs of jeans will the company need to make and sell each month in order to make a monthly profit of $40,000? Explain how you determined your answer.

Functions and Modeling

MATH IN CAREERS

Sky Diving Instructor A sky diving instructor uses math to make models to analyze data and understand the effects of gravity on falling height and location.

If you're interested in a career as a sky diving instructor, you should study these mathematical subjects:
- Algebra
- Calculus
- Statistics

Research other careers that require the use of modeling data with mathematical functions.

ACTIVITY At the end of the unit, check out how a **sky diving instructor** uses math.

Unit Project Preview

Perfecting the Package

The Unit Project at the end of this unit involves finding the least amount of material needed to make a package. You will apply a geometric formula that is represented with a quadratic function. To successfully complete the Unit Project you'll need to master these skills:

- Write equations that describe relationships involving volume and surface area.
- Apply a quadratic function to a geometric problem.
- Measure the dimensions of a three-dimensional object.
- Use technology to find a minimum value.

1. A package of oatmeal comes in a cylindrical container. The container is h cm tall and the base has a radius of r cm. Write an expression for the following:

   a. Volume of cylinder _____

   b. Amount of material needed _____

2. If you substitute a given value for r in the expression and simplify, would the resulting expression be a quadratic expression? Explain.

   _____

   _____

   _____

Tracking Your Learning Progression

This unit addresses important Common Core Standards in the Critical Areas of writing and solving equations and working with functions.

Domain **A.REI** Reasoning with Equations and Inequalities

    Cluster Solve equations and inequalities in one variable.

The unit also supports additional standards.

Domain **F.BF** Building Functions

    Cluster Build a function that models a relationship between two quantities.

Quadratic Functions

? **ESSENTIAL QUESTION**

How do quadratic functions relate to their graphs?

Real-World Video

Projectile motion describes the height of an object thrown or fired into the air. The height of a football, volleyball, or any projectile can be modeled by a quadratic equation.

⊙ my.hrw.com

G⊙ DIGITAL
my.hrw.com

my.hrw.com

Go digital with your write-in student edition, accessible on any device.

Math On the Spot

Scan with your smart phone to jump directly to the online edition, video tutor, and more.

X²
▶

Animated Math

Interactively explore key concepts to see how math works.

Personal Math Trainer

Get immediate feedback and help as you work through practice sets.

Are YOU Ready?

Complete these exercises to review skills you will need for this module.

Symmetry

EXAMPLE   If a figure coincides with itself when folded across a line, it has line symmetry. Use the line of symmetry provided to complete the figure.

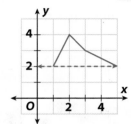 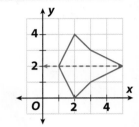

Use the line of symmetry provided to complete each figure.

1.

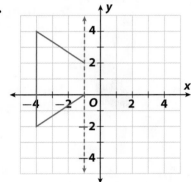

2.

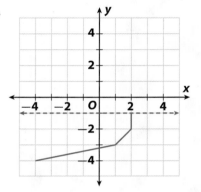

Function Tables

EXAMPLE   Create a function table for $y = 3x + 4$.

x	y
0	4
1	7
2	10

Substitute the x-values into the equation and solve for y.
$$y = 3(0) + 4 = 0 + 4 = 4$$

Function tables example:
$$y = 3(1) + 4 = 3 + 4 = 7$$
$$y = 3(2) + 4 = 6 + 4 = 10$$

Complete the table for each function.

3. $y = 5x - 7$

x	y
−2	
0	
2	

4. $y = -8x$

x	y
−2	
0	
2	

5. $y = x^2 - 3$

x	y
−2	
0	
2	

Reading Start-Up

Vocabulary

Review Words

✔ function
(función)

✔ graph of a function
(gráfica de una función)

✔ symmetry
(simetría)

Preview Words

quadratic function
parabola
vertex of a parabola
maximum value
minimum value
zero of a function
axis of symmetry

Visualize Vocabulary

Use the Review Words to complete the bubble map.

The set of points where *x* is in the domain and *y* = *f*(*x*) is the

When a graph can be rotated or reflected and coincide in a coordinate plane with the original graph, it is said to have

A relation in which every input is paired with exactly one output is known as a

Understand Vocabulary

To become familiar with some of the vocabulary terms in the module, consider the following definitions and select the term from the list of Preview Words that most applies. You may refer to the module, the glossary, or a dictionary.

1. The maximum or minimum value for a parabola.

_____

2. For the function *f*, any number *x* such that *f*(*x*) = 0.

_____

Active Reading

Tri-Fold Note Before beginning the module, create a Tri-Fold Note to help you organize what you learn. Write what you already know about quadratic functions on the first fold and what you want to learn on the second fold. As you read the module, take notes about what you have learned on the third fold to track your learning progress.

GETTING READY FOR
Quadratic Functions
Understanding the standards and the vocabulary terms in the standards
will help you know exactly what you are expected to learn in this module.

COMMON CORE A.CED.2

Create equations in two or more variables to represent relationships between quantities; graph equations on coordinate axes with labels and scales.

Key Vocabulary

equation *(ecuación)*
A mathematical statement that two expressions are equivalent.

What It Means to You

Creating equations in two variables to describe relationships gives you access to the tools of graphing and algebra to solve the equations.

EXAMPLE A.CED.2

A customer spent $29 on wristbands and gel watches. Wristbands cost $2.50 each and gel watches cost $1.75 each.

$w =$ number of wristbands bought

$g =$ number of gel watches bought

$2.5w + 1.75g = 29$

COMMON CORE F.IF.4

For a function that models a relationship between two quantities, interpret key features of graphs and tables in terms of the quantities, and sketch graphs showing key features given a verbal description of the relationship.

What It Means to You

Learning to interpret a graph enables a deep visual understanding of all sorts of relationships.

EXAMPLE F.IF.4

A cliff diver jumps into the ocean from a height of h feet and falls for t seconds before entering the water.

In this equation, the initial height would be the y-intercept and the time at which the diver entered the water would be represented by the x-intercept. As time increases, the height of the diver above the water decreases.

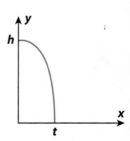

Visit **my.hrw.com** to see all **Common Core Standards** unpacked.

my.hrw.com

Translating Quadratic Functions

COMMON CORE   F.BF.3

Identify the effect on the graph of replacing $f(x)$ by $f(x) + k$, $k\,f(x)$, $f(kx)$, and $f(x + k)$ for specific values of k (both positive and negative); find the value of k given the graphs. Experiment with cases and illustrate an explanation of the effects on the graph using technology. *Also A.CED.2, F.BF.1, F.IF.2, F.IF.4*

ESSENTIAL QUESTION

How does the graph of $f(x) = (x - h)^2 + k$ change as the constants h and k are changed?

EXPLORE ACTIVITY   COMMON CORE   A.CED.2, F.IF.2

The Parent Quadratic Function

A **quadratic function** is a function that can be represented by an equation of the form $f(x) = ax^2 + bx + c$ where a, b, and c are constants and $a \neq 0$. Notice that the greatest exponent of the variable x is 2. The most basic quadratic function is $f(x) = x^2$. It is called the parent quadratic function.

A Complete the table of values for the parent quadratic function.

x	$f(x) = x^2$
−3	$f(x) = x^2 = (-3)^2 = 9$
−2	
	1
0	0
1	
	4
3	

B Plot the ordered pairs, and sketch the graph through the points with a curve.

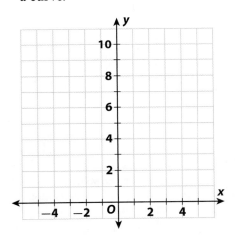

The U-shaped curve is called a **parabola**. The turning point on the parabola is called its **vertex**. The vertex occurs at (0, 0) for this function.

REFLECT

1. a. What is the domain of $f(x) = x^2$? What is the range?

_____

_____

b. Communicate Mathematical Ideas What symmetry does the graph of $f(x) = x^2$ have? Why does it have this symmetry?

_____

_____

Vertical Translations

A **vertical translation** of a parabola is a shift of the parabola up or down, with no change in the shape of the parabola.

Vertical Translations of a Parabola

The graph of the function $f(x) = x^2 + k$ is the graph of $f(x) = x^2$ translated vertically.

- If $k = 0$, the graph is the graph of the parent function, $f(x) = x^2$.
- If $k > 0$, the graph of $f(x) = x^2$ is translated k units up.
- If $k < 0$, the graph of $f(x) = x^2$ is translated $|k|$ units down.

EXAMPLE 1

COMMON CORE F.BF.3, A.CED.2, F.IF.2

Graph each quadratic function.

A $g(x) = x^2 + 2$

x	$g(x) = x^2 + 2$
−3	11
−2	6
−1	3
0	2
1	3
2	6
3	11

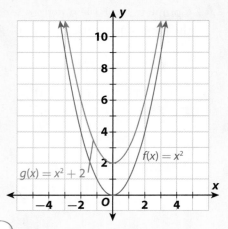

> Plot the points from the table. Notice that the graph is identical to the graph of the parent function $f(x) = x^2$ but translated up 2 units.

B $g(x) = x^2 - 2$

x	$g(x) = x^2 - 2$
−3	7
−2	2
−1	−1
0	−2
1	−1
2	2
3	7

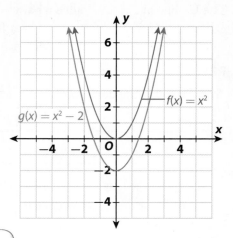

> Notice that the graph is identical to the graph of the parent function but translated down 2 units.

2. Analyze Relationships How do the values in the table for $g(x) = x^2 + 2$ compare with the values in the table for the parent function $f(x) = x^2$?

_____

_____

3. Analyze Relationships How do the values in the table for $g(x) = x^2 - 2$ compare to the values in the table for the parent function $f(x) = x^2$?

_____

_____

YOUR TURN

Graph each quadratic function.

4. $f(x) = x^2 + 4$

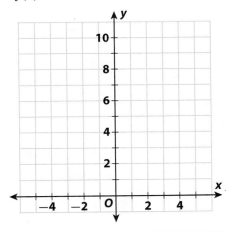

5. $f(x) = x^2 - 5$

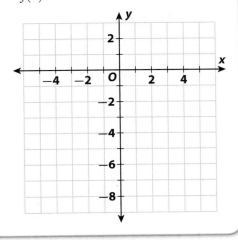

Personal Math Trainer

Online Practice and Help

⏻ my.hrw.com

Horizontal Translations

A **horizontal translation** of a parabola is a shift of the parabola left or right, with no change in the shape of the parabola.

Math On the Spot

⏻ my.hrw.com

Horizontal Translations of a Parabola

The graph of the function $f(x) = (x - h)^2$ is the graph of $f(x) = x^2$ translated horizontally.

- If $h = 0$, the graph is the graph of the parent function, $f(x) = x^2$.
- If $h > 0$, the graph of $f(x) = x^2$ is translated h units to the right.
- If $h < 0$, the graph of $f(x) = x^2$ is translated $|h|$ units to the left.

EXAMPLE 2

COMMON CORE · F.BF.3, A.CED.2, F.IF.2

My Notes

Graph each quadratic function.

A $g(x) = (x-1)^2$

x	$g(x) = (x-1)^2$
−3	16
−2	9
−1	4
0	1
1	0
2	1
3	4

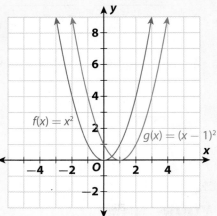

Plot the points from the table. Notice that the graph is identical to the graph of the parent function $f(x) = x^2$ but translated right 1 unit.

B $g(x) = (x+1)^2$

x	$g(x) = (x+1)^2$
−3	4
−2	1
−1	0
0	1
1	4
2	9
3	16

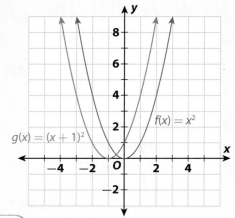

Notice that the graph is identical to the graph of the parent function but translated left 1 unit.

REFLECT

6. Analyze Relationships How do the values in the table for $g(x) = (x-1)^2$ compare to the values in the table for the parent function $f(x) = x^2$?

_____

_____

7. Analyze Relationships How do the values in the table for $g(x) = (x+1)^2$ compare to the values in the table for the parent function $f(x) = x^2$?

_____

_____

YOUR TURN

Graph each quadratic function.

8. $f(x) = (x - 2)^2$

9. $f(x) = (x + 3)^2$

Writing a Quadratic Function Given a Graph

Translating a Parabola

The graph of the function $f(x) = (x - h)^2 + k$ is obtained from the graph of $f(x) = x^2$ by a combination of horizontal and vertical translations.

- If h and k are both 0, the graph is the graph of the parent function $f(x) = x^2$.

- If h is not 0, the value of h shifts the graph to the right or left.

- If k is not 0, the value of k shifts the graph up or down.

- The vertex of the parabola is at (h, k).

Math On the Spot

my.hrw.com

EXAMPLE 3

COMMON CORE   F.BF.3, F.IF.2

Compare the graph of the parabola at the right to the graph of the parent function $f(x) = x^2$. Write an equation of the graph.

STEP 1   Notice the location of the vertex. The parent function has a vertex at (0, 0). This function has a vertex at (3, 2).

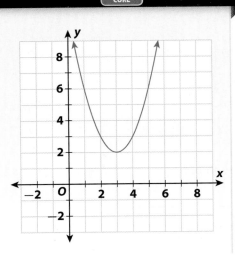

STEP 2 Determine the values of h and k for the function $f(x) = (x - h)^2 + k$.

Since the vertex is at $(3, 2)$, $h = 3$ and $k = 2$. An equation of the parabola is $f(x) = (x - 3)^2 + 2$.

Math Talk

Mathematical Practices

What does the vertex $(3, 2)$ tell you about the graph of the function?

YOUR TURN

10. Compare the graph of the parabola at the right to the graph of the parent function $f(x) = x^2$. Write an equation of the graph.

_____

_____

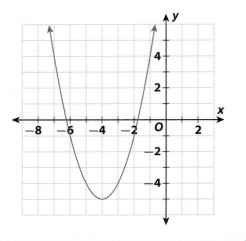

Guided Practice

Graph each quadratic function. (Examples 1 and 2)

1. $f(x) = x^2 + 3$

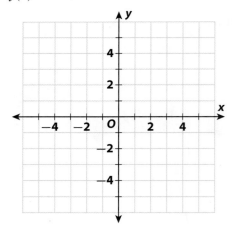

2. $f(x) = (x - 3)^2$

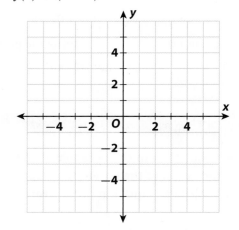

ESSENTIAL QUESTION CHECK-IN

3. How does the graph of $f(x) = (x - h)^2 + k$ change as the constants h and k are changed?

_____

_____

_____

Name_____ Class_____ Date_____

17.1 Independent Practice

Personal Math Trainer

Online Practice and Help

my.hrw.com

COMMON CORE F.BF.3, A.CED.2, F.BF.1, F.IF.2, F.IF.4

Determine the domain and range of the function.

4. $f(x) = (x - 3)^2$

_____

_____

_____

5. $f(x) = x^2 - 7$

_____

_____

_____

6. $f(x) = x^2 + 4$

_____

_____

_____

7. $f(x) = (x + 1)^2 - 6$

_____

_____

_____

8. The parabola shown is a translation of the graph of the parent quadratic function $f(x) = x^2$.

   a. How far has the parent function been translated horizontally? Vertically?

   _____

   b. Write an equation for the function represented by the graph.

   _____

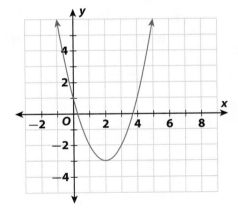

9. The graphs show the heights of two birds as they begin to fly. Both graphs represent quadratic functions.

   a. What is the starting height of each bird?

   _____

   b. What is a possible function for each graph?

   _____

   c. Estimate the time it takes for each bird to reach 60 feet.

   _____

   d. Describe how the two curves are related.

   _____

   _____

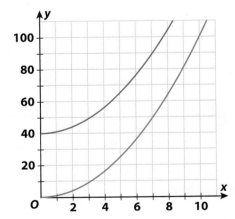

10. **Multiple Representations** Graph the following functions on a graphing calculator. Sketch the results on the coordinate grids provided.

a. $f(x) = (x + 1)^2$

b. $g(x) = (x - 5)^2$.

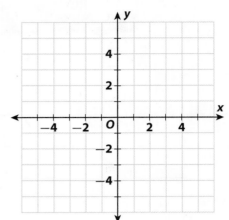

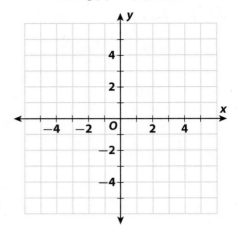

 **FOCUS ON HIGHER ORDER THINKING**

11. **Explain the Error** Nina is trying to write an equation for the function represented by the graph of a parabola that is a translation of $f(x) = x^2$. The graph has been translated 4 units to the right and 2 units up. She writes the function as $g(x) = (x + 4)^2 + 2$. Explain the error.

_____

_____

_____

12. **Critical Thinking** A function is an *even* function if $f(-x) = f(x)$ for all x in the domain of the function. The function $f(x) = x^2$ is an even function since $(-x)^2 = x^2$. Are functions that represent vertical translations of the graph of $f(x) = x^2$ even functions? Are functions that represent horizontal translations of the graph of $f(x) = x^2$ even functions? Explain.

_____

_____

_____

_____

13. **Analyze Relationships** Describe how the effect of k on the graph of $f(x) = x^2 + k$ is similar to the effect of b on the graph of $f(x) = x + b$.

_____

_____

_____

Stretching, Compressing, and Reflecting Quadratic Functions

COMMON CORE F.BF.3

Identify the effect on the graph of replacing $f(x)$ by $f(x) + k$, $k\,f(x)$, $f(kx)$, and $f(x + k)$ for specific values of k (both positive and negative); find the value of k given the graphs. Experiment with cases and illustrate an explanation of the effects on the graph using technology. *Also* A.CED.2, F.IF.2, F.IF.4

? ESSENTIAL QUESTION

How does the graph of $f(x) = ax^2$ change as the constant a is changed?

EXPLORE ACTIVITY COMMON CORE F.BF.3, A.CED.2, F.IF.2

Examining Graphs of Functions of the Form $f(x) = ax^2$

A Complete the table of values for $f(x) = x^2$ and $g(x) = -x^2$.

x	$f(x) = x^2$	$g(x) = -x^2$
−3	9	−9
−2	4	
−1	1	
0	0	0
1	1	
2	4	
3	9	

B Graph the points from the table for $g(x) = -x^2$ and sketch the curve.

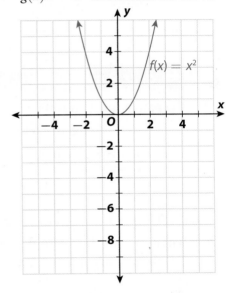

C Complete the table of values for $h(x) = 2x^2$.

x	$f(x) = x^2$	$h(x) = 2x^2$
−3	9	
−2	4	
−1	1	
0	0	
1	1	
2	4	
3	9	

D Graph the points from the table for $h(x) = 2x^2$ and sketch the curve below.

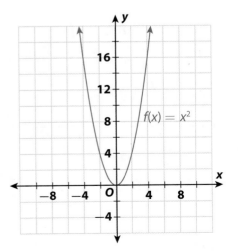

E The axis of symmetry in part A is still the *y*-axis, and the vertex is still (0, 0). How is the new graph different from the old graph?

_____

F The axis of symmetry in part B is still the *y*-axis, and the vertex is still (0, 0). How is the new graph different from the old graph?

_____

REFLECT

1. **Draw Conclusions** Based on the functions in the Explore Activity, how do you think $k(x) = \frac{1}{2}x^2$ differs from the parent function? Use a graphing calculator to verify your answer.

_____

_____

Width of a Parabola

For the parent function $f(x) = x^2$:

- If $|a| > 1$, the graph of $g(x) = ax^2$ is narrower than the graph of $f(x)$.
- If $|a| < 1$, the graph of $g(x) = ax^2$ is wider than the graph of $f(x)$.

Math On the Spot
⏱ my.hrw.com

Graphing $g(x) = ax^2$ when $a > 0$

The graph of $g(x) = ax^2$ is a vertical stretch or vertical compression of the parent function $f(x) = x^2$. When $a > 0$, the graph of $g(x)$ opens upward.

Vertical Stretch	Vertical Compression
$g(x) = ax^2$ when $a > 1$	$g(x) = ax^2$ when $0 < a < 1$

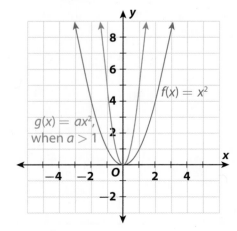

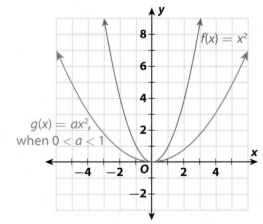

EXAMPLE 1

COMMON CORE   F.BF.3, A.CED.2, F.IF.2

Graph each quadratic function.

A $g(x) = 3x^2$

x	$g(x) = 3x^2$
−3	27
−2	12
−1	3
0	0
1	3
2	12
3	27

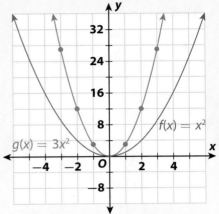

The graph of $g(x)$ is stretched away from the x-axis.
The graph of $g(x)$ is narrower than the graph of $f(x)$.

B $g(x) = \frac{1}{3}x^2$

x	$g(x) = \frac{1}{3}x^2$
−3	3
−2	1.333
−1	0.333
0	0
1	0.333
2	1.333
3	3

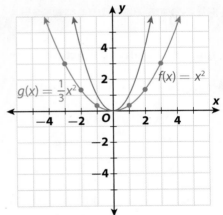

The graph of $g(x)$ is compressed toward the x-axis.
The graph of $g(x)$ is wider than the graph of $f(x)$.

YOUR TURN

Graph each quadratic function.

2. $f(x) = 1.5x^2$

3. $f(x) = \frac{3}{4}x^2$

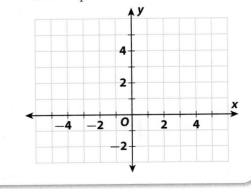

Personal Math Trainer

Online Practice and Help

my.hrw.com

Graphing $g(x) = ax^2$ when $a < 0$

When $a < 0$, the graph of $g(x) = ax^2$ is a reflection across the x-axis of the parent function $f(x) = x^2$, followed by a vertical stretch or vertical compression. The graph opens downward.

Vertical Stretch
$g(x) = ax^2$ when $a < -1$

Vertical Compression
$g(x) = ax^2$ when $-1 < a < 0$

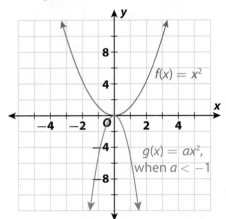
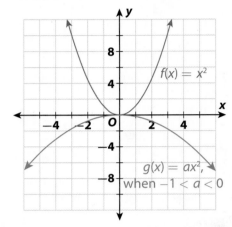

EXAMPLE 2

COMMON CORE F.BF.3, A.CED.2, F.IF.2

Graph each quadratic function.

A $g(x) = -2x^2$

x	$g(x) = -2x^2$
−3	−18
−2	−8
−1	−2
0	0
1	−2
2	−8
3	−18

B $g(x) = -\frac{1}{2}x^2$

x	$g(x) = -\frac{1}{2}x^2$
−3	−4.5
−2	−2
−1	−0.5
0	0
1	−0.5
2	−2
3	−4.5

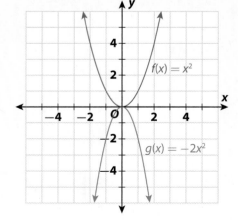

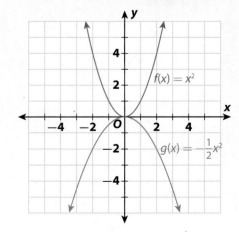

The graph is reflected across the x-axis and then stretched away from the x-axis.

The graph is reflected across the x-axis and then compressed toward the x-axis.

Graph each quadratic function.

4. $f(x) = -3x^2$

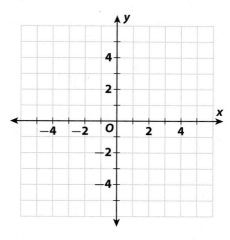

5. $f(x) = -\frac{3}{4}x^2$

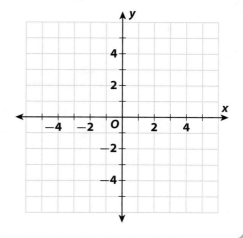

Writing a Quadratic Function Given a Graph

You can write a function rule for a parabola with its vertex at the origin by substituting the x- and y-values for any point on the parabola into $f(x) = ax^2$ and solving for a.

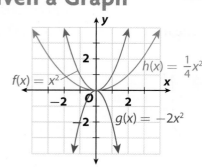

Math On the Spot

my.hrw.com

EXAMPLE 3

COMMON CORE F.BF.3, F.IF.2

The graph below represents a quadratic function of the form $f(x) = ax^2$. Write a rule for the function.

Use the point $(2, -1)$ to find a.

$$y = ax^2$$

$$(-1) = a(2)^2$$

$$-1 = 4a$$

$$-\frac{1}{4} = a$$

The rule is $f(x) = -\frac{1}{4}x^2$.

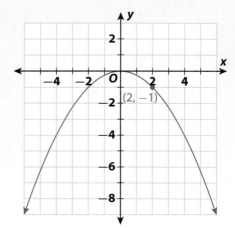

Math Talk

Mathematical Practices

Why can you predict that the value of a is negative?

Personal Math Trainer

Online Practice and Help

⊙ my.hrw.com

YOUR TURN

6. The graph below represents a quadratic function of the form $f(x) = ax^2$. Write a rule for the function.

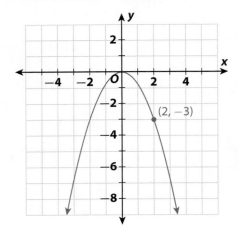

(2, −3)

_____

Guided Practice

Graph each quadratic function. (Examples 1 and 2)

1. $f(x) = 0.6x^2$

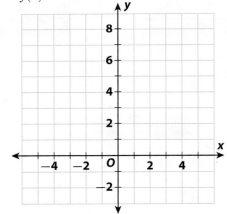

2. $f(x) = -2.5x^2$

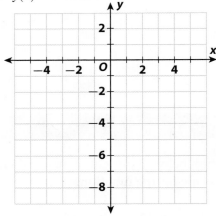

? ESSENTIAL QUESTION CHECK-IN

3. How do the values of the constant a affect the graph of a parabola in the function $g(x) = ax^2$?

_____

_____

_____

_____

17.2 Independent Practice

Personal Math Trainer

Online Practice and Help

my.hrw.com

COMMON CORE   F.BF.3, A.CED.2, F.IF.2, F.IF.4

4. The graph compares the heights of two identical coconuts that fell from different trees.

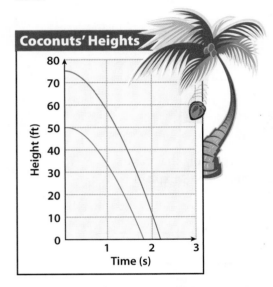

a. Estimate the starting height of each coconut. _____

_____

b. If each graph is represented by a function of the form $f(x) = ax^2$, are the coefficients positive or negative? Explain.

_____

_____

c. Estimate the time it takes for each coconut to reach the ground.

_____

_____

d. Describe how the two curves are related.

_____

_____

_____

Order the functions from narrowest (most vertically stretched) to widest (most vertically compressed).

5. $f(x) = \frac{3}{4}x^2; g(x) = -2x^2; h(x) = -8x^2$

_____

6. $f(x) = -2x^2; g(x) = \frac{1}{2}x^2$ _____

7. **Multi-Step** Give an example of a quadratic function that meets each description. Sketch the graph of your function.

a. Its graph has the same width as the graph of $f(x) = x^2$, but the graph opens downward.

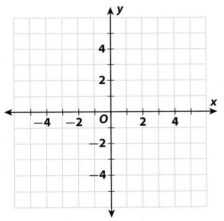

_____

b. Its graph opens downward and is narrower than the graph of $f(x) = x^2$.

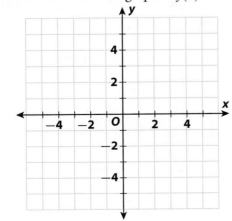

8. Draw Conclusions In general, how does the y-coordinate of a point on the graph of $g(x) = \frac{1}{2}x^2$ compare with the y-coordinate of a point on the graph of $f(x) = x^2$ for the same x-coordinate?

_____

_____

9. Draw Conclusions In general, how does the y-coordinate of a point on the graph of $h(x) = -2x^2$ compare to the y-coordinate of a point on the graph of $f(x) = x^2$ for the same x-coordinate?

_____

_____

H.O.T. **FOCUS ON HIGHER ORDER THINKING**

10. Check for Reasonableness The graph of $f(x) = ax^2$ is a parabola that passes through the point $(-2, 2)$. Kyle says that the value of a must be $-\frac{1}{2}$. Explain why this value of a is not reasonable.

_____

_____

11. Critical Thinking A quadratic function has a minimum value when the function's graph opens upward, and it has a maximum value when the function's graph opens downward. In each case, the minimum or maximum value is the y-coordinate of the vertex of the function's graph.

Under what circumstances does the function $f(x) = ax^2$ have a minimum value? a maximum value? What is the minimum or maximum value in each case?

_____

_____

12. Critical Thinking A function is called an even function if $f(-x) = f(x)$ for all x in the domain of the function. Explain why the function $f(x) = ax^2$ is even for any value of a.

_____

_____

13. Communicate Mathematical Ideas Explain how you know, without graphing, what the graph of $g(x) = \frac{1}{10}x^2$ looks like.

_____

_____

_____

LESSON 17.3 Combining Transformations of Quadratic Functions

COMMON CORE F.IF.7a

Graph linear and quadratic functions and show intercepts, maxima, and minima. *Also, A.CED.2, F.IF.2, F.IF.4, F.IF.7, F.BF.1, F.BF.3*

ESSENTIAL QUESTION

How can you obtain the graph of $g(x) = a(x - h)^2 + k$ from the graph of $f(x) = x^2$?

EXPLORE ACTIVITY   **COMMON CORE** F.IF.2, F.BF.3

Understanding Quadratic Functions of the Form $g(x) = a(x - h)^2 + k$

Every quadratic function can be represented by an equation of the form $g(x) = a(x - h)^2 + k$. The values of the parameters a, h, and k determine how the graph of the function compares to the graph of the parent function, $y = x^2$.

Use the sequence shown to graph $g(x) = 2(x - 3)^2 + 1$ by transforming the graph of $f(x) = x^2$.

A Graph $f(x) = x^2$. Then stretch the graph vertically by a factor of _____ to obtain the graph of $y = 2x^2$. Graph the function.

B Translate the graph of $y = 2x^2$

right _____ units and

up _____ unit to obtain the graph of $g(x) = 2(x - 3)^2 + 1$.

Animated Math

my.hrw.com

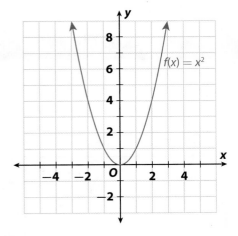

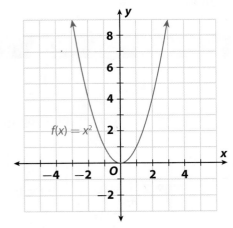

REFLECT

1. The vertex of the graph of $f(x) = x^2$ is _____ while the vertex of the graph of $g(x) = 2(x - 3)^2 + 1$ is _____.

2. Using the equation $g(x) = 2(x - 3)^2 + 1$, find $g(4)$. Is $(4, 3)$ on the curve you plotted?

_____

3. Using the equation $g(x) = 2(x - 3)^2 + 1$, find $g(5)$. Is $(5, 9)$ on the curve you plotted?

_____

4. Using the equation $g(x) = 2(x - 3)^2 + 1$, find $g(2)$. Is $(2, 3)$ on the curve you plotted?

_____

5. Make a Conjecture Describe another sequence of steps for graphing the function $g(x) = 2(x - 3)^2 + 1$.

_____

_____

_____

_____

Math On the Spot

⏱ my.hrw.com

Graphing $g(x) = a(x - h)^2 + k$

To graph a quadratic function of the form $g(x) = a(x - h)^2 + k$, first identify the vertex (h, k). Next, consider the sign of a to determine whether the graph opens upward or downward. If a is positive, the graph opens upward. If a is negative, the graph opens downward. Then generate two points on each side of the vertex. Using those points, sketch the graph of the function.

EXAMPLE 1

COMMON CORE   F.IF.2, F.BF.3

Graph $g(x) = -3(x + 1)^2 - 2$.

STEP 1 Identify and plot the vertex.

The vertex is at $(-1, -2)$.

STEP 2 Make a table for the function.

x	−3	−2	−1	0	1
g(x)	−14	−5	−2	−5	−14

STEP 3 Plot the points and draw a parabola through them.

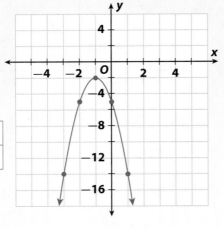

REFLECT

6. List the transformations of the graph of the parent function $f(x) = x^2$, in the order that you would perform them, to obtain the graph of $g(x) = -3(x + 1)^2 - 2$.

_____

_____

7. **Justify Reasoning** Before graphing $g(x) = -3(x + 1)^2 - 2$, would you have expected the graph to open upward or downward? Why?

_____

_____

8. **What If?** Suppose you changed the -3 in $g(x) = -3(x + 1)^2 - 2$ to -4. Which of the points identified in the example would change? What coordinates would they now have?

_____

_____

YOUR TURN

9. Graph $g(x) = -(x - 2)^2 + 4$.

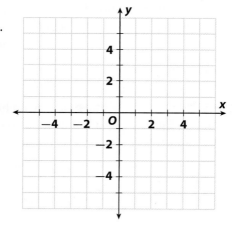

10. Graph $g(x) = 2(x + 3)^2 - 1$.

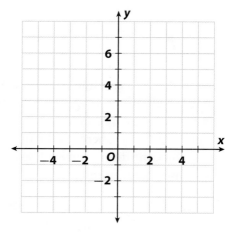

Personal Math Trainer

Online Practice and Help

my.hrw.com

Writing a Quadratic Function Given a Graph

The graph of a parabola can be used to determine the corresponding function.

EXAMPLE 2   COMMON CORE   F.IF.2, F.IF.4, F.BF.1, F.BF.3

A house painter standing on a ladder drops a paintbrush, which falls to the ground. The paintbrush's height above the ground (in feet) is given by a function of the form $f(t) = a(t - h)^2 + k$ where t is the time (in seconds) since the paintbrush was dropped.

Use the graph to find an equation for $f(t)$.

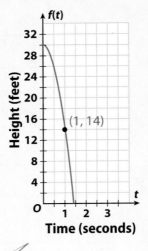

STEP 1   The vertex of the parabola is $(h, k) = (0, 30)$.

Substitute for h and k.
$f(t) = a(t - 0)^2 + 30$, or $f(t) = at^2 + 30$.

STEP 2   You can see that $f(1) = 14$. Substitute 1 for t and 14 for $f(t)$ and solve for a.

$14 = a(1)^2 + 30$

$-16 = a$

STEP 3   Write the equation for the function: $f(t) = -16t^2 + 30$.

> Only Quadrant I is shown because only nonnegative values of t and $f(t)$ make sense in this situation.

REFLECT

11. **Check for Reasonableness**   Estimate how much time elapses before the paintbrush hits the ground. Use the equation for the function and your estimate to explain whether the equation is reasonable.

_____

_____

YOUR TURN

12. A diver jumps off a cliff into the sea below to search for shells. The diver's height above the sea (in feet) is given by a function of the form $f(t) = a(t - h)^2 + k$, where t is the time (in seconds) since the diver jumped. Use the graph to find an equation for $f(t)$.

$f(t) = $ _____

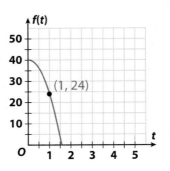

Modeling the Height of an Object in Free Fall

The quadratic function $h(t) = -16t^2 + c$ can be used to approximate the height $h(t)$ in feet above the ground of a falling object t seconds after it is dropped from a height of c feet. This model is used only to approximate the height of falling objects because it does not account for air resistance, wind, and other real-world factors.

Math On the Spot
my.hrw.com

EXAMPLE 3 | COMMON CORE | F.IF.2, F.IF.4, F.IF.7, F.IF.7a, F.BF.1

Two identical water balloons are dropped from different heights as shown in the diagram.

A Write the two height functions and compare their graphs.

> **STEP 1** Write the height functions.
>
> The constant c represents the original height.
>
> $h_1(t) = -16t^2 + 64$ Dropped from 64 feet
> $h_2(t) = -16t^2 + 144$ Dropped from 144 feet

> **STEP 2** Use a graphing calculator.
>
> The graph of h_2 is a vertical translation of the graph of h_1. Since the balloon represented by h_2 is dropped from 80 feet higher than the one represented by h_1, the y-intercept of h_2 is 80 units higher than that of h_1.

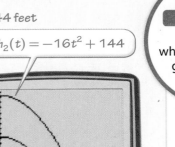

$h_2(t) = -16t^2 + 144$

$h_1(t) = -16t^2 + 64$

Animated Math
my.hrw.com

Math Talk
Mathematical Practices
In part A, why was the window of the graphing calculator set for nonnegative values only?

B Use the graphs to tell how long it takes each water balloon to reach the ground.

The x-intercept of each graph indicates the amount of time it takes for the balloon to reach the ground.

The water balloon dropped from 64 feet reaches the ground in 2 seconds. The water balloon dropped from 144 feet reaches the ground in 3 seconds.

REFLECT

13. **Represent Real-World Problems** Write the function for a water balloon that is dropped from a height of 50 feet. Explain.

_____

_____

YOUR TURN

14. Two baseballs are dropped, one from a height of 16 feet and the other from a height of 256 feet.

a. Write the two height functions.

_____

b. How long does it take each baseball to reach the ground?

_____

Guided Practice

Graph each quadratic function. (Example 1)

1. $f(x) = 2(x - 2)^2 + 3$

2. $f(x) = -(x - 1)^2 + 2$

3. A roofer working on a roof accidentally drops a hammer, which falls to the ground. The hammer's height above the ground (in feet) is given by a function of the form $f(t) = a(t - h)^2 + k$ where t is the time (in seconds) since the hammer was dropped. Use the graph to find an equation for $f(t)$. (Example 2)

_____

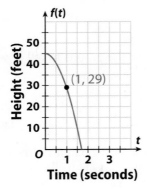

ESSENTIAL QUESTION CHECK-IN

4. How can you use the values of a, h, and k, to obtain the graph of $g(x) = a(x - h)^2 + k$ from the graph of $f(x) = x^2$?

_____

_____

_____

17.3 Independent Practice

COMMON CORE A.CED.2, F.BF.1, F.BF.3, F.IF.2, F.IF.4, F.IF.7, F.IF.7a

Personal Math Trainer

Online Practice and Help

my.hrw.com

Graph each quadratic function.

5. $f(x) = \frac{1}{2}(x - 2)^2$

6. $f(x) = -\frac{1}{3}x^2 - 3$

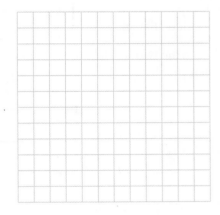

7. $f(x) = 4(x + 2)^2 - 3$

8. $f(x) = -\frac{1}{4}(x - 1)^2 - 3$

9. Two tennis balls are dropped, one from a height of 16 feet and the other from a height of 100 feet.

   a. Write the two height functions and use a graphing calculator to compare their graphs.

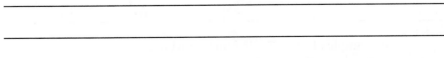

_____

_____

_____

_____

b. Use the graphs of the functions in part a to tell how long it takes each tennis ball to reach the ground.

_____

_____

_____

_____

10. A raindrop falls from a cloud at an altitude of 10,000 ft. Another raindrop falls from a cloud at an altitude of 14,400 ft.

a. Write the two height functions and use a graphing calculator to compare their graphs.

_____

_____

_____

_____

b. Use the graphs to tell when each raindrop reaches the ground.

_____

_____

_____

_____

 **FOCUS ON HIGHER ORDER THINKING**

Work Area

11. **Explain the Error** Kevin says that the graph of the function $f(x) = -(x - 2)^2 + 3$ is a parabola that opens downward and has a vertex at $(3, 2)$. Explain the error.

_____

_____

12. **Make a Prediction** For what values of a and c will the graph of $f(x) = ax^2 + c$ have one x-intercept?

_____

_____

13. **Critical Thinking** Give an example of a quadratic function whose graph is wider than the graph of $f(x) = x^2$, opens downward, and has no x-intercepts.

_____

Characteristics of Quadratic Functions

COMMON CORE **F.IF.4**

For a function that models a relationship between two quantities, interpret key features of graphs and tables in terms of the quantities, and sketch graphs showing key features given a verbal description of the relationship. *Also F.IF.8, A.SSE.3b*

? **ESSENTIAL QUESTION**

How are the characteristics of quadratic functions related to the key features of their graphs?

EXPLORE ACTIVITY COMMON CORE **F.IF.4**

Explore Quadratic Functions

In this activity you will learn how to determine whether a function is a quadratic function by looking at its graph. If the graph of a function is a parabola, then the function is a quadratic function. If the graph of a function is not a parabola, then the function is not a quadratic function.

Use a graphing calculator to graph each of the functions. Set the viewing window to show −10 to 10 on both axes. Sketch the graph that you see on your calculator. Circle "yes" or "no" to tell whether each function is a quadratic function.

A $f(x) = x + 1$

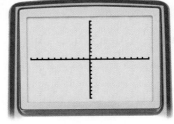

quadratic: yes   no

B $f(x) = -x^2 + 1$

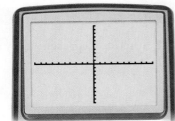

quadratic: yes   no

C $f(x) = 2x^2 - 1$

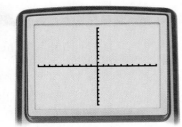

quadratic: yes   no

D $f(x) = x^3$

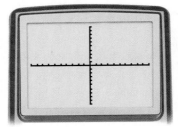

quadratic: yes   no

E $f(x) = \sqrt{x}$

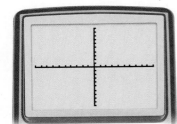

quadratic: yes   no

F $f(x) = 2^x$

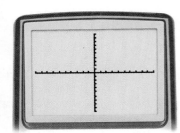

quadratic: yes   no

REFLECT

1. **Communicate Mathematical Ideas** How can you determine whether a function is quadratic or not by looking at its graph?

   _____

   _____

   _____

   _____

2. **Make a Conjecture** Based on your observations, how can you tell if a function is a quadratic function by looking at the equation?

   _____

   _____

Math On the Spot

🔵 my.hrw.com

Identifying Quadratic Functions

If a function is quadratic, it can be represented by an equation of the form $y = ax^2 + bx + c$, where a, b, and c are real numbers and $a \neq 0$. This is called the standard form of a quadratic equation.

EXAMPLE 1

COMMON CORE F.IF.8

Determine whether the function represented by each equation is quadratic. Explain.

A $y = -2x + 20$ 　　　　　Compare to $y = ax^2 + bx + c$.

This is not a quadratic function because $a = 0$.

B $y + 3x^2 = -4$

Rewrite the function in the form $y = ax^2 + bx + c$.

$$y + 3x^2 = -4$$
$$\underline{-3x^2 \qquad -3x^2} \qquad \text{Subtract } 3x^2 \text{ from each side.}$$
$$y = -3x^2 - 4 \qquad a = -3, b = 0, c = -4$$

This is a quadratic function because a, b, and c are real numbers and $a \neq 0$.

C $-y + 2 + 4x^2 = 4x$

Rewrite the function in the form $y = ax^2 + bx + c$.

$$-y + 2 + 4x^2 = 4x$$
$$y = 4x^2 - 4x + 2 \qquad a = 4, b = -4, c = 2$$

This is a quadratic function because a, b, and c are real numbers and $a \neq 0$.

My Notes

REFLECT

3. Critical Thinking Explain why the function represented by the equation $y = ax^2 + bx + c$ is quadratic only when $a \neq 0$.

_____

_____

4. Communicate Mathematical Ideas Why might it be easier to determine whether a function is quadratic when it is expressed in function notation?

_____

_____

YOUR TURN

Determine whether the function represented by each equation is quadratic. Explain.

5. $y - 4x + x^2 = 0$

_____

6. $f(x) = 0.01 - 0.2x + x^2$

_____

7. $x + 2y = 14x + 6$

_____

8. $f(x) = \frac{1}{2}x - 4$

_____

Maximum and Minimum Values

Every parabola has either a highest point or a lowest point, called the vertex. The y-coordinate of the vertex is the maximum value or minimum value of the function represented by the parabola.

Minimum and Maximum Values		
Words	If $a > 0$, the parabola opens upward, and the y-value of the vertex is the **minimum** value of the function. If $a > 0$, the function has no maximum value.	If $a < 0$, the parabola opens downward, and the y-value of the vertex is the **maximum** value of the function. If $a < 0$, the function has no minimum value.

$y = x^2 + 6x + 9$

$y = -x^2 + 6x - 4$

Vertex: $(-3, 0)$
Minimum: 0

Vertex: $(3, 5)$
Maximum: 5

EXAMPLE 2   COMMON CORE   F.IF.4

Determine the maximum or minimum value of each quadratic function from its graph or its equation.

A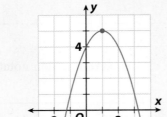

The parabola opens downward, so 5 is the maximum value.

B

The parabola opens upward, so −5 is the minimum value.

C $y = 2(x + 1)^2 - 6$

The vertex (h, k) is $(-1, -6)$. Because $a > 0$, the parabola opens upward.

The minimum value of the function is −6.

D $y = -3(x - 4)^2 + 5$

The vertex (h, k) is $(4, 5)$. Because $a < 0$, the parabola opens downward.

The maximum value of the function is 5.

REFLECT

9. Critical Thinking How could you determine the maximum or minimum value if the equation of a quadratic function is given in standard form $y = ax^2 + bx + c$?

_____

_____

YOUR TURN

Determine the maximum or minimum value of each quadratic function from its graph or its equation.

10.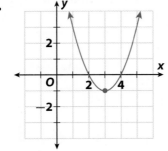

11. $y = -(x - 5)^2 + 8$

_____

12. $y = 4(x + 2)^2 + 3$

_____

_____

My Notes

Personal Math Trainer

Online Practice and Help

⏻ my.hrw.com

Zeros of a Function

A **zero of a function** is a value of x that makes the value of the function 0. The zeros of a function are the x-intercepts of the graph of the function. A quadratic function may have one, two, or no zeros.

> Recall that an x-intercept of a graph is the x-coordinate of the point where the graph crosses the x-axis. The value of y at an x-intercept is 0.

EXAMPLE 3
COMMON CORE F.IF.4

Find the zeros of each quadratic function from its graph. Check your answers.

A $y = x^2 - x - 2$

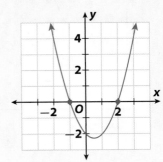

The zeros appear to be -1 and 2.

Check:

$y = x^2 - x - 2$

$y = (-1)^2 - (-1) - 2$

$\quad = 1 + 1 - 2 = 0$ ✔

$y = (2)^2 - (2) - 2$

$\quad = 4 - 2 - 2 = 0$ ✔

B $y = -2x^2 + 4x - 2$

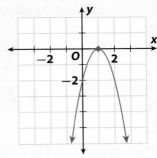

The only zero appears to be 1.

Check:

$y = -2x^2 + 4x - 2$

$y = -2(1)^2 + 4(1) - 2$

$\quad = -2(1) + 4 - 2$

$\quad = -2 + 4 - 2$

$\quad = 0$ ✔

C $y = \frac{1}{4}x^2 + 1$

The graph does not cross the x-axis, so this function has no zeros.

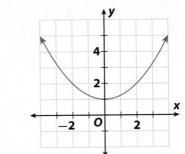

Animated Math
my.hrw.com

REFLECT

13. Critical Thinking If a quadratic function has only one zero, it has to occur at the vertex of the parabola. Using the graph of a quadratic function, explain why.

_____

_____

_____

YOUR TURN

Find the zeros of each quadratic function from its graph. Check your answers.

14. $y = -4x^2 - 2$

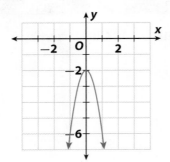

15. $y = x^2 - 6x + 9$

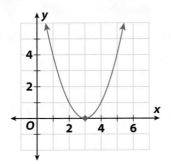

_____   _____

Math On the Spot

⏱ my.hrw.com

Axis of Symmetry

The vertical line that divides a parabola into two symmetrical halves is called its **axis of symmetry**. The axis of symmetry passes through the vertex of the parabola. You can use the zeros of a function to find the equation of the axis of symmetry of its graph.

Finding the Axis of Symmetry by Using Zeros		
Words	**Numbers**	**Graph**
One Zero If a quadratic function has one zero, use the x-coordinate of the vertex to find the axis of symmetry.	Vertex: $(3, 0)$ Axis of symmetry: $x = 3$	
Two Zeros If a quadratic function has two zeros, use the average of the two zeros to find the axis of symmetry.	$\frac{-4 + 0}{2} = \frac{-4}{2} = -2$ Axis of symmetry: $x = -2$	

EXAMPLE 4

COMMON CORE F.IF.4

Sketch the axis of symmetry of each parabola and find its equation.

A

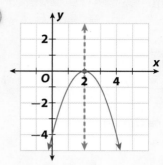

The function has one zero at $(2, 0)$, which is the vertex.

The axis of symmetry is $x = 2$.

B

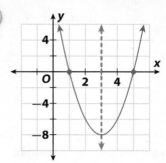

Math Talk
Mathematical Practices

If you are given a quadratic function in the form $y = a(x - h)^2 + k$, how can you determine an equation of the axis of symmetry?

The function has two zeros, at $(1, 0)$ and $(5, 0)$, so use the average of the two zeros to the find the axis of symmetry.

$$\frac{1 + 5}{2} = \frac{6}{2} = 3$$ *Find the average of 1 and 5.*

The axis of symmetry is $x = 3$.

YOUR TURN

Sketch the axis of symmetry of each parabola and find its equation.

16.

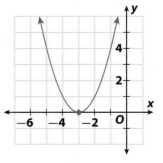

17.

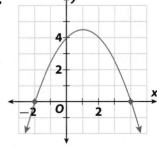

Personal Math Trainer

Online Practice and Help

⏻ my.hrw.com

Determine whether the function represented by each equation is quadratic.
(Example 1)

1. $y + 6x = 14$

2. $2x^2 + y = 3x - 1$

_____

_____

Determine whether each quadratic function has a minimum value or a maximum
value. Then find the minimum or maximum value. (Example 2)

3.

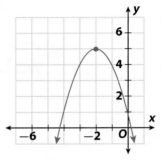

4. $y = (x + 11)^2 + 4$

_____

5. $y = -\frac{1}{2}(x - 1)^2 - 3$

_____

_____

Find the zeros of the quadratic function from
its graph. Check your answers. (Example 3)

Sketch the axis of symmetry of the parabola
and find its equation. (Example 4)

6. $y = 9 - x^2$

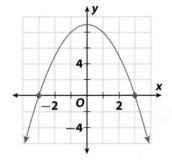

7.

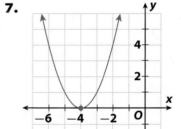

_____

_____

? ESSENTIAL QUESTION CHECK-IN

8. What can you tell about the graph of a parabola when the equation of the
parabola is written in the form $y = a(x - h)^2 + k$?

_____

_____

_____

17.4 Independent Practice

Personal Math Trainer

Online Practice and Help

my.hrw.com

 COMMON CORE F.IF.4, F.IF.8, A.SSE.3b

Determine whether each function is quadratic. Explain.

9. $x - 3x^2 + y = 5$

_____

10. $-2x + y = -3$

_____

For each quadratic function, determine whether it has a maximum value or a minimum value. Then determine the maximum or minimum value.

11. $y = -\frac{1}{3}\left(x - \frac{1}{2}\right)^2 + \frac{1}{4}$ _____

12.

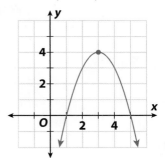

_____

For 13–14, find the zeros of each quadratic function from its graph. Check your answers.

13. $y = \frac{1}{4}(x - 2)^2 + 2$

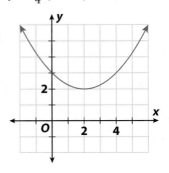

_____

14. $y = x^2 + 10x + 16$

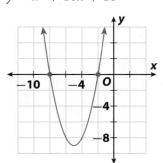

_____

For 15–16, sketch the axis of symmetry of each parabola and find its equation.

15.

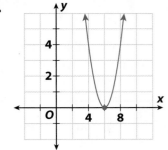

_____

16.

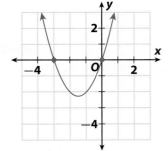

_____

17. Complete the square of the expression in the function $y = 3x^2 + 18x + 30$. Use the result to identify the maximum or minimum of the function and the axis of symmetry of its graph.

_____

_____

_____

18. Factor the expression in the function $y = x^2 - 3x - 4$. Use the result to identify the zeros of the function, the maximum or minimum of the function, and the axis of symmetry of its graph.

_____

_____

_____

_____

 **FOCUS ON HIGHER ORDER THINKING**

Work Area

19. Draw Conclusions Describe the axis of symmetry of the graph of the quadratic function represented by the equation $y = ax^2 + bx + c$ when $b = 0$.

_____

20. a. Critical Thinking You are given the axis of symmetry of a quadratic function and know that the function has two zeros. How would you describe the location of the two zeros? Explain.

_____

_____

b. One zero of a given quadratic function is 6. The axis of symmetry for the graph of the quadratic function is $x = 7.5$. What is the other zero of this quadratic function?

_____

21. Make a Conjecture How could you find an equation of a quadratic function with zeros -3 and 1?

_____

_____

_____

_____

Solving Quadratic Equations Graphically

COMMON CORE **A.REI.11**

Explain why the x-coordinates of the points where the graphs of the equations $y = f(x)$ and $y = g(x)$ intersect are the solutions of the equation $f(x) = g(x)$; find the solutions approximately, e.g., using technology to graph the functions, make tables of values, or find successive approximations. Include cases where $f(x)$ and/or $g(x)$ are liner, polynomial, rational, absolute value, exponential, and logarithmic functions. *Also A.CED.1, A.CED.2, A.REI.4, F.LE.6*

? **ESSENTIAL QUESTION** How can you use the graph of a quadratic function to solve a quadratic equation?

EXPLORE ACTIVITY   COMMON CORE **A.REI.11**

Finding Points of Intersection of Lines and Parabolas

The graphs of three quadratic functions are shown.

Parabola A is the graph of $f(x) = x^2$.

Parabola B is the graph of $h(x) = x^2 + 4$.

Parabola C is the graph of $j(x) = x^2 + 8$.

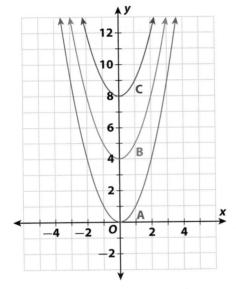

A On the same coordinate grid, graph the function $g(x) = 4$. What type of function is this? Describe its graph.

_____

B At how many points does the graph of $g(x)$ intersect each parabola?

Parabola A: _____ points of intersection

Parabola B: _____ points of intersection

Parabola C: _____ points of intersection

C Use the graph to find the x-coordinate of each point of intersection of the graph of $g(x)$ and parabola A. Show that each x-coordinate satisfies the equation $x^2 = 4$, which is obtained by setting $f(x)$ equal to $g(x)$.

_____

D Use the graph to find the x-coordinate of each point of intersection of the graph of $g(x)$ and parabola B. Show that each x-coordinate satisfies the equation $x^2 + 4 = 4$, which is obtained by setting $h(x)$ equal to $g(x)$.

_____

REFLECT

1. Describe how you could solve an equation like $x^2 + 2 = 11$ graphically.

_____

_____

_____

Math On the Spot

my.hrw.com

Solving Quadratic Equations Graphically, Method 1

You can solve a quadratic equation of the form $a(x - h)^2 + k = c$ by using the expressions on each side of the equation to define a function, graphing the functions, and finding the x-coordinates of the points of intersections of the graphs.

EXAMPLE 1

COMMON CORE **A.REI.4**

Solve $2(x - 4)^2 + 1 = 3$ by graphing.

My Notes

STEP 1 Let $f(x) = 2(x - 4)^2 + 1$.

Let $g(x) = 3$.

STEP 2 Graph $f(x)$.

STEP 3 Graph $g(x)$.

STEP 4 Determine the points at which the graphs of $f(x)$ and $g(x)$ intersect.

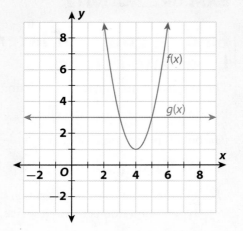

The graphs intersect in two locations: $(3, 3)$ and $(5, 3)$.

This means $f(x) = g(x)$ when $x = 3$ and $x = 5$.

Therefore, the solutions of the equation $f(x) = g(x)$ are 3 and 5.

So the solutions of $2(x - 4)^2 + 1 = 3$ are $x = 3$ and $x = 5$.

YOUR TURN

2. Solve $3(x - 5)^2 - 2 = 10$ by graphing.

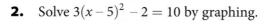

Personal Math Trainer

Online Practice and Help

my.hrw.com

Solving Quadratic Equations Graphically, Method 2

A second method of solving quadratic equations graphically is as follows. First, write the related function for the quadratic equation by rewriting the equation so that one side is 0 and then replacing the 0 with y. Graph the related function and find the x-intercepts of the graph, which are the zeros of the function. The zeros of the function are the solutions of the original equation. Recall that a quadratic function may have two, one, or no zeros.

Solving Quadratic Equations by Graphing

Step 1 Write the related function.

Step 2 Graph the related function.

Step 3 Find the zeros of the related function.

EXAMPLE 2

COMMON CORE A.REI.4

Solve the equation $2x^2 - 5 = -3$ by graphing the related function.

STEP 1 Write the related function. Add 3 to both sides to get $2x^2 - 2 = 0$. The related function is $y = 2x^2 - 2$.

STEP 2 Make a table of values for the related function.

x	−2	1	0	1	2
y	6	0	−2	0	64

Graph the points represented by the table and connect the points.

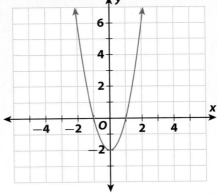

Math Talk

Mathematical Practices

How can you check that −1 and 1 are solutions of the equation $2x^2 - 5 = -3$?

STEP 3 The zeros of the function are −1 and 1, so the solutions of the equation $2x^2 - 5 = -3$ are $x = -1$ and $x = 1$.

YOUR TURN

3. Solve $6x + 8 = -x^2$ by graphing the related function.

_____

Modeling a Real-World Problem

Many real-world problems, particularly those involving the motion of falling objects near Earth's surface, can be modeled by quadratic functions.

EXAMPLE 3

COMMON CORE A.CED.1, A.REI.4

While practicing a tightrope walk at a height of 20 feet, a circus performer slips and falls into a safety net 15 feet below. The function $h(t) = -16t^2 + 20$, where t represents time measured in seconds, gives the performer's height above the ground (in feet) as he falls. Write and solve an equation to find the amount of time before the performer lands in the net.

STEP 1 Write the equation that needs to be solved.

$$-16t^2 + 20 = 5$$

The performer falls into a net that is 15 feet below the tightrope, or 5 feet above the ground.

Math Talk

Mathematical Practices

The graphs also intersect to the left of the y-axis. Why is that point irrelevant to the problem?

STEP 2 A graphing calculator requires that functions be entered in terms of x and y. In terms of x and y, the two functions that must be entered into the calculator are $y = -16x^2 + 20$ and $y = 5$.

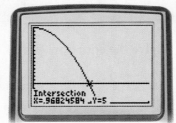

STEP 3 When setting a viewing window, decide what portion of each axis to use for graphing.

Use $0 \le x \le 2$ and $0 \le y \le 20$. Only nonnegative values of x and y are meaningful.

STEP 4 Graph the two functions, and use the calculator's trace or intersect feature to find the amount of time before the performer lands in the net.

The calculator shows an x-value of 0.96824584 for the point of intersection, so a good approximation is $x = 1$.

The performer lands in the net in about 1 second.

REFLECT

4. **Critical Thinking** Why is only the x-value of the intersection point the solution to the equation?

_____

YOUR TURN

5. A squirrel is in a tree 46 feet off the ground and throws a chestnut that lands on a bush 36 feet below. The function $h(t) = -16t^2 + 46$, where t represents time measured in seconds, gives the height of the nut above the ground (in feet) as it falls. Write and solve an equation to find the amount of time before the nut lands on the bush.

_____

Interpreting Quadratic Models

Finding the solutions of a quadratic equation can be helpful in determining other information about the situation modeled by the related function. For example, the solutions can be used to determine how long an event lasted or when a projectile reaches its greatest height.

Math On the Spot
my.hrw.com

EXAMPLE 4 Real World   COMMON CORE   A.CED.1, A.REI.4

A dolphin jumps out of the water. The quadratic function $y = -16x^2 + 20x$ models the dolphin's height (in feet) above the water after x seconds. How long is the dolphin out of the water?

Use the level of the water surface as 0. When the dolphin leaves the water, its height is 0 feet, and when the dolphin reenters the water, its height is 0 feet.

Solve $0 = -16x^2 + 20x$ to find the times when the dolphin leaves and reenters water.

STEP 1   Write the related function for the equation $0 = -16x^2 + 20x$.

$$y = -16x^2 + 20x$$

STEP 2   Graph the function using a graphing calculator.

STEP 3   Use the calculator's trace function to estimate the zeros.

The zeros appear to be 0 and 1.25.

> Substituting 0 for x makes the right side of the equation equal to 0, so 0 is a solution.

Check $-16(1.25)^2 + 20(1.25) = -16(1.5625) + 25$
                $= -25 + 25 = 0$, so 1.25 is a solution.

The dolphin is out of the water for 1.25 seconds.

REFLECT

6. Critical Thinking How would you find the time it takes the dolphin to reach the highest point of his jump?

_____

_____

YOUR TURN

7. A baseball coach uses a pitching machine to simulate pop flies during practice. The quadratic function $y = -16x^2 + 80x + 5$ models the height in feet of the baseball after x seconds. The ball is caught at a height of 5 feet. How long is the baseball in the air?

_____

Personal Math Trainer
Online Practice and Help
my.hrw.com

1. Solve $(x + 2)^2 - 1 = 3$ by graphing. Indicate whether the solutions are exact or approximate. (Example 1)

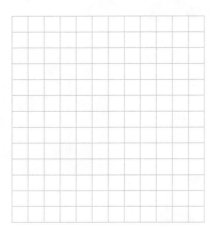

_____

2. Solve $x^2 + 5x + 4 = 0$ by graphing the related function. (Example 2)

_____

3. A man standing at the edge of a cliff 106 feet high, drops a stick that gets caught on a tree limb 42 feet below. The function $h(t) = -16t^2 + 106$, where t represents the time measured in seconds, gives the height of the stick above the ground (in feet). Write and solve an equation to find the amount of time before the stick gets caught in the tree. (Example 3)

_____

4. Yosemite Falls in California consists of three smaller falls. The upper falls are 1430 feet high. The height $h(t)$ in feet of a water droplet falling from the top to the bottom of the upper falls is modeled by $h(t) = -16t^2 + 1430$, where t is time in seconds after it begins falling. Estimate the time that it takes a droplet to fall from the top to the bottom of the upper falls. (Example 4)

_____

_____

? ESSENTIAL QUESTION CHECK-IN

5. How are the solutions of a quadratic equation related to the graph of the related quadratic function?

_____

_____

_____

17.5 Independent Practice

Personal Math Trainer

COMMON CORE   A.CED.1, A.CED.2, A.REI.4, A.REI.11

Solve each equation by graphing.

6. $-\frac{1}{2}x^2 + 2 = -4$

7. $-(x - 3)^2 - 2 = -6$

_____   _____

8. As part of an engineering contest, a student who has designed a protective crate for an egg drops the crate from a window 18 feet above the ground. The height (in feet) of the crate as it falls is given by $h(t) = -16t^2 + 18$, where t is the time (in seconds) since the crate was dropped.

a. Write and solve an equation to find the amount of time before the crate passes a window 10 feet directly below the window from which it was dropped.

_____

b. Write and solve an equation to find the amount of time before the crate hits the ground.

_____

c. Is the rate at which the crate falls constant? Explain.

_____

_____

_____

_____

9. A fireworks shell is fired from a mortar. Its height in feet is modeled by the function $h(t) = -16(t - 7)^2 + 784$, where t is the time in seconds. If the shell does not explode, how long will it take to return to the ground?

_____

10. A baseball is dropped from an airplane 500 feet above the ground. The height (in feet) above the ground is modeled by the function $h(t) = -16t^2 + 500$, where t is the time in seconds.

a. What is the height of the ball after 2 seconds? _____

b. How long will it take for the ball to fall to a height of 100 feet above

ground? _____

c. How long will it take the ball to reach the ground?

_____

 **FOCUS ON HIGHER ORDER THINKING**

11. Counterexamples Pamela says that if the graph of a quadratic function opens upward, then the related quadratic equation has two solutions. Provide a counterexample to Pamela's claim.

_____

_____

_____

12. Critical Thinking Explain why a quadratic equation in the form $ax^2 - c = 0$, where $a > 0$ and $c > 0$, will always have two solutions. Explain why a quadratic equation in the form $ax^2 + c = 0$, where $a > 0$ and $c > 0$, will never have any real-number solutions.

_____

_____

_____

_____

13. Explain the Error Rodney was given the function $h(t) = -16t^2 + 50$ representing the height (in feet) above ground of a water balloon t seconds after being dropped from a roof 50 feet above the ground. He was asked to find how long it took the balloon to fall 20 feet. Rodney used the equation $-16t^2 + 50 = 20$ to solve the problem. What was Rodney's error?

_____

_____

_____

COMMON CORE A.REI.7

Solve a simple system consisting of a linear equation and a quadratic equation in two variables algebraically and graphically. *Also A.REI.4, A.REI.4b, F.IF.4, F.LE.6*

LESSON 17.6 Solving Systems of Linear and Quadratic Equations

? ESSENTIAL QUESTION

How can you solve a system of equations when one equation is linear and the other is quadratic?

EXPLORE ACTIVITY   COMMON CORE   A.REI.7

Determining the Possible Number of Solutions

A system of one linear and one quadratic equation may have zero, one or two solutions.

A The graph of the quadratic function $f(x) = x^2 - 2x - 2$ is shown. On the same coordinate plane, graph the following linear functions.

$$g(x) = -x - 2, \qquad h(x) = 2x - 6, \qquad j(x) = 0.5x - 5$$

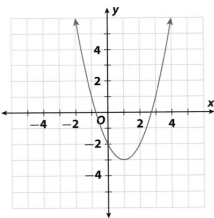

B Look at the graph of the system consisting of the quadratic function and $g(x)$.

How many solutions exist? _____

C Look at the graph of the system consisting of the quadratic function and $h(x)$.

How many solutions exist? _____

D Look at the graph of the system consisting of the quadratic function and $j(x)$.

How many solutions exist? _____

REFLECT

1. A system consisting of a quadratic equation and a linear equation can have

_____ , _____ , or _____ solutions.

Solving Systems Graphically

One way to solve a system is to graph both equations and then find the points where the graphs intersect.

EXAMPLE 1 | **COMMON CORE** A.REI.7

Solve the system represented by the functions graphically.

$$f(x) = (x + 1)^2 - 4, \quad g(x) = 2x - 2$$

My Notes

STEP 1 Graph the quadratic function. The vertex is the point $(-1, -4)$.

The x-intercepts are the points where $(x + 1)^2 - 4 = 0$.

$(x + 1)^2 = 4$

$x + 1 = \pm 2$ *Find the square root of both sides.*

$x = 1 \text{ or } -3$ *Subtract one from both sides.*

STEP 2 Graph the linear function on the same coordinate plane.

The y-intercept is −2 and the slope is 2.

STEP 3 The solutions to the system are the points where the graphs intersect.

The two solutions are $(-1, -4)$ and $(1, 0)$.

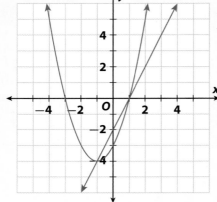

REFLECT

2. If the linear function was $g(x) = 2x - 8$, how many solutions would the system have?

_____

_____

_____

YOUR TURN

Solve each system represented by a pair of functions graphically.

3. $f(x) = -2(x + 2)^2 + 8, \quad g(x) = 4x + 16$ _____

4. $f(x) = (x + 1)^2 - 9, \quad g(x) = 6x - 12$ _____

Solving Systems Algebraically

Systems of equations can also be solved algebraically by using the substitution method.

Math On the Spot

my.hrw.com

EXAMPLE 2

COMMON CORE A.REI.7

Solve the system from Example 1 algebraically.

$$f(x) = (x + 1)^2 - 4, g(x) = 2x - 2$$

STEP 1 Write the related equations.

$$y = (x + 1)^2 - 4, y = 2x - 2$$

STEP 2 Set the right hand sides equal to each other and solve for x.

$$(x + 1)^2 - 4 = 2x - 2$$

$$x^2 + 2x - 3 = 2x - 2 \qquad \text{Simplify the left side.}$$

$$x^2 - 1 = 0 \qquad \text{Use properties of equality to make one side equal zero.}$$

$$(x - 1)(x + 1) = 0 \qquad \text{Factor.}$$

$$x = 1 \text{ or } -1 \qquad \text{Solve for } x.$$

STEP 3 Plug the x-values into the linear equation to find y.

$$y = 2(1) - 2 = 0$$

$$y = 2(-1) - 2 = -4$$

The solutions are $(1, 0)$ and $(-1, -4)$.

REFLECT

5. Why does Step 3 say to plug into the linear equation? What if the x-values are plugged into the quadratic equation?

_____

_____

_____

YOUR TURN

6. Solve the following system of equations algebraically.

$$y = 3x^2 + 4x - 2, y = -20x - 23$$

_____

Personal Math Trainer

Online Practice and Help

my.hrw.com

Solving Systems Using Technology

Systems of equations can be solved by graphing both equations on a calculator and using the Intersect feature.

EXAMPLE 3 (Real World) · COMMON CORE · A.REI.7

A rock climber is pulling his pack up the side of a cliff that is 175.5 feet tall at a rate of 2 feet per second. The height of the pack in feet after t seconds is given by $y = 2t$. The climber drops a coil of rope from directly above the pack. The height of the coil in feet after t seconds is given by $y = -16t^2 + 175.5$. At what time does the coil of rope hit the pack?

STEP 1 Solve the system:
$$y_1 = 2x, \, y_2 = -16x^2 + 175.5$$

STEP 2 Enter the functions into a graphing calculator as Y_1 and Y_2, and graph both of them. Sketch the graphs on the coordinate plane.

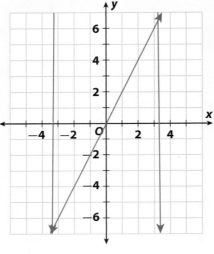

STEP 3 Press 2nd and CALC, then select Intersect. Press Enter to select Y1, then press Enter to select Y2. Move the cursor near one of the intersections and press Enter to make a guess. The display will show the coordinates of the intersection. Repeat for the second intersection.

The intersection points are $(3.25, 6.5)$, $(-3.375, -6.75)$.

The coil hits the pack at $t = 3.25$ seconds.

Math Talk

Mathematical Practices

Why doesn't the other intersection give a solution to the problem?

YOUR TURN

7. A window washer is ascending the side of a building that is 520 feet tall at a rate of 3 feet per second. The elevation of the window washer after t seconds is given by $y = 3t$. A bucket of supplies is lowered to him from above. The height of the supplies in feet after t seconds is given by $y = -2t^2 + 520$. At what time do the supplies reach the window washer?

_____

Solve each system represented by a pair of functions graphically. (Example 1)

1. $f(x) = (x + 3)^2 - 4$, $g(x) = 2x + 2$

The vertex of $f(x)$ is at (⬜ , ⬜).

$f(x)$ has x-intercepts $x =$ _____ , _____ .

$g(x)$ has a slope of _____ and intercept _____ .

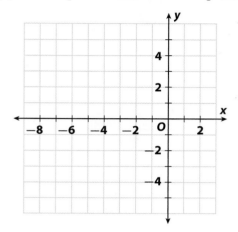

The solutions are _____ .

2. $f(x) = x^2 - 1$, $g(x) = x - 2$

The vertex of $f(x)$ is at (⬜ , ⬜).

$f(x)$ has x-intercepts $x =$ _____ , _____ .

$g(x)$ has a slope of _____ and intercept _____ .

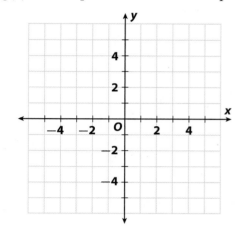

There are _____ real solutions.

3. $f(x) = (x - 4)^2 - 2$, $g(x) = -2$

The vertex of $f(x)$ is at (⬜ , ⬜).

$f(x)$ has x-intercepts $x =$ _____ , _____ .

$g(x)$ has a slope of _____ and intercept _____ .

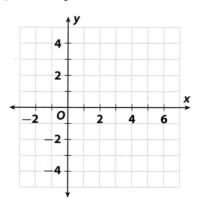

The solutions is _____ .

4. $f(x) = -x^2 + 4$, $g(x) = -3x + 6$

The vertex of $f(x)$ is at (⬜ , ⬜).

$f(x)$ has x-intercepts $x =$ _____ , _____ .

$g(x)$ has a slope of _____ and intercept _____ .

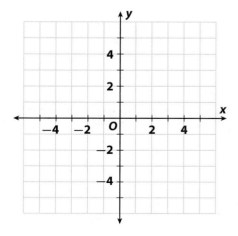

The solutions are _____ .

Solve each system algebraically. (Example 2)

5. $f(x) = x^2 + 1$, $g(x) = 5$

$x^2 + 1 = \boxed{}$

$x^2 - \boxed{} = 0$

$x = \boxed{}$ or $\boxed{}$

The solutions are _____.

6. $f(x) = x^2 - 3x + 2$, $g(x) = 4x - 8$

$\boxed{} = 4x - 8$

$x^2 - \boxed{} x + \boxed{} = 0$

$(x + \boxed{})(x + \boxed{}) = 0$

$x = \boxed{}$ or $\boxed{}$

The solutions are _____.

7. $f(x) = (x - 3)^2$, $g(x) = 4$

$(x - 3)^2 = \boxed{}$

$x - \boxed{} = \pm \boxed{}$

$x = \boxed{}$ or $\boxed{}$

The solutions are _____.

8. $f(x) = -x^2 + 4x$, $g(x) = x + 2$

$-x^2 + 4x = \boxed{}$

$-x^2 + \boxed{} x - \boxed{} = 0$

$x = \dfrac{-b \pm \sqrt{b^2 - 4ac}}{2a}$

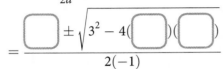

$x = \dfrac{\boxed{} \pm \sqrt{\boxed{}}}{-2} = \dfrac{\boxed{} \pm 1}{-2}$

$x = \boxed{}$ or $\boxed{}$

The solutions are _____.

9. The height in feet of a skydiver t seconds after deploying her parachute is given by $h = -300t + 1000$. A ball is thrown up toward the skydiver, and after t seconds, the height of the ball in feet is given by $h = -16t^2 + 100t$. Use a graphing calculator to solve this system of equations, and then determine when the ball reaches the skydiver. (Example 3)

The two solutions to the system are _____ and _____.

The ball reaches the skydiver at time $t =$ _____

? ESSENTIAL QUESTION CHECK-IN

10. How can the graphs of two functions be used to solve a system of a quadratic and a linear equation?

_____

_____

_____

17.6 Independent Practice

Personal
Math Trainer

Online Practice
and Help
my.hrw.com

Solve each system represented by a pair of functions graphically.

11. $f(x) = -(x-2)^2 + 9$, $g(x) = 3x + 3$

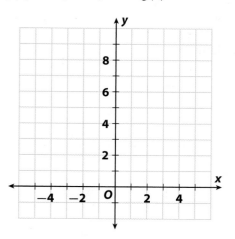

_____

12. $f(x) = 3(x+1)^2 - 1$, $g(x) = x - 4$

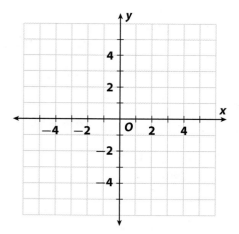

_____

For 13–15, solve each system of equations algebraically.

13. $y = 2x^2 - 5x + 6$, $y = 5x - 6$

_____

14. $y = x^2 + 7$, $y = -9x + 29$

_____

15. $y = 4x^2 + 45x + 83$, $y = 5x - 17$

_____

For 16–17, use a graphing calculator.

16. An elevator in a hotel moves at 20 feet per second. Leaving from the ground floor, its height in feet after t seconds is given by the formula $h = 20t$. A bolt comes loose in the elevator shaft above, and its height in feet after falling for t seconds is given by $h = -16t^2 + 200$.

a. Write the solution(s) to the system of equations which determines when the bolt hits the elevator.

_____

b. At what time does the bolt hit the elevator?

_____

c. At what height does the bolt hit the elevator?

_____

d. Explain why it makes sense for this problem to be modeled with a downward opening parabola?

_____

_____

_____

_____

_____

17. The path of a baseball hit for a home run can be modeled by $y = -\frac{x^2}{484} + x + 3$ where x and y are in feet and home plate is the origin. The ball lands in the stands, which are modeled by $4y - x = -352$ for $x \geq 400$. Use a graphing calculator to graph the system.

a. What do the variables x and y represent?

_____

_____

b. About how far is the baseball from home plate when it lands?

_____

c. About how high up in the stands does the baseball land?

_____

18. **Draw Conclusions** A certain system of a linear and a quadratic equation has two solutions, $(2, 7)$ and $(5, 10)$. The quadratic equation is $y = x^2 - 6x + 15$. What is the linear equation? Explain.

_____

_____

19. **Explain The Error** A student is asked to solve the system of equations $y = x^2 + 2x - 7$ and $y - 2 = x + 1$. For the first step, the student sets the right hand sides equal to each other to get the equation $x^2 + 2x - 7 = x + 1$. Why does this not give the correct solution?

_____

_____

20. **Justify Reasoning** It is possible for a system of two linear equations to have infinitely many solutions. Explain why this is not possible for a system with one linear and one quadratic equation.

_____

_____

_____

21. **Explain the Error** After solving the system of equations in Exercise 16, a student concludes that there are two different times that the bolt hits the elevator. What is the error in the student's reasoning?

_____

_____

Comparing Linear, Quadratic, and Exponential Models

COMMON CORE   F.LE.3
Observe using graphs and tables that a quantity increasing exponentially eventually exceeds a quantity increasing linearly, quadratically, or (more generally) as a polynomial function. *Also F.IF.6, F.LE.1, F.LE.1b, F.LE.1c, S.ID.6a*

? **ESSENTIAL QUESTION**

How can you decide which function type to use when modeling?

EXPLORE ACTIVITY 1   COMMON CORE   F.LE.1

Examining the End Behavior of Linear and Quadratic Functions

The **end behavior** of a function is the behavior of the graph of the function as *x* approaches infinity and as *x* approaches negative infinity. The notation for end behavior is:

$$x \to \infty, f(x) \to ?$$

"As *x* approaches infinity, what does *f(x)* approach?"

$$x \to -\infty, f(x) \to ?$$

"As *x* approaches negative infinity, what does *f(x)* approach?"

A Look at the graph to see which direction the function is headed as *x* approaches positive and negative infinity.

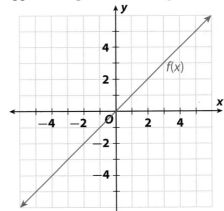
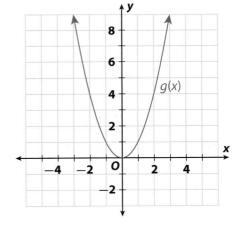

For the linear graph, as *x* approaches positive infinity, *f(x)* is approaching

_____ and as *x* approaches negative infinity,

f(x) is approaching _____.

For the quadratic graph, as *x* approaches positive infinity, *g(x)* approaches

_____ and as *x* approaches negative infinity,

g(x) approaches _____.

B Write the end behavior for both graphs.

Linear:

As $x \to \infty, f(x) \to$ ☐ . As $x \to -\infty, f(x) \to$ ☐ .

Quadratic:

As $x \to \infty, g(x) \to$ ☐ . As $x \to -\infty, g(x) \to$ ☐ .

REFLECT

1. What is the end behavior of $y = 7x - 11$?

_____

_____

_____

2. What is the end behavior of $y = 5x^2 + x - 8$?

_____

_____

EXPLORE ACTIVITY 2    COMMON CORE   F.IF.6, F.LE.3

Examining the End Behavior of Linear, Quadratic, and Exponential Functions

Examining end behavior of a function requires looking at the *x*-values as they become large and positive or large and negative, and looking at their corresponding *y*-values.

A Fill in the missing values in the table.

Linear		Quadratic		Exponential	
x	$L(x) = 5x - 2$	x	$Q(x) = 5x^2 - 2$	x	$E(x) = 5^x - 2$
1	3	1	3	1	3
2	8	2	18	2	
3	13	3	43	3	123
4		4	78	4	623
5	23	5		5	3,123
6	28	6	178	6	15,623
7	33	7	243	7	
8	38	8	318	8	390,623

B We want to determine which function "grows" the fastest. In other words, which function approaches infinity the quickest? To determine rates of growth, determine the successive differences. Fill out the missing parts in the chart below.

Linear		Quadratic		Exponential	
x	$L(x+1) - L(x)$	x	$Q(x+1) - Q(x)$	x	$E(x+1) - E(x)$
1	+5	1	+15	1	+20
2	+5	2	+25	2	
3		3	+35	3	+500
4	+5	4		4	+2500
5	+5	5	+55	5	

C Which function is growing the fastest? _____

D **Make a Conjecture** Will an increasing exponential function eventually always exceed an increasing quadratic function? Explain.

_____

_____

COMMON CORE F.LE.3

Comparing Function Families

Linear, quadratic, and exponential functions are characterized by distinct patterns of increase and decrease over specific intervals.

A Complete the table of values and determine if each linear function is increasing, decreasing, or both.

x	$f(x) = 6x - 5$	x	$g(x) = 2x + 7$	x	$h(x) = -4x + 3$	x	$k(x) = -x + 8$
3		3		3		3	
4		4		4		4	
5		5		5		5	
6		6		6		6	

$f(x)$ increasing $g(x)$ _____ $h(x)$ _____ $k(x)$ _____

B What part of a linear function tells you if it is increasing or decreasing?

_____

Math Talk
Mathematical Practices
If a function is linear, what do you know about the difference in its y-values for constant changes in its x-values?

My Notes

C Complete the table and determine if each quadratic function is increasing, decreasing, or both.

x	$f(x) = 3x^2 - 1$	x	$g(x) = x^2 - x$	x	$h(x) = -4x^2 + 5$	x	$k(x) = -x^2 + 8$
−1	2	−1	2	−1	1	−1	7
0		0		0		0	
1		1		1		1	
2		2		2		2	
3		3		3		3	

$f(x)$ both $g(x)$ _____ $h(x)$ _____ $k(x)$ _____

D Which of the quadratics above are always increasing or always decreasing?

_____

E Explain whether quadratic functions can be characterized as always increasing or always decreasing.

_____

F Complete the table of values and determine if each exponential function is increasing, decreasing, or both.

x	$f(x) = 2^x + 1$	x	$g(x) = -3^x + 4$	x	$h(x) = 5^x - 8$	x	$k(x) = -7 \cdot 3^x + 1$
0		0		0		0	
1		1		1		1	
2		2		2		2	
3		3		3		3	

$f(x)$ increasing $g(x)$ _____ $h(x)$ _____ $k(x)$ _____

G What part of the function tells you if it is increasing or decreasing?

_____

H Will the function $h(x) = 19^x - 10$ always increase or always decrease?

_____

REFLECT

3. Will the function $f(x) = 6^x - 5$ always increase or always decrease?

_____

Choosing a Function Model

Linear, quadratic, and exponential functions can be used in business, medicine, and other fields to model costs of products, disease growth/decay, and so on. You can decide whether a set of data is best modeled by a linear, quadratic, or exponential function by examining the differences and ratios between consecutive output values.

Math On the Spot
my.hrw.com

EXAMPLE 1

COMMON CORE F.LE.1

Analyze each set of data to find the type of function that best represents the data.

A In this table, *x* represents the number of years a company has been in business, and *y* represents profit in thousands of dollars:

x	y
1	3
2	5
3	7
4	9

$> +2$
$> +2$
$> +2$

STEP 1 Find the first differences, the differences between consecutive *y* values.

The first differences are 2, 2, and 2.

STEP 2 Choose the type of function that can be modeled by the points (1, 3), (2, 5), (3, 7), and (4, 9).

The function is linear because the first differences are constant.

B During an experiment, a strain of bacteria is found whose population is modeled by the following data:

Hours, x	Population, y
0	500
1	1000
2	2000
3	4000

$> +500$
$> +1000$
$> +2000$

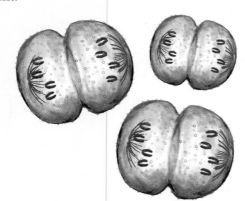

STEP 1 Find the first differences.

The first differences are 500, 1000, and 2000.

STEP 2 The first differences are not constant, so a linear model does not fit. Find the second differences. (These are the differences between consecutive first differences.)

Hours, x	Population, y
0	500
1	1000
2	2000
3	4000

>+500
>+1000
>+2000
>+500
>+1000

STEP 3 The second differences are not constant, so a quadratic model does not fit. Find the ratio of consecutive function values.

Hours, x	Population, y
0	500
1	1000
2	2000
3	4000

>×2
>×2
>×2

There is a constant ratio of 2. An exponential function best models the data.

REFLECT

4. Look at the differences in the y-values. Does the data represent a linear, quadratic, or exponential equation?

x	y
0	1
1	4
2	13
3	28
4	49

>+3
>+9
>+15
>+21
>+6
>+6
>+6

_____

_____

5. A function is found to have a constant second difference of 0. What type of function is it? _____

YOUR TURN

6. Data that is modeled by the points (3, 9), (4, 16), (5, 25), and (6, 36) can be best represented by what type of function? _____

7. Data that is modeled by the points (1, 6), (2, 18), (3, 54), and (4, 162) can be best represented by what type of function? _____

1. Determine the end behavior of $f(x) = 3^x$.

   a. $f(x + 1) = 3^{x+1} = 3^x \cdot 3^1 = 3f(x)$
   Does the value of $f(x)$ increase or

   decrease as x increases? _____

   b. What happens to $f(x)$ as x approaches
   positive infinity?

   _____

2. Tell whether the data is linear by determining
whether the first differences are constant. If
so, give the common difference.

x (weeks)	y (population)
1	5
2	10
3	15
4	20

_____

3. Determine if the data is quadratic:

x	y	First diff.	Second diff.
0	−5		
1	−2	+ 3	
2	7	+ 9	+ ☐
3	22	+ ☐	+ 6
4	43	+ 21	+ ☐

_____

_____

4. Determine the end behavior of
$f(x) = 2x^2 + 3x - 7$.

   a. What type of function is this?

   _____

   b. What is the leading coefficient? _____

   c. What does this say about the end
   behavior?

   _____

   _____

5. The number of nuts produced by a walnut
tree is shown in the table.

x (years)	y (nuts)	Common difference or Common ratio
2	9	> ☐
3	27	> ☐
4	81	> ☐
5	243	> ☐
6	729	

   a. Fill in the boxes next to the table.

   b. Does the data show a common difference
   or a common ratio?

   _____

   c. What type of function models the data?

   _____

? **ESSENTIAL QUESTION CHECK-IN**

6. How can you decide which function type best models a data set?

_____

_____

_____

17.7 Independent Practice

Personal Math Trainer

Online Practice and Help

my.hrw.com

 COMMON CORE F.IF.6, F.LE.1, F.LE.1b, F.LE.1c, F.LE.3, S.ID.6a

Determine if the following are linear, quadratic, exponential, or none of these.

7. $y = x - x^2$

_____

8. $y = 2(x - 3)^2$

_____

9. $y = 3^{x+2} + 12$

_____

10. $y = 7x + 11$

_____

11. $y = \left(\frac{2}{3}\right)^{3x} = 9$ _____

12. $(1, 2), (6, 27), (0, 5), (3, 8), (5, 11)$

_____

13. $(7, 38), (8, 45), (9, 52), (10, 59), (11, 66)$

_____

14. $(-1, 23), (0, 5), (1, 1), (2, 11), (3, 35)$

_____

15. $(1, -11), (2, 4), (3, 29), (4, 64), (5, 109)$

_____

16. $(4, 16), (5, 48), (6, 112), (7, 240), (8, 496)$

_____

17. A cannonball is fired from a stage at time $t = 0$. Its height afterward (in feet) is given by the function $y(t) = -16t^2 + 38t + 2$, where t is measured in seconds. Tell whether the function is linear, quadratic, or exponential. Explain how you know.

_____

_____

18. A rocket is launched, and after t seconds its velocity (in feet per second) is given by the function $y(t) = 112t + 41$. Tell whether the function is linear, quadratic, or exponential. Explain how you know.

_____

_____

19. The population of a colony of bacteria over time is shown in the table.

x (hours)	y (bacteria)	Common Difference or Common Ratio
0	1	> ⬚
1	10	> ⬚
2	100	> ⬚
3	1,000	

a. Complete the column next to the table.

b. What type of function best models the data? _____

20. The amount earned on a certain investment over time is shown in the table.

x (years)	y ($ earned)
1	2
2	6
3	18
4	54
5	162

a. What is the base of the exponential expression in the function that models the data? _____

b. What is the next data point? _____

21. Use the data in the table.

x	y
6	52
7	67
8	84
9	103
10	124

a. What type of function models the data?

_____

b. Explain your answer to part a.

_____

_____

_____

22. The amount of money earned on a $50 investment over time is shown in the table.

x (years)	y (dollars)
0	50
1	150
2	450
3	1,350
4	4,050

a. What type of function models the data?

_____

b. Explain your answer to part a.

_____

_____

_____

23. What type of function models the data?
(10, 51), (11, 57), (12, 63), (13, 69), (14, 75)

_____

24. The amount of money (in thousands) a company spends on advertising is listed in the table by month.

x (months)	y (thousands)
3	14
4	27
5	44
6	65
7	90

a. What type of function models the data?

_____

b. How much is spent in the ninth month?

_____

25. The rainfall (in inches) in a rainforest after x weeks is given by the following data:
(5, 60), (6, 71), (7, 82), (8, 93), (9, 104)

a. What type of function models the data?

_____

b. How much rain will have fallen after the

13th week? _____

26. Jeremy dropped a ball from an initial height of 1.5 meters and measured its height every 0.05 seconds until it hit the floor. The data are shown in the table.

Time x (seconds)	Height y (meters)
0	1.50
0.05	1.48
0.10	1.40
0.15	1.28
0.20	1.11
0.25	0.89
0.30	0.62
0.35	0.30
0.40	0

    a. Do you think the function is linear, quadratic, or exponential? Explain your reasoning.

    _____

    b. Use a graphing calculator to find a regression equation for the data. Explain whether the equation is or is not a good fit.

    _____

    _____

    _____

H.O.T.   **FOCUS ON HIGHER ORDER THINKING**

Work Area

27. Explain the Error To determine if the data represents a quadratic model, Jeff looks at the difference in the consecutive y-values: 50, 56, 62, 68.

x (miles)	7	8	9	10	11
y (cents)	183	233	289	351	419

He decides that since the differences are not constant, the model is not quadratic. Explain the mistake he made.

_____

_____

28. Justify Reasoning Half-life is the amount of time it takes for a quantity to decrease to half of its value. The table shows how much of the original amount of a decaying substance will remain after x hours.

x (hours)	0	1	2	3	4	5
y (amount of original quantity remaining)	1	$\frac{1}{2}$	$\frac{1}{4}$	$\frac{1}{8}$	$\frac{1}{16}$	$\frac{1}{32}$

    a. Is the data linear, quadratic, or exponential?_____

    b. Does the data show a common difference or a common ratio? What is that value? _____

    c. Suppose that you had only the first three columns of data. Could another type of function model the data? Explain.

    _____

    _____

    _____

Ready to Go On?

17.1–17.3 Transformations of Quadratic Functions

1. The function $f(x) = x^2$ is stretched vertically by a factor of 3, translated 2 units to the right, and translated 3 units down.

   Write the equation of the transformed function. _____

17.4 Characteristics of Quadratic Functions

2. Given the quadratic function $f(x) = 2(x + 3.5)^2 - 4.5$, find the equation of the axis of symmetry and the zeros. Determine whether the function has a maximum or minimum value and give that value.

   _____

17.5 Solving Quadratic Equations Graphically

3. Solve $4x^2 + 8x = 32$ by graphing. _____

4. The height of a fireworks rocket launched from a platform 35 meters above the ground can be approximated by $h = -5t^2 + 30t + 35$, where h is the height in meters and t is the time in seconds. Use a graph to find the time it

   takes the rocket to reach the ground after it is launched. _____

17.6 Solving Systems of Linear and Quadratic Equations

Solve each system of equations algebraically.

5. $2x + y = 4; y = x^2 - 2x + 1$

6. $y = 3x - 2; x^2 - y = 6$

   _____   _____

17.7 Comparing Linear, Exponential, and Quadratic Models

7. Describe the end behavior of $y = -x^2 + 3x - 4$ (a) as x increases,

   and (b) as x decreases. _____

   _____

8. What type of function models the data set given by the points $(1, 9)$, $(2, 18)$,

   $(3, 36)$, and $(4, 72)$? _____

ESSENTIAL QUESTION

9. What information does the graph of a quadratic function give you about

   the function? _____

MODULE 17
MIXED REVIEW

Assessment Readiness

Personal
Math Trainer

Online Practice
and Help

my.hrw.com

1. Consider each function. Does the value of the function increase faster than the value of $f(x) = 3x^2 + 6$ as x approaches infinity?

   Select Yes or No for A–C.

   A. $g(x) = 2^x + 6$ ◯ Yes   ◯ No

   B. $h(x) = 5^x + 6$ ◯ Yes   ◯ No

   C. $k(x) = 8x + 6$ ◯ Yes   ◯ No

2. The coordinate plane shows the graph of a quadratic function.

   Choose True or False for each statement.

   A. The function has two zeros.   ◯ True   ◯ False

   B. The maximum value of the function is -2.   ◯ True   ◯ False

   C. The graph is a translation and a vertical stretch of $f(x) = x^2$.   ◯ True   ◯ False

   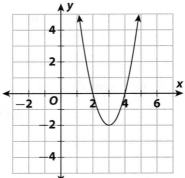

3. The function $h(t) = -16t^2 + 24t + 5$ models the height in feet of a volleyball t seconds after Ashanti hits it. Her teammate Marina spikes the ball from a height of 6 feet as the ball is on its way down. To the nearest tenth of a second, how long after Ashanti hits the ball does Marina spike it? Explain how to use a graphing calculator to solve this problem.

4. The two-way frequency table shows the results of a poll about whether people like a particular television show. Is there any association between a person's age and whether he or she likes the television show? Explain your reasoning.

	Likes Show		
Age	**Yes**	**No**	**Total**
Adult	38	42	80
Child	74	46	120
Total	112	88	200

Piecewise and Absolute Value Functions

? **ESSENTIAL QUESTION**

How do piecewise functions differ from other types of functions?

Real-World Video

Optimizing sales prices is key to running a successful retail business. Cost and pricing structures are rarely linear, instead taking 'jumps' at certain price points.

my.hrw.com

GO DIGITAL
my.hrw.com

my.hrw.com

Go digital with your write-in student edition, accessible on any device.

Math On the Spot

Scan with your smart phone to jump directly to the online edition, video tutor, and more.

Animated Math

Interactively explore key concepts to see how math works.

Personal Math Trainer

Get immediate feedback and help as you work through practice sets.

Are YOU Ready?

Complete these exercises to review skills you will need for this module.

Graph Linear Functions

EXAMPLE Graph the equation $y = -3x + 5$.

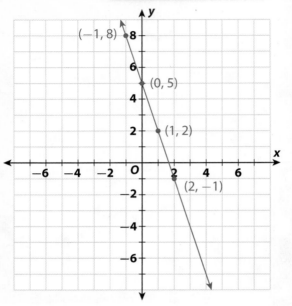

1. Substitute $x = 1$ into the equation.
   $y = -3(x) + 5$
   $y = -3(1) + 5$
   $y = -3 + 5$
   $y = 2$, so the point $(1, 2)$ is on the graph.

2. Repeat step 1 to find other points on the graph. Fill in the table shown.

x	1	0	−1	2
y	2	5	8	−1

3. Graph the points on the scale.

Graph the following equations on the grid shown.

1. $y = 2x + 1$

x	−1	0	1	2
y			3	

2. $y = -4x + 2$

x	−1	0	1	2
y				

3. $y = -2$

x	− 1	0	1	2
y				

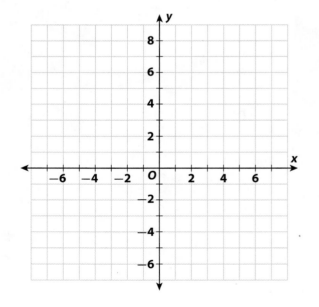

Reading Start-Up

Visualize Vocabulary

Use the Review Words to complete the Pyramid Chart. Write one word in each box.

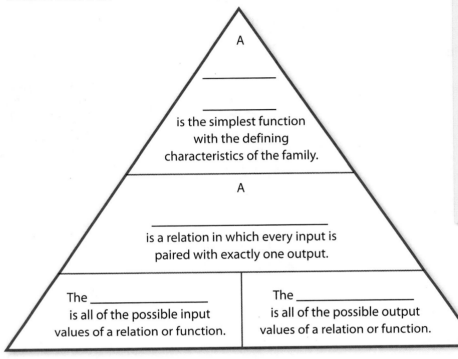

A _____

_____ is the simplest function with the defining characteristics of the family.

A

_____ is a relation in which every input is paired with exactly one output.

The _____ is all of the possible input values of a relation or function.

The _____ is all of the possible output values of a relation or function.

Vocabulary

Review Words

absolute value *(valor absoluto)*

✔ domain *(dominio)*

✔ function *(función)*

integer *(entero)*

✔ parent function *(función de padres)*

✔ range *(rango)*

Preview Words

absolute value function

greatest integer function

piecewise function

step function

vertex

Understand Vocabulary

To become familiar with some of the vocabulary terms in the module, consider the following. You may refer to the module, the glossary, or a dictionary.

1. The word *absolute* refers to an item that is not reduced or diminished in any way. How do you think this definition relates to an **absolute value function**?

_____

2. The *step* is a discrete, discontinuous item that is separate from other items in a relation. What do you think a **step function** might be?

_____

Active Reading

Three-Panel Flip Chart Before beginning the module, create a three-panel flip chart to help you organize what you learn. Label each flap with one of the lesson titles from this module. As you study each lesson, write important information like vocabulary and examples under the appropriate flap.

Piecewise and Absolute Value Functions

Understanding the standards and the vocabulary terms in the standards will help you know exactly what you are expected to learn in this module.

COMMON CORE F.IF.7b

Graph square root, cube root, and piecewise-defined functions, including step functions and absolute value functions.

Key Vocabulary

piecewise function
(función a tramos)
A number or product of numbers and variables with whole-number exponents, or a polynomial with one term.

What It Means to You

You can see what a piecewise function looks like.

EXAMPLE F.IF.7B

The bank gives no interest for any account that has less than $1000 in it. Accounts of $1000 or greater are paid 3 percent interest. How do the rules for the function vary?

The function has two separate rules. Below $1000 one rule of no interest applies. At $1000 or more a, rule of 3 percent interest applies. A function with at least two different rules is a piecewise function.

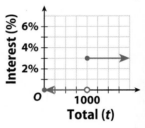

COMMON CORE F.BF.3

Identify the effect on the graph of replacing $f(x)$ by $f(x) + k$, $k\,f(x)$, $f(kx)$, and $f(x + k)$ for specific values of k (both positive and negative); find the value of k given the graphs. Experiment with cases and illustrate an explanation of the effects on the graph using technology.

What It Means to You

Glynnis created the graph shown by graphing $y = \frac{1}{2}x$, $y = x$, $y = 2x$, and $y = 4x$ all on the same grid. What pattern did she observe?

EXAMPLE F.BF.3

Glynnis realized that increasing the coefficient in front of x in the equation for each line increased the slope of the line.

From that, Glynnis could see that, for example, $y = 10x$ would be an extremely steep line, while $y = \frac{1}{10}x$ would be a line that was almost horizontal.

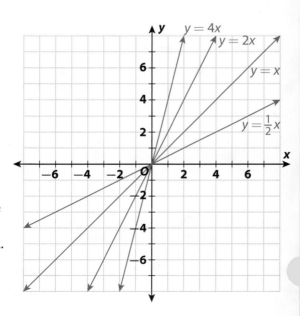

Visit **my.hrw.com** to see all **Common Core Standards** unpacked.

⟳ my.hrw.com

COMMON CORE **F.IF.7b**

Graph square root, cube root, and piecewise-defined functions, including step functions and absolute value functions. *Also A.CED.2, F.BF.1, F.IF.2, F.IF.4, F.IF.5, F.IF.7*

? **ESSENTIAL QUESTION**

How are piecewise functions different from other functions?

Evaluating and Graphing Piecewise Functions

A piecewise function has different rules for different parts of its domain. To evaluate a piecewise function for a given value of *x*, substitute the value of *x* into the rule for the part of the domain that includes *x*.

Math On the Spot

my.hrw.com

EXAMPLE 1

COMMON CORE **F.IF.7b**

A piecewise function is defined by $f(x) = \begin{cases} -x & \text{if } x < 0 \\ x+1 & \text{if } x \geq 0 \end{cases}$.

A brace is used to write a piecewise function.

A Find $f(-3)$, $f(4)$, $f(0.2)$, and $f(0)$.

$f(-3) = -(-3)$ $-3 < 0$, so use the rule $f(x) = -x$.

    $= 3$ Write the value.

$f(4) = (4) + 1$ $4 \geq 0$, so use the rule $f(x) = x + 1$.

    $= 5$ Write the value.

$f(0.2) = (0.2) + 1$ $0.2 \geq 0$, so use the rule $f(x) = x + 1$.

    $= 1.2$ Write the value.

$f(0) = (0) + 1$ $0 \geq 0$, so use the rule $f(x) = x + 1$.

    $= 1$ Write the value.

My Notes

B Make a table of values for the function, then use the table to make a graph.

x	−3	−2	−1	−0.9	−0.1
f(x)	3	2	1	0.9	0.1

x	0	0.1	0.9	1	2
f(x)	1	1.1	1.9	2	3

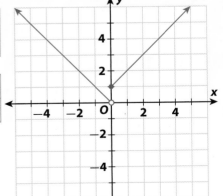

1. Graph the function defined by

$$f(x) = \begin{cases} -x - 2 & \text{if } x < 0 \\ x + 4 & \text{if } x \geq 0 \end{cases}.$$

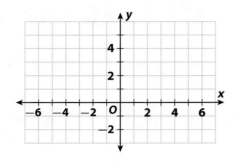

Evaluating and Graphing the Greatest Integer Function

The **greatest integer function** is the piecewise function defined so that $f(x)$ is the greatest integer less than or equal to x, represented by $[x]$. For example, $f(-2.1) = [-2.1] = -3$ since -3 is the greatest integer less than or equal to -2.1.

EXAMPLE 2

COMMON CORE   F.IF.7b

Make a table and graph $f(x) = [x]$.

x	5	3.9	3.1	0.99	−0.2	−0.5	−2.1	−4.8
f(x)	5	3	3	0	−1	−1	−3	−5

Math Talk

Mathematical Practices

Explain why $f(-0.2) = -1$.

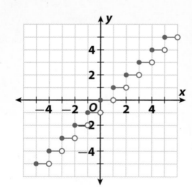

2. Graph the function defined by
$f(x) = -[x]$.

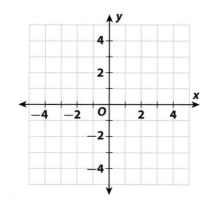

Writing and Graphing a Piecewise Function

Some real-world situations can be represented using piecewise functions.

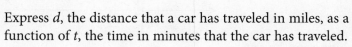

EXAMPLE 3 | COMMON CORE F.IF.4

A team of engineering students have entered a contest for solar-powered electric cars. The cars must travel at a speed of 0.05 miles per minute for 3 minutes to reach a light source to recharge, stop for 1 minute to recharge, then increase their speed to 0.10 miles per minute for the final 2 minutes of their performance. Define and graph a function for the distance and time requirements.

Express d, the distance that a car has traveled in miles, as a function of t, the time in minutes that the car has traveled.

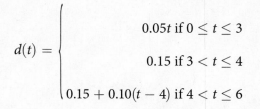

$$d(t) = \begin{cases} 0.05t \text{ if } 0 \le t \le 3 \\ 0.15 \text{ if } 3 < t \le 4 \\ 0.15 + 0.10(t-4) \text{ if } 4 < t \le 6 \end{cases}$$

For the first 3 minutes, the car travels at 0.05 miles/min.

For the next 1 minute, distance is constant ($3 \times 0.05 = 0.15$).

For the final 2 minutes, the car travels at 0.10 miles/min

My Notes

Make a table of values for $d(t)$.

t	1	2	2.5	3	3.5	4	4.5	5	6
$d(t)$	0.05	0.1	0.125	0.15	0.15	0.15	0.20	0.25	0.35

Graph the function.

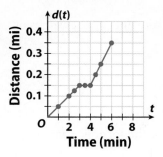

YOUR TURN

3. The cost of admission to a state fair is $4 for children less than 12 years old and $8 for everyone 12 and older. Define and graph a piecewise function that gives the cost of admission for a person who is x years old.

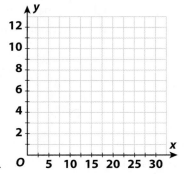

Personal Math Trainer

Online Practice and Help

my.hrw.com

Writing a Piecewise Function for a Graph

To define the piecewise function represented by a graph, write a rule for each part of the graph, and indicate the part of the domain to which each rule applies.

EXAMPLE 4

COMMON CORE · F.BF.1

Define a piecewise function represented by the graph.

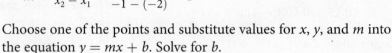

STEP 1   Write an equation for the ray on the left in the form $y = mx + b$.

Find the slope m of the ray on the left. Use the points $(-2, 0)$ and $(-1, 1)$ and the slope formula.

$$m = \frac{y_2 - y_1}{x_2 - x_1} = \frac{1 - 0}{-1 - (-2)} = 1$$

Choose one of the points and substitute values for x, y, and m into the equation $y = mx + b$. Solve for b.

$$y = mx + b$$
$$0 = (1)(-2) + b \qquad \text{Use } m = 1 \text{ and } (-2, 0).$$
$$0 = -2 + b$$
$$b = 2 \qquad\qquad \text{Solve for } b.$$

Write the general form of the equation by substituting the values of m and b into the equation $y = mx + b$.

$$y = mx + b$$
$$y = x + 2$$

STEP 2   Write an equation for the ray on the right in the form $y = mx + b$.

Find the slope m using points $(3, 3)$ and $(2, 3)$.

$$m = \frac{y_2 - y_1}{x_2 - x_1} = \frac{3 - 3}{3 - 2} = \frac{0}{1} = 0$$

Choose one of the points and substitute values for x, y, and m into the equation $y = mx + b$. Solve for b.

$$y = mx + b$$
$$3 = (0)(3) + b \qquad \text{Use } m = 0 \text{ and } (3, 3).$$
$$b = 3 \qquad\qquad\quad \text{Solve for } b.$$

Write the general form of the equation by substituting the values of m and b into the equation $y = mx + b$.

$$y = mx + b$$
$$y = (0)x + 3$$
$$y = 3$$

STEP 3 Determine the domain for each part of the function.

Since the point $(-1, 1)$ is part of the ray on the left, the domain for the part of the function defined by $f(x) = x + 2$ is the set of real numbers less than or equal to -1.

The domain for the part of the graph on the right, which is defined by $f(x) = 3$, is the set of real numbers greater than -1.

This graph jumps from the ray on the left to the ray on the right at $x = -1$. This is called a point of discontinuity, a point where a graph is not continuous.

STEP 4 Define a piecewise function represented by the graph.

$$f(x) = \begin{cases} x + 2 & \text{if } x \leq -1 \\ 3 & \text{if } x > -1 \end{cases}$$

REFLECT

4. **Analyze Relationships** Which rule applies when the graph crosses the y-axis? The x-axis?

_____

_____

_____

YOUR TURN

5. Write an equation for the part of the graph on the left in the form $y = mx + b$.

_____

6. Write an equation for the part of the graph on the right in the form $y = mx + b$.

_____

7. Define a piecewise function represented by the graph.

_____

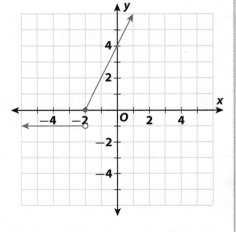

Personal
Math Trainer

Online Practice
and Help

my.hrw.com

For each function, find $f(2)$, $f(1)$, $f(0)$, $f(-2)$, and $f(-3)$.
Then graph the function. (Example 1)

1. $f(x) = \begin{cases} -x + 1 & \text{if } x < 1 \\ x & \text{if } x \geq 1 \end{cases}$

2. $f(x) = \begin{cases} -1 & \text{if } x \leq -1 \\ 2x + 2 & \text{if } x > -1 \end{cases}$

_____

_____

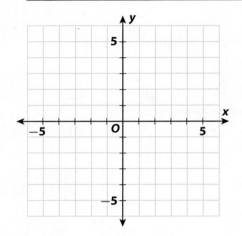

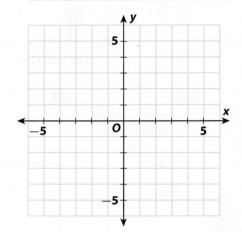

Complete the table for $f(x) = 2[x]$. Then graph the function. (Example 2)

3.

x	1	1.2	0.9	−1.2	−2.1
f(x)	2				

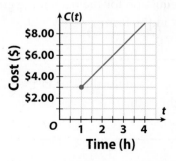

4. A parking garage charges \$3 to park a car for less than 1 hour. The cost for parking for 1 hour or more is shown in the graph. (Examples 3 and 4)

a. Graph the part of the function representing the cost of parking in the garage during the first hour.

b. Use the points $(2, 5)$ and $(3, 7)$ to write an equation for $C(t)$, the cost in dollars for parking t hours, when $t \geq 1$.

_____

c. $C(t) = \begin{cases} \underline{\qquad} & \text{if } t < 1 \\ \underline{\qquad} & \text{if } t \geq 1 \end{cases}$

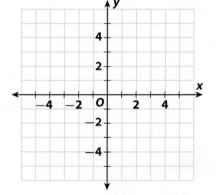

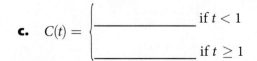

ESSENTIAL QUESTION CHECK-IN

5. How are piecewise functions different from other functions?

_____

18.1 Independent Practice

 COMMON CORE A.CED.2, F.BF.1, F.IF.2, F.IF.4, F.IF.5, F.IF.7, F.IF.7a

Personal Math Trainer

Online Practice and Help

my.hrw.com

Graph each function.

6. $f(x) = \begin{cases} 3 & \text{if } x < -2 \\ x & \text{if } x \geq -2 \end{cases}$

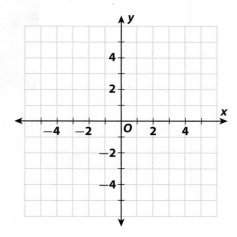

7. $f(x) = \begin{cases} 3x & \text{if } x \leq 2 \\ -3x + 8 & \text{if } x > 2 \end{cases}$

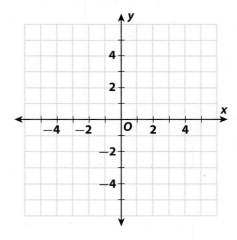

Define a piecewise function represented by the graph.

8. $f(x) = \Big\{$ _____

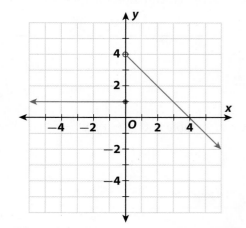

9. $f(x) = \Big\{$ _____

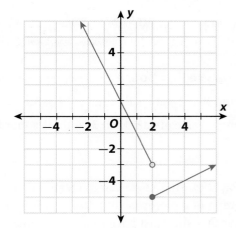

10. **Explain the Error** Deena looked at the functions shown in Exercises 6 through 9 and concluded that the domain of any piecewise function is the set of all real numbers. Is she correct? Explain.

_____

_____

_____

_____

11. Represent Real-World Problems At Maston Lake you can rent a kayak for $16 for the first 2 hours. Time greater than 2 hours is charged a rate of $4 an hour.

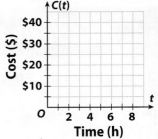

a. Make a graph representing $C(t)$, the cost in dollars of renting a kayak for t hours.

b. Write an equation for the part of the function where $0 < t \le 2$.

_____

c. Write an equation for the part of the function where $t > 2$.

_____

d. $C(t) = \begin{cases} \underline{\hspace{2cm}} & \text{if } t \le 2 \\ \underline{\hspace{2cm}} & \text{if } t > 2 \end{cases}$

12. Create a table and graph $f(x) = -2[x]$. Then graph the function.

x					
f(x)					

x					
f(x)					

H.O.T. **FOCUS ON HIGHER ORDER THINKING**

13. Analyze Relationships Use the piecewise function $f(x) = \begin{cases} 6 & \text{if } x > 3 \\ 5x - 4 & \text{if } x \le 3 \end{cases}$. Find two x-values that have the same value of $f(x)$ with one x-value less than 3, one x-value greater than 3, and the sum of the x-values as 11.

Work Area

_____

14. Explain the Error Margo created this graph of a piecewise function. Emilio told her that she must have made a mistake. Did Margo make a mistake? Explain.

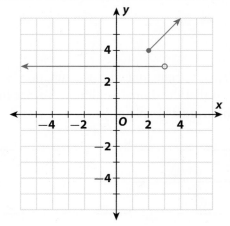

_____

_____

_____

_____

LESSON
18.2

COMMON CORE F.IF.7b

Graph square root, cube root, and piecewise-defined functions, including step functions and absolute value functions. *Also F.IF.4, F.IF.7, F.BF.3*

Absolute Value Functions

? **ESSENTIAL QUESTION**

What are the characteristics of an absolute value function?

EXPLORE ACTIVITY COMMON CORE F.IF.7b

Evaluating and Graphing Absolute Value Functions

As you just learned, a piecewise function has different rules for different parts of its domain. Is the absolute value function a piecewise function? Let's explore the properties of the absolute value function, $f(x) = |x|$.

A When $x \geq 0$: $|x| = x$ — — — — — — — — — — — *Example:* $|3| = $ _____

When $x < 0$: $|x| = $ _____ — — — — *Example:* $|-3| = -(-3) = $ _____

This can be expressed as a piecewise function: $f(x) = |x| = \begin{cases} -x \text{ if } x < 0 \\ x \text{ if } x \geq 0 \end{cases}$

B Complete the tables.

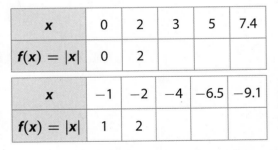

x	0	2	3	5	7.4
$f(x) = |x|$	0	2			

x	−1	−2	−4	−6.5	−9.1
$f(x) = |x|$	1	2			

The function $f(x) = |x|$ is the parent function of absolute value functions. The graphs of absolute value functions are transformations of the graph you drew in part C.

C Graph the absolute value function, $f(x) = |x|$.

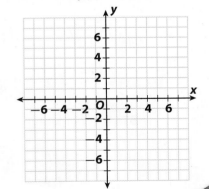

Math Talk
Mathematical Practices

How do you think the "parent function" for absolute value got its name? Discuss.

REFLECT

1. What is the domain and range of the function $f(x) = |x|$? Explain.

_____

_____

_____

2. **Look for a Pattern** With respect to shape and symmetry, what kind of pattern does the graph of $f(x) = |x|$ display?

_____

Characteristics of Absolute Value Functions

The graphs of absolute value functions have some features in common.

- The graphs are composed of two rays that meet at a common point, called the vertex. The vertex for both of the graphs in Example 1 is (0, 2).
- The graphs are V-shaped and symmetrical across a vertical line passing through the vertex.

EXAMPLE 1

COMMON CORE   F.IF.7b

Graph each function.

My Notes

A $f(x) = |x| + 2$

> **STEP 1** Make a table.

x	0	1	−1	2	−2	5	−5
$f(x) = |x| + 2$	2	3	3	4	4	7	7

> **STEP 2** Graph the points.

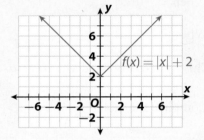

B $f(x) = -|x| + 2$

> **STEP 1** Make a table.

x	0	1	−1	2	−2	6	−6
$f(x) = -|x| + 2$	2	1	1	0	0	−4	−4

> **STEP 2** Graph the points.

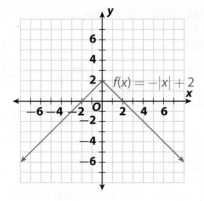

REFLECT

3. **Analyze Relationships** How are the graphs in part A and part B related?

_____

4. Graph $f(x) = -|x| + 1$.

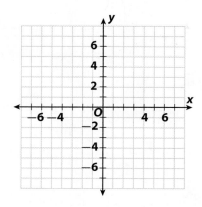

Transformations of Absolute Value Functions

Graphing multiple absolute value functions can help you see how they are related to the parent function $f(x) = |x|$.

EXAMPLE 2
COMMON CORE F.IF.7b

Graph each set of functions on the same coordinate plane. Find the vertex, domain, and range of each function.

Ⓐ $g(x) = |x| + 5$, $h(x) = |x| - 4$, $k(x) = |x| + 1$.

x	0	1	−1	2	−2	7	−7
$g(x) = |x| + 5$	5	6	6	7	7	12	12

x	0	1	−1	3	−3	5	−6
$h(x) = |x| - 4$	−4	−3	−3	−1	−1	1	2

x	0	1	−1	2	−2	5	−5
$k(x) = |x| + 1$	1	2	2	3	3	6	6

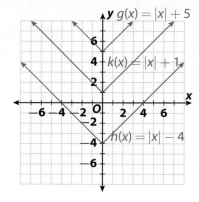

$g(x)$ vertex: $(0, 5)$
domain: all real numbers
range: $y \geq 5$

$h(x)$ vertex: $(0, -4)$
domain: all real numbers
range: $y \geq -4$

$k(x)$ vertex: $(0, 1)$
domain: all real numbers
range: $y \geq 1$

> Each graph is a vertical translation of the parent function.

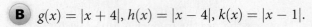

B $g(x) = |x + 4|$, $h(x) = |x - 4|$, $k(x) = |x - 1|$.

x	0	1	−1	2	−2	7	−7
$g(x) = |x + 4|$	4	5	3	6	2	11	3

x	0	1	−1	3	−3	5	−5
$h(x) = |x - 4|$	4	3	5	1	7	1	9

x	0	1	−1	2	−2	5	−5
$k(x) = |x - 1|$	1	0	2	1	3	4	6

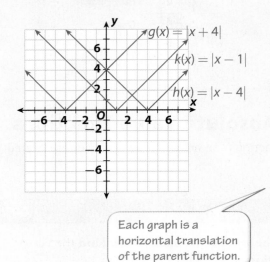

Each graph is a horizontal translation of the parent function.

$g(x)$ vertex: $(-4, 0)$
domain: all real numbers
range: nonnegative real numbers

$h(x)$ vertex: $(4, 0)$
domain: all real numbers
range: nonnegative real numbers

$k(x)$ vertex: $(1, 0)$
domain: all real numbers
range: nonnegative real numbers

REFLECT

5. How does adding a constant value k to the parent function affect the graph?

_____

_____

_____

_____

6. How does subtracting a constant value h from x in the parent function affect the graph?

_____

_____

_____

_____

7. Make a Conjecture Complete the following statements.

For $f(x) = |x| + k$, the vertex is $(0, \boxed{})$.

For $f(x) = |x - h|$, the vertex is $(\boxed{}, 0)$.

YOUR TURN

8. Graph $f(x) = |x| + 3$, $g(x) = |x| - 3$, and $h(x) = |x| - 5$ on the same coordinate plane. Give the domain and range of each function.

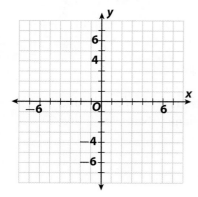

_____

_____

_____

9. Graph $f(x) = |x + 1|$, $g(x) = |x - 5|$, and $h(x) = |x + 5|$ on the same coordinate plane. Give the domain and range of each function.

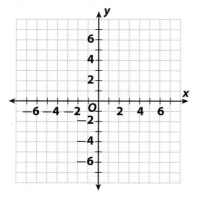

_____

_____

_____

_____

For 1–2, use the same coordinate plane.

1. Complete the table of values for the function $f(x) = |x| + 2$. Graph the function on the coordinate plane. (Example 1)

x	0	1	−1	2	−2
$f(x) = |x| + 2$	2		3		

x	3	−3	5	−5	−7
$f(x) = |x| + 2$					9

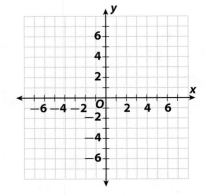

2. Complete the table of values for the functions $g(x) = |x - 3|$ and $h(x) = -|x| + 1$. Graph both functions on the coordinate plane. (Examples 2 and 3)

x	0	1	−1	2	−2	3	−3	4	−4	6
$g(x) = |x - 3|$	3									

x	0	1	−1	2	−2	3	−3	5	−5	6
$h(x) = -|x| + 1$	1									

3. Find the vertex, domain, and range for the function $f(x) = |x| + 2$ from Exercise 1. (Examples 2 and 3)

vertex: _____

domain: _____

range: _____

4. Find the vertex, domain, and range for the function $g(x) = |x - 3|$ from Exercise 2. (Examples 2 and 3)

vertex: _____

domain: _____

range: _____

? ESSENTIAL QUESTION CHECK-IN

5. What are the characteristics of the graph of an absolute value function?

_____

_____

_____

_____

18.2 Independent Practice

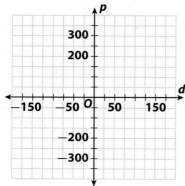

Personal Math Trainer

Online Practice and Help

my.hrw.com

COMMON CORE F.IF.4, F.IF.7, F.IF.7b, F.BF.3

Graph each function. Identify the vertex, domain, and range.

6. $f(x) = |x| - 3$

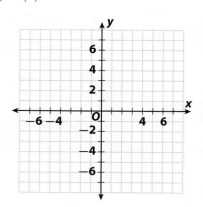

vertex: _____

domain: _____

range: _____

_____

7. $g(x) = |x + 3|$

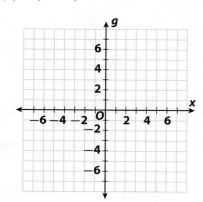

vertex: _____

domain: _____

range: _____

_____

8. Represent Real-World Problems Montague National Bank is running a promotion in which customers get points for any transaction that can be redeemed for prizes. Each transaction is awarded points equal to double the absolute value of its dollar value plus 100 bonus points.

a. Write an absolute value function where $p(d)$ represents the number of points that are awarded when a transaction of d dollars is made.

_____

b. Complete the table of values for $p(d)$.

d	+50	−50	+70	−70	6	−6
p(d)						

c. Graph $p(d)$.

9. The speedometer on a car shows that the car is going 60 miles per hour. The function $e(x)$ defined by $e(x) = |x - 60|$ represents the error in the speed that the speedometer shows, where x is the actual speed of the car in miles per hour. For example, if your actual speed is 70 miles per hour, the error in the speedometer display is $e(70) = |70 - 60| = |10| = 10$ miles per hour. Graph the function.

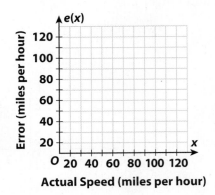

Work Area

10. Explain the Error Terry is checking Randi's work. His comments are in red.

> Name: Randi Manietti
>
> #7 $f(x) = |x| - 5$
>
> $f(3) = -2$
>
> Incorrect! Absolute value functions have no negative values.

Which student is correct? Explain.

_____

_____

_____

_____

11. Critical Thinking Give an example of an absolute value function that has only negative function values. Explain why all function values are negative.

_____

_____

_____

_____

LESSON 18.3 Transforming Absolute Value Functions

COMMON CORE **F.BF.3**

Identify the effect on the graph of replacing $f(x)$ by $f(x) + k$, $k\,f(x)$, $f(kx)$, and $f(x + k)$ for specific values of k (both positive and negative); find the value of k given the graphs. Experiment with cases and illustrate an explanation of the effects on the graph using technology. *Also F.IF.7, F.IF.7b*

ESSENTIAL QUESTION

What is the effect of changing the parameters of an absolute value function?

EXPLORE ACTIVITY 1

COMMON CORE **F.BF.3**

Graphing Absolute Value Functions on a Graphing Calculator

You have learned how to graph an absolute value function by hand using ordered pairs from a table. Now try graphing the parent absolute value function, $f(x) = |x|$, on a graphing calculator.

Recall that the graph of the *parent function* of absolute value functions is a V-shaped graph with its vertex at the point $(0, 0)$.

A Graph the absolute value function, $y = |x|$.

STEP 1 Enter the function as Y_1 by pressing **MATH** and using the Num menu. Choose the absolute value operation.

STEP 2 When you return to the function editor screen, type X after the parenthesis.

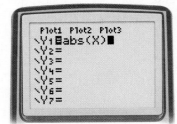

STEP 3 Press **GRAPH** to display the graph of $y = |x|$. Sketch the graph on the screen provided.

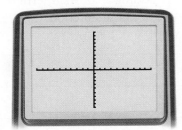

B Now use your calculator to change the parameters of the parent function, $y = |x|$.

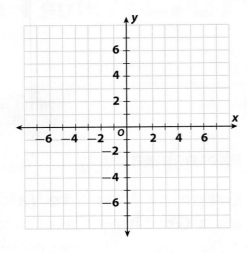

STEP 1 First add a constant to the parent function. Use your calculator to graph $y = |x| + 1$, $y = |x| + 4$, and $y = |x| - 5$, on the same graph. Sketch the graphs on the grid. Make sure that you place the vertex of each graph accurately.

STEP 2 Now add a constant within the absolute value bars. Use your calculator to graph: $y = |x + 2|$, $y = |x - 6|$, and $y = |x + 6|$ on the same graph. Sketch the graphs on the grid.

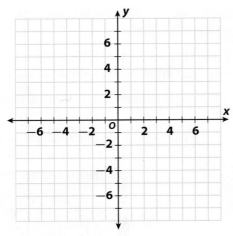

STEP 3 Now choose one of the functions from Step 1 or 2 above, but change the sign of the absolute value term. For example, you might choose to graph: $y = -|x| + 4$ and $y = -|x - 6|$. Sketch the graphs on the grid.

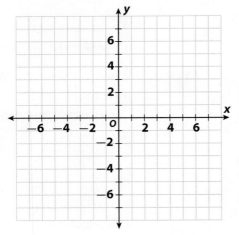

Math Talk

Mathematical Practices

How does changing the absolute value term from positive to negative affect the graph of an absolute value function?

REFLECT

1. **Draw Conclusions** How does adding a constant term outside of the absolute value bars shift the graph of the function?

_____

_____

_____

2. Draw Conclusions How does adding a constant *inside* of the bars shift the graph of the function?

_____

_____

_____

COMMON CORE F.BF.3

Graphing Absolute Value Functions With Coefficients

You have seen how adding a constant to an absolute value function changes the graph of the function. Now you will explore the effects that coefficients of the absolute value term have on the graph.

Math Talk
Mathematical Practices

How are the slopes of the rays that make up the graphs related to the coefficient of $|x|$?

A Use your calculator to graph $y = 2|x|$, $y = -3|x|$, and $y = 5|x|$ on the same graph. Sketch the graphs on the grid.

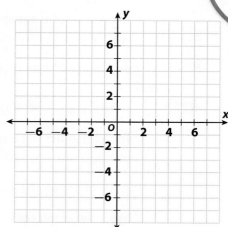

B Now see how fractional coefficients change the graphs. Graph $y = \frac{1}{2}|x|$, $y = \frac{1}{6}|x|$, and $y = \frac{3}{4}|x|$. Sketch the graphs on the grid.

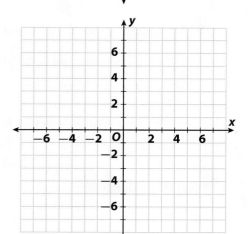

REFLECT

3. Draw Conclusions How do coefficients that are greater than 1 or less than −1 change the graph of an absolute value function?

_____

_____

4. Draw Conclusions How do fractional coefficients between −1 and 1 but not equal to 0 change the graph of an absolute value function?

_____

_____

Writing Equations Using Parameters

If you are given the graph of an absolute value function, you can write a rule for the function by identifying the parameters that have been used to transform the graph of the parent function. Start with the general form $f(x) = a|x - h| + k$ and substitute for the values of a, h, and k.

My Notes

EXAMPLE 1

COMMON CORE F.BF.3

Write a function rule for the graph shown.

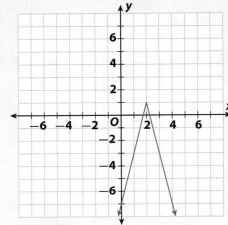

STEP 1 Identify the coordinates of the vertex.

The vertex of the graph is (2, 1).

So $h = 2$ and $k = 1$.

STEP 2 Identify the slope of the rays.

Recall that the slope is the rise over the run.

slope of ray on left $= \frac{4}{1} = 4$; slope of ray on right $= -\frac{4}{1} = -4$

Since the graph opens downward, a is negative. Therefore, $a = -4$.

STEP 3 Substitute for a, h, and k in the general form.

$f(x) = a|x - h| + k$

$f(x) = -4|x - 2| + 1$

So, the function that is graphed is $f(x) = -4|x - 2| + 1$.

YOUR TURN

5. Write a function rule for the graph shown.

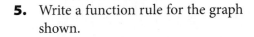

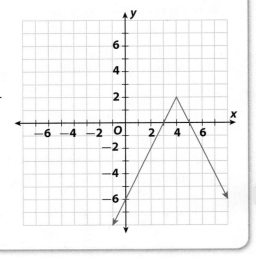

Graphing Using Parameters

EXAMPLE 2

Math On the Spot
my.hrw.com

Graph $f(x) = 2|x + 4| - 3$ without using a calculator or a table of values.

STEP 1 Identify h and k and identify the vertex of the graph.

The general form of an absolute value equation is $f(x) = a|x - h| + k$.

So $h = -4$ and $k = -3$.

The vertex of the graph is $(-4, -3)$.

STEP 2 Plot the vertex.

STEP 3 Identify a and use it to graph the rays.

$a = 2$. So the graph opens upward.

The slope of the ray on the left is -2.

The slope of the ray on the right is 2.

Graph the rays.

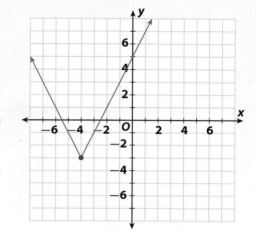

YOUR TURN

6. Graph $f(x) = -3|x - 3| + 5$ without using a calculator or a table of values.

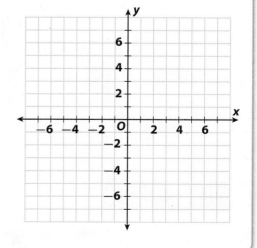

Personal Math Trainer

Online Practice and Help

my.hrw.com

Use a calculator to graph both functions. Then sketch the functions on the coordinate plane. (Explore Activities 1 and 2)

1. $f(x) = |x| - 5$ and $g(x) = \frac{1}{2}|x| - 3$

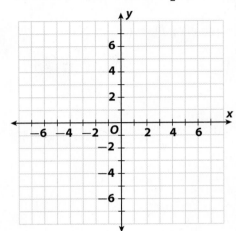

2. $g(x) = -2|x + 3|$ and $f(x) = 3|x - 4| + 1$

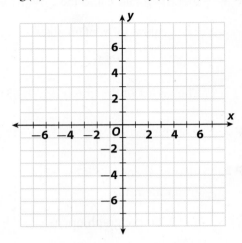

Find the vertex, the value of a, and a rule for the function represented by each graph. (Example 1)

3.

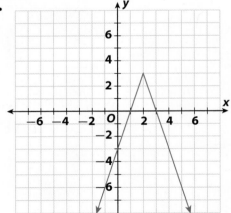

Vertex: _____

a: _____

$f(x) =$ _____

4.

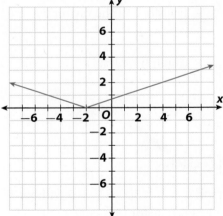

Vertex: _____

a: $\frac{1}{3}$

$g(x) = \frac{1}{3} \cdot$ _____

? ESSENTIAL QUESTION CHECK-IN

5. What is the effect of changing the parameters of an absolute value function?

_____

_____

18.3 Independent Practice

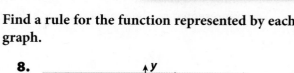

COMMON CORE   F.BF.3

Use a calculator to graph both functions. Then sketch the functions on the coordinate plane.

6. $g(x) = 4|x - 1| - 2$ and
$f(x) = -4|x + 1| + 2$

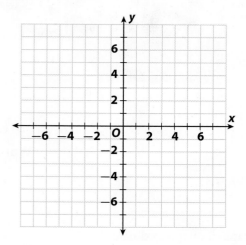

7. $f(x) = f(x) = \frac{1}{5}|x| + 2$ and $g(x) = -\frac{1}{5}|x + 2|$

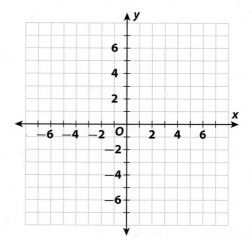

Find a rule for the function represented by each graph.

8.

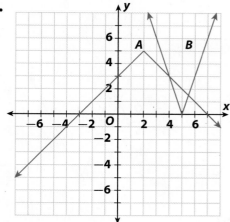

A: $f(x) =$ _____

B: $g(x) =$ _____

9.

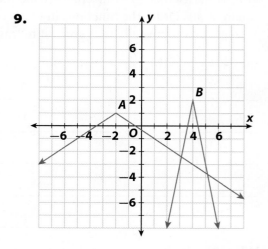

A: $f(x) =$ _____

B: $g(x) =$ _____

10. Explain the Error Ronaldo says that he needs only one piece of information to identify the range of an absolute value function—the constant term added to the absolute value term—such as the 3 in $f(x) = |x| + 3$. Explain Ronaldo's error.

_____

_____

_____

FOCUS ON HIGHER ORDER THINKING

11. **Communicate Mathematical Ideas** Jared drew the diamond shape shown on the coordinate grid by graphing two absolute value functions. What functions are represented by the graphs in Jared's drawing?

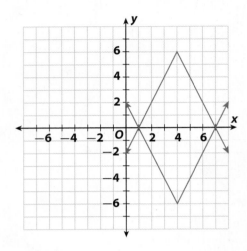

Work Area

12. **Justify Reasoning** Each of the following functions is graphed on a coordinate grid with axes that go from −10 to 10. So the area of the coordinate grid is 400 square units. Order the functions in terms of the amount of area inside the V-shape that is created, from greatest to least. Explain your reasoning.

(a) $f(x) = |x|$ (b) $f(x) = 2|x|$ (c) $f(x) = |x| - 5$ (d) $f(x) = 2|x - 10|$

13. **What If?** Giselle created an absolute value equation whose solutions make a V-shape that opens sideways rather than up or down. How did Giselle do it? Was her equation a function of x? Explain.

LESSON 18.4 Solving Absolute Value Equations and Inequalities

COMMON CORE A.CED.1

Create equations and inequalities in one variable and use them to solve problems.

? ESSENTIAL QUESTION

How do you solve equations and inequalities that involve absolutevalue expressions?

EXPLORE ACTIVITY

COMMON CORE A.REI.11

Solving Absolute Value Equations Graphically

The graphs of three absolute value functions are shown.

Graph A is $f(x) = |x|$.

Graph B is $h(x) = |x - 2|$.

Graph C is $j(x) = |x + 3|$.

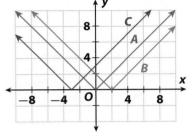

A On the same coordinate grid, graph the function $g(x) = 5$. What type of function is this? Describe its graph.

_____

B At how many points does the graph of $g(x)$ intersect each graph?

Graph A: _____ points of intersection

Graph B: _____ points of intersection

Graph C: _____ points of intersection

C Use the graph to find the x-coordinate of each point of intersection of the graphs of $h(x)$ and $g(x)$. Show that each x-coordinate satisfies the equation $|x - 2| = 5$, which is obtained by setting $h(x)$ equal to $g(x)$.

_____

D Use the graph to find the x-coordinate of each point of intersection of the graphs of $j(x)$ and $g(x)$. Show that each x-coordinate satisfies the equation $|x + 3| = 5$, which is obtained by setting $j(x)$ equal to $g(x)$.

_____

REFLECT

1. Describe how you could solve an equation like $|x + 4| = 9$ graphically.

_____

_____

_____

2. How many points of intersection exist for the graphs of $m(x) = |x| + 3$ and $n(x) = 3$? How many solutions does the equation $|x| + 3 = 3$ have? Explain.

_____

_____

_____

3. How many points of intersection exist for the graphs of $p(x) = |x| + 10$ and $q(x) = 2$? How many solutions does the equation $|x| + 10 = 2$ have? Explain.

_____

_____

_____

Math On the Spot

my.hrw.com

Solving Absolute Value Equations

To solve absolute value equations, perform inverse operations to isolate the absolute value expression. Then you must consider two cases.

Solving an Absolute Value Equation

1. Use inverse operations to isolate the absolute value expression.

2. Rewrite the resulting equation as two cases that do not involve absolute values.

3. Solve the equation in each of the two cases.

EXAMPLE 1

COMMON CORE A.REI.3

Solve each equation.

A $|x| = 4$

$|x| = 4$ *Think: What numbers are 4 units from 0?*

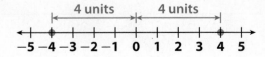

4 units   4 units

$$-5\ -4\ -3\ -2\ -1\ \ 0\ \ 1\ \ 2\ \ 3\ \ 4\ \ 5$$

Case 1	Case 2	*Rewrite the equation as two cases.*
$x = -4$	$x = 4$	

The solutions are -4 and 4.

B $4|x + 2| = 24$

$$\frac{4|x + 2|}{4} = \frac{24}{4}$$ Divide both sides by 4.

$$|x + 2| = 6$$ Think: What numbers are 6 units from 0?

Case 1	Case 2
$x + 2 = -6$	$x + 2 = 6$
$\underline{\quad -2 \quad -2}$	$\underline{\quad -2 \quad -2}$
$x \quad = -8$	$x \quad = 4$

Rewrite the equation as two cases.
Subtract 2 from both sides.

The solutions are -8 and 4.

YOUR TURN

Solve each equation. Check your answer.

4. $|x| - 3 = 4$

5. $8 = |x - 2.5|$

_____   _____

Special Cases of Absolute Value Equations

Not all absolute value equations have two solutions. If the absolute value expression equals 0, there is one solution. If an equation states that an absolute value is negative, there are no solutions.

EXAMPLE 2   COMMON CORE   A.REI.3

Solve each equation.

A $|x + 3| + 4 = 4$

$$|x + 3| + 4 = 4$$
$$\underline{\qquad\quad -4 \quad -4}$$ Subtract 4 from both sides.
$$|x + 3| \quad\; = 0$$

$$x + 3 = 0$$
$$\underline{\quad -3 \quad -3}$$ There is only one case. Subtract 3 from both sides.
$$x \quad\; = -3$$

B $5 = |x + 2| + 8$

$$5 = |x + 2| + 8$$
$$\underline{-8 \qquad\qquad -8}$$ Subtract 8 from both sides.
$$-3 = |x + 2| \;\text{✗}$$ Absolute value cannot be negative.

This equation has no solution.

Solve each equation.

6. $2 - |2x - 5| = 7$

7. $-6 + |x - 4| = -6$

_____

_____

Solving Absolute Value Inequalities

Absolute value inequalities are solved using the same steps as for solving absolute value equations. However, if you divide by a negative number, you must reverse the inequality symbol.

EXAMPLE 3

COMMON CORE A.REI.3

Solve each inequality. Graph the solution.

A $|x| + 3 < 12$

$|x| + 3 - 3 < 12 - 3$ Subtract 3 from both sides.

$|x| < 9$

$x > -9$ AND $x < 9$ Write as two cases.

$-9 < x < 9$

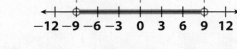

9 units   9 units

−12 −9 −6 −3 0 3 6 9 12

B $|x - 8| + 5 \geq 11$

$|x - 8| + 5 - 5 \geq 11 - 5$ Subtract 5 from both sides.

$|x - 8| \geq 6$

$x - 8 \leq -6$ OR $x - 8 \geq 6$ Write as two cases.

$x - 8 + 8 \leq -6 + 8$ OR $x - 8 + 8 \geq 6 + 8$ Add 8 to both sides.

$x \leq 2$ OR $x \geq 14$

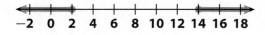

−2 0 2 4 6 8 10 12 14 16 18

Solve each inequality.

8. $2|x| \leq 6$

9. $|x| + 10 > 12$

_____

_____

Solving Real-World Problems

Absolute value equations can be used to model and solve real-world problems.

EXAMPLE 4   COMMON CORE A.REI.3, A.CED.1

Sydney Harbour Bridge in Australia is 1149 meters long. Because of changes in temperature, the bridge can expand or contract by as much as 420 millimeters. Write and solve an absolute value equation to find the minimum and maximum lengths of the bridge.

First convert millimeters to meters: 420 mm = 0.42 m.

The length of the bridge can vary by 0.42 m, so find two numbers that are 0.42 units away from 1149 on a number line.

You can find these numbers by using the absolute value equation $|x - 1149| = 0.42$. Solve the equation by rewriting it as two cases.

Case 1

$x - 1149 = \quad -0.42$

$\underline{+ 1149 \quad + 1149}$

$x \quad = \quad 1148.58$

Case 2

$x - 1149 = \quad 0.42$

$\underline{+ 1149 \quad + 1149}$

$x \quad = \quad 1149.42$

Add 1149 to both sides of each equation.

The minimum length of the bridge is 1148.58 m, and the maximum length is 1149.42 m.

YOUR TURN

10. Sydney Harbour Bridge is 134 meters tall. The height of the bridge can rise or fall by 180 millimeters because of changes in temperature. Write and solve an absolute value equation to find the minimum and maximum heights of the bridge.

_____

_____

11. The diameter of a valve for the space shuttle must be within 0.001 mm of 5 mm. Write and solve an absolute value equation to find the minimum and maximum acceptable diameters of the valve.

_____

_____

Personal Math Trainer

Online Practice and Help

my.hrw.com

Guided Practice

Solve each equation by graphing. (Explore Activity)

1. $|x + 1| = 3$

Graph the functions $f(x) = |x + 1|$

and $g(x) =$ _____ .

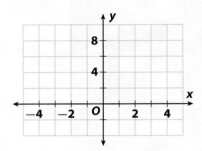

The solutions are $x =$ _____ .

2. $2|x| = 4$

Graph the functions $f(x) =$ _____

and $g(x) =$ _____ .

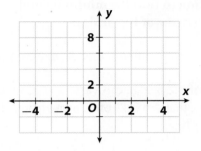

The solutions are $x =$ _____ .

Solve each equation. (Examples 1 and 2)

3. $9 = |x + 5|$

_____

4. $|3x| + 2 = 8$

_____

5. $|x - 3| - 6 = 2$

_____

6. $|x + 4| = -7$

_____

7. $7 = |3x + 9| + 7$

_____

8. $5|x + 7| + 14 = 8$

_____

Solve each inequality. (Example 3)

9. $|3x| + 2 \leq 8$

_____

10. $|x + 2| > 7$

_____

11. $|x - 3| + 2 \geq 4$

_____

12. **Communication** Barry's walkie-talkie has a range of 2 mi. Barry is traveling on a straight highway and is at mile marker 207. Write and solve an absolute value equation to find the minimum and maximum mile marker from 207 that Barry's walkie-talkie will reach. (Example 4)

_____

? ESSENTIAL QUESTION CHECK-IN

13. How do you solve absolute value equations and inequalities?

_____

_____

_____

18.4 Independent Practice

COMMON CORE A.REI.3, A.CED.1

Personal
Math Trainer

Online Practice
and Help

my.hrw.com

Solve each equation or inequality.

14. $|2x - 4| = 22$

15. $18 = 3|x - 1|$

16. $3|x| - 12 = 18$

17. $|x| + 6 = 12 - 6$

18. $|x - 3| + 14 = 5$

19. $3 + |x - 1| = 3$

20. $|x| - 6 > 16$

21. $|x + 1| - 7.8 \leq 6.2$

22. $|x - 5| + 1 \leq 2$

23. The two numbers that are 5 units from 3 on the number line are represented by the equation $|n - 3| = 5$. What are these two numbers? _____

24. Write and solve an absolute value equation that represents two numbers x that are 2 units from 7 on a number line.

_____

25. A brick company guarantees to fill a contractor's order to within 5% accuracy. A contractor orders 1500 bricks. Write and solve an absolute value equation to find the maximum and minimum number of bricks guaranteed.

_____

26. Fill in the missing reasons to justify each step in solving the equation $3|2x + 1| = 21$.

Statements	Reasons
1. $3|2x + 1| = 21$	**1.** Given
2. $|2x + 1| = 7$	**2.**
3. $2x + 1 = -7$ or $2x + 1 = 7$	**3.** Definition of absolute value
4. $2x = -8$ or $2x = 6$	**4.**
5. $x = -4$ or $x = 3$	**5.**

27. A machine prints posters and then trims them to the correct size. The equation $|l - 65.1| = 0.2$ gives the maximum and minimum acceptable lengths for the posters in inches. Does a poster with a length of 64.8 inches fall within the acceptable range? Why or why not?

_____

_____

28. A nutritionist recommends that an adult male consume 55 grams of fat per day. It is acceptable for the fat intake to differ from this amount by at most 25 grams. Write and solve an absolute value inequality to find the range of fat intake that is acceptable.

_____

29. The thermostat for a sauna is set to 175 °F, but the actual temperature of the sauna may vary by as much as 12 °F. Write and solve an absolute value inequality to find the range of possible temperatures.

_____

_____

30. The minimum and maximum sound levels at a rock concert are 90 decibels and 95 decibels. Write an absolute value equation to model the situation.

_____

H.O.T. FOCUS ON HIGHER ORDER THINKING

Work Area

31. Analyze Relationships Tell whether each statement is sometimes, always, or never true. Justify your answer.

a. The value of $|x + 4|$ is equal to the value of $|x| + 4$.

_____

_____

b. The absolute value of a number is nonnegative.

_____

_____

32. Critique Reasoning Do you agree with the following statement: "To solve an absolute value equation, you need to solve two equations." Why or why not?

_____

_____

_____

_____

33. Critical Thinking Is there a value of a for which the equation $|x - a| = 1$ has exactly one solution? Explain.

_____

_____

_____

18.1 Piecewise Functions

1. Graph the function $f(x) = \begin{cases} -2x & \text{if } x < 2 \\ -2x + 2 & \text{if } x \geq 2 \end{cases}$.

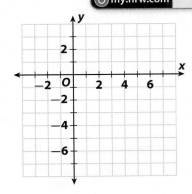

18.2–18.3 Absolute Value Functions/Transforming Absolute Value Functions

2. Graph $f(x) = 3|x| - 5$.

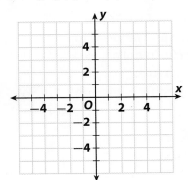

3. Write a rule for the graphed function.

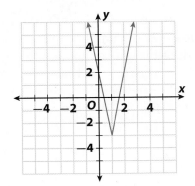

$g(x) = $ _____

18.4 Solving Absolute Value Equations and Inequalities

Solve each equation or inequality.

4. $|2x - 1| = 11$

_____

5. $3|x + 5| < 24$

_____

? ESSENTIAL QUESTION

6. How do piecewise functions differ from other types of functions?

_____

_____

MODULE 18

MIXED REVIEW

Personal
Math Trainer

Online Practice
and Help

my.hrw.com

Assessment Readiness

1. Consider the functions $f(x) = |x|$ and $g(x) = |x - 1| + 3$.

   Which combination of transformations below could be applied to the graph of $f(x) = |x|$ to produce the graph of $g(x) = |x - 1| + 3$? Select all that apply.

   ○ horizontal translation   ○ vertical translation
   ○ reflection across the x-axis   ○ vertical stretch

2. Consider the absolute value function $f(x) = -2|x + 2| + 3$.

   Choose True or False for each statement.

   A. The maximum value of the function is 3.   ○ True   ○ False

   B. The graph is symmetric about the
   line $x = 2$.   ○ True   ○ False

   C. The y-intercept of the function is -1.   ○ True   ○ False

3. To rent a camera, there is a flat fee of $10 plus a daily charge. For the first 3 days, the daily charge is $22 per day. For each day over 3, the daily charge is reduced to $11 per day. Write a piecewise function that gives the total cost $c(d)$ in dollars to rent a camera for d days. Explain how you determined the function rule.

4. The table shows how the number of members in an outdoor club has changed over time. Use a calculator to find an exponential function model for the data. Explain how you know that the model is a good fit.

Month	1	2	3	4	5	6	7	8	9	10
Members	17	22	24	30	39	49	55	68	85	100

Square Root and Cube Root Functions

ESSENTIAL QUESTION

How do the square and cube root function families relate to their graphs?

my.hrw.com

Real-World Video

An audio engineer uses radical functions to calculate sound intensity, which decreases faster than linearly with distance.

GO DIGITAL
my.hrw.com

my.hrw.com

Go digital with your write-in student edition, accessible on any device.

Math On the Spot

Scan with your smart phone to jump directly to the online edition, video tutor, and more.

Animated Math

Interactively explore key concepts to see how math works.

Personal Math Trainer

Get immediate feedback and help as you work through practice sets.

Are YOU Ready?

Complete these exercises to review skills you will need for this module.

Squares and Square Roots

EXAMPLE   Find the square root of 16.
$n = 4$ because $n^2 = 16$.

Finding the square of a number is the inverse operation of finding the square root.

Find the squares of the following numbers.

1. 8

2. -13

3. 50

_____   _____   _____

Find the square roots of the following numbers.

4. 9

5. 144

6. 225

_____   _____   _____

Function Tables

EXAMPLE   Create a function table for $y = 4x - 1$.

x	y
0	−1
1	3
2	7

Insert the x values into the function and solve for y.
$y = 4(0) - 1 = 0 - 1 = -1$

7. Create a function table for $y = \sqrt{x} + 1$.

x	y
0	
1	
4	

8. Create a function table for $y = x^2 - 3$.

x	y
−2	
0	
5	

9. Create a function table for $y = 85$.

x	y
−4	
−2	
9	

10. Create a function table for $y = 5x + 4$.

x	y
−5	
−1	
3	

Reading Start-Up

Vocabulary

Review Words

✔ domain (*dominio*)

✔ inverse (of a function) (*función inversa*)

  parameter (*parámetro*)

  parent function (*función madre*)

✔ range (*rango*)

✔ reflection (*reflexión*)

  translation (*traslación*)

Preview Words

  cube root function

  square root function

Visualize Vocabulary

Use the Review Words to complete the bubble map. You may put only one word in each bubble.

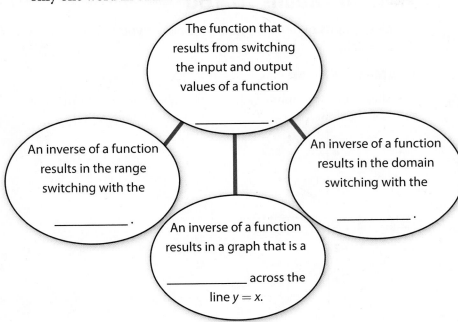

The function that results from switching the input and output values of a function _____.

An inverse of a function results in the range switching with the _____.

An inverse of a function results in the domain switching with the _____.

An inverse of a function results in a graph that is a _____ across the line $y = x$.

Understand Vocabulary

To become familiar with some of the vocabulary terms in the module, consider the following. You may refer to the module, the glossary, or a dictionary.

1. A function whose rule contains a variable under a square-root sign.

_____

2. A function whose rule contains a variable under a cube-root sign.

_____

Active Reading

Layered Book Before beginning the module, create a Layered Book Note to help you organize what you learn. The four flaps of the layered book can summarize information into four pages, one for each lesson. Write details of each lesson on the appropriate flap to create a summary of the module.

Square Root and Cube Root Functions

Understanding the standards and the vocabulary terms in the standards will help you know exactly what you are expected to learn in this module.

COMMON CORE | F.IF.7b

Graph square root, cube root, and piecewise-defined functions, including step functions and absolute value functions.

Key Vocabulary

function *(función)*
An input-output relationship that has exactly one output for each input.

What It Means to You

Creating graphs of different functions allows you to compare them visually.

EXAMPLE F.IF.7B

The shapes of the graphs of square and cube root parent functions are shown below.

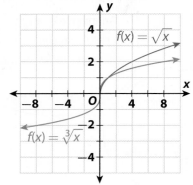

COMMON CORE | F.BF.3

Identify the effect on the graph of replacing $f(x)$ by $f(x) + k$, $k\,f(x)$, $f(kx)$, and $f(x + k)$ for specific values of k (both positive and negative); find the value of k given the graphs. Experiment with cases and illustrate an explanation of the effects on the graph using technology.

Key Vocabulary

function notation *(notación de función)*
The notation used to describe a function.

What It Means to You

You can change a function by adding or multiplying by a constant. The result will be a new function that is a transformation of the original function.

EXAMPLE F.BF.3

The graph below shows examples of vertical translation of the function $f(x) = \sqrt{x}$ which occurs when a constant is added or subtracted to the function.

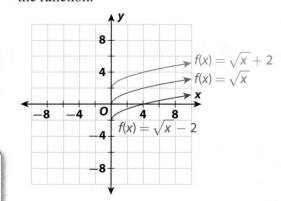

Visit **my.hrw.com** to see all **Common Core Standards** unpacked.

my.hrw.com

19.1 Square Root Functions

COMMON CORE   F.IF.7b

Graph square root, cube root, and piecewise-defined functions, including step functions and absolute value functions. *Also F.IF.7, F.IF.9*

? **ESSENTIAL QUESTION**

What function is the inverse of a quadratic function?

EXPLORE ACTIVITY Real World   COMMON CORE   F.IF.9

Understanding One-to-One Functions

A function is **one-to-one** if each output of the function is paired with exactly one input. Only one-to-one functions have inverses that are also functions.

Recall that in an inverse function, the x- and y-values are switched. This means that the graph of $f^{-1}(x)$ is the reflection of the graph of $f(x)$ across the line $y = x$.

Sketch the inverse of each function graphed below.

A

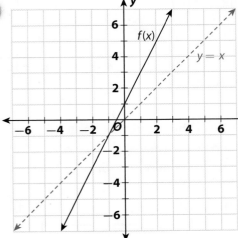

B

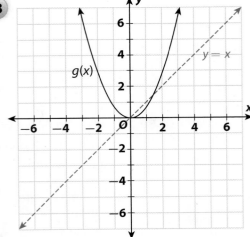

Linear functions with nonzero slopes are always one-to-one,

so their inverses [**are / are not**] functions.

Quadratic functions are not one-to-one. The reflection of the parabola labeled $g(x)$ across the line $y = x$

[**is / is not**] a function.

Math Talk
Mathematical Practices

Why is the quadratic function $g(x)$ not one-to-one?

REFLECT

1. Explain why the reflection of the graph of $g(x)$ (a parabola) across the line $y = x$ is not a function.

_____

_____

_____

Graphing the Inverse of a Quadratic Function with Restricted Domain

EXAMPLE 1

COMMON CORE · F.IF.7b

Graph the function $f(x) = 0.5x^2$ for the domain $x \geq 0$. Then graph its inverse, $f^{-1}(x)$, and write a rule for the inverse function.

STEP 1   Make a table of values to graph $f(x)$ for nonnegative values of x. Then use the table to graph the function.

x	$f(x) = 0.5x^2$
0	0
1	0.5
2	2
3	4.5
4	8

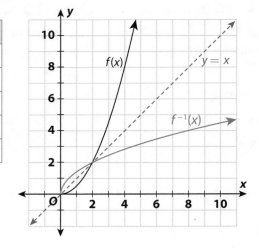

STEP 2   Make a table of values for $f^{-1}(x)$ by finding the image of each point on the graph of $f(x)$ after a reflection across the line $y = x$. To reflect a point across $y = x$, switch the x- and y-coordinates of the point.

Points on the graph of $f(x)$	(0, 0)	(1, 0.5)	(2, 2)	(3, 4.5)	(4, 8)
Points on the graph of $f^{-1}(x)$	(0, 0)	(0.5, 1)	(2, 2)	(4.5, 3)	(8, 4)

STEP 3   Use the table from Step 2 to graph $f^{-1}(x)$ on the grid in Step 1.

STEP 4   Write the rule for $f^{-1}(x)$.

$f(x) = 0.5x^2$

$y = \frac{1}{2}x^2$ Replace 0.5 with $\frac{1}{2}$ and $f(x)$ with y.

$2y = x^2$ Multiply both sides by 2.

$\sqrt{2y} = x$ Take the square root of both sides. Use the definition of positive square root.

$\sqrt{2x} = y$ Switch x and y to write the inverse.

$\sqrt{2x} = f^{-1}(x)$ Replace y with $f^{-1}(x)$.

The rule for the inverse function is $f^{-1}(x) = \sqrt{2x}$, for $x \geq 0$.

2. Graph the function $f(x) = x^2 + 2$ for the
domain $x \geq 0$. Then graph its inverse, $f^{-1}(x)$,
and write a rule for the inverse function.

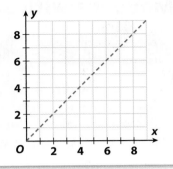

_____

Domain of Square Root Functions

A quadratic function of the form $f(x) = ax^2$, where
$x \geq 0$, is a one-to-one function, so its inverse is
also a function. With this limited domain, the
inverse of $f(x) = ax^2$ is the *square root function*
$g(x) = \sqrt{\frac{x}{a}}$.

A square root function is a function whose rule
involves $\sqrt{x}$. The parent square root function is
$g(x) = \sqrt{x}$. The graph shows that $g(x) = \sqrt{x}$
is the inverse of $f(x) = x^2$ for $x \geq 0$.

A square root function is defined only for values
of x that make the expression under the radical sign nonnegative.

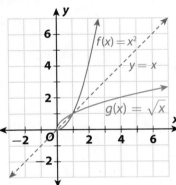

Math On the Spot

my.hrw.com

Math Talk

Mathematical Practices

What are the domain and
range of the square
root function $g(x) = \sqrt{x}$?
Explain.

EXAMPLE 2

COMMON CORE   F.IF.7b

Find the domain of the square root function $f(x) = \sqrt{x + 4} - 3$.

$f(x) = \sqrt{x + 4} - 3$

$x + 4 \geq 0$ *The expression under the radical sign must be
greater than or equal to 0.*

    $x \geq -4$ *Solve the inequality. Subtract 4 from both sides.*

The domain is the set of all real numbers greater than or equal to -4.

Find the domain of each square-root function.

3. $f(x) = \sqrt{3x - 5}$ **4.** $f(x) = 3\sqrt{x + 1}$

_____   _____

Modeling with Square Root Functions

EXAMPLE 3 Real World

COMMON CORE F.IF.7b

The function $d(t) = 16t^2$ gives the distance d in feet that a dropped object falls in t seconds. Write and graph the inverse function $t(d)$ to find the time t in seconds it takes for an object to fall a distance of d feet. Then estimate how long it will take a penny dropped into a well to fall 48 feet.

My Notes

STEP 1 Write the inverse function.

The original function is a quadratic function with a domain restricted to $t \geq 0$. The function fits the pattern $f(x) = ax^2$ for $x \geq 0$, so its inverse will have the form $g(x) = \sqrt{\frac{x}{a}}$.

Original Function	Inverse Function
$d(t) = 16t^2$ for $t \geq 0$	$t(d) = \sqrt{\frac{d}{16}}$ for $d \geq 0$

STEP 2 Complete the table of values and use it to graph the function $t(d)$.

d	0	4	16	32	64	100
t	0	0.5	1	1.4	2	2.5

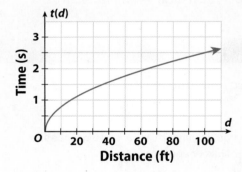

STEP 3 Use the function $t(d)$ to estimate how long it will take a penny to fall 48 feet.

$$t(d) = \sqrt{\frac{d}{16}} \qquad \text{Write the function.}$$

$$t(48) = \sqrt{\frac{48}{16}} \qquad \text{Substitute 48 for } d.$$

$$t(48) = \sqrt{3} \qquad \text{Simplify.}$$

$$t(48) \approx 1.73 \qquad \text{Use a calculator. Round to the nearest hundredth.}$$

It will take about 1.73 seconds for a penny to fall 48 feet.

REFLECT

5. Explain why the domain is restricted to $t \geq 0$ for the original function $d(t) = 16t^2$.

_____

_____

6. Describe another way that you could find the time it would take a penny to fall 48 feet.

_____

_____

YOUR TURN

7. A company manufactures square tabletops that are covered by 16 square tiles. If s is the side length of each tile in inches, then the area A of a tabletop in square feet is given by $A(s) = \frac{1}{9}s^2$.

a. Write and graph the inverse function $s(A)$ to find the side length of the tiles in inches for a tabletop with an area of A square feet.

_____

b. What is the side length of the tiles that make up a tabletop with an area of 4 square feet?

_____

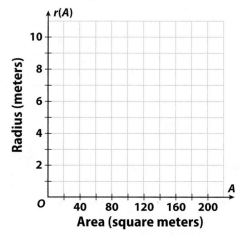

8. The function $A(r) = \pi r^2$ gives the area A in square meters of a circle with a radius of r meters.

a. Write and graph the inverse function $r(A)$ to find the radius in meters of a circle with an area of A square meters.

_____

b. Find the radius of a circular swimming pool that has a surface area of 120 square meters. Round to the nearest tenth.

_____

Personal Math Trainer

Online Practice and Help

my.hrw.com

1. Complete the table of values to graph the function $f(x) = x^2 + 1$ for $x \geq 0$. Next, use the table to find four ordered pairs on the graph of the inverse function and draw its graph. Then write a rule for the inverse function. (Explore Activity and Example 1)

x	f(x)
0	1
1	
2	
3	

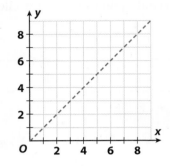

Ordered Pairs $f^{-1}(x)$
$(1, 0)$
$(2, \qquad)$

$f^{-1}(x) = $ _____

Find the domain of each square root function. (Example 2)

2. $y = 2\sqrt{4x - 1}$

$\boxed{} \geq 0$

$4x \geq \boxed{}$

$x \geq \boxed{}$

3. $y = \sqrt{3(x - 3)} + 1$

$\boxed{} \geq 0$

$\boxed{} \geq 0$

$3x \geq \boxed{}$

$x \geq \boxed{}$

4. The function $a(r) = 3.14r^2$ approximates the area a in inches for a circle with radius of r inches. (Example 3)

   a. Write the inverse function $r(a)$.

   _____

   b. Use the inverse function to find the radius of a circle with an area of 94.2 in^2. Round to the nearest tenth.

   _____

? ESSENTIAL QUESTION CHECK-IN

5. What is the inverse of a quadratic function?

   _____

   _____

   _____

19.1 Independent Practice

Personal
Math Trainer

Online Practice
and Help

my.hrw.com

COMMON CORE F.IF.7, F.IF.7b, F.IF.9

Graph the function $f(x)$ for the domain $x \geq 0$. Then graph its inverse, $f^{-1}(x)$, and write a rule for the inverse function.

6. $f(x) = 2x^2, f^{-1}(x) = $ _____

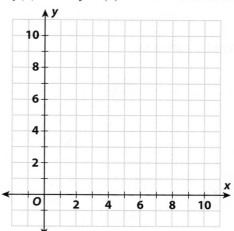

7. $f(x) = -x^2, f^{-1}(x) = $ _____

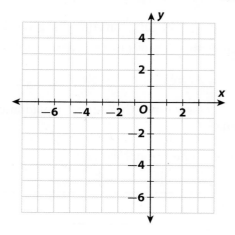

8. $f(x) = \frac{1}{3}x^2, f^{-1}(x) = $ _____

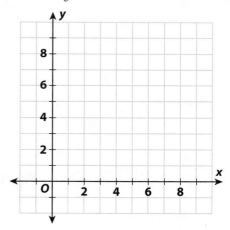

9. $f(x) = -\frac{1}{2}x^2, f^{-1}(x) = $ _____

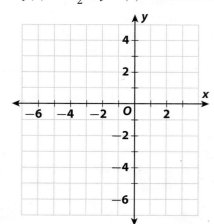

Find the domain of each square root function.

10. $f(x) = \sqrt{x - 1},$ _____ **11.** $f(x) = \sqrt{2x + 3} + 5,$ _____ **12.** $f(x) = \sqrt{2(x + 1)},$ _____

13. $f(x) = 4 - \sqrt{3x - 12},$ _____ **14.** $f(x) = \sqrt{2x - 5},$ _____ **15.** $f(x) = \sqrt{4 - 3x},$ _____

16. Communicate Mathematical Ideas Explain how to find the domain of a square-root function. Why is the domain restricted for some square root functions?

_____

_____

_____

17. The function $d(t) = 16t^2$ gives the distance d in feet that a dropped object falls in t seconds. Use the inverse of the function to find how long it will take an apple to fall 32 feet. Round to the nearest hundredth.

_____

18. The function $A(s) = \pi r^2$ gives the area A in square feet of a circle with a radius of r feet. What is the radius of a circle with an area of 16π square feet?

_____

19. **Multi Step** The function $A(s) = s^2$ gives the area A in square meters for a square with a side of s meters. Write a formula for perimeter of a square in

terms of its area. _____

20. **Justify Reasoning** Consider the quadratic function $f(x) = x^2$.

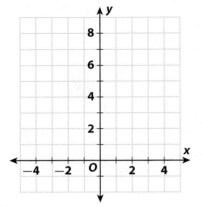

   a. Is $f(x)$ one-to-one? Explain.

   _____

   _____

   b. How could you restrict the domain of $f(x)$ so that the inverse function, $f^{-1}(x)$, is one-to-one? Explain. Graph the function for the restricted domain.

_____

_____

_____

Work Area

21. **Represent Real-World Problems** The formula for converting temperatures from degrees Fahrenheit F to degrees Celsius C is $C = \frac{5}{9}(F - 32)$. What is the inverse of this function? How can you use the inverse to find where the Celsius temperature equals the Fahrenheit temperature?

_____

_____

22. **Justify Reasoning** Why is a linear function not one to one if the slope is 0?

_____

_____

_____

Transforming Square Root Functions

COMMON CORE   **F.BF.3**

Identify the effect on the graph of replacing $f(x)$ by $f(x) + k$, $k\,f(x)$, $f(kx)$, and $f(x + k)$ for specific values of k (both positive and negative); find the value of k given the graphs. Experiment with cases and illustrate an explanation of the effects on the graph using technology. *Also F.IF.9.*

ESSENTIAL QUESTION

How can you transform the parent square root function?

EXPLORE ACTIVITY 1   COMMON CORE   F.BF.3

Stretching and Compressing Graphs

For a function in the form $g(x) = a\sqrt{x}$, the value of a will transform the parent function $f(x) = \sqrt{x}$

A Complete the table for $g(x) = 3\sqrt{x}$.

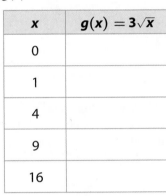

x	$g(x) = 3\sqrt{x}$
0	
1	
4	
9	
16	

B Graph $g(x)$.

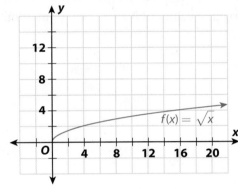

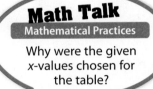

Math Talk
Mathematical Practices

Why were the given x-values chosen for the table?

C The graph of $g(x) = 3\sqrt{x}$ is a vertical *stretch* of the graph of the parent function. The stretch is by a factor of 3 since each output is _____ times the output of the parent function.

D Complete the table for $h(x) = 0.5\sqrt{x}$.

x	$h(x) = 0.5\sqrt{x}$
0	
1	
4	
9	
16	

E Graph $h(x)$.

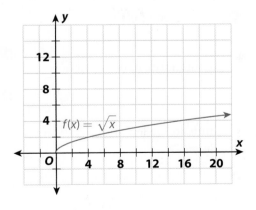

F The graph of $h(x) = 0.5\sqrt{x}$ is a vertical *compression* of the graph of the parent function. The compression is by a factor of 0.5 since each output

is _____ times the output of the parent function.

REFLECT

1. Interpret the Answer Complete the sentences for $f(x) = a\sqrt{x}$.

a. When $|a| > 1$, the graph of $g(x)$ is a vertical _____ of the graph of the parent function.

b. When $|a| < 1$, the graph of $g(x)$ is a vertical _____ of the graph of the parent function.

EXPLORE ACTIVITY 2

COMMON CORE   F.BF.3, F.IF.9

Translating Graphs

In the previous activity, you explored how values of a in the function $f(x) = a\sqrt{x}$ affect the graph of the parent square root function. In this activity, you will explore how the values of h and k in the function $f(x) = \sqrt{x - h} + k$ affect the graph of the parent square root function.

A Complete the table for $g(x) = \sqrt{x + 4} - 3$.

x	$g(x) = \sqrt{x + 4} - 3$
−4	
−3	
0	
5	
12	

Notice that the table uses x-values that result in perfect squares.

B Graph $g(x)$.

C The graph of $g(x) = \sqrt{x + 4} - 3$

is a _____ of the graph of the parent function.

The _____ is _____

units to the left and _____ units down.

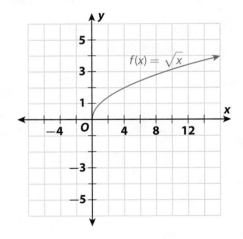

D Give the domain and range for $g(x)$.

Domain: $x \geq$ _____

Range: $y \geq$ _____

E Complete the table for $h(x) = \sqrt{x - 2} + 4$.

x	$h(x) = \sqrt{x - 2} + 4$
2	
3	
6	
11	
18	

Notice that the table uses x-values that result in perfect squares.

F Graph $h(x)$.

G The graph of $h(x) = \sqrt{x - 2} + 4$

is a _____ of the
graph of the parent function. The

translation is _____ units to

the _____ and _____

units _____ .

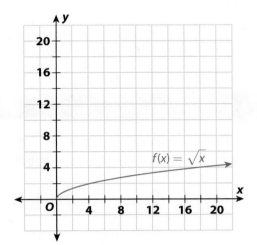
$f(x) = \sqrt{x}$

H Give the domain and range
for $h(x)$.

Domain: $x \geq$ _____

Range: $y \geq$ _____

REFLECT

2. Draw Conclusions How can you determine the domain of $m(x) = \sqrt{x + 4} - 3$
by looking at its function rule?

_____

_____

_____

_____

3. Make a Conjecture Predict how different values of a in the function
$f(x) = a\sqrt{x - h} + k$ will affect the range.

_____

_____

Writing the Equation of a Square Root Function

If the shape of the graph is stretched or compressed and the graph moves left or right and/or up or down, this is a combination of transformations.

Transforming a Square Root Function

Any transformation has an equation of the form $f(x) = a\sqrt{x - h} + k$.

- If $a = 1$, $h = 0$, and $k = 0$, the graph is $f(x) = \sqrt{x}$.
- If h is not 0, then the value of h moves the graph right or left along the x-axis.
- If k is not 0, then the value of k moves the graph up or down along the y-axis.
- If a is not 1, then the graph of $f(x)$ is a compression of the parent function if $a < 1$ and a stretch if $a > 1$.

EXAMPLE 1

COMMON CORE F.BF.3, F.IF.9

Write the function rule for the function represented by the graph.

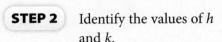

STEP 1 Identify the function type.

The shape of the graph indicates a square root function.

STEP 2 Identify the values of h and k.

The endpoint $(0, 0)$ from the parent square function was translated to $(1, 3)$. So, $h = 1$ and $k = 3$.

The equation has the form $f(x) = a\sqrt{x - 1} + 3$.

STEP 3 Use the point $(5, 7)$ to identify a.

$f(x) = a\sqrt{x - 1} + 3$ Substitute for x and y.

$(7) = a\sqrt{(5) - 1} + 3$ Simplify the radical.

$7 = a\sqrt{4} + 3$

$7 = a(2) + 3$ Subtract 3 from both sides.

$4 = a(2)$ Divide both sides by 2.

$2 = a$

Substitute $a = 2$, $h = 1$, and $k = 3$ into the general function $f(x) = a\sqrt{x - h} + k$. The function is $f(x) = 2\sqrt{x - 1} + 3$.

REFLECT

4. The point $(0, 0)$ is on the graph of the parent square root function. How can you find the point on the square root function to which $(0, 0)$ is translated?

_____

_____

5. **Interpret the Answer** Does the graph in Example 1 represent a vertical stretch or a vertical compression of the graph of the parent function? Does this agree with the value of a that you found? Explain.

_____

_____

_____

_____

YOUR TURN

Write the rule for the function represented by each graph.

6.

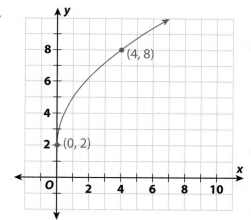

_____

7.

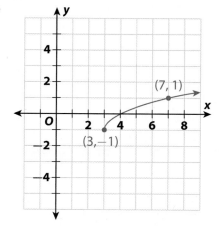

_____

Personal Math Trainer

Online Practice and Help

my.hrw.com

Graph each square root function. Then describe the graph as a transformation of the graph of the parent function, and give its domain and range.
(Explore Activities 1 and 2)

1. $g(x) = 0.5\sqrt{x} + 2$

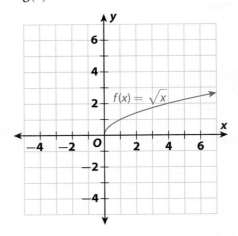

_____

_____

_____

2. $g(x) = -\sqrt{x} + 5$

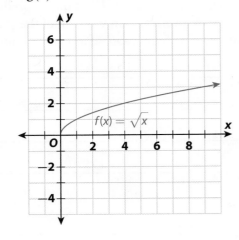

_____

_____

_____

3. Kyle drew this translation of the graph of the parent square root function. (Example 1)

a. How far has the graph of the parent function been translated horizontally? _____

b. How far has the graph of the parent function been translated vertically? _____

c. Write a rule for the function represented by the graph.

_____

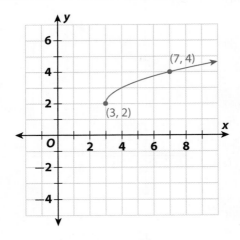

ESSENTIAL QUESTION CHECK-IN

4. What do the values of a, h, and k tell you about how the graph of $f(x) = a\sqrt{x - h} + k$ is related to the graph of the parent function $f(x) = \sqrt{x}$?

_____

_____

_____

_____

19.2 Independent Practice

COMMON CORE   F.BF.3, F.IF.9

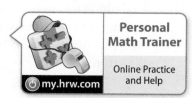

Personal Math Trainer

Online Practice and Help

my.hrw.com

Determine the domain and range of each function.

5. $f(x) = \sqrt{x - 3} + 2$

_____

_____

6. $f(x) = 3\sqrt{x + 2} + 1$

_____

_____

7. $f(x) = \sqrt{2x + 3}$

_____

_____

8. $f(x) = \sqrt{6 - 2x} + 3$

_____

_____

9. $f(x) = 5\sqrt{x + 0.5} + 3$

_____

_____

10. Multi-Step Write the function represented by the given transformation of the graph of $f(x) = \sqrt{x}$.

a. The graph is translated 3 units down.

_____

b. The graph is translated 3 units down and 2 units left.

_____

c. The graph is stretched by a factor of 5, translated 3 units down and 2 units left.

_____

11. Bill is a house painter. The graph shows the relationship between the number of square feet of paint, x, needed to cover a square wall, and the length in feet, y, of the square wall. The graph accounts for some paint that Bill may spill.

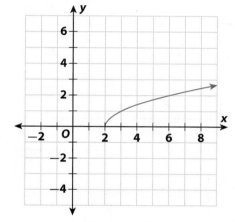

a. How much spillage is taken into account?

_____

_____

b. What function is represented by the graph?

_____

c. Estimate the length of the sides of the wall if enough paint was purchased to cover 40 square feet.

_____

d. Describe how the graph is related to the graph of the parent function.

_____

_____

_____

12. Explain the Error A student was trying to find the function for a graph of a translation of a square root function. She found the value of h to be 2 and the value of k to be 4. She writes the function as $f(x) = \sqrt{x - 4} + 2$. Explain the error.

_____

_____

13. Critical Thinking What is the limitation of considering the square root function $f(x) = \sqrt{x}$ to be the inverse of the quadratic function $f(x) = x^2$? Refer to a table or graph to explain your answer.

_____

_____

_____

_____

_____

_____

14. Analyze Relationships Describe how the effect that the value of k has on the graph of $f(x) = \sqrt{x} + k$ is similar to the effect that the value of b has on the graph of $f(x) = x + b$.

_____

_____

_____

15. Multiple Representations Which function has a greater minimum value, $f(x) = \sqrt{x - 4} - 1$ or the function whose graph is shown?

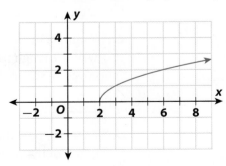

_____

_____

_____

LESSON
19.3 Cube Root Functions

COMMON CORE   F.IF.7b

Graph square root, cube root, and piecewise-defined functions, including step functions and absolute value functions. *Also F.IF.7, F.IF.9*

? **ESSENTIAL QUESTION**

What is the inverse of a cubic function?

EXPLORE ACTIVITY   COMMON CORE   F.IF.7b

Understanding Cube Root Functions

The following activity will introduce you to the cube root function and its graph.

A Complete the table of values for the parent cubic function, $f(x) = x^3$, and use the table to complete the graph.

x	$f(x) = x^3$
−2	
−1	
0	
1	
2	

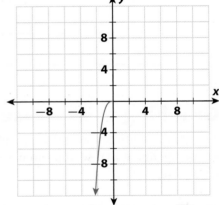

B Because $f(x)$ **is / is not** a one-to-one function, its inverse is also a function.

The inverse of $f(x) = x^3$ is the *cube root function* $g(x) = \sqrt[3]{x}$.

A **cube root function** is a function whose rule involves $\sqrt[3]{x}$. The parent cube root function is $g(x) = \sqrt[3]{x}$.

C Complete the table of values for the parent cube root function, $g(x) = \sqrt[3]{x}$. Use the table and the fact that the graphs of inverse functions are reflections across the line $y = x$ to graph the function $g(x)$.

x	$g(x) = \sqrt[3]{x}$
−8	
−1	
0	
1	
8	

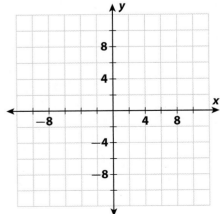

REFLECT

1. **Communicate Mathematical Ideas** Explain how the values in the tables for $f(x) = x^3$ and $g(x) = \sqrt[3]{x}$ show that the graphs of these functions are reflections of each other across the line $y = x$.

_____

_____

2. Is $g(x) = \sqrt[3]{x}$ also a one-to-one function? Explain.

_____

_____

3. **Analyze Relationships** What are the domain and range of $f(x) = x^3$? What are the domain and range of $g(x) = \sqrt[3]{x}$?

_____

_____

Graphing the Inverse of a Cubic Function

The graph of a function and the graph of its inverse are reflections of each other across the line $y = x$, so you can use the graph of a function to sketch the graph of its inverse.

Math On the Spot

my.hrw.com

EXAMPLE 1

COMMON CORE F.IF.7b

Graph the function $f(x) = 0.5x^3$. Then graph its inverse, $f^{-1}(x)$, and write a rule for the inverse function.

STEP 1 Make a table of values and graph the function $f(x) = 0.5x^3$.

x	f(x)
−2	−4
−1	−0.5
0	0
1	0.5
2	4

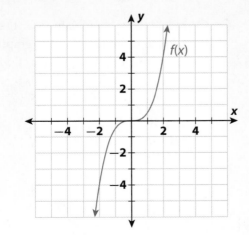

My Notes

STEP 2 Find points on the graph of the inverse of $f(x)$ by finding the image of each point after a reflection across the line $y = x$.

Points on the graph of $f(x)$	(−2, −4)	(−1, −0.5)	(0, 0)	(1, 0.5)	(2, 4)
Points on the graph of $f^{-1}(x)$	(−4, −2)	(−0.5, −1)	(0, 0)	(0.5, 1)	(4, 2)

STEP 3 Use the table from Step 2 to graph $f^{-1}(x)$.

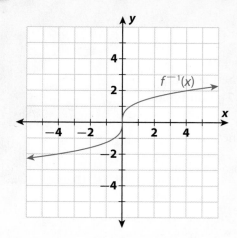

STEP 4 Write a rule for $f^{-1}(x)$.

$y = 0.5x^3$ Replace $f(x)$ with y. Solve for x.

$2y = x^3$ Multiply both sides by 2.

$\sqrt[3]{2y} = x$ Take the cube root of each side.

$\sqrt[3]{2x} = y$ Switch x and y to write the inverse.

$\sqrt[3]{2x} = f^{-1}(x)$ Replace y with $f^{-1}(x)$.

Math Talk
Mathematical Practices

How is the graph of a cube root function different from the graph of a square root function?

YOUR TURN

4. Graph the function $f(x) = 0.25x^3$. Then graph its inverse, $f^{-1}(x)$, and write a rule for the inverse function.

_____

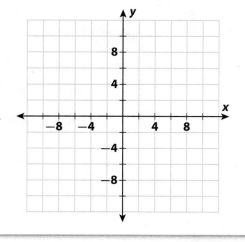

Personal Math Trainer

Online Practice and Help

my.hrw.com

Modeling with Cube Root Functions

As with other types of functions, cube root functions can be used to model real-world situations.

EXAMPLE 2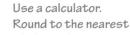

COMMON CORE   F.IF.7b

A pike is a type of freshwater fish. The function $w(L) = \frac{L^3}{3500}$ gives the approximate weight $w(L)$ in pounds of a pike with length L inches.

Write and graph the inverse function $L(w)$ to find the approximate length $L(w)$ in inches of a pike weighing w pounds. Then use your function to find the length of a 7-pound pike.

STEP 1 Write the inverse function.

The original function is a cubic function.

It can be written in the form $f(x) = ax^3$ where $a = \frac{1}{3500}$.

Its inverse will have the form $g(x) = \sqrt[3]{\frac{x}{a}}$.

Original Function	Inverse Function
$w(L) = \frac{1}{3500}L^3$	$L(w) = \sqrt[3]{3500w}$

STEP 2 Make a table of values and use it to graph the function $L(w)$. Because you are asked for an approximation, you can round the values of $L(w)$ to the nearest whole number.

w	0	1	2	3	4	5
L(w)						

STEP 3 Use the function $L(w)$ to estimate the length of a 7-pound pike.

$L(w) = \sqrt[3]{3500w}$ Write the function.

$L(7) = \sqrt[3]{3500(7)}$ Substitute 7 for w.

$L(7) = \sqrt[3]{24,500}$ Simplify.

$L(7) \approx 29$ Use a calculator. Round to the nearest whole number.

So, a 7-pound pike will be about 29 inches long.

My Notes

5. What is the reasonable domain and range of $L(w)$?

_____

_____

_____

_____

6. Interpret the Answer What is the meaning in the context of the problem of the point at approximately $(6, 28)$ on the graph of $L(w)$?

_____

_____

7. Communicate Mathematical Ideas Describe what happens to the graph of $L(w)$ as the values of w increase. Is this true for all cube root functions?

_____

_____

_____

_____

YOUR TURN

8. For another type of fish, the relationship between the weight $w(L)$ in pounds and the length L in inches is given by the function $w(L) = \frac{L^3}{2500}$. Write and graph the inverse function $L(w)$ to find the approximate length $L(w)$ in inches of a fish of this type weighing w pounds. Then find the length of a fish of this type that weighs 10 pounds.

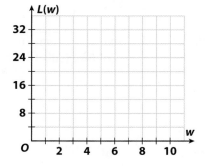

_____

A 10-pound fish would be approximately _____ inches long.

Personal Math Trainer

Online Practice and Help

my.hrw.com

Graph the function $f(x)$. Then graph its inverse, $f^{-1}(x)$, and write a rule for the inverse function. (Explore Activity and Example 1)

1. $f(x) = 2x^3$

$$y = 2x^3$$

$\boxed{} = x^3$

$\boxed{} = x$

$\boxed{} = y$

$f^{-1}(x) = $ _____

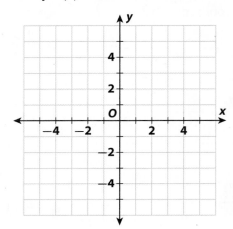

2. $f(x) = -x^3$

$$y = -x^3$$

$\boxed{} = x^3$

$\boxed{} = x$

$\boxed{} = y$

$f^{-1}(x) = $ _____

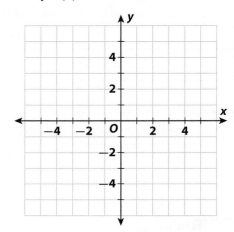

3. The function $V(r) = \frac{4}{3}\pi r^3$ gives the volume $V(r)$ in cubic inches of a sphere with a radius of r inches. (Example 2)

a. Write and graph the inverse function $r(V)$ to find the radius in inches of a sphere with a volume of V cubic inches. _____

b. To the nearest inch, what is the radius of a basketball with a volume of 455 cubic inches? _____

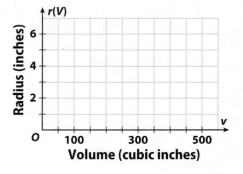

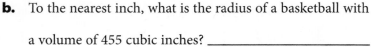

ESSENTIAL QUESTION CHECK-IN

4. If you are given the rule for a cubic function, $f(x)$, what are two ways that you can graph its inverse function?

_____

_____

_____

19.3 Independent Practice

Personal Math Trainer

Online Practice and Help

my.hrw.com

COMMON CORE   F.IF.7, F.IF.7b, F.IF.9

Graph $f(x)$. Then graph its inverse, $f^{-1}(x)$, and write a rule for the inverse function.

5. $f(x) = \frac{1}{4}x^3$

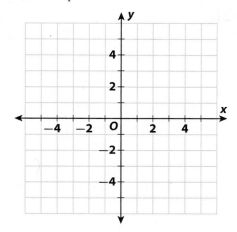

$f^{-1}(x) = $ _____

6. $f(x) = -\frac{1}{3}x^3$

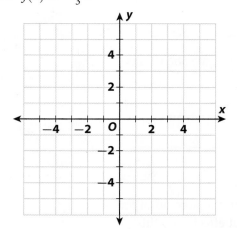

$f^{-1}(x) = $ _____

For each function, write a rule for the inverse function.

7. $g(x) = \sqrt[3]{\frac{x}{5}}$

_____

8. $h(x) = \sqrt[3]{\frac{5x}{2}}$

_____

9. A company manufactures water tanks in the shape of rectangular prisms. The length of each tank is 3 times the width, and the height of each tank is twice the width.

a. Given that 1 cubic foot ≈ 7.48 gallons, write a function $c(w)$ that approximates the capacity in gallons of a tank with a width of w feet.

_____

b. Write and graph the inverse function $w(c)$ to find the width in feet of a tank with a capacity of c gallons.

_____

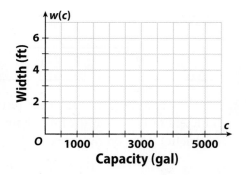

c. To the nearest foot, what is the width of a tank that has a capacity of 3000 gallons?

_____

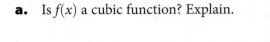

FOCUS ON HIGHER ORDER THINKING

10. Communicate Mathematical Ideas
The graph of $f(x) = x(x + 1)(x - 1)$ is shown.

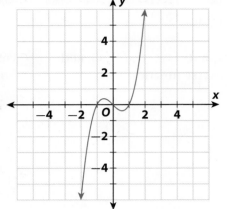

a. Is $f(x)$ a cubic function? Explain.

_____

_____

_____

_____

b. Is $f(x)$ a one-to-one function? Explain.

_____

_____

c. Does an inverse function for $f(x)$ exist? Explain.

_____

d. Give one way to restrict the domain of $f(x)$ so that an inverse function exists.

_____

11. Justify Reasoning Ellie is determining the inverse of $g(x) = \frac{27}{8}x^3$. She thinks that $g^{-1}(x) = \frac{2}{3}\sqrt[3]{x}$. Is she correct? Justify your answer.

_____

_____

_____

12. Critical Thinking Consider the restriction that you made to the domain of $f(x)$ in Exercise 10 so that the inverse function would exist. What effect does this restriction have on the range of the inverse function? Explain.

_____

_____

_____

_____

_____

_____

Transforming Cube Root Functions

COMMON CORE F.BF.3

Identify the effect on the graph of replacing $f(x)$ by $f(x) + k$, $k\,f(x)$, $f(kx)$, and $f(x + k)$ for specific values of k (both positive and negative); find the value of k given the graphs. Experiment with cases and illustrate an explanation of the effects on the graph using technology. *Also F.IF.9*

? ESSENTIAL QUESTION

How can you transform the parent cube root function?

EXPLORE ACTIVITY 1   COMMON CORE F.BF.3

Stretching and Compressing Graphs

$f(x) = \sqrt[3]{x}$ is the parent function from which other cube root functions are formed. You can transform the parent cube root function by changing the values of a, h, and k in the general form of cube root functions.

$$f(x) = a\sqrt[3]{x - h} + k$$

A Complete the table for $g(x) = 3\sqrt[3]{x}$.

x	$g(x) = 3\sqrt[3]{x}$
-8	
-1	
0	
1	
8	

B Graph $g(x)$.

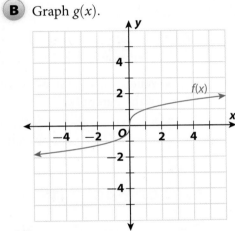

C The graph of $g(x)$ is a vertical _____ of the graph of the parent

function by a factor of _____ .

D Complete the table for $h(x) = 0.5\sqrt[3]{x}$.

x	$h(x) = 0.5\sqrt[3]{x}$
-8	
-1	
0	
1	
8	

E Graph $h(x)$.

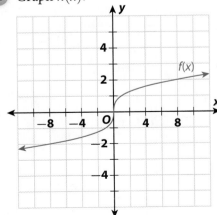

F The graph of $h(x)$ is a vertical _____ of the graph of the parent

function by a factor of _____ .

REFLECT

1. **Justify Reasoning** Explain how you know in part D that the graph of $h(x)$ is a vertical compression of the graph of the parent function.

_____

_____

_____

_____

_____

_____

2. **Make a Conjecture** Complete the sentences for $f(x) = a\sqrt[3]{x}$ based on your observations from Explore Activity 1.

   • When $|a| > 1$, the graph of $f(x)$ is a vertical _____ of the graph of the parent function.

   • When $0 < |a| < 1$, the graph of $f(x)$ is a vertical _____ of the graph of the parent function.

EXPLORE ACTIVITY 2　　COMMON CORE　F.BF.3

Translating Graphs

New functions may also be formed by translating or reflecting the graph of the parent function.

A Complete the table for $g(x) = \sqrt[3]{x - 2} + 4$.

x	$g(x) = \sqrt[3]{x-2}+4$
−6	
1	
2	
3	
10	

B Graph $g(x)$.

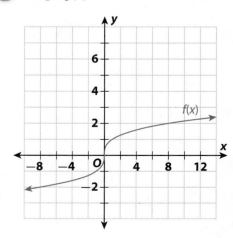

C The graph of $g(x)$ is a translation of the graph of the parent function

2 units _____ and _____ units up. The domain

is _____ . The range is _____ .

D Complete the table for
$h(x) = \sqrt[3]{x + 3} - 2$.

x	$h(x) = \sqrt[3]{x+3} - 2$
−11	
−4	
−3	
−2	
5	

E Graph $h(x)$.

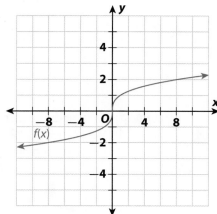

F The graph of $h(x)$ is a translation of the graph of the parent function

3 units _____ and _____ units down. The domain is

_____ . The range is _____ .

REFLECT

3. What are the values of h and k in $g(x) = \sqrt[3]{x - 2} + 4$? What effect do h and k have on the graph of the function?

_____

_____

_____

_____

_____

_____

4. **Make a Conjecture** Complete the sentences for $f(x) = \sqrt[3]{x - h} + k$ based on your observations from Explore Activity 2.

- The graph of $f(x)$ is a translation of the parent function $|h|$ units

  _____ if $h < 0$ and h units _____ if $h > 0$.
- The graph of $f(x)$ is a translation of the parent function $|k|$ units

  _____ if $k < 0$ and k units _____ if $k > 0$.

Writing the Equation of a Cube Root Function

You can write the cube root function represented by a graph by identifying the values of a, h, and k.

EXAMPLE 1   COMMON CORE   F.BF.3

Write the function rule for the function whose graph is shown below.

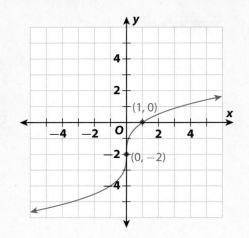

STEP 1   Identify the function type.

The shape of the graph indicates a cube root function.

STEP 2   Identify the values of h and k.

The point $(0, 0)$ from the graph of the parent cube root function was translated to $(0, -2)$.

Therefore, $h = 0$ and $k = -2$. So, the function is of the form $g(x) = a\sqrt[3]{x - 0} - 2$.

STEP 3   Use the point $(1, 0)$ to identify a.

$g(x) = a\sqrt[3]{x - 0} - 2$ Function form

$0 = a\sqrt[3]{1 - 0} - 2$ Substitute 0 for $g(x)$ and 1 for x.

$0 = a\sqrt[3]{1} - 2$

$0 = a(1) - 2$

$2 = a$

Substitute $h = 0$, $k = -2$, and $a = 2$ into the general function $f(x) = a\sqrt[3]{x - h} + k$. The function is $g(x) = 2\sqrt[3]{x} - 2$.

REFLECT

5. The point $(0, 0)$ is on the graph of the parent function. How can you find the point on the cube root function to which $(0, 0)$ is translated?

_____

_____

_____

_____

6. **Check for Reasonableness** Does the given graph represent a vertical stretch or a vertical compression of the graph of the parent function? Does this agree with the value of a that was found? Explain.

_____

_____

_____

_____

YOUR TURN

7. Write the rule for the function represented by the graph.

_____

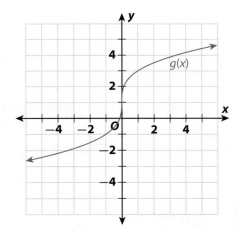

8. In the graph of the cube root function shown, are h and k positive or negative?

_____

_____

_____

_____

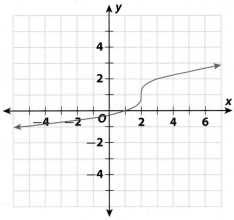

Personal Math Trainer

Online Practice and Help

⊙ my.hrw.com

1. Graph the cube root function
   $g(x) = 2\sqrt[3]{x} - 4$. Then describe the graph
   as a transformation of the graph of the
   parent function shown, and give its domain
   and range. (Explore Activities 1 and 2)

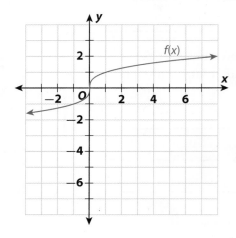

_____

_____

Domain: _____

Range: _____

2. Write the rule for the function represented
   by the graph. (Example 1)

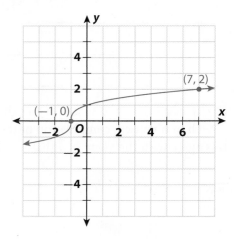

$f(x) =$ _____

3. Explain how the graph of $g(x) = 2\sqrt[3]{x+1} - 2$ is a transformation of the
   graph of the cube root parent function. (Explore Activities 1 and 2)

_____

_____

 ESSENTIAL QUESTION CHECK-IN

4. What do the values of a, h, and k tell you about how the graph of
   $f(x) = a\sqrt[3]{x - h} + k$ is related to the graph of the parent function $f(x) = \sqrt[3]{x}$?

_____

_____

_____

_____

_____

_____

19.4 Independent Practice

COMMON CORE F.BF.3, F.IF.9

Personal
Math Trainer

Online Practice
and Help

my.hrw.com

Graph each cube root function. Then describe the graph as a transformation of the graph of the parent function shown.

5. $g(x) = 0.2\sqrt[3]{x}$

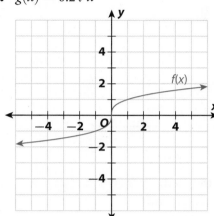

6. $g(x) = \sqrt[3]{x - 3} + 1$

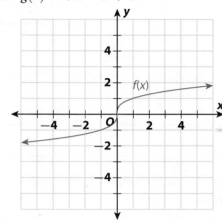

_____

_____

_____

_____

Write the rule for the function represented by each graph.

7.

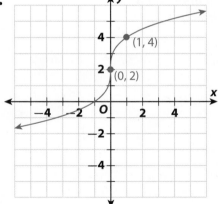

$f(x) =$ _____

8.

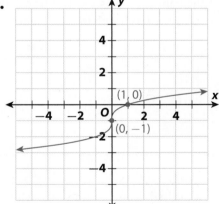

$f(x) =$ _____

9. What are the values of a, h, and k in the following function: $g(x) = 3 + \sqrt[3]{x + 2}$?

_____

_____

_____

H.O.T. FOCUS ON HIGHER ORDER THINKING

10. Explain the Error Kristen incorrectly described the graph of $g(x) = 0.3\sqrt[3]{x}$ as a vertical stretch of the graph of the parent function $g(x) = \sqrt[3]{x}$ by a factor of 0.3. What was her error?

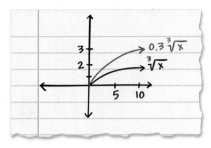

_____

_____

11. What if? If the graph of the parent function, $g(x) = \sqrt[3]{x}$, is stretched vertically by a factor of 2 and translated 2 units right and 3 units down, what would be the point where the curvature of the graph changes on the resulting graph?

_____

_____

12. Explain the Error To graph the function, $f(x) = \sqrt[3]{x-4}$, Dalton determined that the value of h was -4 and translated the graph of the parent function 4 units to the left. Explain why Dalton's translation was incorrect.

_____

_____

_____

_____

13. Communicate Mathematical Ideas Explain why square root functions have a limited domain and range while both the domain and the range of cube root functions consist of all real numbers.

_____

_____

_____

_____

_____

Ready to Go On?

Personal
Math Trainer

my.hrw.com

Online Practice
and Help

19.1 Square Root Functions

Find the domain of each square root function.

1. $f(x) = \sqrt{x + 5} - 2$

2. $f(x) = \sqrt{2x - 6} - 1$

_____

_____

_____

_____

19.2 Transforming Square Root Functions

Describe the graph of each function as a transformation of the
graph of the parent function.

3. $f(x) = 2\sqrt{x - 2}$

4. $f(x) = \frac{1}{3}\sqrt{x + 1}$

_____

_____

_____

_____

19.3 Cube Root Functions

Write a rule for the inverse of each function.

5. $f(x) = -2x^3$

6. $f(x) = \frac{1}{6}x^3$

_____

_____

19.4 Transforming Cube Root Functions

7. Write the rule for the function
represented by the graph.

_____

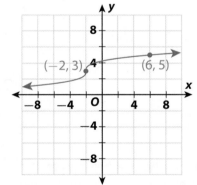

? ESSENTIAL QUESTION

8. What does the rule for a square root function
or a cube root function tell you about its graph?

_____

_____

_____

_____

_____

MODULE 19

MIXED REVIEW

Assessment Readiness

Personal Math Trainer

my.hrw.com

Online Practice and Help

1. Look at each expression. Is the expression equivalent to $2x^2 - 2$?

   Select Yes or No for A–C.

   A. $(4x^2 + 6x + 3) + (-2x^2 - 6x - 5)$ ○ Yes ○ No

   B. $(x^3 - 2x^2 + 8) - (x^3 + 4x^2 + 10)$ ○ Yes ○ No

   C. $2(x + 1)(x - 1)$ ○ Yes ○ No

2. Consider the cube root function $f(x) = \sqrt[3]{x - 4}$.

   Choose True or False for each statement.

   A. The domain of $f(x)$ is $x \geq 4$. ○ True ○ False

   B. The function $f(x)$ is the inverse of $g(x) = x^3 + 4$. ○ True ○ False

   C. The graph of $f(x)$ is a translation 4 units to the right of the graph of $h(x) = \sqrt[3]{x}$. ○ True ○ False

3. The function $f(x) = \sqrt{3x}$ gives the voltage in volts of an electric circuit with a power of x watts and a resistance of 3 ohms. Graph the function, and explain what its y-intercept represents in this situation.

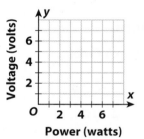

Power (watts)

4. Regina makes square quilts out of green and white fabric. The graph shows the relationship between the amount of green fabric used in a quilt and the side length of the quilt. Write the equation of the square root function shown in the graph. Describe how the graph is related to the graph of the parent function.

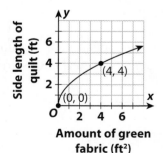

Amount of green fabric (ft²)

Study Guide Review

Key Vocabulary

quadratic function (*función cuadrática*)

parabola (*parábola*)

vertex of a parabola (*vértice de una parábola*)

maximum value (*valor máximo*)

minimum value (*mínimo de una función*)

zero of a function (*cero de una función*)

axis of symmetry (*eje de simetría*)

? ESSENTIAL QUESTION

How do quadratic functions relate to their graphs?

EXAMPLE 1

Use the graph of the quadratic function $g(x) = 4(x + 0.5)^2 - 9$. Find the minimum or maximum, zeros of the function, and the axis of symmetry.

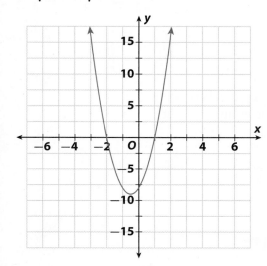

The vertex is at (h, k) which is $(-0.5, -9)$. The graph opens upward, so it has a minimum at the vertex.

The zeros of the function are the x-values where the function intersects the y-axis. These appear to be at $(-2, 0)$ and $(1, 0)$. These can be verified by substituting the x-values into the function.

The axis of symmetry of a parabola goes through the vertex. On this graph, the axis of symmetry is at $x = -0.5$.

EXAMPLE 2

Use the graph to write an equation for the function.

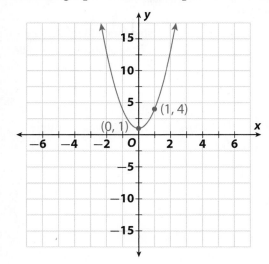

You need to find a, h, and k in the equation $g(x) = a(x - h)^2 + k$. The vertex (h, k) is at $(0, 1)$. Substitute these values into the equation.

$g(x) = a(x - 0)^2 + 1$

$g(x) = ax^2 + 1$

Notice that $(1, 4)$ is on the graph. Substitute the values into the equation, and solve for a.

$g(x) = ax^2 + 1$

$4 = a(1)^2 + 1$

$4 = a + 1$

$3 = a$

The equation is $g(x) = 3x^2 + 1$.

EXERCISES

1. Graph solutions of the equation $f(x) = -(x + 2)^2 - 3$. Find the minimum or maximum, zeros, and axis of symmetry. *(Lesson 17.4)*

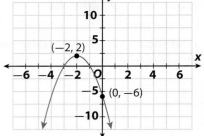

_____

_____

_____

2. Given the graph of the function, write the equation of the function. *(Lessons 17.1, 17.2, 17.3)*

_____

_____

_____

3. A coconut tree is 64 feet tall and is dropping its fruit to the ground below. The function $h(t) = -16t^2 + 64$, where t represents time measured in seconds, gives the coconut's height above the ground (in feet) as it falls. How long does it take the coconut to reach the ground?

(Lesson 17.5) _____

Piecewise and Absolute Value Functions

Key Vocabulary
absolute value function *(función de valor absoluto)*
greatest integer function *(función de entero mayor)*
piecewise function *(función a tramos)*
step function *(función escalón)*
vertex of an absolute-value graph *(vértice de una gráfica de valor absoluto)*

? ESSENTIAL QUESTION

How do piecewise functions differ from other types of functions?

EXAMPLE 1

Write the equation for the function whose graph is shown.

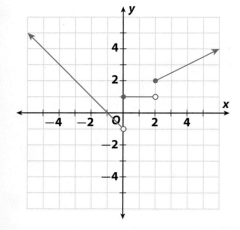

Write a rule for each part.

When $x < 0$: $y = -x - 1$

When $0 \le x < 2$: $y = 1$

When $x \ge 2$: $y = 0.5x + 1$

Write in bracket form.

$$f(x) = \begin{cases} -x - 1 & \text{when } x < 0 \\ 1 & \text{when } 0 \le x < 2 \\ 0.5x + 1 & \text{when } x \ge 2 \end{cases}$$

EXAMPLE 2

Graph each function.

A $g(x) = 4|x|$ Create a table of values for the function.

x	−2	−1	0	1	2
g(x) = 4|x|	8	4	0	4	8

Graph the function on a coordinate plane.

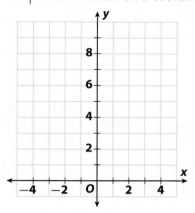

B $g(x) = |x - 5| + 1$ Create a table of values for the function.

x	1	3	5	7	9
g(x) = |x − 5| + 1	5	3	1	3	5

Graph the function on a coordinate plane.

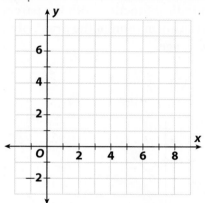

EXERCISES

1. On a trip, the Martez family travels at an average speed of 50 miles per hour for 3 hours, stops for 1.5 hours to eat, and resumes at an average speed of 60 miles per hour for 2 hours. Write an equation for the function $d(t)$, where d is distance and t is time in hours. (Lesson 18.1)

_____

2. Graph the function $g(x) = -\frac{3}{4}|x|$. (Lesson 18.2)

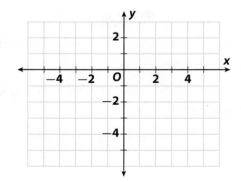

3. Write an equation for the function shown. (Lesson 18.3)

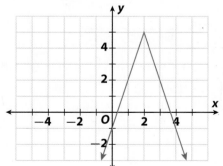

_____

Solve each equation or inequality.

4. $2|x| + 3 = 17$

_____

5. $|x| - 5 < -2$

_____

Square Root and Cube Root Functions

Key Vocabulary
cube root function
   (función de de raíz cúbica)
square root function
   (función de raíz cuadrada)

? ESSENTIAL QUESTION

How do the square and cube root function families relate to their graphs?

EXAMPLE 1

Graph each radical function with the parent function. Then describe the graph as a transformation of the graph of the parent function, and give its domain and range.

A $f(x) = 3\sqrt{x+1} - 2$

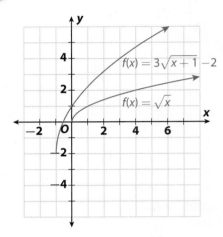

This is a square root function. Identify the values of h, k, and a in $f(x) = a\sqrt{x-h} + k$.

   $h = -1$, a translation to the left 1 unit

   $k = -2$, a translation down 2 units

   $a = 3$, a stretch with a factor of 3

Domain: $\{x \mid x \geq -1\}$ Range: $\{y \mid y \geq -2\}$.

B $f(x) = -2\sqrt[3]{x-2} + 2$

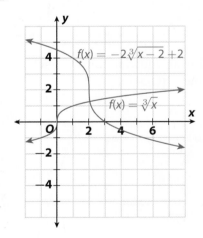

This is a cube root function. Identify the values of h, k, and a in $f(x) = a\sqrt[3]{x-h} + k$.

   $h = 2$, a translation to the right 2 units

   $k = 2$, a translation up 2 units

   $a = -2$, a stretch with a factor of 2 and a reflection

The domain is all real numbers and the range is also all real numbers.

EXERCISES

Graph each radical function with the parent function. Then describe the graph as a transformation of the graph of the parent function, and give its domain and range. (Lessons 19.2, 19.4)

1. $f(x) = 3\sqrt{x+1}$

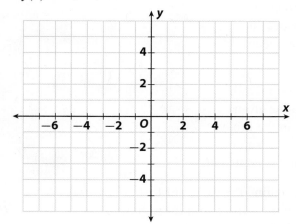

_____

_____

_____

_____

_____

2. $f(x) = 0.5\sqrt[3]{x} + 2$

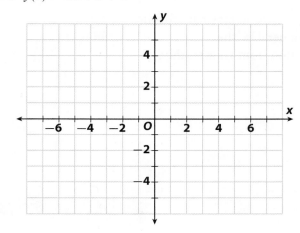

_____

_____

_____

_____

_____

Graph each function. Then graph the inverse of the function, and write a rule for the inverse function. (Lesson 19.1 and 19.3)

3. $f(x) = 2x^2 + 3$ for $x \geq 0$, $f^{-1}(x) = $ _____

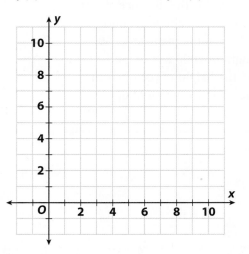

4. $f(x) = -3x^3$, $f^{-1}(x) = $ _____

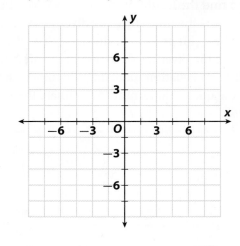

Perfecting the Package

Find a package that is cylindrical in shape—a container of oatmeal, a tube of chips, or a can, for example. Measure the height of the container to the nearest millimeter, and record the volume given on the label.

In this project, you will determine if the manufacturer used the least possible amount of material needed to contain the given volume. Using the quadratic expressions you wrote in the Project Preview, write a function $M(r)$ that gives the amount of material needed in terms of r. (*Hint*: use the volume given on the container.)

Using the MINIMUM feature of a graphing calculator, find the value of r that minimizes M. Round to the nearest millimeter. Then measure to find the radius of your container and determine whether the manufacturer used the least possible amount of material for the container.

Report your findings, and include any recommendations you may have for the manufacturer regarding the dimensions of the container. Use the space below to write down any questions you have or important information from your teacher.

MATH IN CAREERS ACTIVITY

Sky Diving Instructor Objects fall with an acceleration rate of -32 feet per second squared. A sky diving instructor needs to know how long it will take for the diver to reach the height at which the parachute should be opened. The formula he will use to find the height of the diver is $y = -16t^2 + h_0$, where y is the distance above the ground, t is the time since the diver jumped, and h_0 is the height above ground when the diver jumped out of the plane. The diver jumped out of the plane at 12,500 feet. Assume the diver needs to open the parachute at a height of 2000 feet to land safely. Write an equation modeling the time in seconds and the height of the diver in feet. Use the quadratic formula to estimate the time at which the diver should open the chute.

UNIT 5
MIXED REVIEW

Assessment Readiness

Personal Math Trainer

Online Practice and Help

my.hrw.com

1. Consider the functions. Which one(s) represent translations of the parent square root function $f(x) = \sqrt{x}$?

   Select Yes or No.

   A. $g(x) = \sqrt{x + 5}$ ○ Yes   ○ No

   B. $g(x) = 6\sqrt{x}$ ○ Yes   ○ No

   C. $g(x) = \sqrt{x} - 3$ ○ Yes   ○ No

   D. $g(x) = -\sqrt{x}$ ○ Yes   ○ No

2. Look at each point. Does the point lie on the graph of the piecewise function $f(x) = \begin{cases} -0.5x + 2 & \text{if } x < 1 \\ 2x - 1 & \text{if } x \geq 1 \end{cases}$?

   Select Yes or No.

   A. $(0, 2)$ ○ Yes   ○ No

   B. $(1, 1)$ ○ Yes   ○ No

   C. $(4, 0)$ ○ Yes   ○ No

3. Ashley makes and sells wedding invitations. The function $f(x) = 0.005x^2 + 3.15x - 75$ models her profit in dollars for an order of x invitations. How many invitations must be included in an order for Ashley to earn a profit of $200? Explain how to use a graphing calculator to solve this problem.

4. A cornfield maze is in the shape of a square. This year, the side length of the square is being increased by x meters compared to last year. The new area of the maze will be equal to $(x^2 + 300x + 22{,}500)$ square meters. What was the side length of the maze last year? Explain your reasoning.

Performance Tasks

★ **5.** The coordinate plane shows an arch that forms part of a bridge. Each unit represents 1 foot. Write the equation of the quadratic function that models the arch, where x is the horizontal distance in feet from the left end and y is the height in feet for a given value of x. Explain your answer.

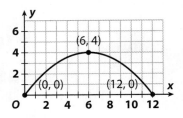

★★ **6.** A highway rest stop is at mile marker 25. The function $f(x) = |x - 25|$ gives the distance of a car at mile marker x from the rest stop.

  a. Graph the function.

  b. What is the vertex of the function, and what does it represent in this situation?

  c. A hotel on the highway is at mile marker 47. Write a function $g(x)$ that gives the distance in miles of a car at mile marker x from the hotel. Describe $g(x)$ as a transformation of $f(x)$.

  d. A car is at mile marker 36. How far is it from the rest stop? How far is it from the hotel? Explain how you know.

★★★ **7.** The table shows the amount a company has budgeted for software for the first 6 months of the year. Write an equation that can be used to predict the amount y in dollars that the company has budgeted for software in the xth month of the year. Justify your choice of model (linear, quadratic, or exponential), and use it to predict how much the company will budget for software in October.

Month	Amount Budgeted($)
Jan	1126
Feb	1720
Mar	2182
Apr	2512
May	2710
Jun	2776

The Pythagorean Theorem

COMMON CORE 8.G.7

Apply the Pythagorean Theorem to determine unknown side lengths in right triangles in real-world and mathematical problems in two and three dimensions. *Also 8.G.6*

ESSENTIAL QUESTION

How can you prove the Pythagorean Theorem and use it to solve problems?

EXPLORE ACTIVITY COMMON CORE 8.G.6

Proving the Pythagorean Theorem

In a right triangle, the two sides that form the right angle are the **legs**. The side opposite the right angle is the **hypotenuse**.

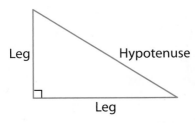

Leg   Hypotenuse

Leg

The Pythagorean Theorem

In a right triangle, the sum of the squares of the lengths of the legs is equal to the square of the length of the hypotenuse.

If a and b are legs and c is the hypotenuse, $a^2 + b^2 = c^2$.

A Draw a right triangle on a piece of paper and cut it out. Make one leg shorter than the other.

B Trace your triangle onto another piece of paper four times, arranging them as shown. For each triangle, label the shorter leg a, the longer leg b, and the hypotenuse c.

C What is the area of the unshaded square?

_____

Label the unshaded square with its area.

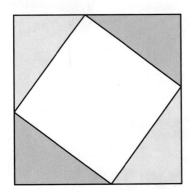

D Trace your original triangle onto a piece of paper four times again, arranging them as shown. Draw a line outlining a larger square that is the same size as the figure you made in **B**.

E What is the area of the unshaded square at the top right of the figure in **D**? at the top left?

_____

Label the unshaded squares with their areas.

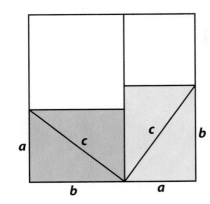

F What is the total area of the unshaded regions in **D**?

_____

Reflect

1. Explain whether the figures in **B** and **D** have the same area.

   _____

2. Explain whether the unshaded regions of the figures in **B** and **D** have the same area.

   _____

   _____

   _____

3. **Analyze Relationships** Write an equation relating the area of the unshaded region in step **B** to the unshaded region in **D**.

   _____

Math On the Spot

🔘 my.hrw.com

Animated Math

🔘 my.hrw.com

Math Talk

Mathematical Practices

If you are given the length of the hypotenuse and one leg, does it matter whether you solve for *a* or *b*? Explain.

Using the Pythagorean Theorem

You can use the Pythagorean Theorem to find the length of a side of a right triangle when you know the lengths of the other two sides.

EXAMPLE 1

COMMON CORE **8.G.7**

Find the length of the missing side.

A
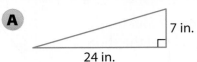
7 in.
24 in.

$$a^2 + b^2 = c^2$$

$$24^2 + 7^2 = c^2 \qquad \text{Substitute into the formula.}$$

$$576 + 49 = c^2 \qquad \text{Simplify.}$$

$$625 = c^2 \qquad \text{Add.}$$

$$25 = c \qquad \text{Take the square root of both sides.}$$

The length of the hypotenuse is 25 inches.

B
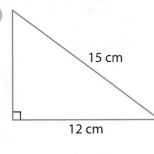
15 cm
12 cm

$$a^2 + b^2 = c^2$$

$$a^2 + 12^2 = 15^2 \qquad \text{Substitute into the formula.}$$

$$a^2 + 144 = 225 \qquad \text{Simplify.}$$

$$a^2 = 81 \qquad \text{Use properties of equality to get } a^2 \text{ by itself.}$$

$$a = 9 \qquad \text{Take the square root of both sides.}$$

The length of the leg is 9 centimeters.

Personal Math Trainer
Online Practice and Help
⏻ my.hrw.com

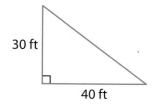

Find the length of the missing side.

4.

30 ft

40 ft

_____

5.

41 in.

40 in.

_____

Math On the Spot
⏻ my.hrw.com

Pythagorean Theorem in Three Dimensions

You can use the Pythagorean Theorem to solve problems in three dimensions.

Animated Math
⏻ my.hrw.com

EXAMPLE 2

COMMON CORE 8.G.7

A box used for shipping narrow copper tubes measures 6 inches by 6 inches by 20 inches. What is the length of the longest tube that will fit in the box, given that the length of the tube must be a whole number of inches?

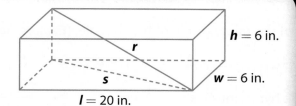

$h = 6$ in.

$w = 6$ in.

$l = 20$ in.

r

s

STEP 1 You want to find r, the length from a bottom corner to the opposite top corner. First, find s, the length of the diagonal across the bottom of the box.

$$w^2 + l^2 = s^2$$

$$6^2 + 20^2 = s^2 \qquad \text{Substitute into the formula.}$$

$$36 + 400 = s^2 \qquad \text{Simplify.}$$

$$436 = s^2 \qquad \text{Add.}$$

STEP 2 Use your expression for s to find r.

$$h^2 + s^2 = r^2$$

$$6^2 + 436 = r^2 \qquad \text{Substitute into the formula.}$$

$$472 = r^2 \qquad \text{Add.}$$

$$\sqrt{472} = r \qquad \text{Take the square root of both sides.}$$

$$21.7 \approx r \qquad \text{Use a calculator to round to the nearest tenth.}$$

The length of the longest tube that will fit in the box is 21 inches.

> **Math Talk**
> Mathematical Practices
>
> Looking at Step 2, why did the calculations in Step 1 stop before taking the square root of both sides of the final equation?

YOUR TURN

6. Tina ordered a replacement part for her desk. It was shipped in a box that measures 4 in. by 4 in. by 14 in. What is the greatest length in whole inches that the part could have been?

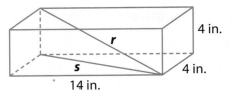

4 in.

r

s 4 in.

14 in.

Guided Practice

1. Find the length of the missing side of the triangle. (Explore Activity 1 and Example 1)

$a^2 + b^2 = c^2 \rightarrow 24^2 + \boxed{} = c^2 \rightarrow \boxed{} = c^2$

The length of the hypotenuse is $\boxed{}$ feet.

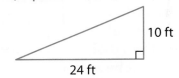

10 ft

24 ft

2. Mr. Woo wants to ship a fishing rod that is 42 inches long to his son. He has a box with the dimensions shown. (Example 2)

$h = 10$ in.

$w = 10$ in.

$l = 40$ in.

a. Find the square of the length of the diagonal across the bottom of the box.

_____

b. Find the length from a bottom corner to the opposite top corner to the nearest tenth. Will the fishing rod fit?

_____

? **ESSENTIAL QUESTION CHECK-IN**

3. State the Pythagorean Theorem and tell how you can use it to solve problems.

_____

_____

_____

_____

A.1 Independent Practice

COMMON CORE 8.G.6, 8.G.7

Personal
Math Trainer

Online Practice
and Help

my.hrw.com

Find the length of the missing side of each triangle. Round your answers to the nearest tenth.

4.

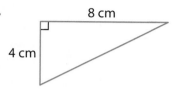

8 cm

4 cm

_____

5.

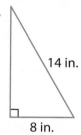

14 in.

8 in.

_____

6. The diagonal of a rectangular big-screen TV screen measures 152 cm. The length measures 132 cm. What is the height of the screen?

_____

7. Dylan has a square piece of metal that measures 10 inches on each side. He cuts the metal along the diagonal, forming two right triangles. What is the length of the hypotenuse of each right triangle to the nearest tenth of an inch?

_____

8. **Represent Real-World Problems** A painter has a 24-foot ladder that he is using to paint a house. For safety reasons, the ladder must be placed at least 8 feet from the base of the side of the house. To the nearest tenth of a foot, how high can the ladder safely reach?

_____

9. What is the longest flagpole (in whole feet) that could be shipped in a box that measures 2 ft by 2 ft by 12 ft?

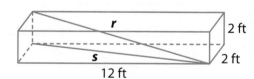

r

s

12 ft

2 ft

2 ft

_____

10. **Sports** American football fields measure 100 yards long between the end zones, and are $53\frac{1}{3}$ yards wide. Is the length of the diagonal across this field more or less than 120 yards? Explain.

_____

11. **Justify Reasoning** A tree struck by lightning broke at a point 12 ft above the ground as shown. What was the height of the tree to the nearest tenth of a foot? Explain your reasoning.

12 ft

39 ft

_____

_____

_____

H.O.T. **FOCUS ON HIGHER ORDER THINKING**

12. Multistep Main Street and Washington Avenue meet at a right angle. A large park begins at this corner. Joe's school lies at the opposite corner of the park. Usually Joe walks 1.2 miles along Main Street and then 0.9 miles up Washington Avenue to get to school. Today he walked in a straight path across the park and returned home along the same path. What is the difference in distance between the two round trips? Explain.

_____

_____

_____

13. Analyze Relationships An isosceles right triangle is a right triangle with congruent legs. If the length of each leg is represented by x, what algebraic expression can be used to represent the length of the hypotenuse? Explain your reasoning.

_____

_____

14. Persevere in Problem Solving A square hamburger is centered on a circular bun. Both the bun and the burger have an area of 16 square inches.

a. How far, to the nearest hundredth of an inch, does each corner of the burger stick out from the bun? Explain.

_____

_____

_____

_____

b. How far does each bun stick out from the center of each side of the burger?

_____

c. Are the distances in part **a** and part **b** equal? If not, which sticks out more, the burger or the bun? Explain.

_____

_____

Converse of the Pythagorean Theorem

COMMON CORE 8.G.6

Explain a proof of the Pythagorean Theorem and its converse.

? ESSENTIAL QUESTION How can you test the converse of the Pythagorean Theorem and use it to solve problems?

EXPLORE ACTIVITY COMMON CORE 8.G.6

Testing the Converse of the Pythagorean Theorem

The Pythagorean Theorem states that if a triangle is a right triangle, then $a^2 + b^2 = c^2$.

The *converse* of the Pythagorean Theorem states that if $a^2 + b^2 = c^2$, then the triangle is a right triangle.

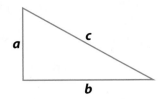

Decide whether the converse of the Pythagorean Theorem is true.

A Verify that the following sets of lengths make the equation $a^2 + b^2 = c^2$ true. Record your results in the table.

a	b	c	Is $a^2 + b^2 = c^2$ true?	Makes a right triangle?
3	4	5		
5	12	13		
7	24	25		
8	15	17		
20	21	29		

B For each set of lengths in the table, cut strips of grid paper with a width of one square and lengths that correspond to the values of a, b, and c.

C For each set of lengths, use the strips of grid paper to try to form a right triangle. An example using the first set of lengths is shown. Record your findings in the table.

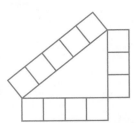

Reflect

1. **Draw Conclusions** Based on your observations, explain whether you think the converse of the Pythagorean Theorem is true.

_____

_____

Identifying a Right Triangle

The converse of the Pythagorean Theorem gives you a way to tell if a triangle is a right triangle when you know the side lengths.

EXAMPLE 1

Tell whether each triangle with the given side lengths is a right triangle.

A 9 inches, 40 inches, and 41 inches

Let $a = 9$, $b = 40$, and $c = 41$.

$$a^2 + b^2 = c^2$$

$9^2 + 40^2 \stackrel{?}{=} 41^2$ Substitute into the formula.

$81 + 1600 \stackrel{?}{=} 1681$ Simpify.

$1681 = 1681$ Add.

Since $9^2 + 40^2 = 41^2$, the triangle is a right triangle by the converse of the Pythagorean Theorem.

B 8 meters, 10 meters, and 12 meters

Let $a = 8$, $b = 10$, and $c = 12$.

$$a^2 + b^2 = c^2$$

$8^2 + 10^2 \stackrel{?}{=} 12^2$ Substitute into the formula.

$64 + 100 \stackrel{?}{=} 144$ Simpify.

$164 \neq 144$ Add.

Since $8^2 + 10^2 \neq 12^2$, the triangle is not a right triangle by the converse of the Pythagorean Theorem.

My Notes

YOUR TURN

Personal Math Trainer

Online Practice and Help

my.hrw.com

Tell whether each triangle with the given side lengths is a right triangle.

2. 14 cm, 23 cm, and 25 cm

3. 16 in., 30 in., and 34 in.

4. 27 ft, 36 ft, 45 ft

5. 11 mm, 18 mm, 21 mm

Using the Converse of the Pythagorean Theorem

You can use the converse of the Pythagorean Theorem to solve real-world problems.

EXAMPLE 2

COMMON CORE 8.G.6

Katya is buying edging for a triangular flower garden she plans to build in her backyard. If the lengths of the three pieces of edging that she purchases are 13 feet, 10 feet, and 7 feet, will the flower garden be in the shape of a right triangle?

Use the converse of the Pythagorean Theorem. Remember to use the longest length for c.

Let $a = 7$, $b = 10$, and $c = 13$.

$$a^2 + b^2 = c^2$$

$$7^2 + 10^2 \overset{?}{=} 13^2 \qquad \text{Substitute into the formula.}$$

$$49 + 100 \overset{?}{=} 169 \qquad \text{Simpify.}$$

$$149 \neq 169 \qquad \text{Add.}$$

Since $7^2 + 10^2 \neq 13^2$, the garden will not be in the shape of a right triangle.

> **Math Talk**
> Mathematical Practices
>
> To what length, to the nearest tenth, can Katya trim the longest piece of edging to form a right triangle?

YOUR TURN

6. A blueprint for a new triangular playground shows that the sides measure 480 ft, 140 ft, and 500 ft. Is the playground in the shape of a right triangle? Explain.

_____

_____

7. A triangular piece of glass has sides that measure 18 in., 19 in., and 25 in. Is the piece of glass in the shape of a right triangle? Explain.

_____

8. A corner of a fenced yard forms a right angle. Can you place a 12 foot long board across the corner to form a right triangle for which the leg lengths are whole numbers? Explain.

_____

_____

Personal Math Trainer

Online Practice and Help

⏻ my.hrw.com

1. Lashandra used grid paper to construct the triangle shown. (Explore Activity)

   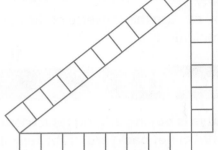

   a. What are the lengths of the sides of Lashandra's triangle?

      _____units, _____units, _____units

   b. Use the converse of the Pythagorean Theorem to determine whether the triangle is a right triangle.

   $$a^2 + b^2 = c^2$$

   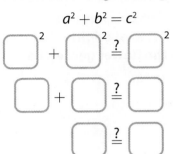

   The triangle that Lashandra constructed **is / is not** a right triangle.

2. A triangle has side lengths 9 cm, 12 cm, and 16 cm. Tell whether the triangle is a right triangle. (Example 1)

   Let $a =$ _____ , $b =$ _____ , and $c =$ _____ .

   $$a^2 + b^2 = c^2$$

   ☐² + ☐² $\overset{?}{=}$ ☐²

   ☐ + ☐ $\overset{?}{=}$ ☐

   ☐ $\overset{?}{=}$ ☐

   By the converse of the Pythagorean Theorem, the triangle **is / is not** a right triangle.

3. The marketing team at a new electronics company is designing a logo that contains a circle and a triangle. On one design, the triangle's side lengths are 2.5 in., 6 in., and 6.5 in. Is the triangle a right triangle? Explain. (Example 2)

   _____

? ESSENTIAL QUESTION CHECK-IN

4. How can you use the converse of the Pythagorean Theorem to tell if a triangle is a right triangle?

   _____

   _____

A.2 Independent Practice

Personal Math Trainer

Online Practice and Help

my.hrw.com

Tell whether each triangle with the given side lengths is a right triangle.

5. 11 cm, 60 cm, 61 cm

_____

6. 5 ft, 12 ft, 15 ft

_____

7. 9 in., 15 in., 17 in.

_____

8. 15 m, 36 m, 39 m

_____

9. 20 mm, 30 mm, 40 mm

_____

10. 20 cm, 48 cm, 52 cm

_____

11. 18.5 ft, 6 ft, 17.5 ft

_____

12. 2 mi, 1.5 mi, 2.5 mi

_____

13. 35 in., 45 in., 55 in.

_____

14. 25 cm, 14 cm, 23 cm

_____

15. The emblem on a college banner consists of the face of a tiger inside a triangle. The lengths of the sides of the triangle are 13 cm, 14 cm, and 15 cm. Is the triangle a right triangle? Explain.

_____

16. Kerry has a large triangular piece of fabric that she wants to attach to the ceiling in her bedroom. The sides of the piece of fabric measure 4.8 ft, 6.4 ft, and 8 ft. Is the fabric in the shape of a right triangle? Explain.

_____

17. A mosaic consists of triangular tiles. The smallest tiles have side lengths 6 cm, 10 cm, and 12 cm. Are these tiles in the shape of right triangles? Explain.

_____

18. History In ancient Egypt, surveyors made right angles by stretching a rope with evenly spaced knots as shown. Explain why the rope forms a right angle.

_____

_____

_____

19. Justify Reasoning Yoshi has two identical triangular boards as shown. Can he use these two boards to form a rectangle? Explain.

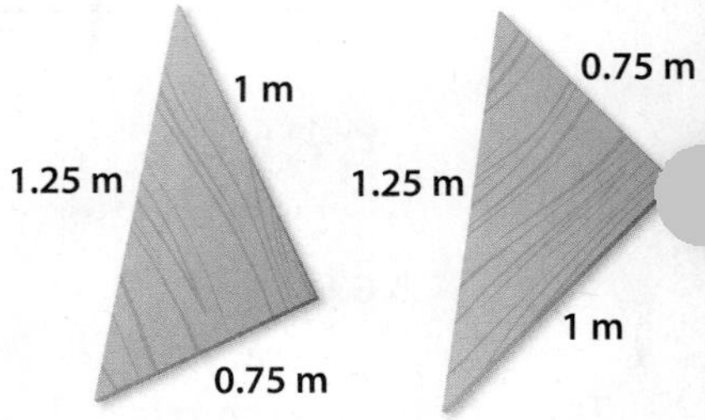

_____

_____

_____

20. Critique Reasoning Shoshanna says that a triangle with side lengths 17 m, 8 m, and 15 m is not a right triangle because $17^2 + 8^2 = 353$, $15^2 = 225$, and $353 \neq 225$. Is she correct? Explain.

_____

_____

H.O.T. FOCUS ON HIGHER ORDER THINKING

Work Area

21. Make a Conjecture Diondre says that he can take any right triangle and make a new right triangle just by doubling the side lengths. Is Diondre's conjecture true? Test his conjecture using three different right triangles.

_____

_____

_____

_____

22. Draw Conclusions A diagonal of a parallelogram measures 37 inches. The sides measure 35 inches and 1 foot. Is the parallelogram a rectangle? Explain your reasoning.

_____

_____

_____

_____

23. Represent Real-World Problems A soccer coach is marking the lines for a soccer field on a large recreation field. The dimensions of the field are to be 90 yards by 48 yards. Describe a procedure she could use to confirm that the sides of the field meet at right angles.

_____

_____

_____

_____

Distance Between Two Points

COMMON CORE 8.G.8

Apply the Pythagorean Theorem to find the distance between two points in a coordinate system.

How can you use the Pythagorean Theorem to find the distance between two points on a coordinate plane?

Pythagorean Theorem in the Coordinate Plane

EXAMPLE 1

COMMON CORE 8.G.8

Math On the Spot
my.hrw.com

The figure shows a right triangle. Approximate the length of the hypotenuse to the nearest tenth using a calculator.

STEP 1 Find the length of each leg.

The length of the vertical leg is 4 units.

The length of the horizontal leg is 2 units.

STEP 2 Let $a = 4$ and $b = 2$. Let c represent the length of the hypotenuse. Use the Pythagorean Theorem to find c.

$$a^2 + b^2 = c^2$$

$$4^2 + 2^2 = c^2 \qquad \text{Substitute into the formula.}$$

$$20 = c^2 \qquad \text{Add.}$$

$$\sqrt{20} = c \qquad \text{Take the square root of both sides.}$$

$$\sqrt{20} \approx 4.5 \qquad \text{Use a calculator and round to the nearest tenth.}$$

STEP 3 Check for reasonableness by finding perfect squares close to 20.

$\sqrt{20}$ is between $\sqrt{16}$ and $\sqrt{25}$, so $4 < \sqrt{20} < 5$.

Since 4.5 is between 4 and 5, the answer is reasonable.

The hypotenuse is about 4.5 units long.

YOUR TURN

1. Approximate the length of the hypotenuse to the nearest tenth without using a calculator.

_____

Personal Math Trainer
Online Practice and Help
my.hrw.com

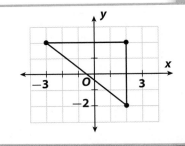

Finding the Distance Between Any Two Points

The Pythagorean Theorem can be used to find the distance between any two points (x_1, y_1) and (x_2, y_2) in the coordinate plane. The resulting expression is called the Distance Formula.

Distance Formula

In a coordinate plane, the distance d between two points (x_1, y_1) and (x_2, y_2) is
$$d = \sqrt{(x_2 - x_1)^2 + (y_2 - y_1)^2}.$$

Use the Pythagorean Theorem to derive the Distance Formula.

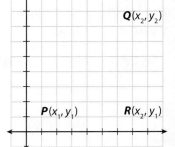

A To find the distance between points P and Q, draw segment $\overline{PQ}$ and label its length d. Then draw horizontal segment $\overline{PR}$ and vertical segment $\overline{QR}$. Label the lengths of these segments a and b. Triangle

PQR is a _____ triangle, with hypotenuse _____.

B Since $\overline{PR}$ is a horizontal segment, its length, a, is the difference

between its x-coordinates. Therefore, $a = x_2 -$ _____.

C Since $\overline{QR}$ is a vertical segment, its length, b, is the difference between

its y-coordinates. Therefore, $b = y_2 -$ _____.

D Use the Pythagorean Theorem to find d, the length of segment $\overline{PQ}$. Substitute the expressions from **B** and **C** for a and b.

$$d^2 = a^2 + b^2$$

$$d = \sqrt{a^2 + b^2}$$

$$d = \sqrt{\left(\boxed{} - \boxed{}\right)^2 + \left(\boxed{} - \boxed{}\right)^2}$$

Math Talk
Mathematical Practices

What do $x_2 - x_1$ and $y_2 - y_1$ represent in terms of the Pythagorean Theorem?

Reflect

2. Why are the coordinates of point R the ordered pair (x_2, y_1)?

_____

_____

_____

Finding the Distance Between Two Points

The Pythagorean Theorem can be used to find the distance between two points in a real-world situation. You can do this by using a coordinate grid that overlays a diagram of the real-world situation.

EXAMPLE 2

COMMON CORE 8.G.8

Francesca wants to find the distance between her house on one side of a lake and the beach on the other side. She marks off a third point forming a right triangle, as shown. The distances in the diagram are measured in meters.

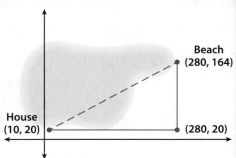

Beach
(280, 164)

House
(10, 20)

(280, 20)

Use the Pythagorean Theorem to find the straight-line distance from Francesca's house to the beach.

STEP 1   Find the length of the horizontal leg.

The length of the horizontal leg is the absolute value of the difference between the x-coordinates of the points (280, 20) and (10, 20).

$$|280 - 10| = 270$$

The length of the horizontal leg is 270 meters.

STEP 2   Find the length of the vertical leg.

The length of the vertical leg is the absolute value of the difference between the y-coordinates of the points (280, 164) and (280, 20).

$$|164 - 20| = 144$$

The length of the vertical leg is 144 meters.

STEP 3   Let $a = 270$ and $b = 144$. Let c represent the length of the hypotenuse. Use the Pythagorean Theorem to find c.

$$a^2 + b^2 = c^2$$

$$270^2 + 144^2 = c^2 \qquad \text{Substitute into the formula.}$$

$$72{,}900 + 20{,}736 = c^2 \qquad \text{Simplify.}$$

$$93{,}636 = c^2 \qquad \text{Add.}$$

$$\sqrt{93{,}636} = c \qquad \text{Take the square root of both sides.}$$

$$306 = c \qquad \text{Simplify.}$$

The distance from Francesca's house to the beach is 306 meters.

> **Math Talk**
> Mathematical Practices
>
> Why is it necessary to take the absolute value of the coordinates when finding the length of a segment?

Reflect

3. Show how you could use the Distance Formula to find the distance from Francesca's house to the beach.

_____

_____

_____

Personal Math Trainer

Online Practice and Help

⏻ my.hrw.com

YOUR TURN

4. Camp Sunshine is also on the lake. Use the Pythagorean Theorem to find the distance between Francesca's house and Camp Sunshine to the nearest tenth of a meter.

_____

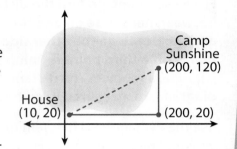

House (10, 20)

Camp Sunshine (200, 120)

(200, 20)

Guided Practice

1. Approximate the length of the hypotenuse of the right triangle to the nearest tenth using a calculator. (Example 1) _____

2. Find the distance between the points (3, 7) and (15, 12) on the coordinate plane. (Explore Activity) _____

3. A plane leaves an airport and flies due north. Two minutes later, a second plane leaves the same airport flying due east. The flight plan shows the coordinates of the two planes 10 minutes later. The distances in the graph are measured in miles. Use the Pythagorean Theorem to find the distance shown between the two planes.

(Example 2) _____

(1, 80)

Airport (1, 1)   (68, 1)

? ESSENTIAL QUESTION CHECK-IN

4. Describe two ways to find the distance between two points on a coordinate plane.

_____

_____

_____

A.3 Independent Practice

Personal Math Trainer

Online Practice and Help

my.hrw.com

5. A metal worker traced a triangular piece of sheet metal on a coordinate plane, as shown. The units represent inches. What is the length of the longest side of the metal triangle? Approximate the length to the nearest tenth of an inch using a calculator. Check that your answer is reasonable.

_____

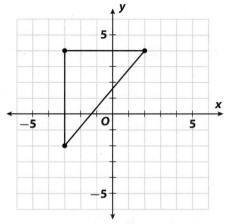

6. When a coordinate grid is superimposed on a map of Harrisburg, the high school is located at (17, 21) and the town park is located at (28, 13). If each unit represents 1 mile, how many miles apart are the high school and the town park? Round your answer to the nearest tenth.

_____

7. The coordinates of the vertices of a rectangle are given by $R(-3, -4)$, $E(-3, 4)$, $C(4, 4)$, and $T(4, -4)$. Plot these points on the coordinate plane at the right and connect them to draw the rectangle. Then connect points E and T to form diagonal $\overline{ET}$.

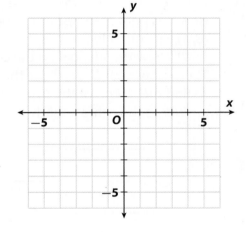

   a. Use the Pythagorean Theorem to find the exact length of $\overline{ET}$.

   _____

   b. How can you use the Distance Formula to find the length of $\overline{ET}$? Show that the Distance Formula gives the same answer.

   _____

   _____

   _____

   _____

   _____

   _____

8. Multistep The locations of three ships are represented on a coordinate grid by the following points: $P(-2, 5)$, $Q(-7, -5)$, and $R(2, -3)$. Which ships are farthest apart?

_____

9. Make a Conjecture Find as many points as you can that are 5 units from the origin. Make a conjecture about the shape formed if all the points 5 units from the origin were connected.

_____

_____

_____

10. Justify Reasoning The graph shows the location of a motion detector that has a maximum range of 34 feet. A peacock at point P displays its tail feathers. Will the motion detector sense this motion? Explain.

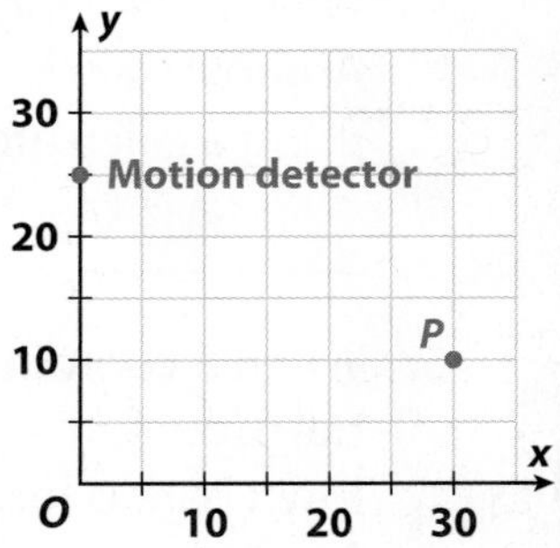

_____

_____

_____

H.O.T. FOCUS ON HIGHER ORDER THINKING

11. Persevere in Problem Solving One leg of an isosceles right triangle has endpoints (1, 1) and (6, 1). The other leg passes through the point (6, 2). Draw the triangle on the coordinate plane. Then show how you can use the Distance Formula to find the length of the hypotenuse. Round your answer to the nearest tenth.

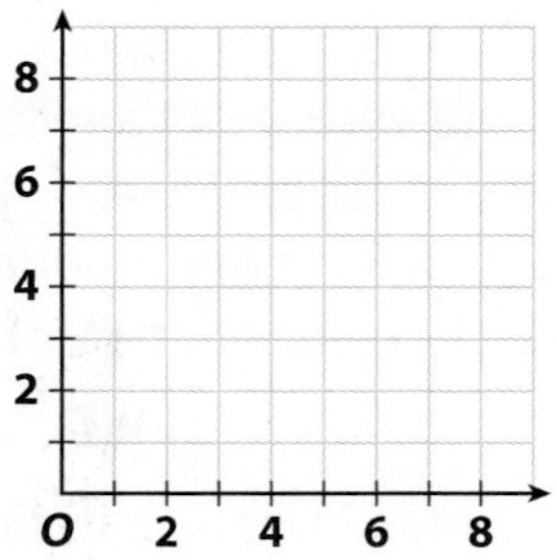

_____

_____

_____

12. Represent Real-World Problems The figure shows a representation of a football field. The units represent yards. A sports analyst marks the locations of the football from where it was thrown (point A) and where it was caught (point B). Explain how you can use the Pythagorean Theorem to find the distance the ball was thrown. Then find the distance.

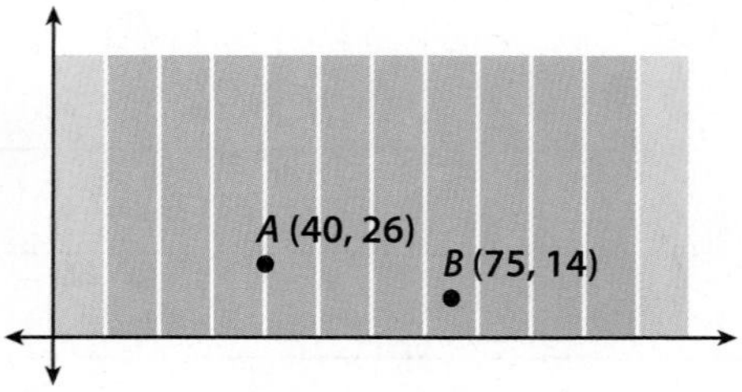

A (40, 26)

B (75, 14)

_____

_____

_____

_____

_____

Index

Index

Index

© Houghton Mifflin Harcourt Publishing Company

Index

Index

vocabulary, 5, 27, 49, 87, 117, 153, 211, 245,
    275, 335, 379, 409, 429, 483, 521, 561, 625,
    691, 729
  Key Vocabulary, 6, 28, 50, 88, 118, 154, 212,
      246, 276, 336, 380, 430, 484, 522, 562, 626,
      692, 730
  Understand Vocabulary, 5, 27, 49, 87, 117, 153,
      211, 245, 275, 335, 379, 409, 429, 483, 521,
      561, 625, 691, 729
  Visualize Vocabulary, 5, 27, 49, 87, 117, 153,
      211, 245, 275, 335, 379, 409, 429, 483, 521,
      561, 625, 691, 729

W

weather, 189, 250, 266, 434

X

***x*-intercept,** 164, 655

Y

***y*-intercept,** 164

Z

zero
    as exponent, 337
    finding axis of symmetry using, 656
    of a function, 571, 655–656
    significant digits and, 9
zero product property, 571–578, 579, 580

© Houghton Mifflin Harcourt Publishing Company

Index

TABLE OF MEASURES

LENGTH

1 inch = 2.54 centimeters

1 meter ≈ 39.37 inches

1 mile = 5,280 feet

1 mile = 1760 yards

1 mile ≈ 1.609 kilometers

1 kilometer ≈ 0.62 mile

MASS/WEIGHT

1 pound = 16 ounces

1 pound ≈ 0.454 kilograms

1 kilogram ≈ 2.2 pounds

1 ton = 2000 pounds

CAPACITY

1 cup = 8 fluid ounces

1 pint = 2 cups

1 quart = 2 pints

1 gallon = 4 quarts

1 gallon ≈ 3.785 liters

1 liter ≈ 0.264 gallons

1 liter = 1000 cubic centimeters

SYMBOLS

≠	is not equal to		π	pi: (about 3.14)
≈	is approximately equal to		⊥	is perpendicular to
10^2	ten squared; ten to the second power		∥	is parallel to
			$\overleftrightarrow{AB}$	line AB
$2.\overline{6}$	repeating decimal 2.66666...		$\overrightarrow{AB}$	ray AB
$\lvert-4\rvert$	the absolute value of negative 4		$\overline{AB}$	line segment AB
$\sqrt{}$	square root		m∠A	measure of ∠A

FORMULAS

Triangle	$A = \frac{1}{2}bh$	Cone	$V = \frac{1}{3}\pi r^2 h$
Parallelogram	$A = bh$	Pyramid	$V = \frac{1}{3}Bh$
Circle	$A = \pi r^2$	Pythagorean Theorem	$a^2 + b^2 = c^2$
Circle	$C = \pi d$ or $C = 2\pi r$	Quadratic Formula	$x = \dfrac{-b \pm \sqrt{b^2 - 4ac}}{2a}$
General Prisms	$V = Bh$	Arithmetic Sequence	$a_n = a_1 + (n-1)d$
Cylinder	$V = \pi r^2 h$	Geometric Sequence	$a_n = a_1 r^{n-1}$
Sphere	$V = \frac{4}{3}\pi r^3$		